Shakespeare on the American Stage

From Booth and Barrett to Sothern and Marlowe

Sir Johnston Forbes-Robertson, painted for *Theatre* magazine, July 1914.

Shakespeare on the American Stage

From Booth and Barrett to Sothern and Marlowe

VOLUME 2

Charles H. Shattuck

Folger Books
Washington: Folger Shakespeare Library
London and Toronto: Associated University Presses

Associated University Presses
440 Forsgate Drive
Cranbury, NJ 08512

Associated University Presses
25 Sicilian Avenue
London WC1A 2QH, England

Associated University Presses
2133 Royal Windsor Drive
Unit 1
Mississauga, Ontario
Canada L5J 1K5

The paper used in this publication meets the requirements of the American National Standard for Permanence of Paper for Printed Library Materials Z39.48-1984.

Library of Congress Cataloging-in-Publication Data
(Revised for volume 2)

Shattuck, Charles Harlen, 1910–
Shakespeare on the American stage.

Vol. 2 has imprint: Washington : Folger Shakespeare Library ; London : Associated University Presses.
"Folger books"—V.
Includes bibliographical references and indexes.
Contents: [1] From the Hallams to Edwin Booth—v. 2. From Booth and Barrett to Sothern and Marlowe.
1. Shakespeare, William, 1564–1616—Stage history—United States. 2. Theater—United States—History. 3. Actors—Biography. I. Title: Folger Shakespeare Library. II. Title.
PR3105.S5 792′.0973 75-43999
ISBN 0-918016-77-0 (v.2) (alk. paper)

Printed in the United States of America

Contents

Illustrations

Preface

THIS VOLUME is the inevitable sequel to *Shakespeare on the American Stage: from the Hallams to Edwin Booth* (Folger Books, 1976). During the summer of 1974 Dr. O. B. Hardison, Director of the Folger Shakespeare Library, proposed that in anticipation of the nation's Bicentenary I prepare a history of Shakespeare's two hundred years on the American stage. It was easy to accept this assignment, impossible to fulfill it in the time available. The subject proved so rich that I could cover only the first of two centuries, and I could do even that much only by omitting quantities of detail and focusing a set of essays around major figures and events confined, for the most part, to the eastern seaboard.

As I attempt now to advance the history, the matter thickens. In this volume I cover a mere half-century, down to the end of World War I. As our nation expanded, its theatres multiplied by the hundreds, its performers by thousands, and theatre-goers, from coast to coast, by many hundreds of thousands. Again I must omit much, and only occasionally can I remind readers that in the generation before cinema usurped public attention, live theatre (and Shakespeare) was everywhere.

What I find especially rewarding during this period is the vast growth of theatrical criticism. A city like Boston or Philadelphia would be served by well over a dozen daily or weekly journals, each employing from one or two to a battery of theatre reporters and critics. From the city of New York there emanated more than *three dozen* journals—some like the *Dramatic Mirror* devoted exclusively to theatre, but all covering theatre with professional and generally expert writers.

Theatre meant so much to the public then that editors allowed their critics all the space they needed to say what must be said. Reviews were detailed and literate, and they represented every shade of opinion, from the irredeemable (sometimes glowing, sometimes peevish, even vituperative) Victorianism of William Winter (known then as the "Dean of Critics") to the rowdy muscularity of A. C. Wheeler (pseudonym "Nym Crinkle"), the most eloquent spokesman of the cigar-and-whiskey school of theatrical evaluators; from the solid scholarship of John Ranken Towse, most judicious of the firm-set conservatives, to such willing promoters of modernism as Norman Hapgood, James Huneker, and Walter Prichard Eaton.

Boston was blest with the measured wisdom of Henry Austin Clapp of the *Advertiser,* often declared to be the fairest, soundest, best-informed theatre critic of his time; Edward Fuller and Professor Charles Copeland of the *Post;* and the grand constellation of writers who gathered at the *Transcipt*—Edwin Edgett, Evelyn Sutherland, others anonymous, later Kenneth Macgowan and Hiram Moderwell, culminating in the distinguished career of Henry Taylor Parker. Famous across the country were such critics as L. Clarke Davis of Philadelphia, Robinson Locke of Toledo, George Goodale of Detroit, Elwyn Barron and James O'Donnell Bennett and Percy Hammond and W. L. Hubbard of Chicago, Oliver Sayler of Indianapolis, and Peter Robinson of San Francisco.

At their best these professional witnesses bring us more vivid images of—and warmer feelings for—Shakespearean performers at their work than does perhaps any body of American critics before or since. In some cases their testimony sharply qualifies—elevates or diminishes—artistic reputations that have seemed, from constant repetition, immutably fixed. Occasionally, when these critics disagree, their clashes of opinion may prove more entertaining and illuminating than the subjects they are quarreling about. I have offered generous samples of their writing, and only wish there were time and space to do thorough justice to their insights, their prejudices and follies, their wisdoms. A massive study needs to be made of the state of theatrical criticism as the nineteenth-century theatre was entering its autumnal flowering, soon to wither and make way for the theatre that we think of as "modern."

For a decade or so after the Great War our attention in America was diverted from Shakespeare to the products of our own much-heralded "dramatic renaissance"—the emergence of Rice, Odets, O'Neill, and their like. Shakespeare production—detached from tradition, fitting awkwardly into the new "naturalism" of acting, and even awkwardly (to some it seemed) into scenery styled by the "New Stagecraft"—became occasional, tentative, sporadic. Probably not until our re-education from the mother-country by Margaret Webster and Maurice Evans in the 1930s did we find our way back to Shakespeare-as-he-ought-to-be.

My indebtedness to dozens of critics, biographers, and historians is acknowleged piecemeal in footnotes throughout the essays. But I must record special gratitude to a number of young scholars working in this period who have most generously made available to me, for information and ideas, their new and for the most part unpublished findings. These include Tori Haring-Smith (on modern productions of the *Shrew*), James R. Miller (on Lawrence Barrett), Tice L. Miller (on the critic Towse), John A. Mills (on Fechter and other modern Hamlets), Alex Pinkston (on Mansfield), Joan Saliskas (on Julia Marlowe), John Chase Soliday (on the Booth-Barrett tours), Gary Williams (on modern productions of the *Dream*), and Thomas Key Wright (on the critic "Nym Crinkle"). I have gained much, too, from conversation or correspondence with, among others, Doris Adler, Dennis Bartholomeusz, James Ellis, Attilio Favorini, Alan Hughes, Edward Moore, John Ripley, Denis Salter, and Daniel Watermeier.

To Jeanne Newlin and Martha Mahard of the Harvard Theatre Collection, to George Nash, former director of the Gabrielle Enthoven Collection, to the staff of the Theatre Collection of the New York Public Library, to the Research Board of the University of Illinois, I am much indebted for aid in gathering material for this study. Jean Miller, keeper of the Art Collection of the Folger Shakespeare Library has been ingenious and tireless in plumbing the archives for illustrations. Nora Tracy, editorial assistant for the *Shakespeare Quarterly,* and Lena Cowen Orlin, now Executive Director of the Folger Institute and Associate Director of Academic Programs at the Folger, have served as traffic managers on this project, keeping countless problems of manuscript handling, placing of illustrations, collecting permissions, etc. steadily on track. The Society of Authors, on behalf of the Bernard Shaw Estate, has granted permission for quotation of passages from the critical writings of Bernard Shaw.

Much of the photographing of materials located in Urbana was done by my friend and neighbor, the late Carolyn Pape (Mrs. Mark Netter), whose sudden death interrupted her exactly when she was happiest in her work on the project. I am grateful to my colleague, John Friedman, for carrying the photography to completion. Marlyn Ehlers and Sherri George, both of the secretarial staff of the University of Illinois Department of English, have typed my crude manuscript into readable copy. I am indebted to Katharine Turok, managing editor of Associated University Presses, and to her staff, for their extraordinarily judicious and thorough attention to matters of style as well as technical preparation of the manuscript for the printer.

I owe most to Dr. John Andrews, formerly the editor of Folger Books, and Director of Academic Programs at the Folger, for his firm insistence that this history be carried forward, and for his extraordinary patience over the years while my essays and revised essays drifted slowly to his desk. My wife Susan, too, who has been my best helper and critic, has been more than humanly forgiving for the time I have spent in finishing this work, and is even willing to contemplate my engagement on its sequel. American Shakespeare of the twentieth century (which in fact got under way in the 1890s) must be attended to next.

Shakespeare on the American Stage

From Booth and Barrett to Sothern and Marlowe

Introduction

IN 1920 George C. D. Odell concluded his stage history of Shakespeare with an impassioned Epilogue. For Odell the late Beerbohm Tree's massive reconstructions of Shakespeare—*Richard II, Antony and Cleopatra, Henry VIII* and the rest—these, for Odell, were the last word, the supreme achievement, in the staging of Shakespeare. "Let us," he cried, "here lay a wreath on the tomb of the brave believer in Shakespeare and theatre."[1] Without Tree there seemed to Odell no one of sufficient authority to protect Shakespeare from the new wave of meddling experimentalists—Gordon Craig and his disciples, exponents of the "New Stagecraft." Victims, all of them, of "German and Russian dyspepsia," they would no longer offer honest pictures of the scenes Shakespeare had in his mind's eye. They even declined to be called "scene painters." They were "stage decorators." They would not show us literal castles or hollyhocks, but in the post-impressionist manner would *suggest the essences* of what lies in Shakespeare's words. Odell was dismayed. And indeed for the thirty more years that he lived he would never be reconciled to the loss of his old-time visions of Elsinore or Illyria or that magic "wood a league without the town."

The most threatening of the experimentalists had been Granville Barker, whose London production of *The Winter's Tale* in 1912 was described in the *Athenaeum* as "that mingling of discordant, ill-related elements, that impossible jangling of different keys, which can never be removed from vulgarity." In 1915 his *Midsummer Night's Dream* had been transported from London to New York, where Odell himself had flayed it with many column inches of ridicule. To demonstrate the shame into which Shakespeare's play had been plunged, Odell quotes at length his own review for us. Then he adds, to cap the disaster, "I hope also that this silly and vulgar way of presenting Shakespeare died with all the other vain, frivolous, un-simple things burnt up in the great war conflagration."[2]

It is dangerous to prophesy. What the great war conflagration burned up was not the New Stagecraft, but rather what Odell dearly loved, what Beerbohm Tree stood for, and beyond Tree a whole century of misguided striving to express Shakespeare by stripping away his most suggestive poetry and "realizing" it in wood and paint and canvas. This is not to say that Tree and the scene-painters of his nineteenth-century predecessors did not achieve countless miracles of picture-making—verdant meadows and scarred battlefields, awesome tombs, exalted throne rooms in majestic castles, stormy skies and sunlit skies, visions of Egypt, visions of Venice, moonlight falling on banks of flowers—all to serve "Shakespeare." But the more elaborate and "real" the scenery was, the more often it ate up time and attention that would have been better spent on Shakespeare's language. In any case, as Odell might have guessed, within a decade the newborn art of cinema would relieve the Shakespeare *theatre* of scenic realism and provide "the real thing" (if that was what we truly wanted) a hundred times more effectively than could be accomplished with wood and paint and canvas on narrow stages.

As a matter of fact, several modern techniques of staging Shakespeare were in use long before Odell wrote those final pages. In England in the early 1890s William Poel mounted his campaign against Henry Irving's overblown splendors at the Lyceum by reviving the platform and balcony stage of the Elizabethans and banishing scenery altogether; he never relaxed his efforts nor for half a century ceased publicizing them. Within a year his scheme was taken up as a pedagogic device by Professor George Pierce Baker at Harvard, and a "Globe staging" was used

Illus. 1. Viola Allen as Viola in *Twelfth Night.*

there for student performances of Elizabethan and Jacobean plays. Soon after the turn of the century Gordon Craig and his New Stagecraft were much talked about, occasionally put to use, and by 1910 were widely effective. If Barker's extravagantly *nouveaux* techniques were too highly spiced for Odell's palate, what could Odell have made of all the other modern arts? In drama itself how could he have put up with *Peer Gynt* or *A Dream Play?* To what extent he traveled in Europe and encountered the ballet, the new music, the modern painting, I do not know; but Nijinsky was in America and Stravinsky was performed in New York and post-impressionism was practiced by American painters long before the Great War. Odell surely could not have missed the famous Armory Show of 1913 with its display of Cézanne, Gaugin, van Gogh, Matisse, and hundreds of canvases of avant-garde Americans. There were Duchamp's *Nude Descending a Staircase* and everything else to tell him what was happening to art in the twentieth century. But Odell's ideas about the art of staging Shakespeare grew in a separate walled garden, so deeply rooted there after over thirty years of playgoing that he never learned to endure the thought of change.

I do not intend in this study to explore in detail these early manifestations of modernism in Shakespeare staging, but mainly to report the culmination of "Victorian" methods in America up to the Great War. Scenic investiture, stimulated by the example of Henry Irving, who brought his entire Lyceum productions to America on several occasions, grew more elaborate. "Historical accuracy" continued to be a guiding principle. In spite of a steady increase of textual scholarship in the academies, the plays in performance continued to suffer extremes of bowdlerization, and were ripped apart, condensed, and reorganized to fit them to the scenic stage or to satisfy the whim of a producer.

The actors, on the other hand, began to abandon time-honored histrionic methods. A great many young actors cast in supporting roles—and some older ones, too, who presumed to the status of stars—had unfitted themselves for Shakespeare. The special vocal elevation and sustainment appropriate to verse-speaking had come to be regarded as pretentious, bombastic, and "old school," and actors tended to flatten out verse so that it was barely distinguishable from prose. Posture, gesture, and movement became with some actors so domesticated, so "natural" in a sidewalk-and-drawing-room manner that they bore no relation to the rhythms dictated by language written and actions conceived three hundred years earlier. Some actors no longer attempted to impersonate prescribed dramatic characters, but merely warped the characters into likenesses of themselves. Tragedy lost ground during this period, and there was a steady rise of interest in the comedies, especially those that strongly feature women—young, beautiful women, whose managers (and sometimes the actresses themselves) traded less on the appeal of Shakespeare than on the appeal of good legs.

As in the first volume of this study *(From the Hallams to Edwin Booth),* I do not intend to produce an "annals" of Shakespeare production, mentioning every interesting actor or event that appeared. I regret certain omissions—the lovely Viola Allen, for instance, who in the 1880s days supported McCullough and Salvini; in the first decade of this century played Viola, Imogen, Rosalind, Juliet, Desdemona, and the doubled roles of Hermione and Perdita; and as late as 1915 played Lady Macbeth to the Macbeth of James K. Hackett. Edith Wynne Matthison made a brilliant success when Ben Greet brought her to America in 1903 to play Everyman, which she followed with a fine Rosalind. Married to the scholar-playwright Charles Rann Kennedy, she specialized in his plays; but dur-

Illus. 2. Some of Miss Allen's romantic roles: as Juliet, as Viola, as Hermione, as Imogen, as Desdemona, and as Perdita.

Illus. 3. Stuart Robson and William Crane as the two Dromios.

Illus. 4. Nat Goodwin as Shylock.

ing Irving's final seasons she had been a worthy successor to Ellen Terry as Portia to Irving's Shylock, in 1908 she played Portia in New York to the Shylock of Albert Bruning, and in 1916 the Queen Katherine to Beerbohm Tree's Cardinal Wolsey.

Stuart Robson and W. H. Crane were a partnership of comedians whose *Comedy of Errors* was famous in the 1870s and 1880s, and Crane was often called on for his Falstaff. Louis James was an all-round tragedian, not one of the first class but one who toured extensively from the 1890s on as Hamlet, Richard III, and other "heavy" roles. Nat Goodwin, a much loved comedian, made a surprisingly successful effort as Shylock in 1901. Frederick Warde, whose experience was mainly in the country circuits, mastered a huge repertory, from Caliban to King Lear, and left an entertaining set of reminiscences, *Fifty Years of Make Believe* (1920).

To name these few is to sin against dozens of other Shakespeareans and part-time Shakespeareans who kept the plays alive when commercial managers were persuading themselves that Shakespeare was used up, out of favor with the public, impractical for the "modern" scenic theatre—"no money in it." My purpose is not to count the troops, but rather to sort out the major figures, forces, and movements of the time that brought the old way with Shakespeare, the "Victorian way," to its climax, ushered it toward oblivion, and thus cleared the ground for the new.

Since my first volume, *From the Hallams to Edwin Booth,* concluded just past the height of Booth's career, leaving one grand resurgence for him, it is appropriate to begin the present study with his final years—his partnership with Lawrence Barrett and their Shakespeare tours of the nation.

I think it fair to call the Booth-Barrett way with Shakespeare, in comparison with much that came after them, the "classic" way. By this I mean mainly

Illus. 5. Edith Wynne Matthison as Rosalind.

that they followed, knew that they followed, and were proud to follow, a long line of Shakespeareans dedicated to the projection of poetic drama (tragic, but comic and romantic as well) for its own sake. Booth and Barrett remembered the past and revered it. Of course, as children of their age, they shared in what was the obligatory fashion, the Victorian overloading of the stage with scenery. But as for their acting, they were heirs of the methods of the Kembles and Cooper, of the Keans and the elder Booth, of Macready and Forrest and Cushman. They were proud of that heritage, would modify but preserve it. Their theatre was an established art, mutable perhaps in surface detail, but deeply rooted in tradition. Their repertory was a body of acknowledged masterpieces—rarely a new play qualified for admittance. They themselves were gifted, fine-tuned instruments for performing those masterpieces. It was not their business to revolutionize the theatre (though building upon it as they received it, they might refine and improve it): their purpose was to communicate the *play* and the *dramatic experience* as skillfully as their elders had done hundreds of times before them.

When Booth built his great theatre on Twenty-third Street he meant it to be a temple of art, something perhaps like the Comédie Française or the great municipal theatres of Germany, to house forever the finest actors and scenic artists who would maintain the great repertory. But he could only look backward. He knew nothing about revolutionary movements in

Illus. 6. Louis James.

Illus. 7. Frederick Warde as King Lear and his son as the Fool.

science, thought, politics, economics, art, and theatre itself, which, beginning to stir in Europe, would one day render his theatre (had it lasted) an anachronism. He could not have imagined a Chekhov, a Wedekind, a Kaiser. He could not in his wildest nightmares have conceived the *Six Characters* of Pirandello ridiculing his whole enterprise. Seen in historical perspective, Booth, much as we admire him, is a fly in amber. And Barrett, too, a "lesser Booth," is another. Throughout his later years Barrett wanted above all else to build a theatre exactly like the one Booth had lost, and with Booth's same ideals. Death took him before he could make that mistake. Like another great actor-manager before him, William Charles Macready, Barrett wanted to create a body of masterpieces for his own time—but not by Ibsen! not by Zola!—by American playwrights, in blank verse, on historical-classical subjects, just like *Julius Caesar,* Bulwer's *Richelieu,* or Boker's *Francesca da Rimini.*

By 1890 the rising generation of actors, some critics, many of the public, the commercial-minded theatre managers (especially those city-centered) looked upon what was left of Booth and Barrett as outmoded, artificial, more declamatory than theatrical, used up—to be venerated perhaps, as relics of the "palmy days," but not to be preserved or imitated. What the younger generation in America wanted in the 1890s was novelty—in Shakespeare new personalities, new interpretations, new stage business, and ever more gorgeous scenery. They had already been titivated by the new ways and new faces of Fechter, Salvini, Irving and Terry—even Lillie Langtry, Margaret Mather, and Mrs. Brown Potter; more was on the way from Sarah Bernhardt and Beerbohm Tree. Never mind the old vehicles: personality was the thing.

Against this crowd of flash-figures Booth and Barrett, no longer "news," swiftly faded from view. Early in 1891, in fact, Barrett collapsed during a performance and died a few days later. Booth withdrew from the stage and lived on in retirement for a couple of years longer. The world rushed on without them.

Others will arrive in these pages whose conservative approach to their art resembles that of Booth and Barrett and whom I would also count as "classic" actors. Johnston Forbes-Robertson was one. Through his education and associations he was doubtless more sophisticated, intellectual, and susceptible to modern ideas than Barrett or Booth, but like them he was modest, unpretentious, and unselfseeking. When he played Hamlet his only desire was to express Shakespeare's Hamlet, not some special idiosyncratic Hamlet bred out of his own fancy. Nothing marks his selflessness more certainly than his eagerness night after night for the final fall of the curtain. Helena Modjeska is of this company of selfless artists, too, passionately devoted to the play and to no other objective. And Julia Marlowe—innocent, devoted, almost childlike in her eagerness to make Viola and Juliet live in the minds of her hearers—was utterly indifferent to what hostile critics said or what strangers might take exception to.

If Booth and Barrett in their last great swings from coast to coast displayed to the whole nation their ideal development of classic tragedy, then what had become of Shakespeare's comedy? In the last three decades of the nineteenth century, many actors and actresses played Shakespeare's comedy, but the comic center held, or was assumed to hold, wherever Augustin Daly—examined in chapter II—stood and issued his commands. Daly must have been a terrible person to deal with unless one had something he needed and were willing to give it to him. Humorless and dictatorial, insatiably egocentric, he seems on the record less a play-director than a lion-tamer. Yet he knew exactly what comic effects, what heavy dosage of sentiment, would please his public. His Shakespeares (after 1886 they were *all* comedies) were mixed among plays of modern vintage: melodramas that he wrote himself; adaptations of French society drama, some of them mildly risqué; and Americanized German farces heavily laced with American slang.

It would not appear from such a bill-of-fare that his actors were regularly immersed in any style appropriate to Shakespeare. Yet in everything they did, they were enormously popular—especially the "Big Four": Ada Rehan, John Drew, Mrs. G. H. Gilbert, and James Lewis. Mrs. Gilbert, then in her seventies, had seen or played everything in her time, but the other three were not experienced Shakespeareans. The adorable Ada Rehan was simply a puppet in Daly's hands, and without character, will, or ideas of her own, simply did everything Daly told her to do—adorably. Lewis was a brilliant little comedian whose antics fitted in wherever antics were called for. John Drew was a straight man and romantic, but so little committed to Shakespeare that when he realized Miss Rehan's popularity outshone his, he withdrew from the company, joined the Frohman management, specialized in parlor drama, and became a famous matinee idol. He did not touch Shakespeare again for twenty years. When he played Benedick in 1913 he had forgotten how.

Daly's professional ethics were questionable. He bullied actors and tried to prevent their advancement. He published under his own name translations of plays from languages he could not read. He hired or bribed some critics and so intimidated others that except for his last couple of years his productions were critically overpraised and rival productions were critically dismissed. His hostility to Julia Marlowe and the shabby tricks he used to prevent her success in New York are notorious. He butchered play texts freely: a study of his version of *Twelfth Night* is a revelation of his high-handedness with Shakespeare.

A comment of George Meredith's can increase appreciation of my third essay, "The Feminization of Shakespeare." In the second half of the nineteenth century women in great numbers emerged into positions of equality with men on the Shakespeare stage, and in a number of cases even took control. Up to Meredith's time (the *Essay on Comedy* was delivered as a lecture in 1877) women, for the most part, had been petted and adored by the sentimentalists—or in coarser society had been made to walk behind. In the Muslim world to this day women may not show their faces in public. And the proud Arabian male, said Meredith, "insists on the prudery of the veil as the civilizing medium of his race." Under this condition, Meredith allowed, there may have been fun in Bagdad, *"but there never will be civilization where comedy is not possible; and that comes of some degree of social equality of the sexes."* It is only *"where women are on the road to an equal footing with men, in attainments and in liberty . . . there, and only waiting to be translated from life to the stage, or the novel, or the poem, pure comedy flourishes."*[3]

In theatre (and dance, of course), more than in almost any other sphere of artistic activity, women have long been "on the road to an equal footing with men," and at times in the nineteenth century they actually took over management. In England from the 1820s Eliza Vestris was a power. In America Laura Keene opened her own New York theatre in 1856: occasionally she staged Shakespeare. And there was the indomitable Charlotte Cushman, half-woman, half-man, fiercest of Ladies Macbeth, who could cross the gender line, too, as the most passionate of Romeos and an imperious Cardinal Wolsey. The Cushman did not manage theatres but she managed managers.

In the 1870s and later many actresses assumed leadership, established companies, hired the best-looking males in the trade to support them as leading men, and packed them in with the rest of their baggage. They won control by determination, intelligence, sharp business sense, and their own drawing-power as beauties and artists. Meredith based his case of the importance of women in comedy upon the intelligence of Molière's Célimène and the wit of Congreve's Millamant. He seems not to have noticed that these same qualities in Rosalind and Juliet and Beatrice are enriched by a humanity and charm even more compelling than the sheer braininess of French court ladies and cool Restoration belles. The third chapter introduces a wide range of actresses, from true artists to mere sexpots, but all of them by one means or another asserting the eminence of women as Shakespeareans—a position they have never surrendered and never will.

With improved speed and comfort of transatlantic travel and American rail service, and with an increasingly vast theatre market, the United States was visited during this period by hordes of European entertainers, including the most eminent Shakespeareans of England, Germany, Italy, and France. As discussed in chapter IV, the variety of interpretations and styles of acting they brought us doubtless broadened our perceptions of histrionic possibilities, and freed our actors of certain ossified ways. At the same time, though, the extremely colloquial manners of a Fechter, the "personality acting" of Irving and Terry, the animalism of Salvini, the free-wheeling flamboyance of Beerbohm Tree may have led some American artists astray and disturbed without improving the taste of American audiences. Irving, who came oftenest of them all, brought—for better or worse—certain marvelous gifts: if not that of acting, that of physical staging. As long as illusionist scenery was the vogue he showed the ultimate that could be achieved in full-fashioned realism—in cunning design and illusionist painting toned with atmospheric lighting, far beyond anything American scenic artists had ever achieved. He showed, too, masterpieces of ensemble acting, casts ideally chosen and behaving with that clock-work precision which only a master régisseur like Irving could bring about. As he had done in London, he raised the social tone of the American theatre. Not to have seen Irving in all of his roles and be ready with enthusiastic opinions about them at the next fashionable gathering quite cut one out of polite social intercourse. For men of affairs or of the arts to be invited to one of Irving's breakfasts at Delmonico's was an honor to boast about for weeks afterward. And best of all, he brought the most adored actress of her time, Ellen Terry.

It is questionable whether Miss Terry was truly much of an actress in the absolute sense. Shaw said of her that "she never needed to perform any remarkable feat of impersonation: the spectators would have resented it: they did not want Ellen Terry to be Olivia Primrose: they wanted Olivia to be Ellen Terry."[4] And Miss Terry came close to confessing in her *Memoirs* that her acting was not truly acting but simply being herself in the guise of Portia and Ophelia and Viola and above all as Beatrice. Shaw, who made a special study of her, and in one sense knew her better than anybody, drew her complete portrait: her wisdom and her wit masked under seeming naïveté, her fearlessness, her compassion, her mothering instinct, her understanding of male pride and male folly, her loving heart—it is all there in Lady Cicely Wayneflete in *Captain Brassbound's Conversion.* In a sense Shaw did her acting for her: when she played the part she simply *was* Cicely. Audiences worshiped her.

Among other actors who came repeatedly from abroad was the most famous Hamlet at the turn of the century, the well-nigh faultless Johnston Forbes-Robertson, the actor for whom Shaw wrote the great role of Caesar, "because he is the classic actor of our day, and had a right to require such a service from me." Forbes-Robertson reminded insistently colloquializing actors what the English language should sound like, and how to read verse. Beyond that he brought a fresh, authoritative interpretation of Hamlet, full of surprising and right revelations. And, amazingly, by playing Hamlet in Brooklyn in no more scenery than gray curtains, and at Harvard repeatedly on Professor Baker's "Globe staging" he drove home the lesson that the play, not its trappings, conveyed the essential dramatic experience.

My fifth chapter brings together as unlikely a pair of American Shakespeareans as the age could offer—Richard Mansfield, the educated, sophisticated, many-talented artist, one of the most publicized actors of the time and sometimes then acclaimed America's greatest; and Robert Mantell, rough, irregular, a social outsider, at times just above the status of bankrupt vaudevillian, certainly unfortunate in his living. For half of the years when Mantell should have been rising in the profession he was banished by the courts (for nonpayment of alimony) from the sovereign state of New York and its great city, forced to practice his profession as best he could, unknown to fame, in the provinces. Yet which of these was the greater Shakespearean?

Mansfield brought a wide range of talents to the stage. A skilled musician, he sang many leading Gilbert and Sullivan roles. He was expert in dialect parts. Physically versatile, he could astound audiences with instantaneous transformations from Dr. Jekyll to Mr. Hyde. He was America's first Cyrano de Bergerac. A friend of Shaw's, he introduced Shaw to America in *Arms and the Man* and *The Devil's Disciple.* Trained as a painter, learned as an archaeologist, he loaded the stages of *Richard III* and *Henry V* with marvelously beautiful recreations of historical scenes. Yet near the end of his career he was labeled by one critic "Our Worst Actor," and by another "The Greatest."

Mansfield died in 1907 at the age of fifty-five. Mantell was not allowed to begin his New York career as a Shakespearean until 1904, when he was fifty. When he came back from court-imposed exile, he crept into the city, so to speak, through one of the least reputable theatres on Broadway, during the least profitable three weeks of the season. The more distinguished critics did not bother to attend his opening, for if they remembered him at all they would have dismissed him as an aging provincial has-been. Within three weeks they would learn that an earnest, perhaps coarse, but certainly powerful tragedian was at hand. During the next fifteen years Mantell returned to the city many seasons, bringing nearly a dozen major tragic roles. Even William Winter ("Dean of Critics"), who at first treated him with utter contempt, became his admirer, advocate, and personal friend.

Chapter VII, devoted to Julia Marlowe (and incidentally to her partner and husband Edward H. Sothern), is as much a tribute to Miss Marlowe's courage as to her art, her beauty, and her dedication to Shakespeare. At the age of twelve she left home to join a traveling theatre company—a children's company of *H.M.S. Pinafore*— in which she quickly rose from the chorus to the leading role of Sir Joseph Porter. This was in 1878. While still in her early teens, as an extra in the professional theatre of Cincinnati she observed at close hand, and *critically,* all the major Shakespeareans of the day as they passed through that theatrical sub-capital of the Midwest. Her young sensitivity and unspoiled brain found much to criticize. At eighteen, chaperoned, fed, and housed by an older actress who believed in the girl's possibilities, she went to New York, where for three years she devoted herself to private study of the ingenue roles she would begin her career with—Juliet, Viola, and Rosalind, of course, and certain popular roles from the modern repertory. When she was twenty-one, a manager put her successfully through a tryout tour of New England towns, a "professional matinee" in New York, a week's stand at the Star Theatre in New York, and a whirlwind tour of the Midwest. At twenty-two she engaged her own company of experienced actors (a troupe superlatively trained by Helena Modjeska) and was on her way to triumphant recognition in Washington, Boston, Philadelphia—everywhere but New York.

When she ventured into New York she was snubbed by the critics and outmaneuvered by the most powerful manager in the city, Augustin Daly. In all innocence she had offended Daly and Daly's most strident ally among the critics, William Winter. They drove her out of the city, and it was several years before she dared compete with Daly again. From about 1897 she was taken up by the Syndicate (the newly organized Theatre Trust, or monopolistic booking agency) and entered upon a period of financial prosperity and artistic starvation; for the Syndicate featured her everywhere in popular but trashy plays but would not permit her to do Shakespeare ("no money in it"), which was all she longed to do. Finally in 1904 she was, so to speak, set free. Charles Frohman, an associated of the Syndicate, recognized the immense possibilities (financial as well as artistic) in teaming her with E. H. Sothern, who had recently emerged from years of work as a popular entertainer and both produced and played a surprisingly effective Hamlet. It was an ideal combination, and for three years Miss Marlowe realized her long-postponed ambition—to play Juliet, Beatrice, Ophelia, the Shrew, Viola, Portia, (and later Rosalind) to the finest audiences in the land.

The pattern was broken in 1907 when she and Sothern, both now out of the Syndicate and under the management of the Shuberts, agreed to separate for a while. Presumably she expected to play her own repertory, but the Shuberts, as aggressively commercial-minded as the Syndicate had been, compelled her to grub money in two dreadful plays that surely tried her spirits.

What seemed salvation to her was the call to rejoin Sothern in 1909, to open and to direct the classical part of the program at the grandest theatre ever built in America—the millionaire's New Theatre at Columbus Circle. They failed spectacularly. They had committed themselves to *Antony and Cleopatra,* for whose leading roles neither of them was "right." And they were *not* to direct the classical part of the program. And the theatre itself was an architectural betrayal. At the earliest opportunity they withdrew.

This set them free again to resume their Shakespeare repertory, augmenting it with *Macbeth,* for a number of seasons. In 1914 Miss Marlowe was forced to retire because of illness, and then the Great War intervened. In 1919 they returned to the stage, where they persisted intermittently until final retirement in 1924.

Sothern was generally a less skilled, less attractive Shakespearean than Miss Marlowe, but he supported her loyally, and as Benedick and Malvolio, roles that somehow fitted him best, he was superb. He also loved directing and had a keen sense for set design. Though trained in the old illusionist systems of design (as late as 1912 he ridiculed the "faddism" of the New Stagecraft[5]), yet by the end of the war he came to recognize what marvels of charm, liveliness, and efficiency had been achieved by the "stage decorators" in musical entertainments. Following their lead he devised a system of simplified staging—a compromise between "representational" and "suggestive" scenery which served him and Miss Marlowe very nicely during their last seasons. Thus he carried Shakespeare staging one small step toward the "modern" way.

The Epilogue to this set of essays contains a report of the celebrations in New York and abroad in the spring of 1916 marking the tercentenary of Shakespeare's death. Here, too, I have taken note of the remarkable surge of Shakespeare production during the decade just before America's entrance into the Great War.

The Syndicate

In order to understand the workings of the American theatre in the early decades of this century, and especially to understand what happened to Shakespeare and other classic drama, or significant modern drama, in those days, one must be aware of the effect and after-effect of a bomb that burst over the scene in 1896–97—the Theatrical Trust, which came to be known as the Syndicate.[6]

We tend to forget, when we think about theatres and actors and plays and shifting fashions of theatre art, especially in times long past, that theatre has always been not only an art, but a business. If the heart of theatre beat behind the curtain and footlights, its blood was the money that flowed through the box office. By the end of the nineteenth century, American theatre had become a business of unbelievable complexity. Many hundreds of theatre buildings were spread across the country, some catering to educated and sophisticated audiences, many more peddling run-of-the-mill melodrama and simple farce-comedy to a naïve clientele; and every one of them needed to provide some thirty weeks of constantly varying entertainment. And dozens and dozens of companies were offering every level of show, from trained animal acts to Shakespeare—and every one of them was seeking some thirty weeks of uninterrupted employment.

Time was when the booking of engagements, at least for well-established companies, could be almost automatic. When the Booth and Barrett companies made their rounds during a season, the company manager, Arthur Chase, would simply arrange return dates for the following season. But suppose a newly organizing company, let's say in Worcester, Massachusetts, wanted to establish a route for its first (say, 1879–80) season. The company manager would set his opening week in Worcester for mid-September 1879. Then, during the preceding spring and summer months he would visit New England towns within easy reach of each other, picking up all the weeks, split-weeks, or one-night stands that he could capture. Then he or his advance man would cross the Hudson and work New York state, Pennsylvania, and so forth until his calendar was as full as he could make it. But there would be a few patches of dead time to be arranged for later.

Meanwhile a theatre owner or manager in Galesburg, Illinois, had been entertaining advance men from all directions. Some he accepted, some he rejected because the weeks they asked for were committed, some he rejected because their repertory was too highbrow or too lowbrow or too expensive or too similar to others already contracted. By the end of the normal booking season he might be left with three or four dark weeks.

The company manager from Massachusetts and the theatre manager from Illinois might then entrain for New York and head for Union Square, where on the sidewalks and benches they would find dozens of booking agents with notebooks listing needs and supplies all over the country. If lucky the managers would go home with their cards well filled. Or perhaps they must await the luck of the draw—accidental opportunities that would open as the season progressed. For many (perhaps most) in the profession it was a risky, nerve-wracking, expensive system. Sharp brains would one day put it all in order.

Illus. 8. Abraham Erlanger, a principal partner in The Theatrical Trust, called the Syndicate.

Just "by chance" one day in 1896 a group of "theatrical magnates" (powerful booking agents) happened to meet for lunch at the Holland House in New York. Abe Erlanger and Marc Klaw, partners, owned or "controlled" (by agreement, that is, they regularly booked) a good many theatres in and near New York, plus a string of theatres through the South. Another pair, Nixon and Zimmerman, controlled Philadelphia solidly, and regularly handled many first-rate houses farther west. Charles Frohman owned or controlled so many theatres from New York to Omaha (and controlled so many top-flight performers) that he could afford to work independently or, when convenient, join in with the agreement reached at lunch that day at the Holland House. He had a partner, too, Alf Hayman, who covered a string of theatres reaching from Omaha to the Pacific and up and down the West coast. Harris and Rich, who controlled Boston and environs, were not present that day, but joined the group later on. What the half-dozen agreed upon was presently announced as the Theatre Trust (cf. the sugar trust, the steel trust, the oil trust)—a monopoly of the theatre booking business—the Syndicate. All bookings aranged by these four sets of partners were to be routed through the central New York office of Marc Klaw and Abe Erlanger.

Illus. 9. Marc Klaw, a principal partner in the Theatrical Trust, called the Syndicate.

For theatre managers across the country this was

apparently a boon and a blessing. They simply sent in their requests to whichever set of partners they dealt with regularly, their requests were sorted through the exhaustive files at Klaw and Erlanger's office, and they got what they asked for or the nearest best substitutes. As the season progressed they regularly paid in to the Syndicate 5 percent of the box office gross, said to range from $25 to $250, probably no more than smaller agents had exacted from them earlier. They were satisfied. When Harrison Grey Fiske, husband of Minnie Maddern the actress, and editor of the *Dramatic Mirror,* who opposed the Syndicate, asked sixty-five managers to comment on the new arrangement, he got only six replies. When Joseph Jefferson, by-passing the Syndicate, agreed to go directly to two old-time managers because they complained that the "octopus" was strangling them, he found when he got to their theatres that they had by then surrendered to the "octopus."

It was only the actors, and as it turned out only a handful of the most popular (hence most independent) actors, who howled in outrage, for it was they who were most threatened. Nat Goodwin, Francis Wilson, Richard Mansfield, James Herne, James O'Neill, and Minnie Maddern Fiske, being much in demand, had always been able to arrange their own bookings, choose the first-rate theatres they wished to occupy, and obtain favorable times and terms from the local managers, who were of course glad to have them. But suddenly they were no longer their own masters. No first-rate theatres would be available to them unless they booked through the Syndicate, and they would go where and when the Syndicate sent them. Apparently, too, the Syndicate could set their financial terms—at least it is said that they drove Modjeska and Fanny Davenport out of the profession because they were getting old and losing their box office appeal: "the Syndicate would not cart old women about the country unless it could do so at a profit." The Syndicate was so ruthless that once they actually broke up a marriage when they sent word to Julia Marlowe that she was welcome to play with star-billing in any of their theatres, but Robert Taber, her husband at the time, could not. Only Augustin Daly had the power or bravado to thumb his nose at them and send his *Ada Rehan Tour* (which had become an annual event) wherever he pleased. But only once, I think. He died in 1899 before the battle could be joined whether he or the Syndicate was the stronger.

When the Syndicate began to lay out its policies, Fiske of the *Mirror* refrained from editorializing, but simply printed news and opinions as they came to him. This meant a good deal of *hostile* comment from the offended actors. One day Fiske's office door flew open and there was Alf Hayman shouting at him, "Fiske, I order you not to make another mention of the Theatrical Syndicate in your paper! What the Syndicate does is my private business and no concern of the theatrical profession or the public." When Fiske pointed out that actors, managers, and the whole public needed to know what was happening in the theatre, and that he would continue to print such news as came to him, "without fear or favor," Hayman was crazed with rage. "You go and do that," he yelled, "and I'll kill the *Mirror,* break you, and drive Mrs. Fiske from the stage!"[7]

From that day Fiske took up his rhetorical clubs and belabored the Syndicate without stint. Out-of-town papers joined him for a while, but since they were remote from the scene, their effectiveness was negligible. For a while the New York *World* supported Fiske by exposing Syndicate lies,—for a while, but when the cause was lost, it fell silent. Other New York papers were frightened off by threats from Klaw and Erlanger that if they continued to report or comment they would be sued for libel. The American News Company was forbidden to distribute any copies of the *Mirror* that so much as mentioned Klaw and Erlanger. When Fiske invented a separate publication called the *Theatrical Trust Supplement* (November 13, 1897)[8], the Syndicate entered a $100,000 suit against him. He was not intimidated.

At the urging of the editor of the *World,* early in 1898 the offended actors agreed to found an "Association for the Promotion and Protection of an Independent Stage in the United States." The members would play only in theatres whose managers would accept them directly, without intervening agents of any kind. They elected Richard Mansfield, the most distinguished of their number, president, and all met at his office one evening at the time he appointed. Half an hour later Mansfield sent in a letter excusing his non-attendance. The Association never met again, and by the end of the year all but one of the signers had gone over to the enemy. Minnie Maddern Fiske was the conspicuously heroic hold-out. She toured to Chicago in *Tess of the D'Ubervilles,* returned to rent the non-Syndicate Fifth Avenue Theatre, and carried on defiantly for many months with *Becky Sharp* and other significant (but non-Shakespearean) plays.

The Syndicate was accused of being unscrupulous money-grubbers, coarse-minded outsiders—Jews who, like Jews in banking, real estate, the clothing trade, or wherever money made money, would use sharp practice to line their pockets. Much of this was true. Obviously by their tactic of funneling all, or nearly all, the booking fees in America into their own coffers, they grew rich fast: it was common to car-

Illus. 10. Minnie Maddern Fiske, determined foe of the Syndicate. Poster by Ernest Haskel.

icature them as bearded, bald, big-nosed "Izzys" glittering with diamond rings, diamonded watch-fobs, diamond stick-pins.[9]

But when it was alleged that they knew nothing about theatre and cared less, that was not true. They certainly knew, as gentile managers and actors also knew, that theatre was a business and it could not thrive as an art if it were not successful as a business. Henry Irving and many another foreign artist came to America for a number of reasons, but one compelling reason was to make enough money to support their theatres at home. Booth and Barrett in their last great tours of America in the 1880s drove many "Jewish" bargains with local managements (sometimes carrying away 90 percent of the take): even when it was realized that they were amassing money for charitable or public purposes, or to provide for retirement, their "greed" seemed astonishing. But unquestionably the masters of the Syndicate knew the business of theatre from the ground up and they would be sure that from their point of view it would thrive.

Abe Erlanger had been involved in theatre from boyhood.[10] He began in the hat-check department of a Cleveland theatre in the early 1870s; by his quick wits he rapidly worked his way up as chief usher, as box office keeper, and as stage manager. When the Euclid Street Opera House was built he was made treasurer, then business manager. In 1884 he moved to the West coast as advance man, then co-manager, of a company trouping Bronson Howard's *Baron Rudolph.* The next year he began a five-year stint as manager of Joseph Jefferson's immensely successful tours of *Shadows of a Great City.* By then no one knew more than Erlanger about problems of the road. Marc Klaw, a few years younger, earned a law degree and in 1878 was admitted to the Kentucky bar; to learn a living, however, he also took up journalism, including play-reviewing, and became deeply interested in the legal and financial problems of the theatre. Early in his career the Frohman brothers, Charles and Daniel, hired him to prosecute a set of play-pirates who were bootlegging productions of *Hazel Kirke,* a valuable Frohman property. Klaw became the Frohmans' regular legal counsel, and learned everything about contracts, schedules, royalty payments, and many other legal aspects of the far-flung American theatre scene. In 1887 he became advance man for Effie Ellsler's production of *Aladdin,*

Illus. 11. Harrison Grey Fiske, husband of Minnie Maddern, editor and publisher of the New York *Dramatic Mirror,* which fought the Syndicate.

Illus. 12. "Our Old Friend the Octopus in His Character, The Theatrical Trust," *Life,* December 10, 1897.

met Erlanger, and joined in partnership with him.

Together, and gradually, they developed the notion of a systematized, centralized system of the booking business. They took over a large office in New York where they gathered and pooled all available information about the vast and rapidly expanding network of "the road" in the United States—the theatres, their stock of scenery, lighting systems, backstage personnel, train connections, hotel accommodations, restaurants, everything of interest to companies on tour. As they expanded their own controls over theatres and companies, they rented desk space to booking agents of lesser stature, and even shared information with them (while gleaning more). But finally, after that "chance" luncheon meeting in 1896, the Syndicate announced itself the sole power in the booking business and froze the others out.

Their hegemony was not absolute, of course. There were towns and villages too remote or poor to be worth their attention, and companies too feeble in talent to qualify for their sponsorship. There were barns, converted grange halls, abandoned churches, and run-down theatres notorious for the vulgarity of their offerings, where anyone could play who was willing to sink so low. In 1905 and 1906 Sarah Bernhardt gleefully defied the Syndicate by playing around the country, first in a series of skating rinks, and then in Texas and thereafter in a gigantic tent.

Unquestionably the Syndicate harmed the American Theatre in many ways. Their bad manners, as much as their merciless monopoly, created much ill feeling, mutual distrust, rifts of friendship in the profession. They dictated what plays could be played. There would be no more experimenting with the "heavy" new drama from overseas: no Ibsen, Hauptmann, Maeterlinck, Sudermann—advice from the field told them that the good American public would not pay money that did not bring quick money's worth in "entertainment." Their best actors were to concentrate on the "sure things"—comedy, ripping farces, fashionable dress shows, sensation drama (decent, of course) in well-worn molds. These were the money-makers. Shaw would not do (not until 1904 when "Candidamania" swept the country). Since

Illus. 13. Charles Frohman, theatre manager and agent, associate of the Syndicate, on board The Lusitania.

it was a truism that "the Bard does not pay," Shakespeare (except, of course, as performed by international celebrities) was out. Poor Julia Marlowe, who would have dedicated every moment of her life to Shakespeare, played almost none of him for half a dozen years before and after the turn of the century until Charles Frohman cunningly teamed her with E. H. Sothern and for a couple of seasons backed them to the hilt in Shakespeare. The public expected to see Forbes-Robertson's famous Hamlet when the Syndicate brought him over, but for Syndicate reasons, never made public, he was forced into modern plays for several weeks. Perhaps he rebelled. At any rate he did play Hamlet, to enormous success, and returned to play it again in sequent seasons. But after 1908, when the public got a taste of *The Passing of Third Floor Back,* he was forced to suffer through that maudlin morality play at least as often as they let him display his best art in Shakespeare. Over and over again the Syndicate suppressed, perverted, and wasted acting talent by forcing actors into long runs of unworthy plays simply to feed the box office.

It was particularly unfortunate that most of the members of the Syndicate were Jewish, the acting profession being almost uniformly gentile. In a period of rising xenophobia and anti-Semitism this provoked an especially virulent hatred of the "octopus." *Life* magazine, under the editorship of Charles Metcalfe, produced cartoons of the Syndicate that stand high among the most viciously racist statements in the whole history of American journalism.

Whether they knew it or not, few at the time would acknowledge that the Syndicate was conferring certain lasting benefits upon the theatre. They regularized the booking system, to the great advantage of theatre owners and performers alike. They built many new theatres and improved older ones so that they were fit for actors to act in and spectators to attend. They enforced contracts, so that both theatre owners and performers could count on the terms and rewards they had bargained for. They strengthened copyright laws and reduced plagiarism and the bootlegging of plays. They prevented the rise of amusement taxes. Such benefits were lost sight of in the firestorm of outrage when "art" and "artists" were subjected to laws of the market-place. Eventually, of course, the performers would redress the balance, would protect themselves from the tyranny of the market place by founding Actors Equity (1919); but in popular memory, the original members of the Syndicate are still regarded as a piratical gang of vicious profiteers.

One man among the "rapacious Jews" escaped the most savage censure. This was Charles Frohman, a man of taste, vision, culture, and fundamental decency, who truly loved the theatre, its art and artists, as much as he enjoyed power and money. And he was much loved in return.[11] Among playwrights of the day he was a trusted friend of Jones and Pinero, of Gillette and Fitch, of Barrie and Shaw. Among performers he fostered the careers of Maude Adams, Annie Russell, Margaret Anglin, Ethel Barrymore, William Faversham, Henry Miller, Sothern and Marlowe, and countless others during this troubled, directionless time in the American theatre. His death in the sinking of the Lusitania in 1915, when he was at the peak of his international career as a seeker out and promoter of plays and players, was a sorry loss.

It takes one fire to blow out another. Soon after the turn of the century a second business organization invaded the theatre scene and set itself up in rivalry to the Syndicate. This was the brothers Shubert—Sam and Lee and Jacob—who came to New York in 1900

Illus. 14. Lee Shubert, brother of Sam and Jacob, whose Independent Movement rivaled The Syndicate.

after some experience in theatre and some success in the clothing business in Syracuse. They took over the Herald Square Theatre, acquired a few others in and around New York, and calling themselves the Independent Movement, began buying or building first-class houses from coast to coast. Whether from the beginning they displayed any less commercial, more enlightened and art-oriented attitude toward drama and theatre than the Syndicate is probably debatable, but at least in business terms they fought the Syndicate and broke its strangle hold. By 1910 or thereabouts these mighty opposites declared an armistice and learned to cooperate. I do not know that either organization can be especially credited with advancing the Shakespeare program in America, except in a business way. When the Shuberts opened their Shubert Theatre in 1913, they had the good taste to call in Johnston Forbes-Robertson to dedicate it with his Hamlet. But both organizations, on the whole, have devoted their efforts to the advancement of the modern American drama rather than to concern for the classics.

Perhaps one of the most striking effects of both these commercializing groups—the Syndicate and the Shuberts—was to help bring into focus the scattered cries long heard up and down the land for an "art" theatre, a "national" theatre; or, considering the enormousness of the country, a dozen or more permanently established "municipal" theatres. Germany, perhaps, was the model most often referred to, where in every city a stock company of competent actors could settle down for long, even life-time engagements, prepared to revive all of the valuable classics and introduce into repertory all the best contemporary plays; where, too, visiting stars could pay welcome visits. One such theatre in America was the Boston Museum, whose splendid history of continuous playing ran from 1841 to 1893. Booth meant his great theatre, opened in 1869, to function in this way, but he lost it in bankruptcy in a very few years and it was demolished in 1883.

The cry for a national theatre was raised over and over by America's road-weary stars, and most eloquently by foreign visitors. Salvini, who loved to come to America, finally could not endure the ceaseless wandering—theatre, railroad, hotel room, over and over—gave up, and came no more. Helena Modjeska, who came from Poland and wandered throughout the states for nearly thirty years, pled most eloquently for true theatres in place of mere entertainment shops where ignorant landlords presented *Julius Caesar* one night and trained monkeys the next in brainless succession. But at about the turn of the century, out of dozens of such public cries—then exacerbated by the apparent sterilization of our theatre when the Syndicate and the Independents took over—there arose one mighty effort in New York to create an art theatre as splendid in appointments, as perfect in administration, and artistically as ideal as the Burgtheater in Vienna, the Théâtre Français in Paris, the Boston Symphony, or the Metropolitan Opera. This turned out to be the multi-million-dollar New Theatre at Columbus Circle, which opened in 1909. A disaster. I need say no more of it here. Its faulty planning, overblown imperial architecture, its sorry opening, and its speedy decline and fall are sketched fully enough in my seventh chapter.

The American theatre was not to be saved that way—not in multi-million-dollar marble palaces—but, ironically, in a modest and earnest, half-amateur, professionally despised, almost subterranean theatre movement well under way by the end of this period: the Little Theatre. Here vital seeds would send down roots and send up shoots of America's own drama of the twentieth century.

As for the future of Shakespeare after the Great War, that is another story.

Miss Julia Marlowe; a portrait executed in 1901 by Irving R. Wiles. Presented to the National Gallery of Art, Washington, D.C., by Julia Marlowe Sothern in 1951. Courtesy of the National Portrait Gallery.

Chapter I

Classic Acting of Tragedy
The Partnership of Booth and Barrett

When Edwin Booth put himself under the management of Lawrence Barrett in the latter half of the 1880s, and those "loving brothers," as they came to be called, carried their acting to every important theatre town across the country, those years were the sunset glow and twilight of Shakespearean tragedy in nineteenth-century America.

When Booth and Barrett ended their careers in 1891, some were glad to be rid of them, and to be rid of Shakespearean tragedy in the classic manner also. Only a year earlier the New York critic Andrew Carpenter Wheeler (his common pseudonym as a reviewer was Nym Crinkle) had published a manifesto entitled "The Extinction of Shakespeare."[1] He argued that the fastidious (effete?) modern public had "outgrown Shakespeare"—Shakespeare's tragedies, that is. They were insensitive to his poetry, had no tolerance for his stupendous passions and declamatory style, could not stomach his cruelty or his fatalism. Tragedy was dead. Our modern playwrights had invented Melodrama as a comfortable substitute and were already fashioning Comedy-Drama as a further descent from Tragedy's awful height. And as for Shakespeare's classical practitioners, especially Booth and Barrett. Nym Crinkle wanted them gone. In the *World* newspaper of March 8, 1891, he called them "mummified actors, who are enduring by reason of packed spice and frankincense, that keep them in an unchangeable and antiseptic condition." He declared that "nowhere but at a public funeral and a public performance of Shakespeare do we parade the relics of departed worth." Ten days later Barrett collapsed in the middle of a performance, languished for two days and died. Two weeks later, informally, but finally, Booth retired.

The actors, both of them ill and aging, had not needed Nym Crinkle to tell them that the end was at hand. In December of 1890 when they went to Boston to play at the Boston Theatre, the manager paid them a bonus to take their Shakespeare elsewhere. He could not afford to interrupt the run of *The Soudan,* a sensational British melodrama which crowded his house nightly. Booth wrote to his daughter Edwina, "It would seem that what is called 'legitimate drama' is about 'played out' in classical Boston."[2]

The end was at hand and they were kings without heirs—as a matter of fact, without kingdoms. Booth's own theatre, which he had built to house the finest actors and the noblest of the Standard Drama for generations to come, had long since been pulled down. Barrett, lacking capital and health, had postponed indefinitely the home theatre he wanted to build, where he could mount a classical and modern repertory. They could not find among the younger men in the profession any with art enough to follow in their traces. Their protégé Mary Anderson was supposed to perpetuate their kind of theatre, but in 1890 she left the stage to marry and live abroad. Barrett put his faith in Julia Marlowe, and after Mary Anderson's defection Booth, too, thought that Miss Marlowe was "the only hope we have."[3] Eventually, to a degree, she justified their faith, but only long after both men were dead.

Booth and Barrett had been a long time arriving at their partnership as "loving brothers." When they first met at Burton's Theatre in New York in 1857, Booth at twenty-four, blessed with the Booth name and gen-

Illus. 15. Edwin Booth in the 1850s.

ius and fortified by five years' experience in the Far West, had broken loose from stock work and set his course as a star; Barrett at nineteen, the self-educated son of a Detroit tailor, was just coming on as a supporting actor in Burton's company—Laertes to Booth's Hamlet. From the beginning they were attracted to each other and they would remain on friendly terms for the next fifteen years. But Barrett would be second to Booth as an actor—Laertes to his Hamlet—to the end of the story. Booth's career, centered in the metropolis, rose meteorically. Barrett's career developed outside the metropolis—in New Orleans, San Francisco, and dozens of cities of the South and Midwest.[4] Competent as actor and manager, he acquired a widespread following, yet from the metropolitan point of view, he would always be something of an outsider, respected for energy and ambition, but hardly in competition with Booth as "America's greatest living actor." It is probable, indeed, that his prolonged exposure to provincial and Western audiences during the 1860s encouraged him, as it did John McCullough, Louis James, and many lesser "country stars," to over-energize his acting, to broaden and coarsen it, and to fix certain vocal mannerisms which later on the New York critics would take exception to.

New York was Barrett's Mecca, of course. He had watched from far off Booth's rising accomplishments—the "Hundred Nights *Hamlet,*" the celebrated stagings of *Richelieu* and *The Merchant of Venice* at the Winter Garden, and capping all these the 1869 opening of Booth's Theatre, the most splendidly equipped theatre in America, dedicated, so Booth assured him, to "The True, the Beautiful and Good." He longed to share in its program, and Booth had promised him that its doors would always be open to him.[5]

When he decided the time had come to brave New York, he did not go directly to Booth's but to Niblo's, engaged by Jarrett and Palmer for a month in the late summer of 1870. There, with his explosive Cassius in *Julius Caesar,* he startled the critics into admiring him. He "rolled upon the stage like a red-hot bomb," declared a critic for the *World.*[6] According to the *Leader,* he "possesses the acting instinct, a quick, vigorous mind, a virile body attuned with a splendid voice, and a passionate nature which needs the curb rather than the spur. These are things not to be slighted in this day of Chesterfield tragedians. Cassius was, therefore, a manly success."[7]

Booth took notice. He engaged Barrett to support him in several plays during the second half of the 1870–71 season.[8] As a special privilege, Barrett was to have the theatre entirely to himself on Saturday nights to stage plays of his own choosing. And when Booth left town in late April, Barrett was to star in Leontes, a role that he coveted, in a brand-new production of *The Winter's Tale* which Booth had prepared for himself but never used. After Leontes he would bring out for the first time in America *The Man o'Airlie,* a play already famous in London. Furthermore, Booth was planning a grand revival of *Julius Caesar* for the 1871–72 season, and he would of course engage Barrett to play Cassius.[9]

Nothing, it would seem, could have been more propitious for Barrett than these arrangements, and when he left New York in February of 1872, after the gratifying success of *Caesar,* he and Booth were on the best of terms. Yet pressures were building that would dynamite their friendship. For one thing, Barrett's salary of $250 per week was at once more than Booth

Illus. 16. Lawrence Barrett.

could afford to pay and barely half what Barrett could expect to earn on the road.

Toward the end of 1872 it began to dawn on Barrett, then in New Orleans, that Booth was not re-engaging him. (He seems to have forgotten that Booth had told him soon after *Caesar* that "I cannot give you time next season.")[10] Then, too, he heard that Booth was about to star another actor in a play called *Marlborough*—a play that Barrett had brought from England, had shown to Booth, and expected Booth to star him in.[11] His temper flared. He accused Booth of breaking his word about this year's engagement and of usurping the rights to *Marlborough*. Booth's temper blazed. "Your accusation is utterly false and you well know it," he wrote. "You have no engagement with me—nor even a promise of one since you closed with Cassius." In his wrath Booth said other cutting things, the cruelest being this: "You are, physically, so unsuited to the character of Marlborough that I regarded your proposition to perform it as simply absurd."[12] Simply absurd!

Barrett responded to this insult with one long eruption of ice-cold anger—even his handwriting, usually illegible, is for once clear as print. He asserted his own eminence in the profession, ascribed Booth's so-called eminence to the toadyism of paid followers, and put an absolute end to their relationship.[13] Booth penciled on the letter, "Preserve this as a souvenir of the blackest ingratitude." For six or seven years they shunned each other.

Booth's affairs were on the verge of collapse. By 1874 he lost his theatre and declared bankruptcy. A year later he began the long slow labor of reestablishing himself and paying his debts. In 1875 Augustin Daly mounted two significant Shakespeares for him—on November 8 *Richard II,* which Booth had never played before; on November 16 *King Lear* in a "restored" version, the first Lear-without-Tate to be performed by any important American actor. Then he took to the road, where the money was, and set about improving his reputation as a "national" and not merely an "East coast" star. He toured the South, for instance, delivering 52 performances in 14 cities.[14] In 1876 he responded to John McCullough's invitation to San Francisco, his first visit there in twenty years. The Western critics welcomed him home, but being used to the robust acting of McCullough, the ringing oratory of Barry Sullivan, the fiery attack of Barrett, they hardly knew what to make of the quieter, more subtle, "gentlemanly" style which Booth had been developing for his more sophisticated Eastern audiences. Their praise was laced with hesitations. The San Franciscan women loved him, however, for his beauty of face, velvety voice, and gentility. His profit for the eight-week stand there was $50,000.[15]

In the early 1880s Booth crowned his reputation in excursions overseas. In 1881, after a generally disappointing season at the Princess's in London, he won glory enough during a month-long engagement at the Lyceum, alternating Iago and Othello with his host Henry Irving. In 1882 he successfully toured the British provinces. In 1883 he played his best Shakespearean roles in the principal cities of Germany and Austria, winning "laurels and ribbons galore," gold and silver wreaths, the admiration of German audiences, and the affection of the German actors.

But he came home exhausted, both health and bank account drained to the lees. Though he was not yet fifty, his hair was graying, he was dyspeptic, and his addiction to long black cigars (twenty or more a

Illus. 17. Lawrence Barrett as Cassius. Courtesy of the University of Illinois Theatre.

day) was wrecking his nerves. Careless of professional arrangements he fell in with wretched companies and cheap-john managements. Just then, too, in 1883–84 Henry Irving brought to America his superbly trained Lyceum company and carloads of elegant scenery for some half-dozen world-famous Lyceum productions. The critics used Irving as a stick to beat Booth with. Why, they demanded, had not our own "greatest living actor" done as much for the American theatre? Why did he let his plays be "merely pitchforked upon the stage"? And why did he act so badly, shambling about ungracefully, muttering indistinctly? A critic of one shabby performance of *Hamlet* declared that "the King had the best of it and was fully justified in trying to put such a Hamlet out of the way."[16] For two seasons (1884–86) Booth took refuge, so to speak, at the Boston Museum, which in earlier times he had deplored as a "grave of talent."[17] The company there was not distinguished for tragic acting, but at least it was a balanced company of respectably trained professionals.[18] Booth could feel at home with them, as with a family, and several of them were in fact old friends. He was at home with Boston audiences, too, who were honored to have him permanently among them. And he was spared the rigors of travel.

Barrett meanwhile was driving himself relentlessly. At first after the estrangement from Booth he kept to the country. In 1873–74, according to James Miller's count, he played 248 performances in 65 cities; in 1874–75, 210 performances in nearly 50 cities.[19] In the fall of 1875 he did a month in San Francisco and a national tour eastward. On December 27, 1875, Jarrett and Palmer brought him into New York again to repeat his Cassius in what was to be the most spectacular *Julius Caesar* that America had ever seen.[20] This was at Booth's Theatre, which Jarrett and Palmer now leased, and the scenery was basically that which Charles Witham had designed for Booth's 1871 production, only refurbished and improved upon by a scene painter named William Voigtlin. The cast was augmented by some 160 supernumeraries. The Senate scene, inspired by Jean Léon Gérôme's famous painting, was even more elaborate than Booth and Witham had made it. A final scene was added in which the body of Brutus was consumed on a funeral pyre. In a very long review of the production in the *Spirit of the Times,* by what one takes to be a elderly and very erudite observer, the "historical accuracy" of the staging is given highest marks.[21] To be sure, the low-cut gowns of Calphurnia were unacceptable, for "Roman matrons did not expose their bosoms and arms until the time of Nero, when the Empress Poppœa, that monster's wife, first gave offence to Roman ideas of modesty by baring her neck and arms." The scenery, however, was splendid, and our learned reporter identifies in the sets a dozen or more Roman buildings as attested to by "the most learned of living archaeologists, Baron Visconti." He approved Barrett's acting, especially his management of the toga, but it was E. L. Davenport's Brutus that threw him into ecstasy. "He might have been the statue of old Brutus himself, which, after a marble existence of nineteen hundred years, by supernatural grace was permitted to live for a brief space of time, like the effigy in Don Juan, or the Galatea of Pygmalion, and to enact by night in this master tragedy." One senses that this reviewer's love of "history" quite overmasters his interest in Shakespeare. "The illusion is often so complete that an hour or so at Booth's is like passing a short time in the company of those old heroes who delighted our boyhood." This *Caesar* production ran for 103 performances, and by touring it through 26 nearby cities the management extended the run to 166.

In December of 1876 Jarrett and Palmer set Barrett up in a grand spectacular of *King Lear;* but this time, lacking archaeological authority, they spread more quantity than good judgment upon the stage. As was customary in the nineteenth century they showed Lear's throne room as a "Saxon Hall," and they peopled it with a hundred or so extra figures—lords and ladies by the dozen, knights, guards, pages and *druids.* The *Spirit of the Times* critic was amused by the presence of druids, pointing out learnedly that druids had disappeared centuries before Saxon architecture was

Illus. 18. Lawrence Barrett as King Lear. Courtesy of the Hampden-Booth Library at The Players.

brought to England; amused, too, by the mistletoe wreaths "suggesting a German grocer's shop at Christmas"; and by a painting hung above the throne, "a really good specimen of the modern German school of Overbeck and Cornelius." At the beginning of the third act, while the storm raged, a thunderbolt struck a huge tree and sent it crashing down. Never mind that on that heath "for miles about there's scarce a bush": the falling tree effect had delighted theatregoers in other spectacles aforetime and would again, and it gave the old king something to sit on. In the fourth act Cordelia arrived at the battlefield sidesaddle on a real horse. But spectacle could not carry the tragedy. Though Barrett's Lear was generally recognized as intelligent, eloquent (except for such vocal defects as falsetto tones, sniffing, and asthmatic breathing), fierce when fierceness was called for, yet it lacked warmth in the pathetic passages. "It never moves the spectator to sympathy, much less to tears, not even in the painful scene on the heath," wrote the *New York Times* critic. "It is, in brief, an eminently respectable performance and nothing more."[22] It disappeared after thirteen performances. Booth happened to be in town, at the Lyceum, and his much more appealing Lear, revived a few week later, dimmed whatever luster there was in Barrett's work.

Illus. 19. Edwin Booth in the early 1880s.

For the next three seasons Barrett avoided New York, but toured with incredible energy—60 cities in one year, 103 cities the next, 82 cities the next.[23] About the end of the decade (probably in 1880) he apologized to Booth for his "mad" letter of 1873, and Booth proposed that they "consider it never was writ."[24] Their relationship thus renewed—cemented, incidentally, by the affection between their daughters—gradually developed into the easy friendship of the old days.

By 1885 Booth had so slowed his pace that he contemplated retirement. He knew, of course, that he would "have to make a tour of the South and West pretty soon for a final visit, and to replenish a purse which of late has been pretty well drained;" and one June day in 1885 in Barrett's home in Cohasset he said just that. Barrett, to whom retirement was unthinkable, responded, "By Jove! I'd like to manage a tour for you; it would help me very much and I'd feel a great pride in it."[25] On July 1 a contract was signed.[26] For the season of 1886–87 Barrett agreed to plan Booth's route, book theatres, provide equipment, actors, and a company manager. All that Booth had to do was *act.*

Barrett loved management almost as much as performing, and his talent for "running the show" was doubtless more valuable than his actorship.[27] Though he played a great many roles—far more than Booth—and was competent in them all, he was superlative in very few. His small stature (an inch or two shorter than Booth's five foot seven) somewhat limited his range, and his face, though good to look at, was not easily disguisable. Clara Morris recalls his "enormous brow. . . , and how beneath his great, burning eyes his cheeks hollowed suddenly in, thinning down to his sensitive mouth." She speaks of his "hungry eyes," and Otis Skinner of his "deep-set and burning eyes."[28] It might have been the face of a monk, says Skinner, and whether the role was Richard III or Romeo, Richelieu or Jamie Harebell in *The Man o'Airlie,* the same monk's face was always visible. His speech, especially in verse drama, was mannered. The critic Alfred Ayres, after allowing his mastery of stage technique, physical strength, earnestness, and a good voice, attacked every aspect of his elocution: he is always artificial, said Ayres, he never seems to think, he speaks his lines like a lesson conned, he is sing-songy and preacher-like, he breathes gaspingly, he never pauses, he misplaces emphases—and, to sum up all, "the actor that gets into the elocutionary slough Mr. Barrett is in is irretrievably lost."[29] Ayres was a notoriously harsh critic, but his was only an extreme way of putting Otis Skinner's more genial summation of Barrett's style: "There was a tempestuous, torrential character to his acting in many of his parts that swept his audiences into enthusiasm. In a high pitch of nervous intensity he would often shoot through these parts like a race horse."[30] Though far more ambitious than Booth, yet he lacked the one all-important quality with which Booth was naturally endowed, a warm stage personality. He earned the admiration of audiences, but not their "love." A certain steely hardness in him—Clara Morris called it "cold enthusiasm"—reduced his popular appeal.[31]

In every aspect of management, though, he was in his element. In 1869 when a group of San Francisco businessmen built the California Theatre for him and McCullough, his was the hand and mind that set that theatre on its course. He traveled to London to obtain fine costumes, established a sound repertory of plays and mounted them handsomely, and brought attractive stars to the California to share the stage with McCullough and himself. In his own words he "established a first class theatre on a solid basis."[32] At the New Orleans Varieties, which he also managed, he daringly hired a double company in order to have the best possible performer for every role. This innovation was disastrously expensive, but he revived the Varieties from what the *Picayune* called "almost a theatrical corpse" and put the drama "upon that high footing it held in older times."[33] By the 1880s he no longer traveled alone on starring tours, but like Booth, marched at the head of his own company. The telling difference was that whereas Booth hired actors randomly and left them to play their parts pretty much as they pleased, Barrett planned balanced companies, sought able actors, and drilled them into smooth performance with dictatorial precision.

He loved fine stage pictures. He hired extras by the dozens to build crowd scenes; he employed the most skillful scene painters, carpenters, and costumers to dress his plays to best advantage. His dearest hope, never realized, was to revive in a theatre of his own that grand productional program that Booth abandoned when he lost Booth's Theatre. He attempted during their partnership to persuade Booth to invest in his dream-theatre, but Booth spent his surplus fortune on a clubhouse for The Players instead.

Like the English Macready in earlier decades, Barrett endeavored to foster a dramatic renascence: he encouraged writers to bring him plays of "literary significance," advised them in matters of dramatic structure, and staged their works. The most distinguished American writer he drew into his net was William Dean Howells (*A Counterfeit Presentment,* 1877; *Yorick's Love,* 1878), but others whose works he staged included George Boker, William Young, and Steele MacKaye. In the last year of his life he produced Oscar Wilde's *Guido Ferranti.* His "renascence" contributed nothing to our store of dramatic masterpieces, for the best of his plays were blank verse costume dramas on historical or legendary subjects, grounded in an outmoded esthetic, mere imitations of imitations of Shakespeare. Yet as a manager and producer he won great esteem for his efforts.

Barrett managed Booth in five national tours. In the first of these, while Barrett toured separately, Booth was sole star of his company; in the second, third, and fifth Booth co-starred with Barrett; in the fourth with Helena Modjeska. The first three tours extended from coast to coast, the fourth was confined to the eastern half of the country, the last to a very few cities in the East. The following chart shows at a glance the extent to which the actors bombarded the country with their classic repertory, and what rewards it brought them.[34]

	Profits	Booth's Share	Barrett's Share
1886–87: 35 weeks Booth alone 232 performances in 60 cities	$ 265,554.66	$212,443.78	$ 53,110.93
1887–88: 36 weeks Booth and Barrett 255 performances in 73 cities	416,493.59	249,896.15	166,597.44
1888–89: 36 weeks Booth and Barrett 224 performances in 35 cities	249,749.17	149,849.50	99,899.67
1889–90: 31 weeks Booth and Modjeska 215 performances in 35 cities	207,987.84	124,792.70	83,195.14
1890–91: 12 weeks Booth and Barrett 79 performances in 7 cities	58,640.59	35,184.35	23,456.24
	$1,198,425.85	$772,166.43	$426,259.42

First Season: 1886–87

Barrett's management of Booth in 1886–87 was a marvelously effective rescue operation.[35] Booth had intended only to make a leisurely farewell tour and retire, but after Barrett sent him looping back and forth some 14,000 miles across the country, playing 232 performances in 60 cities, he emerged with improved health, firmly redeemed reputation, over $212,000 profit, and willingness to tour again. Barrett had planned the itinerary cunningly. It would expose Booth to all the best-paying parts of the country (only

Illus. 20. Edwin Booth as Bulwer's Richelieu. From the painting by John Collier, R.A.

the Deep South was omitted). It would cover certain well-populated areas with one-night stands (but never more than two weeks of these at a time), and after each of these sets of bone-rattlers it would come to rest in a major city for a week or longer.

The company manager, Arthur Chase, was a masterly conservator of Booth's well-being. Booth hated night travel: as much as possible Chase confined traveling to daylight hours. He booked special trains when they were needed for Booth's comfort, and after New Orleans (midway in the season) Booth luxuriated in a private car, the *David Garrick*. Booth was inclined to hole up in his quarters when not working: Chase would arrange for him to take the ladies of the company to visit Minnehaha Falls near Minneapolis or Shaw's Gardens in St. Louis or the Garden of the Gods out of Denver.[36] He watched over Booth's diet and saw to it that he ate in company: when principal meals were served on board the train, the ladies shared Booth's table. These, of course, were Chase's lesser duties. He paid bills, issued salaries, kept accounts, arranged hotel accommodations, bargained with theatre owners over future reservations and with railroad officials over rates, buttered reporters and told them the right kind of lies, wired ahead or gave to the Associated Press all especially favorable notices, talked up Barrett's concurrent tour, and during the season wrote at least ninety letters to Barrett reporting Booth's progress.

The tour began in Buffalo on September 13, 1886. After three nights there the company sped through Detroit and other Michigan towns to Minneapolis-St. Paul, their farthest point northwest. In more leisurely fashion they moved east again—two weeks in Chicago, a week in St. Louis, a week in Cleveland. They settled in New York for the whole month of November and extended their stay by a further week in Brooklyn. The first half of December was given to Boston, the second half to one-nighters in a dozen smaller cities of the East. They spent two weeks of January in Philadelphia, after which a series of five week-long stands carried them from Baltimore westward to Memphis, then south to New Orleans. In the last week of February they hurtled through five cities of Texas. A nonstop journey across the desert states brought them to Los Angeles for a four-night stand—then on to San Francisco where they settled for most of March. By the end of April they had done a week in Salt Lake City, a week in Denver, and a half week each in Omaha and Kansas City. That was the end of the tour as first projected, but Barrett and Chase between them set up a dozen one-nighters to bring the company home—from Des Moines, Iowa, to New Bedford, Massachusetts, where they disbanded on May 14.

The tour had been so thoroughly advertised that its very opening in September was auspicious. All that the Buffalo reporters wanted to know in advance was, "Is he all right?" Chase assured them, of course, that Mr. Booth was never in better health. No fears that Booth might fail diminished the box office: *Richelieu* opened at $1,374, nearly $500 more than Booth had taken in at his last appearance in that place.[37]

Richelieu was one of Booth's favorite and most useful roles, which he had played so often and so brilliantly that, for all its humdrum verse and claptrap moments, many of his audience probably could not distinguish it from *echt*-Shakespeare. He played it 46 times this season and used it in most cities to open a run. Its excitements provided a sort of a warm-up for the customers and himself. At the grand climax when, clad in scarlet satin and white ermine, he raised his right hand high above his head and stood on tiptoe to hurl against his enemies the "Curse of Rome," he dominated the stage like a flaming exclamation mark.[38] The play was a kind of front-of-the-tent come-on. Typically this season it would draw about $1,100; *Hamlet* a night or two later would draw from $1,600 to $2,000. At Buffalo, on the third night, Hamlet drew $1,900, which was $500 more than Booth had ever drawn in any performance at Buffalo.[39]

He offered Hamlet, his mainstay role, 88 times this season. It was not, we must remember, the vibrant Hamlet that he played for 100 nights in 1864–65, nor the impassioned though indecisive Hamlet of 1870. It was a more "level" Hamlet, somber and philosophical, burdened with doubt, reconciled to death—the Hamlet that Hamlin Garland called "the good man enduring."[40] Once he took up the burden of avenging his father's murder he moved relentlessly to that end, his emotions under firm control. Booth kept his voice low, deep, and musical, with few startling changes of energy or pitch.

He was too old, of course, to fit anyone's notion of what Hamlet ought to look like. Unluckily an English actor named Wilson Barrett (no kin to our Barrett) was just then Hamletizing in America and persuading newspaper writers far and wide that the true Hamlet was a bouncing juvenile. Midway in the season Lawrence Barrett sent Booth some of the English Barrett's printed opinions, apparently as a gentle hint that Booth should rejuvenate his Hamlet with make-up and a wig. Booth did not accept the hint:

> I return the W. B. bosh—recd. yesterday. Since his oft published comments of Hamlet's age the "critics" have gone for my thin grey pate & wrinkled face with a vengeance—even the friendly ones have been aroused to these disappointments. Well, I presume I must begin to shelve my inky cloak & rely on Lear and Richelieu.[41]

Illus. 21. Edwin Booth as Hamlet. Drawn by W. J. Hennessy. Folger Shakespeare Library.

The actress Kitty Molony, who had been placed in Booth's company by Barrett as a sort of secret agent, tells how, at Barrett's direction, she persuaded Booth to wear a Hamlet wig during the San Francisco run of the play;[42] but it appears from the first-night reviews there, which mention Booth's "silver streaks" and "glints of grey," that her persuasion was ineffective.[43] Sometime later he did succumb to the wig, but not until after San Francisco.[44]

The season prospered from the beginning. Business at the Twin Cities was "way in advance of any previous done in Minnesota."[45] In Chicago, even at low prices ($1.50 top), the nightly receipts usually exceeded $2,300, and there, for the first of many times, Chase would speak of "over a thousand people turned away."[46] One night in St. Louis *Hamlet* drew $2,621, "a regular crush," and about this time Chase was convinced that a "Booth boom" was in the making. By October 20 he could boast that " 'Mr. Booth's greatest tour' is now mentioned weekly from Portland Me. to Portland Ore."[47]

But disaster hung in the air. The day Booth took his actresses to Minnehaha Falls he caught a bad cold, and he could not shake it off. By the time he got to St. Louis he thought it had turned to malaria.[48] In Cleveland it worsened. And there lay ahead his month-long New York engagement at the Star Theatre, which he hated to go into. The Star was a wretched house—too far down town, too expensive to rent, too dirty and malodorous. "The Star stinks of mortality—dead cats & *sich*," he wrote Barrett; "maybe the buried hopes of decayed actors; some old Polonius perhaps lied rotting there—you can nose him as you go up the lobby; or mayhap it be the ghost who *scents* the air. . . ."[49] A week into his New York run he complained of "torturing gripes," and twenty-four hours later he was confined to his bed, threatened by pneumonia and suffering something like inflammation of the bowels.[50] Whether it was food-poisoning, the climax of his cold exacerbated by a chill caught in his unheated dressing room, or as Kitty Molony suggests, the psychic aftermath of her breaking her dressing-table mirror, he was deathly ill for three or four days. The theatre was dark for a week.[51]

Booth's illness broke the back of the New York run. The first week's receipts had risen from $1,100 to an almost respectable $1,600, but when he resumed playing the receipts were but little over $600 and they barely approached $1,600 at the end of the run two weeks later.[52]

Boston welcomed Booth with its old affection. For the *Hamlet* matinee at the end of the first week Chase predicted a $2,000 house, but for once he seems to have underestimated. According to Kitty Molony the orchestra had to play behind the scenes, their pit being filled with chairs to accommodate the overflow crowd. This was regarded as a "miracle" at the Boston Theatre, which seated 3,000.[53]

The river of dollars rose to a flood as the company moved westward. At Pittsburgh "the week's business was the largest in the history of the Smoky City."[54] At Cincinnati Chase had persuaded the railroads to run special trains from a hundred miles around, and in spite of torrential rains the week was "the greatest on record by considerable." One night of *Hamlet* there produced $2,749, another "perfect crush."[55] The word from New Orleans was that the bottom had dropped out of theatrical business, that Fanny Davenport was playing to $100. But Booth opened to $1,220.[56] Five cities in Texas yielded "the largest profit so far of the season," and more time should have been allotted to them.[57] The four-day stand in Los Angeles brought $11,000.[58] Chase instructed Al Hayman, the San Francisco manager, to *auction* seats for the opening night, a gambit which earned $1,500

Illus. 22. Edwin Booth takes the ladies of his 1886 company to Minnehaha Falls. *(Top)* Arthur Chase, manager; *(upper row)* Mrs. Baker, Kitty Molony, Booth; *(middle row)* Mrs. Doud, Emma Vaders, Augusta Foster; *(bottom)* Ida Rock.

over and above the regular prices. At the end of the first week in San Francisco he handed Booth a check for $10,324.73, which Booth thought was "a good deal of money for a week's work."[59] The four weeks' profit was $63,000, "the largest four weeks ever done in Frisco."[60]

The climax of the San Francisco run, at least for Kitty Molony, was Booth's Othello. Although he carried his Othello costume on the tour, he always entrusted that role to his leading man, Charles Barron—because, he insisted, Othello was "too hard work"—and chose Iago for himself. The great Tommaso Salvini had recently passed through San Francisco, and the critics, willing to allow Booth's supremacy in every other role, would seem to suggest that he could not match the Italian actor's Moor. Kitty Molony could not allow supremacy in anything to pass from her idol. So she hinted and pled, and perhaps because "Mr. Booth was already convinced that his acting was my chief pleasure in life," he consented: he would play Othello once and once only, especially for her. He would buy her a private box, send her roses and sweets—and on the night, just before she went to take her place, he said, "I shall act to you!" If even half her story is true she earned these ecstatic memories of his performance:

> And what a lesson *in method* his Othello was—for in this performance Edwin Booth utilized so very, very much of his art. Passion swept from him seemingly uncontrollable as wild fire, yet to the student observer right here was his art most calculated. He not only made us feel that chaos was come again, but he left us in no doubt what chaos is. In the big scene with Iago, I could only think of the crescendo of a great orchestra. His agonized fury mounted higher and higher until it did seem as if the gates of heaven alone could halt him, and if they did—what difference would it make? Did we not see him carry hell up with him? I was sure I saw tiger jaws shake Iago, for Othello was all tiger now. Then he flung Iago from him! Oh, his contempt for Iago! It was fearful. He played upon us in this scene. This word is misleading of his strength and sense of doom. He conducted his audience crash upon crash, until it could bear no more. Mercifully the curtain fell. The audience sat shrinking, gasping. It stayed quiet—until it remembered it was an audience—and then it gave way.
>
> Calls for "Booth! Booth!! Booth!!!" Flowers were flying through the air to the stage. "Bravo! Bravo!! Bravo!!!" No one thought at all of Salvini—not if those shouts and flower hurlings told their story true. Here was no longer a contest for the crown of Othello. Here was sheer adoration of genius.
>
> The death scene is a blank in my memory. I do not know what Mr. Booth did in this act. I only know what I felt. He had reduced me to an unthinking state. I was nothing but feeling.[61]

It was Chase's business, of course, to be avid about profits for his masters, and to measure the "Booth boom" in terms of dollars in the coffers. For him the "Banner Night" of the season was not measured by any one of Booth's especially excellent performances: it was a night in Kansas City when *Hamlet* brought in an incredible $3,668. The audience that night was "the most brilliant audience I ever saw, everybody in full dress & not one lady in ten with a bonnet on."[62] Chase was impressed on another night by a Mr. Garrett of Kansas City who brought to the theatre a party of a hundred and twenty-seven. He fed them a supper at $15.00 a plate, graced with six-page satin menus, and sent thirty guests who came from Leavenworth home by special train. The evening's bill for this "man of taste," as Chase calls him, was over $2,600.[63]

From the very beginning of the season Barrett was determined not to lose his hold on Booth. Before the tour was two weeks old, Barrett proposed that in 1887–88 they should share acting honors in a single company.

Booth was dumbfounded:

> "Thou torturest me, Tubal!" I have hardly yet recovered from the shock your letter gave me. My dear boy—I have barely set my foot upon the road, which I thought to travel for the last time, when you appal me . . . by your proposition to prolong the agony another weary year![64]

All the same, "a tour together would be jolly," and after a good many ifs and buts, on October 15, in Chicago, he signed the contract for the "B & B Combination."[65]

The burden of planning the next year's tour fell upon Chase, who began settling terms with theatre proprietors as he encountered them. Booth's only assignment was to assess his present company and recommend which of them to hire again. The task was a delicate one, for although Barrett was supposed to have given him a first-rate company yet it seemed to Booth "no better than others I've had the past few years."[66] He did admire his Ophelia, Emma Vaders—the best Ophelia he had ever seen. He actually applauded her from the wings one night, and frequently spoke of her as a genius. Offstage, to be sure, she seemed "off her head a bit"—carried a revolver, laughed hysterically at matters quite unfunny—but as Booth would say, "such nervous temperaments make good actresses."[67]

Among the rest he could find few prizes. Sarah Baker as Regan "looks antique enough to spank old Lear" and quite justified the Fool's quip about Lear's making his daughters his mothers.[68] Charles Barron, who played Othello, Macduff, the Ghost, Richmond, and Edgar—although he was half a dozen years younger than Booth—was labeled "old style" by Chase

Illus. 23. Edwin Booth as Othello. Drawn by W. J. Hennessy. "Put up your bright swords . . ." Folger Shakespeare Library.

Illus. 24. Edwin Booth as King Lear. Drawn by W. J. Hennessy. Folger Shakespeare Library.

and "slow and preachy" by Booth. He improved as the tour progressed. During the New York engagement Booth could report that Barron played Othello excellently: "he gets a regular call each night—which is genuine & deserved; he *belches* here & there somewhat harshly, but not often."[69] John Malone, the Claudius, could not suppress a foolish grin: "A star danced the night Malone was born—'twas far below zero and as the baby smiled at the twinkler he 'froze so' and ever since he has smiled—he even murders while he smiles: *vide* his King Claudius."[70] Carl Ahrendt played Polonius and other old men with a harsh German accent.[71] John Sullivan, the Laertes, was a "hard" actor, and Chase called him a "pantaloon."[72]

The case of Kitty Molony was embarrassing. Booth knew perfectly well that she was a pet of Barrett's but he could see no good in her acting: "Miss Molony is not at all capable—even for the parts she has played. I sincerely regret it, for she is a pretty & good little body; her case is hopeless." Early in the tour he pretended that he had forgotten to bring certain of his costumes, so that certain plays in which she had been assigned parts had to be dropped from the schedule. "In my paternal weakness I concluded to omit the plays rather than break her aspiring heart by casting others for them; she would have d——d both."[73]

Of Booth's company only Charles Hanford (Horatio, Lorenzo), Owen Fawcett (First Gravedigger, Fool, Grumio), and three small part players survived the winnowing and were retained for the 1887–88 season.

Illus. 25. Edwin Booth as Macbeth. Drawn by W. J. Hennessy. Folger Shakespeare Library.

Second Season: 1887–88

The bill of plays that the "B & B Combination" offered in 1887–88 was exclusively Shakespearean—six plays that starred Booth and starred or featured Barrett. In *Julius Caesar* (108 performances) and *Othello* (61) their roles were balanced: Barrett's Cassius to Booth's Brutus, Barrett's Othello to Booth's Iago. In the plays less frequently performed Barrett supported Booth's lead: Laertes or Ghost in *Hamlet* (37), Bassanio in *The Merchant of Venice* (24), Macduff in *Macbeth* (13), Edgar in *King Lear* (12). Besides acting in every play, Barrett, aided by the efficient Arthur Chase, carried the burden of management. Under this arrangement his share of the profits was raised from 20 percent to 40 percent.

The acting company, made up largely from Barrett's group, was much stronger than Booth's had been.[74] Barrett himself replaced "old style" Charles Barron. John Lane took over Claudius and Banquo from smiling Malone, and Ned Buckley, a promising young Californian, took Malone's Cassio and Edmund. Ben Rogers was far better "first old man" than the German Ahrendt had been. If Minna Gale, Barrett's leading lady, was less high strung than Emma Vaders, she was more reliable and more versatile—a capable Portia (in *Caesar*), Desdemona, Ophelia, Portia (in *The Merchant*), and Cordelia. Elizabeth Robins, just beginning her many-sided career in theatre and literature, played Calphurnia, Nerissa, and Regan. Gertrude Kellogg was a strong Emilia, Gertrude, Lady Macbeth, and Goneril. There was no Kitty Molony to tell afterward what happened or might have happened behind the scenes.

In spite of Booth's complaints about the pains of travel and the strain of nightly performing, this tour was more extensive than the first. They worked one week longer, traveled 2,000 miles farther, played 23 more performances in 13 more cities. To offset all these labors and make life on the road somewhat less killing, they retained the private car, now christened the *Junius Brutus Booth,* from beginning to end of the season and the partners made their home in it.[75]

The geography of the tour resembled that of the preceding year. They began in Buffalo on September 12 and played Detroit, Minneapolis, Duluth, and through Wisconsin to Chicago. After three weeks in Chicago they dropped down to Kansas City, expecting, of course, to attract the same munificent audiences that had greeted Booth in April. A new manager there, an entrepreneur named Colonel Warder, had engaged them for the week of October 24 to open his new Warder Opera House.[76] The day they arrived the house was not yet quite built. The walls were up but unroofed, and half the flooring of the auditorium and stage was not laid. Moreover, winter had set in early: it was freezing cold, and that afternoon while carpenters sawed and hammered, an inch of snow covered the interior. The Monday performance was canceled. On Tuesday, the carpenters stretched tarpaulins over the auditorium, moved in huge stoves, and finished flooring enough of the stage so that they could erect a three-walled set. This canvas box was supposed to protect the actors from icy winds as they went through the motions of *Othello*. By eight o'clock some 2,000 patrons were waiting to be admitted, and by ten o'clock, when enough scaffolding had been removed from the house to make room for them, a few hundred remained. Heavily coated, huddling near the stoves, they watched the show. Some stayed to the end.

As the week dragged on, the weather softened somewhat, and the company got in enough performances to complete their contract, collect their guaranteed $18,000, and be on their way. On the Thursday night there was joy in the house when Macbeth's Porter sang out his line, "This place is too cold for hell."

After Kansas City they worked across the Midwest and through Pittsburgh in a month. Philadelphia, Boston, and New York were each allotted two weeks. Baltimore, with influx from Washington, was good for one week.[77] Then from January 16 through February 11 they swept through the South, touching 12 cities from Richmond to New Orleans.

The practice of "scalping," then less harshly termed "speculation," was common enough in the wake of any successful show, but as Booth and Barrett traversed the South it rose to epic dimensions.[78] In Atlanta over one hundred men and boys, black and white, waited in line all night before the box office opened, each ready to buy the maximum number of seats (10) allowed him for each performance, which he would then sell for as much as twice their value. At Nashville, where the Booth-Barrett engagement was the greatest ever recorded, hundreds were lined up for two days, and $20 became the street price for a $5.00 ticket. In Memphis the speculators set up tents across the street from the theatre a week before the sale began, each man and boy wearing a number to indicate his place in line. One speculator, known to be an employee of the Memphis Theatre, profited hundreds of dollars by hiring eight men to buy tickets on his behalf. The boldness of this maneuver was surpassed later in the season when real estate agents of Salt Lake City advertised in the newspaper that they would suspend regular business for a few days while they bought and sold Booth-Barrett tickets. The actors' profit from this tour exceeded what Booth alone had brought in by about $151,000, but the public probably paid much more than that amount into the pockets of speculators.

Following Chase's advice the company devoted two weeks instead of one to Texas, covering 8 cities, and a full week of Los Angeles. Since both stars had recently visited San Francisco, the time there was reduced from four weeks to three. The flight eastward paused for a week at Denver and three nights at Omaha. Then followed a mad canter through lesser cities of Missouri, Iowa, Illinois, Indiana, Michigan, and Ohio. An eccentric but ingenious promoter who called himself "Daniel Quilp" detained them in Louisville for three days with a guarantee of $10,000.[79] He rented a vast Exposition Hall, brought in scenery and temporary seating, and advertised a "Dramatic May Festival." The actors delivered four of their tragedies to holiday crowds, most of whom could see the stage even if they could not hear the dialogue. Quilp paid the guarantee, pocketed $10,000 for himself, and invited the actors back for the fall of 1889 for double the money. From Louisville the company proceeded to Williamsburgh on Long Island, where the tour ended on May 19.

This season of the "B&B Combination" marks the summit of Shakespearean tragedy in the theatres of nineteenth-century America. Here, as had never happened before, America's "two greatest living actors," supported by a company of better than average talent, were playing Shakespeare's greatest tragedies to packed houses from coast to coast. Critics, especially early in the run, indulged in hyperbolic praise: Booth and Barrett were the peers of Irving and Salvini if not their superiors, and one Toledo writer would only grudgingly allow Irving a place beside them.[80] Critics also marveled at the fact that *two* such masters of their craft were not jealously competing with each other but were working together in mutual respect and fellow-feeling to promote the best interests of theatre art. In the light of their past relationship this was indeed remarkable. Barrett was cheerfully willing to accept second honors on the stage, taking his main satisfaction in feats of management. Booth admired Barrett's producing skill and was deeply grateful for it. "He is an excellent stage manager & not only executes his own ideas but carries out whatever I suggest," he wrote William Winter; and "Barrett & I get along cozily; keeping very much to ourselves & working harmoniously in every respect."[81]

Barrett usually scheduled *Julius Caesar,* in which the leading roles were so nicely balanced, as the opening play in any city. He knew as well as the Duke of Saxe-Meiningen that well-drilled crowd scenes compel respect; they also teach an audience that they are witnessing an entire play and not merely a virtuoso exhibition by one or two stars. At the Buffalo opening, the whole company rose to the occasion, and at the end of the performance, as Booth reported to his daughter, Barrett was in seventh heaven. Booth was somewhat rusty in his own part, and had to "feel" his way through it, yet near the close he was tendered an unexpected tribute. When Ned Buckley as Antony came to the eulogy of Brutus, he touched one word in it with an emphasis that it had perhaps never before received: "This *was* the noblest Roman of them all." The audience took his meaning—a compliment to the actor who had just played the part—and an approving rustle of applause ran round the house.[82]

But Booth did not always fare well in Brutus. As the tour progressed and he worked his way deeper into the part, he made it quieter, more meditative, more brooding and "philosophical"—more, indeed, like his Hamlet. This development was strategically dubious, especially when poised against Barrett's fiery Cassius; for although Brutus does resemble Hamlet tonally, once the Assassination Scene is past, he is left (unlike Hamlet) without much "dramatic work" to do. Barrett's Cassius blazed away as in popular conception tragic heroes should, and in effect left Booth's Brutus far behind. John Chase Soliday, who has collected notices from every city they played in, has found dozens of tributes to Barrett and many a disappointed report of Booth. In city after city his Brutus is dismissed as "cold" or "conversational" or "perfunctory" or even "dull and mechanical." A Cincinnati critic seemed to understand the situation and put the case clearly: "Brutus doesn't give one a chance to tower. And people last night wanted to see Booth tower. . . . The part of Brutus did not give him any opportunity to electrify his audience. That was disappointing. Everyone went to the theatre expecting to be thrilled."[83]

Along the way, it appears, Barrett learned to bank his fires and relate his Cassius closer to Booth's Brutus. A San Francisco critic observed that whereas his Cassius used to be nervous, feverish, and rather petty, he now showed "just enough and no more of that." By now "firm, controlled, dignified, he seemed not a kind of peevish conspirator, but a patriotic, short-tempered Roman."[84] Another San Franciscan recognized in the production as a whole a general toning down of energies consistent with modern subtilization of theatre art. In the old days, he observed, actors represented all Roman tyrants and patriots as "big lunged fellows who orated instead of talked and made speeches to each other in lieu of conversation; something like the lower strata of our present day politicians." Booth and Barrett had changed all that, so that "last night we witnessed a few Roman gentlemen quietly considering the best means to remove a danger that menaced their country." In this quieter ambience the critic could be charmed by the "extraordinary simplicity and gentleness" of Booth's Brutus, its "kindly, gentle side, and the almost religious feeling that Booth makes prominent."[85]

Caesar being their featured play of the season, they devoted a solid week to it in each major city—Chicago, Philadelphia, Boston, San Francisco—and in New York they showed nothing but *Caesar* for their entire two weeks. On the swing through the South, though, they gave *Caesar* infrequently, offering instead their second strongest "double star" play, *Othello.* Perhaps they feared that the Assassination Scene might stir up Rebel memories or even provoke Rebel yells from unreconstructed Southerners. Yet to present a "miscegenation" play was not, as a Richmond critic put it, "calculated to enthuse the southern heart."[86] When they played *Othello* in Montgomery, Alabama, a critic there made every effort, "vile as the play is," to do justice to the skill of the actors. But *Othello* "cannot, in the nature of things, be appreciated by a Southern audience," he declared, and if Iago is to be hanged, "the black-a-moor murderer of the fair haired, blue eyed Desdemona . . . should be hanged, and drawn and quartered too."[87] No serious confrontations arose, however, and as we have seen, the thriving business in ticket speculation indicates that the "best people" were more eager to receive the famous players than to make trouble over the race issue. At Charleston, "Even the social season suspended its operations . . . balls and parties were omitted or postponed and beaux and belles thronged to witness the play."[88]

On May 21, 1888, three nights after their tour ended, Booth and Barrett took part in one of the most famous events in American theatre history—the benefit performance for the aged and ill Lester Wallack, who had been one of New York's most beloved actor-managers. The play was *Hamlet,* the place was the Metropolitan Opera House, the cast was All-Star. Booth played Hamlet, Barrett the Ghost, Joe Jefferson and Billy Florence the Gravediggers, Frank Mayo the King, Eben Plympton Laertes, and John Gilbert Polonius. Helena Modjeska's Ophelia was so inspiring that it roused Booth, after his lethargic early scenes, to an impassioned performance. In every court or public scene some 130 "extras," every one of them an actor of great or rising reputation, crowded the rear and sides of the stage. "It was a stupendous affair," said Edwin Milton Royle in *Edwin Booth as I Knew Him*, "and probably the worst performance of the play ever given."[89] Wallack died a few months later, but his widow had the benefit of the $20,000 which the performance realized.

Third Season: 1888–89

When Barrett was planning the first tour of the "B&B Combination" he yielded to the persuasions of Booth and Arthur Chase not to prepare special scenery.[90] All the principal theatres, they argued, were well equipped to mount their classical repertory. This, however, was to reckon without the great many theatres in the schedule that were not so equipped. Audiences everywhere, especially at advanced prices, expected something dazzling to look at, and since it was known that the actors carried away nine-tenths of the box office receipts, they were soon reminded by the press that local managers could ill afford to build new scenery for them. "How will Booth and Barrett be remembered in succeeding ages?" wondered a writer in the Cincinnati *Times-Star*. "As two talented men who loved the almighty dollar more than their art."[91] The protests became especially shrill during short stands toward the end of the season. "All the plays were poorly mounted," was the cry in Indianapolis, "the scenery and accessories being absolutely shabby."[92] In Terre Haute, where Barrett had squabbled with the management about scenic arrangements on previous occasions, the manager this time grudgingly provided what was called for, but got his revenge by making noisy disturbances in the lobby during the performance and by turning Barrett's portrait, which hung there, face to the wall.[93] In Lafayette a disgruntled newspaper editor got the notion that the actors had insulted his city by using stock sets instead of the proper sets locked up in their baggage car. He sent word of this to Fort Wayne, their next stop, where it was published, and threatened to follow them and see that they were "brought to terms" if they insulted Fort Wayne also.[94]

Stung by these attacks, Barrett determined to mount the plays of the 1888–89 tour as carefully as he would mount them for a theatre of his own. He dropped *Macbeth* and *King Lear* (both of which Booth found too exhausting), thus reducing the repertory from six plays to four.[95] *Hamlet* was so universally popular that he could gamble on adequate scenery for it anywhere. He needed then to provide sets for only three plays—*The Merchant of Venice, Othello,* and *Julius Caesar.*

He gave his first attention to *The Merchant.* For years that play had been shorn of its final act, cut to half its length, and billed, together with another short piece, under the title of *Shylock.* But in 1884 Henry Irving had shown America his splendid production of the *whole* play, after which Barrett realized he could no longer offer the docked version. In Chicago in 1887 he had made a tentative restoration of it which greatly pleased Booth. The production "was superb and finely acted," Booth wrote his daughter, "and Miss Gale's Portia made the comedy delightful, while the beautiful scenery and costumes gave exquisite effect to the casket scene and the last act in the moonlight garden."[96]

The scenery that Barrett prepared for 1888 rivaled Irving's. Designed and built in Chicago (where it was first seen) by Ernest Albert, with the assistance of scene painters Noxon and Toomey, it was guaranteed to be "historically correct." Act I began on the Piazzetta of St. Mark's along the south side of the Palace of the Doges, whose columned facade filled the side of the stage to the audience's right. In the foreground stood the tall gray column bearing St. Mark's winged Lion, beyond it the red column bearing St. Theodore and the Crocodile. In the distance, across the Grand Canal, rose the distinctive facade and dome of the church of Santa Maria della Salute. To the left could be seen part of the sail and prow of a ship tied to the quay, and in the middle distance gondolas came and went over the waters. Act II, beginning with the first Portia scene at Belmont, featured a view from the house overlooking a terrace. The major actions of Acts II and III took place in the street before Shylock's house, which stood beside a canal. A huge bridge arched over the canal, its span so high that a gondolier could pass under it standing in his boat. Shylock's house occupied the foreground to the audience's right, its moldy and crumbling walls attesting to the stinginess of its owner. Jessica communicated with Lorenzo from a balcony of the house, and of course they eloped in a gondola. This set was said to have been modeled on a painting by Martin Rico (1833–1908), a popular impressionist who specialized in Venetian scenes.

The Casket Scene of Act IV *(sic)* took place in a magnificent octagonal domed room in Portia's house

Illus. 26. Edwin Booth as Shylock. Courtesy of the Harvard Theatre Collection.

at Belmont. The columns supporting the dome were of delicately colored marble, gray and gold, and in the arches between the columns great pots of greenery stood in relief against amber hangings. Through the center arch one looked out over blue waters to the skyline of Venice, dominated by the Campanile. The Trial Scene, called Act V, took place in a Council Chamber of the Doge's Palace: a reproduction of Tintoretto's fresco, "The Glory of Paradise," which Ruskin had declared the greatest painting in Venice, covered the far wall. Act VI returned to Belmont, a "dreamy Italian garden by moonlight, with rose-colored lamps and twinkling stars."[97]

It must not be thought that this scenic enrichment of the play, together with the restoration of the charming last act, in any degree softened or sentimentalized Booth's conception of Shylock. Into this atmosphere of romance and gallantry, Booth projected a greasy old man in a scraggly wig and worn clothes, the passion of greed stamped on his face. This was by no means the idealized representative of a persecuted race such as Macready conceived and Irving almost ennobled; it was a grasping, fawning, revengeful money-lender—the blood-thirsty Shylock of an older tradition, hated by Christians, despising their hatred, and hating *them.* Booth never "liked" Shylock, or thought he ought to like him, any more than he "liked" Sir Giles Overreach in *A New Way to Pay Old Debts.* Without reference to any issue of racial tolerance-intolerance, he simply took up the vicious wretch that he found in the book and presented him as he thought Shakespeare intended.[98] Such a reading was perhaps insensitive. Sociologically it was probably harmful. At a time when immigration of Europe's tired, poor, huddled masses, especially central European Jews, was at flood-tide, xenophobia and anti-Semitism were rising to fever-pitch among the Gentile Establishment of America. Booth's presentation of Shylock may well have heightened that fever in crude minds, and Booth was aware of the possibility. As he once wrote to Richard Mansfield, "It is not easy to estimate how much the antipathies to the Jewish race have been sharpened by those portrayals of the wolf-like ferocity of the one great figure that typifies the spirit of usury."[99] Regarding it as a specimen of acting, however, no thoughtful person could deny its integrity; no one could deny its power.

Othello and *The Merchant* were bracketed as the "Venetian Nights" plays. The Senate Scene in *Othello* of course used the identical Council Chamber set in which Shylock received judgment. Act I began in a Venetian street before Brabantio's house, "with its quaint perspective and its picturesque and seemingly solid mansions." This was followed by another Venetian street scene—often omitted—in which Brabantio confronts Othello. Act II began at the port of Cyprus, "with its view of the calm and sunlit sea stretching far into the distance, and of the curving walls of the fort, against which the waves seem to be softly breaking." Then came "the living room in Othello's palace, with its Oriental splendor of color and furnishings, its gorgeous furniture, its stained glass, its silken hangings." And finally, "the chamber in which the tragedy culminated, darkly bright with the soft and poetic radiance of a southern moon, with its bedstead raised aloft like a throne, and covered with trappings befitting the state of an eastern prince."[100]

The scenery for *Caesar* was modeled after Jarrett and Palmer's 1875 production, which Barrett had recreated at various times since then. The three unforgettable scenes were, of course, the great Roman square at the beginning, the Senate Scene based on Gérôme's painting, and the cremation of Brutus at the end. Booth was amused to see the "excellent representation of myself in papier-maché . . . made by our property man" . . . consumed in the flames of the funeral pyre.[101]

These three productions—*The Merchant, Othello,* and *Caesar*—probably constitute the ultimate best in "historically accurate" staging of Shakespeare, combined with superb acting, that ever toured the entire nation. From a twentieth-century point of view they may seem unnecessarily, even wastefully, overburdened, but in the judgment of their time they were simply "right." As the Boston *Post* put it, "Booth and Barrett are among the few artists left who play Shakespeare instead of merely "mounting" him. For this moderation let us be thankful."[102]

The acting company, except for the loss of Ned Buckley and Elizabeth Robins, was essentially the same strong team that had served so well in 1887–88. The tour lasted the customary 36 weeks and completed 251 performances. *The Merchant* and *Othello* each played 71 times, *Caesar* 51 times, *Hamlet* 31 times, and two bills of modern plays 26 times. The shape of the tour was radically different, partly by plan and partly by force of circumstances. It would play longer engagements in fewer towns—35 towns instead of 73—and only about a dozen one-nighters.

The tour began, curiously, with a week at the Warder Opera House in Kansas City, where they had nearly been frozen out the year before. They opened on September 10, 1888, in balmy weather, and apparently the week was prosperous.[103] From Kansas City the company made a seven-week loop to Minneapolis, Chicago, Cincinnati, and back to St. Louis. At that point, it appears, they were scheduled to invade the South, but an epidemic of fever forced cancellation of

Illus. 27. Edwin Booth as Iago. Folger Shakespeare Library.

all engagements below the Ohio River.[104] For two weeks they vacationed, and then settled into New York, where they extended their run to a leisurely but not particularly profitable eight weeks. Theatre-goers of the metropolis were losing interest in their aging heroes, who in fact at this point needed rest more than money. Barrett was afflicted with swollen glands on his neck; Booth was increasingly weary, poisoning himself increasingly with his twenty or more cigars a day.

On April 3, in Rochester, New York, after twelve weeks of playing through the East, Booth collapsed during a performance, partly paralyzed.[105] Barrett, in panic, announced to the audience "the beginning of the end" of "the greatest actor who speaks the English tongue." The news flashed everywhere on the telegraph; obituary notices were readied in hundreds of newsrooms. Fortunately these were premature. Ten days later Booth was well enough to rejoin the company in Cleveland.

The next 25 performances took them across the country to San Francisco, where they dedicated the new California Theatre (the second of that name). It was a gala night. Barrett told the audience they were "as splendid as any I ever saw in any city, not excepting the capitals of Europe," and described the auditorium (inspired by the architecture of the Taj Mahal) as "more beautiful than any I have ever seen."[106] The box office take for that evening was $5,980—by far the largest ever recorded for a performance by "The B&B Combination." The tour would come to an end, however, sooner than they had planned. Both men were too weary and ill to carry on. They reduced their San Francisco engagement from four weeks to three, canceled all further engagements up and down the coast, and made for home—Barrett to the health spas of Germany seeking a cure for the swollen glands on his neck.

Fourth Season: 1889–90

The last two seasons of Barrett's management added little significant accomplishment to the record. It appeared that the public had seen enough of them in the few plays in which they could share top billing, so for the 1889–90 season they divided forces. Barrett, taking Minna Gale as leading lady, went to Chicago, where on October 9 he produced a new play by William Young called *Ganelon.* It was handsomely reviewed, and it might have earned back the $30,000 or more that Barrett spent on it, but he had hardly begun his tour of it when the glandular affliction struck again. By December he had to cancel further engagements and undergo an operation. In late January he returned to the German spas to recuperate. His season had been a dead loss.

Booth retained most of the preceding year's strong company, but he could offer only the stale old round of Richelieu and Hamlet, Shylock and Macbeth. His drawing card was a new leading lady—Helena Modjeska, the Polish actress whose Ophelia had astonished everyone at the Wallack benefit. Although her speech was strongly marked with foreign accent, her physical beauty and emotional appeal had attracted an ardent following all across the country.

Unfortunately her repertory and Booth's had little in common, and she had to support Booth in roles almost entirely new to her. The Ophelia at the Wallack benefit which won her this engagement had been only her second Ophelia in English. She had never played Lady Macbeth or Portia or Bulwer's Julie de Mortemar in *Richelieu* (a role she despised). Booth could not conceivably play Romeo to her famous Juliet or Orlando to her Rosalind. He hated the role

Illus. 28. Edwin Booth as Hamlet. Drawn by W. J. Hennessy. Folger Shakespeare Library.

of Benedick,[107] but could do it, and since Beatrice was one of Modjeska's favorites he reluctantly let *Much Ado* be scheduled for some of the Saturday matinees.

In his letters to Barrett, Booth rarely commented on Modjeska's acting—or, if he praised her work in one line the next was likely to carry a qualification: "Modjeska's Ophelia was a superb performance—really *great,* but Julie & Portia were not satisfactory;" or, "I'm inclined to think Beatrice will be a fine performance; but her accent is terrible & I doubt if she can be understood."[108] Arthur Chase, who had to put up with her occasional displays of temperament and temper, thought poorly of her: "The Mme. is *slow* and is 'no chicken'." Or he would send Barrett clippings that suggested she was far inferior to Minna Gale. "There is no enthusiasm here & the plays go with little applause," he wrote; "last night in Hamlet she did not get a hand on her mad scenes."[109]

On February 8, in Brooklyn, she fell during a performance of *Macbeth* and sprained her ankle so badly that she was out of the company for three weeks. Luckily Minna Gale was not only available but ready in every role of Booth's plays, and we may be sure she made the most of the opportunity. After Modjeska returned, Booth had to conclude "that Modjeska's playing this season has thrown Gale into bold & most favorable prominence."[110]

Probably Modjeska was more attractive to the public than these comments from behind the scenes suggest. Her Ophelia, for instance, appealed so strongly to Edward Tuckerman Mason that he compiled a record of every aspect of her interpretation as he perceived it: in the scene with Laertes, for instance, her "smile of sisterly love," her "half-playful tone," the sadness and anxiety in her face as she listened to his warnings about Hamlet; the pathos of her mad scenes as her voice broke from singing to smothered laughter to loud full laughter to hysterical weeping.[111] It did happen that the box office receipts declined by a few hundred dollars a week from the

Illus. 29. Helena Modjeska as Ophelia to Booth's Hamlet in his 1889–90 season. Folger Shakespeare Library.

preceding season, but that may have been as much Booth's fault as Modjeska's. His energy was certainly at a low ebb. Late in November, after an exhausting week of Macbeth, he used health as an issue to argue down some of Barrett's ambitious plans for the *next* season:

There must be no more Matinees, no more one night jumps for me—I can't stand it. Yesterday I acted Richelieu—barely able to force myself through it, owing to the previous night's fatigue, and in the evening I suffered tortures throughout Macbeth. The vertigo which afflicts me & the lack of physical strength are apparent to all, & to me it (the vertigo) is dangerous as well as distressing. The vigor that I occasionally manifest is nervous force merely which, like a stimulant, leaves me in a collapsed condition.[112]

In his report to Barrett after the New York opening of *The Merchant,* Chase included a graphic account of between-the-acts behavior of certain critics:

The papers here are very severe on Modjeska and not favorable to Mr. B. Joe Howard came in the box office last night between the acts, he had been drinking and talked loud, he said the house was d—— bad and he was d—— glad of it. I simply asked him *why* he was glad, he replied because it showed that the public would not patronize a queer performance, that Mr. B. no longer tried to act but walked through his parts, and was again surrounded with a "lot of sticks," and that it was high time he retired. I told him the season's statement told a very different story. Alfred Ayres a few nights since gave me the same argument. I told him he had the right to criticise the performances in his newspaper work but for him to come to me in the front of the house . . . to tell me how bad he considered the attractions, I thought it very bad taste on his part and I was tired of listening to it.

Nym Crinkle (the *World*) was complaining, too, and the *Herald* critic was downright hostile. They sounded like hounds moving in for the kill.[113]

Whatever their weaknesses, though, the company fought along to May 10, completing 214 performances in 31 weeks, visiting 41 cities of the northern and eastern states. For the first time under Barrett's management Booth did not venture farther west than St. Louis.

Fifth Season, 1890–91

The final season of the partnership was brief and disastrous. Home from Germany in the summer of 1890, healthy (he thought) and, as always, ready for the fray, Barrett booked a tour for the whole season. He began in Milwaukee in late September. Booth, who had declined to perform more than fifteen weeks, joined him in Baltimore on November 3, and they played their standard joint repertory for seven weeks in 4 cities. On December 20, Booth went into hibernation for the ten winter weeks. Barrett took the Broadway Theatre in New York, and through January and February exhibited a whole series of his modern plays. He revived *Ganelon* and *Francesca da Rimini,* got up for the first time Oscar Wilde's hitherto unproduced *Guido Ferranti,* and then, as if reviewing his whole career as a champion of contemporary playwrights, revived several of his favorites, including *Yorick's Love* and *The Man o'Airlie.*[114] He was killing himself with overwork.

Soon after March 2, when Booth rejoined him, Barrett caught a severe cold. On March 18, midway in his performance of de Mauprat in *Richelieu* he whispered to Booth, "I can't go on." Another actor finished the play for him while attendants got him to his hotel and to bed. Pneumonia set in. On the evening of March 20 he died.

Booth carried on for a few nights to fill out contractual agreements, and on April 4, at the Brooklyn Academy of Music, he played his last Hamlet. Or murmured it: many in the audience could barely hear him. At the final call he spoke a few words of farewell and, without fanfare or formal announcement, left the stage forever.

The theatre historian George Odell began his playgoing when Booth was still "the greatest actor in the world, certainly in the English-speaking world," and Barrett was "a noble, if less brilliant associate." Half a century after their careers ended, he pronounced upon their decline and fall with what seems to us now appropriate generosity: "The passing of Booth and Barrett closed an epoch in American theatrical history. If, as Garrick is said to have said, tragedy died with Mrs. Cibber, in America it died with Booth and Barrett. . . . The grand style was gone, leaving us poor indeed."[115]

Chapter II

Augustin Daly and the Shakespeare Comedies

Although it was not literally true that as Nym Crinkle insisted in 1890, "tragedy was dead," yet public appetite was turning away from Shakespeare's tragedies toward his comedies and romances. The principal American purveyor of these was Augustin Daly (1835–1899).[1]

Daly never acted. Unlike Booth and Barrett, the actor-managers, Daly was solely a manager, dedicated to gratifying his own sense of what was "good theatre." When he took up management he announced that he would support whatever, in his lights, was novel and entertaining in contemporary drama, and revive whatever, in his lights, was rare and worthy in the legitimate drama of the past.[2] Anything seen or heard upon his stage had to be sentimentally appealing and morally unobjectionable, for "his lights" were blinkered by the restraints which society and the theatre world imposed upon him. At one time, perhaps in defense of some mildly "dangerous" play, he insisted to William Winter that "everyday life is as proper . . . to discuss upon the stage as it is in the pulpit, the Senate chamber, or the columns of a paper"—but he did not, of course, define how much of "everyday life" was publicly discussable in any forum, and in any case, as he assured Winter, on his stage the terrible lessons that life teaches us would be softened by "gentle contrasts."[3] As for staging Shakespeare, he said, "We want to make Shakespeare attractive to the masses, and to that end . . . we must concede something to them." He meant, in fact, that we must mount and dress Shakespeare prettily; he also meant that we must make him "clean."[4]

From his boyhood days, the theatre was Daly's all-consuming preoccupation. His devotion to the theatre was cleverly explained by the English artist W. Graham Robertson, who saw it as wholly a matter of self-fulfillment: "Daly must have been a great actor who could not act. He was rough and uncouth, with harsh utterance and uncultured accent; a singer without a voice, a musician without an instrument." So he used his performers to do what he himself longed to do but could not. A performer who did not respond to his direction as a fine violin to a master fiddler would not thrive in his company. In the long run it was only through Ada Rehan, with whom, says Graham Robertson, he played out in real life the Svengali-Trilby drama of du Maurier's romance, that he found the perfect means of self-expression that he craved.[5]

Nym Crinkle understood this relationship very clearly. In one of his feuilletons for the *Dramatic Mirror,* he passed a series of remarks on Miss Rehan's Helena in *A Midsummer Night's Dream.* "It is malapropos," he wrote, "to ask if Miss Rehan plays Helena with the slightest variation from the other parts she has played. . . . Miss Rehan plays Helena as Mr. Daly wants her to play it." Then he generalized: "Obedience is the first law in Mr. Daly's theatre." Mr. Daly, Nym Crinkle said, controls every movement of every actor, every fairy, every super, the angle of every piece of furniture in his production of the *Dream.* "There isn't a hairpin that doesn't get its point from him." And as for Miss Rehan, she is

> a ductile comedienne, and her ductility is as uniform as the phrases it elicits. She was delightful and sweet as Katherine (in the *Shrew*), and she is sweet and delightful as Helena. She is a perpetual amalgam of sweetness and light. But really I wonder if she thinks it is her light, or if she has come . . . to understand that she is the moon and Daly is her sun.[6]

Bernard Shaw came to a similar conclusion—or, rather, the question—whether Miss Rehan was an

Illus. 30. Augustin Daly, manager. Folger Shakespeare Library.

Illus. 31. Ada Rehan, Daly's leading lady. Folger Shakespeare Library.

actress or an automaton. In 1897 he was speaking of her Rosalind: "If *As You Like It* were a typical Shakespearean play, I should unhesitatingly declare Miss Rehan the most perfect Shakespearean executant in the world." But when he thinks of the roles she doesn't play—Helena in *All's Well,* Isabella in *Measure for Measure,* Cressida, those characters in which Shakespeare makes serious attempts to hold the mirror up to nature—then he wonders.

> Rosalind is not a complete human being: she is simply an extension into five acts of the most affectionate, fortunate, delightful five minutes in the life of a delightful woman. . . . I cannot judge from Miss Rehan's enchanting Rosalind whether she is a great Shakespearean actress or not: There is even a sense in which I cannot tell whether she can act at all or not. So far I have never seen her create a character: she has always practised the same adorable arts on me, by whatever name the playbill called her. . . . I have never complained. . . . In Shakespear (what Mr. Daly leaves of him) she was and is irresistible: at Islington on Monday she made me cry faster than Mr. Daly could make me swear. But the critic in me is bound to insist that Ada Rehan has as yet created nothing but Ada Rehan. She will probably never excel that masterpiece; but why should she not superimpose a character study or two on it![7]

Shaw would return to this theme again, recognizing with some indignation that Daly controlled her and used her and prevented her from the full use and development of her natural gifts.

Miss Rehan joined Daly's company in 1879, became his leading lady, ultimately his "star" and partner, and almost certainly his mistress.[8] Daly had her in his mind's eye when he described the heroine of his book about Peg Woffington: "She was possessed of the tempting beauty of eye and mouth, the glowing health, the flashing wit, the sprightly humor and the quick intelligence of the native-born Irish girl."[9] She was tall, well-built (a little on the heavy side), handsome rather than pretty, velvet-voiced, warm-hearted with friends though shy and silent among strangers. She became one of the most admired actresses, or personalities, of her day—not, it appears, by her own initiative and volition but by surrendering herself totally to Daly. When Daly died, her actorship died, and she knew it. "This has been a great blow to me," she wrote to William Winter. "I am very indifferent to the future. If I ever go on again with my work, I fear it will be more of the machine than the artiste. . . . I was fully alive to all he ever did for me and he knew my

Illus. 32. John Drew, Daly's leading man. Folger Shakespeare Library.

Illus. 33. James Lewis, Daly's principal comedian. Courtesy of the University of Illinois Theatre.

devotion to him and his ambitions. It was so well understood between us that we had really grown into being One."[10] Though she lived for many more years, her artistic life was ended. When she went on the road in 1904–5 in her favorite old parts—Katherine the Shrew, Portia, and Lady Teazle, her co-star Otis Skinner reports that "the exquisite comedienne with whom I had the happiest memories of five years' association was no more. . . . Augustin Daly was dead and without him she was helpless."[11]

Daly's actors generally referred to him as "The Governor." Those who left his service were wont to describe him as a god in his little heaven or a despot in his kingdom. For although he could be genial, generous, and affectionate with the few friends he had time for, in the theatre he drove his actors with whip and spur. Self-centered, willful, austere, abrupt in decision and certain of his rightness, he brooked no resistance to his directions, which were commands. When Charles Fechter once insisted on having his own way in a certain scene, said Daly, "I turned to him and told him what I thought of him and of his acting and his conduct, and I made it perfectly clear that I intended to be, *at all times and in all circumstances,* the manager and absolute master of my theatre. We never had any trouble after that."[12]

Daly made every effort to control the New York press.[13] He practically bought and paid for William Winter of the *Tribune,* known as the "Dean of Critics." He paid Winter for arranging acting versions of classic plays, for vetting the texts of plays about to be produced, for writing introductions to the Daly acting editions. He lent Winter money. He paid Winter's expenses to Europe when the Daly company was taking a production abroad. He engaged Winter to write a book about Ada Rehan. Of course he did not pay Winter for writing up his productions in the *Tribune.* These gigantic reviews, obviously prepared in advance, were labors of love, for Winter believed in Daly devoutly, and especially in Daly's handling of Shakespeare and the classics. And Winter adored Ada Rehan and would exalt her above any rival.

Daly's relations with Edward Dithmar of the *New York Times* were less intimate, but he had Dithmar in his pocket. The *Times* reviews, if less magniloquent than Winter's, were highly celebrational. Dithmar produced a book called *Memories of Daly's Theatres* in praise of Daly and his company. In 1888 half a dozen critics were persuaded by Daly to collaborate in *A Portfolio of Players,* glorifying actors in his company. He hired critics to scout for useful plays in foreign

Illus. 34. Mrs. George Gilbert, Daly's comic Old Lady. Folger Shakespeare Library.

Illus. 35. Edward A. Dithmar, theatre critic for the *New York Times,* 1884–1901.

languages and translate them for him.

Occasionally a hostile review would so enrage him that he would ban, or attempt to ban, the critic from his theatre. This happened to Charles Meltzer of the *Herald* for objecting to Daly's *School for Scandal.* It happened to Norman Hapgood of the *Commercial Advertiser* for preferring Julia Marlowe's Rosalind over Ada Rehan's. Daly, furious, announced that the *Commercial Advertiser* would no longer be favored with Daly's advertisements, and the paper itself would no longer be found in "Daly's Theatre's reading room." Hapgood amused himself by printing comments on Daly's bluster, culled from a half a dozen newspapers across the country.[14] The Chicago *Evening Post* used the occasion to point out that "It has long been a matter of common knowledge that Augustin Daly has attempted to control the dramatic criticism in New York." The most laughable item Hapgood included was:

At first this created great consternation in newspaper circles, all editors warned their dramatic critics to go gently with Mr. Daly's Miss Rehan, lest a like calamity should befall their publications. They lived in mortal fear of being debarred from the Daly reading room until it was found that there was no reading room at Daly's.

Daly's bullying of the press did have its certain effect, and we cannot know how many worthy young actors and actresses suffered from press attacks which Daly suborned or inspired. The case of Julia Marlowe, as we shall see, is well documented.

Daly was feverishly secretive about his work, his plans, his methods. Members of his company were enjoined "never to allow a reporter to interview us on any pretext whatever." Rehearsals were strictly closed.[15] No one could bring up a matter of business with him except in his office and by appointment—in fact no one was permitted to say so much as "good morning" to him unless Daly spoke first. The actors were instructed not to walk along Broadway lest they be recognized as members of the company and be accosted by strangers.[16]

By most accounts Daly was a great teacher of acting, with a knack for spotting talent in novices, especially

Illus. 36. William Winter, "Dean of Critics," theatre critic for the New York *Tribune,* 1865–1909. Folger Shakespeare Library.

young women, and bringing their art to fulfillment. "I believe he could teach a broomstick to act," said Dora Knowlton, who had once spent a season as a "Daly Debutante"; "he shows everyone just how to move, to speak, to look; he seems to know instinctively just how everything should go to get the best effect." Miss Knowlton describes vividly his manner of conducting rehearsals:

> Mr. Daly usually sits in one of the orchestra chairs during rehearsals, about five rows back, with folded arms, hat on the back of his head, watching everything with those keen blue eyes; suddenly he will stop someone in the midst of a speech and request that person to repeat the lines or perform some bit of business in a different manner. Then, if the change does not suit him, he springs to his feet and rushes up on the stage, striding over the backs of the chairs and along a plank laid from the orchestra railings across the footlights. He darts about the stage, with his coat-tails fairly flying, while he talks fast, gesticulates emphatically, and assumes the most peculiar attitudes to illustrate his meaning, winding up with "Now do you see?" Then he strides over the chairs again, sits down and the rehearsal goes on.

It took Miss Knowlton (a delicately nurtured young lady) some weeks to get used to the "very strong language" Daly used with his carpenters and scene painters when *their* work went awry.[17]

Illus. 37. Dora Knowlton, a "Daly Debutante" for one season, wrote a book about it. Later a publisher's editor and translator.

Daly wanted to abolish the actors' traditional concepts of "lines" and "stars." When an applicant began his interview with "My line is . . .," Daly would cut him off with, "There is no line in this theatre; you do everything."[18] The dictum was easier to pronounce than to enforce, and he sometimes damaged the work of his performers by compelling them to play roles outside their ability. It is said that the death of James Lewis—a bony, chirrupy little man—was brought on by the anxiety he suffered when Daly assigned him the impossible role of Falstaff.[19] As for the "star" system, Daly's efforts to put an end to it were mainly frustrated. "I don't want individual successes, sir, in my theatre," he once declared to a reporter. "I put them all in a line, and then I watch, and if one head begins to bob up above the others, I give it a crack and send it down again!" Thus, when Clara Morris made a hit in her first play with him, in the next play he cast her as "a walking lady of second quality."[20] But two or three years later when, as Cora the Creole in *Article 47*, she established her reputation as an emotional actress of extraordinary power, she abandoned Daly to find fortune and glory under other management. This sort of thing happened so often that Daly became known as a *maker* of stars. Eventually, too, as Ada Rehan, John Drew (Rehan's romantic opposite number), Mrs. Gilbert (specialist in "old woman" roles), and James Lewis (low comedy lead) came to be known as "The Big Four," there was little question with the public that these were the "stars" at Daly's own shop. And after Miss Rehan's creation of Katherine the Shrew and Rosalind, and Daly's deepening emotional involvement with her, and John Drew's secession from the company, Daly had no choice but to stake his fortune on Miss Rehan and actually give her star billing.[21]

Between 1869, when he first took up management at the Fifth Avenue Theatre, and 1877, when he suffered financial failure, he was particularly interested in staging "Old Comedy" ranging from Cibber and Farquhar to Sheridan Knowles, melodramas of his own devising (*Under the Gaslight* and the like), and farces and dramas which he adapted from German and French originals. Yet he did not altogether overlook Shakespeare. Three times he engaged Shakespearean stars for limited runs. In 1869 it was Mary Scott-Siddons, whose repertory included *Twelfth Night, As You Like It,* and *Much Ado.* In the fall of 1875 he was host to Edwin Booth, and for almost the only time in his managerial career he turned his actors to

Illus. 38. Daly reading a play to his company. Courtesy of the University of Illinois Theatre.

labor at classic tragedy, supporting Booth in *Hamlet, Othello, Richard II,* and *King Lear.* In May of 1877 the lovely Adelaide Neilson came to town (her third visit to America) and played Viola, Imogen, and Juliet with Daly's company. None of these events (except Booth's *Richard II* and *King Lear,* both new creations) was remarkable except for the presence of a famous actor in the central role.[22]

During the 1870s Daly produced four Shakespeare comedies with his own company. In his fourth season, the autumn of 1872, he got up *The Merry Wives of Windsor,* of which E. A. Dithmar of the *New York Times* would later declare, "It is not likely that the play has ever been as well acted in our time." It ran for three weeks.[23] In August of 1873 he offered *A Midsummer Night's Dream* with handsome woodland scenery, a moving panorama, a ballet of fifty children, and a rendition of Bottom the Weaver by the famous stage clown George Fox. Unfortunately the financial panic of 1873 struck just when the run should have gathered momentum so that it closed prematurely.[24] In February of 1874 he staged *Love's Labors Lost,* which had never been seen in New York. Though it was well performed and beautifully mounted, the public cared so little for the play that it was withdrawn in its second week.[25] Two and a half years later he presented Fanny Davenport and Charles Coghlan in *As You Like It.* The forest scenery was beautiful: "leafy vistas in the woodlands . . . suffused with continuously changing light, the hues of dawn and the glowing colors of sunset, fading into dark." Fanny Davenport was arch and gamesome as Rosalind, but she failed to convey the "superb mentality, rich womanhood, sensuous yet spiritual . . . and the passionate, affectionate heart of Rosalind." Coghlan's Orlando was "a kind of rural Hamlet, mooning in the woods, as listless as idleness, and lethargic to the verge of sleep." The expensive revival lasted only three weeks.[26]

When Daly resumed management in the fall of 1879, after bankruptcy and an enforced sabbatical, he refrained from staging Shakespeare until he had rebuilt his company, his reputation, and his treasury. Yet all the while he was preparing a Shakespearean campaign. Between 1886 and 1899 he staged ten of Shakespeare's comedies, with plans at the end of his life for still more to come.[27] Each production was worked up with extraordinary care: an original acting version, prepared by William Winter or himself or his brother Joseph and almost always vetted by William Winter; new scenery, dresses, and musical arrangements; a privately printed edition of the acting version, with an elegantly turned Introduction by Winter—who also composed in advance a very long, learned, and flattering review to be published in the

Tribune the morning after the opening night.

Daly had originally invited Winter to prepare all the acting versions, but except for *The Merry Wives,* Winter could not work fast enough to keep up with Daly's needs.[28] He did, however, enunciate certain "principles of emendation" which served Daly well. Of course, he declared, one must be reluctant "to touch, even in the most reverent spirit, the work of 'the divine William.'" It was "presumption," it was "sacrilege." Yet recognizing how poorly Shakespeare had put his plays together for use on the modern stage, one might proceed quite comfortably in the necessary work of improving them. "It is impossible to act Shakespeare *precisely* as the text is written," Winter noted. "Not a single one of his plays—as we both know—is ever acted in that manner. A servile fidelity to the original text is not in my opinion a sign of either good judgment or practical scholarship."[29] Every play must be cut to a playing time of three hours at most (and this means three hours in *Daly's* slow-paced theatre, not in Shakespeare's theatre, or ours); all "foul or vulgar" language must be suppressed; descriptive passages, which only duplicate what the scene painter can express better, are dispensable; and merely "literary" passages, which impede action, must go.[30]

Daly began his Shakespearean campaign in 1886 as he had begun in 1872 with *The Merry Wives.*[31] Winter labored hugely over the text, revising his revision of it four or five times, and his methods served as a model for Daly's own operations in the future. He shaped the play into four acts and reduced the scene changes from twenty-two to sixteen. All things considered, the narrative that he provided is a reasonably sound one. Of course he got rid of the mysterious scenes concerning the Germans and the stolen horses, and the scene of Master William's Latin lesson. He speeded the ending by cutting some thirty-five lines of poetry in the fairy scene at Herne's Oak. He cut about thirty lines from IV.2, in which the wives decide to tell their husbands what pranks they have been playing; and some eighty lines from IV.5, during which Simple consults Falstaff about the loss of a chain. He "improved" the story lines by transposing a scene or two so that Falstaff's first two tribulations (the Buckbasket Scene and the beating of Mother Prat) are brought closer together, and so that the Fenton-Anne love story is presented in one sequence instead of two.

He fattened certain roles. Ada Rehan's Mrs. Ford took over a few lines from Mrs. Page. Mrs. Gilbert's Dame Quickly usurped some of the functions of the Host. In I.3 a brief speech of Falstaff's was moved down the page so that Falstaff (Charles Fisher) could take the curtain. The other three act-endings were so manipulated that John Drew's Master Ford would have the last word.

Winter enlivened the text by certain small additions. According to old custom, when in I.4 Dr. Caius says, "Follow my heels, Rugby," Rugby would follow too closely, and Caius would shout, "Ah, Jack-a-dandy, I tell you follow my heels, not tread on my heels." The fairies in Act V, deprived of their song about "lust and luxury," were awarded Oberon's jingle from the *Dream,* "Trip away, make no stay, meet me here by break of day." And near the end of the play Evans was given the pretty line from the Bad Quarto, "I will dance and eat plums at your wedding." Daly himself concocted an Epilogue for Falstaff to speak, a neat collection of lines from *2 Henry IV* in which Falstaff boasts of his wit and his nobility.[32]

Winter's sternest task was expurgation. The job had mainly been done by others before him, but he attacked it afresh, and he was the man for the job. He

Illus. 39. John Drew and Ada Rehan as The Fords in *The Merry Wives of Windsor.* Courtesy of the University of Illinois Theatre.

Illus. 40. Ada Rehan *(left)* and Virginia Dreher as the two Merry Wives reading Falstaff's love letters. Folger Shakespeare Library.

truly felt that he was relieving Shakespeare of an unwelcome burden. "There is an intended verbal coarseness in part of the text," he wrote, "a straining after vulgarity. It was neither natural nor easy to Shakespeare; but he seems to have thought it harmonious with the gross subject of Falstaff's mercenary lust. I have pruned out the more obvious of those expressions."[33]

All terms even remotely connected with religion had to go: *God, py'r Lady, Jack-priest, of the Church, given to prayer, bless my soul, resurrection, day of judgment, damnation, hell, the devil, the dickens.* Ungenteel references to the body and any reference to excretory functions would not do. *Belly* became *person. My parts* became *me.* And these words were suppressed: *entrails, urinals, foul, stinking, fretted in grease, sweating and blowing, mock-water, make-a-de-turd, barrow of butcher's offal, guts made of puddings, tuns of oil in his belly.* And, of course, Winter canceled every word suggestive of sex organs or activity. *Lust* became *vice. Enjoy her* became *victory. Lie with* became *sup with.* These words were suppressed: *fornication, boarding, keep him above deck, cuckold, cornuto, Actaeon, buck, horn-mad, horum, whore, bitch, my doe with the black scut, lecher, stones, erection, pullet-sperm, take up your wife's clothes, pills to cool the reins, when gods have hot backs, a cool rut-time, piss my tallow.* All earlier Victorian and even eighteenth-century acting versions had been cleansed of the boldest of these terms, but Winter's text was unquestionably the "cleanest."

In congratulating Daly on the beauty of the production, Brander Matthews wrote, "Beautiful were both the Merry Wives and beautiful was sweet Anne Page—indeed I do not think I ever saw three prettier women on the stage together than Miss Rehan, Miss Dreher and Miss Kingdon. Beautiful too were the costumes and the scenery." Matthews also congratulated Daly that Shakespeare was not a contemporary American playwright. If he had been, the critics would have accused him of flippant cheap humor and farcical incident.[34]

But in essential effect, Winter and Daly between them had *made* the play a contemporary American one. As Dithmar noticed in his *New York Times* review:

> The fashion which has long prevailed of making a notable revival of Shakespearean comedy the excuse for the display of rich fabrics and handsome painting, a feast of color and a marvel of expense, has been faithfully adhered to. The worthy but somewhat coarse middle class English men and women of the fourteenth [*sic!*] century were exhibited last night in satins and silks and velvets of graceful shape and agreeably harmonized tints, dresses such as the counterparts of the poet's robust characters never dreamed of wearing. . . . Modern audiences would be shocked if Ford and Page, and that precious old body Dame Quickly, and the rest of them came on the stage as Shakespeare drew them and spoke his lines as he intended those lines should be spoken. The text is shorn of all its vulgarity. . . . Daintiness and gracefulness are the characteristics of the performance now, not the boisterous frolic and the hearty animalism of old England, its men and its literature.[35]

If Dithmar is here protecting his (somewhat shaky) knowledge of "history," he is all the same approving the "modernizing"—even "Americanizing" of Daly's production. None of the characters but Falstaff, he notes (and he "was never more than a faint outline sketch of that rare old genius") was "cast in a Shakespearean mold." In short, between Winter's cuts and Daly's actors, *The Merry Wives* was as jolly and innocent as a set of chapters out of Dickens.

Daly's casting violated Shakespeare's intentions quite as thoroughly as Winter's blue pencil had done. Charles Fisher, his Falstaff, was "singularly handsome—with a rosy face, snow-white hair, clear, merry gray eyes, and gay attire"[36]—a veritable Father Christmas in appearance and as free of Falstaffian grossness as that kindly saint. He was played, said William Winter, "as a good-natured, amiable old fellow, who really does not seem to mean any especial mischief, but is just a donkey in his besotted folly."[37] The wives, well past their holiday time of beauty, were played by Ada Rehan and Virginia Dreher, both in their mid-twenties—"a pair of dazzling young beauties, in their silks and laces and sparkling gems," whom Shakespeare would never have recognized as the middle-aged country women he had intended. The husbands, said John Ranken Towse, looking back thirty years later, were similarly transformed: "The fiery, jealous Ford, in the hands of John Drew, was a pretty fellow, an exquisite in dress, and a courtier in behavior. . . . The Master Page of Mr. Otis Skinner was a swaggering young prig, who might, for all his apparent years, have been the lover of his own daughter, Sweet Anne." The style of their acting was all wrong, too, said Towse, "their modern manners contrasting strangely with the old costumes and vigorous speech. They used to play the warm-blooded farce as if it were an anemic social comedy of the present."[38]

Daly's brother Joseph attempted to defend the actors' style, if not their youth, on the grounds that Daly deliberately trained them to be *natural* in speech and action, and thus, he argued, they were truer to the play as Shakespeare *meant it to be played* than if they had adopted an "artificial method"—which he dismissed as the "rhythmical chant once adopted by some performers in delivering blank verse, and referred to by Cibber in his 'Apology,' Chapter IV."[39] In that chapter Colley Cibber did indeed condemn "straining vociferation" (rant) and the "dangerous af-

Illus. 41. Charles Fisher as Falstaff in *The Merry Wives of Windsor.* Folger Shakespeare Library.

fectation of monotone." But what brother Joseph forgot is Cibber's *positive* description of proper verse speaking: "The Voice of a Singer is not more strictly ty'd to Time and Tune, than that of an Actor in Theatrical Elocution. The least Syllable too long, or too lightly dwelt upon, in a Period, depreciates it to nothing; which very Syllable, if rightly touch'd, shall, like the heightening Stroke of Light from a Master's Pencil, give Life and Spirit to the whole."[40] Though *The Merry Wives* is largely a prose play, its prose is that of a poet, like Congreve's prose or Vanbrugh's—rhetoric cunningly styled, loaded with images and sound effects which must be delivered with energy, precision, and the utmost obedience to what Cibber calls "Time and Tune." Only thus can the actors "Act" the comic music which subtends the comic action. Daly had better have trained his actors by the Cibber method, or sent them to school to old James Murdoch, the actor-elocutionist, than let them smother Shakespeare's word-music under the colloquial chatter which, quite appropriately, they had developed for the "anemic social comedy" of their modern repertory."

The critic of the *Herald* dared to enter mild caveats. He admitted, to begin with, that it would have been audacious, even risky, for most companies who ordinarily deal in popular farce-comedies to step "from the ridiculous to the sublime"—from *A Night Off* to the height of Shakespeare's *Merry Wives*.[41] But Daly has dared it, and even greatly pleased a brilliant first night audience. It is true, though, that the actors, especially the men, were not quite ready for it. "By training and experience they are exponents of the coat-and-waistcoat drama. Their doublet and hose were not worn with that absence of self-consciousness which distinguishes the actor accustomed to exercise his powers in what is known in theatrical jargon as the "legitimate." Nor were their Elizabethan sentences uttered as trippingly from the tongue as could be wished. Sometimes too glib they lost their bright points; sometimes too heavy and slow they spoiled them. Yet on the whole they were much applauded, said the *Herald,* and Daly should be encouraged to effect more Shakespeare revivals. The *Spirit of the Times* was firm in its opinion that Charles Fisher was so lacking in Falstaffian humor that he threw the whole performance askew,[42] and Towse of the *Post* declared that old Mrs. Gilbert (Dame Quickly) was the only member of the company sufficiently "old school" to know how to handle this kind of comedy.[43]

Attendance dwindled, and after 35 performances (January 14 to February 13, 1886) Daly withdrew it. He would revive it once more, on January 11, 1898, at the end of his career. By then only Miss Rehan and Mrs. Gilbert were still playing their accustomed roles. George Clarke, an old-timer, resembled Falstaff considerably more effectively than Charles Fisher had. But by this time Verdi's opera was on hand, and for a true Falstaff one went to hear the great Victor Maurel.[44]

A year later, with *The Taming of the Shrew,* Daly caught the public's fancy.[45] In its first run *The Shrew* netted 121 performances (January 18 to April 30, 1887); in the summer of 1888 it took a place of honor in the Shakespearean revival going on in London; it played at Stratford and around the English provinces; Daly took it to Paris, rather to the puzzlement of most French observers. It became a fixture in Daly's repertory.

Part of the reason for the failure of *The Merry Wives* was the fact that the play demands brilliant execution of a wide range of roles, and apart from the principals (who, as we have seen, were themselves not right for their roles) Daly did not have enough actors capable of the tasks assigned them. In *The Shrew,* on the other hand, the all-absorbing central action was sustained by Ada Rehan and John Drew, the best pair of romantic comedians that Daly ever owned. The Bianca subplot required only straightforward comic playing, easily within the range of Virginia Dreher, Otis Skinner, Frederick Bond, and others of Daly's second team. Drew and Rehan, who had shared innumerable comical, farcical, and romantic pairings during their years of service with Daly, were exactly ready for Petruchio and Kate. "What the wonderful pair did with the play," wrote Graham Robertson, who saw them when they came to London, "how they contrived that the brutal tale of the bullying, starving and frightening of a virago into a spiritless drudge would become the delightfully amusing love story of two charming people I have never been able to find out; but nevertheless the miracle was wrought."[46] To Joseph Daly the wonder was that John Drew could commit so much violence and yet fuse with it the charm and polish he had developed for drawing-room plays.[47] The crowning wonder, though, was the transformation of gentle Ada Rehan into a raging tiger.

Daly provided her a "delayed entrance" (a favorite device) in order to heighten the appeal of his favorite actress. By cutting her few lines in the first act he kept her out of sight while expectations grew. And then, as the curtain rose on the second act, "a voice raised without, a pause of expectancy, and there swept on to the stage a figure that will never be forgotten by any there present—Ada Rehan as Katherine the Shrew."[48] She came unencumbered, not driving Bianca before her, but "Enter Katherine in a rage, sweeping round the stage, and Bianca following." George Odell would remember it half a century later as "The most magnificent stage-entry I have ever seen."[49] She was a pillar of fire—"a woman of the passionate red Italian loveliness to which the Venetian school of painting has accustomed us."[50] Her dress was dark red, the underskirt red velvet and the red overdress of heavy silk brocade, the deep sleeves lined in flame color. Her shoes were dark red satin, and she wore a flat red cap over her curling auburn hair.[51] She opened her performance, says Towse, "at the highest pitch of quivering indignation," and she kept up this level of intensity in every exchange with Bianca, her father, and Petruchio until Petruchio hauled her off the stage after the wedding.[52] "Not a whit of her shrewishness did she spare us," says Graham Robertson; "her storms of passion found vent in snarls, growls, and even inarticulate screams of fury; she paced hither and thither like a caged wild beast, but her rages were magnificent, like an angry sea or a sky of tempest; she blazed a fiery comet through the play, baleful but beautiful."[53]

Throughout the "taming" at Petruchio's house she displayed pride, anger, shame, amazement—and when Petruchio's rages at his servants rose to their wildest—she displayed terror. The more he bewildered and bullied her, the more sympathy she drew from the audience. Gradually, and with touches of humor, she began to join Petruchio's game: smilingly she melted into submission, to serenity, to her own natural loveliness. "And when the storm passed," says Robertson, and at the end of the play "in the last great speech she showed her happy love, her voice took on an unimagined music. The words fell softly, slowly, like the last drops of a clearing shower."[54]

One feature of the production that excited especial interest was that this was the first time that American audiences ever saw the play "as Shakespeare wrote it." From 1766, when the Douglas-Hallam troupe introduced Garrick's three-act reduction called *Catharine and Petruchio,* down to Daly's bold stroke, the Garrick version was the only one known to American stages.

Of course it was not *quite* "as Shakespeare wrote it." Daly, who prepared the acting version himself, restored the wooing of Bianca and restored the Induction.[55] But he shaped the play into four acts instead of five, and made vast cuts—fifty-five lines of a Tranio passage in I.2; fifty lines of a Tranio passage in IV.2; sixty lines from the final scene, and so forth. He expurgated thoroughly, of course, at times replacing Shakespeare's bawdry with patches borrowed from Garrick. Thus the passage between Kate and Petruchio about the wasp's sting and where it lies, whether in tongue or tail, became the following:

Petruchio. The fool knows where the honey lies, sweet Kate.
Kate. 'Tis not for drones to taste.
Petruchio. That will I try. *(Offers to kiss her; she strikes him.)*

Eight or ten such softenings were achieved under the authority of Garrick.

Daly spoiled the structure and sense of the second half of the play by high-handed transposition of scenes. Shakespeare developed the grand taming in three separate scenes: in IV.1, on a cold stormy night Petruchio brings Kate to his house in the country, bullies his servants, and send her to bed without supper; in IV.3, the next morning, he lets her eat but refuses to let her have a new cap and gown; in IV.5, some hours later, along the road to Padua, he quarrels with her about the sun, the moon, and the age and gender of old Vincentio, whom they meet along the way. Shakespeare provided time *between* these three actions by inserting units of the Bianca story (IV.2 and IV.4). To have preserved the Shakespearean order would have cost Daly four scene changes, so he pulled out the Bianca scenes, tacked them together, and presented them *before* the taming sequence. The result is that the Petruchio-Kate night scene, the morning after scene, and the scene along the highway all take place without change of time and all of them inside Petruchio's house. Old Vincentio is absurdly made to poke his head inside the door, "as if enquiring the way." Kate's rapid breakdown from outrage to submissiveness in a single scene was admired by some as a histrionic *tour de force,* but others found it difficult to believe.

Daly was no feminist, but he was sentimental about women, and he could not bear to see his heroine defeated. At every possible point he evened the score between the adversaries. In the second act, just before Petruchio's triumphant exit line, "We will be married a' Sunday," Daly borrowed from Garrick a patch of seven speeches in which Kate refuses to give Petruchio her hand, Petruchio attempts to kiss it, and she gives him a box on the ear. Borrowing again from Garrick, he arranged for Kate to bring down the second act curtain with a prophecy of victory. Her father warns her that she must accept Petruchio's offer, for "'twill be the last." "Is't so?" she cries:

Then watch me well and see the scorned Katherine
Make her husband stoop unto her lure.

With flaming resolution she foretells that she will tumble Petruchio from his perch:

> Katherine shall tame this haggard; or if she fails,
> Shall tie her tongue up, and pare down her nails.

In the final scene Daly laid on his "happy ending" with a trowel. The setting, by the way, was a gorgeous picture of wealth and well-being, modeled on Veronese's painting, "The Marriage Feast at Cana."[56] On the porch of a Renaissance palace a banquet is laid out. Behind the banquet tables is a low marble gallery. Beyond that we see classic temples and pavilions in a romantic landscape. From the gallery a soprano and a boys' chorus open the scene with a song by Sir Henry Bishop (1786–1855), "Should He Upbraid." Bishop had adapted Petruchio's lines

> Say that she rail, why then I'll tell her plain
> She sings as sweetly as the nightingale.

He reversed the gender of the pronouns—"Katherinized" it, so to speak—and turned the point of it against Petruchio. The song as Daly uses it here teasingly promises what is to come. When Kate has spoken about half of the lecture on what women owe their husbands, Petruchio breaks in with a speech from Garrick, announcing that all his lordly bullying has only been "An honest mask, which I throw off with pleasure." He kneels then to kiss her hand and prophesies that their future lives will be "one gentle stream of mutual love, compliance, and regard." She declares herself ashamed of her former behavior, raises him up tenderly, and takes the curtain with a couplet or two of authentic Shakespeare. Thus, sentimentally, Petruchio himself is tamed, and the match ends in a draw.

The public and critical reception was all but unanimously celebrational. William Winter led off with congratulations that Daly had restored this "piquant and bustling comedy" as it had never been seen in America—"in its original form." (In London Ben Webster had staged the "whole play" in 1844 and Samuel Phelps in 1856, but it had not been done in America.) Winter praised Daly for restoring the Induction, for cutting the rest of the play to reasonable playing time, and, of course, for judicious suppression of all coarse words and vulgar innuendo. It was an article of faith with Winter that "no one of Shakespeare's plays ever is given upon the stage, or ever should be given there, word for word, as Shakespeare wrote it."[57] Now it was time for everyone to join in the denunciation of Garrick's version as an "abomination" under which "our stage has so long groaned" and to thank Daly for bringing the "antidote to this poisonous farce."[58] (Winter himself may have groaned a bit at the exuberance of this denunciation, since only a decade before he had approved and polished the Garrick version for inclusion in Edwin Booth's "Prompt Book" edition of Shakespeare's plays.)

Dithmar of the *New York Times* perhaps outdid Winter in flattering Daly's achievement. First he produced a column-long review praising everything and listing forty or more distinguished citizens and their parties in the boxes and the parquet. To this he added a half-column stage history of the play and Garrick's reduction of it.[59] Four days later in a second notice he proclaimed the *Shrew* "the greatest hit" of Daly's career, noted the approval of General Sherman and the governor of Michigan, and explained how Daly could cast every role superbly because of his generous policy of keeping on his payroll what nearly amounted to a double company of character actors, ingenues, etc., to be ready as understudies or to rehearse plays yet to be put on the boards.[60] Finally, after the hundredth night Dithmar explained how much the extraordinary success of the *Shrew* owed to Daly's unerring supervision of every minute detail, his direction of every "movement, glance, finger motion, and word" that occurred on stage. He noted, too, that on this hundredth night every lady in the audience was presented an elegantly printed souvenir book of the play as Daly staged it.[61]

Winter had dared to suggest a slight defect in Miss Rehan's Katherine—"that it did not give the requisite hint of any woman-like softness underneath that virago exterior"—so that her final submission at the end seemed "a little sudden and a little insincere." Dithmar found no such shortcoming:

> The Katherine of Miss Rehan . . . was of greater merit than any other individual performance. In appearance she was a superb figure, and the gradations of tempos in her earlier scenes with Petruchio, her simulation of fright in the stormy episode that begins the honeymoon, and the delicate art with which the submission of the woman to the man was depicted demonstrated the constantly increasing skill of this fine actress and her keen insight. Katherine, at beginning the personification of shrewishness, was in the denouement a sweet and sympathetic personage.[62]

John Drew, who, to be sure, was generally satisfying as Petruchio—was occasionally, as in the Boston *Transcript,* awarded the honors of the evening[63] yet had to compete with ghosts of Petruchios by actors greater than himself—Garrick's Woodward, the Kembles, Macready, Booth, and many others who had used the Garrick farce to crack a whip in. He had not the "virile, masterful strength" that older critics expected of Petruchio, said the Boston *Home Journal,* but he made up for it by the grace, humor, gallantry, and

Illus. 42. John Drew as Petruchio in *The Taming of the Shrew.*

Illus. 43. Ada Rehan as Katherine the Shrew.

cleverness of "a man of breeding."[64]

So far as I know there was but one sour note. For some reason there was at that time bad blood between Daly and Harrison Grey Fiske, editor of the *Dramatic Mirror,* and for some years the *Mirror* would not notice Daly's productions. In 1887, however, Nym Crinkle was contributing to the *Mirror* a weekly feuilleton, in which he freely expressed his most extravagant enthusiasms and his pet aversions. On February 26 he acknowledged that of all the plays in New York Daly's *Shrew* was "doing a good business." The streets around his theatre were nightly blocked with carriages and the box office was turning people away. And then Nym Crinkle struck a low blow:

> But I don't think any Shakespearean critic would deliberately sit down and conscientiously say this was an entirely worthy performance of the great comedy. . . . Certainly it is not my idea either of Katherine or Petruchio. . . . It is not Shakespeare in the best sense, but has a modern cut glass novelty that tickles. It glitters. It is overladen with jewelry and flounces. People have very little to say about the Petruchio, but they talk for hours about the banquet scene and the cut glass. In a word, the production is a triumph of Mr. Daly's, not of Shakespeare's, and I suppose Mr. Daly has copyrighted it.[65]

When two years later Daly revived the *Shrew* as an item in a spring festival, the attack was renewed, and this time in a bolder, more bludgeoning manner. On March 30, 1890, the *Mirror* featured a special article entitled "Daly's *Taming of the Shrew.*" It is two columns long, signed, and except for half a sentence of praise of Miss Rehan's performance, it systematically damns everyone and everything in the production. It is not in Nym Crinkle's style and I can only guess the author was Fiske himself. A sampling of its main points are the following.[66]

The Induction, says the writer, should never have been undertaken: it is spurious and it is dull, and furthermore the ineptitude of the players rendered it intolerable. The company, trained in Americanized German farce, should not presume to play Shakespeare. Until we have a company capable of such high work we ought regretfully to part company with that worthy author and content ourselves with works of lesser value. The clowning at Petruchio's house was show-shop buffoonery, vulgar and valueless. Mr. Drew understands nothing of the high comedy in Petruchio: he might play it "a great deal better than he did if he would ask his esteemed mother to tell him what some of the old actors, with whom she has so often acted, did with the character." The waits between the acts were fearfully long, and though Mr. Widmer's band plays remarkably well, we can have too much of these dreamy, long-drawn-out waltzes. The Banquet Scene was most disappointing, and the chorus of little boys, after having so credibly sung their choruses, had to stand staring like a Sunday-school class through all the final action. The costumes, though expensive, were ugly. The programs, badly printed, were unreadable in the dim lighting of the auditorium. The house is so badly ventilated that after an hour the aroma is "most distressing to ladies, and even the sterner sex could dispense with it."

The heavy-handedness of Fiske's attack, if indeed it was his, can hardly have done Daly any harm, especially in light of the established popularity of his production. It may, however, have served warning to Daly that the *Mirror* could be neither bullied nor bought. In any case, Fiske seems eventually to have called off his dogs. In a few years he would be publishing reasonable, sometimes favorable, reviews of Daly, and Daly would place advertisements in the *Mirror.*

As the production ran its course, it appears that Miss Rehan truly did respond to William Winter's suggestion and Dithmar's encouragement. Without abandoning her tigerish opening and her shows of resistance, she won total affection of the audiences, and, indeed, "took over the play." According to Justin McCarthy, when Daly took the production to London, society there "went wild" over her, in drawing-rooms as well as from the stalls: "the ambition of every man and every woman was to meet Ada Rehan, to look upon her face, to touch her hand, and to listen to the music of one of the loveliest voices that have ever given a new grace to poetry."[67] This social lionizing must have sorely strained the nerves of so private and shy a person as Miss Rehan is known to have been, but for Daly's sake and the *Shrew's* sake she would endure it. Daly commissioned J. Scott Hartley to do a bust of her as Katherine, once in marble and once in bronze. Her portrait by Hillary Bell hung in the foyer of Daly's theatre. Her portrait by Eliot Gregory hangs permanently in the picture gallery of the Royal Shakespeare Theatre at Stratford-upon-Avon.[68]

A Midsummer Night's Dream always invites spectacle: Daly's *Dream* was probably the most spectacular of the century. He brought it out in the winter of 1888 (January 31 to April 17), revived it in March of 1890, took it to London in the summer of 1895, and toured it throughout America in 1895–96.[69]

William Winter called Daly's arrangement of the play "an excellent working version,"[70] and early critics flattered Daly for his "loving reverence of the poet," declaring that he "takes the play as Shakespeare wrote it, follows the text with conscientious

Illus. 44. Banquet Scene at end of *The Taming of the Shrew.* Folger Shakespeare Library.

care."[71] The fact is, he followed the text with a carving knife, eviscerating the poetry with murderous care. In the opening scene he lopped out the charming stichomythic exchanges between Hermia and Lysander that follow "The course of true love never did run smooth" (those "silver-sweet antiphonies," as William Archer called them[72]), and half of Hermia's pretty "swearings" that she will meet Lysander in the wood. He canceled Titania's famous poem about stormy weather; large sections of bitter snip-snap between the quarreling lovers (many of these lines that Daly actually printed in his souvenir edition were penciled out by the prompter as omitted in performance); some twenty-five lines of delightful fooling when Bottom, in the arms of Titania, orders a honeybag for breakfast (also printed but struck out by the prompter); the entire scene of Bottom's reunion with his fellows; and at least fifty lines of the fairies' verses at the end of the play. In 1895 Bernard Shaw raged against such abuse of the text, and William Archer remarked grimly that "there is much in a name, and *Daly* is fatally suggestive of *Dele*."[73]

The modern reader will not readily recall "indecencies" in the *Dream*, but Daly and Winter did. Puck's recital of his pranks did *not* include a fat and bean-fed horse beguiling a filly foal with sexy neighing; nor did he slip a stool from an old lady's "bum," but from "beneath" her. Titania's pregnant friend did not run down the strand imitating the "big-bellied" sails of passing ships. Theseus did not order the lovers "to bed" but to "now list." Who would sniff obscenity in Thisbe's line to Wall: "My cherry lips have often kissed thy stones"? Daly expunged it.

The casting went somewhat askew. After Ada Rehan's storming Shrew and Virginia Dreher's mild Bianca, Daly reversed the assignments: that is, he gave the tiny vixen Hermia to tall Virginia Dreher and the tall but gentle Helena to less tall Ada Rehan. Miss Rehan salvaged something by her first entrance when she "came bounding on in her love mania," and she showed a flash of fire in the third act when she rounded on her "moonstruck, herb-bewitched adorers."[74] But for the rest she had nothing to do but read poetry, and she did so rather badly. Jeannette Gilder in *The Critic* found both the actresses "floored, to speak figuratively, by the blank verse."[75] John Ranken Towse faulted Miss Rehan in particular for monotonous reading, and declared that throughout the company "the poetry suffered severely in its delivery by unaccustomed lips."[76]

Illus. 45. Ada Rehan as Helena in *A Midsummer Night's Dream.* Courtesy of the University of Illinois Theatre.

On the other hand, Bernard Shaw, who like most Londoners adored Miss Rehan, praised her reading without reservation. Considering the demands he usually put upon stage speakers, his tribute to her vocal skills is, to say the least, out of character.

> She gives us beauty of tone, grace of measure, delicacy of articulation; in short, all the technical qualities of verse music, along with the rich feeling and fine intelligence without which those technical qualities would soon become monotonous. When she is at her best, the music melts in the caress of the emotion it expresses, and thus completes the conditions necessary for obtaining Shakespear's effects in Shakespear's way.[77]

When we take Shaw's passage in context, however, we find it reaching toward a darker meaning, a warning: beauty of speech and youth charm are not enough to make a great actress. Unless she moves on to Shakespear's Imogen, Shaw said, unless like Duse and Janet Achurch she takes up Sudermann and Ibsen, her appeal will be gone when youth is gone. Just as Shaw longed to rescue Ellen Terry from Henry Irving so too he would rescue Ada Rehan from Augustin Daly: "With grandfather Daly to choose her plays for her, there is no future for Ada Rehan."[78]

Daly's production of the *Dream* recalled almost every flashy effect and device that had accreted to the play during the past half-century. His stage manager, old John Moore, had seen Eliza Vestris's Covent Garden *Dream* in 1840, had prompted William Burton's New York *Dream* in 1854, and had recorded in his promptbook masses of information about traditional scenic arrangements and stage business: the stage history of the play with all its devices was at Daly's elbow.[79]

As was the custom, Daly assigned the role of Oberon to a woman, thereby earning a sneer from Shaw, who seems never to have heard of the "feminized" Oberons of Mme Vestris, Fanny Ternan, Charlotte Cushman, and many another. "It must not be supposed that he does this solely because it is wrong," said Shaw, "though there is no other reason apparent. He does it partly because he was brought up to do such things, and partly because they seem to him to be a tribute to Shakespear's greatness, which, being uncommon, ought not to be interpreted according to the dictates of common sense."[80] In Charles Kean's production, Puck (Ellen Terry, age eight) made his first entrance seated on a mushroom which sprang up through a trap. Daly did not repeat that device, but he remembered it: *"Enter a fairy plucking flowers. With her wand she switches at a mushroom growth near C. and from it Puck appears."*[81] Puck used to embark upon his "girdle round the earth" by flying: Daly wired up little Bijou Fernandez for that feat—though on opening night "Puck had misadventures in his early efforts to whirl about the stage, but we presume the carpenter will do better tonight."[82]

The Indian boy that Oberon and Titania quarrel about was actually brought upon the stage and then made to disappear magically. Two bearers in Moorish dress carried in a curtained palanquin within which the boy lay on a silver couch. When Oberon begged Titania to give him the boy, she signaled the curtains to be closed. When Oberon tore the curtains open, the boy was gone. According to John Moore, one of the bearers had released a spring, and boy and couch flew upward and were concealed in the roof of the palanquin.

Sunset, darkness, moonlight, and dawn were effects that Daly could execute far better than earlier producers because by 1888 he had both electricity and calciums (gas) to work with. He could make mists rise and clear them away by manipulation of gauzes. By change of light upon gauzes he could reveal scenes or wipe them out. Thus, at the end of the first workmen's scene "the house of Peter Quince disappears as though drawn into airy nothingness," and again in the fourth act, "the glen and tangled wood appear to dissolve." One of the prettiest effects occurred at the end of the third act when the lovers one by one lay down to sleep. As the darkness thickened around them and the air was filled with music, a crowd of goblins and fairies danced about in the mist, singing and flashing tiny battery-powered lamps on their wands and in their hair. *Fireflies!* Audiences were delighted. In London, however, the effect went for nothing, for fireflies are unknown in England. Shaw scorned the business as only one more unaccountable Daly foolishness.[83] William Archer fretted through a long paragraph at "the disorderly and meaningless flashing and fading of the electric lamps." He thought they could at least have been made to "follow the rhythm of the song instead of flitting and flickering in chaotic discordance."[84]

To bring his fourth act to a grand climax, Daly merged two traditional elements—a moving panorama and travel by boat. In an 1867 production in New York a panorama, imported from London, exhibited scene after scene of landscape along the lovers' route as they strolled back to Athens. In two 1854 productions, despite the fact that Athens is miles from the sea, the play opened with the arrival of a Grecian galley bearing Theseus and Hippolyta to the steps of Theseus's palace.[85]

Daly combined boat and panorama in an operation of extraordinary complexity. Just after Bottom wakes from his dream and rushed off to find his fellows,

> Daybreak begins to appear. The air is tremulous with joyous song, and the first red flare of sunlight burns down a woodland glen. . . . As the sun rises higher, as the crimson of dawn melts into the golden splendor of early morning, the mist ascends, the glen and the tangled wood appears to dissolve, and a bright open scene with a luminous river in the background bursts into view. On the bare earth lie the four lovers, locked still in slumber. . . . Suddenly, from a distance, sounds the echoing note of a huntsman's horn, and the barge of Theseus glides down the stream.[86]

From upstage left the barge moves to upstage center, and Theseus, Hippolyta, and company disembark, come forward to discuss the pleasures of the hunt, and presently discover the sleeping lovers. Then the grand scenic marvel ensues. The entire party enters the barge, and while the orchestra plays Mendelssohn's music, they sail from this mile without the town to Theseus's palace.

What in fact happened was that the barge sat still in its "stream" at upstage center while the panorama behind it and the ground row on the nearer shore moved from audience right to audience left so that the barge seemed to move from audience left to right through everchanging landscape until it reached the crowd of waving welcomers at the palace steps.[87]

Did this panoramic journey "call forth applause"? Did the spectators "cheer lustily"? Was it "a feast of color and truly a marvel of illusion; and as you gaze upon it your senses are bewitched . . . and you realize indeed the ecstasy of a happy dream"? So certain American reviewers tell us.[88] Or was the passage "justly jeered at by the first-night gallery"? Did the galley appear "an ambidextrous barge . . . seen threading its way, obviously on dry land, through an epileptic forest, jerked spasmodically along like a freight train in the act of shunting"? Was it "more absurd than anything that occurs in the tragedy of Pyramus and Thisbe"? Thus certain witnesses in London.[89]

The New York audiences and critics were, for the most part, simply amazed at the ingenuity and beauty of Daly's stagecraft. As Maurice Minturn put it in the *Herald,* "Mr. Daly may be said to have realized what Wagner taught to be the perfection of stage art, where music, scenery, poetry and prose in their highest degree should be combined, and no one branch sacrificed to the other."[90] Minturn failed to notice that Daly was less concerned than Wagner about the libretto. He actually asserts that Daly was conscientiously faithful to the text, quite overlooking the omission of famous passages and minor violations of Shakespeare's language.

Nym Crinkle was very much aware that, triumph as it was, neither Shakespeare nor the actors had much share in it. It was a triumph, he said, of Daly and stage scenery. He called it only "a prime example of good housekeeping. Mr. Daly is the best Dame Trot of a manager that we have. And when Shakespeare is in question let us by all means give our attention to Mr. Daly's neatness, and industry, and cleanliness, and propriety."[91] Winter and Dithmar, like Minturn, were uncritically enthusiastic over this "remarkably able production of one of the great plays . . . mounted and clothed in scenery and attire as rich and beautiful as any that has ever been used to dress a play on the American stage."[92] It meant nothing to them that Daly had a blind eye and a tin ear when it came to the uses of dramatic poetry.

One of the surprising castings was that of James Lewis as Bottom. Anyone in those days who remembered the Bottom of portly William Burton or of Ben DeBar would turn for Bottom to the Falstaffian W. F. Owen, an actor of the size and the unctuous, rubicund order that the part seems written for; but Daly chose instead—perversely or cunningly—an actor of the exact opposite mold—"thin, dry, quaint, and chirrupy." Such was Lewis, and he reveled in the part.

Illus. 46. Duke Theseus and company arrive by barge through the wood "a mile without the town" in *A Midsummer Night's Dream.* Courtesy of the Theatre Collection of the New York Public Library.

Illus. 47. The moving scenery has brought them part way home to Athens. Courtesy of the Theatre Collection of the New York Public Library.

Illus. 48. The moving scenery brings them another quarter-mile toward home. Courtesy of the Theatre Collection of the New York Public Library.

Illus. 49. They arrive and dock at Theseus' palace. Courtesy of the Theatre Collection of the New York Public Library.

"The manner that he imparts to Bottom is not that of slow sapience and ruminant gravity, but that of nimble and eager delight in himself and all his faculties and deeds," said Winter. "He made a separate entrance, crying 'Ready,' and he struck the keynote then of his whole impersonation. It was received from first to last with the keenest enjoyment."[93] Even Jeannette Gilder, who protested that it was "not in the least Shakespearean—is, in fact, nothing but broad burlesque without insight or significance," gave in to it, for "it is funny all over, and excites so much merriment that it would be useless to criticize it."[94] Someone noticed that after he awoke from his dream, and approached his exit, Lewis gave a donkeyish kick that was "preposterously exuberant."[95]

To George Odell, writing as late as the 1940s, this production of the *Dream* was "the best within my experience of half a century."[96] To the English, however, the actors, with the possible exception of Miss Rehan, seemed little above the ordinary, and as for Daly's aerial flights, trick palanquins, and panoramic barge journeys, every English Christmas or Easter pantomime offered many more and far more ingenious gimcracks. The London *Athenaeum* was scandalized by the indiscriminate scissoring and the "Transatlantic squeamishness" of the bowdlerizing, acknowledged Daly's work at best as "pretty," and dismissed the whole affair as a "triviality."[97]

Daly's most satisfactory Shakespeare was his *As You Like It.* It opened in New York in December of 1889 for a healthy run (December 17 to February 10), triumphed in London in the summer of 1890, toured America in 1892, and was kept in repertory to the end of Daly's career.[98] Ada Rehan and John Drew led the company as Rosalind and Orlando, but Rehan's Rosalind (they pronounced it Rose-a-lined)[99] inevitably took the honors. Drew's eminence in the company was declining as his partner's rose. Unable to compete with the attraction of Miss Rehan's "womanliness," Drew would soon desert Daly and enlist under a rival management.[100]

Daly prepared his own acting version,[101] basing it pretty closely on the restoration (and expurgation) of the text prepared for Drury Lane in 1842 by William Charles Macready. Macready had never published his arrangement, but stage manager John Moore had long ago acquired a transcription of it.[102] Following Macready, Daly restored to the First Lord the description of Jaques' moralizing over the wounded deer, a passage which for a century before Macready and decades after him Jaques had taken for himself. Like Macready, he discarded the "Cuckoo Song" borrowed from *Love's Labors Lost,* which from the days of Kitty Clive had been sung by Rosalind (or Celia) at that point in the fourth act when Rosalind speaks of the infidelity of wives. He restored the dialogue between Rosalind and Jaques at the beginning of the fourth act, brought Jaques in as an observer of Touchstone's wooing of Audrey, restored some of the Masque of Hymen, and, to the annoyance of William Winter, who thought it a vulgar excrescence, restored the Epilogue.

Daly rejected two common preconceptions of the play. Down through the nineteenth century a tradition had developed, abetted to a degree by the gentle, lady-like, ultra-poetical performances of England's best-loved Rosalind, Helen Faucit, that the play was tinged with a kind of sweet sadness, shaded under "melancholy boughs," perhaps nostalgic for an edenic world.[103] Daly would have none of that. His production was to be joyous, and his Rosalind more healthy than genteel. He directed his painters to create a Forest of Arden in springtime colors with plenty of sunshine and greenery. The forest sets consisted of sliding panels and a panorama, so that scenes could change without interruption, with no let-down of liveliness or stalling of forward movement.[104] He engaged Signor Bianchini of the Paris Opera to design cheery dresses. He instructed his musicians to quicken the tempo of the songs.[105] He ordered his band of exiles to be "as merry as gypsies."

It was received, for the most part, as Daly intended. Dithmar of the *New York Times* praised everyone and everything, although, as if he were not in top form, his observations are rather platitudinous.[106] Winter was at his most exuberant. Half of his very long review marvels at the extraordinary happiness of life in the forest—"the brightest, the gayest and the loveliest production of *As You Like It* that our stage has ever known." Even Jaques, as interpreted by George Clarke, was in no sense a Hamlet, for not only did he not suffer, he took the keenest delight in his contemplative rumination and cynical satire. "Rosalind is the comedy," though, and much of Winter's essay is devoted to Miss Rehan's Rosalind. He can hardly stem the flow of vibrant terms that describe the character and the actress—"spiritually pure, intellectually brilliant, physically handsome, lithe, ardent and tender. . . . She is exultant in her physical life, her heart is full of tenderness, and what her heart feels her tongue must speak." And Miss Rehan discriminated perfectly, says Winter, between the lovely woman, the woman playing the boy, and the boy playing the woman. In the first act she revealed amply "the sweetness, the passion and the buoyancy of Rosalind's nature, and . . . the bewildered tremor naturally incident to the first love of a girl's heart." Then

Illus. 50. Ada Rehan as Rosalind in *As You Like It.* Folger Shakespeare Library.

in the second act, "in her state of liberty and not of banishment in the forest of Arden, Miss Rehan's gleeful animal spirits soon began to irradiate the performance, and from that time onward the inspiriting glow of happy-hearted raillery never flagged." The knowledge that she gleans from Orlando's verses that her love is reciprocated "liberates her into a gentle frenzy of pleasure, and this condition is expressed . . . by incessant frolic." Winter is insistent, too, on the utter perfection of Miss Rehan's speaking of Shakespeare's language—a matter that proved subject to debate. "No one acts a poetic part with more flexibility; no one speaks blank verse with more of the fluency of perfectly natural utterance; and no one delivers prose with a nicer perception of the melody inherent in our language."[107]

Turning to the *World* to discover what petard rascally Nym Crinkle has discovered this time to blow Daly once more at the moon, we are amazed to find an entire column of unmitigated praise. Daly had tried his favorite *As You Like It* twice before, in the 1870s, once with Mary Scott-Siddons, once with Fanny Davenport, with only mild success. But now in Ada Rehan he has found "the perfect Shakespearian maiden" for Rosalind. The production he presents her in is commendable for "the elaborate care and minute adjustment of the beautiful work and for the exquisite good taste . . . in every detail of the pastoral picture." He praises Daly for restoring the text. He praises him for the joyous springtime feeling of the setting, for keying the play to the gladness of Rosalind, and not to the conventional gloom of Jacques and "melancholy boughs." Jaques, too, tickled him by his comic, not oppressive reading of his cynical speeches. But above all, there was "the generous display of a beautiful woman," Ada Rehan. "Our generation go to see the Maid of Arden in her doublet and hose." Farther on "I suppose Rosalind is the sweetest and gentlest transcript of womanliness that Shakespeare has afforded us." But Shakespeare "clothed her about with the doublet and hose of another sex merely to show that her disposition has no doublet and hose in it."[108] Ten days later (December 29) he wrote again to congratulate New York on having two Shakespearean triumphs simultaneously—Daly's *As You Like It* and Richard Mansfield's *Richard III*—and the precipitate cancellation, because of "very vehement criticism," of Mrs. Mansfield's second performance of a play of the "Ibsen school," then called *Nora, or a Doll's Home.*

A similar "conversion" (I think I may call it so) is the editorial policy of Harrison Grey Fiske in the *Dramatic Mirror.* His attacks on Daly, often written by Nym Crinkle, had, of course, angered Daly, and in these times, so far as I have noticed, Daly did not advertise in the *Mirror.* And Fiske did not review *As You Like It* in mid-December when it opened. But its popularity was such that it had to be noticed. On January 4, 1890, in an unsigned column called "Unconsidered Trifles," occur several paragraphs of warm compliment to Miss Rehan. In the first place, when she became Ganymede she dressed herself to look like a boy. Marie Wainwright, who had lately played Viola-Cesario, so corseted herself to emphasize her feminine curves. But when Miss Rehan becomes Ganymede, "her figure is that of a thin, lithe young stripling. She has even dispensed with that rotundity of calf which most women called upon to appear in shortened skirts find it necessary to supplement by art, if nature has not vouchsafed it to them." Farther along appear compliments to Miss Rehan's reading:

> Except by Booth, I have never heard Shakespeare's words made so rich in meaning, nor rendered with such infinity of intonation. In this respect Miss Rehan has reached a point far beyond that which she touches in society drama. Nor have I seen speech given with such a running accompaniment of rhythmic gesture.

And over all, the graceful expressiveness and appropriateness of her movements:

> Her first falling in love with Orlando was a revelation of grace, a succession of beautiful movements that would have been the hope and despair of an artist. As Ganymede she flashes from one pose to another; none are conventional; often they are highly unconventional, but they are always restrained within the bounds of girlishness and always attractive.[109]

It is strange to find such eloquent admiration of Miss Rehan in a journal still generally hostile to Daly.

Others there were to whose ears Miss Rehan sounded a very different tune. Jeannette Gilder of *The Critic* did not like her at all. Daly's *production,* she thought, was "one of the most pleasing representations of the play seen in this city for a good many years." But as for Miss Rehan, she "played Rosalind in a style peculiarly her own. It was not Shakespearean, and it was not poetic to any marked degree." It was "animated, piquant, and feminine, but it lacked personal distinction and delicacy of sentiment." And Miss Rehan spoke her lines badly. "Her intonation was faulty, and her imperfect powers of elocution made her rebuke to the tyrant Duke . . . much less impressive than it ought to have been."[110]

Charles Meltzer, newly come to the *Herald,* condemned Daly's production out of hand:

Illus. 51. John Drew as Orlando. Folger Shakespeare Library.

Well, there's no denying it. Mr. Daly's comedians are modern comedians. Shakespeare does not fit them. The poetical gifts have been denied them. . . . When Miss Rehan and Mr. Drew and the rest were trying hardest to give the illusion of poetry, the thought would obtrude itself that they were only mummers.[111]

Stephen Fiske, in the *Spirit of the Times,* declared the play far beyond the capacity of Mr. Daly's "very light comedians," simply because their principal traffic and training was in "German farcicalities" rendered by Daly into "American slang."[112]

Rosalind's "incessant frolic," which so pleased Winter, did not please everyone. Henry Clapp of the Boston *Advertiser* found that as soon as she dressed for the woods she dissipated her force in random action. Her voice became high-pitched, he said, her manner hysterical, her gesturing excessive. She took up half the stage in "eye-fatiguing perambulations"—or, as an English critic later put it, in "steeple-chasing."[113] Many years afterward, Alfred Ayres would blame Daly for "Dalyizing" Miss Rehan in this very matter. All that Daly knew about acting, in Ayres's opinion, was summarized in his three-word motto: "Acting is action." He understood nothing of the art of repose. So his actors were forever on the run, "moving about and sawing the air . . . doing things for which there was no discernible reason."[114]

Charles Copeland of the Boston *Post* was one of the first to complain of a tasteless bit of stage business which critics would scold Miss Rehan for to the end of her career but could never persuade her to abandon. At the line "Alas the day! what shall I do with my doublet and hose?" every Rosalind in those days made a point of forgetting for an instant that she was "a man" and would make some shy and amusing gesture to cover her legs. But Miss Rehan overdid it, expressing, as Copeland put it, "an exaggerated horror" that Orlando would see her skirtless. She not only tugged at her tunic in vain effort to conceal her knees, but seized Celia's skirt and tried to hide her legs behind it. Besides being displeased by this gesture of false modesty, Copeland and others heard in her voice a squeal of shame that augmented the vulgarity of the gesture.[115] Graham Robertson, who knew her well enough to quiz her on the matter, discovered that she made such a conspicuous fuss over the business only because Daly told her to. Robertson gave her a reasoned explanation why it was artistically wrong. That made no difference. Even if he could convince her, she would still do what Daly ordered: "I should still feel sure that he was right and I was wrong." For Robertson this was proof conclusive that she was a real-life Trilby to Daly's Svengali.[116]

The general manners of the whole company—how they walked, gestured, spoke, rose and sat, wore their garments—seemed to many out of key with the text. "Put Mr. Drew in a nineteenth century drawing room and he is at home in it," said Charles Meltzer. "Set Miss Rehan in a Fifth Avenue conservatory and who can be more natural? But in the Forest of Arden they like most of Mr. Daly's clever artists, go astray, go unreal and uneasy. Rarely last night could I bring myself to take any of them *au sérieux.*"[117] Something very like this, though cast in more general terms, was intended by the reviewer for the Boston *Transcript.*

As might have been foreseen, a company . . . which has for many years expended its energies upon very different dramatic material from "As You Like It" . . . such a company does not show itself completely at home in this new dramatic and poetic atmosphere. Some of the old methods which have long been successfully relied on for effect are

Illus. 52. George Clarke as Jaques. Folger Shakespeare Library.

here found to be futile, and apart from the purpose. Some old, ingrained and inveterate stage habits do not quite fit the new demands.

By way of illustration this critic points out that Miss Rehan, though in her court costume of the first act was ideally beautiful, graceful, and dignified, as

soon as she doffs her female attire, and appears in the forest, she is miles away from the character. Effective she always is—that is to say, she delivers her lines in a way to make you laugh at their wit. But she is effective in such a small mimminy-pimminy, almost farcical way! She is so terribly mannered and artificial; you see the machinery so plainly at work![118]

In short, she carried into the Forest of Arden far too much of the social manners—styles of moving and speaking—that she had developed so efficiently for cute turns in comedies of contemporary fashionable life.

When Daly took *As You Like It* to Henry Irving's Lyceum in the summer of 1890 it fared vastly better with both public and critics than at home. London went wild over it. The *Daily Telegraph,* for instance, found the American actors' speech remarkably good—far more listenable, indeed, than London audiences were used to hearing from their native born and bred performers:

On our own stage it is rare to hear Shakespeare's lines spoken with such dignity, distinctness, and musical force. Here was just the happy mean between the modern familiar and flippant style and the frothy rhetoric of the old school. The text was spoken so clearly that everyone in the house understood it, but still with that sonorousness that Shakespeare's text demands. . . . English audiences go to sleep over Shakespeare because, as a rule, the text is delivered with such slovenliness. Last night all remained in their seats delighted until half-past eleven, and even then the majority were disinclined to go.[119]

Perhaps we should suspect in this flattery of the Americans an implied dispraise of England's own Henry Irving, who, for all his managerial skills, was usually accounted a poor speaker. And surely the *Illustrated London News* had Irving in its sights when it held up Daly as an object-lesson in the controversy over the actor-manager system. Daly is *not* an actor-manager, it argued—not an actor at all, but a *director.* He is a man of letters, a Shakespearean student, a book-collector, a man of culture, and under his firm, intelligent guidance his company behaves as an artistic commonwealth, each member concerned not merely for his personal advantage, but for the play: "The play is the very first consideration."[120]

As everyone in London knew, Irving ought to have staged *As You Like It* long before this for Ellen Terry's sake, but he had never done so, and after Daly's astonishing triumph that summer night in 1890, he could hardly have risked comparisons. Not that he liked what he saw. According to Graham Robertson, who shared a box with him, he grumbled at scene after scene. All that he had to say about Miss Rehan was, "How long d'you suppose those silk tights would last in the forest?" When the huntsmen entered to sing "What shall he have that killed the deer?" he objected to their "dancing along on their toes to the music," and snorted, "Does he think he's doing a comic opera?" When two girl singers, dressed like principal boys in a pantomime, tripped gaily on in polka step to sing "It was a lover and his lass," it was more than Irving could endure. "*Good* God!" he exclaimed, and departed."[121] He sent in his politeness note though. "A delightful performance, and Miss Rehan beyond praise. . . . It's a pity you can't play it more than six nights. It would grow and grow."[122]

Illus. 53. James Lewis and Isabel Irving as Touchstone and Audrey. Courtesy of the University of Illinois Theatre.

Daly did play it more than six nights. The reviews compelled him to. Streams of rapturous prose flowed through the London presses all that night and for two weeks thereafter. Daly was praised, the production was praised, Miss Rehan and the company were praised: "The conquest achieved by Miss Rehan over the audience was complete, and the enthusiasm was untiring and unbounded."[123] Now and then a critic would remember that long ago England had known an Age of Comedy, when one generation had rejoiced in the Irish wit of Peg Woffington and another in the silvery laughter of Dora Jordan. Perhaps that great age would return again. The audiences of 1890 could not have stomached the spiced dishes of those earlier times, and were certainly not ready for the *whole* text of the play, but they were grateful for Miss Rehan's discreet mixture of "womanliness" and romp, which was probably as much as they deserved.

Letters of congratulation poured in in a flood. William Winter, who had followed the company to England, could not sleep after the performance, and well after midnight was downstairs at Daly's hotel scribbling a report for the master. "There cannot be the least doubt of the success achieved this night. I heard the usual thing about the 'poetic' Rosalind—but there was but one opinion about Ada. 'We have left off criticizing her,' one man said—'We are enslaved by her.' " Squire Bancroft told Winter that Ada's was the best Rosalind he'd seen since Helen Faucit's twenty years earlier. Mrs. Bancroft said it was the best she had *ever* seen—so fresh and bright and new. "What I saw in Ada's performance," Winter went on, "was a beautiful symmetry—the building up of it and the rounding of it! Wonderful in everybody—*lovely in her.* And another thing—*your stage management, the detail, the completeness!* Mr. Bancroft said, 'I see one *guiding mind* in all this, and that of course is Daly's'. Well—that is the truth. No man knows it better than *I* do. This night has made me very glad."[124]

Mrs. Thomas Hardy wrote, reminding Miss Rehan that her husband had prophesied this triumph.[125] Sir Theodore Martin, husband to Helen Faucit, wrote Daly that he would prefer somewhat less frolicsomeness in the love scenes, but allowed that he had never seen the play presented with greater spirit of life.[126] Miss Faucit herself congratulated Miss Rehan and initiated an exchange of photographs.[127] Ellen Terry sent her a long scarlet feather—the one Irving had worn as Mephistopheles, to "give *vim* to yr. cap."[128]

The novelist Justin McCarthy wrote her that "Rosalind never lived till tonight & I never understood the fantastic divine comedy till tonight. . . . I have it in my heart to wander all over Kensington Gardens tomorrow carving the name of Rosalind upon every tree trunk. But London is not Arden & I, alas, am not Orlando—but only the humblest, the most devoted of your servants."[129]

The next Sunday after the London opening was Daly's birthday, and Miss Rehan sent him a loving cup and a loving letter.

> My dear Gov:
>
> Many many happy returns of the day. I send you a cup that cannot be easily broken, with the hope that it may always be as full of happiness & success as your life has been for the last few days, & that the days may grow into years. May I add the selfish wish that I may be with you to share them. I also wish to acknowledge your generous assistance for the high position I hold today in my profession. May God bless you.
>
> Sincerely & most affectionately
> Ada.[130]

The week may well have been the most gratifying in Ada Rehan's entire career—professional triumph before the London audience and a feast of friendship, happiness, and love.

For 1893 Daly determined to surpass all his previous Shakespearean accomplishments: in *Twelfth Night* he found stuff that appealed with extraordinary intensity to his "creative" instincts. He disassembled the play and rebuilt it, cleansed it of every grossness, doubled the amount of music that Shakespeare called for (but canceled that too gloomy song "Come away death"), hired Graham Robertson to costume it in the high esthetic mode,[131] and invented the most striking scenic effects, from violent storm to rose garden by moonlight. By cutting more than six hundred lines he got rid of everything that might endanger the "poetry" and "beauty." His efforts hit popular taste exactly as he intended. In New York *Twelfth Night* ran for six weeks (February 21 to April 8); it finished the season in Boston; a year later it enjoyed over 100 performances in London; it stayed in Daly's repertory to the end.[132]

Most of the publishing critics echoed or even promoted the popular enthusiasm. Yet there were deep divisions. Consider only the responses to Miss Rehan's Viola. Out of William Winter's review (some two thousand words, all evidently composed in advance) we may cull such sentences as these:

> Viola is a woman of deep sensibility: and that way Miss Rehan has comprehended and reproduced her, permitting a certain wistful sadness to glimmer through the gauze of kindly vivacity with which, otherwise, her whole bright and gentle figure is artfully swathed. . . . The great underlying cause of her brilliant success was the profound sincerity of

her feeling—over which her glee was seen to play, as moonlight plays upon the rippling surface of the ocean depth. . . . Lovely reserve and aristocratic distinction blended in the performance, and dignified and endeared it. The melody of Shakespeare's verse—especially in the passage of Viola's renunciation—fell from her lips in a strain of fluent sweetness that enhanced its beauty and deepened the pathos of its under significance. In such tones the heart speaks. . . . Her elocution was at its best—concealing all premeditation, and flowing, as the brook flows, with continuous music. . . . Her performance was as natural and as sweet as the opening of the rose.[133]

Jeannette Gilder of *The Critic* thought quite otherwise:

Miss Ada Rehan, when in her proper element, which is one of archness, or frolic or pretty petulance, is a most charming actress who need fear no rival; but in characters whose very essence is romantic, poetic and sentimental she is misplaced. Her defects are those of temperament, not of intelligence. Her delivery of verse is monotonous and unsympathetic, and her style of acting lacks the delicacy, refinement and grace necessarily associated with the heroines of poetry and imagination. In interpreting them she is compelled to restrain her own natural vivacity, and to substitute for it a colorless demeanor which is necessarily ineffective and often dull.[134]

These opinions confronted each other everywhere in the press. Dithmar of the *New York Times* wrote two long reviews praising every aspect of the production, defending Daly from "the jibe and the jest and the sneer" so often directed against him, and declaring that "surely the actress never before seemed so lovely as she did in her page's garb, or spoke so well, or mingled in her acting archness and sentiment, the passion of womanhood, the unquenchable spirit of youth so deftly." Against this Towse of the *Evening Post* declared that "in the more delicate, sentimental and purely poetic interludes her droning singsong robbed the familiar lines of almost all their familiar beauty." In Boston Arthur Warren of the *Herald* found nothing to blame; Clapp of the *Advertiser* and Mrs. Sutherland of the *Transcript* were reluctant to praise.[135]

In *The Critic* Miss Gilder isolated one weakness of the production very clearly: "the general richness of the setting excites expectations with regard to the acting which, unfortunately, are not always realized." Daly's company, or what was left of it, was not right for the play. John Drew, who might have played Orsino, had defected. Otis Skinner was gone. Arthur Bourchier rehearsed Orsino but quarreled with Daly and resigned. The part was then taken on short notice and played without distinction by Creston Clarke (a nephew of Edwin Booth). Perky little James Lewis would be nobody's idea of a proper Toby Belch, but Daly padded his thighs and belly and instructed him to be jolly but not at all vulgar: the "carousal scenes" passed very tamely, said *The Critic*. Except for Winter, not even friends of the management were much amused by these scenes.[136] George Clarke's Malvolio started off well enough, but his Yellow Stockings Scene lost its point because he was dressed in a dainty costume of pastel colors, pretty but not ridiculous: his cross-gartering consisted of bands of white ribbon on pale yellow hose.[137] Feste, which Lewis might have made a good thing of, was relieved of most of his speeches and assigned to a sweet-voiced singer, Lloyd Daubigny, who was no comedian and was hardly called upon to "act" at all.[138]

As for Miss Rehan's Viola, it appears that although she was adored for her personal beauty, she had great difficulty at first in finding what to make of the part. Her situation was much the same as that when Daly cast her as Helena in the *Dream.* There was no room in Viola for the explosiveness of her Katherine nor for the wit and merriment of her Rosalind. Viola, confined to a dramatic situation which she cannot dominate, has to be rescued from it; and Miss Rehan, thus prevented from lifting and carrying the play, was subdued by it.[139] Happily, there are signs that in time her performance improved. When the production went to London, William Archer, A. B. Walkley, and Shaw—though they could not abide Daly's arrangement of the text—were all delighted by her Viola. The *Athenaeum* called it "bewitching." Archer took mild exception to the slowness of her speaking, her exaggerated pauses and excessively lengthened vowels, but both he and Walkley actually preferred her Viola to her Rosalind. For Shaw, "the moment she strikes up the true Shakespearian music, and feels her way to her part altogether by her sense of that music, the play returns to life and all the magic is there."[140] When Clapp of Boston saw the play a second time in the autumn of 1894, he withdrew his initial objections and declared she had "accomplished a wonderful advance," was now "almost beyond praise."[141] By 1898, Norman Hapgood, a hard man to please, sounded as deep in love with her Viola as everyone else: "As Viola her varied voice is kept at its sweeter, easier, more natural tones, her face is quiet with a sad love, an expression across which the lighter humor flits from moment to moment. . . . It stands as one of the best Shakespearean interpretations of the time."[142]

Daly was far more interested in creating spectacular stage effects than concerned for Shakespeare's play, and his tamperings were so outrageous as to deserve the compliments of a certain philistine critic named Vance Thompson, who declared that "he is doing what Colley Cibber did for his generation, and he is doing it quite as well." According to this Thompson, Daly's "method of ameliorating and remodeling the Shakespearean plays is the only feasible one." Every generation must take from the plays those qualities which are "in the line of its own fashionable modes of amusement," and what the modern amusement hunter wants is "pretty faces, pretty music, pretty pictures." Thompson is aware that the attitude he is expressing is not that of a superior person: "but you and I, it is to be hoped, are not superior persons and have learned that when we cannot get the moon it is well to put up with the substitute of wholesome green cheese."[143]

Shakespeare's opening scene sets theme and tone for the play as Duke Orsino, accompanied by sweet music, broods over his unrequited love for the lady Olivia; next Shakespeare presents Viola at the sea shore, just rescued from shipwreck, hoping desperately that her beloved brother has not been drowned. Daly was not the first nor would he be the last to "improve" the play by reversing these two scenes, but his improvement is the most radical that anyone ever perpetrated. He had read *The Tempest* and discovered there how to get the evening going with a bang. With darkened stage and Storm Music he worked up his theatre's full potential of thunder, lightning, wind, and rain. Gradually the storm subsided, the music calmed, the rising dawn revealed through mists a boat lying alongside the rocky shore. The mists cleared. A Chorus was heard in the distance singing Ariel's song, "Come unto these yellow sands." When the lights were up to full, who should arrive but Viola's brother Sebastian and his rescuer Antonio, who were not supposed to be seen until Shakespeare's second act. When they explained themselves and went their ways, the Chorus, a band of happy Illyrian peasants, danced across the stage singing "Come unto these yellow sands" at top volume. Then at last came Viola with her Captain, sailors, and baggage, the Captain singing another snatch from *The Tempest*—Stephano's "I shall no more to sea, to sea. Here shall I die on shore." Viola's worry about her brother may have seemed a bit pointless, since the audience had just seen him in perfect health, but probably at that moment the audience was less concerned with plot than Viola's glorious costume. Though just arrived out of the stormy ocean, she appeared to be on her way to a fashionable soirée—a white gown embroidered with delicate gold patterns, the deep sleeves trimmed with wide gold fringe, a full-length rose-red cape draped from her shoulders.

When she heard about Orsino, and went off to "serve this duke," Daly then turned back to Shakespeare's opening scene. Probably he was uneasy about the boldness of his "improvement," for he consulted the leading American Shakespearean, H. H. Furness, about it. Furness's response must have gratified him hugely, and encouraged him to commit even further violations of the text:

> In the name of sanctity why do you think I'll be shocked at any changes which a modern playwright thinks best to make in the omission or transposition of scenes in Shakespeare? His stage is not our stage, his audiences are not our audiences. 'Tis only additions like Dryden's, Tate's or Garrick's that are lèse majesté. Your partial combination of the two seacoast scenes strikes me as excellent.[144]

Furness urged him, too, to eliminate the final appearance of Malvolio, a suggestion which Daly would accept and improve upon.

When he finally got round to the Orsino Scene he had quite lost sight of its Shakespearean significance, and after the Storm Scene it must have seemed to him impossibly thin and feeble. He glamorized it. When the curtain rose on the love-lorn bachelor in his palatial quarters, he did not strike one as love-lorn at all: nine pretty girls—musicians, singers, and dancers—stood or knelt or lay about the stage. When he called for music they treated him not to a brief strain with a dying fall, but a full concert rendition of Sir Henry Bishop's setting of the twenty-fifth stanza of *Venus and Adonis,* "Bid me discourse, I will enchant thine ear." After the song they performed an Oriental dance.[145]

There was a technical reason for thus stretching out this first Orsino scene. At the end of it Orsino would cut ahead to scene four, calling for Cesario, and Miss Rehan had to be ready at the entrance in her green doublet and hose (identical with the costume in which we have already seen her brother). As Shakespeare arranged his narrative, she would have had the long Sir Toby scene (I.3) in which to make the costume change, but in order to reduce the amount of scene-shifting Daly postponed the Sir Toby scene and tacked together two Orsino scenes (I.1 and I.4). Thus, in order to give Miss Rehan time enough in her dressing room he had to pad the first Orsino Scene with song and dance.

The "carousal" scenes (Shakespeare's I.3 and II.3, also tacked together) were not played below stairs, as had long been the custom, but in Olivia's beautifully appointed drawing room—dainty furniture, a bronze chandelier, gilt statues on tall pedestals—and through a wide archway at the back a view of a pretty garden. It was hardly the ambience for Shakespeare's low comedy. But Daly did not want it to be *very* low. William Winter had urged from the beginning that "Sir Toby will not be made a foul & dirty Sir Toby—for that is not necessary."[146] Business with tobacco

Illus. 54. Orsino in *Twelfth Night* surrounded by his entertainers. Folger Shakespeare Library.

Illus. 55. Herbert Gresham as Aguecheek, Lloyd Daubigny as Feste, and James Lewis as Sir Toby in *Twelfth Night.* Folger Shakespeare Library.

pipes and flagons was kept to a minimum and nobody got very drunk or very amusing. In the second of these scenes, the late night one, there was a great deal of singing of "catches," all those named by Shakespeare—"Hold thy peace," "Three merry men be we," and "There dwelt a man in Babylon." Daly added two more that had crept into the play a century earlier:

Christmas comes but once a year
And therefore we'll be jolly

and this one, probably sung as a round:

Which is the properest day to drink,
Saturday, Sunday, Monday?
Each is the properest day I think.
Why should I name but one day?
Tuesday, Wednesday, Thursday, Friday,
Saturday, Sunday, Monday.[147]

Feste did not sing "O mistress mine" in this scene but at Orsino's court in place of "Come away, death."

The gulling of Malvolio—the Letter Scene—took place in a spectacularly beautiful garden in front of Olivia's house. The house, a two-story structure, which one entered by mounting steps at either end of a high porch, stood at an angle at stage right. Downstage of the porch and near it was a garden chair, and across at stage left a stone bench. While Malvolio strolled about center stage, musing and preening himself, the pranksters hid behind a massive bank of very pink roses at upper left center. Across the back of the garden was a kind of picket fence with an arched opening at center, beyond which lay another flowered garden and beyond that the sea.

To mark the transition between the Letter Scene and Cesario's second visit to Olivia, which followed without intervening dialogue, Feste sang the first stanza of "It was a lording's daughter," the fifteenth item in Shakespeare's *The Passionate Pilgrim.*

The sentimental climax of the play was entirely a Daly intervention—a tableau sustained by a serenade. After the farcical violence of the Cesario-Sir Andrew duel, Viola heard words from Antonio that intimated that her brother was alive. Sinking into the garden chair near the porch she soliloquized, "O, if it prove, Tempests are kind, and salt waves fresh in love." Dusk was gathering, the new moon rose over the sea (in the west!), and music sounded. Through the archway up center came Orsino, followed by his band of girl-musicians, who half-hidden behind the bank of roses sang "Fair Olivia, what is she?" (Schubert's setting of the Sylvia song from *The Two Gentlemen of Verona*). Olivia appeared on her high porch, and looking down discovered Orsino gazing up at her. Turning away in annoyance, she discovered Cesario, and fixed her gaze lovingly on *him*—who was, of course, gazingly lovingly at Orsino. "The garden was all in moonlight," wrote William Winter; "The delicious music flowed on, and over that perfect pageant of romance the curtain fell."[148] Even Bernard Shaw allowed that this Dalyism was both permissible and seductive, "thanks to Schubert and to the conductor, Mr. Henry Widmer, who has handled the music in such a fashion as to get the last drop of honey out of it."[149]

All that remained of the play (Acts IV and V) after this feast of music and moonlight Daly packed into a single act. Not much remained that served Daly's purpose: a bit of sword play between Sir Toby and Sebastian, Olivia's drawing Sebastian offstage to marry him, the recognition between brother and sister, and Orsino's taking Viola for his "fancy's queen."

There was no room for Malvolio in this world of happy lovers. Everything after his Yellow Stockings Scene—the Prison Scene, his demand for retribution, his furious exit ("I'll be revenged on the whole pack of you")—was eventually canceled. Furness had urged Daly to omit Malvolio's very last appearance: "We really do not want to see Malvolio again—the laugh has died out & it can with difficulty be revived."[150] Furness as much as Daly appears to have been oblivious to the ambivalence, the irony, the weight of the Malvolio story: Malvolio was a joke or he was nothing. And Daly objected to Malvolio even more strongly. As he told Winter, Malvolio's ordeal was painful and tiresome. He had got all the laughs that could be got out of the foolish gull, and these bitter passages only undercut and destroyed the "poetical" climax which he had so cunningly created. Though he printed the Prison Scene, he cut it from the performance. He sped the love affairs to their joyous conclusion, and while Feste and Maria sang the three most "innocent" stanzas of "Hey, ho, the wind and the rain," the company of lovers danced a galliard.

Of the many reviews of this *Twelfth Night* that I have seen, surprisingly few have been troubled that Daly smashed the play in order to turn it into a musical entertainment. Arthur Warren of the Boston *Herald* offered an apologetic nod to those devoted Shakespeareans who might regard it as sacrilegious to cut lines, dispense with scenes, and subordinate characters in order to suit the tastes of modern audiences. "Malvolio has been somewhat slighted," Warren admitted, "and he is not as prominent a figure in the comedy as the author intended he should be, but, after all, there is much matter concerning this character which usually has the effect of wearying an audience."[151] That idiot, before mentioned, who

Illus. 56. George Clarke as Malvolio delivering a ring to Ada Rehan's Viola (Cesario). Folger Shakespeare Library.

Illus. 57. Catherine Lewis as Maria laying the bait for Malvolio: Folger Shakespeare Library.

would give up the moon for wholesome green cheese, defended Daly with the argument that "it is no compliment to Shakespeare to make art dull."[152] When the play got to England, William Archer reminded us that he disapproved of Daly's method, but as if weary of the struggle he only cited a few absurd misreadings and omissions (Feste was denied his "Ginger shall be hot i' the mouth too"), and borrowed a few neat whacks from Shaw, who, as Corno di Bassetto, was responsible only for covering the music.[153]

Only Henry Clapp of Boston, after a second viewing, was sufficiently annoyed to enter sustained complaint. The best parts of the performance, he acknowledged, were "almost beyond praise," but there was "much which could scarcely be endured." The singing was abundant and excellent, and the choral rendition of "Bid me discourse" was pleasant to the ear—"even if the eye was a little amused by the resemblance of the court of Orsino, the 'bachelor' duke, to a Turkish seraglio." But in order to make room for so much music, and as a concession to scenic arrangements, "characters are made to march in and out with utter unreason," and Daly

> found it necessary to tear and pare and clip and snip Shakespeare's text . . . with a frankly insolent recklessness which would not have discredited Colley Cibber or Nahum Tate. Passages memorable in every line are presented in scarcely recognizable fragments; many of the most familiar are sacrificed altogether; and not seldom a cruel telephone abridgement is practised upon splendid pieces of wit, and the audience are treated to an exact half of some immortal world-famous joke. Turning *Twelfth Night* from a comedy into an operetta, even in a half dozen scenes, is certainly illegitimate. But the most extraordinary defeat of the spirit of comedy achieved by this version must not escape being noted. For the first time in who can say how many centuries, the entire revels of Sir Toby, Sir Andrew and the Clown are

conducted without the assistance of apparent drinking and smoking,—perhaps for fear of spoiling the scenery.

The revelry concluded with a noisy dance and no words: it was useless for Sir Toby to shout "it's too late to go to bed now" when there was neither wine nor tobacco to stay up for.

But not even Clapp takes exception to the dismissal of Malvolio from the play after the Yellow Stockings Scene. All that seriously mattered, even to Clapp, was that "the evening was made beautiful and delightsome by Miss Rehan's Viola."[154]

And that, of course, was Daly's whole intention—to feed the public appetite for prettiness and sentiment. He gave them lovely scenery bathed in atmospheric sweetness, pretty costumes designed by the delicate artist Graham Robertson (and to Robertson's dismay, *re*designed them to make them prettier), beautiful women, nothing to embarrass or worry anyone, and over all a wash of lovely music gathered *ad libitum* from anywhere. And Daly was rewarded. The historian and diplomat John Hay, for instance, thanked him for "this beautiful and masterly presentation of one of Shakespeare's most poetical works." Hay had come up to New York from Washington especially to take his children to it, and his own delight had been heightened by theirs. "It is hard to estimate the good you are doing in putting before the public such a magnificent result of combined industry, liberality, intelligence, and taste," he wrote. "Your 'Twelfth Night' is saturated with beauty and poetry; the most enchanting dreams of fairyland are there, incarnate before our eyes. I hardly see how scenic art can go farther."[155]

Of the half-dozen other Shakespeares that Daly attempted after 1890, not one achieved genuine success. In 1891 (March 29 to April 11), before Drew left him, he offered a new production of *Love's Labors Lost* (it had failed him in 1874), doubtless counting on the team of Rehan and Drew to bring it off. He wasted them, however, by casting them as the Princess of France and the King of Navarre instead of as Rosaline and Berowne, where there was strong comic work to do. Rehearsals, he found, were like "trying to squeeze juice out of a stone,"[156] and the production failed in two weeks. In 1895 he undertook *The Two Gentlemen of Verona* (February 21 to March 19, plus a week in London), depending for box office appeal upon productional effects, Miss Rehan's Julia heightened into a star part, and the fact that the play had not been seen in New York since Charles Kean's three nights of it in 1846. He made his own acting version, "on the usual principles," said Bernard Shaw, "altering, transposing, omitting, improving, correcting, and transferring speeches from one character to another."[157] But not even Miss Rehan's pleasing exhibition of herself in page-boy costume, nor the moonlit lake Daly invented for the environs of Milan, nor a thunderstorm in the final act could make up for the tenuousness of the narrative. In New York it played only 26 performances.

The year 1896 found Daly waging an ugly little campaign against Julia Marlowe, who with her husband Robert Taber was bringing her company into New York City for the first time in five years.[158] His own company was to be on tour when she came, but hearing that she would open with *Romeo and Juliet,* he quickly engaged the fashionable Mrs. James Brown Potter and Kyrle Bellew and set them up at Daly's Theatre in a handsome staging of the same play. They opened on March 3 but failed, deservedly, in three weeks.[159] Miss Marlowe's main hope was to conquer New York with her transvestite rendition of Prince Hal in *Henry IV.* Accordingly, Daly planned a *Henry IV* with Miss Rehan as Hal. When Marlowe's production failed, Daly aborted his, although toward the end of the year he did put his acting version into print.

In December of 1896, Daly produced *Much Ado About Nothing,* which ran for a comparatively successful seven weeks (December 21 to February 7). It might have done much better had he staged it five years earlier, when John Drew could have partnered Miss Rehan, and James Lewis would have led the comics; but Drew was gone and Lewis was dead, and, as Towse says, Daly had little left of his old company but the scene painters. And even Miss Rehan never really "got into the skin" of Beatrice, said Towse. She fell back upon her old impersonation of Katherine the Shrew, and "imparted a bitterness, not to say a rudeness, to the sallies of the fair disputant which does not belong to them.[160]

The Tempest (April 6 to 23, 1897) was reduced to a raree show. Half of the text was omitted,[161] and the evenings were largely turned over to the musicians and the stage machinists. William Winter loyally pretended to be "calmed, ennobled, and refreshed" by "the high influence of poetry that proceeds from the heart of it."[162] But young Norman Hapgood, newly come to the drama desk of the *Commercial Advertiser,* was puzzled that anyone could be taken in by the

awkwardly moving canvas clouds, rickety rocks that are too plainly made of cloth and wooden frames, supers with animals' heads that do not fit at the neck, and girls swinging in midair on obvious wires. Prospero cannot be believed in as a magician, when you see all the machinery that works his miracles, and can actually hear an impatient voice tell the moving rocks, sundered by a wave of Prospero's wand, to "Hurry up there!"[163]

Illus. 58. Sidney Herbert as Shylock in the opening scene of *The Merchant of Venice.* Folger Shakespeare Library.

Illus. 59. Carnival outside Shylock's house during the elopement of Jessica. Folger Shakespeare Library.

Illus. 60. After the Trial, Portia welcomes the company to Belmont. Folger Shakespeare Library.

Remarkably, Miss Rehan was not in the starting company, but she did fill in as Miranda during the final week.

Daly's last major effort, a costly one, was spent on *The Merchant of Venice* (November 19, 1898 to January 2, 1899). Scenically it was gorgeous, but except for Miss Rehan the actors were by no means up to the demands of the text. Charles Richman spoke and posed and moved so badly as Bassanio that one critic claimed to have been as fearful as Portia herself that he would choose the wrong casket.[164] Sidney Herbert looked like Shylock, but was simply too young and inexperienced—"a stock actor in a star part," as Joseph Daly defined him[165]—to realize either the fury or the pathos of the role. The text was cut and disarranged as usual, partly to build up the role of Portia with delayed entrances and give her the curtain lines, partly in a frenzied effort to make the play "clean." Lines containing such words as "stake" and "pen" and "ring" were dropped because to Daly's nice mind they were obscene. The Act I set, though unmistakably Venetian, was an inadequate imitation of the set invented for Booth and Barrett ten years earlier—a view from the Riva degli Schiavoni across the water toward Santa Maria della Salute.[166] The action began with pantomime, Hapgood reports, "various people silently guying each other"; and as the dialogue sets in, "to keep the speeches from boring the audience, property Venetians pass to and fro, and particularly efficient work is done by a troupe of small children, who chase one another about the street, running and laughing."[167] The Elopement Scene, with Shylock's house and a great bridge crossing a canal, likewise echoed but "improved upon" scenic arrangements of earlier producers. Whereas the house in the Booth-Barrett production was "mouldy and crumbling," Daly painted it prettily and covered it with roses. Jessica was serenaded with a song from *Cymbeline,* "My lady, sweet, arise," and a horde of carnival revelers performed an elaborate dance to celebrate the joy of the elopement. This was too much even for William Winter, who declared it "ludicrous and incredible."[168] The final scene outside Portia's mansion in Belmont was all too beautiful, according to John Corbin—"good enough to distract attention from Shakespeare's lines." In fact, so many lines were cut from the act that it took as long to set the scene as to play what lines were left, and, said John Corbin, "any sensible man would put on his coat at the end of the fourth act and go home and read them unhampered in his study."[169]

One fine personality actress, plus pretty pictures, would not suffice. Most of the critics were forgiving, but not enthusiastic, and by December 1 Daly knew he was losing his audiences. "I think I am more discouraged over the results of this production than any that I have yet experienced."[170] The production came too late in the history of the company. A few months later he was dead, his theatre was sold, and the production had no chance to grow. When Miss Rehan tried to revive it in 1904 with Otis Skinner, her own art had also died and the attempt was a gloomy failure.

Chapter III

The Feminization of Shakespeare

During the last quarter of the nineteenth century and throughout the Edwardian era, society in America, in England, and all of Western or Westernized Europe experienced an extraordinary intensification of woman-worship. This had nothing to do with the simultaneous rise of women's rights movements—its impulse, indeed, was quite the opposite. What the fashion magazines of, say, the 1890s demonstrate with their displays of Professional Beauties in party gowns—exposed glowing shoulders, conspicuous bosoms, constricted waists, swelling hips, and long sweeping trains as astonishing as peacocks' tails—is that women were being dressed and paraded, coveted by men and envied by women, for their attractiveness as sex-objects.

Proper Englishmen and Americans blamed the French for generating the new eroticism and for promoting it in literature, art, and the theatre. Thus, for instance, when Dumas's novel *La Dame aux Camélias* became a stage play *(Camille)* in 1853, it was not allowed on British stages, or in its original form, in America. But what was too wicked to be said in English could be sung in languages audiences did not understand: Verdi's operatic version, *La Traviata,* was embraced at once. Presently, though, English-speaking audiences began to accept the play itself—in bleached versions under fumigating titles. In Jean Davenport's version, labeled *The Fate of a Coquette* (1863), Camille was rather carelessly flirtatious but no one could doubt that she was at bottom a "good woman." She really loved Armand, and for his sake she gave up her "dissipations." In spite of good intentions, however, she contracted a pulmonary disorder and died as "tragically" as Dumas intended. In Laura Keene's version, subtitled *A Moral of Life* (1856), Camille's naughtiness happened but did not happen: it was all a play-within-a-play, a dream. Camille, a common serving girl who was in love with Armand, longed for polkas and champagne. Her good mother fairly warned her where sin would take her, but all unheeding, Camille went her way, which, of course, led straight to consumption and death. But as the catstrophe drew near, she awoke. The tragic but redemptive part of the story had been only a dream. The beloved Armand was alive and available. She married him and lived happy ever after.

In Britain, audiences were protected against corruptive influences in the theatre by official censorship operating under the Office of the Lord Chamberlain. In America from the late 1860s the unofficial but equally stringent censorship by Anthony Comstock, self-appointed Secretary of the Society for the Suppression of Vice, insulated theatre-goers—and book readers and gallery-goers too—from anything suggestive of sex. Between 1868 and World War I, Comstock is credited with impounding and destroying 160 tons of books and pictures conducive to sin.[1]

Comstock could destroy objects, but with all his confiscatory powers he could not suppress the public's natural delight in seeing pretty women in their parlors and on their stages. And as public taste in Shakespeare drew away from the great masculine tragedies—*Caesar, Macbeth, Othello,* and *Lear*—and turned "to favor and to prettiness" of the lighter plays, flocks of young actresses, sweet to look upon and sometimes good to hear, came fluttering from the wings. After the death of Charlotte Cushman in the mid-1870s, Amazonian overwhelmers were rarely featured in the bills. Emma Waller, Fanny Janauschek, Mrs. D. P. Bowers and others remained available when "heavies"

Illus. 61. Mrs. D. P. Bowers as Lady Macbeth.

Illus. 62. Madame Fanny Janauschek.

were needed, but Queen Katherine, Constance, and Volumnia were seen but rarely; and Lady Macbeth no longer "pitched into" Macbeth in the old Cushman manner: she seduced him, as in England Ellen Terry seduced Henry Irving's Macbeth, with womanly allure.

The cleverest of this new breed of "womanly women" often took command of the profession. Many of them hired and led their own companies, chose and directed their own plays, were featured on posters and in newspaper advertisements, and usurped the attention of the critics, who lavished paragraphs upon the lady stars and saved a few sentences at the end to mention the Romeos, Malvolios, Orlandos, and Benedicks who acted "in support." Audiences flocked to adore these much advertised tender Juliets, sparkling Rosalinds and Beatrices, and gentle Violas.

Augustin Daly's whole managerial career, as we have seen, turned more and more to woman-worship. Throughout the 1870s he surrounded himself with adorable young ladies, some of whom occasionally filled Shakespearean assignments—Ada Dyas, Nina Varian, Sara Jewett, and Agnes Ethel among them—and in at least one season he carried a troupe of "Daly Debutantes," pretty girls from good families whose business was to lounge or stroll or dance about the stage in elegant dresses. In the 1880s Virginia Dreher, a charming girl from the South, worthily seconded Ada Rehan as Mistress Page, Bianca, and Hermia. Then as public affection for Miss Rehan grew into almost a cult (and Daly's affection for her grew into a personal passion), Daly promoted her above everything else. His theatre became a temple where the people gathered to worship the beloved Ada, a secular Madonna.

There were hosts of these adorables on our stages. When Fanny Davenport (1850–98), always given to plumpness, emerged as Rosalind in the mid-1870s, William Winter described her as "first a buxom beauty, and then a saucy boy."[2] Frederick Schwab of the *New York Times* was quite delighted with her "Swinburnean opulence of charms," and fancied that in her "floss of satin and sheen of pearls" in the court scenes she had stepped right out of Tennyson's *Dream of Fair Women*.[3] Everyone agreed, though, that in the

Illus. 63. Mrs. Emma Waller.

Illus. 64. Sara Jewett, Ada Dyas, and Nina Varian, typical young beauties of the day, many of whom played for Daly.

forest scenes she was far too hoydenish—pert and piquant and jolly, but altogether forgetting the tender side of Rosalind—her affectionateness, timidity, and touches of melancholy. In Imogen and Viola, too, she put plenty of bravado into her scenes in male disguise, but lacked the delicacy that belongs to those characters. And so, long before her career ended, Miss Davenport faded from public favor.

Rose Eytinge (1835–1911), "a handsome brunette, with brilliant dark eyes, an ample figure, a strong, melodious voice," usually starred in modern society drama, but in 1877 she played a Cleopatra in New York that William Winter would later single out as the best he had ever seen in his sixty or seventy years of playgoing. He declared "her temperament ardent and passionate, her character formidable, her knowledge of all the arts of female coquetry complete, and her comprehension at least of Cleopatra's waywardness, caprice, and fiery temper thorough and exact."[4]

Two attractive visitors from England found their way into Shakespeare after beginning their stage careers in London burlesque (comic and satiric take-offs of currently successful serious plays). Ada Cavendish (1847–95), slender, graceful, golden-haired, and Rose Coghlan (1851–1932), a handsome, black-haired Irish girl, were both accounted delightful to see and listen to, though both, owing to their early training in broad comedy, were criticized at first for too much exuberance and not enough sentiment. William Winter thought that the Cavendish brought the right level of power to Juliet's Potion Scene and Tomb Scene, and that her skill at banter made her a better Beatrice than a Rosalind.[5]

When Miss Coghlan first played Rosalind in 1880, Winter found her to be handsome but lacking "refinement."[6] She remained in America (became a citizen), and eventually her Rosalind became a genuine American favorite: "Hers is no rose-petal Rosalind," said a Boston critic, "all nerves and no blood. She is brimming with animal spirits, fantastic in a wholesome

Illus. 65. Fanny Davenport as Rosalind. Folger Shakespeare Library.

Illus. 66. Ada Cavendish. Courtesy of the University of Illinois Theatre.

Illus. 67. Rose Coghlan.

Illus. 68. Rose Eytinge.

way. . . . She shows a healthy sense of humor—a thing no fool ever yet possessed—which prevents her sentiment from becoming flimsy or shallowly sentimental."[7] In 1887 she played Rosalind in a famous outdoor production at Manchester, Massachusetts.[8] This affair, perhaps inspired by Lady Archibald Campbell's production in the forest of Coombe in Surrey three years earlier, was arranged by Agnes Booth Schoeffel (herself a sometime successful Rosalind) to raise money for the Actors' Fund of America. In 1891 Miss Coghlan again played Rosalind out-of-doors for a charity at Castle Point, Hoboken.[9]

A beautiful and dependable, if not brilliant, actress who began as a sorely untutored Juliet when she was nineteen, was Marie Wainwright (1853–1923). She developed steadily during the next decade, and by January of 1889 her Rosalind was praised by New York critics for its straightforwardness and sincerity. On this occasion, defying the management, she discarded the high boots prescribed for her Ganymede costume and went into the forest in maroon stockings. Nym Crinkle was gratified by the sight of "her shapely and spring-time limbs in their entirety."[10] Teamed now with Louis James, whom she married, she starred in the romantic comedies, and played Ophelia, Desdemona, and so forth in support of James's tragic heroes.

One remarkable event in the feminization of Shakespeare was an *As You Like It* with an all-female cast. The wife of A. M. Palmer, the theatre manager, wanting to establish a fund in aid of unemployed actresses, got up this performance, which took place at her husband's theatre on November 21, 1893.

Illus. 69. Marie Wainwright as Viola.

Strange as it must have seemed to hear the formidably whiskered Duke Frederick pipe his threats in a girlish treble, yet the affair netted $2,500 for the cause and was accounted an artistic success. Joe Jefferson said he had never seen the play so well done in all its parts. Mary Shaw was the Rosalind, Maude Banks the Orlando, Fanny Janauschek (a natural heavy) the Jaques. Kate Davis's Touchstone was enthusiastically applauded, and May Robson as Audrey chewed turnips to everybody's satisfaction. Besides the regular cast, 106 actresses served as courtiers, halbardiers, guards, pages, shepherds, and shepherdesses. House management was taken over by twenty-seven actresses and society belles. Palmer's crew of stage carpenters shoved the sets about, keeping discreetly out of sight.[11]

Adelaide Neilson

Throughout the 1870s by far the most enchanting Shakespearean actress on the American stage was the young Englishwoman Lillian Adelaide Neilson (1846?–80), who visited America during four seasons.[12] In 1872 and 1873 she brought Juliet and Rosalind; in 1874 she added Beatrice; in 1876–77 Viola and Imogen, in 1879–80 Isabella. Of these, the universal favorite was Juliet. "Forever and forever, as long as history endures, Miss Neilson will be the Juliet most enthralling to lovers of the stage." So wrote George Odell half a century after her death—though, to be sure, he had never seen her. "Her rich, dark-eyed beauty, her grace, her pensive charm, her intensity, her golden voice—these are the spells by which she still takes the imagination captive."[13]

In 1865, when as a novice of nineteen she first played Juliet in London, a romantic legend sprang up to account for her apparently un-English beauty and origin. She was born in Spain, near Saragossa, so the story went, her father a Spanish nobleman, her mother an English governess, and she was educated in the finest schools of Italy and France. The facts are quite otherwise. She was born out of wedlock, at Leeds, in Yorkshire, to an obscure actress on the Northern Circuit, a Miss Annie Browne. Nobody will ever know who her father was. The year of her birth was probably 1846.

In 1848 Miss Browne married a local paper-hanger named Bland, a hard-drinking man, moved to the village of Guisely, and bore some dozen more children before Bland succumbed to the bottle. The glamorous Lillian Adelaide Neilson was known in her childhood as Lizzie Ann Bland.

In her fifteenth year she ran away from home, her decision precipitated, it appears, by her drunken stepfather's attempt to molest her sexually. She made her way to London and somehow got a place in the ballet of a London theatre, for she was determined, like her mother before her, to become an actress.

Someone—perhaps it was young Philip Henry Lee, a clergyman's son, or perhaps a naval officer named Henry Carr Glyn, who took a romantic interest in her—removed her from the theatre and entered her in a young ladies' academy where in two years, it is said, she learned everything a fine lady needed to know—including mastery of seven languages! When she was seventeen Lee married her and began to guide her toward stardom in the profession. John Ryder, an old actor who was reputed to be the "best

Illus. 70. Adelaide Neilson as Juliet. Courtesy of Harvard Theatre Collection.

Juliet-maker" of his time, took her in hand. "Do your tears come quickly?" he asked her. She lifted her face toward him and "her soft eyes welled with tears." "You will do, my dear," said Ryder. "I will teach you, and, what is more, I will make you."[14]

In 1865 she took her stage name and began to play Juliet. In a very few years she became one of London's leading actresses, with a salary said to be £400 per week. Even the jewels she ordinarily wore were valued at $50,000, and the diamond solitaires at her ears were said to have been gifts from the Russian and Austrian ambassadors.

In the decade of the 1870s, in spite of embarrassing events in her personal life, her fame as an actress rose to highest pitch on both sides of the Atlantic. Although in later years her admirers attempted to veil the facts, it is evident that offstage she was as impetuously amorous as she appeared to be in Juliet. In 1874 a Mrs. Eleanor Birch of Manchester, England, won a divorce on the grounds that her husband had committed adultery with Miss Neilson many times at many places. In 1877 Miss Neilson obtained an American divorce from Philip Lee (who had turned out to be a fool and bounder), having proved in court that he had enjoyed "intimate relations with notorious women in the city of New York." Yellow journalists played up the lurid details of these events, but even with the meanest intentions, they could not diminish the beauty of her Juliet.[15]

When Edwin Booth brought her to New York to his own theatre in 1872, some critics thought her unready. One claimed that in the Potion Scene she quite overdid the grisly *postmortem* conditions that she imagined she would wake up to in the Capulet tomb. Yet everyone acknowledged her personal beauty—her slender, graceful figure, her extraordinarily lovely face, her chestnut hair, large dark eyes, sensitive mouth, and clear, warm, exquisitely musical voice. "The sweet naïveté, the flower-like freshness of her earlier scenes are very winning," wrote Henry Sedley in the *New York Times;* and he declared flatly that this was the "best representation of *Romeo and Juliet* that we have anywhere seen in some years, or have ever seen in New York at all." This may have cost Booth and his young wife Mary McVicker a twinge or two, for only three years earlier he had *opened* his theatre with *Romeo and Juliet,* in which both he and Miss McVicker failed badly. William Winter, at that first viewing of Miss Neilson, defined her femininity in terms exactly typical of a woman-worshiping American gentleman of the day. "Feminine softness pervades the whole personality that was expressed through the medium of her art," he wrote; and then he added, "She does not, in other words, appear to be the kind of woman who wishes to go to Congress or to drive an omnibus."[16]

Year after year her Juliet continued to charm audiences. As the *New York Times* noted in 1874, she had played Juliet nearly 800 times in England and America, but "she depicts her with as much freshness of color, spirit, and care as if she were her newest creation."[17] Critics recorded many of her "points": her graceful movements during the minuet at the Capulet ball; the pathetic foreboding of "If he be marrièd / My grave is like to be my marriage bed"; the pretty way she kissed the spot on her hand which Romeo had kissed in parting from her; the alternations between archness and passionate impulse with which she teased the nurse for news of Romeo; her taking the vial from Friar Lawrence not with a crescendo of terror, but a cry of joy; the controlled delirium of her Potion Scene; and at the moment of death the beautiful action of drawing her dead husband's arm under her head.[18] By 1880, according to Henry Clapp, the Boston critic, all had come together in near perfection, and her Juliet was scarcely to be recognized as the work of the same artist who played it there some seven years ago, so changed was it for the better in every respect. She was teamed then with Edward Compton, whose attractive Romeo "was better, indeed, than any other assumption of the part which it was ever our fortune to see." What the critics did not then know was that this Juliet was deeply in love with this Romeo and by 1879 had probably married him.[19]

The Rosalind which she brought us in 1872 was never one of her best or more characteristic parts, apparently because she had not quite the stature or quickness or sense of fun to bring off the Ganymede scenes. Certain affectionate moments, as when she dropped her head against Orlando's shoulder and said, "Come, woo me, woo me," were pretty enough; but when she attempted to make the more comic points, she lapsed into mere coquettishness, or broke the bounds of taste by overdoing them. As the London *Observer* once put it, "The manner and bearing of the actress suggest to us a high-spirited school girl, who, having nerved herself for a freak of thoughtless daring, abandons herself unreservedly to the reckless fun of its consequences."[20]

Beatrice, which she attempted at the Lyceum in New York in 1874, was simply outside her range. Her Beatrice was "pleasing," said the *Telegram;* "it is gracious, full of tenderness and womanliness, but it hardly fulfils the ideal which Shakespeare has so clearly presented of a gay, witty, clever, and somewhat shrewish damsel, who falls in love against her will, and even then has doubts whether to acknowledge the fact."[21] The *Herald* records that in the "Kill

Illus. 71. Miss Neilson as Viola. Folger Shakespeare Library.

Claudio" passage she provoked laughter. Many actresses have inadvertently fallen into that trap, but the *Herald* critic asserts that she did so deliberately. On the line, "I would eat his heart in the marketplace," she "turned this magnificent explosion of rage into comedy—nay, burlesque—provoking insignificant, nay, impertinent laughter, and making the judicious grieve."[22] If this is fair reporting, Miss Neilson quite mistook her Beatrice. In any case, after this one trial she did not play the part again in America.

Probably her very finest role was Viola, which she played with Augustin Daly's early company at the Fifth Avenue Theatre on May 7, 1877. The role was perfectly suited to her person. It called for no strong bursts of energy (which, in fact, sometimes failed her in certain passages of Juliet), no spitfire sharpness as in Beatrice, and except for the "duel" with Sir Andrew no occasion for extravagant prankishness. "It is an exceedingly poetical performance, very tender, very refined and modest, and, withal, extremely free and natural," said Frederick Schwab in the *New York Times;* and in her four or five especially lyrical passages Schwab paid tribute to her "so pure, elegant, and expressive" delivery of the text.[23] William Winter dwelt upon the subtle admixture of sadness and joy which permeated her Viola. But Winter was so enraptured by the very presence of Miss Neilson as Viola that his review is a soft explosion of metaphors—especially floricultural. The heroine's name puts him in mind of violets. A few inches down the column he doses us with the perfume from a garden of blown roses; still farther with "the dreamy, dying odor of the jasmine"; and presently, to cap a miscellaneous cluster of pretty figures, with "the odor of blossoms on the soft winds of night."[24]

Three years later Henry Clapp of Boston declared that "We can remember no representation of comedy so perfect as this, none which so gratified the taste, bewitched the imagination, sank into the memory, and transported from the present. The spell seemed to be cast over every listener, and to maintain its sway

Illus. 72. Miss Neilson as Beatrice.

in face and speech long after the curtain had fallen upon the fifth act."[25] However quietly she worked her magic as Viola, she must often indeed have hypnotized whole audiences. When Winter returned to the subject in 1880, he happened for once to stop listening to the throbbing of his own pulse and looked about him: "During certain moments of her presence last night . . . the effect upon the great multitude that saw her was so profound and entrancing that the great theatre grew hushed and solemn as some cathedral aisle."[26]

A week after *Twelfth Night,* Daly produced *Cymbeline* for her (May 14, 1877), and her Imogen was generally accounted yet another advance in her art of wooing and winning "the softer sympathies." The better critics, who knew the play intimately in the study, though few had seen it performed, understood, as Clapp put it in the Boston *Advertiser,* that "Of all Shakespeare's women she is the most womanly, the most complete, the most satisfying. Less impassioned than Juliet, less fascinating than Rosalind, less dainty than Viola, less intellectual than Portia, less imposing than Hermione, she somehow seems made up of every one of these 'beautiful creatures' best', and certainly overtops any one of them." She is also, said Clapp, "the most wifely of wives."[27] Miss Neilson seems to have measured up to every dimension of Clapp's prescription—serenely affectionate toward Posthumus Leonatus in her first parting with him, genuinely outraged at Iachimo's attempts to seduce her, powerfully convincing in her insistence that Pisanio obey his master's command and slay her, utterly charming in her pretty trepidations as she entered Belarius's cave. When she played the boy with Guiderius and Arviragus, she was "the most winsome boy that ever trod the boards." When, like Juliet, she woke from her drug-induced sleep and found beside her the dead body of Cloten, which she took to be Leonatus, she performed an intensely agonizing scene over the corpse—a vocal performance more demanding in tragic terms than anything called for in Juliet. Her life in the role was brief (she never played it in London), but it may well have topped any of her performances in America.

She revived *Measure for Measure* in London as early as 1876, and played it here and there in America thereafter, but she did not exhibit her Isabella to New York audiences until May 24, 1880, and then only two scenes of it as the climax in a farewell potpourri of favorite passages from Shakespeare. Perhaps she was wise to withhold it from the major American theatre centers, for the leading metropolitan critics, who fancied themselves guardians of public morals, commonly held *Measure for Measure* to be "in many of its aspects essentially repulsive to the best taste of our time." The Boston *Courier* thought it should be kept on the shelf, like Shelley's *The Cenci*—something perhaps to "be read in the closet with profit and pleasure," but "not altogether savory when partaken of in a mixed company at a public performance."[28] No one questioned the morality, the nobility of Isabella, but the company she necessarily keeps—the bawds and pandars of the comic scenes—and, of course, the indelicate "bed-trick"—were simply intolerable. When Miss Neilson did perform the evening of Shakespearean scenes, William Winter was disposed to dwell upon the beauty of the whole program rather than upon moral matters. To pass, he observed, "from the girlish glee and artless merriment of Viola to the romantic, passion-touched tremulous entrancement of Juliet, thence to the ripe womanhood of Imogen, and so finally to the grandeur of Isabella, was to fill the imagination with an ideal of all that is excellent in woman."[29]

Illus. 73. Miss Neilson as Imogen. Folger Shakespeare Library.

In July of 1880, after her fourth American tour, Miss Neilson and Edward Compton sailed for England, and thence to Paris for a vacation. On a Saturday in mid-August, during a drive through the Bois de Boulogne, they stopped in the Pré Catalan for refreshment. Miss Neilson drank a glass of iced milk.

Presently she was attacked with acute stomach pains, and Compton took her to a *cabinet particulier* in a nearby restaurant. A physician relieved her temporarily with laudanum and warm poultices. When the pains renewed, a second physician administered certain pills which induced profuse vomiting and then seemed to bring relief. During the night, however, the pains again grew violent and by three in the morning she was dead. A ruptured vein in the Fallopian tube had disgorged several pints of blood into the abdominal cavity. She is buried in London's Brompton cemetery, the cross on her grave inscribed "Gifted and beautiful. Resting."

The mystery of her origins, the beauty of her performing, the half-hidden streak of scandal running through her life, the horror of her death—all these told and retold, exaggerated, distorted, contradicted by medical experts, spiritualist mediums, scandalmongers, and genuine Neilson worshipers—have fused into a myth that we can never forget.

Mary Anderson

If Adelaide Neilson may be taken as the archetypal romantic actress, the American Mary Anderson (1859–1940), unlike the Neilson in every way, was at her best an ideal actress of the classic kind.[30] She was tall, strong, statuesque. Her beauty was cool rather than seductive. Her approach to her roles in Shakespeare seems to have been studied rather than instinctive and emotional. And, as William Winter would say, she was "as noble . . . in her private life as she was beautiful, fortunate, and renowned in her public pursuits." Like the Neilson she made her stage debut when in her teens, and similarly, too, her career lasted barely fifteen years. It did not end in disaster, however. In 1889, weary of labors that had come to feel like enslavement, she withdrew from the profession, married an English solicitor, and settled in the village of Broadway, a few miles south of Stratford-upon-Avon. She would live there happily for the next fifty years.

Although Mary Anderson appeared in only three Shakespeares—*Romeo and Juliet, As You Like It,* and *The Winter's Tale*—she not only acted them, she produced them. Furthermore she produced all three in England, two at Henry Irving's Lyceum, where they would be measured against the high production standards set by Irving himself, and her stagings seem not to have fallen short of the Irving model. When she brought these productions to America they were admired across the country. During the last half-dozen years of her career she was generally recognized as one of the major performers of her time.

Born in Sacramento in 1859, "Our Mary" grew up in Louisville, Kentucky, where her family had settled in order to be near her mother's uncle, a Franciscan priest named Anthony Miller. Pater Anton put her into a nun's school, apparently intending for her some variety of religious life. When she was about ten, however, her mother, who had been widowed during the war, married a Dr. Hamilton Griffin, who in the years to come would strongly encourage the child's awakening interest in the stage.

When she was twelve she saw the attractive Edwin Adams play Richard III; when she was fourteen Edwin Booth came to Louisville in *Richelieu, Hamlet, Richard III,* and the rest of his classical repertory. Her mind was made up. She persuaded her mother (though Pater Anton disapproved) to let her with-

Illus. 74. Mary Anderson. Folger Shakespeare Library.

draw from school, study her "regular subjects" in private, and devote most of her time to elocution and the memorizing of dramatic roles. She specialized in such heavy fare as Schiller's Joan of Arc, and tragic *male* roles in imitation of Edwin Booth. These seemingly misguided efforts doubtless strengthened and enriched her voice, which John Ranken Towse would one day describe as one of her "most potent weapons . . . a rich contralto, thoroughly feminine, but uncommonly full, deep, supple, and melodious."[31]

When she was about fifteen she got a hearing with Charlotte Cushman, who urged her to continue practicing in private, and when she entered the profession "to begin at the top," as a star, rather than work her way up through lesser roles in a stock company. The actor-barrister George Vandenhoff, who coached her briefly, turned her away from male roles and directed her toward such female heavies as Bianca in Milman's *Fazio* and Sheil's Evadne, and for lighter work Pauline in Bulwer's *Lady of Lyons.* These "modern" but rapidly fading roles would be the mainstays of her first decade in the profession.

On November 27, 1875, when she was sixteen, she made her debut in a single performance of Juliet at Macauley's theatre in Louisville, and then spent two years learning her business in starring engagements—often unsuccessful—in New Orleans, St. Louis, San Francisco, and other cities throughout the South and West.

When she first dared New York in November of 1877, playing mostly non-Shakespearean roles, her work was still pretty raw. Yet everyone acknowledged her beauty. "Tall, willowy and young," said the *Herald,* "a fresh, fair face, short and rounded, a small, finely chiselled mouth, large, almond shaped eyes of dark gray or blue, hair of a light brown, a long white throat, a slender person . . . good looking, with a singularly sweet, organ-toned voice."[32] Her costumes were painfully unbecoming, and after her Juliet the *Spirit of the Times* declared that no one but herself could have succeeded in "such dreadfully inartistic garments."[33] Yet her dignity of person commanded respect. She reminded this same critic of a Greek statue, a Juno, a Calypso; Angelica Kauffman or Benjamin West could have chosen her for a model; she called to mind Sir Joshua Reynolds's portrait of Mrs. Siddons as the Tragic Muse. At this time too, though, we begin to hear intimations of what will swell to a critical chorus—complaints about her "coldness." The *New York Times* put it as her "lack of facial expression, her want of the magnetism known . . . as the 'sympathetic quality,' and above all, a need of warmth and tenderness."[34]

Illus. 75. Miss Anderson as Juliet.

Strangely enough, this complaint of the critics seems not to reflect the response of professional colleagues or of the general public. As she played back and forth across America for the next half-dozen years she earned the admiration of many leading actors of the older school—Booth and Barrett and McCullough and Jefferson—and won the affection of armies of playgoers. Her reputation crossed the Atlantic; and in 1883 she accepted Henry Abbey's invitation to occupy Irving's Lyceum for the following season. (In the event, she occupied the Lyceum for most of *two* seasons.)

That first season in London she avoided Shakespeare altogether and acted only nineteenth-century material. She opened as Parthenia in a pseudo-classical play called *Ingomar,* advanced to W. S. Gilbert's *Pygmalion and Galatea,* in which she played the animated statue, and revived *The Lady of Lyons.* The London critics, like the Americans, strove to put her down. She is handsome, they allowed, in a classic

Grecian way. She is clever and artistic (but lacks the art of concealing art). Her acting is polished and in correct taste. What she wants altogether is freshness, spontaneity, *abandon.* She has not a spark of the *feu sacré* of a Rachel or a Bernhardt. She is not inspired. She has talent but not genius.[35] These sentiments, which greeted her opening in early September, spread like a rust throughout the season. And they damaged her not at all. By mid-December, as a reporter for *The Graphic* pointed out, she had become "the rage." All London flocked to see her. "The Lyceum is crowded nightly with fashionable folk whose carriages block the way; and those who would secure places to witness her performances are met at the box office with the information that all the seats have been taken long in advance."[36]

She was patronized by the Prince and Princess of Wales, was befriended by Lord Tennyson, Robert Browning, Wilkie Collins, the Edmund Gosses, and Mrs. Humphrey Ward; was painted by George Frederick Watts and done in marble by the court sculptor, Count Gleichen. Lawrence Alma-Tadema became her close friend and artistic adviser, and Lewis Wingfield, John O'Connor, and other of the first scenic artists of London put themselves at her disposal.

For her second season at the Lyceum she chose to offer Juliet. The fact that Irving himself had mounted a splendid production of the play with Ellen Terry only two years earlier posed a special challenge. She rose to it enthusiastically. With true archaeological zeal she visited Verona, accompanied by an Italian artist who made careful sketches of every building, room, and vista there she could possibly use. Working from these sketches, John O'Connor, Hawes Craven, and other scene painters created an authentic Verona on the Lyceum stage. "All the scenes were . . . beautiful," wrote William Winter, who happened to be in London to cover the first London excursion of the Augustin Daly company. These scenes were "invested with an atmosphere so beguilingly poetic that the spectator who looked on them saw Verona itself, and realizing Italy and golden joys, seemed to hear the rustling of leaves in the languorous air of Southern night, and the song of the nightingale, mourning in the dusky Italian woods."[37] As a matter of fact, it was more stage decoration than Miss Anderson really wished for: during the hundred nights run of the play, "we found the cumbersome scenery more a drawback than an aid." The worry and labor of preparing it had exhausted her, too, and prevented her from readying her own performance as she should have done. In order to get through the opening night (November 1, 1884), she apparently lapsed into crudities that thoughtful fresh study could have prevented. Years afterward she would write that her disappointment in her first London performance was extremely painful.[38]

The critics let fly at her. The London correspondent to the Philadelphia *Evening Bulletin* could find only two reasonably friendly notices to send home for American readers.[39] The correspondent to the *Spirit of the Times* listed the *Times, Telegraph, Standard, St. James Gazette, Pall Mall Gazette, Saturday Review, Truth,* and *World* as "not by any means altogether cordial."[40] The *Times* epitomized this Juliet as "the gushing but empty rapture of a schoolgirl who has dabbled in poetry, and inspired herself with the second-hand sentiment of the circulating library." The *Standard* found that in this role we "more than ever feel the inability of the American actress to portray passion."[41] The *Saturday Review* would allow her nothing: she was all poses and attitudinizing and girlish playfulness when she should be radiant with the glow of passion; she lapsed into *an American accent* and she was utterly ignorant of how to speak blank verse; she was loud instead of powerful in tragic scenes, and her

Illus. 76. Miss Anderson and Mrs. Stirling as Juliet and the Nurse.

lament over Romeo's banishment was mere rant; she vulgarized the Potion Scene by crude stage business—running from Tybalt's ghost and hiding behind a table, shrieking, indulging in foolish pantomime as she foresaw herself madly playing with her forefathers' joints. "There was no reason to suppose that Miss Anderson *could* play Juliet, and consequently there is no reason to be surprised at the demonstration that she *cannot* do so."[42]

The Earl of Lytton ("Owen Meredith"), a friend of Miss Anderson, was so astonished at the virulence of the attacks that he took a jury of friends to see her Juliet; and having received their unanimous opinion that the critics had been unfair, he published in *The Nineteenth Century* a twenty-two page analysis of her performance and a critique of the critiques.[43] He acknowledged that she committed errors, notably her violence in the Potion Scene; but on the whole his conclusion was "Put not your trust in newspaper criticism." Her acting, he declared, far from revealing an inability to portray passion, "was full of feeling and tenderness." In this respect, he said, her Juliet was far superior to Ellen Terry's. Of the many Juliets that Lytton had seen, this was the only one that drew tears from him. He detected nothing specifically or blamably "American" in her accent or intonation. Indeed, she spoke blank verse "rather better than worse than we are accustomed to hear it spoken by our best actors." He called attention to many lovely moments throughout her performance: her first entrance at the call of the Nurse, which was not really an entrance but a revelation (at "Madam, I am here," she thrust aside a curtain and was seen standing on a stair framed in an arched doorway); her breaking into a little dance movement when she first heard far-off strains of music from the ballroom; her leaning from the balcony toward Romeo "in an attitude of passionate but tender yearning, her hair falling loose over her neck, and her arms folded as already clasping the dear prize of her bosom"; her grace and playfulness in the scene in which the Nurse brings the first news from Romeo; her fall in the Potion Scene (she managed to fall across the bed with her head hanging down, the face upturned toward the audience, the eyes yet open).

Lytton spent pages on the second Balcony Scene, where "Miss Anderson's acting rises into the purest poetry of tenderness and passion"; and on the scene that follows with mother, nurse, and father. This was her masterpiece: the "weary lassitude" and "indescribable dejection" with which she admitted her mother to the room; the "touching simplicity" of her words, "Mother, I am not well"; the explosion of courage, the scorn of lip and flash of steady eye, the gathering of strength throughout her figure as she denied that she would marry Paris; the sobbing appeal to her mother and the Nurse after Capulet flung her to the floor; the burst of passion against the Nurse's perfidy as she cried out, "Ancient damnation! O most wicked fiend!"

In the Death Scene, Lytton noticed, she introduced a master touch: just before Romeo took the poison, but unobserved by him, she made a slight gesture as if waking—startling and thrilling to the beholders. The death itself, in part reminiscent of Neilson's, was managed beautifully: "having fallen at a little distance from Romeo, she raises her head faintly, searches with a look, as of eyes that are fast growing dim, for his dead body; creeps softly close up to it, tenderly lifts the dead man's arm, and places it around her neck, nestling her head into the fold of it; then, with a satisfied sigh of infinite tenderness, expires."

Lytton asserted emphatically what it was habitual with others to deny, that she had great power of facial expression. "She has a play of countenance which, without the aid of voice or gesture, expresses in rapid alternation, tenderness, scorn, sorrow, terror, and dream reverie." And further, almost unique among actors of the day, was her ability to stand still. Most actors "seem incapable of expressing emotion without movement, and whenever they are not in movement they are awkward. Miss Anderson is able to express strong feeling without moving a limb."

When she brought *Romeo and Juliet* to America in the fall of 1885, it was received in high favor. No finer scenery had ever been seen in Boston or in Chicago, not even Irving's best, and the critic of the Boston *Transcript* lamented that such paintings could not have a permanent place in a gallery of art, but must be doomed to the ephemeral life of the stage.[44] Here and there, to be sure, someone would still complain of her lack of "divine fire." Nym Crinkle called her "a great white rose that the gods have deprived of fragrance."[45] A Brooklyn critic, in extraordinarily bold terms, would like to have Juliet played by "a sensuous woman" who could express "sexual love," "the mad frankness of desire," "an Oriental delirium," "the very mania of passion."[46] Most observers, however, like Elwyn Barron of the Chicago *Inter Ocean,* were glad to recognize Miss Anderson's "new powers and new excellences," how graciously she had modified her former loudness, had brought dignity in place of coquettishness to the Balcony Scene, had informed the tragic scenes with "the majesty of sorrow, the dignity of courage." For William Winter, who could claim to have seen her Juliet in many different places some thirty-five times, it was by far the finest: "More than that of Adelaide Neilson, Helena Modjeska, Ellen Terry, or any other actress whom I have ever seen in the part, it was saturated with the force and color of *tragedy*."[47]

During the summer of 1885 the artist John O'Connor happened to meet Miss Anderson in Stratford-upon-Avon, and after showing her the Memorial Theatre (built in 1879 but not yet quite finished) he persuaded her that she ought to get up *As You Like It*, the play most firmly rooted in woody Warwickshire, and perform it there. He himself would prepare the scenery. The proposal was especially welcome, for Miss Anderson and Henry Abbey, her manager, were ready for her return to America in the fall, and a second Shakespeare in her repertory would strengthen her appeal to the American public. The company that they assembled and began rehearsing included young Johnston Forbes-Robertson for Orlando and Romeo, Francis Macklin for Jaques and Mercutio, Zeffie Tilbury for Celia, and J. G. Taylor for Touchstone and Peter.

The performance, on August 29, was a great event for Stratford. Special trains brought crowds from all directions. All the principal London critics were brought down by Abbey in his special train, and with them the faithful William Winter.[48] The nine hundred seats were all sold at advanced prices, and Miss Anderson decreed that the profits would go to the theatre's building fund. A fresh-slain deer, to be carried across the stage during the hunters' glee, was brought from Charlecote Park; Audrey was provided a whole basket of turnips dug from the garden at Ann Hathaway's house. After the play the critics gathered for supper at the Red Horse Hotel, where Joseph Knight of the *Athenaeum* delivered an elegant toast to Miss Anderson's enterprise in bringing about this beautiful occasion, and the company feasted until the small hours.

How polished the performance was is doubtful. One or two critics, probably coached by Abbey, emphasized that this was a first performance, briefly rehearsed, and that it should be judged as a sort of preparation for other English cities yet to be visited, and for America.[49] Repeatedly one reads that Miss Anderson had never seen any other actress's Rosalind.[50] William Archer explained that for Miss Anderson's benefit Abbey had lured the metropolitan critics into the wilds in order to obtain their most helpful judgments uncolored by the response of hypercritical London audiences.[51] (The fact of the matter, as we have seen, is that in the case of Miss Anderson it was the critics rather than the audiences who were hypercritical.) Be that as it may, the audience response at Stratford was enthusiastic: the native Stratfordians were flattered by the occasion, and the heavy infusion of American tourists cheered and applauded for patriotism's sake.[52] Abbey's net had brought in a wasp or two, of course, mere reporters from *The Sporting Times* and the like, who saw the event as nothing but a publicity stunt, mere Barnumism. The reporter for *The Bat* confessed to an impulse to demand his money back until he remembered that as Abbey's guest he hadn't spent any.[53]

But most of the critics drew in their claws. The *Daily Chronicle*, the *Morning Post*, the *Daily Telegraph*, and the *Sunday Times* turned out glowing tributes.[54] Sidney Lee maintained his scholarly integrity by giving the performance a courteous but restrained review in the *Academy*: charmed by Miss Anderson's comic spirit, vivacity, and womanly dignity in the Forest Scenes, but thinking poorly of most of the supporting actors, and positively deploring the choice of acting version, which over forty years after Macready's restorations was still giving Jaques the First Lord's *description* of Jaques.[55]

The critic for *St. Stephen's Review* thought Miss Anderson lacked "the knack of self-effacement," but enjoyed her personality. He liked especially her handling of the comedy scenes with a sort of "what a day we are 'aving" air—and "truly she was fair to look upon, the fairest Rosalind I have ever seen."[56]

William Archer wrote it up at once for the *World* newspaper and again later in a full essay for *The Theatre*, in which he reviewed all the work she had done in England.[57] On the whole he preferred her Rosalind, however briefly prepared, to her often performed Juliet, on the grounds that her comic gift was superior to her tragic gift. She is wonderfully clever, and she charms, Archer said, but she does not enrapture. "Her beauty . . . is not of the Circean order, enthralling the senses and perverting the judgment. It is good, honest, healthy comeliness, a precious gift, but not a talisman to conjure with." Her Rosalind will doubtless be one of her best parts:

> It is a work of a most intelligent artist, who happens to possess some peculiar qualifications for this very character . . . a very rare combination of beauty, grace, and what may be called physical as well as mental talent. . . . Youth, health, and high spirits form the charm of her performance. Had it been a little less graceful we should have had to call it bouncing, but the actress's consummate charm of pose and movement saves it from this reproach.

William Winter took the occasion to assure his home readers in the *Tribune* that "Americans . . . have but a faint idea of the great popularity of Miss Mary Anderson in England, or the sincere, fervent interest that is felt, by the best classes of English people, in all her professional movements." During her two seasons on the English boards "she has surpassed the achievement of any American performer in legitimate drama who preceded her in this land. . . . The beautiful and brilliant woman who came here so modestly, who so well represents the best in the American stage, and who has so richly adorned by her personal worth the laurels gained by her genuine merit, possesses the affectionate good will of the whole people, and thus stands in exceptional repute."[58]

After a quick tour of the English provinces to rehearse *As You Like It* further, she sailed home, and on October 12, 1885, she offered it as a novelty to open her New York season. She was greeted at her first entrance with prolonged applause and cheers—a rousing welcome home for "Our Mary"—but as the evening wore on, the audience wearied of the play and turned cold, and she had to accept the verdict that for the moment at least her Rosalind had failed. She kept it on for only a week, then turned to non-Shakespearean roles and to Juliet for a month before going on the road.[59] After so generous a send-off from Stratford, why did her Rosalind at first displease both audience and critics at home?

The *New York Times* called *As You Like It* a failure, as did Nym Crinkle in the *World.* Jeannette Gilder in *The Critic* thought her Rosalind merely mechanical and accused the actress of relying on youth and good looks and not really working at her art. The *Dramatic Mirror* decided that she was not capable of comedy, that in Rosalind she was "a tragedy queen ineffectually endeavoring to suppress her natural grandeur beneath an ill-fitting assumption of romp and jest."

Only the faithful Winter placed her Rosalind above all others. (Four years later, of course, he would award first place to Ada Rehan.) It is only Winter who records enough "points" to give us a fair impression of the whole. He reports that in her first-act appearances, clad in a long gown of flowered gold, she was certainly "more than common tall"—a necessary but often neglected attribute of Rosalind. When she defended herself and her father against Duke Frederick's accusation of treason, she did indeed look and sound like a princess. Winter found unique expressions of sentiment in her early scenes. Thus her question to Celia, "What think you of falling in love?" was not merely sportive: it hinted also at "a heart full of passionate tenderness, hungry for the right object on which to bestow itself." Her manner of giving Orlando her chain was a "new business." She did not place it around his neck, as other Rosalinds did (and do): she let it fall slowly from her hand to his hand "as though she would caress the hand into which it fell."

Her forest costume was handsome and appropriate: hose and doublet of russet brown, the sleeves slashed with white puffs; a skirt of brown leather

Illus. 77. Miss Anderson as Rosalind. Folger Shakespeare Library.

belted at the waist; and down her back a long claret-red cloak which at the line "What shall I do with my doublet and hose?" she would modestly but unostentatiously swing across her legs. She forestalled the leers of sensualists (which some Rosalinds were wont to invite) by wearing long leather boots—sensible garb for a young man to wear into a thorny wilderness. In this costume, with boar spear in hand and curtle-axe on thigh (she wore a hatchet, though, and not a short sword as she should have done), with her tall stature and long stride, her masculine disguise was almost entirely convincing.

Rosalind provided Miss Anderson her first opportunity on stage to use her singing voice, which was so rich and true that it was often remarked that she could have made a career as a vocalist. It had been traditional from the days of Kitty Clive for Rosalind to insert in the fourth act (at "your wife's wit going to your neighbor's bed") the "Cuckoo Song" from *Love's Labors Lost.* This uncalled-for embellishment of the cuckoldry theme had come to be regarded as indelicate, and in 1842 Macready suppressed it. But it continued to be printed in acting editions and more often than not it was heard. Miss Anderson used it—or the innocent opening lines of it—in an unexpected place. Early in the third act, on her way to find Orlando's verses, she was heard from offstage as she came wandering through the trees, singing "When daisies pied, and violets blue, / And lady-smocks all silver-white. . . ." The effect surprised and delighted everyone.

When she asked Orlando if he is as much in love as his rhymes speak, she pressed one hand to her bosom, where we have seen her hide a sheet of his verses. When he, turning thoughtfully away, said, "Neither rhyme nor reason can express how much," she reached out as if to caress him, and withdrew her hand just before he turned to look at her. In the scene with Silvius and Phebe she roughened her voice and exaggerated her mannish swagger as she scolded Phebe for rejecting "a good man's love." The mock-marriage was a delicious mixture of sentiment and glee. In the scene of the bloody napkin, after she swooned and then awakened, she uttered the line "I would I were at home" in such desolate and pathetic tones that she nearly broke her disguise.

When her American tour ended in May of 1886, she took a long vacation. Most of the winter of 1886–87 she spent in Paris, improving her French, studying music, and reading. Learning that Irving was to visit America again in 1887–88, she arranged once more to occupy the Lyceum, and as a bold stroke to revive the rarely performed *The Winter's Tale.* As an even bolder stroke she would herself play both Hermione and Perdita, taking for authority a couple of lines that comment on the close resemblance of mother and daughter.[60] Since the two are never on stage together except in the Statue Scene, where Perdita has only a couple of tiny and dispensable speeches, it needed only a silent stand-in for Perdita to make the doubling at least possible. In the spring of 1887 she assembled a company and performed *The Winter's Tale* for one night only, on Shakespeare's birthday, in Nottingham. According to the provincial audience and her many London friends who came to see the production, it was immensely successful; but when she opened it at the Lyceum on September 11, 1887, she was shocked by the coldness of the first-night audience and the extreme hostility of the press.[61]

The scenery was generally praised as worthy of the Lyceum, especially Hawes Craven's setting for the fourth act in Bohemia. At stage right a wooded hillside descended toward center stage, so that entering characters came down a steep path through leafy branches and alongside a stream trickling over rocks; at stage left a peasant cottage nestled among tall trees; in the middle distance one caught a glimpse of the blue Aegean. Miss Anderson, whose youth and beauty served her perfectly as Perdita, joined in the shepherds' dance with such extraordinary grace that the dance was regularly encored. As Perdita she was much praised.

As Hermione, though, she was found wanting. It was allowed, to be sure, that she played the little scene with Mamillius prettily; that when she heard of the death of Mamillius her way of suddenly wrapping her cloak about her face and falling senseless was brilliantly executed; and, of course, that her gradual coming to life and descending the steps in the Statue Scene was superb pantomime. But most of the critics condemned her behavior in the Trial Scene. The *Daily Chronicle* was perhaps alone in reporting sympathetically her conception and execution of that scene: "She does not make Hermione a 'tragic queen,' whose eyes flash fire and hurl defiance at her accuser as he sits in his chair of state. . . . Miss Anderson's Hermione is, on the contrary, a gentle loving woman. . . . Nothing could well be more delicately emotional or tenderly sympathetic than her rendition of this scene. Hermione's words are as eloquent as they are true, but she has not the strength for declamatory display." Against this opinion we must weigh the following: that she "fails in the attempt to impart passion or pathos to her speeches" *(Standard);* that "there are no tears in her deep-toned voice . . . there is nothing convincing in her violent display of grief" *(Morning Post);* that "her muffled and monotonous enunciation, sinking at times almost to a whine, jarred unpleas-

Illus. 78. Miss Anderson as Hermione in *The Winter's Tale.* Folger Shakespeare Library.

antly on the ear" *(Morning Advertiser);* that "there is something of the virago in the deep masculine tones which the actress brings forth from her chest in pathetic moments" *(Times).*

Few of the critics would accede to the doubling of mother and daughter, the meaner of them accusing her of mere professional vanity in taking both roles for herself. A probably well-founded complaint was that in the final scene one could hardly pay attention to the Statue and the miraculous animation of it, being distracted by the stand-in Perdita posed so conspicuously with her back to the audience and so unnaturally silent.

Miss Anderson's arrangement of the text drew (and deserved) positively virulent attacks, and whoever advised her (she names several persons, including Lord Lytton and Henry Irving) did her ill service. She published her version, so that her crimes against the text are a matter of record. Her Preface tells us what to expect. The First Folio, she declares, is so full of blunders that "any scrupulous reproduction of this mutilated text would be mere pedantry," and "a literal adhesion to the text as it has been handed down to us would in any case savour of superstition."[62] So she cut the play by half, and delivered few more more than 1,500 of Shakespeare's 3,075 lines. Her verbal inaccuracies are unbelievable: in a portion of the Mamillius scene in which she spoke five short speeches, William Archer detected five omissions, additions, or errors. And her bowdlerizing was absurd. In the Trial Scene she could not make herself say, "The bug which you would fright me with . . ." but substituted "That which you would fright me with. . . ." Archer speculated that she understood "bug" to mean the *cimex lectularius!* For the word "strumpet" she substituted "wanton." She could not refer to her child as the "firstfruits of my body," but "of our marriage." She could not mention "the innocent milk" that she fed the baby with. She suppressed several lines referring to "the child-bed privilege." In

Illus. 79. Miss Anderson doubling as Hermione's daughter Perdita. Folger Shakespeare Library.

the early scenes she showed no physical sign of pregnancy, and none of her attendants spoke lines referring to it.[63]

The critic for the *Saturday Review* opened his devastating attack with the assertion that "Miss Mary Anderson at the Lyceum has again done what in her lay to bring Shakespeare into disrepute," and he prophesied that "such miserably inadequate and utterly mistaken attempts" would necessarily "drive educated audiences from the theatre." As a prophet he could not have been farther off the mark. *The Winter's Tale* became the most celebrated and most popular play in Miss Anderson's repertory. She performed it 164 nights running, and, she wrote, if her lease had not expired she could have run it 100 nights longer.[64]

When she brought it to America in the fall of 1888 (November 13), it was heralded as her finest accomplishment.[65] Her feat of doubling Hermione and Perdita was taken as an artistic triumph. "As Hermione," wrote Dithmar of the *New York Times,* "Miss Anderson is stately, dignified, queenlike, majestic in her grief, touching in the moment of forgiveness. As Perdita she is at first a lovely picture of innocent girlhood, surprisingly airy and gleesome; and afterward, in the brief period of Perdita's sorrow, she expresses the gentleness and sincerity of the girl's nature with charming delicacy. We have not often heard Shakespearean verse spoken on our stage as well as she speaks it." Even Nym Crinkle, who had always held out against her, surrendered to her charm this time: "In Hermione and Perdita I think she has found her metier."[66] Clapp of Boston, a hard task-master, actually thought her acting version was "to be highly commended, and though he withheld approval from her Hermione, like everyone he praised Perdita's tenderness with Florizel, and thought her dancing a "miracle of airy grace."[67] George Odell claimed, over fifty years later, that he could never forget

> the magnificence of her appearance as the statue, revealed when Pauline drew the red curtain, standing at the top of a great flight of marble steps. Mary Anderson's descent of those steps, arrayed as she was in inconceivable beauty of feature, form, and costume, was a sight to be experienced but rarely in this life. I have, in fact, never seen anything like it, before or since. A scene of contrasted loveliness was the dance that brought Perdita to our notice; she, with the other boys and girls of the harvest scene, came, a group of revellers, swinging hand in hand down a grassy incline, round a great tree, and arriving in the foreview, as radiant a group of happy dancers as the stage has ever known. . . . This dance became the talk of the town; old playgoers still talk of it with something like reverential awe as a manifestation of supreme art in the theatre."[68]

Was "Our Mary" a great actress, or only an admirable person and a splendid figure of a woman? Bernard Shaw denied that she was truly an actress at all, but only a very beautiful woman with so strong a character of her own that she could neither sink herself into the characters she enacted nor give herself away nightly to be stared at by the public.[69] "Before her the art of acting fled abashed," as Shaw once put it.[70]

Yet our own greatest American actors of the generation just passing from the stage—Edwin Booth and Lawrence Barrett—admired her immensely, expected her to carry their classic style into the future, and were saddened in 1889 when she abandoned the profession. Perhaps she should have been born a generation earlier, before the rise of sentiment and subtlety in end-of-the-century acting. She might with her beautiful face, contralto voice, and fine figure have out-rivaled Charlotte Cushman, companioned Edwin Forrest, or queened it well with Barry Sullivan and John McCullough. A heroic actress, she was too big for the actors of her age: she needed giants to stand up to.

Anna Cora Mowatt

A not uncommon occurrence during the middle and later half of the century was the intrusion into the profession of lady amateurs who, without talent or training or anything to recommend them but determination and personal beauty, set themselves up as stars. Women of fashion, dissatisfied with their butterfly existence or escaping from unbearable husbands, would accept social ostracism and even risk public derision by the critics in their effort to win fame and independence "on the boards." One of the first to show the way (and to succeed at it!) was Anna Cora Mowatt (1819–70), who made the break in the 1840s.[71] As the daughter of Samuel Ogden, a prominent New York merchant, she had been born into the world of fashion, but when her husband James Mowatt failed in health and in business she turned to the theatre simply to earn a living. Fortunately she had the intelligence and talent for it. In 1841 she began a "semi-theatrical" platform career, doing public recitations of poetry. She wrote a clever comedy of manners, called *Fashion,* which began its New York run at the Park Theatre in March of 1845. In June that year she turned actress, her first professional performance being Pauline in *The Lady of Lyons.* In the fall of 1846 she established a partnership with E. L. Davenport, one of the wisest young actors of the day. With his coaching and support she won a solid reputation as Rosalind, Beatrice, Juliet, and a range of non-Shakespearean roles, hailed in England as well as at home. Her husband died in 1851. In 1854 she

Illus. 80. Anna Cora Mowatt as Beatrice.

withdrew from the stage and reentered society as the wife of one William Ritchie, a Virginia gentleman of good standing in the social world. Toward the end of the 1850s, though, as political tensions rose between North and South, her relations with Ritchie became unbearably strained. She left him before the war broke out and went abroad to spend her last years in retirement in Italy and England.

Margaret Mather

Margaret Mather (1859–98) was certainly not a refugee from high society when she entered the profession, but of her incurable amateurism there is no denying. Born and brought up in poverty, the daughter of a Detroit innkeeper, at the age of nineteen she ran away to New York, passionately determined to become an actress. Very beautiful, but emotionally unstable, uneducated, and apparently not very bright, she fell into the hands of an unscrupulous producer, John M. Hill, who offered to make a star of her. Hill's methods were to advertise, to promise, to promote, to puff. Months before her debut as Juliet, the *Spirit of the Times* was reporting that the news it had received of this "miracle of tragic genius" were "so excessively eulogistic as to seem almost burlesque." With tongue in cheek the writer notes that "she fairly frightens the professionals who rehearse with her, and no one can listen to her without tears."[72]

Hill kept her in rehearsal for an entire year, during which time he learned from her inability to take instruction that he had better not expose her to the attention of the New York critics. Her debut, on August 28, 1882, was at McVicker's in Chicago, and for three years Hill ran her about the provincial circuits, advertising her extravagantly, until the country managers declined to book her any longer until her reputation had been proven in the metropolis. Accordingly, having loaded the New York press with advertisements, having plastered the town with pictures of the beautiful Mather, and having spent nearly $23,000 on the most gorgeous mounting of *Romeo and Juliet* that New York had ever seen, on October 13, 1885, Hill let the curtain of the Union Square Theatre rise on his "miracle of tragic genius."[73] He even hired a claque to applaud uproariously, at right places and wrong, on the opening night. It was a mixed success. The *Spirit of the Times* was reminded of the old joke about *Hamlet* with Hamlet left out, and declared that Miss Mather had not starred as Juliet but that the scenery had starred her. In the early love scenes her delivery was mechanical and sing-song. In the later tragical scenes she displayed quite overwhelming passion, shrieking hysterically as she snatched the vial of potion from Friar Lawrence, and tumbled acrobatically down a flight of steps when the potion took effect. William Winter tried to be fair to the newcomer in his first notice, but he had to conclude that she exhibited more force than sweetness, more physical recklessness than spiritual beauty, more animal storm and tumult than intellect and controlled emotion. Even so, the affair was spectacular enough to run past the first of the year, and Hill could advertise that Miss Mather was "the only actress who ever starred as Juliet seventy-six times in any country."[74] After this achievement, and with his impressive new *mise-en-scène* he could renew his profitable campaign throughout the country.

Otis Skinner, who was Miss Mather's leading man and manager for part of the 1890–91 season, recalled how, as she left the stage after a violent emotional scene, waves of hysteria would pass over her: "her fingers would snap; nervous laughter on her lips, and the pupils of her eyes dilating to an entire blackness. Then, in a moment, her body would be stretched upon the floor of her dressing-room, rigid as iron, and unconscious. The condition would last five or ten minutes, then she would come out of it as weak as a kitten."[75] This was not acting, of course, but simply "tearing a passion to tatters, to very rags, to split the ears of the groundlings." In 1890 and again in 1897 she played a rather coarse Imogen in *Cymbeline*.[76] From time to time she won praise for her Rosalind, although the role offered her little occasion for the outbreaks of passion she loved to indulge in. She rarely played it in New York. Between 1892 and 1896 she withdrew from the profession, having married Gustave Pabst, scion of the wealthy family of brewers in Milwaukee. The family snubbed her. She quarreled with her husband and horse-whipped him, and he divorced her. It is said that she obtained a settlement of $100,000, enough to finance a sumptuous revival of *Cymbeline*. In April of 1898, while touring *Cymbeline* in West Virginia, she suddenly died.[77]

Illus. 81. Margaret Mather.

LILLIE LANGTRY

Illus. 82. Lillie Langtry.

The most famous—or notorious—woman of fashion to invade the American stage was Lillie Langtry (1853–1929), the Jersey Lily.[78] Born in 1853, daughter of the Reverend William Le Breton, Dean of the Isle of Jersey, she brought to the world such resources of energy, intelligence, ambition, physical beauty, and bravado that she was bound to make her mark somehow. At the age of twenty she married the scion of a moneyed family of Belfast, one Edward Langtry—not, as she explained in later years, because she loved him, but because she loved his yacht and wanted to possess it. Langtry was a dull man, a wastrel, in the long run a permissive cuckold and sullen drunkard, who could not gratify her socially, intellectually, or sexually. And what was worse, his moneyed family disowned him.

Having settled in London, for about a year the Langtrys lived in social obscurity, but by a chance encounter they picked up an invitation to a fashionable garden party. Lillie wore her only decent dress, a severe black, a mourning outfit her family had given her following the death of her young brother. At the garden party they knew no one but their host, and sat by themselves, but Lillie's beauty in the black dress was much noticed. To their great surprise they found themselves invited to an At Home at Lady Sebright's a few nights later. Lillie wore the same black dress, with no jewels or any other ornaments that would distract attention from her face and auburn hair. Artists were present, and suddenly John Everett Millais, Lord Leighton, Frank Miles, and James McNeill Whistler descended on her, all begging her to sit for her portrait. Invitations thereafter streamed in upon the Langtrys, to Lillie's delight and Edward's mounting annoyance, and in a matter of weeks Lillie was recognized throughout London society as a P.B.—a Professional Beauty. George Frederic Watts, Edward Burne-Jones, William Morris, the Rossettis, Algernon Swinburne, Oscar Wilde, Henry Irving, and even Prime Minister Gladstone, all paid homage to her charm and beauty, and it was a short way to the Prince of Wales's bed.

In 1880 Lillie separated from Langtry, with whom she had had no sexual relations for over a year, and retired to Jersey, where in early 1881 she gave birth to a daughter. The common assumption has long been that the Prince was father of the child, but it is now known that while Lillie served the Prince's pleasure she was carrying on a passionate love affair with young Louis Battenberg, the Prince's nephew. Louis was the father. The social and political situation was impossible. The Battenbergs would not have permitted Louis to marry Lillie had marriage been possible; and it was not possible in any case, for Langtry would not give Lillie a divorce. So Louis was sent off to the navy; the child Jeanne-Marie was brought up by Mrs. Le Breton and was taught to call her mother her aunt. The Prince of Wales, partly out of generosity, partly out of considerations of family and the state, let gossiping tongues credit the paternity to him. He continued to be a good friend of Lillie.

And Lillie, without husband or income, was determined to support herself by way of the stage. Coached by the former actress Henrietta Hodson, then wife of Henry Labouchère, the editor of *Truth* and liberal Member of Parliament, in December of 1881 she appeared as Kate Hardcastle in a charity performance of *She Stoops to Conquer.* As soon as it became known that she was joining the profession, Society dropped her, but His Royal Highness did not. Accompanied by Princess Alexandra, he regularly occupied the royal box on Mrs. Langtry's opening nights. She played a run at the Haymarket and a prosperous tour through the provinces. Whether or not she could act, everyone had to pay attention to the Prince's mistress, one of the most beautiful and most talked about women in England.

London first saw her in Shakespeare on September 23, 1882, when she presented herself as Rosalind, supported by a scratch company which she was about to take with her to America.[79] Most of the critics dismissed the company as mediocre or downright bad, but by a considerable majority they treated Mrs. Langtry sympathetically, reckoning her a coming artist who would have to be taken seriously after she returned from her experience in America.[80] Judgments in the main ran as follows. Certainly she was clever, handsome, and graceful. She spoke the language brilliantly—sometimes too rapidly but always accurately and with significance and point. She was not yet an *ideal* Rosalind: she had learned the surfaces but not the depths of the character. But her accomplishment was amazing in light of the fact that she had been at her trade less than a year, and was still laboring "to master the grammar of the art to which her life was to be devoted."[81] And she could not have adopted a more able tutor than Mrs. Labouchère (who, as a matter of fact, had accompanied her throughout her provincial tour and made every performance a study). If at times, as a result of strenuous coaching, her performance seemed mechanical, doubtless as she grew into the role, ease and spontaneity would displace the effect of lessons faithfully conned.

Illus. 83. Lillie Langtry as Rosalind.

The two most common objections to her Rosalind were, first, that she had "no heart," and second, that once into her Ganymede dress she overindulged in comic romp. Many critics took note of her seeming lack of emotional involvement during the first act. Here, according to the *Era,* she failed to realize the refinement, delicacy, and romance of the character. During the wrestling scene she seemed more concerned for the arrangement of her train than for the danger to Orlando. In her speeches to Orlando one heard mere words and sensed little affection in them. Her response to the Duke's charge of treason lacked spirit. At the end of the act she appropriated Celia's lines and "threw them at the heads of the audience" like "a bread-and-butter miss just escaped from a modern boarding school."[82]

Here it must be remembered that in the English theatre there had been two very different Rosalinds. The Rosalind of Peg Woffington (1741), of Dora Jordan (1787), and of Louisa Nisbett (1842) was a merry creature, rather a hoyden, getting all the fun she could out of her masculine disguise. But this, said the *Daily Telegraph* in 1882, was a "strange heresy," a total misreading of Shakespeare's intentions. "Our forefathers believed it religiously before it was dissipated and crushed by Helen Faucit, the most ideal and enchanting of Rosalinds."[83] Miss Faucit, now Lady Martin, had just published her essay on Imogen and was perhaps already at work on her "Rosalind" essay, in which she would dwell upon "the glad rapture of the tender passion," "the sweet little womanly question," and "her pretty womanly waywardness playing like summer lightning over her throbbing tenderness of heart."[84] This sentimental, genteel Rosalind was the only Rosalind that the critic at the *Telegraph* could bear to see. To him and many another, Mrs. Langtry's reversion to the "comic" Rosalind was a shocking lapse of taste. Even the *Era,* which recorded that her triumph began when she put on her Ganymede dress and commenced to speak and move freely and naturally, was upset by her treatment of "Alas, the day! What shall I do with my doublet and hose?" Evidently she tossed the line directly at the audience as a flippant aside, "in the tone and action of burlesque."[85]

Eventually she abandoned this somewhat crude

effect, for as her friend Graham Robertson insisted, she was *not* hoydenish and she "carefully avoided all vulgar clowning in passages referring to her male attire." Robertson credited her indeed with one bit of stage business of extraordinary wit and delicacy: "When she spoke the line—'Here, on the skirts of the forest, like fringe on a petticoat,' she put out her hand with a perfectly natural gesture to pick up her own petticoat, and finding none, paused awkwardly for half a second."[86]

The *Era* was careful to remind its readers that when Mrs. Langtry first appeared on the stage, it had been among the first to point out her shortcomings, "and to denounce the fashionable folly which proclaimed her a heaven-born actress." But by now "hard work, hard study, earnestness of purpose, and great natural intelligence have combined to bring about a result which a few short weeks ago we should have thought impossible." And so, "*fiat justitia:* let justice be done though the heavens fall. Mrs. Langtry, during the short time she has been upon the stage, has given undeniable proof that she has taken up acting, not as a mere toy to be dropped when tired of, but with serious intent."[87] The *Morning Post* (a Tory paper) whose adulatory review must have gratified her royal patron as well as herself, addressed the question of how her Rosalind would be received in America: "If refinement of manner, graphic characterization, and a melodious delivery of the text be appreciated at their proper worth, Mrs. Langtry's Rosalind will be even more popular in the principal American cities than her Miss Hardcastle or Hester Grazebrook."[88] But *Bell's Life in London,* no friend to the lady, observed more coolly, and as it turned out, more accurately, "In England a certain leaven of friends and acquaintances leavens the whole lump. In America this will be changed. Vulgar curiosity will probably also supply audiences there, but prejudice will be strong, and criticism plainer."[89]

From October 23, 1882, the day Mrs. Langtry landed at New York, that city was aflame with Langtry fever. The day after her arrival, seats for her opening in a play of Tom Taylor's, called *An Unequal Match,* scheduled for October 30 at the Park Theatre, were sold by auction, realizing $10,000. But on the afternoon of the scheduled opening, the Park burned to the ground. Throughout the next week while arrangements were made to move the opening elsewhere, excitement mounted. On November 6 an audience of the wealthiest and most fashionable playgoers of the city assembled to inspect this internationally famous Professional Beauty. They were disappointed. As Stephen Fiske declared in the *Spirit of the Times,* "There were in the audience at least a hundred ladies with whom Mrs. Langtry cannot compare as a beauty," and he went on to catalogue her deficiencies: her hands and feet were too big, her eyes too light, her hair artificially colored and waved, her voice high and harsh in impassioned speeches, and her walk awkward.[90]

By November 13, her first night as Rosalind, the Langtry fever had broken. Fashion stayed at home, there were many empty chairs, and speculators hawked tickets in the street for a dollar apiece. In Mrs. Labouchère's box Oscar Wilde, a one-man - claque, attempted to stir up applause, but the audience declined to follow his signals. By now, in fact, Mrs. Langtry's "beauty" had become a sort of town joke. An enterprising showman who ran a museum nearby staged an exhibition of "American Beauties": customers paid at the door to inspect each Beauty on her stand, and having made the rounds, were invited to vote for their favorites.[91]

By then certain journalists were saying that in sponsoring the Langtry visit, manager Henry Abbey had counted on neither her artistry nor her beauty, but merely on her notoriety. So at least the reporter for the *Dramatic Mirror* understood it:

> The people had gathered [at *As You Like It*] for the sole purpose of seeing how Mrs. Langtry looked in tights. . . . Before Mrs. Langtry came on in Act Two every lorgnette was leveled upon the stage. Necks were craned and heads held high up so that nothing should be lost. Here the real interest of the evening was focused, for the great question of Mrs. Langtry's legs was to be decided by an intelligent American public. When she made her entrance, garbed as Ganymede, the house was as still as death. Then there was a reaction and a buzz of comment in all parts of the auditorium. The agony was over—men and women looked at one another blankly. There was no denying it; Mrs. Langtry's legs were a total failure.

The reporter rattled on in a crude account of the shape and dimensions of those legs—ankle, calf, and knee.[92] Stephen Fiske affected to deplore such rude and indelicate writing. "But what are the critics to do?" he wondered. "Mrs. Langtry does not pretend to be an actress; she cannot play Rosalind, and she openly challenges attention to her limbs by leaving off the trunks and boots which she wore in London and showing herself in brown silk hose."[93] It was simply not true that she had altered her costume in this way. She had never worn boots. Her Ganymede dress had always consisted of a gray or lavender tunic which came almost to her knees, and her legs were clad in claret-color hose. Throughout the London reviews runs the opinion that her tunic was unusually long, and the overall effect of her dress was modesty. But in New York the lie was out that she was deliberately exposing her legs, and scandal-mongers deliberately repeated it.

The major daily papers—except for the *World,* which printed a glowing puff by the notoriously purchasable William Stuart—condemned Mrs. Langtry's Rosalind almost without reservation. Critics for James Gordon Bennett's *Herald* and *Telegram* had been instructed to support Mrs. Langtry, but they could not accept her Rosalind. The *Herald* reluctantly declared it "a great disappointment"; the *Telegram* acknowledged her beauty but was certain that "she cannot play Rosalind at all." The *New York Times* was left with "the dreary consciousness of something futile and wasted." The *Post* felt called upon "to speak out plainly, when an entire populace runs mad and stultifies itself by the blind adoration of a pretty face." The *Sun* even asserted that she "reads her lines badly."[94] William Winter, who was trapped by manager Abbey into an "accidental" encounter with Mrs. Langtry, was thought to have been seduced by her into writing nothing about her that was not complimentary, but he could not subscribe to her "hoydenish" interpretation:

Illus. 84. Lillie Langtry as Juliet.

> This Rosalind is never passionate, never ideal, never touched with a passing shadow of mournfulness, never depressed, never "out of suits with fortune," never, beneath her mask of banter, even momentarily anxious about the fate of her love. . . . Mrs. Langtry understands . . . the character, not as a complex web of thought, passion, sentiment and archly simulated coquetry, but as that of a merry and rather unrefined girl who is romping in the woods, and whose business it is to be as mischievous as possible. She puts on the garments of a boy, and she dashed in for a frolic. . . . We have seldom seen so charming a woman in Rosalind; we have never seen a weaker performance of the part.[95]

Jeannette Gilder in *The Critic* minced no words: "Of course, her Rosalind was a fiasco. . . . Let the professional beauties of England keep within their own domain. The American stage wants none of them."[96]

During the week of December 9 the Langtry scandal broke upon the town. Mrs. Labouchère suddenly issued a public announcement that she disapproved of Mrs. Langtry's personal behavior, was at once dissociating herself from Mrs. Langtry's professional affairs, and would return to England without delay.[97] For several weeks past, Mrs. Langtry had been seen everywhere with a dashing young man-about-town named Frederick Gebhard. As a matter of fact, she had not yet submitted to him sexually (that would come before the season ended), but appearances gave substance to Mrs. Labouchère's veiled charges. Mrs. Langtry, following advice given her long since by Prime Minister Gladstone, denied nothing. Unfortunately Freddie denied everything. In an ill-spelled letter to the *Sun* he declared that Mrs. Langtry had done nothing wrong and challenged Mrs. Labouchère to produce marriage lines of her own. As the pot came to a boil, the *Spirit of the Times* smugly expressed its pity for "the poor gushers on both sides of the Atlantic, who, in defiance of the facts, have painted Mrs. Langtry as a model of loveliness," lamented the harm that her behavior had done to the profession, and prophesied that "a flood of London gossip, hitherto dammed up by princely patronage, will soon inundate the society paragraphers."[98] When she left town for her tour of the country, her reputation was so besmirched that it would have sunk another woman—her sheaf of reviews so damaging as to have ruined another actress. But not this one. Her fortunes battened on gossip and hostility. Wherever she went, often with Freddie in tow, crowds stormed the box office. By April of 1883 when she had swept across the country and back, she arrived in New York with a clear profit of well over $100,000.

Illus. 85. Lillie Langtry as Rosalind.

During the 1880s she would spend four more seasons in America, drawing *many* hundreds of thousands of dollars. She acquired a New York mansion on West Twenty-third Street, a luxurious private railroad car, a ranch in California, and a stable of racehorses. (Racing would become one of her most profitable vocations.) A town in Texas was named for her.

From the beginning she had vowed that in the long run she would be recognized not merely as a beauty but as a successful actress,[99] and to the world's steadily rising amazement she achieved that goal. By 1886, for instance, the *Spirit of the Times,* which during her first American seasons had simply sneered at her, was declaring her Pauline in *The Lady of Lyons* the finest that had ever graced the stage.[100] When the *Spirit of the Times* critic caught a performance of *As You Like It* in February of 1889, he could not imagine "a more charming, piquant, and dainty Rosalind."[101]

When word got out in New York in 1888 that she was planning to do *Macbeth,* the town suffered a shock of disbelief, for her "line" was surely confined to the light, the charming, the socially graceful. Lady Macbeth was quite outside the Langtry range. But many who came to scoff on January 21, 1889, remained to cheer. It was a "new" Lady Macbeth, which American audiences had never imagined. "The time has gone by," wrote Nym Crinkle, "for chromos of Mrs. Siddons."[102] What Mrs. Langtry offered was not the traditional virago, bullying her husband to action, but a womanly, wifely, loving Lady Macbeth, certain of purpose, for her husband's sake steeling herself to do what must be done—seducing Macbeth rather than driving him. This "feminization" of Lady Macbeth was happening simultaneously in London. Ellen Terry's womanly, wifely, loving Lady Macbeth had been revealed only three weeks earlier, on December 29, 1888.

Nym Crinkle was delighted with it. He labeled her method "naturalism." He reported that "she read the letter very much as any intensely interested woman would have read it, without enforced gesture or grimace or exaggeration; but with an earnest purpose, a deep significance, and a mental strain apparent in her manner."[103] Further, in the dagger scene, "she preserved the same mean of naturalness. There was no attempt to 'mug' or to 'pump' the lines. She never attempted to create theatrical thrills at her climaxes, but only to make her meaning and purpose unmistakable." Charles Coghlan's Macbeth was dismissed by many critics as dull and colorless, but Nym Crinkle saw it as matching perfectly with Mrs. Langtry's overall conception of the play: like her performance, Coghlan's, too, was naturalistic. "I have never heard the dagger scene so deliberately, so accurately reduced to a soliloquy. I never heard it . . . so like what a human being would have said and done, while it was so utterly unlike what an actor would have done. It defied in its lingering precision every canon of the footlights. But it had a realness, nevertheless, that was new."[104] The *Spirit of the Times* marveled at Lady Macbeth's femininity—for instance, at "the wonderfully winning way in which she crept into Macbeth's arms while whispering to him her plan for the assassination." When Lady Macbeth returns from Duncan's room and cries "I shame to wear a heart so white," Shakespeare intended her to mean "so white as yours": she is rebuking Macbeth for cowardice. But Mrs. Langtry read it otherwise. Trembling, panting, leaning against a pillar, she turned the line into an apology for her own weakness, her revulsion at the sight of blood. In the Sleepwalking Scene she

> gets as far away as possible from the Siddons tradition. . . . She does not attempt to thrill the audience, but to arouse pity for the poor, weak, dying woman. Dressed all in

Illus. 86. Lillie Langtry as Lady Macbeth. Courtesy of the Harvard Theatre Collection.

Illus. 87. Charles Coghlan, who played Macbeth with Mrs. Langtry.

white . . . she glided in through a turret door in the moonlight like a corpse prepared for burial. The whole scene was played in a feeble whisper until the distraught lady began to react the murder of Duncan. Then when she thought she heard the knocking at the gate, she put out the light and made a quick exit in the ghostly grey of the moon, as if dragging off Macbeth. This is new business; but it is natural; it is Shakespearean.[105]

It is doubtful that Ellen Terry or any other actress has created finer effects in the Sleepwalking Scene.

Not everyone approved, of course. Harrison Grey Fiske of the *Dramatic Mirror,* irrevocably hostile to Mrs. Langtry, declared smartly on January 26 that "Age cannot wither her, nor custom stale her infinite—monotony;" and, "Her tempting would not rouse a village schoolboy to 'play hookey' or burgle the jam-closet." But in the same issue of this journal "Nym Crinkle's Feuilleton" celebrated the production as a triumph of ensemble acting and modern "naturalism."[106] And the *New York Times,* the *Tribune, The Graphic,* the *Post,* the *Press,* and the majority of responsible journals were by now ready to acknowledge that her Macbeth production and her own performance in it succeeded far beyond their expectations.[107] As the *Spirit of the Times* judged the case, "Those who have hitherto sneered at her as a society amateur will now hide their diminished heads or join in the general chorus of congratulations. Society amateurs do not produce such plays as *Macbeth* nor act such difficult characters so as to win golden opinions from professionals, critics, and public."[108]

This was Mrs. Langtry's last major Shakespearean effort in America. It is worth noting that a year later, on February 24, 1890, she capped her London reputation as a Shakespearean in a superb production of *As You Like It* designed by the Honorable Lewis Wingfield. Eight years had passed since London had seen her Rosalind. Society, led by the Prince and Princess of Wales and their daughter, turned out to welcome her, and, as the *Era* put it, "a more delightful impersonation of Rosalind . . . the most critical could not desire, the most exacting could not expect."[109]

Mrs. Brown Potter

America's most remarkable woman of fashion to take to the stage was Mrs. Brown Potter (1857–1936).[110] Born Cora Urquhart, the petted and pampered daughter of a New Orleans banker and cotton grower, she grew up pretty and clever, but willful, vain, and thoroughly undisciplined. Almost from childhood she developed a talent for parlor recitations, her memory stocked with poems, stories, and scenes from popular and classic plays to entertain her society friends.

When she was twenty, a Mr. James Brown Potter, son of a New York millionaire and a member of the fashionable "400," came to New Orleans, met Miss Urquhart during a croquet game, loved her copper-colored hair and almond eyes, and three months later married her. She stayed with Potter for about nine years and bore him a daughter. But apparently marriage meant little more to her than a prolongation of her party life, now among the New York "400." She would claim long afterward that she could not remember how or why she drifted into the engagement with Potter, and it is said that in a fit of pique during their honeymoon trip she threw her wedding ring out the train window.

Throughout her years with Potter she continued her parlor recitations (including at least one "naughty" ballad called *'Ostler Joe,* which, by telling the story of a fallen woman, shocked some proper listeners and drove the sister of President Cleveland out of the room), participated in amateur performances of plays for charity, and let herself be persuaded by drawing room admirers that she was as accomplished

Illus. 88. Mrs. Cora Brown Potter.

an actress as any professional of the day. Nothing would do at last but that she abandon husband and child, and in defiance of his family and indifference to the concern of friends, go on the stage. In 1886 she went to London, where her cachet as a member of the "400" was a passport into the highest social circles. She became a particular favorite of the Prince of Wales, and when on March 28, 1887, she made her stage debut at the Haymarket in Wilkie Collins's *Man and Wife,* the Prince occupied the royal box.

In the fall of 1887 she returned to America, accompanied by the attractive young English actor Kyrle Bellew, and presented herself to New York audiences and elsewhere in plays of contemporary vintage. Midway in her second season, on January 8, 1889, at Palmer's Theatre, she undertook the most difficult and controversial woman's role in Shakespeare, Cleopatra.

The *mise en scène* was utterly magnificent. The Abbey management spared no expense in calling in New York's finest scenic artists to create "glowing pictures" to sustain "such voluptuousness of movement and gorgeousness of color as are seldom enjoyed, even in this era of spectacular Shakespeareanism. . . . It is dazzlingly, sensuously beautiful. It is as voluptuous as lithe-limbed dancers, dreamy incense, lascivious chants and oriental richness can make an exhibition."[111] According to the Chicago *Tribune,* "there were pictures of Egypt that stimulated the imagination—interiors of palaces and temples, glimpses of antique idols, and pageants of love and military glory—and these views were contrasted with the severity of Roman architecture and the marble coolness of Roman homes."[112]

The audience augmented the glamour of the occasion. The "400" were there in vast numbers and so were hundreds more who "enviously hang upon the ragged edge of that charmed circle." The standing room was crowded with "cloaked beauties" and "even the top gallery . . . where a woman was never seen before, was bright with ostrich tips and the gay colors of feminine attire." For the whisper had gone out that this sometime "queen of the inner circle" was about to

Illus. 89. Kyrle Bellew.

"make a fuller display of her physical possessions" than was ever permitted in ordinary society drama. "Society was scandalized at the suggestion and immediately with an expectant thrill of delight secured seats in order that it might be horrified by the reality."[113]

Bellew arranged the acting version, cutting and reorganizing Shakespeare's forty-two scenes into a tidy package of fourteen scenes divided into six acts.[114] He took up the curtain not on the lovers in Alexandria, but on Caesar in Rome—that is to say, he spotted that fourth scene of Shakespeare's first act as exactly the sort of actionless expository opening common to well-made plays of the day. After this exposition he combined all the "useful" Egyptian matter of Shakespeare's first act into a single scene leading up to Antony's departure. Thus his Act I reduced five scenes to two. His second act followed the same geographical order: first, a Roman scene (Shakespeare's II.2) in which Caesar and Antony meet, quarrel, and are reconciled under the agreement that Antony will marry Caesar's sister; second, a gathering of Egyptian scenes which Shakespeare scattered over three acts, in which Cleopatra longs for Antony, gets news of him, beats the messenger, and calls back the messenger to find out more about Antony's new wife. A ballet of Nautch dancers was introduced to liven up this "Egyptian life and times." Bellew's third act, omitting much, carried through the first defeat of Antony and the whipping of Caesar's messenger. The fourth act covered Antony's victory by land and his joyous reunion with Cleopatra. The fifth act recounted Antony's defeat at sea and showed his attempt at suicide. In the sixth act, within the Monument, Cleopatra received the dying Antony and killed herself. A simple tableau of Caesar standing over the dead lovers closed the play. Much Shakespeare was lost, of course, but "the version is symmetrically compacted for theatric purposes," said Nym Crinkle in the *World,* congratulating Bellew for having "done this work intelligently, bravely, and conscientiously."

Illus. 90. Kyrle Bellew as Antony. Folger Shakespeare Library.

Of all the spectacular elements of the production provided by Manager Abbey, what drew most attention was Mrs. Potter's six Egyptian-style dresses.[115] The first was of white silk gauze, with a yellow sash encrusted with diamonds and black pearls; the second, yellow gauze with a lavender sash ornamented with rubies; the third, bronze-green gauze heavily jeweled suggesting the colors of a serpent; the fourth, in the battle scene, a corslet of armor enameled blue, a white gauze skirt, and of course a plumed helmet; the fifth, blue and pink gauzes, a headdress of roses, a belt or zone made of feathers of the sacred vulture, and a vulture's two wings framing her face; the sixth, in the Monument Scene, black gauzes studded with gold and a mulberry mantle embroidered with peacock feathers. What fascinated her beholders even more than the display of color and jewelry was the see-through effect of her skirts. Whenever she moved one could make out the whole shape of her legs, and though the reporters were careful to point out that she wore tights, they were flesh-colored tights, so that the illusion of nudity was often nearly perfect. One review, naughtily entitled "Mrs. Potter's Legs,"[116] tells us that the men in the audience "dart forward as one man. They never are confident. They are kept on tenter hooks, always on the eve of a satisfactory and thorough view and never getting it."

Mrs. Potter's voice in Cleopatra was her weakest point. It was harsh, metallic, monotonous. Franklin Fyles in the *Sun* tells us that she spoke between teeth that seemed clenched sometimes and that bit off words at others.[117] A Chicago critic reports that "she moaned and whined, but never spoke clearly, distinctly, or impressively. . . . When in the gorgeous robes of Cleopatra she uttered some splendid line, it was either an indistinct murmur or a shriek, so that

Illus. 91. Mrs. Brown Potter as Cleopatra. Folger Shakespeare Library.

one could not help thinking of Juno's bird, whose gorgeous plumage ravishes the eye, but whose voice makes one long for the healing balm of silence."[118] She could never express love (or any other amiable passion) vocally. Except for her voice, however, she exhibited the whole art of lovemaking with every part of her. Her dark eyes would "roll and flirt, and gleam and wink, and are now half-closed and serpentine, and now full-orbed and bottomless." Her bosom rose and fell, her lithe body "winds and waves in the seeming stress of passion's influence. . . . A sigh escapes her, and there is a simultaneous movement over, rather than of, her whole body that is as difficult to explain as the passing of a wave over the surface of the sea. . . . She twines and coils and twists around Marc Antony, now stabbing him with her eyes, now drinking in his gaze, now panting and hanging limp and languid on him."[119] As she bent over the dying Antony she tore open her bodice, exposing the flesh-colored silk cloths covering her bosom. In her own death scene, at least at Palmer's on the first night, she became so rapt that she tore away the concealing silks and literally laid bare her breast for the audience to see and the asp to bite. It is said that her husband watched this performance from the back of the house, fled horrified, and never laid eyes on her again.

Such carryings-on were altogether too much for the establishment critics, who, without exactly charging the performance with immorality, denounced the actors on artistic grounds. In William Winter's opinion Bellew and Mrs. Potter were "experimental triflers." And when such great characters as Antony and Cleopatra were assumed, he said, "the one by an effeminate stage stripling and the other by a belle of the drawing room, it becomes needful to protest again an obvious desecration of Shakespeare's poetry." Winter acknowledged that Bellew in his proper range as a light comedian could be excellent, but as Antony he was "simply absurd." He was "no more in harmony than a flute would be with a thunderstorm."[120] As Winter's indignation rose over the years, he would declare that from this pair of actors "the emotions of Antony and Cleopatra were in no way more impressive than would be the stridulous loves of a couple of grasshoppers in a cabbage leaf."[121] Dithmar of the *New York Times* half approved of Bellew, but thought his situation helpless:

> He was associated with a Cleopatra who would have been a heavy burden for any Antony to bear, a Cleopatra with a beautiful face, whose expression was as devoid of passion as the painted expression on the face of a doll, a Cleopatra who paced the stage incessantly, swung her long arms wildly, talked or shouted most of the time in an inflexible monotonous voice, and was as unlike the Serpent of the Nile . . . as any pretty Anglo-Saxon woman could be.[122]

According to the *Spirit of the Times,* Bellew and Mrs. Potter "can no more act tragedy than they can fly. They substitute weakness for strength, bombast for majesty, rant for elocution."[123] Metcalfe of *Life* magazine labeled the whole affair "The Triumph of the Tawdry."[124]

The virulence with which Winter and others of the establishment attacked the Potter-Bellew production is in part, at least, a measure of their allegiance to Mrs. Grundy. It is refreshing, then, to come upon the opinions of Nym Crinkle, who loved nothing better than to bait Mrs. Grundy—and to bait bardolators, too. He wrote several reviews, one of them for the *World* and later a feuilleton for the *Dramatic Mirror.* As we have noted he flattered Bellew for reshaping Shakespeare's forty-two scenes into an almost "well-made" modern play. He praised Bellew's acting, too, though somewhat guardedly, labeling him more Grecian than Roman (more graceful than stalwart) in method. But mainly he was delighted with Mrs. Potter's Cleopatra, because she neither "virginized" her nor made a heroine of her; she did not "etherealize" her but "sensualized" her. Shakespeare's Cleopatra "with amorous pinches black and wrinkled deep in time" is no Juliet. She is a "remarkable transcript of passion and voluptuousness," and so, he said, Mrs. Potter showed her. Thus he continued, she jarred on the sensibilities of our namby-pamby critics who write for our namby-pamby society. Just as Tommaso Salvini revealed to us that *Othello* is a cruel play, not a sentimental one, and its central character is an "elemental ruffian," a "sweating beast," so Mrs. Potter has taught us that Cleopatra is "a blaze of passion blown by the wind of caprice and fed with selfishness."

> It would have been a very nice thing . . . if we could have had Cleopatra in pantalettes and properly infibulated; it would have been still better if some Boston adapter had fixed the text so that she could have married Antony and thus made things proper. But Mr. Kyrle Bellew was not from Boston. He refused to make a nice society play of it. . . . He stuck to Shakespeare's badness like a brick. . . . I am glad of it. If we are going to have Elizabethan dramas, suppose we preserve the spirit as well as the color of them. If you want to do something more consonant with the age and its five o'clock teas—don't do *them.*

The conventional problem, he declared, is "how to get Shakespeare into a dress coat." Our evening critics would make Othello a kind of priest, "smothering Desdemona from some high, abstract, transcendental, Brahminical motive." They would "squeeze the hot blood out of Cleopatra and give us the turnip of propriety."[125]

Later in the month George Edgar Montgomery of New York sent a further review to the Boston *Post* in which he vigorously seconded Nym Crinkle's position, praising Mrs. Potter's "bravely right" conception of Cleopatra.

> What is there in the nature, in the dream, in the speech of Cleopatra to suggest queenliness, much less poetry? So wanton a creature has seldom been painted. She is base in her passion, mean in her temper. She is heartless and soulless. Vanity, self-love, self-gratification—these are the things she cherishes. She loves Antony with bestial blood, and betrays him in the mood of a harlot. She is cruel, vindictive and shallow. A generous thought in behalf of others, of her country and duties, does not enter her passionate brain. She is a fine physical combination of the shrew and wanton, and she is very little more.

Montgomery even suggested that a clique of New York critics had conspired to write down Mrs. Potter while writing up Mary Anderson and Lillie Langtry (whose reputation was then steadily on the rise).[126]

Whether she liked it or not Mrs. Potter found herself championed by a shabby little journal called *The Theatre* (to which, by the way, Nym Crinkle contributed one of his reviews),[127] which in one issue declared that her critical enemies "after long records of prevarication, hypocritical quibbling, and humble pliability to contemptible circumstance, have drawn themselves up now in the biliousness of their might and struck one woman as a butcher would strike an ox." And:

> Mrs. Potter should not shut herself in her rooms and weep over the scourging she has lately received, as I am told she does. There are places where the cry of the fawn, as the wolves pull her down, dies unheard, but New York is not such. Perhaps if the shortcomings of the actress had been treated with the gentle spirit of rebuke that they deserve, no one would have felt the duty of lifting his shield above her; but now she may rest assured that somewhere and at all times there will be blades opposed to those that are raised to slay her.[128]

Another writer in another issue of *The Theatre* somewhat more wittily set up Mrs. Potter as representing the aspirations and preferences of the young and the aspiring, and labeled such old school critics as Winter, Dithmar, and Towse as "The Dodo Kings".[129]

The literary manners of these Nym Crinkles and John Carboyses and Montgomerys and Joe Howards and C. McLellans and "Trophoniuses" who wrote for *The Theatre*—all of them rebels against the stringent moral codes of the latter decades of the century—do put one off by their crude belligerency. But no revolution was ever won in silk gloves.

Whether the theatre-going public was more interested in "the truth about Cleopatra" or in "Mrs. Potter's legs," the production enjoyed a five-week run at Palmer's theatre and a three-and-a-half month tour of the country. For the most part, critics in other cities followed the Winter-Dithmar line of attack, and this *Antony and Cleopatra* is remembered to this day as a *succès de scandale* and a vulgar profanation of the play.

The Potter-Bellew combination next made a world tour, barnstorming in India, Australia, China, and Japan. In 1891 they leased the Strand Theatre in London, to occupy it for the next decade except for forays to other cities and other lands. In the fall of 1895 Augustin Daly brought them to America to perform a dramatization of Dumas's *The Queen's Necklace,* and on March 3, 1896 (in competition with Julia Marlowe), he presented them in a splendid new production of *Romeo and Juliet.*

That play had been in their repertory for years, but at Daly's it was not successful. A note in Daly's playbill declared that the acting version was "founded on

Illus. 92. Madame Helena Modjeska. Folger Shakespeare Library.

Horace Howard Furness's Variorum Edition"—a bit of pretentiousness which only called attention to the ridiculous gaps in the text.[130] The entire scene which begins with Juliet's "gallop apace, you fiery footed steeds" and builds to the climactic line "O serpent heart, hid with a flowering face" was omitted. Juliet did not speak the passage beginning "O, bid me leap, rather than marry Paris, / From off the battlements of any tower." Apparently anything was dropped that called for more vocal skill than Potter possessed. She got through the Potion Scene only with the support of music from the orchestra. The sorry fact is that after nearly a decade in the profession she had learned little about how to use her voice in poetic drama: she spoke in thin monotonous tones, emphasized wrong words, and conveyed little of the emotional content of the role. "Frivolity, self-consciousness, weakness, and affectation are not the attributes of Juliet," wrote William Winter with predictable severity, "nor have they ever been considered to be the attributes that constitute an actor of Shakespearean tragedy."[131] A few puffs appeared, but they could not save the production from an early closing. Daly, who had spent a fortune on the mounting, was on the road with his regular company. From New Orleans he wrote his brother, "I cannot understand its dreadful failure."[132] Old hand though he was in judging women, he had been quite taken in by the charms of Mrs. Potter, which could draw infatuated crowds to Cleopatra, but would not do for Juliet at all.

Mrs. Potter continued to act, however, and with some successes in London, as in Beerbohm Tree's *The Three Musketeers,* and (against the will of the author, but *by* the will of the new king) in Stephen Phillips's *Ulysses.* Soon thereafter, her appeal declined; she drifted into vaudeville, failed there, and eventually withdrew from public appearance altogether.[133]

Helena Modjeska

America's most distinguished actress of Shakespeare during the last quarter of the nineteenth century was neither American-born nor British, but a native of Poland. This was Helena Modjeska (1840–1909).[134] At the age of thirty-six, after a career of sixteen years in the highly exigent theatre of Poland, she abandoned her place at the top of the profession there and, with her husband Karol Chlapowski ("Count Bozenta") and a small band of followers, came to America, intending to establish a Polish farming commune near Anaheim in southern California. They sank all their capital in this colonizing venture, and when it failed (for they knew next to nothing about farming methods) they could not even buy passage home.

Modjeska rose to the emergency. Though she knew very little English—never to the end of her days, indeed, would she be able to sound all our vowels and consonants quite as they ought to be—she embarked upon a new stage career in this foreign land.

Leaving her husband in charge of the failed farmstead (incidentally, they would always retain a residence there, called "Arden"), she went up to San Francisco, which was not only the theatrical capital of the West but also the home of a sizable Polish community upon which she could depend for company and counsel. For some months she worked with a language coach, Johanna Tuholsky—amateur but expert and devoted—and by mid-summer of 1877 she persuaded Barton Hill and John McCullough, proprietors of the California Theatre, to give her a hearing. On August 20, 1877, she made a successful debut in Eugène Scribe's *Adrienne Lecouvreur.* At the end of that week she played Ophelia to McCullough's Hamlet, and in her second week Juliet. These approaches to Shakespeare were but tentative, however.

For several seasons her mainstays in American theatre were *Adrienne Lecouvreur,* Dumas's *Camille,* Halévy's *Frou-Frou,* and other adaptations of French sensation dramas in which her foreign accent could add a grace to her foreign characterization.

Modjeska's origins, including even the evolution of the name by which we know her, are a tangle almost impossible to unravel. She was the love-child of one Jozefa Benda, widow of a long dead merchant of Cracow, and she was fathered, it is believed, by Prince Wladislaw Sanguszko, a member of one of Poland's most illustrious families. At birth she was called Jadwiga Benda, but sometime later, under the sponsorship of another of her mother's companions, a musician named Michael Opid, she was christened Helena Opid. In her later teens she married, or became the mistress of (and took the name of), one Gustave Sinnmayer Modrzejewski, who supervised her education, encouraged her and certain of her Benda siblings to indulge in amateur theatricals, and assisted her in obtaining early professional engagements.[135] She had two children by him before they separated in 1865. In 1868 she married Karol Bozenta Chlapowski ("Count Bozenta"), though being by that time an actress of reputation (and to spare the annoyance of the proud Chlapowski clan) she retained "Modrzejewska" as her stage name. In 1877 John McCullough simplified it to "Modjeska" before sending her first American bill of the play to the printer.[136]

Several of Jozefa Benda's offspring became actors or musicians,[137] but Helena, daughter of a prince, far surpassed the others in accomplishment, and it is commonly assumed that her finest qualities were genetically inherited. However that may be, when she reached adulthood, her lovely features capable of great range of expression, her graceful carriage, her extraordinarily lovely voice, and above all her quick sensitivity and keen intelligence speedily elevated her to high rank in the Polish national theatre. But after sixteen years of rising success, for reasons partly political and partly social—even though it apparently meant sacrificing her career—she chose exile. During the later half of the nineteenth century many distinguished foreign language actors visited and toured America, usually to make money and go home, but Modjeska, the most brilliant of them, was the only one to seek a homeland in America.

Although she played Juliet with some frequency from 1878, she worked her way into Shakespeare gingerly. Not until 1882, when she had been playing in English for six years (including one season in London), did she dare offer herself as Rosalind and

Illus. 93. Modjeska's home in California, called "Arden."

Illus. 94. Modjeska's husband, Karol Chlapowski, Count Bozenta.

Viola, and thereafter gradually dared to add Imogen, Desdemona, Julia, Isabella, and Beatrice. When she joined Edwin Booth for a season in 1889, he required her to revive Ophelia and to get up Portia and Lady Macbeth. Subsequently she added Queen Katherine and Cleopatra to her repertory, and briefly even Constance in *King John.* The total number of her Shakespearean roles during the thirty-year span of her career in America was fourteen,[138] exceeding in range as well as in number the repertory of any other American actress of her time. And she carried this repertory, along with her many non-Shakespearean roles, to every corner of the nation. She played in over 225 towns and cities in thirty-nine of the then forty-five states, and in five provinces of Canada.[139] She was always on the road. More truly than any other Shakespearean actress of her time, she served the entire country.

The first significant notices of her Juliet recognized that here was a novel and interesting interpretation. As Jeannette Gilder remarked in the New York *Herald,*[140] Modjeska had studied in a new school of acting, and avoiding (probably not knowing) the traditional "points" in the role as performed in the English-speaking theatre, she studied the role afresh, moved in new grooves, and invented points of her own which wonderfully brightened Juliet. In wheedling the Nurse for news of Romeo, for instance, she alternately wept in anxiety and laughed for joy. At the line "Vile earth to earth resign" (III.2, when she first hears of the brawl in the streets and Romeo's slaying of Tybalt), she subtly displayed her dagger, thus foreshadowing her own death by dagger thrust. At the conclusion of III.5 ("Myself have power to die") she again handled the dagger significantly. When she heard her mother approaching in III.5, she hurled herself upon the bed, thus adding credibility to the line, "Madam, I am not well." In the Potion Scene, horrified at the prospect of meeting Tybalt's ghost, she did not run about or hide herself, but simply dropped into a deep chair and leaned back in it as if frozen with terror. When she came to the actual self-stabbing, she set the handle of the dagger against a stone pillar and bore down upon the point with her whole weight, then threw herself upon the body of Romeo for one last embrace.

Illus. 95. Modjeska as Juliet. Courtesy of the University of Illinois Theatre.

In Boston, Clapp of the *Advertiser* took exception to excessively sentimental touches in her Balcony Scene. He thought she made far too much fuss over the danger to Romeo ("the place death . . . if any of my kinsmen find thee here"), thus signaling to the audience that something dreadful is about to happen which in fact does not happen; and she concluded the scene altogether too prettily by showering Romeo with handfuls of rose petals.

The *Spirit of the Times* among others objected to her reading of Juliet as far too "modern" and "French," as if it had been infected by Camille. Nearly everyone was troubled by her ineradicable foreign accent. Her voice, as musical instrument, was certainly beautiful to listen to, but sometimes whole lines were unintelligible, and she could not altogether master the rhythmical system of English blank verse. As Jan McDonald speculates in an interesting account of Modjeska's Juliet in London,[141] her "failure in verse delivery in Juliet may well be of the same origin as the failure of the Moscow Art Theatre actors to find a satisfactory Shakespearean style, or indeed of more recent actors who, in an attempt to convey emotional truths rather than the old fashioned 'voice beautiful' tend to mumble their way through highly charged poetic passages." Modjeska's life-long problem was that of anyone not born to the language—to discover the tunes and tones of "standard" English. In an effort to produce clear meaning, she would often reduce verse to prose.

A further objection to her Juliet was that at thirty-seven she was too old for the part. Her beauty carried her, however, and sensible reviewers accepted this shortcoming in exchange for her grace, intelligence, and professional skill. She vowed that she would play Juliet when she was a grandmother, and she did so. Her last recorded Juliet was at the Fourteenth Street Theatre in New York on February 11, 1888, six months after the birth of her grandchild Felix. She was forty-eight.

When she first played Rosalind in America in the fall of 1882, she had just returned from three years abroad, the last of them spent mainly in London acting her American repertory at the Royal Court Theatre, striving to improve her pronunciation. As befitted a woman of her social rank and professional distinction, she mingled in the best of London society. Of the literary circle she came to know Tennyson, Arnold, Browning, and Wilde. She visited the studios of Millais, Watts, Alma-Tadema, Leighton, and Burne-Jones. Henry Irving and Ellen Terry befriended her, Wilson Barrett managed her productions at the Royal Court, Forbes-Robertson acted with her, and she knew the Kendals and Sarah Bernhardt. On at least one occasion she sat at dinner beside the Prince of Wales, face to face with Lillie Langtry, and when she was visited by Mrs. Langtry in her dressing room, she was one of the first to encourage Lillie to join the profession.[142]

The Rosalind that she offered America (in Boston, Brooklyn, Troy, Philadelphia, and Washington before opening at Booth's Theatre in New York on December 11, 1882) surprised as well as delighted most spectators, who had known her only as a strongly "emotional" actress, and had never seen her in an outright comic role. Here and there a critic like Clapp of Boston or Fiske of the *Dramatic Mirror* held out for the Rosalind of the late Adelaide Neilson, but others had recently been so offended by Mrs. Langtry's Rosalind that they praised Modjeska perhaps more than her performance deserved. Her command of English was still flawed, of course, and as the critic at the New York *Herald* observed, "Shakespeare was one of those exacting fellows who expect their lines to be clearly enunciated"—yet "if we don't understand her words she understands their meaning, to the delight of all."[143]

She brought to Rosalind's first act an unusual earnestness, dignity, queenliness. She made plain that the banishment of her father hangs heavy upon Rosalind, and as Jeannette Gilder pointed out,[144] she is "the poor relation" at the court: "Her naturally merry humor is overshadowed; she is 'out of suits with fortune.' If she jests with Touchstone, it is for Celia's sake; so unselfish is she that she puts her own sadness aside and sports with the clown to enliven her comrade. . . . Her banter seems always ready to end with a sob. Her laughter runs perilously nigh to tears." Her falling in love with Orlando is conspicuous in her few words and her looks, and love gives her strength to weather her immediate trial. When Duke Frederick orders her into exile, "she rears her head resolutely. She is no longer alone in the world. If she pleads, it is with calm and dignity." She defies the Duke boldly, "with concentrated scorn," yet so controlling her voice and temper as not to "make a point" in the conventional theatrical manner. (In a lecture to the Goethe Club Modjeska once explained that some actresses attempt here to produce a melodramatic effect, "but it is a mistake. Rosalind is never loud. Shakespeare himself told us that she is smooth, patient, and silent. Even in her indignation she is not disrespectful.")[145] As soon as the Duke departs, she "falls womanlike on her knees in a flood of tears." Then, says Miss Gilder, "Once more love comes to her aid. It prompts her to a sudden resolve. It irradiates her with a great joy. She will dress as a man, with curtle-axe and boar-spear. She will wear a swashing

Illus. 96. Modjeska as Rosalind. Folger Shakespeare Library.

appearance. She will go 'to liberty and not to banishment.' The scene lasts for a few brief minutes, and in it Modjeska plays on every note of emotion. Her range is wide; her touch unerring."

Once into the forest "all is comedy," says Miss Gilder, "and Modjeska is singularly brilliant. She sparkles with merriment. She throws off epigrams like a spray of diamonds. . . . Never had these foresters, fleeting the time carelessly, as they did in the

Illus. 97. Modjeska as Viola. Folger Shakespeare Library.

golden world, had among them a youth so trim of limb, so dapper in bearing, so merry in humor." The humor of it, or the wit rather, could only be defined by reference to something French, according to Miss Gilder—to the plays of Marivaux, for instance, or the *proverbes* of Alfred de Musset.

In studying the role, Modjeska turned to Shakespeare's source in Thomas Lodge's *Rosalynde,* and she attempted to find a middle ground between the extreme refinement of Lodge's conception and the boldness of Shakespeare's, which after all was written to be played by boy actors. If the style of Lodge is "sickly," she said, that of Shakespeare is "sharp, energetic, and strong"—perhaps "a little too strong for whatever woman you might be creating." She would not make Rosalind a hoyden, and on that score she deserves credit for rejecting the commonly interpolated Cuckoo Song, though it is evident that she did so for purity of manners rather than for purity of text. Like everyone else of the day she suppressed certain "crude sentences" which she held fitter for Shakespeare's time than for her own. Yet she lost nothing of the joyousness of Rosalind, and John Ranken Towse declared her characterization the best it had ever been his fortune to see: "it was arch, tender, elegant, intellectual, highly bred, and womanly, perfectly consistent, and executed with a technical perfection possible only to the complete artist.[146] George Odell, who began his Modjeska-worship in 1886, insisted half a century afterwards that "a lovelier Rosalind in grace, charm, sensitive and imaginative interpretation, it would be impossible to conceive of."[147] The role was always Modjeska's favorite and, appropriately, Marion Coleman entitled her biography of Modjeska *Fair Rosalind.*

Modjeska's Viola, which followed Rosalind a week later at Booth's Theatre (December 18), seemed to its first critics inferior to her Rosalind. To William Winter it was "so finical and flustered," as well as verbally indistinct, that he could not make out what idea of the character she intended," and thought it "could be called by any other name than Viola."[148] To Montgomery of the *New York Times* it was but a faint version of Rosalind.[149] Only Joseph Clarke of the *Herald* responded to it sympathetically, recognizing that Viola is a less commanding role than Rosalind, sensitive and beautiful but lacking both the will-power and the opportunity to control the events and shape her destiny. Clarke noted in her first scene, when she landed from a storm-tossed boat, her nice transitions from terror of the storm to sorrow for the loss of her brother to bright resolution to "serve the duke." In her Act II scene with the Duke, remembering her own words, "For I can sing / And speak to him in many sorts of music," she herself sang "Come away, death," accompanying herself sweetly with a harp. She spoke the passage "She never told her love" with great care and tenderness—"but not [Clarke cannot forget Neilson] with the melody that made it golden from the lips of a Viola, now, alas, no more."[150] Towse declared flatly that Modjeska was the equal of Ellen Terry in the role, if not her superior;[151] and Odell remembered her Viola of 1886 and after as "incomparably the finest I ever saw."[152]

By 1886 she had gathered a superb company for this and all her plays. W. F. Owen as Sir Toby was "jovial and winesoaked to good purpose." Maurice Barrymore's Orsino was properly courtly and lovelorn, Mary Shaw was a sprightly Maria, Grace Henderson was graceful and interesting as Olivia. "Mme. Modjeska's Viola, thus surrounded," said Dithmar of the *New York Times,* "seemed more beautiful than ever. The tenderness, joyousness, and inherent humor of the girl's nature were all revealed with exquisite art, and the performance was as nearly perfect in expression, in its gradations of light and shade, and pictorial effect, as we can hope to have performances of Shakespearean comedy nowadays."[153]

In the first two weeks of February, 1888, Modjeska presented three Shakespeare heroines to New York audiences—Imogen, Isabella, and Beatrice. She had been playing *Cymbeline* all across the country since September of 1883, but not with startling success, and only now she chose to test it on the metropolitan critics. Unfortunately, the scenery (apparently stock sets at the Fourteenth Street Theatre) was shabby, the stage management execrable, the acting version (in seven acts!) wearisome, her then supporting company, except for Robert Taber's excellent Pisanio, was poor, and Modjeska's own Imogen, though finely tuned in every scene, was reckoned less successful than Neilson's a decade earlier. The outrage Modjeska displayed at the insinuations of Iachimo, her anguished insistence that Pisanio kill her, her charming performance as the boy Fidele all gratified the critics. But bad casting and bad staging diminished Modjeska's own worth, and though she kept *Cymbeline* in her touring repertory a while longer it added minimally to her reputation.[154]

Except for the selected scenes that Adelaide Neilson had used to climax her farewell to New York in 1880, New York audiences had never seen *Measure for Measure* until Modjeska offered one performance of it on February 6, 1888. As Towse says, it was a "hazardous experiment."[155] From various corners whimpers were heard that it was too "unpleasant" a play to inflict upon a polite public, that it had been too heavily expurgated so that what remained was hardly intelligible, or, on the contrary, that it had not been expurgated enough. Yet strong voices championed it. Dithmar of the *New York Times* declared it "one of the most distinctly moral plays ever written," likening Angelo to that Pharisee of the New Testament who thanked God that he was not as other men. Except for certain "impure expressions," which Dithmar was pleased to note were excluded from this production, he was firm in the opinion that this play of Shakespeare's is morally far superior to Dumas's specious *La Dame aux Camélias* and "dozens of other modern plays that it is quite the fashion for youths to take their sweethearts to see."[156] Of Modjeska, Dithmar observed that she never looked handsomer than in the white robe of the novitiate; and Charles Meltzer of the *Herald* praised her "harmonious picture of a sister's devotion and a woman's chastity. Marked with delicate, delightful art was all her lighter work, while in the stronger scenes she was powerful, and above all things, natural."[157] Jeannette Gilder was struck by Modjeska's genuinely nun-like feeling, and wondered whether "only a sincere Catholic like Modjeska could have so delicately and naïvely conveyed the chaste, religious nature of the grief-stricken nun."[158]

When she took the play to Boston late in March, Edward Fuller of the Boston *Post* observed that her "characterization has all those qualities of delicacy, grace, and absolute naturalness and sincerity which we have long since learned to expect from her; and it has besides a brilliancy and a force to which she has sometimes not been equal."[159] Clapp of the *Advertiser* found that her "declamation was the best that has been heard from the fair lady's mouth on the English-speaking stage."[160]

She was fortunate in having young Robert Taber to play Claudio, for in the Prison Scene he depicted fear of death and desperate pleading with such startling fervor as to excite Modjeska herself to unexpected intensity of indignation, and at the end of their scene audiences called them before the curtain again and again. Others of the company were less effective. Eben Plympton, in his effort to make Angelo the center of interest, put on such a Nero-like face and manner—arrogant and lustful from the beginning—that it was incredible that the Duke would have trusted him for a moment; and the Duke, too, sustained by Charles Vandenhoff, seems to have taken his cue from Curio's slanderous description of him as "the fantastical duke of dark corners" and converted him into a skipping, mischievous, sadistic prankster.

Modjeska's Isabella appears to have been one of her very finest impersonations. She did not play it often, but she kept it in her touring repertory, and was still being praised for her rendition of this "deep-souled, high-hearted, clear-spirited heroine" ten years later when she had turned fifty-eight.

Modjeska's first attempt at Beatrice occurred in Chicago in November of 1887, and she offered it in nine cities—westward to Kansas City, south to New Orleans, northeast to Buffalo and Toronto—before trying it on New York on February 7 and 8, 1888. Dithmar was delighted that she had added so fine a role to her repertory and found her "thoroughly happy in scenes of badinage and banter" with Eben Plympton's red-bearded soldierly Benedick. In the "Kill Claudio" passage he thought her only slightly behind Ellen Terry.[161] In Boston, where Modjeska made a stand late in March, Mrs. Sutherland of the

Transcript was particularly delighted that an actress with no drop of Anglo-Saxon blood in her could so cunningly suppress her innate sensibility and imitate the coolness, even the hardness, of an Anglo-Saxon Beatrice: "The intellectual brilliance and vivacity of temperament of Beatrice, what may be called her over-brimming moral healthiness, find in Mme. Modjeska an admirable exponent. She delivers her witty speeches with a snap and sprightliness that make you fairly tingle, and with a grace and charm that are unspeakable. And over the whole she throws that mantle of distinction and high breeding without which Beatrice would not be Beatrice."[162] Edward Fuller of the *Post* thought her in the main not snappish enough, and preferred a reading of the part much closer to that of Katherine the Shrew; but in the "Kill Claudio" passage he found her "quick and passionate demand" was exactly as it should be, far surpassing the "pretty pet" of Ellen Terry, and rising to genuine passion as she continued to rage against the infamous behavior of Claudio.[163]

When Modjeska teamed with Edwin Booth for the season of 1889–90 (he wanted her mainly for the Ophelia she had contributed to the Wallack benefit a year earlier), Booth occasionally permitted *Much Ado* to be scheduled. He hated to act Benedick ("This fellow is a lover," he once snarled to Otis Skinner as they waited in the wings. "I loathe the whole pack of them. Always did."),[164] yet he owed it to Modjeska to let her take an occasional turn at one of her favorite roles. At the beginning of their season he let Benedick down so badly that the *Dramatic Mirror* labeled the play *Much Ado About Nothing Worth Speaking Of* and called Booth's work "just such a careless performance as that gifted actor can give when he does not choose to waste his energies."[165] He could, of course, rise to it when his spirits were up. Later, in Chicago, he was "almost incomparably delightful as Benedick. . . . It was his Benedick of old, spirited, graceful and magnetic, toned down by the refinement of his artistic development, a Benedick who never oversteps the bounds of naturalness and who is always the courtly gentleman of the sixteenth century."[166] He was aging and ailing, of course: a year later, worn out at fifty-seven, he would withdraw from the stage and three years beyond that would be dead. Modjeska meanwhile, at the age of fifty seems to have reached a peak of vitality and charm. She reveled in the fun of Beatrice, and apart from the difficulty of making the words understood, continued to delight audiences whenever *Much Ado* was billed.[167] She would play her last Beatrice in San Francisco on January 19, 1906, when she was sixty-six.

To accommodate Booth, Modjeska had to get up three Shakespeare roles practically from scratch. Ophelia she had played once at the beginning of her American career, and re-invented it for the Wallack benefit, but of course she had to study it thoroughly now to match it to Booth's favorite and most popular role of Hamlet. Portia in *The Merchant of Venice* and Lady Macbeth were entirely new to her.

Her first Portias were on September 30, 1889, in Pittsburgh and in New York on October 28. In *The Merchant* the two stars were perhaps most evenly and pleasingly balanced. Booth's Shylock, as William Winter saw it, was the "fiend-like man, cold and deadly in outward seeming . . . fiercely impelled by the pent-up fires of human hatred, malice, and cruelty."[168] If to others a tone or gesture here or there seemed to claim something like compassion or pity, Booth did not see it that way. As he made plain to H. H. Furness, he opposed the sentimentalization of Shylock as "the venerable Hebrew the Martyr," and regarded him pretty severely as a stage villain, set in contrast to the free and joyous doings at Belmont.[169] Against this bleak figure Modjeska played a pretty range of attractive attitudes. To the early scenes, in which she describes the long series of ridiculous wooers, she brought the brightness of her Rosalind—and spoke her English rather better than usual. In the Trial Scene she introduced at least three novel effects which were found pleasing. Instead of the scarlet robes affected by Ellen Terry and other recent Portias, she wore a black cloak and hood, black velvet trunks, and black silk tights: thus, presumably, she meant to focus attention on the reality and earnestness of Portia rather than on flashy stage effects.[170] She opened the scene in deepened, almost mannish tones, but gradually warmed her voice so that the audience would feel, beyond her disguise, the compassionate pleading of a life-loving woman.[171] And finally, quite by accident, she invented a bit of interplay which at first startled and annoyed Booth, but then delighted him. In the "quality of mercy" speech, she began at the podium, but

> as I talked I left my place and came down to where Shylock stood, and at the lines, "It is an attribute of God himself," I touched Mr. Booth on the shoulder. He started back, and in a whisper cried to me, "That is all wrong, all wrong"; and his horror of my innovation quite distorted his face. It made him start back, and the act got him a round of applause.

At supper after the play he apologized for rebuking her, and when Dithmar declared it "a new business, appropriate and effective," Booth adopted it permanently.[172]

When Modjeska was about to appear as Ophelia, the *Spirit of the Times* anticipated the event with a sneering reference to the racetrack, where "aged horses are not allowed to run in races for two and three years olds"—yet here was grandmother Modjeska being sent out in roles for ingenues. She was 49.[173]

No one else sneered. The usually caustic Nym Crinkle found this opening "a gala night for the Booth season." He hinted at certain reservations about Booth, though was grateful for Booth's diamond-like precision of speech: "Curious, isn't it, that we have got to come to an American actor to discover the consonants in the Queen's English?" But it was Modjeska's Ophelia that truly charmed him.

Nothing she has done this season came so near to replacing her in the good opinions of her innumerable friends. At all events, nobody ever saw the great pathetic mad scene so pathetically done. The rest was a vision, not an interpretation. Modjeska reminds me of Thorvaldsen's Venus in her length and delicacy of limb, her clear-cut intellectuality and her sinuous grace. You couldn't vulgarize her if you put her on the rack, for, like that heroic martyr that they buried alive, she would think more of her delicacy than of her life."[174]

Something very human, touching, and "modern" in Modjeska's Ophelia sweetened Nym Crinkle's temper, for his praise of actors in the classic drama was rare and sparing.

Some critics—William Winter was one—found her too mature, too passionate, too experienced an actress for Ophelia: "she overweights the fragile loveliness and meek surrender of the Rose of May."[175] But "Harlequin," a New York correspondent to the Boston *Home Journal,* was delighted to find her looking much younger than he had expected. Slenderly built, she bore her years with grace, and a flaxen wig hanging loose down her neck and covering her forehead in a fluffy bang was expressive of girlishness. If she showed too much emotional power to be the easy tool of the elders, yet the public would not object to that, since "every bit of emotion that can be put under the skin of a Shakespearean play is to them so much gained in interest." Harlequin appreciated the familial warmth in the scene of Laertes' leave-taking—the affection between Modjeska and Otis Skinner and their indulgent sympathy for the Polonius of old Ben Rogers. Through the Play Scene Modjeska's behavior was quite unlike the doll-like imperturbability of most Ophelias: she watched Hamlet continually, "with a visible fright dawning on her face; and her exit at the end of the scene, when the king calls for lights, was very effective, with its stumbling steps and its backward look of terror." In the Mad Scene she was neither merely melancholy nor harshly raving: "There is a suspicion of a mad gurgle of laughter running behind her voice all the time, and occasionally it breaks out into a sad appeal more painful than tears." She did not sing the songs to fixed tunes, as was the custom: "she starts a tune, and rambles into a chant, or an intonation, and ends sometimes by mumbling the lines, and sometimes by laughing them out. It was altogether a most effective rendition." Her dressing of the Mad Scene was a startling innovation. She abandoned the white robe which all Ophelias had gone mad in, and wore a dress of grass green china silk similar to the dresses she had worn throughout the play—"and ever hereafter," said Harlequin, "the white-decked Ophelia will seem an affectation."[176]

Illus. 98. Modjeska as Lady Macbeth. Folger Shakespeare Library.

She played Ophelia forty-five times during the season, but after separating from Booth she never played it again.

When in the fall of 1889 Booth brought Modjeska to her first New York performance of Lady Macbeth, she had experienced only one trial of it—a matinee in Pittsburgh. No one expected her to make much of the part, for the Lady Macbeth that most people knew was simply outside her range. In a sympathetic but half-apologetic review, Jeannette Gilder explained that Modjeska could not feign because she could sympathize with "the emotions which make Lady Macbeth an exception to her sex. Her own art has always been distinguished quite as much for its womanly grace and charm as for its bright intellectuality, and she cannot, with all her finished skill, identify herself with a character which is in its essence . . . unfeminine."[177] And Nym Crinkle, similarly disposed to be friendly, could not resist likening her performance to a translation of Milton by Béranger.[178] Modjeska herself, before she began to study the role, confessed to an interviewer that she could hardly see herself—or rather, hear herself—as Lady Macbeth: "There must have been hard tones sometimes in the voice of Lady Macbeth. I cannot hear in my voice those hard tones. . . . She is so sharp, like a knife, and I am so round like a spoon. So you see it would be like a fat Camille."[179]

It was no such thing of course. Like Ellen Terry in London a year earlier (like Mrs. Langtry in New York then also) she worked cunningly and persistently with those feminine powers which came naturally to her. She received Macbeth home affectionately, wooed and tempted him, rather than drove him, and, as would eventually be recognized, grounded her characterization on the prescription for Lady Macbeth that Sarah Siddons spelled out but never performed—"fair, feminine, nay, perhaps, even fragile" with "a charm of such potency as to fascinate the mind of a hero so dauntless, . . . to seduce him to brave all the dangers of the present and all the terrors of the future world."[180] In her first performances she was perhaps *too* tender, too pretty, too amiable in the opening scenes, with only occasional flashes of anger or contempt. Later she learned to deepen the tone of these scenes.

The most interesting thing that emerges from the critics' reports over the years is that unlike the bold-hearted criminal Ladies Macbeth of tradition who growled and stormed their way through three acts and then almost unaccountably collapsed into remorseful dreams and death in Act V, Modjeska planned her entire performance as a steady progression toward the Sleep-walking Scene.[181] Time and again as the action passed the audience would see her nerves begin to give away. Thus, when she started toward Duncan's chamber, clutching the bloody daggers, she was seized with a sudden terror and had to brace herself to face the horror beyond the wall. When the murder was discovered and the alarm sounded, she did not put on a show of fainting from pretended horror, but seemed *really* to faint from terror of being found out. In the Banquet Scene, according to Siddons's suggestion, she as well as Macbeth seemed to see the ghost of Banquo. Certainly, as Miss Gilder reports, "she exhibited a terror only less painful than that of her spectre-ridden lord." Through such moments as these she prepared her audience for the Sleep-walking Scene and heightened the agony of it. In that scene she confirmed her triumph. There, said Charles Meltzer, she rose to the height of tragedy: "Remorse was stamped on every line of her pallid face. Her movements were tragic, and she spoke her lines with an intensity of woe that thrilled." On the opening night the curtain rose and fell repeatedly on the scene so that she could acknowledge the applause.

Macbeth was not one of Booth's best or favorite roles, and since Booth arranged the scheduling, Modjeska played Lady Macbeth only 24 times during the season, as against Julie de Mortemar in Bulwer's *Richelieu* 38 times and Ophelia 49 times. The latter two she would never play again, but, teamed with Joseph Haworth and others she would play Lady Macbeth some 220 times during the years to come. In her final season of 1906–7 she played Lady Macbeth over 60 times, and except for an occasional Camille or Mary Stuart, nothing else.[182]

The three further Shakespeare roles that she assumed after 1890 add little of interest to her record. On October 10, 1892, she produced *Henry VIII* in New York, ostensibly to add one more "mature" figure to her gallery. Predictably she omitted the final act, so that the performance closed with the death of Queen Katherine, which, says Towse, "she made beautifully tender and solemn."[183] Yet she lacked the strength to bring off Katherine's towering dignity or her few moments of scorn and defiance, and without these and, except for Otis Skinner as King Henry, without interesting actors in supporting roles, this rather bland play could hardly become a public favorite. She offered it for two weeks in New York, and then, after a week in Philadelphia, a week in St. Louis, a week in Denver, and a week at the end of the season in Boston, she shelved it. Nine years later, in 1901–2, under a management that provided her a handsome physical production and a fine cast, she revived it for nearly 50 performances in some 25 towns and cities, from the East coast to the West and back again. By the end of that run even she was bored with its lack of variety, and she never played it again.

From her earliest days in San Francisco studying English with Johanna Tuholsky, Modjeska was determined to act Shakespeare's Cleopatra.[184] Every few years word would come out that her production of

Illus. 99. Modjeska as Queen Katherine. Folger Shakespeare Library.

Antony and Cleopatra was in preparation. But not until September 21, 1898, at the Baldwin Theatre in San Francisco, did it come to pass. Cleopatra at age fifty-eight! That would seem indeed "wrinkled deep in time." But not so with Modjeska. She was never more girlish. The Chicago *Tribune* put the case in these terms:

> One expects in Cleopatra a dark-browed, swarthy, voluptuous woman, with an all-conquering will power and dauntless courage. She must rule Antony by all the wiles of her sex, but chiefly by witchery of the senses. Modjeska's Cleopatra is almost bland, and bland not only in outward appearance but in character. She plays on the sensual part of Antony's nature, but she herself suffers from a passion which is of a far more ethereal kind. She is light, fanciful, almost elf-like. . . . Like a wayward child she plays upon the feelings of men because it is pleasant to have her way, and especially so when Emperors and dictators kiss her hand. . . . It is a charming, fairylike Cleopatra that Modjeska gives us, even if it is not Shakespeare.[185]

It is almost as if she had got the role rewritten by Sir James Barrie. There was not an ounce of sensuality in her make-up, and as the Chicago *Chronicle* put it, she "seeks to make Cleopatra a very proper person."[186] Although she played *Antony and Cleopatra* some two dozen times across the country, she never took it into New York, and it is perhaps best that we have no record of what our regular battery of metropolitan critics would have made of it.

The last role that she would add to her gallery was Shakespeare's Constance in *King John,* with R. D. MacLean as the villainous king. They opened on October 17, 1900, in Syracuse, New York, and played it on tour 27 times, alternating it with *Macbeth* and Schiller's *Mary Stuart.* Constance is a brief role, limited to only three scenes in the first half of the play, and one wonders why Modjeska elected it.[187] Again in this season Modjeska did not enter the city of New York—prevented by the Syndicate—and the critical record of her Constance is meager.[188]

In 1892, in a splendid essay in the *Forum* entitled "Endowed Theatres and the American Stage," Modjeska addressed herself to the ailments of the theatre in America and prescribed for their cure.[189] "It seems to me," she wrote, "that there is no danger in America which can be said to threaten the future existence of the stage." New theatre buildings, new stars, and new companies proliferate. The *stage* will exist. But these proliferations have nothing to do with the advancement of dramatic literature and the dramatic art. The trouble with theatre in America, she said, is that it is becoming grossly commercialized. With few exceptions it is controlled by theatre landlords collecting vast rents, and theatre managers with little or no artistic or literary training, whose sole motive is to fill their pockets while providing "amusement" to the greatest number of customers. Under the profit system *Julius Caesar* must compete with shows of acrobats and trained monkeys.

In every city of Continental Europe, she reminded her readers, theatres are public buildings, handsomely designed, standing in open squares with space about them. They are built and sustained by public money and are scrupulously cared for. In America, on the other hand, theatres are crowded between or even behind shops in business streets, and though their facades may be decorated, their insides are wretched: the actors' quarters behind the scenes are more often than not cramped, airless, shabby, and unclean.

Modjeska noted that every European theatre has its

own permanent company. The actors and other artists have long contracts (even life-long appointments), regular salaries, pensions after retirement, and permanent homes. American stars and their companies are wanderers—forever on the road, lucky to settle in any city for a week or two.

> But how can one feel able to perform the difficult tasks of the stage after twenty-four hours of travelling or after a number of weeks of so-called "one-night stands"? Still in spite of fatigue the actor has to obey the prompter's bell; no matter whether he feels well or ill, he must "go on" . . . . Scarcely has he time to unpack his trunk and eat a cold supper in a hurry before he must appear on the stage with a radiant countenance. Where is art then? Art has covered her face and flown away, ashamed of those who cease thus to be priests at her altar and simply become commercial travellers in art, changing the stage to a sample-room where the public has only a vague idea what the article might have been if it had been shown under the best conditions.

European theatres avoid long runs, which are so detrimental to the actor's art. If a new play is successful at the Burg Theatre in Vienna it is placed in the permanent repertory, to be played as often as it holds interest, in alternation with other good new plays and the standard classics. In America a starring actor may be condemned to repetition of a single successful play for weeks or months at a time, or be sent on tour with a very limited repertory.

"There is no remedy except in the establishment of endowed theatres independent of the money question"—that is, without regard to profit. She understood that under the American mode of government (and considering attitudes of the people, most of whom regard the theatre as "amusement" and some of whom regard it as the gate to hell) national or municipal monies cannot be used for this purpose.

> The only chance is to find among the rich, the very rich, of this country men both enlightened and generous enough to endow such theatres with private donations. I say *very* rich, because it would be unfair to conceal that the cost of the establishment of such a theatre would run not merely into tens or hundreds of thousands, but into millions.

Noting finally that our millionaires have already generously established religious and educational institutions, symphonic orchestras, and museums of the fine arts, she trusts that they will serve the theatre also.

Within a decade of this writing, plans were stirring among wealthy New Yorkers to build just such a theatre as she described. In the last pages of her *Memories and Impressions* she wrote, "I welcome with joy the advent of the National Theatre in New York, which will, like the Théâtre Français have in connection with it a dramatic school. . . . The establishment of the National Theatre is in itself a great event in the annals of the American stage, and will undoubtedly have a beneficent influence on the dramatic art in the United States."[190]

It was called the New Theatre, and stood at West Sixty-second Street, near the bottom of Central Park West. It opened only a few months after her death, and it soon failed. It is well that she did not survive to witness the decline and fall of that Millionaires' Folly.

Sarah Bernhardt

It was no great contribution to the history of Shakespeare on the American stage, but it was a striking moment in the late century "feminization" of Shakespeare when Sarah Bernhardt (1845–1923), "the greatest actress in the world,"[191] brought us her transvestite Hamlet.

America (and Europe too) had known many a female Hamlet before hers—in 1911 William Winter listed twenty-one that he had seen or known of.[192] The best of them, like Charlotte Cushman, Alice Marriott, and Emma Waller, were big-boned, big-voiced rather mannish women, who had worn out their interest in Lady Macbeth and Volumnia and Hermione or whatever "heavy" female roles were available, and simply needed to test their strength on one or another of the tragic heroes. Except for Romeo, which Cushman played for years, Hamlet was the most accessible. None who tried it was conspicuously successful.

Awareness of the "femininity" of Hamlet was in those days widespread. As early as 1866, the poet-critic E. C. Stedman in an appreciative essay about Edwin Booth noted that Booth was least fitted for the Othellos and Macbeths of the Shakespeare repertory because of their overpowering masculinity, but that he was supremely gifted for Hamlet because of the feminine qualities in his style—subtlety, tunefulness, gentleness, mobility.[193] About 1881, an American Shakespearean named Edward Vining plucked out the heart of Hamlet's mystery by announcing that Shakespeare had originally intended to write the drama of a *woman* caught up in this tragedy—a woman in disguise, a Rosalind at Elsinore.[194]

But that a French-speaking French woman, Sarah Bernhardt—slender, fragile, the quintessence of femininity—should undertake Hamlet, and let it be known that she would troupe it to England and America, sent shock waves through the Anglo-Saxon world. The London *Era* reported it for English readers when she opened it in Paris on May 20, 1899.[195] Alan Dale of the *Journal* reported it for New York

Illus. 100. Sarah Bernhardt.

readers when she opened it at the Adelphi in London on June 12, 1900,[196] and the American critics had made up their minds about it long before she first revealed it to America in the Garden Theatre in New York on Christmas night, 1900.

She had commissioned a new translation by Eugène Morand and Marcel Schwob—a prose translation, avoiding the swinging alexandrines and jingle of rhymes common to earlier French versions. This was sensible enough, although the publication and wide distribution of the translation gave opportunity to every English-speaking critic to examine the text and quote to his readers the occasional oddities ("Wormwood" became "Absinthe") and above all, the inadequacy of clear French prose to convey the metaphorical suggestiveness of Shakespeare's poetry ("One woe doth tread upon another's heels" became "Un malheur marche sur l'autre").

The French were delighted by her performance. Edmond Rostand, for instance, declared that now he was "able, for the first time, to comprehend Shakespeare's masterpiece."[197] The correspondent to the London *Era* treated it on the whole fairly, describing some of Bernhardt's new stage business and approving much of it, but taking care to warn his home audience that this new Hamlet "is a vivacious, excitable, almost fidgetty stripling, whose febrile agitation bears no resemblance to our ideal of the musing, melancholy Dane. . . . The performance is more emotional than impressive; feminine in its feverish restlessness and excessive juvenility." The scenery and costumes, he said, are handsome; the acting company mediocre.

In London, when she got there, critical opinion was split. The *Times* critic regarded it an "interesting *tour de force* . . . worked out with care and intelligence and with consistent grip upon the character as the actress conceives it." It was unconventional, of course, and certainly no melancholy philosopher,

> but a pleasant, humorous, very gay prince, who in happier circumstances would have been the life and soul of the Court—a merry trifler with old Polonius, the first to welcome any diversion such as the travelling players afforded, a companion Yorick would still have delighted to consort and jest with. . . . Little wonder that French critics have declared that it has been left to Mme. Bernhardt to show Paris a living Hamlet.

Illus. 101. Sarah Bernhardt as Hamlet.

Besides listing her many "clever, original touches," the *Times* critic declared that from her first scene the house was completely under her spell: "The keen questioning looks she cast into her informer's faces, her eager, disjointed questions, brought out the full dramatic value of the fateful communication."[198]

Max Beerbohm, on the other hand, had to keep an iron control on his lips the whole time in order not to smile, for if he smiled he would have laughed, and "one laugh in that dangerous atmosphere, and the whole structure of polite solemnity would have toppled down, burying beneath its ruins the national reputation for good manners." He titled his review, "Hamlet, Princess of Denmark," and the only compliment he could pay her was that her Hamlet, from first to last, was *"très grande dame."*[199]

Alan Dale's report from London to America was an unmitigated sarcasm. He had adored the "divine Sarah" in many roles for many reasons, but here, as Hamlet, he thought her simply a freak. "The spectacle of an elderly lady encased in black silk tights, supplemented by a sable fur-trimmed tunic, wearing a fuzzy Titian-tinted wig, chattering away at Shakespeare done into French could scarcely be very edifying." All the talk about her wonderful new conception of the part is absurd: her Hamlet is nothing but Sarah—Sarah-Tosca, Sarah-Camille, Sarah-Lecouvreur. "This remarkable looking woman-youth, with the abdomen thrust forward, the thin, gaunt legs in untutored positions, and the utterly unmasculine gestures, was a parody upon a character that we have been taught to look upon as almost sacred. . . . To ask an Anglo-Saxon audience to accept such Gallic spasms as characteristic of Hamlet is to ask too much."

In November of 1900 Bernhardt brought a considerably improved company and an expanded repertory to America, and began with a five-week stand at the Garden Theatre in New York. *Hamlet,* opening on Christmas night, would occupy the final week before she set off on a three-and-a-half month tour of the country. She had engaged the great Constant Coquelin to join her, agreeing to support his Cyrano de

Illus. 102. Forced out of their regular theatres by The Syndicate, Sarah Bernhardt obtained a tent. After Dallas, where this picture was taken, she played all around the country in her tent.

Bergerac with her Roxane—he to play the First Gravedigger to her Hamlet.

Again, as in London, the reviews were mixed and contradictory. The New York *Herald*, while distinguishing it as a Latin, not a Gothic interpretation, pronounced it unquestionably a triumph—"thoroughly intelligent and consistent. It was throughout a marvelous exhibition of elocutionary power, of facial play and bodily grace."[200] H. T. Parker came down from Boston to report to the *Transcript* a long, measured, and on the whole approving review.[201] Dithmar, like his London counterpart, went overboard with enthusiastic approval.

This new Prince of Denmark, so low of stature, so wonderfully graceful in every motion and gesture, so agile, and so restless most of the time, but so incomparably effective in repose; this Hamlet of the short tunic, the daintily molded limbs, the broad pale forehead surmounted by yellow hair; the strangely mobile face of a Pre-Raphaelite, or decadent cast—whichever one chooses to call it—this odd, pathetic, eloquent, courtly, gracious, lithe, explosive, grotesque, hysterical Hamlet of splendid contradictions, will please the few, the art-loving, the appreciative, if not the multitude. . . . The dignity, grace, and feeling of Mme. Bernhardt's acting in Hamlet's first scene made one forget the "eternal womanly" in her appearance that costume cannot hide. From the Prince's first reply to Claudius to the emotional outburst after the exit of Horatio and his friends, the commingling of princely grace and dejection in her acting was admirable. No Hamlet has ever made more, and with less fuss, out of the message of the soldiers and his college friend.[202]

J. Ranken Towse wrote a well-tempered and discriminating paragraph on the subject for *The Critic*.[203]

It remained to William Winter to turn upon her the whole artillery of critical abuse.[204] From first to last, he declared, her "ideal of Hamlet is radically and absolutely wrong"—interesting only to connoisseurs of freaks. Never in Winter's long remembrance had Hamlet been "more effectively crucified than he is in the French play and by the French actress." The Morand-Schwob prose version, he admitted, is written in respectable French, but it imparts "as clear a perception of Shakespeare's poetry as might be derived from listening to the whistle of the wind through a bunghole." He described Bernhardt's black costume fairly enough, but the flaxen wig infuriated him. It had been introduced by Charles Fechter, who was simply wrong: Danes are not necessarily blond, and every evidence in the play indicates that Hamlet's hair was dark. The costume was padded somewhat to make her look like a man, but she was plainly "a thin, elderly woman, somewhat disguised." She presented, in sum, a Hamlet that was "dapper, shrill-voiced, anaemic, vapid, and yet full of fussy, shrewish energy; a splenetic, loquacious stripling, now gloomily glowering, now chattering like a parrot, at all points whimsical and at no moment impressive." When she first exhibited this Hamlet in Paris "it was a great night for Gaul, and thereupon the victorious Mme. Bernhardt, much encouraged, invaded England with her popinjay Hamlet, and actually exhibited him in the Shakespeare Memorial Theatre at Stratford-upon-Avon."

The most frequently mentioned novelties of stage business in Bernhardt's performance are the following. First of all, there was the blond wig. At a moment when Hamlet was particularly exasperated at the behavior of Rosencrantz and Guildenstern he knocked their heads together. When Polonius brought him news of the arrival of the Players, Hamlet not only kicked him in the shins, but plucked an imaginary fly off the old man's nose and chased it around the stage, "buzz-buzzing" through Polonius's following speeches. When he asked if the actors could play *The Murder of Gonzago*, the First Player handed him a copy of it, as if he carried the company's whole repertory in his belt. In the Play Scene, instead of shielding his face with a fan, as was customary, Hamlet draped his face in the long tresses of Ophelia's hair. The royal party watched the play from a raised balcony at stage left. At the climactic moment Hamlet scrambled up the side of the balcony, held a torch close to the King's face to observe the King's expression, and laughed violently throughout the royal exit. When Hamlet stabbed Polonius through the arras and should have turned wonderingly to Gertrude with the question "Est-ce le roi?" Bernhardt leaped back, raised her sword and cried triumphantly, "C'est le roi!" so that for an instant the play appeared to be over.[205] One extraordinary effect (and a touching one) was worked out in the scene between Hamlet and his mother. Portraits of the two kings were painted on the walls, as indicated in Nicholas Rowe's edition. But the portrait of Hamlet's father was painted on a transparent gauze, so that by a change of lighting the figure of M. Durce, who played Le Spectre, would displace the painting. When Le Spectre disappeared and only the painting remained, Hamlet passed his hands over it in a desperate effort to bring his father back.

The Graveyard Scene was so arranged that it concluded with Hamlet reclining mournfully on the pile of earth beside the grave. In the dueling scene Hamlet received his wound in his sword hand. He first observed the gouts of blood, then the look of remorse on Laertes' face. By a furious assault on Laertes he disarmed him and forced the exchange of weapons. He died standing, his falling body caught by Horatio, and was borne off on a huge shield—"to the general relief," declared the implacable William Winter.

Illus. 103. Caricature of Bernhardt's Hamlet, drawn in Paris for *La Rampe* by C. Leandre.

Probably the most sensitive response to Bernhardt's Hamlet is that of Elizabeth Robins, actress and novelist, which appeared in the *North American* magazine some weeks before Bernhardt's New York appearance.[206] Miss Robins had seen Bernhardt in London, and in the early 1880s she had acted with Edwin Booth in America. Although she treats Bernhardt's performance with sympathy and respect, she sees it in terms of a tragic hero only as a boy—even a rather mischievous one. Limited by sex, size, and temperament, Bernhardt could achieve nothing more than that. She could not possibly rise to the earnestness of tone or the profound thoughtfulness for which Booth was famous. "Sitting in the Adelphi Theatre, I heard again the voice of Edwin Booth soaring out beyond Madame Bernhardt's, and filling the distances she made no attempt to sound. . . . Although I saw her yesterday, and that other Hamlet years ago, the old performance is still vivid from end to end, and the new one only here and there."

Chapter IV

Foreign Visitors and the New Realism

WHENEVER THE ACTING PROFESSION and the theatre-going public seem to have settled into agreement as to the "right" way to perform Shakespearean tragedy and verse drama generally, "Nature"—ever-changing Nature—intrudes and the whole art of acting is challenged. Thus, for instance, in early eighteenth-century England, the tribe of actors led by Barton Booth and Robert Wilks believed that they had perfected the magnificent art of Thomas Betterton, but it appears that they had merely strait-jacketed it into elegant posturing and a vocal recitatif known as the "Tone." Charles Macklin changed all that. In 1725, in his first London engagement, he "spoke so familiar," with so little of "the hoity-toity tone of the tragedy of that day" that his manager broke with him and advised him to "go to grass for another year or two."[1] He did go to grass—to the provinces—for several years as a matter of fact; but eventually he returned, and in 1741 he astounded everybody with the savage realism ("Nature") of his Shylock. A few months later David Garrick seconded him with a thrilling performance, full of "natural" touches, of Richard III. Next, by way of preparation for his King Lear, Garrick quite literally "went to Nature"—to study the maniacal shrieks and the lapses into sodden gloom of a poor Londoner who had gone mad after accidentally killing his beloved girlchild. Garrick's Lear—his masterpiece—was no statuesque model of the then fashionable notion of what a tragic hero ought to be, but a "little, old, white-haired man . . . with spindle-shanks, a tottering gait, and great shoes upon his little feet."[2] Yet this diminutive, unheroic figure could horrify audiences by his cursing of Goneril, and in the Tent Scene reduce them to tears as he awoke from madness and was reunited with Cordelia.

Again at the beginning of the nineteenth century, after John Kemble and Sarah Siddons had labored to perfect Coriolanus and Volumnia, the Macbeths, and the rest of their tragic repertory into the grand monuments that Sir Joshua Reynolds had approved of, the general public deserted all that they stood for and turned its favor to the "natural" starts and flashes of Edmund Kean and the romantic sensibility of Eliza O'Neill. Or again in our own generation, as a number of great speakers of Shakespeare move through their seventies, their famous roles are often taken over by untrained, unmusical, but "natural" voices—or by actors who deliberately shun all that we have long assumed to be appropriate to "Shakespeare." At Stratford-upon-Avon, for instance, we have witnessed a Hamlet so utterly anti-heroic that, anticipating the next notion of the Polish critic Jan Kott, he died snickering.[3] Another Hamlet, at the Roundhouse Theatre in London (later in America) delivered the language of Hamlet in a harsh North-of-England accent, and typically assumed the slump-shouldered posture of a shopclerk leaning over the counter to make a sale. The time will come when the recorded Shakespeare of our own classic masters, say John Gielgud, Maurice Evans, Peggy Ashcroft and Laurence Olivier will sound as archaic, "unnatural," and slightly absurd as the recordings of Irving and Terry or of Sothern and Marlowe sound to us now. "Nature" and "Time" are merciless revisionists of histrionic art.

In the lag-end of the nineteenth century our American Shakespeareans were sharply reminded of their responsibility to "Nature" by a number of visiting European actors who played Shakespeare with a difference. Coming from their separate national and cultural backgrounds, they interpreted Shakespeare from different perspectives. Those who played in foreign languages often missed significant nuances in Shakespeare's vocabulary, poetry, and rhetoric, and substituted ideas and emphases of their own. In any case they had not emerged from the American tradition (perhaps we should say convention) developed by the elder Booth, Forrest, Davenport, Edwin Booth, McCullough, and Barrett, so that what they did often seemed new and strange. The American observers generally labeled it—and hailed or hated it—as "realism" or "naturalism."

The crowd who came, mostly tragedians, included the Germans Daniel Bandmann, Ludwig Barnay, Adolph von Sonnenthal, and the Saxe-Meiningen troupe; the Czech Fanny Janauschek; the Italians Tommaso Salvini, Adelaide Ristori, Ernesto Rossi, and Ermete Novelli; the Polish Helena Modjeska; the Anglo-French Charles Albert Fechter; the English Henry Irving, Wilson Barrett, Johnston Forbes-Robertson, and Herbert Beerbohm Tree; the French Jean Mounet-Sully, Sarah Bernhardt, and Coquelin *aîné*.

Charles Albert Fechter

Of these, the first to make a striking effect was Fechter (1824–79), who arrived in 1870.[4] Born in London of an English mother and a German father, he spent two-thirds of his life in Paris, where as an actor at the Comédie Française, the Odéon, the Porte-Saint-Martin, and various lesser theatres (a quarrelsome man, he frequently moved from one management to another), for twenty years he specialized in contemporary melodramas and romances, acquiring an enviable reputation as a *jeune premier*. High on his list of favorite vehicles were *Ruy Blas, Monte Cristo, The Duke's Motto,* and *The Corsican Brothers*. He spoke English fluently though with a Gallic intonation, and thus, after a quarrel with the French government over bureaucratic interference with his work, he abandoned Paris and crossed the Channel to treat London to his authoritative interpretations, in English, of modern French plays. And then, to everybody's amazement, he offered *Hamlet*.

His performance was revolutionary and it was a triumph. He would show the English people and their theatrical profession what their favorite tragic masterpiece ought to look like and sound like. It seemed to Fechter that what most English tragedians were doing in those drab and leaderless days (Macready was gone, Charles Kean was gone, and only Samuel Phelps, aging and weary and still sustaining the Kemble-Kean-Macready traditions of acting, remained conspicuous on the London scene)—what

Illus. 104. Charles Fechter. Courtesy of the University of Illinois Theatre.

most English tragedians were doing was sterile, unreal, inhuman—mere imitations of outworn conventions. The English critic George Henry Lewes understood all this and brilliantly encapsulated it in a few lines about the "conventional" actor who hasn't the imagination or emotional power to *be* the part and can only go through the well-known motions of *acting* it.

> Instead of allowing a strong feeling to express itself through its natural signs, he seizes upon the conventional signs . . . his lips will curl, his brow wrinkle, his eyes be thrown up, his forehead be slapped, or he will grimace, rant, and "take the stage," in the style which has become traditional, but was perhaps never seen off the stage; and thus he runs through the gamut of sounds and signs which bear as remote an affinity to any real expressions as the pantomimic conventions of ballet-dancers.[5]

I do not believe that Lewes meant this list of "actions that an actor might play" to describe Phelps, nor would it apply to the Booth-Barrett-McCullough-Davenport leadership of the American stage, into which Fechter would move in 1870. But doubtless it fairly describes many a yount tyro or aging ham actor

Illus. 105. Fechter as Monte Cristo.

of the day, and in rough exaggeration it parodies the finest exponents of the then accepted "Shakespearean manner." And the style in which Fechter played Hamlet (and became the rage of London) was so utterly novel that for the moment at least the "Shakespearean manner" was quite discredited.

One of Fechter's most celebrated creations had been the gentlemanly Armand Duval in *La Dame aux Camélias,* and it was his intention to make Shakespeare's heroes, beginning with Hamlet, resemble Armand Duval as nearly as possible—colloquial, suave, genteel, domesticated to drawing room and boudoir. With Hamlet he could fairly well succeed with this plan, for much of the time Hamlet can be construed as a gentleman, a polished courtier, a cultivated scholar, an ardent lover, a wit, a good companion[6]—an easy transplant from the Scribean *pièce bien faite* of the day. Fechter made Hamlet such a dashing, naturally joyous man of the world that Clapp of Boston would one day remark, "We scarcely recognize our old familiar friend, the melancholy Prince of Denmark."[7] Fechter startled his spectators with such novelties of line-reading and stage business that few would regret the loss of moodiness and introversion which they had always expected in Hamlet.

To begin with, Fechter's appearance: his Hamlet was not slender and dark-haired, according to tradition, but—as Goethe had proposed in *Wilhelm Meister* (1796)—blond. Fechter, a plumpish man in 1861 (quite fat when he came to America in 1870), wore a shoulder-length blond wig, a mustache, and a short beard. Some recognized that he resembled the famous self-portrait of Albrecht Dürer;[8] some thought he was imitating the conventional image of Christ.[9]

For a hero with so many burdens on his mind, this Hamlet was remarkably light-hearted. When he responded to Horatio, "I pray thee, do not mock me, fellow-student; I think it was to see my mother's wedding," one heard not a trace of sarcasm, but only an amiable little joke. In the "words, words" scene, he chaffed Polonius merrily, without satiric bite. He was hail-fellow-well-met with Rosencrantz and Guildenstern, relaxed and easy with them even after he had learned that they were agents of Claudius. Thoroughly egalitarian, he threw his arm around the neck of the First Player—although in the first act he had permitted Horatio to kneel to him and kiss his

Illus. 106. Fechter as Hamlet. Folger Shakespeare Library.

hand.[10] When he was called to his mother's apartments after the Play Scene, according to an amused New York critic, he marched up to her, saying "with a jaunty, good-natured, bantering impudence, 'Now, mother, what's the matter?' much as a lad of the period, our period, might address his old lady when he expected her to scold him for staying out too late at night." For his colloquy with the Gravedigger, he plumped himself down on a gravestone, laid one leg across the other knee, idly nursed his foot—"and falls a-chaffing with the fellow as if he were a New York politician courting popularity with a gentlemanly barkeeper."[11]

He introduced curious readings and bits of stage business, apparently from not quite understanding Shakespeare's language. For the midnight assignation to await the Ghost he did not enter *with* his friends, but came from the opposite side of the stage and *met* them: the reason for this, he explained, was that he had said, "I'll *visit* you." He did not permit Horatio to cross the Ghost's path, as all Horatios wise in demonology had done: his Horatio, a good Catholic, made a Sign of the Cross.[12] When a critic once proposed to him that he ought to tone down the brightness and vigor of his playing because it was incredible that such a Hamlet would delay so long in killing the king, Fechter responded that his characterization was squarely based on the language of the text. "Do you not recall the words of Hamlet's father in the queen's closet, 'I come to *wet* thy almost blunted purpose'?" Apparently he thought "whet" was only a variant spelling of "wet," and "blunted" did not mean "made dull" but "made firm" or "forthright." Thus he understood that the Ghost came to "dampen down" Hamlet's too zealous pursuit of vengeance.[13] Left alone at the end of the Closet Scene, he stepped to the arras, lifted it, and pointing down at the dead Polonius, said, "and worse remains behind," suggesting to some observers that he thought "remains" was not a verb but a noun—the *remains* of Polonius.[14]

He made a good many damaging cuts, one of the most perverse being, at the end of the play, his omission of the command to Horatio to "absent thee from felicity awhile," to live on and "tell my story." Here Fechter's Hamlet forgot all about Horatio, Denmark, and the truth about himself, and substituted a totally irrelevant sentimental effect—forgiveness of Laertes. When the poison felled him, he crawled to Laertes, took his hand, looked in his face, and died on his breast.[15] Many a Juliet would use this exact business to conclude her very different tragedy.

Exception was taken—even by some of Fechter's admirers and by admirers of the rising school of realism—to the conversational tone and torrential rush of Fechter's speaking, which canceled the meditative side of Hamlet's makeup and quite destroyed the "march and majesty" of Shakespeare's verse.[16] So impetuous a speaker, "after his interview with the Ghost, would have gone straightway to the palace and, taking the King by the throat wherever he could have found him, would have cut his heart out and flung it in the face of his mother, and immediately have given orders for his own wedding with Ophelia."[17] He suppressed the scene of the King defenselessly praying, for such a hurry-up Hamlet as his could not possibly forego so easy an opportunity to take his revenge and stop the play then and there.[18]

The "To be, or not to be" soliloquy is of course not an oratorical set-piece, as conventional actors were wont to make it, but it is a "slow" piece. With its careful balancing of yea against nay, its precise measuring of the evils of this life against the unknown evils of life after death, it is a sober meditation. But Fechter spun it off at breakneck speed, drawn sword in hand, ready, it appeared, to commit suicide then and there.[19] "He chatters in the graveyard as though he had no thought but of bagatelles, rattles through his soliloquies like problems in metaphysics, and wears lofty passions like temporary annoyances."[20]

In spite of all such exceptions Lewes in London could declare that Fechter's Hamlet "was one of the very best . . . I have ever seen." It was the nearest approach in Lewes's experience to a realization of Goethe's idea of "a burden laid on Hamlet too heavy for his soul to bear." Lewes admired Fechter's "refinement, the feminine delicacy, the vacillation of Hamlet;" and "it is only in the more tragic scenes that we feel any shortcoming." Lewes hastened to add that Fechter's Othello was "one of the very worst" he had ever seen, and he demonstrated in great detail how in attempting to make Othello natural he made him merely vulgar.[21] Since Fechter did not bring Othello to America, we need not concern ourselves with the details of it, but only recognize that in America Hamlet alone among the tragic heroes was subjected to Fechter's method of coat-and-waistcoat domestication. Fechter's basic error, said Lewes, was that "he has allowed the acting manager to gain the upper hand. In his desire to be effective by means of small details of 'business,' he has entirely frittered away the great effects of the drama. He has yet to learn the virtue of simplicity; he has yet to learn that tragedy acts through the emotions, and not through the eye; whatever distracts attention from the passion of the scene is fatal."[22]

In the *Atlantic Monthly* for August 1869, there appeared a three-page announcement by Charles Dickens that his intimate friend, the distinguished artist Mr. Fechter, was about to make a tour of the United States. Dickens described Fechter's romantic qualities in Armand Duval and the *Lady of Lyons,* his picturesqueness in *Ruy Blas,* his remarkable control of the English language, the brilliance of his Iago (but no mention of Othello, which Fechter had failed in and had shelved), and climaxed his "introduction" with a paragraph on the famous Hamlet.

> Perhaps no innovation in Art was ever accepted with so much favor by so many intellectual persons pre-committed to, and preoccupied by, another system, as Mr. Fechter's HAMLET. I take this to be the case (as it unquestionably was in London), not because of its picturesqueness, not because of its novelty, not because of its many scattered beauties, but because of its perfect consistency with itself. . . .

This puff extraordinary of the "natural" Hamlet runs on for well over a column.[23]

Fechter arrived in New York in the first days of 1870, and set up shop at Niblo's on January 10. The timing of his arrival was unfortunate, especially if he intended to astonish a New York audience with his Hamlet, for just five days before his debut, Edwin Booth opened his master-production of *Hamlet* at Booth's Theatre. So Fechter bided his time with two weeks of *Ruy Blas* and two weeks of *The Duke's Motto.*

The rival geniuses paid each other the proper honors, of course: on Booth's opening night Fechter and his leading lady Carlotta Leclercq were guests in Booth's own box. Fechter applauded Booth generously, and Booth's audience applauded Fechter for applauding Booth. Meanwhile, one can be sure, Fechter was taking the measure of Booth's performance, which, however fine in itself, was very much the "ideal" and "traditional" Hamlet that Fechter had effectively routed from popular favor in London. He would not be able to rout this one, of course. For most Americans then and for decades to come, Booth *was* Hamlet; and in this season of 1870, at the top of his form, Booth would carry his grand production of *Hamlet* without interruption to the middle of March, would revive it from time to time thereafter, and would continue to play the role, by popular demand, until his retirement twenty years later.

Toward the end of Fechter's first month in New York he yielded to the urging of "interested citizens" and announced six performances of *Hamlet* during the next (last) week of his engagement. It certainly caused a stir.[24]

The critics were in disarray. The *Herald* did not review it at all. The *New York Times* labored its way through a long and thoughtful essay, likening the difficulty of accepting so iconoclastic a performance to the difficulty we first had in accepting the pre-Raphaelite painters, praising bits of it and blaming bits, denying him "princeliness" and "repose," observing that he acts from "without" rather than from "within"—and finally declaring him the best Hamlet this critic had ever seen. Comparison with Booth was obligatory: Booth, said the *Times,* is only a high-grade eclectic artist; Fechter is a genius! Mr. Fechter "is the pre-Raphaelite of his art, and his career and influence in it indicates a complete parallel illustration. We mean to say that we have strayed in the interpretation of our higher drama so far away from nature, that the abrupt presentation of nature's self comes upon us with a kind of shock."[25]

William Winter, Booth's most devoted advocate, went underground. He did not review Fechter's Hamlet in the *Tribune.* On January 11 he had acknowledged Fechter's American debut in *Ruy Blas* politely but coolly, with a sentence or two reminding his readers that a number of American actors were every bit as remarkable as the distinguished visitor. On Saturday, February 19, the last day of Fechter's brief run of Hamlet, in a simple listing in the *Tribune* of current theatrical events, occurred this sentence, unquestionably from Winter's pen: "Mr. Booth's Hamlet . . . may be seen today, at the matinee,—and our people should know how to prize it, after what they have seen and suffered elsewhere." Considering the calendar of the week, those last words, "what they have seen and suffered elsewhere," can speak of nothing but Winter's contempt for Fechter's performance. I believe, too, that I hear Winter's voice in a pseudonymous notice in *Turf, Field, and Farm* (another of those curious nineteenth-century papers that review drama, music, and the arts alongside stock-breeding, horseracing, hunting, and various sports). If it is Winter's voice it is in his snarling mode. It declares that "Carping criticism [any criticism that favors Fechter over Booth] loses its point when ninety-nine hundredths of the best minds of the country have endorsed Mr. Edwin Booth's Hamlet as the true Hamlet of Shakespeare." It denounces "the utter folly of any critic in assuming that Hamlet . . . was three or four inches taller than Edwin Booth, and that because the ancient Danes were a tow-headed people, the representative of the Prince of Denmark should wear a carrotty wig, with eyebrows to correspond, and have blue or gray eyes"; et cetera.[26] Winter's ultimate put-down of Fechter, written years later, may be found in his *Shakespeare on the Stage.*[27]

Most of the New York reviewers, having just subscribed to Booth's production and performance of *Hamlet* as the wonder of the age, had to hold their

Illus. 107. Fechter as Hamlet at grave of Ophelia.

ground, and, however amazed or delighted they were with Fechter's innovations, had to relegate him, however respectfully, to second place. Two long studies, in *The Nation* and the *Galaxy,* which I have drawn upon in describing Fechter's Hamlet as a whole, manage to measure the actor against the role, and to "place" him fairly. In the November *Atlantic Monthly,* Kate Field, who would eventually become Fechter's biographer, published a detailed and unquestioningly admiring "appreciation" of his Hamlet. Valuable for certain facts, it is so partisan in its judgments, praising Fechter even for his mistakes, that one can hardly take it seriously.

From New York Fechter went directly to Boston, where he displayed his Hamlet at once. There, out of the shadow of Booth's new production, he was much more favorably received. "It appears to have been the fashion in New York," said the Boston *Traveller,* "to compare the Hamlet of Mr. Fechter with that of Edwin Booth, to the manifest detriment of the former. Our judgment . . . rebels at this." According to this writer, Booth in Hamlet, and indeed in all his parts, is simply an imitative actor. His Hamlet is a mosaic—here a bit of his father, here a trace of Barry Sullivan or Charles Dillon or Davenport or Vandenhoff or Wallack—nothing really of his own. Against this the *Traveller* presents Fechter as a truly original creator.[28]

In a very long review by Henry Clapp in the *Advertiser,* we find an even-handed balancing of the comparative worth of the two actors' opposing methods, and Clapp comes down on the side of Fechter.

> The quality of Mr. Fechter's genius is manifestly positive and aggressive rather than negative and receptive; he must reproduce Shakespeare, not reflect him. The Hamlet of this actor is great, at all events:—great in conception and in execution; its fervor is intense, its love and its passion are grand, wonderful and magnetically thrilling; it moves the heart by its splendid genuineness, and quickens the fancy by its vivid picturesqueness. Mr. Booth's Hamlet is a marvellously clever composition: Mr. Fechter's is an unquestionable inspiration. Mr. Booth's impersonation is like an elaborate and finished oration; Mr. Fechter's is like a flaming lyric poem. We are charmed with the fine performance of Mr. Booth as Hamlet; we forget that the Hamlet of Mr. Fechter is a piece of acting.[29]

It is better, Clapp is saying, to "reproduce" (recreate) Shakespeare than merely to repeat his words and obviously indicated actions. "A genius like Fechter can neither be desired nor expected to represent the thought of another mind without changing and coloring it by an alchemy of its own." Fechter's method—his deliberate imposition upon the plays of images and ideas external to them—would profoundly affect the staging of Shakespeare in later times. Not the play, but the interpreter, would all too often usurp our interest. Spreading down the years the Fechter method has rendered "Shakespeare" fair game for any sort of "originality." Clapp could not have known that what he was applauding was the opening of a Pandora's box; he could not have imagined the thousand wild tricks that would be played upon the Shakespeare texts in the generations to come.

Tommaso Salvini

Of Tommaso Salvini (1829–1915), who visited the United States five times between 1873 and 1889, playing always in Italian, it was customary to say that he was the greatest actor of the day, or the greatest since Garrick, or the greatest the world had ever seen.[30] Born into a family of actors but orphaned in his teens, he received his early training in the company of Gustavo Modena, a powerful actor and a no-nonsense tutor of those under him. Modena rarely explained a character that one of his actors was to play, but simply said, "Do it this way."[31] Young Salvini was clever enough to acquire Modena's technical skills without merely imitating him, and he advanced so rapidly that he was playing major tragic roles with the young but already distinguished Adelaide Ristori before he was twenty.[32]

He tells us that he desired to excel in everything, and it appears that except for his inability to master foreign languages, he succeeded.[33] At sixteen he took singing lessons and developed so rich a baritone that when he once performed with two of the finest vocalists of the day—a tenor and a soprano—"I venture to say that I was not third best in that triad." Coming to realize, however, that the techniques of voice production for singing and for declamation were incompatible, he gave up music, though he was fully confident that he could have achieved a distinguished career in opera. He taught himself to swim by hurling himself from a high place into the sea where he could not touch bottom. He became so skilled a dancer that he always delighted his partners. For five years he practiced fencing, and took part in public exhibitions for the benefit of his teachers. "In like manner I became one of the best billiard-players in Italy, and so good a horseman that no horse could unseat me. My muscular strength, fostered by constant exercise, was such that with one arm I could lift a man seated in a chair and place him on a billiard table." An ardent republican, in 1849 he enlisted in Garibaldi's forces and served in the Defense of Rome; when the republicans were defeated he was captured by the French and briefly imprisoned.[34]

It is not surprising that in 1853 when Giulio Carcano's translations of Shakespeare came into his

Illus. 108. Tommaso Salvini.

hands, he fixed upon Othello, the most muscular and soldierly of the tragic heroes, as the first Shakespearean role he wished to study.[35] He immersed himself in the play; he read all the criticism of it he could find (including English and German critiques in translation); he read Giraldi Cinthio's *Il Moro di Venezia,* studied the history of Venice, and investigated in depth the nature of the Moors—their art of war, their social practices and religious beliefs, and their passions.[36] Knowing so much more about the Moorish people than Shakespeare knew, or all the generations of actors since Shakespeare, he imposed a notorious "improvement" upon the ending. Because, he said, according to Moorish custom only enemies or criminals were executed by cutting into their vital organs, his Othello did not stab himself, but seized a scimitar and slashed his throat.

He first produced *Othello (Otello)* at Vicenza in June of 1856. It was not much liked—possibly, Salvini suggests, because the audience could not accept a play that was not faithful to the Aristotelian unities. In Venice, too, although the audience applauded his acting vociferously, their considered response to the play was, "This is not the kind of thing for us." In spite of this, he repeated it several times in Venice, and forced it on the public in Rome and elsewhere, always selecting it for his own benefit nights, until his Italian audiences not only accepted it but demanded to see it again and again.[37] When he first performed it in Naples, he tells us,

> It seemed that evening as if an electric current connected the artist with the public. . . . Actor, character, and audience felt the same impulse, were moved as one soul. I cannot describe the cries of enthusiasm which issued from the throats of those thousands of persons in exaltation, or the delirious demonstrations which accompanied those scenes of love, jealousy and fury; and when the shocking catastrophe came . . . a chill ran through every vein, and, as if the audience had been stricken dumb, ten seconds went by in absolute silence. Then came a tempest of cries and plaudits, and countless calls before the curtain. When the demonstration was ended, the audience passed out [of the theatre] . . . and collected in groups of five, eight, or a dozen at various spots near the theatre; then, reuniting as if by magnetic force, they came back into the theatre, demanded the relighting of the footlights, and insisted that I come on the stage again, though half undressed, to receive a new ovation.[38]

When he had mastered Othello he next undertook the "strange but fascinating" character of Hamlet, but even though "my Hamlet was judged more than flatteringly by the most authoritative critics," Othello would always be his one certain Shakespearean triumph.[39]

Though not an especially tall man, he needed only to step onto any stage to command it. Broad-shouldered and heavyset (yet amazingly lightfooted, quick, and graceful), he could not be *not* paid attention to. His large features and flashing black eyes expressed every emotion, from ferocity to rapture to tenderness, that lay within the tragic-heroic range. He obviously belonged in no other range: the enormous black mustache which he let grow in his twenties and never dispensed with was a clamorous declaration of his masculinity. His greatest attribute was his voice, which Towse of the New York *Post* called "one of the most powerful, flexible, and mellifluous organs ever implanted in a human throat."[40] He could bark commands, out-thunder thunder, laugh with heartwarming good fellowship, gush with affection, and project whispers to the farthest reaches of any auditorium. His stage presence was so powerful that he dwarfed everyone around him, and for that reason, it is said, other actors were reluctant to engage in his companies.[41]

On September 16, 1873, Salvini presented himself as Othello (in Italian, of course) at the Academy of

Music in New York City, supported by an all-Italian company, with the lovely Isolina Piamonti as Desdemona. He took the town by storm. The *New York Times* critic could not begin his review until he had delivered a kind of grand hurrah: "To live in New York is to live where the mountains come, and where all the things one's heart longs for in their turn come around." Salvini, he declared, was the greatest of all Othellos, born to play the part, of face and figure exactly right to embody the martial Moor. He congratulated Salvini for choosing *Othello* rather than one of his Italian plays to open his engagement, for the audience knew *Othello* so well that they could easily follow it even in a language they did not understand.[42]

As the season wore on he added *Hamlet* and some of his Italian pieces—*La Morte Civile, Francesca da Rimini, Il Gladiatore*—and he performed in some 15 cities from Boston to New Orleans. In 1880 he came to the United States again, but then and thereafter with an American manager, John Stetson, and a supporting company who spoke English. The "macaroni" or "mish-mash" effect was ridiculed at first, but audiences soon realized that when they could hear and understand the lesser characters without effort it was much easier to concentrate on Salvini and his acting. It seemed, indeed, to Stephen Fiske at the *Spirit of the Times,* that once the play got under way "it was as if Salvini alone were speaking English, and all the other characters talked some unknown tongue. . . . During Salvini's longest and quietest speeches, his perfect art conveyed the exact meaning of every word to the mind of the auditor."[43] Such was the skill of "the greatest actor the world has ever produced." During this second visit he added *Macbeth* to his repertory. In 1882–83 he added *King Lear,* and in 1885–86 *Coriolanus.* In the spring of 1886 he, the world's most powerful Othello, teamed with Edwin Booth, America's most cunning Iago, for a series of performances in New York, Philadelphia, and Boston that drew widespread critical attention. In his fifth and final visit in 1889–90, he added no more Shakespeares, but played Othello 36 times, out of a total of 103 performances, from coast to coast. He loved America deeply, and "if I had been ten years younger I should have returned thither ten times more." But at the age of sixty he found the exhaustion of the road *(teatro, strada ferrata, e locanda)* too much for him and he dared not come again.[44]

Salvini's physique was so impressive and his voice so rich that in Othello's early scenes he hardly needed to exert himself to establish the character in its full dimensions. The *New York Times* critic was astonished at the simplicity and quietness of his opening: "he is far above point-making or attitudinizing for effect."[45] Certain that right was on his side, Salvini's Othello could respond to Brabantio's attacks with dignity and serene good humor. Thus, reports Edward Tuckerman Mason in his book about Salvini's performance, at the line "Keep up your bright swords for the dew will rust them," he delivered the first half of the line as a loud command, then paused, smiled, and made a pleasantry of "for the dew will rust them."[46] His address to the Senate was a model of frankness, modesty, and assurance. At "Rude am I in my speech," he smiled, and spoke on then "in a very smooth and melodious manner, using the finest, and most musical tones in his voice."[47] The charge that he had used drugs or magic to win Desdemona he dismissed with good-natured smiles and amused contempt. Throughout Desdemona's testimony he listened apprehensively, then joyously, and at its close he went to her rapidly, "raising her from her knees and encircling her with his arm."[48] The *New York Times* critic attested to Othello's tenderness toward Desdemona throughout this scene, "his whole soul melting with fondness in his face"—and then added this curious qualifier: "but as no Christian gentleman ever looks at a woman."[49]

At the reunion of the lovers on the quay at Cyprus, free from the restraints of the Senate chamber, Othello could at last express the depth and intensity of his love. Embracing Desdemona and leading her to the front of the stage, he delivered the great love poem ("O my soul's joy") with impetuous utterance. It was wholly exultant. There was no premonition of the tragedy to come. He embraced and kissed her repeatedly, and after the obligatory bits of exposition and giving of orders, he led her into the castle.

Mason is most emphatic on the "naturalness" of Salvini's performance, contrasting it to the artificiality of certain other tragedians Mason had known. Salvini, he says, "is never afraid to be colloquial, when the situation demands colloquial treatment. Where other actors declaim, he talks. . . . I can still hear the voice of a famous American actor, saying 'Come, Desdemona,' with solemn, sonorous declamation, as though he were leading her off to instant execution—instead of taking her in to supper."[50] And yet another point of Mason's:

> When the situation warrants, Salvini introduces exquisite high-comedy effects; and this in places where no other tragedian, whom I have seen, would dream of doing such a thing. . . . It is, perhaps, not too much to say, that in the first three acts of this play, before Othello's suspicion is aroused, Salvini gives more of the essential spirit of high comedy than could be found in the Mercutio of some noted actors who have played that part.[51]

Illus. 109. Tommaso Salvini as Othello.

Many Othellos lapsed into jealousy almost immediately upon hearing Iago's "Hah? I like not that" (III.3.35). Salvini disregarded, or smiled away, Iago's insinuations as long as possible—at least until Iago's "Look to your wife" (III.3.197). For he was "not easily jealous." But once the fires were lighted they burned hotter and hotter until at "Villain, be sure thou prove my love a whore *(una vil druda)*" (III.3.359) he vented his wrath upon Iago:

He rushes upon Iago, clutches him by the throat, and forces him down upon his knees. The rest of this speech, and the following two speeches, he delivers holding Iago by the throat, at times menacing him with his clenched right hand while he holds him with his left hand, at times seeming almost to twist Iago's head from his body. These speeches are given with the utmost rapidity of utterance, and very loudly. At the end, "For nothing canst thou," etc., he twists Iago violently from left to right, and flings him prostrate upon the stage, Iago lying upon his back, with his head toward the right. Then, with clenched hands upraised, with distended eyes, and passion-contorted face, he raises one foot, as if to stamp out Iago's life. He restrains himself, perceiving that he has gone too far, and retires a few steps backward, raising his hands and exclaiming "Oh, no, no, no!" He then advances again, quickly, to the prostrate Iago, who raises his left hand, as if to ward off a fresh attack upon him. Othello grasps Iago's hand, and raises him to his feet, with an inarticulate sound, expressive of grief, shame, regret, and then staggers blindly up the stage to the lounge, upon which he throws himself, exhausted.[52]

This violence seemed to be a climax which could not be surpassed, but for Salvini it was only a beginning. As the "proofs" of Desdemona's perfidy mounted—Iago's narration of Cassio's dream, Desdemona's insistence that Cassio be forgiven, her failure to produce the handkerchief—Othello's fury seethed until he resembled a volcano about to erupt. When Desdemona cried, "In sooth, you are to blame" (III.4.97) and threw her arms around his neck, he repelled her violently, for her very touch had become downright loathsome to him.[53]

As was customary in nineteenth-century stage versions, the action was accelerated by the omission of several passages: Othello did not fall into a trance, he did not overhear the dialogue between Iago and Cassio, and Bianca did not appear to return the handkerchief to Cassio. Othello's passions were fueled enough without these extra demonstrations. In the Lodovico scene he struck Desdemona across the face with the letter from Venice.[54] In the Brothel Scene, he called her *vituperata, infame druda, adultera,* and *astuta Veneta cortigiana,* and paid Emilia for her service as a bawd.[55] Well before this point the smiles and sunny laughter of the early scenes had turned into horrid grimaces and vicious cachinnations.[56]

The Willow Song Scene was retained to provide that necessary relaxation of tensions before the catastrophe, and from it Desdemona retired into the curtained alcove upstage center which contained the fatal bed. One candle was burning on a table downstage. A thunderstorm was brewing.

Othello entered slowly, locked the door behind him, muttered "It is the cause, my soul," and went up to the curtains, sword in hand, as if to commit his bloody act. He partly opened the curtains, paused on "I'll not shed her blood," came downstage to the table, and laid his sword there. At "I'll smell it on the tree," he went into the alcove and spoke a few lines, sobbing, behind the curtains: it does not appear from his lines that he kissed her, and in any case he was concealed from the audience's view. Presently he came out and stood at a window at stage right to watch the lightning.

Desdemona rose, parted the curtains, and called, "Will you come to bed, my lord?" Othello showed by his facial expression and a low mutter his abhorrence of bedding with a proven *puttana,* and demanded to know if she had prayed that night. Desdemona, alarmed, emerged from the curtains and came down to Othello at stage right. During the following dialogue he would not look at her but went upstage and paced back and forth in extreme agitation.[57]

John Ranken Towse is the most eloquent witness to the scene as it was played in 1873:

Desdemona, not yet disrobed, alarmed by the menace in Othello's look and manner, gradually retreated as she replied to his interrogations until she reached the left-hand corner of the stage by the footlights. As played by Piamonti—a lovely woman and magnificent actress—she was the personification of pitiful, protesting love gradually resolving into speechless terror. Salvini, convulsed, with fixed and flaming eyes, half-crouched, slowly circled the stage toward her, muttering savagely and inarticulately as she cowered before him. Rising at last to his full height with extended arms, he pounced upon her, lifted her into the air, dashed with her across the stage and through the curtains, which fell behind him. You heard a crash as he flung her on the bed, and growls as of a wild beast over his prey. It was awful—utterly, abominably un-Shakespearean, if you will, but supremely, paralyzingly real—only great genius, imaginative and executive, could have presented such a picture of man, bereft by maniacal jealousy of mercy and reason, reduced to primeval savagery.[58]

Lesser horrors—the slaying of Emilia and the wounding of Iago—follow.

Then comes the ultimate violence of Othello's suicide. In Mason's words:

He seizes the point of the curved sword with his left hand, grasps the blade, just below the hilt, with his right hand, and, leaning backward as he says "thus" *(così),* he draws it violently across his throat, sawing backward and forward. His head falls back, as if more than half-severed from his body; he drops the sword and staggers backward (his full front to the audience) toward the alcove; but before he can reach the bed, he falls backward, and dies, in strong convulsions of the body and the legs. Quick curtain.[59]

It was horrible, says Towse, and it was "realism."

Mason and Towse admired the art and passion of Salvini's Othello without reservation: Nym Crinkle revelled in it. For years he used Salvini's "realism" as a rebuke to nineteenth-century sentimentalism and false gentility, and in October of 1889 he rejoiced in the opportunity that Salvini's last visit afforded him to renew his campaign:

Thousands of people have been attending a spectacle in New York City of ferocious lust and barbaric cruelty, night after night, and have thrilled with horror and protested with their nerves, at a representation which was so strangely out of keeping with the taste and the mood of our era.

In Nym Crinkle's eyes, and to his vast delight, Salvini had once more revealed Othello in the manner and spirit which Shakespeare intended. Shakespeare "was not only a sensational writer, but a sensational writer at a time when the dull sensibilities and brute apprehension of the people required an order of entertainment and a bloody method of enhancing it which our age and temperament will not tolerate." The play of Othello is "terrible and cruel," and its cruelty should be respected. Some months earlier, while congratulating Mrs. Brown Potter for exhibiting Cleopatra not as a grown-up Juliet but as a voluptuous harlot, Nym Crinkle reminded his readers that Shakespeare was no modern drawing-room gentleman and Othello was no priestly protector of marriage laws, but was in fact what certain hostile critics had labeled him, an "elemental ruffian" and a "sweating beast."[60] All of Edwin Booth's efforts to idealize Othello and find the means to kill Desdemona without being a butcher had only robbed Shakespeare of his frank intention. Of all American actors only Edwin Forrest, whose killing of Desdemona reminded Nym Crinkle of an abattoir, had got the character right. It was in no sense nice. But Edwin Forrest, Nym Crinkle declared, was a stranger to the nineteenth century.[61]

William Winter, in the long run, could hardly find language strong enough to express his disapproval of Salvini's Othello and all the rest of Salvini's Shakespearean impersonations. I must speculate that in 1873, when Salvini first came to town, for some reason Winter was prevented from seeing and reviewing the first performance of *Othello.* A substitute, highly literate (except that he calls the actor Thomas instead of Tommaso), and capable of imitating the yea-saying style that Winter would use in praising an Irving or an Ada Rehan, simply poured on for well over a column the superlatives of approval. Knowing as we do what Winter really felt about Salvini once he saw him, it is astounding to read, in this first review, such statements as the following. The writer called this Othello "a noble achievement in dramatic art . . . one of the most victorious that has been made within our knowledge." "If ever this tremendous tragedy was offered in a fitting spirit, it was so offered last night." "We have little save acceptance and applause for Salvini's Othello." Except for the lack of "sweetly sad benignity," it was "superlatively excellent." He declared "with emphasis" that it was "profoundly poetical in spirit, and entirely symmetrical in form," and declared further that "He never descends into prose, however vital be the permeating humanity of his embodiment. Along the whole line of the work there flows an ideal glow. It is—as in acting Shakespearean tragedy it always ought to be—a poetic creation interpreted by an artist of poetic temperament and poetic skill."[62]

Winter would have to revise that assessment on every possible occasion over the years in order to square himself with his own artistic and moral conscience, as well as with the *Tribune* readers who put their faith in his judgments. He would always acknowledge that Salvini's *acting* was superb, but insisted that his conception of Othello was radically and ruinously false. "He makes him an animal—and very little else," he wrote in 1886 on the occasion when Salvini and Booth played together. "He is at his best in the ferocity." This was to take "a low view of the character, squarely at odds with the text." Salvini's Othello's love for Desdemona is not ideal love but lust, carnal passion, lacking refinement, lacking poetry. The *true* Othello is not a "snorting barbarian," who converts this great poem into a "blood and thunder melodrama." His killing of Desdemona, which should be a majestic sacrifice, is in Salvini's hands only an act of retribution by a raging fiend.[63] In *Shakespeare on the Stage* Winter flatly rejected the grisly murder of Desdemona and the suicide by throat-cutting, and further emphasized the animalism, sensuality, and total lack of poetry in Salvini's performance. "Offered as Shakespeare's Othello, it was repugnant equally to judgment, scholarship, and taste. In fact, it was a desecration of the poetic original."[64]

Although Salvini was fascinated by the character of Hamlet and thought highly of his own performance, he was aware that the public regarded him as physically too stalwart for the role. It was wrong of the public, he implied, to insist upon a "slender" *(esile)* Hamlet, for surely the Queen said that he was "fat" *(adiposo).* She also said that he was "scant of breath," which went into Italian as *affannoso,* and thence back into English as "asthmatic."[65] The emendation of "fat" to "faint" had not come Salvini's way; the Elizabethan meaning of "fat" as "sweaty" had not yet been recognized.

The public was right, of course. Not only in size but in energy and temperament Salvini was ill-suited to play Hamlet. The role rarely afforded him outlet for the vocal and physical power that had astounded audiences at his Othello, and within the restraints of the role he seemed monotonous and the play tedious. When he first offered it in New York on October 2, 1873, with his all-Italian company, he was blamed for the text he used, an early adaptation by Giulio Carcano. The *Herald* called it a thing of shreds and patches, and claimed to detect a hundred examples of alterations, interpolations, transpositions, and omissions.[66] By 1880, playing with an English-speaking company, he had perforce to use a much improved version; but the better the text, the less able Salvini was to make it work. The *New York Times* critic, to be sure, who always praised Salvini, announced that his Hamlet "revealed new depths of his genius" and declared that his "natural method—a method that is illustrated both by his manner and by his elocution—is employed with affluent effect in this performance."[67] But not even the new "naturalism" could save him in this role. Many critics recommended that he abandon Hamlet.

Certain bits of his stage business were frequently noticed. At the end of the Play Scene, like Fechter before him, he tore up the promptbook that he was holding and threw the pages into the air. In the Closet Scene (following the invention of Henry Irving) at "Look here upon this picture and on this" he imagined the double portraits in the air. At the death, a remarkable business, which Salvini appears to have invented, was much admired: his eyesight dimming, he searched feebly for Horatio's face, drew it down to him, and kissed it.[68]

One of William Winter's accounts, written many years after the event—pejorative, playing for laughs—sharply pinpoints Salvini's general unfitness for the role:

> The spectacle presented by Salvini as Hamlet was preposterous. His Prince had the aspect and apparent muscularity of a bull. The dominant attribute of him was executive force. Such a man would have tossed Uncle Claudius into the sea; slain Rosencrantz and Guildenstern by the simple method of smashing their heads together; placed Mother Gertrude in a nunnery; married Ophelia offhand; spanked brother Laertes, and kicked Fortinbras down the castle stairway—and would have attended to all that business before breakfast.[69]

In short, to adapt Goethe's metaphor of the acorn in a fragile vase, there was too much Salvini for the slender form of Hamlet.

Salvini's own notes on the role contain two curious thoughts: that the Ghost should never appear to the audience but only his voice be heard; and that Hamlet strongly hopes that Ophelia's prayers for him will win God's pardon for all his sins.[70]

It is difficult to assess Salvini's Macbeth, for which, of course, he had the voice and figure to perform superbly. He first played it in America at Booth's Theatre in New York on February 10, 1881. The *Spirit of the Times* sneered that he could no more play Macbeth than Hamlet, but that is surely unfair.[71] Howard Ticknor of the Boston *Daily Advertiser,* as thoughtful a

Illus. 110. Salvini as Macbeth.

critic as any, could write that "No impersonation of the character which we have ever seen can compare with this. In no part which Signor Salvini has played here are his immense physical power, his magnificent ease in motion, his superb dignity of carriage, his perfect capacity for soldiership and kingship so effective and effectual as in Macbeth."[72]

In order to look like a primitive Scot, he wore a tousled, shoulder-length red wig and a bristly red beard, and he reddened his very black mustache. His massive barbaric costumes were designed by Gustave Doré, who visited Scotland in order to arrive at "historical accuracy."[73]

For the most part, his Macbeth was well received. If what the spectators wanted was a display of physical power, an unsympathetic character, selfish, relentlessly evil, sensual and conscienceless, physically courageous but morally weak, committing crime after crime and unrepentant to the end, then his performance was gratifying. Advocates of realism must have been pleased, too, as one gathers from the fretful complaints of William Winter, who thought the entire performance "distinctly inharmonious with poetical tragedy." Among Winter's objections was that Macbeth's manner toward Lady Macbeth was as "merely domestic, commonplace" as would befit John Mildmay, the businessman hero of Tom Taylor's *Still Waters Run Deep.*[74] If you expected signs of "supernatural soliciting," of the haunted man, of any inner struggle of conscience, doubt, or remorse, you were disappointed. "The external Macbeth was perfectly portrayed, not the inner," said Towse of the *Post,* who called it melodramatic rather than truly tragic. "His impersonation was luridly pictorial—perfect in execution—but he did not give Shakespeare's Macbeth."[75]

In Salvini's essay on the play there occur two inexplicable assertions.[76] First, "in my version, I always omitted the ghost of Banquo, in the banquet scene, because I thought it more impressive to make my audience feel that I alone saw the ghost." But Winter reports that the ghost, "gory and besmirched, was, in the Banquet scene, produced in the King's chair and likewise brought up through a trapdoor." Second, "I do not believe that Shakespeare meant the sleepwalking scene for Lady Macbeth." She was far too evil, according to Salvini, to collapse into remorse, and Shakespeare probably meant the scene for Macbeth himself. "I found this scene so unnatural that I cut it out of my version." He may have done so in his own country, but not in America. Neither audiences nor actresses would have tolerated this omission, and the critics would have cried murder at so gross a violation.

Salvini's Lear may have been one of his most attractive roles, though, as Towse says, for various reasons it did not receive the appreciation it deserved.[77] With the yet well-remembered Lear of Edwin Forrest one knew from the start and never forgot that Lear was the *king,* but Salvini, with his penchant for realism, emphasized the human attributes of *old man*—William Winter called him "an *ordinary* man."[78] The Boston *Transcript* on one occasion observed the lack of sublimity in his performance; on another "that want of elevation above *everyday humanity.*"[79]

He established his kind of humanity with Lear's first entrance, moving up the steps to his throne with the slow, heavy steps of a man who is very old but still sturdy. When an attendant stepped forward to take his arm, he rejected the assistance impatiently, thus making the point that he could very well take care of himself. He announced the divisioning of his kingdom without the rhetorical fanfare that was (still properly is) customary, but in curt business tones, as if he were merely formalizing arrangements that had already been decided on. When Goneril delivered her hyperbolic declaration of "love" he positively chuckled, and he chuckled again when Regan topped her elder sister's speech. It was as if they were acting a play, and he was tickled that they knew their parts so well. Cordelia's unexpected "Nothing" simply amazed him. It angered him, of course, but he did not storm at her. He renounced her in low tones, harshly, decisively, and one knew that his dismissal of her was irrevocable. Only when Kent attempted to intervene did his voice turn to thunder. Yet he caught himself, stood silent for several seconds (Winter says, incredibly, "for almost a minute"), then uttered the words of banishment with cold, controlled, absolute emphasis.

This mode of opening the play can be justified, logically and psychologically, especially if one does not read English very well and if one speculates too closely upon how a "real" Lear might behave in "real life." It is, however, to rewrite the play, to smother Lear's violent rhetoric ("The barbarous Scythian, / Or he that makes his generation messes / To gorge his appetite"), and to disregard Shakespeare's habitual practice of opening a tragedy with something instantly exciting—a ghost at midnight, a brawl in the streets, and the like. Salvini's restrained Lear could be thought-provoking, but it was not "Shakespearean."

Whether right or wrong it was deeply considered. He knew exactly what he was doing. He claims to have studied the role for five years before attempting to play it, and once he knew his plan he never changed it. A Boston reviewer of 1885 underscores the fact that "His Lear is now, in all important respects, quite what it was three years ago." He moved through the play in clearly defined emotional stages.

Illus. 111. Salvini as King Lear, drawn by John W. Alexander. Folger Shakespeare Library.

After his iron-hard if low-keyed opening, he shed the cares of kingship and reverted to an almost boyish delight in life, trading quips with his Fool and the disguised Kent; in the second act, as his daughters turned against him, he forgot kingship altogether, lost his royal dignity and became merely a domestic victim, a brokenhearted father; in the third act, as madness overtook him, he became neither king nor father but a rebel against all nature and all order. After the great Mad Scene somewhere near Dover (IV. 6), his capture by Cordelia's soldiers, and his waking in Cordelia's tent, he regained his sanity but not his physical strength. He continued to act the feeble man to the end of the play; and arguing that Lear would not have strength enough to carry the dead Cordelia, he dragged her body on, showing by facial expression the terrible effort it cost him.[80] This persistent enfeeblement was novel, doubtless pathetic, and wonderfully "real," but surely it scanted Shakespeare's intention of providing a "lightning before death"—the miraculous resurgence of health and strength and even joy that Lear experiences when reunited with Cordelia. It makes nothing of Lear's

> "No, no, no, no! Come let's away to prison.
> We two alone will sing like birds i' th' cage . . .

> Wipe thine eyes;
> The good-years shall devour them, flesh and fell,
> Ere they shall make us weep! We'll see 'em starv'd first."

It enfeebles Lear's

> "Howl, howl, howl! O, you are men of stone."

It forgets the fact that

> "I kill'd the slave that was a-hanging thee."

It disregards the plain stage direction of the Folio: "Enter Lear with Cordelia in his arms." It is not easy to reconcile this mishandling of the ending with Salvini's claim that he studied the role for five years; but perhaps he studied only what Giulio Carcano, his translator, gave him; and, according to Towse, the Italian version was irretrievably bad.

Jeannette Gilder evidently saw his first American Lear in Boston, for she published a detailed "pre-review" in *The Critic* just before his New York opening on February 21, 1883. She wanted to call it "the greatest Lear of the time," but she knew that preconceptions would prevent many from accepting so absolute a valuation. Among the novelties she called attention to was Lear's extraordinary joyousness in the passage when he returns from hunting (I.4). "His nature expands; broad beams of laughter gleam over the snows of his face. Every gibe [of the Fool] adds to his mirth, and the more foolish the jest, the more impertinent the rhyme, the more he relishes it . . . He is all sunshine." But then Goneril comes in and the tempest bursts. "These sudden transitions, as everybody knows, are Salvini's greatest effects. Men of the Anglo-Saxon race do not thus break loose; Italians, however, know no restraint, and the extraordinary passions of Lear are surely better expressed by the fervor of Italy than by the chill of the North."[81]

Towse attributes Salvini's comparative lack of success in Lear not only to the badness of the text but to the wretched inadequacy of the supporting company. He suggests, too, perhaps not unfairly, that critics who declared Salvini's performance "un-Shakespearean" may have meant only that he failed to make many points that had become traditional on English and American stages.

> Whether or not the interpretation was Shakespearean, it was grand, imaginative, and profoundly affecting. Nothing could be more touching than his recognition of Cordelia or his lament over her corpse. The whole embodiment was worthy of association with this masterwork of human genius.[82]

Indeed, said Towse elsewhere, "there seemed to be no limit to the range of his emotional expression. He exhibited the power of an Edwin Forrest with the delicacy and subtlety of a Duse. He could overwhelm with a thunderous outburst—free from all suspicion of rant—or electrify with the mute manifestation of suppressed passion."[83] "In these days of stage pygmies," said Jeannette Gilder, "to see an actor of Salvini's greatness is an opportunity not to be lost."[84]

Henry Irving and Ellen Terry

"Irving is on the sea." Thus on October 17, 1883, Stephen Fiske of the *Spirit of the Times* trumpeted to his readers that Henry Irving (1838–1905)[85] was about to arrive in America. "He comes like a king, with avant couriers to announce him, courtiers to accompany him, and a distinguished following to bring up the rear of the procession."

Fiske had taken his information, if not his jocular tone, from Joseph Hatton, London correspondent of the New York *Tribune,* who had arrived in advance, "his brown eyes bright with the assurance of Irving's success." Austin Brereton, who had written a book about Irving's early career and who much later would become his official biographer, had been sent over by a syndicate of London newspapers to follow Irving everywhere and report his triumphs by telegraph. The *Illustrated London News* despatched an artist to furnish sketches of Irving on stage and in society.

"Irving is expected to land here next Sunday," Fiske rattled on, "saluted by a military band, and escorted up the Bay by a fleet of steamboats and steam yachts. . . . The ordinary business of the metropolis will be suspended and the streets cleared of the usual traffic. The bells of all the churches will be rung at 10:30 A.M., but no steam whistles nor firecrackers will be permitted. It is arranged that the day shall be cool and sunshiny." According to Fiske, no omnibuses would run on Broadway and Fifth Avenue, and Irving would drive up those streets to the Brevoort hotel "between sidewalks crowded with our citizens in their best clothes."[86]

A week later, Fiske called the arrival of Irving, Ellen Terry, and Irving's London company "the dramatic event of the week, of the season, of the century." No actor in history, he said, ever held so high a place on the English stage as Irving held at that moment. Not only was he worthy successor to the great line of English tragedians, he had revolutionized all regular methods of company management and the staging of plays. No actor before him had played so many parts (nearly 700, Fiske had been told), or played a Shakespearean role for so many consecutive nights (200 nights of Hamlet, 210 of Benedick, 250 of Shylock), or played to so much money. No other actor had come to America with so high a purpose: not for money, being already rich, not for fame, being already famous, but to win the approval of America and thus earn the right to be called "first actor in the English-speaking world." And finally, no actor before Irving ever held so high a place in society. Past generations of English nobility had *patronized* Garrick, Kemble, Macready, and Charles Kean, but the present nobility "welcome Irving as an equal," or even "defer to him as a superior."

Fiske did not much exaggerate Irving's position as a social lion. When it became known in London in the summer of 1883 that Irving planned to tour America, a grand banquet was given for him in St. James's Hall, with Lord Chief Justice Coleridge in the chair and five hundred and twenty gentlemen in attendance, representing law, medicine, art, music, drama, and society; in the galleries some four hundred ladies listened to speeches by Coleridge, James Russell Lowell (then the American ambassador), and Irving himself. He was feted at the Garrick Club by Squire Bancroft and eighty of the first men in the theatre profession.[87] In New York the Lotos Club welcomed him with a ceremonial dinner attended by over two hundred distinguished citizens. At the Clover Club in Philadelphia he was presented a watch that had belonged to Edwin Forrest. At the Somerset Club in Boston he met William Dean Howells, Samuel Clemens, and Thomas Bailey Aldrich among a host of literary and social lights. President Arthur entertained him at the White House. Shortly before his departure the following April, Edwin Booth gave a breakfast for him at Delmonico's, and on April 25 Irving himself gave a breakfast there for a hundred American friends. On this final occasion William Winter, who had welcomed him in the autumn with a short poem, now bade him godspeed with a long one—praised him, thanked him, blessed him, and (somewhat prematurely) wished him a restful grave beneath England's roses.[88]

Although Irving was not a particularly gregarious person—indeed, rather a loner—celebrations of this sort, and special honors, were a way of life with him. Once firmly established as leader of the profession, he deliberately used public celebration, playing upon the self-esteem of "society," to enhance his eminence. He gave a banquet on every thinkable occasion—opening nights of major productions, hundredth nights, closing nights—calling in a hundred or more guests from the social and professional upper crust to feast with him in the Beefsteak Room or on the stage of the Lyceum Theatre, and to listen to congratulatory addresses. Bernard Shaw tells us that although as a theatre critic he was always invited to opening night banquets ("Chicken and Champagne," he called them, "lordly bribes"), he always stayed away.[89] For outsiders to the profession, however, an invitation from Irving was a prized honor, and few would decline the great man's bidding.

As head of the profession he was called upon to officiate at theatrically historical events—to dedicate the Shakespeare Fountain in the market-place at Stratford, to dedicate the Sarah Siddons monument in Paddington. As an accredited "intellectual" (in 1887 in collaboration with a friend who did most of the editing he brought out the eight-volume *Henry Irving Shakespeare*), he received honorary doctorates from the universities of Dublin, Cambridge, and Glasgow. In America he lectured at several major universities. He was member of a half dozen exclusive London clubs, and no less a patron than the Prince of Wales put him up for the Marlborough. In 1889 the Queen invited him and his company to perform for her at Sandringham, and in 1895 she elevated him (the first actor to be so honored) to the knighthood.[90]

We think of Irving as a major Shakespearean. Indeed, if it were not for his work in Shakespeare we should probably not think of him often, for as he himself declared to Ellen Terry, "No actor or actress who doesn't play in 'the classics'—in Shakespeare or old comedy—will be heard of long."[91] His record as a Shakespearean is certainly extensive. Between 1856 and 1871, before he came to the Lyceum, he played 47 Shakespearean roles (all but one or two of them secondary or minor) in 18 plays. At the Lyceum, between 1871 and 1905, at first under the Bateman management and then under his own, he played 14 *leading* roles in splendid productions of 13 plays.[92] During his eight visits to America, between 1883 and 1904, he transported 6 of these roles—Shylock, Benedick, Malvolio, Hamlet, Wolsey, and Macbeth—each supported by its Lyceum company and *mise-en-scène*.

If in the long run Shakespeare was what saved Irving's reputation, it was not what he played most often, nor was it what he was really best equipped for. When he first presented himself to America in 1883, meaning, surely, to put his best foot forward, it was not so much the Shakespearean that he showed us, but the specialist in contemporary melodrama. Except for *The Merchant of Venice,* the plays he offered during his four-week opening run in New York were popular pieces of recent vintage which, except for their titles, are by now well forgotten. He began on October 29 with his notorious thriller, Mathias in *The Bells*—in which, according to William Winter, "by giving this murderer a human heart, by making paternal

Illus. 112. Sir Henry Irving, from a painting by Sir J. E. Millais, Bart. P.R.A. Folger Shakespeare Library.

tenderness the motive and passion of his life, and then by depicting, with consummate skill, those agonies of the soul which only such a soul can suffer, he creates an image not less pitiable than horrible of that forlorn humanity which evil has conquered and which inexorable justice must now destroy."[93] (The *New York Times* called the play "a tawdry melodrama.")[94]

For contrast he followed Mathias with W. G. Wills's sentimental tragedy, *Charles I,* in which he played the role of the Martyr King, "richly complex in its elaborately courtly manners; and fraught equally with sombre gravity and tender feeling" (William Winter again).[95] Next came black villainy, crumbling senility, and horrible death in Boucicault's *Louis XI.* He got around to Shakespeare on November 6—Shylock, with Ellen Terry's Portia. When in mid-month he turned to Charles Reade's *The Lyons Mail,* doubling as Dubosc and Lesurques, the look-alike villain and victim, he came near to losing certain friends in the press. "He is attracting the largest, the most fashionable audiences ever assembled in New York," observed Stephen Fiske, "and he suddenly presents them with an old Bowery melodrama of the school which passed out of popularity when Kirby died. . . .[96] A dozen better pieces are brought out every month at the unadvertised theatres on the East side, without attracting the slightest critical attention. . . . The play is not worth the footlights."[97] If Irving made partial amends later by presenting Miss Terry and himself in an "old comedy"—a cut-down version of Hannah Cowley's *The Belle's Stratagem*—nonetheless Fiske and other critics were put off by the cheap diet he was serving them and clamored for more Shakespeare.

He promised that when he returned in the spring he would give them *Hamlet,* but in the event, although he played Hamlet occasionally during his tour of the country, he withheld it from the metropolis until another season. Hamlet was "his" character in London, but in America it belonged to Edwin Booth. What the critics of New York wrote was what went home by cable, and it would not do, at the end of the season, to risk spoiling his conquest of America with any chilling comparison. His decision to delay Hamlet was strategically correct.

Of all Irving's Shakespeare roles, Shylock, which he played over one thousand times during this career, was obviously the most successful. Irving thought highly of it himself: once in private, and "in all humility," he said that his was *"the only great Shylock."*[98]

This did not necessarily mean that it was Shakespeare's Shylock. Basic to Irving's philosophy of acting, like Fechter's, was his insistence on the primacy of the actor as creative artist: the actor's interpretation of a part, what he made of it by filtering it through himself, was more important than the part as it appears "in the book." Only a "mummer" would seek to *be* the character; the true actor would "adapt the part to his own personality" (to paraphrase Ellen Terry, whose ideas about acting were very like Irving's), and thus would reveal something about the character that would be new, unique, and valuable.[99]

Illus. 113. Ellen Terry.

Irving's Shylock is a fair (and not extravagant) example of how his theory worked. As William Winter once heard him declare, "Shylock is a bloody-minded monster—but you mustn't play him so if you wish to succeed; you must get some sympathy with him."[100] And sympathy Irving got, through personal magnetism, powerful acting, stage management, and fiddling with the text—more sympathy than was good for the romantic love stories with which the play begins, climaxes, and ends—against which (ideally) Shylock plays a harsh but limited counter-balance. In Irving's production Ellen Terry as Portia had her innings as one of the most delightful personalities ever seen on the English-speaking stage, but the rest of the players, though well directed, hardly mattered and

Illus. 114. Irving as Shylock. Folger Shakespeare Library.

Irving's Shylock swamped the lot of them.

His desire to produce *The Merchant of Venice* did not arise so much out of interest in the *play* as out of chance encounters with a special breed of Jew. During a Mediterranean cruise in the summer of 1879 he became aware of Jewish merchants from the Levant—not the filthy, grasping, contemptible villains of English stage tradition, but romantically costumed patriarchs moving with dignity and assurance (yet fawning obsequiously when challenged) among the natives of Tunis. Rethinking Shylock with this image in mind, remembering too the Sephardic Jews of Spain, and Baron Rothschild and Benjamin Disraeli of his own day and nation, he could imagine Shylock "a proud man, respected on the Rialto, the leader of his synagogue and conscious of his moral superiority to . . . the Christians who baited him." Surely he could fit this Shylock into the dramatic situation Shakespeare had contrived. He could transpose Shylock from villain to hero, from Christian-killer to inspired avenger of the centuries-long oppression of his race, a martyr in that noble if defeated cause.[101]

Pruning the text would help. He would not, of course, like Edwin Booth and others in the old-fashioned American tradition, drop the curtain on Shylock's exit from the Trial Scene. He let the love story play to its ending, and was properly praised for this major restoration. But by *trimming* the love story—cutting out Morocco's first scene, omitting Arragon altogether, reducing Bassanio's Casket Scene by more than a third—he saved a maximum of stage time for Shylock. He also deleted scenes or lines that are prejudicial to Shylock's character: for instance, II.3, in which Jessica describes Shylock's home as a hell, confesses how ashamed she is to be daughter to such a father, and longs to become a Christian and Lorenzo's wife; and III.5, in which the Clown warns Jessica that because she is the Jew's daughter she will certainly be damned.

Appearance would help. His costume was at once sober, splendid, and meaningful. It consisted of a rust-brown tunic reaching to his ankles and over that a dark brown gaberdine edged with fur. The sleeves of the tunic fitted closely from elbow to wrist, setting off his long, expressive hands. He leaned upon a heavy walking stick. From his black brimless cap one black forelock dropped down his forehead, and at the back and sides of his head cascades of gray hair tumbled over his collar. He wore a curly beard and thin mustache. Three spots of color brightened and gave meaning to the dark ensemble: on the front of his cap a vertical bar of yellow proclaimed his Jewishness; round his waist a broad sash, cross-striped with red and yellow, repeated that fact; glittering through his gray locks gold earrings bespoke his wealth.

He could draw sympathy through pantomime, through wordless actions that Shakespeare never dreamed of. Twenty years ealier Charles Kean had brought the scene of Jessica's elopement to a joyous climax by the addition of a street carnival. As the lovers departed by gondola, sailing down a canal under a great bridge, a band of masked revelers spilled onto the stage, dancing, singing, tumbling, and bringing down the act drop with a burst of glad music.[102] Irving kept that romantic improvement, but he cunningly topped it and reversed its effect by adding one episode more. A moment after the curtain touched the floor (to a roar of applause, of course) it rose again on an empty and nearly silent stage. And there appeared on the arch of the bridge, climbing up out of the farther darkness, the grim figure of Shylock, with lantern and crutch-stick, coming home late from Bassanio's dinner:

> For an instant he paused, his seamed, cruel face, visible in a gleam of ruddy light, contorted by a sneer as he listened to the sound of revelry dying away in the distance. Then he descended the steps, crossed to his dwelling, raised his right hand, struck twice upon the door with the iron knocker, and stood like a statue, waiting—while a slow-descending curtain closed in one of the most expressive pictures that any stage has ever produced.[103]

Thus Irving stole the scene and the curtain for Shylock. With one firm stroke of silent business he *rewrote* the scene, so to speak, converting the happy fulfillment of a love story (and the rescue of a captive maiden from the Jew-dragon's den) to the pitiful story of a decent, careful father betrayed by a heartless daughter. Irving's innovation was widely acclaimed, and throughout the next generation nearly all Shylocks adopted it or "improved" it farther.

Another effective pantomimic addition enriched the Trial Scene. Among the spectators Irving posted a cluster of bearded Jews who followed Shylock's rising triumph and ultimate defeat with excited responses. The Duke's final order that Shylock forsake his religion and turn Christian fell upon these Jews "like a thunderbolt": Shylock's tragedy became the tragedy of their nation, Shylock their scapegoat and their hero.[104]

On one very public occasion Irving was smartly rebuked for his all too sympathetic reading of Shylock. After the Lyceum banquet on the hundredth night of *The Merchant,* while soft music sounded and souvenir books of the play were being distributed, surrounded by "some three hundred and fifty gentlemen, every one of whom was a celebrity," Irving settled back to hear Richard Monckton Milnes, Lord Houghton, toast his production and performance. Houghton led off with a few witty, slightly acidulous allusions to theatrical "centenaries," then detoured, oddly, into a discussion of a certain new school of historians who seemed determined to rehabilitate all the great villains who ever lived: Nero, Tiberius, Richard III ("a most amiable sovereign, particularly fond of nephews"), Marat, Robespierre ("only prevented from regenerating the human race by their dislike to shedding human blood"). And now, Houghton continued, on this very stage, the old Jew Shylock, usually regarded as a ferocious monster, had become a fine gentleman of the Hebrew persuasion, afflicted with a stupid servant and a pernicious daughter, frustrated in his efforts to avenge the centuries of wrongs heaped upon his race, retiring at last "accompanied by the tears of women and the admiration of men." If Iago should fall into Mr. Irving's hands, "he would be regarded, not as a violent, but as a very honest man, only devoted to the object of preserving the honour of his wife." When the speaker concluded with the obligatory flourish of compliments to his host, the company rose to drink Irving's health and to cheer him with *more* than customary enthusiasm.[105]

Milnes's speech was regarded as "not a happy one, nor in good taste for such an occasion," but it by no means diminished the box office for the next 150 nights of *The Merchant*'s run.

In fairness to Irving it must be acknowledged that, as Shylock, he won audiences not merely by playing tricks on the text, but by cunning and convincing acting.[106] He played his first scene—against all precedent and to everybody's wonderment—very quietly. His Shylock entered slowly, leaning on his stick, mulling over the request that Bassanio had initiated in the wings: "Three thousand ducats, well." Rubbing thumb and fingers together, calculating, with nothing in mind but the proposed loan, the odds, the interest, he resembled whatever proudest, most distinguished Jewish merchant Irving had encountered that summer in the Mediterranean. He would raise his voice in anger only twice in the scene—first to reject Bassanio's ill-advised invitation to dinner ("Yes, to smell pork . . ."), and again to rebuke Antonio for having spat on him and called him dog. When Antonio rounded on him, he withdrew in fawning tones, pretending friendship and service.

There is good reason for this initial restraint. Shakespeare does not announce Shylock as a bad lot. He does not even mention his name or his existence before we see him. There is no reason, then, for the actor to come upon the stage glowering and snarling, threatening all Christendom with Shylock's first utterances.

Shylock's fawning response to Antonio's attack upon him (at I.3.137) is "Why, look you how you storm! I would be friends with you, and have your love." Then as he invited Antonio to accompany him to a notary to "seal me there your single bond," Irving introduced a novel stage business: he laid his forefinger on Antonio's breast. Antonio recoiled, wrapping his cloak about him, disgusted by the physical contact. Shylock drew back in shocked silence, measured his hurt, and in that instant envisioned a knife laid to that "fair flesh." He stepped forward smilingly to offer his "kind" proposal. Once his offer was accepted, his exit, says Laurence Irving, was "almost jaunty."

From the moment of Jessica's elopement to the beginning of the Trial Scene, Shylock's anger rose and hardened in carefully planned stages, justified at every turn. In the great Street Scene (III.1), he entered to Salarino and Salanio on the run. "His hair streaming, without a cap, his shirt torn open, he gesticulated wildly at them and was evidently frantic with grief." He repeated the line "Let him look to his bond" in cold fury; and when asked what use he could make of Antonio's flesh, he positively screamed, "To bait fish withal," launching then into his passionate declaration of a Jew's right to vengeance. A moment later, reminded of Jessica's thievery and her waste of diamonds and ducats, he wished her "dead at my foot," "hears'd at my foot." But then, as if shocked by his own wish, he abruptly reversed it, improving the text with an interpolated appeal for sympathy: hiding his face in his hands, he sobbed "No, no, no, no, no!"

At the news of Antonio's loss of ships he instantly hardened again. He called for Antonio's arrest. He cried, "I will have the heart of him if he forfeit." His eyes blazed, his jaws snapped shut, he rolled up his right sleeve to the elbow, "and the fingers of the right hand stretched forth . . . quivering, as if already they were tearing out the heart of his hated enemy."

Irving restored one scene that earlier managers customarily omitted (III, 3)—the scene in which Shylock taunts Antonio, berates the jailer for permitting Antonio to walk the streets, and again and again declares, "I'll have my bond." The reason for this restoration was certainly not that which William Winter quaintly suggested—to provide time offstage for Portia and Bassanio, Nerissa and Gratiano, to get properly married! Irving needed this scene to keep Shylock in the foreground. He had been absent for some two hundred lines, and as the play moved toward the Trial Scene, he wanted to mark one more stage in the hardening of Shylock's resolution.

In the Trial Scene, says Irving's grandson, he "gave the finest performance of his life." He entered this scene as he had entered his first, dignified and quiet. But under his quietude he was not now incipiently malevolent, he was burningly so. Under the controlled surface, murderous determinations were seething. Deferential to the court, contemptuous of his enemies, rejecting offers of two or three times the sum of the loan, utterly untouched by the young lawyer's pious lecture on the subject of mercy, he clung maniacally to his demand for blood and justice. *Blood,* however, was not written in the bond, and when he broke control, when he shrieked, "A sentence! Come, prepare!" and leaped toward Antonio to slash him, the phrase "no jot of blood" was the trap that Portia caught him in.

Defeated, he dropped the scales and the life went out of him. His voice became heavy and thick. His eyes dimmed and he could barely keep them open. "I am not well," he pled, and struggled toward the door. Gratiano's crude jibe stopped him. "He turned," says Laurence Irving. "Slowly and steadily the Jew scanned his tormentor from head to foot, his eyes resting on the Italian's face with concentrated scorn. The proud rejection of insult and injustice lit up his face for a moment, enough for the audience to feel . . . that, in that glance, Shylock had triumphed." At the door, seized with weakness, he nearly fell, but with a fierce effort he drew himself up to full height, glared back defiantly, sighed, and stalked out of sight.

The *mise-en-scène* of Irving's *Merchant* had been created at the Lyceum on short notice, almost hastily, and by Lyceum standards it was regarded as comparatively simple (evidently more painted drops than built scenes"). Yet up to 1883 American audiences had never been treated to anything so satisfying. "It was the very poetry of the scene-painter's and stage-manager's art," declared the critic of the Boston *Evening Transcript.* It showed signs of wear, to be sure, but it still retained its gorgeousness and beauty, and like a well-aged painting from Renaissance times, it was perhaps more suggestive than when its colors came fresh from the brush.[107] Everybody praised the good taste, the discretion, of Irving and his aides. It was "not so much the opulence of the costumes, the picturesqueness of the groupings, or the beauty of the scenery," said the critic of the New York *Herald,* as "the poetic tact with which these are applied."[108] The *Spirit of the Times* was gratified that the stage was not overcrowded with scenery, properties, or people: "and yet the impression left upon the audience is that they have seen the real Venice, with its quaint and crowded streets, its narrow canals, its picturesque gondolas; that they have mingled with the masquers and listened to the moonlight serenades."[109] The living reality of Irving's Venice so impressed the young George Odell, who spent the greater part of his long life resisting twentieth-century developments of scenic art, that as late as 1940 he would be exclaiming that Irving's stagings "make the staging of modern impressionists and depressionists, fifty years later, seem like the vague and pointless wanderings of lost children in a maze of unimaginative gloom."[110]

In the early 1880s the esthetic of scenic realism was so firmly grounded, and Irving's application of it provided such delightfully easy recognitions, that only an intransigent visionary like William Poel would think of challenging it. Poel, then a very young man, hardly known in England and utterly unheard of in America, would spend the next half-century "proving" that Shakespeare's plays should be stripped of all scenic embellishment and restored to the bare platform stage for which they were written. He would, in fact, succeed to the degree that no one preparing Shakespeare for the stage in our time would resurrect the scenic methods which Irving brought to perfection. Only on film, of course, scenic realism far more "real" than Irving could have hoped for is taken for granted. So in our time we are pulled between the extremes of minimal, suggestive scenery for Shakespeare on stages and total, full-statement scenery on film. Not so in 1883. Then there was only the one way, which everyone (but Poel) agreed upon. George Montgomery of the *New York Times* could assure his readers that Irving's *The Merchant* represented not only "everything as it might have happened in Venice," but (with a wild leap) everything "as it did appear in Shakespeare's imagination."[111]

The heightened realism of Irving's scenery was held to be a perfect complement to Irving's style of acting and *therefore* to the "realism" of Shakespeare. In 1884 the critic of the *Evening Transcript* expected no objection when he observed that "Shakespeare is so admirably true and human, so searching and exhaustive in his delineation of character, that the more closely his interpreters adhere to a true representation of real life, the more in harmony they will be with his conception." This critic withdrew from the suggestion that Shakespeare was a forerunner of "the modern, so-called naturalistic literary school" with its excessive emphasis upon the forces of environment, the study of *"l'homme dans son milieu."* He would point out, however, that the character-drawing of Shakespeare and that of the French classicists—say Racine—are at opposite poles. The characters of the classicists are developed "too much *in abstracto* for their material surroundings to be of vital importance." *Mise-en-scène* can add to their splendor, but it hardly serves to illustrate them. Shakespeare's characters, on the other hand, "are studied so close to life, the influence of time, place, and social atmosphere is so strong upon them, that emphasizing these surroundings in a scenic way has really an illustrative force. A carefully-studied and truthful *mise-en-scène* becomes an actual functional part of the drama itself, and gives additional vitality and intelligibleness to the action."[112]

However warmly the American critics responded to Irving's meticulous stage decoration and management, their temperature lowered as they turned to his person and performance. Most of them would admit that he was an extraordinarily "interesting" actor and doubtless a brainy one, and as the years passed and Irving came to America again and again, winning ever-increasing popular acclaim, many of them accepted and even promoted the faith that he was the greatest actor in the world. But from the beginning there were obstacles to critical acceptance—above all, his physical and vocal eccentricities, his mannerisms.

Those critics who had done their homework had read a notorious pamphlet called *The Fashionable Tragedian,* by William Archer and Robert Lowe, which had appeared in England in 1877. These authors opened their attack on Irving with a devastatingly insinuating set of premises: "The first requisite for histrionic greatness is power to move and speak like a normal and rational human being. A man may have intellect, 'picturesqueness,' taste, and all the rest of it, but if he walks like an automaton whose wheels need oiling, and speaks alternately from the pit of his stomach and the top of his head, he will never be a great, or a good, or even a passable actor."[113]

Even forewarned by Archer and Lowe, many Americans were astounded at what they saw and heard when Irving appeared before them. After his opening in *The Bells,* young Harrison Grey Fiske wrote the following in the *Dramatic Mirror:*

> Nothing that has been said about Mr. Irving's celebrated "mannerisms" has exaggerated them. They are almost past belief. . . . If any other man in God's creation went on the stage before an audience of intelligent people and walked and talked as Irving does, he would be set down at once as a harmless crank of the Count Joannes stamp or a presumptuous fellow whose audacity was an insult to the sense and understanding of his listeners. . . . His mannerisms . . . consist of a remarkable style of walking and gesticulating, a hitherto unknown perversion of the English tongue, and a delivery which is like no other in the whole world. . . . His walk is as ungainly as if he were stumbling over a swamp. His legs describe eccentric circles; they seem to be independent of each other and entirely at variance with the rest of his body. When he crosses the stage those legs halt, shamble, and waver horribly. When he stands still they execute awkward *pirouettes* and strange meaningless movements. When he makes a "point," one foot stomps the inoffensive boards. Irving's arms and head seem to be in sympathy with his lower extremities. His elbows jut out at various angles, and his hands toy with the air. Except when he remains in one position, his head sinks between his shoulders and wags in all directions. . . .
>
> As for his vocal play—even in moments when passion or emotion should quicken the flow of words, his utterance is slow and fitful, sentences being pumped out, with evidences of awful effort, in short sections. The voice at times in one word quaveringly runs the entire gamut from the highest to the lowest note, or *vice-versa.* Stress is laid on the wrong syllables, emphasis is given to wrong words, and the meaning of lines is frequently perverted. Not only is the significance of certain passages completely lost by false elocution, but the words themselves are often rendered unintelligible by inexplicable mispronunciations.[114]

Offstage, one gathers, Irving spoke the language of his friends and neighbors, but when he got excited behind the footlights every vowel he encountered became another vowel, and an occasional consonant suffered strange warping too. Gordon Craig, in his curious "defense" of Irving, preserved some useful specimens of Irving-words. "For *good,* Irving said *god—sight* was *seyt—stood* was *stod—smote* became *smot—hand* was often *hond* or *hend.*" Shylock's "cut-throat dog" became something like "cut-thrut dug"; in *The Bells* Mathias's "Take the rope from my neck" became "Tack the rup frum mey nek"; and so forth.[115]

In a full-dress article in the *Atlantic Monthly* the Boston critic Henry Clapp expressed his amazement that "the most successful and cultivated of English actors should not have mastered the rudiments of his art. . . . He has not learned how to sit, stand, or move with the ease, repose, vigor, and grace which are by turns or altogether appropriate to attitude or action; and, worse even than this, he does not know how to speak his own language." When he first came to America he is said to have apologized for his "English" mannerisms of speech, but, says Clapp, his peculiar *patois* is no more English than Choctaw. (A fellow critic would liken it to Volapük.) What Clapp thought more hopeless than faulty pronunciation was his incurably bad voice—high-pitched, of narrow range, and so lacking in resonance that his declamation was weak and ineffectual. Then, too, everything was staccato: "There are no sweeps or long strokes in it, but everything is accomplished by a series of light, disconnected touches, or dabs." He has "no capacity for displaying vigorous, sustained passion," and when he comes to a passionate speech of any length he resorts to "rhythmic nod of the head, the dull stamp of the foot, and the queer clutch of the breast." He could startle and thrill audiences at certain moments, Clapp admits—for instance, at the end of the Mousetrap Scene in *Hamlet,* when he leaped up and hurled himself into the King's chair, screaming in rage and triumph. But, Clapp observes, he produced the *thrill* by noise and action only, not by use of comprehensible language.[116]

Irving's insistence on the primacy of the actor—his right to "interpret" roles rather than merely to declaim the lines set down for him—not only set him free from "the book" (which in effect meant from the author of the book), but set him free from "tradition"—from what other actors had done with the roles before him. Irving adamantly rejected tradition. In the fall of 1884, one week before reviewing Irving's Hamlet in the *Spirit of the Times,* Stephen Fiske declared that his favorite Hamlet had been E. L. Davenport's:

> It was gentle, scholarly, refined, impressive, and complete. Mr. Davenport did not indulge in any new readings: he gave the acting version so clearly and musically that none of his audience was bothered about a siege or sea of troubles or about the distinction between a handsaw and a heronshaw. He had no theory about Hamlet's insanity to elucidate, but stayed sane or went mad according to Shakespeare's words. He left the apparent contradictions of the text to explain themselves. . . . To listen to him was an unalloyed delight, and, when the final curtain fell, the audience was pleased and pensive rather than puzzled and perplexed.[117]

Fiske knew what he was doing. This description of Davenport is a précis of nearly everything in the tradition that Irving set himself firmly against. Davenport's handsome face and figure, his physical ease, vocal clarity and sonorousness, his lack of "ideas" to impose upon the part would mean to Irving that the actor was contributing nothing, or at most a comfortable, probably soporific "beauty." In his own performance, loaded with ideas, bits of business, and a thousand "delicate touches," he meant to startle the audience into paying attention to the "real" Hamlet. He even set himself up against Shakespeare's rhetoric—rejecting the patterns of sound and meaning which Shakespeare created within his blank verse, and the graceful play of phrase against phrase in his prose. He broke up the flow with interpolated repetitions, grunts, and exclamatory noises—anything to force attention upon the dramatic moment. He would say that "it was of more importance to present the thing the words stood for than merely to sing the music of periods." All language spoken on the stage must be spoken, as it were, for the first time—instantaneously improvised thought. In his essay on Irving's theory of acting, Stephen Schultz concludes that Irving doubted it was possible to read verse properly and present a character at the same time.[118]

In a curious many-columned feuilleton in the *Dramatic Mirror,* signed J. M. M., Irving is labeled a "manufactured" actor and a "great *artist,*" in contrast to Edwin Booth, who, though careless in his work, is a "born" actor, a "great *actor.*" Irving is an "intellectual actor"; he has created himself by intelligent concern for every detail of his characterizations, by taking infinite pains with scenic arrangements and the work of his supporting actors. He leaves us pleased but unexcited, the writer continued. Booth will never take seriously his responsibility as director or producer, yet in spite of his shabby surroundings, mean accessories, and commonplace support, audiences are thrilled by his performance. The fact is, according to J. M. M., Irving is not a tragic actor, but only an esthete, a Grosvenor Gallery type of artist. What Oscar Wilde is to literature, Irving is to dramatic art. What Burne-Jones, with his "sallow women of angular form, dressed in bilious costumes of sage green and mustard plasters," is to the art of painting, Irving is to dramatic art. So Irving gave London a Hamlet in the Grosvenor style—"that is, one which should create surprise instead of admiration." No one is more conscious than Irving himself "of his inability to portray heroic characters, and therefore, instead of trying to raise Irving to the altitude of Macbeth or Othello, he seeks to drag these magnificent creations down to the level of a character actor."[119]

In *Much Ado About Nothing,* which was Irving's principal offering to New York during April 1884, the last month of his first tour of America, Ellen Terry always carried off the honors. Irving's Benedick was generally regarded as only tolerable, but Miss Terry's Beatrice was so much loved that Irving would bring *Much Ado* to America twice more, in 1884 and 1893. "A more charming performance of a Shakespearean heroine we have not seen since Neilson passed away," wrote young Fiske in the *Dramatic Mirror,* ". . . a personality so charming that she wins all hearts. Her methods are perfectly natural, and one forgets that she is acting, so deftly does she conceal the means whereby she produces her effects."[120] One senses that the realism that Irving strove for and spoiled by mannerisms, Miss Terry achieved without effort. The Boston *Transcript* speaks of the "thousand little delicate touches" in her performance, and to illustrate, mentions "the way in which she made the little page hand her her fan properly, after he had offered it awkwardly," and "her unostentatious brushing the tears away from her eyes as she leaves the forlorn Hero after the scandal in the church."[121]

Like Irving, she felt unconstrained by tradition or even by "the book," and her Beatrice is a novelty. In Victorian eyes Beatrice was a bit "unwomanly," perhaps at times something of a virago. But nothing

Illus. 115–19. Five studies of Irving's dramatic attitudes from *The Fashionable Tragedian,* by William Archer and Robert Lowe, 1877.

Illus. 120. Ellen Terry as Beatrice. Folger Shakespeare Library.

shrewish or mannish was apparent in Miss Terry's performance. William Winter observed approvingly that she "transfigured" Beatrice.[122] As a certain Boston critic put it, she had simply reshaped the role so that it was "quite too much like Rosalind, entirely reconstructed on a nineteenth century plan, obviously more feminine and gentle than Shakespeare intended." All the same, he continued, not ten persons in the audience would care a button that she so misconceived the part, for she was "about as bewitching as it is given to any mortal to be upon the stage."[123]

Irving's Benedick, likewise "transfigured," seems to have puzzled or annoyed more critics than it gratified. Winter, scrambling for language to approve of it as a comic characterization, defined it as a kind of "subtle playfulness . . . an odd, quaint fellow, eccentric though elegant . . . quizzical, fond of sagacious rumination, and slightly saturnine . . . a complex nature, based on goodness, merely pretending to cynicism."[124] The Boston *Transcript* surrendered to Irving completely. Acknowledging Irving's "extraordinary eccentricities, confessing his own "state of sin" in approving so much that is wrong, yet, this critic declared, "he *is* the man Benedick with all his high breeding, his courtly gallantry, his wit, humor, and knightly singleness and warmth of feeling," and "we, for one, can call it nothing but genius."[125]

So highly chivalric a reading of the role appeared to no one else that I have noticed. The *New York Times,* having called Irving picturesque in his fine costumes, had to mention that he walked "as though he were dangled by invisible wires" which produced "the queer motions of his knees and the spasmodic jerks of his body." The *Herald* observed the "certain stiffness" in his purely comic scenes and his inability to laugh and be gay without artificiality. Clapp of the Boston *Advertiser* grudgingly admitted his "intellectual quality" but found him "absurdly unsuited" to the

Illus. 121. Irving as Benedick. Folger Shakespeare Library.

part and objected to his farcical actions, unwarranted repetition of words, and "interpolations of grunts and inarticulate sounds."[126]

One would not expect "historical accuracy" to count for much in staging *Much Ado,* but it did so in those days. The action was thought to have taken place in 1535, when the Spaniards were returning from an expedition to Tunis, and Irving was complimented for having costumed the play (the male characters) in patterns from the era of Henry VIII.[127] Although the scenery, as Ellen Terry remarked, was for the most part nothing extraordinary, the fourth-act Church Scene astounded everyone by its beauty, grandeur, and totally realistic effect. In Irving's own words it was "Telbin's masterpiece, with its real built-out round pillars thirty feet high, its canopied roof of crimson plush from which hung the golden lamps universally used in Italian cathedrals, its painted canopy overhanging the altar, its great ironwork gates, its altar with cases of flowers and flaming candles rising to a height of eighteen feet, its stained glass windows and statues of saints."[128] Happily, the Claudio of the company, young Johnston Forbes-Robertson, was a skilled painter, and he preserved this scene, with all the characters in place, in a handsome canvas.

Not every aspect of the stage-management, though, was as it should have been, and certain Boston critics kept score on the lapses. The clown scenes were so reduced (no Trial Scene) that the actor of Dogberry could make little of his part. In the Garden Scene the conspirators against Benedick behaved in "such silly and self-conscious farcicalness of tone and action" that even a Dogberry would have seen through the game they were playing.[129] And, almost incredibly, Irving insisted on using the traditional additions to the "Kill Claudio" Scene. When Benedick should take his exit on "Go comfort your cousin. I must say she is dead. And so farewell," Irving made Miss Terry say,

Illus. 122. The Church Scene in Irving's *Much Ado,* painted by Johnston Forbes-Robertson, who played Claudio and may be seen here at center, a little back. Irving, as Benedick is nearer us. Ellen Terry is between us and the altar. Courtesy of the Hampden-Booth Theatre Library at The Players.

"Benedick, kill him, kill him if you can," to which Irving responded, "As sure as I'm alive, I will." The actress had to put up with this dull gag for a dozen years or more, relieved only that no critics or Shakespeare scholars noticed it. So she thought. Critics in Boston noticed it, and were as annoyed as she by the blot on the text.[130]

Irving's *Twelfth Night* was unfortunately short-lived. At the end of the first London performance (July 8, 1884), the unbelievable happened: when Irving stepped forward to deliver his customary opening night address to the audience, he was interrupted by a scattering of boos and hisses. Startled and angered, he treated the audience to a scolding, which of course helped not at all. Some of the critics, attempting to account for the audience's displeasure, blamed Irving's Malvolio as "too tragical." Irving himself, speaking to friends, blamed the "failure" on the lack of great comedians to play Sir Toby and his circle—indeed, he replaced half a dozen of the company before bringing *Twelfth Night* to America.[131] Secretly, though, he seems to have doubted his own rendition of Malvolio. This was a pity, for by many accounts his Malvolio was superb. Joseph Knight of the *Athenaeum* called it "the best Malvolio the stage has seen." According to William Winter, Irving was the first in modern times to make Malvolio "an actual human being, capable of feeling passion and suffering pain as well as causing mirth."[132]

He made himself up to look as much as possible like Don Quixote—his tall gaunt figure clad in close-fitting black satin with gold stripes, with diamonds in his ears, the chain of office around his neck, and in his hand a long slender staff which he swung erratically. He was nearly bald; his eyebrows, painted high on his forehead, gave him a constant look of superciliousness (or surprise); his cheeks were sallow and sunken; he wore a skimpy brown mustache twisted at the ends, and a narrow pointed beard. Malvolio being such an extravagant creature, Irving's naturally grotesque physical movements and vocal quirks could enhance his characterization rather than damage it. And since Malvolio is utterly self-centered, deliberative—"alone," so to speak—Irving could move through the language of the part freely and according to his own patterns, without destroying Shakespearean patterns of pentameter verse or speedy-witty prose. Malvolio is a "slow" role, affording countless opportunities for the "delicate touches" of behavior that were central to Irving's ideas about acting. This Malvolio was a man of parts and breeding, intensely aware of his superiority. Irving did not gag or play for easy laughs, but was desperately in earnest at every moment, and thus profoundly amusing. Unfortunately, as a result of his self-distrust, Irving not only abandoned *Twelfth Night* after its run in America, but never again undertook a comic role in Shakespeare.[133]

Illus. 123. Irving as Malvolio

Ellen Terry, who played the boy Cesario charmingly in her cream-colored satin tunic and a little blue cap that rode perkily on her golden curls, was not unhappy when the play was dropped from Irving's repertory. She thought the production as a whole was "dull, lumpy, and heavy." She may have noted the wonderment of several American critics that she and Irving had both let themselves be consigned to such relatively "unimportant" parts,[134] and this would have confirmed her own recognition that Viola cannot take command of the situation she is thrust into. Then, too, in America at least, she was bested by a ghostly competitor—Adelaide Neilson, so lately dead, whose lovely Viola haunted the memory of the reviewers. The *Herald* critic thought it fair to note that Miss Terry had other parts "more exacting, more pathetic, and even more merry."

Scenically this *Twelfth Night*—with its array of seascapes, ravines, luxurious gardens, mansions *à la* Palladio, and a gloomy dungeon for Malvolio's imprisonment—was not only splendid in itself, but occasion for the *Spirit of the Times* to attempt to shame our American managers into emulating Irving's production methods.[135] Nothing like it had ever been seen upon the New York stage until Mr. Irving came—but "the public will hereafter insist that the same completeness of accessories and unity of action shall be displayed by all professionals, and the sooner the Irving system is generally adopted the better for all concerned. . . . Mr. Irving has shown us that what our own managers have claimed to be impossible is easily done with the requisite tact and taste and skill."[136]

If Irving's most enduring role in Shakespeare was Shylock (he could play Shylock at any age), his most daring, celebrated, characteristic, and controversial role was Hamlet. In Hamlet, the role in which tragic actors generally compete for supremacy, Irving most conspicuously defied playhouse tradition (many would say he defied the art of the play) by imposing on the role his new-found "realism," his "natural treatment and colloquial style." He intended to realize a Hamlet who was no mere play actor or declaimer, but a deeply troubled and thoroughly believable human being. As Clement Scott said of Irving's first London performance in 1874, his Hamlet was infected with "moral poison." For two entire acts, Scott observed, he almost prevented the audience from applauding him while he wove about them a mysterious, indescribable spell. A few of Scott's excited sentences put the case clearly:

> Those who have seen other Hamlets are aghast. Mr. Irving is missing his points, he is neglecting his opportunities. . . . But Mr. Irving's intention is not to make points, but to give a consistent reading of a Hamlet who "thinks aloud". . . . We can almost realize the workings of his brain. His soliloquies are not spoken down at the footlights to the audience. Hamlet is looking into a glass, into "his mind's eye, Horatio!" His eyes are fixed apparently on nothing, though ever eloquent. He gazes on vacancy and communes with his conscience. . . . He is not acting, he is not splitting the ears of the groundlings; he is an artist concealing his art; he is talking to himself; he is thinking aloud.[137]

The English critic Edward R. Russell observed of Irving's soliloquies that he blended them into the fabric of the character, that he conceived them "with so little attention to their essentially declamatory traditions that he did not even study to end them with the usual perorative inflections, which gave a distinct and satisfying sense of something concluded."[138] Years later William Winter would illustrate Russell's point by noting that at the end of "To be or not to be" Irving would utter "Soft you now," not as if he were already seeing "the fair Ophelia," but as if he was about to add a further thought to his meditation on life and death.[139] Such "purism of reality," Russell observed, since it violates the structure and tone of Shakespeare's play, would be highly dangerous if attempted by an actor less compelling than Irving.

It appears that Irving would have liked to open his American campaign with Hamlet, but postponed it until he could accustom the American (New York) audiences to his "natural treatment and colloquial style" through other, mainly modern plays. He promised New York at the of his autumn engagement that he would give them Hamlet when he returned in the spring. Moving out into "the country" he tried Hamlet in Philadelphia, Boston, Chicago, and elsewhere, and he satisfied himself that it went very well. In a letter home to one of his London aides, L. F. Austin (March 2, 1884), he could declare that "Hamlet has never been so enthusiastically received in England." Yet he had to tack on to that sentence, "it is a bitter pill to certain Americans that any actor but *one* can be accepted in it." The *"one,"* of course, was Edwin Booth, and we read between the lines that whether fairly or unfairly Irving had all too often been made aware that Americans preferred their own great, somewhat more conventional, more "Shakespearean" Hamlet.[140]

When he did return to New York, as we have seen, he filled most of the month of April with *Much Ado,* and still postponed Hamlet, shaken, it may be, by the fact that in 1883 three powerful metropolitan critics had followed him to Philadelphia to take the measure of his Hamlet, and had sorely belittled it. George Montgomery of the *New York Times* acknowledged the excitement generated in the Play Scene ("one of those thrilling effects of eccentric acting for which we forgive him so much"); acknowledged, too, the intelligent interpretation of the character—but owing to

Illus. 124. Irving as Hamlet. Folger Shakespeare Library.

Irving's lack of "histrionic method," the evening offered not a play but "an illustrated lecture." The first two acts, while Irving scrupulously avoided "points" but wove his spell, were for Montgomery "unquestionably and without relief very dull." The elocution was "singsong," the movements "galvanic," the soliloquies "monotonously mouthed." W. S. Gilbert's *Patience* had recently come to town, and Montgomery declared, as Irving's "lengthy and lugubrious legs assumed the function of a pair of flexible dividers, upon the one fixed foot of which, as upon a pivot, he slowly revolved into one after another of the stained-glass attitudes, it did bring Bunthorne to mind." In Hamlet's advice to the Players, according to Montgomery, Shakespeare had accurately foretold practically all of Irving's vices, but Irving delivered that speech with special ease and grace, quite unaware of its relevance to himself.[141]

Henry Clapp of the Boston *Advertiser* and John Ranken Towse of the New York *Post* held their fire until March of 1884, when each brought out in a national magazine a long essay in which he analyzed and evaluated Irving's art.[142] Neither was satisfied with the Hamlet. Of the two, Clapp was the less abrasive. He credited Irving with full appreciation of Hamlet's swift wit, wondrous imagination, affectionateness, and superfine sanity hovering so dangerously near to madness. The soliloquies, though badly spoken, were lucidly thought out and delivered *like thinking* and not like "speaking a piece." The performance was picturesque. What Irving lacks is tragic power, the "capacity for displaying vigorous, sustained passion." He is a light actor, a character actor. He can get away with Hamlet, as he surely could not with Othello or Lear, because Hamlet is not really a heroic or tragic part: it is a picturesque character part!

Towse's opinion resembled Clapp's, but he would not soften it with so prettily quibbling a re-definition of Hamlet. He could not understand why Irving's Hamlet excited a storm of controversy in England, for he could see little room for difference of opinion about it. "It exhibits all the virtues and weaknesses which would naturally be expected by all observers of Mr. Irving's acting." His eccentricities and affectations, "grievous blots as they are at all times, become almost unbearable in Shakespearian tragedy, and could nowhere be more offensive or anomalous than in Hamlet." Irving so busies himself creating pictorial effects and illustrating certain scenes with elaborate artifice that the result is mental confusion. One cannot tell, for instance, whether his Hamlet is mad or not mad. But that question and others of the same weight are unimportant: "for the entire absence of tragic passion effectually relegates the performance to the second class." In his major scenes—with the Ghost, with the Queen, at his death—"there was not a gleam of tragic fire; and it is scarcely too much to say that the tragic side of Hamlet's character received no representation at all. . . . It is plain now, not only that he cannot be included in the first rank of living tragedians, but that he has scarcely any right to the name of tragedian."

Irving was stung by this. "Towse—Lowse I shall spell it," he wrote in his March letter to Austin. He postponed a New York trial of *Hamlet* to another season.[143]

When he did reveal it to New York in five performances beginning November 26, 1884, toward the end of his month-long autumn engagement, the critical response was predictable. The *New York Times* reviewer (no longer George Montgomery, but E. A. Dithmar, new in the chair, and aware of what Montgomery had written a year before) turned in a nervously mixed report: the performance was "distinguished by many excellencies"; it was "so marked by the actor's mannerisms . . . as to produce an almost grotesque effect"; it was "more suggestive . . . of melodrama than tragedy." And finally, "Mr. Irving's acting in Hamlet is great acting, and it should be seen by everybody who finds enjoyment and instruction in the spoken drama."[144] Nym Crinkle in the *World* used Irving as an occasion to take another nip at Edwin Booth. Somewhat perversely he described Irving's as a "flesh and blood" Hamlet, contrasting it to Booth's way with the character, which is "to look as pretty and feel as bad as he can."[145] For William Winter, of course, "the night was a golden one," and his 3,500-word essay in the *Tribune* rises to a grand climax of approbation in these sentences:

> A man who acts greatly is, doubtless, a great actor, without reference to what it is that his acting is specifically designed to exhibit; but the man who acts a great part, like Hamlet, so as to put us into possession of it, has accomplished more, and risen to a higher intellectual station than is possible to even the most perfect executant. This is Mr. Irving's victory—and it is a brilliant one; unequivocal; permanent; not to be denied; and safe beyond the reach of disparagement.[146]

Needless to say, the disparagers were at work before Winter's violet ink was dry.

Stephen Fiske, who could usually be expected to praise Irving, noted in the *Spirit of the Times* that the critics of Philadelphia, Boston, and Chicago did not much like this Hamlet, and though the New York public seemed to have accepted the production as Irving's greatest, yet to Fiske it appeared not so much a tragedy as a melodrama. And Irving, far from the handsome, graceful Prince of Ophelia's description, presented "a quaint, weird, saturnine Hamlet, with a long cloak which he wears constantly, in and out of doors, using it as a drapery for his poses." Fiske then offered, *seriatim,* twenty-five or thirty observations of moments in the performance and of items in the stage management, some approving but most of them corrective.[147] The younger Fiske (Harrison Grey), in the *Dramatic Mirror,* would allow Irving nothing. Except among the small circle of Irving-worshipers, he said, "the personation has excited astonishment or mirth rather than admiration." There is nothing kingly about this middle-aged Hamlet; he is a venomous yet vacillating crank. He snatches at every opportunity to introduce melodramatic effects for no other reason than to attract attention and to violate established interpretations. With all his "peculiarities and fol-de-rols" he would reduce the soliloquies to the level of the fustian speeches of Edmund Dantes or Mathias the Burgomaster.[148]

According to the *Herald* (presumably the critic Felix de Fontaine), "Mr. Irving's Hamlet will not be popular in America. . . . It is forcible, picturesque, melodramatic, grim and weird. But it will not be popular in America. . . . Instead of the lightly satirical Hamlet . . . there is presented a gaunt, pallid figure, in whose mouth the shafts of raillery become poisoned darts. He crouches in the moonlight before his father's ghost, uttering strange cries, contorting his features into extraordinary shapes. It is Mathias of *The Bells,* not Hamlet. . . . Mr. Irving will do well to remove it from his series."[149]

And so Irving did. In his return visit to New York in the spring, he played Hamlet once more, on March 26, 1885, but after that season never again in America.

As Irving aged into his middle fifties, he added a brace of cardinals to his repertoire—Shakespeare's Wolsey at the Lyceum on January 5, 1892, and Tennyson's Becket on February 6, 1893. Both became him well, as did also Bulwer's Cardinal Richelieu, which he had been playing for two decades. The dignity, composure, and power of these characters seemed almost a projection of his own matured sense of command as leader of his profession. William Archer—once upon a time Irving's harshest critic, but by the 1890s an admirer—declared after Becket, "Nature designed him for a prince of the church"; and Irving's grandson has written, "He came, like Becket, to regard the Augustinian habit which he assumed as the vestment of an officiating priest. . . . he persuaded himself that in the performance of Becket, spanning the gulf between Church and Stage, he and his audience united in an act of worship."[150] In the fall of 1893 he brought both scarlet-robed dignitaries—the arrogant, self-seeking Wolsey, and Becket the martyr hero—in a repertory of nine plays, for his fourth tour of America.

Everybody recognized that of all Irving's Shakespeares the *mise-en-scène* of *Henry VIII* was thus far the finest.[151] Irving meant it to be so. "In my judgement," he said, "*Henry VIII* is a pageant or it is nothing." If the play was weak dramatically, he would gratify popular appetite for Renaissance glamour by the richest possible overlay of colorful and authentic upholstery. He assembled a superb cast, called in Sir Lawrence Alma-Tadema to supervise the scene painters, Edward German to compose incidental music, and Seymour Lucas and Alice Comyns Carr to design costumes based on the paintings of Holbein. He spent on the production several thousand pounds more than the box office could possibly recover.

To demonstrate his infinite care for correctness, no matter what the cost, he liked to tell the story of the making of his cardinal's robe. Someone lent him an actual robe from Cardinal Wolsey's time to use as a model. Irving had silk cloth woven especially, in order to get the right texture, and sent it to Rome to be dyed by the dyers to the College of Cardinals. It came back with the word that the exact tone of red that he requested could no longer be had. He then commissioned chemists at Coventry to recreate the color and dye it there. He was enormously proud of the result and took from it inspiration for his acting: "When you are getting into the skin of a character", he said, "you need not neglect his wardrobe."[152] Sometime later he wore it to a fancy dress ball at Devonshire House. Ellen Terry reports that "as the Cardinal swept up the staircase, his 'cappa-magna' trailing behind him at its full magnificent length, a sudden wave of reality seemed to sweep up with him, submerging the pretty make-believe of that aristocratic masquerade."[153]

"As scene after scene was unfolded," wrote the critic for the *Dramatic Mirror,* "and as the teeming life of the period of the burly king was reproduced with marvelous realism, the spectator for the nonce seemed to live in that time, for of such power is the illusion created by the wizard Irving. The procession, the masque in the Cardinal's palace, the ecclesiastical court—these were pictures of a kind not often seen upon the stage, and not soon to be forgotten."[154] We for whom the literal realism of sound and color cinema is commonplace can only guess at the measure of this critic's rapture in the presence of "historically accurate" and "real" stage scenery. We have no photographs of Irving's scenery. In souvenir books of the play that Irving sometimes issued, there are splendid

Illus. 125. Irving as Cardinal Wolsey

drawings of scenes by Bernard Partridge and other artists, but Irving did not permit cameras to record his stagings. Much of the beauty of the paint work of Hawes Craven, Joseph Harker, and William Telbin was created by low lighting, by glooms and shadows, all of which would be lost, depth and distance lost, color lost, and magic lost, as seen under hot white light through the merciless flattening eye of cameras. The critic's romantic dream of seeming "to live in that time" would be shattered if every photographer's window offered him inescapably real copies of what in the warm darkness of the stalls he thought he dreamed.

In New York Irving opened his 1893 season on November 8 with three weeks of Tennyson's Cardinal Becket, then a week of Shylock, then two weeks of Shakespeare's Cardinal Wolsey. Tennyson's play took the honors, even over Shakespeare's, not because it was a better play, but because of universal curiosity to see this production of the greatly admired poet's finest closet drama. Then, too, Irving played Becket with a peculiarly intense identification with it, as if he were conducting a priestly rite, a secular sacrifice of the Mass.[155]

Since the two roles were played within a short period of time, critics had the opportunity to assess Irving's ability to distinguish each role from the other. Irving's Becket, said William Winter, is spiritual, appeals to your soul—irradiates your whole being with a sense of sublimity. His Wolsey is brainy, hard-headed, crafty and sensuous; he alerts your intellect to comprehend what he is doing; through half his role he wakens your distrust, dislike, and awe as he hypocritically manipulates all about him—then at his fall he inspires sympathy and pity. It is the triumph and glory of Becket, said Winter, to perish in quest of the kingdom of heaven; it is Wolsey's misery to perish in a vain struggle for the kingdom of earth.[156] Becket, the more lyric character—all of a piece, so to speak—rises steadily and nobly toward his glorious death. Wolsey is far more dramatic and "human"; until he falls he is always playing a part—always in control of events, or hiding behind them, shifting his position from reality to artifice to reality with never a betrayal of what he is really up to. After his conference with the Queen he would watch her depart with the mask of false pity frozen on his face. Then his mobile features thawed and changed: his face turned hard, inscrutable. With a shrug of the shoulders he dismissed all concern for her and haughtily followed her off.[157]

In the reviews of these Cardinals we find fewer complaints about Irving's mannerisms—partly, it may be, because Irving had mastered some of the worst of them, partly because the scarlet robes constantly reminded him of the need for restraint and dignity.

When William Archer reviewed Irving's London Becket, he called upon the printer to serve up full capital letters to celebrate Irving's DICTION. "Here he gives us . . . clear-cut, beautiful English speech in smooth flowing, delicately cadenced, poetic periods. Many of his lines and sequences of lines were a joy to the ear."[158] In America, William Winter, reviewing Wolsey, said that Irving delivered "the famous farewell not with the glib facility and hollow mouthing of a sonorous elocutionist, but in the faltering accents of a breaking heart."[159] That sounds very well, leaving behind only one unsatisfied question: did his accents falter, his heart break, too much? When we turn to E. A. Dithmar of the *New York Times* we read that Irving's elocution was "beautifully simple" until he came to the lines at the end of the Farewell Scene:

> O Cromwell, Cromwell,
> Had I but serv'd my God with half the zeal
> I serv'd my king, He would not in mine age
> Have left me naked to mine enemies.

"This he delivers in his worst manner—or his best. Which is it? It is in defiance of all the rules of pronunciation. It is assuredly effective, but in a strange sort of way. But no one else in the world ever spoke so but Henry Irving."[160]

The last Shakespeare production that Irving introduced to America was *Macbeth,* a revival of his Lyceum production of 1888. It opened in New York on October 29, 1895, was shown five times in that week, then gave way to a run of *King Arthur,* and was brought out for two more nights near the end of the engagement in mid-December. According to the *New York Times,* the first-night audience wanted to be enthusiastic, but their attempts fell flat.[161]

As was to be expected, Irving's concept of Macbeth ran counter to stage tradition. According to most critics of the day, it also violated the text. Given the bleeding sergeant's account of Macbeth's splendid conduct in battle—given, too, King Duncan's praise of him, trust of him, and affection for him—we can hardly doubt that Shakespeare intended to present Macbeth from the first as a man of immense physical power, a brave soldier, a loyal subject to the King—in short, to qualify him for the role of tragic hero. His fall from grace, it is true, sets in at once. When the weird sisters tempt him with the prophecy that he will be King, waveringly but inevitably he surrenders to temptation: "Stars, hide your fires; / Let not light see my black and deep desires." There is nothing wavering about his lady, however. She needs only to see the words in his letter, "Hail, King that shalt be!" to be transformed at once into an angel of destruction, a whip to drive Macbeth up to the throne and down to damnation, a murderer herself if need be. Macbeth will be a child at her direction.

But Irving rejected out of hand this traditional concept of Macbeth as "a good man who has gone wrong under the influence of a wicked and dominant wife," and took to the lecture platform to explain his own concept. Macbeth, he said, is "one of the most bloodyminded, hypocritical villains" that Shakespeare ever invented. He not only had thought of murdering Duncan before he met the witches, but had broached the subject to his wife before the curtain rises ("What beast was't, then, / That made you break this enterprise to me?"). Far from being influenced by his wife, Irving said, "it is quite possible that Macbeth led his wife to believe that she was leading him on. It was part of his nature to work her moral downfall in such a way." "Figs," he said, "do not grow on thistles, and there is no virtue in him." Macbeth is a great poet, to be sure, and Irving insisted that he is "brave."[162] Yet at the front of his study book he had written these three words: LIAR, TRAITOR, COWARD.[163]

Unquestionably it was a cowardly Macbeth that Irving enacted, and he overdid it. Albert Steinberg of the New York *Herald* thought there was "no need of making Macbeth quite such an abject pusillanimous creature." After the murder "not only does he tremble, he positively sobs with remorse." For James Huneker in the *Morning Advertiser* it was merely a replaying of Mathias of *The Bells,* and after the murder it became "a squeaking, mouthing imbecile . . . a superior degenerate . . . a poor driveling wretch overcome by his conscience-kindled fears in the most approved footlight fashion. . . . It is not Macbeth that he gives us; only a stage creature, infirm of vitality, not a warrior, but a weak-kneed, hysterical madman."

Clapp of Boston saw this Macbeth as "a subtle, crafty, craven soul, introverted, superstitious, sneakish, almost devoid even of corporal courage." According to most commentators, Clapp said, after the murder "Macbeth grows harder and harder, tougher and tougher." But Irving so slurred the better elements in Macbeth's nature, as exhibited in the first two acts, that one could not perceive in him any struggle between the powers of good and evil—and "instead of growing firmer of fibre he grows more and more hysterical and spasmodic, more inordinate in grimace and snarl. . . . In short, the heroic element, the physical potency, the solid force of nature, which in a better view of Macbeth would be displayed . . . suffer a total eclipse."[164] Both Clapp and Towse understood the reason for this "new" Macbeth. Towse speaks of Irving's want of "heroic dimensions." Clapp says that Irving knew that his limitations of body and voice disqualified him for "a larger and stronger and more Shakespearean scheme." Thus, as in most of his other classic roles, he adapted Macbeth to his own person.

Nym Crinkle, who liked above all things to take the other side, looked upon Irving's perversion of the character and found it good. This "new" Macbeth, "without the measured tread and pompous mystery of old-time tragedy," delighted him because it fell in with his pet notion that Shakespeare's plays change with the times, that we would not have him on our stage at all if he did not come down off his eminence and accommodate our modern taste. He said that Irving had, with "masterful realism," devoted "all his marvelous talent and skill in the accentuation of one side of Macbeth's character, and that side the negative one. The personage becomes in his poignant delivery of him an instantly intelligible coward and little else." Thus, it appears, Irving converted tragedy into melodrama. But to say this, Nym Crinkle insists, is not to disparage Irving's effort, for Shakespeare, though a "fixed quantity" in literature, must always on the stage "be adjustable to the increased discernment, the widened knowledge and the advanced taste of the people." Nym Crinkle did not, as with Irving's Hamlet, use the phrase "flesh and blood," but he meant the same thing when he spoke of the "inimitable realism" of this Macbeth, of his stepping "out of poetry into life," of how he "flung himself, so to speak, at the sensibilities," of how his thought "transmitted itself unmistakably and instantly along the muscles."[165]

According to Irving's English friends, by the nineties he had scrubbed away his eccentricities and developed an unexceptionable style. William Archer was converted. Even Bernard Shaw would now and then toss out a word of approval. Long afterwards Graham Robertson would write:

> His artistic life was one long struggle towards perfection; fault after fault he conquered, one by one he laid by his mannerisms, line by line he modelled the beautiful, sensitive face that he had evolved from the original immobile and rather ordinary features. To the hour of his death he worked incessantly, his whole career was a progression, and those who witnessed his last performance probably saw him at his best.[166]

But America was not convinced. Jeannette Gilder of *The Critic* wanted to admire his Macbeth, but she had to declare that her "enjoyment of it was marred by his own indulgence in deplorable vocal mannerisms and eccentricities, which made a great part of his performance wholly unintelligible. . . . he so mouthed and mumbled his lines that their sense was entirely

Illus. 126. Irving as Macbeth. Folger Shakespeare Library.

lost. He could not be understood even by persons as familiar with the text as he is himself . . . and more than once, at great crises in the action, ripples of half-suppressed laughter ran around the house." Laurence Hutton of *The Mail* declared that his utterance was "never worse," and noted that his grimaces were laughed at. Joseph Howard of the *Sun* thought it too bad that Queen Victoria had knighted him, for his English was now worse than ever. Dithmar of the *New York Times* reported an exchange between an elegantly clad lady ("Why does he mumble his words so? Could you understand him?") and her disgruntled escort fingering his expensive ticket stubs ("Not I.").

The "funniest incident" of the New York opening night, according to Joseph Howard (a notoriously irreverent critic), was the last speech of the evening. After several curtain calls, while the audience was filing out, Irving came to the footlights to deliver a curtain speech. Many of the audience returned and stood at the rear to listen. Those who had opera glasses assured those who had none that Irving's lips were moving, but only now and then a syllable could be heard. Suddenly an explosive noise was heard from the wings. An actor rushed onto the stage, looked embarrassed, bowed, and retreated. Irving's lips moved a minute longer, then he left too. A crowd of reporters sought out Bram Stoker, one of Irving's agents, to find out what Irving had said. Stoker went off to ask Irving. And he returned: "Really this is too bad, gentlemen. I have seen Mr. Irving and Mr. Irving seems to be as much in the dark as anyone else. He says he hasn't the least recollection of what he said."[167]

While Nym Crinkle was working up his earnest, if somewhat specious, recommendation of Irving's Macbeth for the Sunday edition of the *World,* his colleague Charles Meltzer, who wrote the regular first-night reviews, was taking Irving's measure by another yardstick. Of all the accounts that I have read of Irving's peculiarities of stage behavior, from *The Fashionable Tragedian* of 1877 to Gordon Craig's spirited defense in his 1930 "little book" about Irving, Meltzer's description of the first six lines of the Dagger soliloquy provides the most sustained and perhaps most accurate record. Meltzer withheld it until December 18, 1895, after Irving had completed his autumn engagement and left town.

> As a fair example of Mr. Irving's faults of utterance and manner, take the scene wherein the master has conceived Macbeth to see the ominous air-drawn dagger. . . . This is what he does.
>
> First he throws his chest and head far back and seems to regard a point in the air behind him. Then he twists his body to one side, to the other side, waves both arms vaguely in the air, ruffles his hair and groans. Then he gasps painfully. Then he spreads his legs far apart, teeters for a moment like one getting "a good ready" to run a race, and groaning again, begins:
>
> "Is this a dagger"—groans—"that I see before me"—groan and dropping the voice—"um umthing um me hand?"—more groans. "Come"—shrieking and waving both hands uncertainly above his head—"let me clutch thee"—lifting his eyebrows four inches six times. "I have thee not"—looking fixedly at the upper gallery—"and yet"—prodigiously rolling and expectorating that "t"—"I see thee still." Long pause while Mr. Irving's legs give way under him. "Art thou not, tum-tum, dum-tum, sensible to feeling as to sight?"—very loud; then sinking his voice to a hoarse whisper "or art thou but a dum tum tum tum tum tum"—and so forth, mumbling some words so that at ten feet they were undistinguishable and hurling others at that mysterious point in the upper gallery which Mr. Irving makes ever his weird confidant.[168]

In 1954–55 a young English actor brought audiences even nearer to Irving's presence. A play

Illus. 127. Another view of Irving's Macbeth. Folger Shakespeare Library.

called *The Diary of a Nobody* (based on the Grossmith novel and set in the 1890s) contained a middle-class evening party with parlor entertainments, including "imitations." Alan MacNaughtan's imitation of Henry Irving's Mathias was wonderfully amusing, but so extravagant in posture, gesture, and sound that one took it for a far-fetched caricature. But the late W. McQueen Pope, who claimed to remember Irving well, assured me it was a very accurate recovery of Irving's style. And Mr. MacNaughtan has told me that he not only read everything he could find about Irving but also was coached by several old-timers who knew and had played with Irving.

Ellen Terry's performance came off much better than Irving's. When she first played Lady Macbeth at the Lyceum in 1888, those who disliked it, she said, were those who did not want a fresh reading of the character—"who hold by the 'fiend' reading."[169] In America she encountered such objections as "weak but conscientious . . . handicapped by physical limitations" *(The Critic);* "tender and tearful" (New York *Sunday Herald*); and "a want of depth and tragic fulness" (Boston *Advertiser*). Or her too careful speaking troubled some hearers: she is "the opposite extreme from Mr. Irving in her distinct and too strongly divided enunciation" *(Life).* But most critics accepted her joyously. She was "a pictorially majestic queen—gilded throughout by her golden art of pleasing" *(Dramatic Mirror);* "positively charming in a medieval picture of an amber-haired beauty" (Boston *Globe*); "the reading of her lines is probably the best ever given them" *(The Mail and Express);* "her sleepwalking scene touched the point of rare beauty and pathos at the utterance of her long-drawn sighs" (Boston *Advertiser*); and "her performance was the most satisfying feature of the night" (New York *Sun*).[170]

Of course she played the Lady in her own manner, as numerous critics pointed out—"the only conception of her role nature allowed her," said James Huneker. She had considered the "tradition" of Lady Macbeth, from Mrs. Siddons through Charlotte Cushman—the powerful, masculine, and fiendish overwhelmer. She had also studied Mrs. Siddons's essay on the subject in which she conceives the Lady as of the kind "most captivating to the other sex—fair, feminine, nay, perhaps, even fragile." She recognized that Siddons's way of *playing* the part would be wonderfully effective—if one could do it, but she herself could not. She also believed that Siddons's view of the part in *writing* was at once closer to Shakespeare ("she was *not* a fiend, and *did* love her husband") and that it was within her own range. She chose to "play to the best of one's powers—one's own possibilities. Adapt the part to my own personality . . ."[171]

In 1888 when she first played it at the Lyceum, Henry Labouchère, the editor of *Truth,* teased Irving with a friendly leg-pull. Thirteen years earlier, Labouchère said, Irving had believed that Lady Macbeth, in the person of Kate Bateman, "was a shrew of the most determined type, the kind of woman to be carefully avoided." But now he thinks she is "the sweetest and most affectionate character who ever drew breath." In the person of Ellen Terry we have "an aesthetic Burne-Jonesy, Grosvenor Gallery version of Lady Macbeth, who roars as gently as any sucking dove!. . . . The artistic and the cultured are prepared to bow before the divinity, and to believe, or make believe, that lady Macbeth has been very much maligned, that the very thought of murder would draw tears from her eyes, that she can exhibit in this character playfulness, tenderness, affection, and conjugal rapture."[172]

Irving may have persuaded the audience at his lecture that the plan to murder Duncan originated with Macbeth, not with his lady, and that only by his connivance did she come to believe that she was the driving force behind that plan—but so intricate a *schema,* running counter to common preconceptions, was nearly impossible to communicate from the stage. Dithmar of the *New York Times* flatly rejected it (and the *Herald* critic agreed), declaring that this Macbeth "depends wholly on Lady Macbeth for his "bloody instructions, as all Macbeths will to the end of time." Nor does it appear that Miss Terry conceded the initiative to her lord and master. She did not bully him, of course, in the old Cushman manner: she seduced him, and there are few if any signs among the many dozens of jottings in her rehearsal copies that she needed or knew any motivation except burning ambition for herself and her beloved husband. In Roger Manvell's words, "she beguiles him into murder in order to fulfill their secret longing for the throne, and uses every feminine device at her command to goad him into the single, necessary action."[173]

Alongside Macbeth's first words to her—"Duncan comes here tonight"—she wrote in her study book, *R hand eagerly on his breast. Action first. Slow* and *smile;* and smiling she said, "And when *goes* hence?" After a considerable pause, in tones insinuating much, Macbeth answered, "Tomorrow, as he purposes." She understood at once: *Draw back R arm quickly to shoulder—head up.* She *breathes "Ah";* then her energetic response—"O, never / Shall sun *that* morrow see!"

Through the next nine to twelve lines, while she laid out the beginnings of her plan, the notes read *bright—quick—aflame—I clap my hand on his mouth and smile at him. Smile, smile.* At "he that's coming / must be

Illus. 128. Ellen Terry as Lady Macbeth. Folger Shakespeare Library.

provided for," she wrote *keep it fierce, give it time, give it time;* then presently, *simmer down.* When, convinced, he said, "We will speak further," she *turns him, puts her arm around his neck.* As the scene concludes with "Leave all the rest to me," *Closer in, she too plotting. Charm. Serpent.* He put his arms around her and they left the stage in a loving embrace. In his brooding soliloquy, "If 'twere done when 'tis done . . ." Macbeth talks himself out of the murder: "We will proceed no further in this business." Lady Macbeth must counter his funk and rebuild his determination; in the space of forty-five lines she does so. Miss Terry wrote, *I love this scene,* and at her entrance she called herself *the spur.* Along the margins she jotted many sharp words: *severely, sarcasm, cold, distant, dangerous, accusing,* but the distinctive words were *quiet, low voice, no rant, only amaze,* and *low down voice always.* Her "We fail" was given with a *strong downward inflection;* then at "Screw your courage to the sticking place" it was *slow change developing into great change.* As the plan develops to blame the murder on the sleeping chamberlains, Miss Terry wrote, "Now see—here is a beautiful plan which your wife has thought out (the hell-cat)", and she mesmerized him with *slow——ly———play with his hands and charm him.* Caressing him with hands and voice, rousing him sexually, she lured him back to the necessary action.

"The true protagonist of the fugued tale of passion and bloody murder became a woman all graciousness," said James Huneker, "for Ellen Terry could turn hell itself to prettiness. She was an alluring wretch. . . . She was tender—oh, so divinely tender when she spoke of that suckling babe. You ne'er believed her awful threat."[174] Her motto for the role was *"Be damned CHARMING."*

"Some people hate me in it," she said; "some, Henry among them, think it my best part." It is curious that this actress, who spent nearly her entire career making people laugh at her comedy and weep gentle tears at her pathetic roles, should be remembered most vividly as the tragical Lady Macbeth of John Singer Sargent's majestic portrait. There she stands, seemingly nine feet tall, in a dress of soft green wool and blue tinsel overlaid with real green beetles' wings, and a cloak of heathertoned velvet embroidered with flame-colored griffins. She holds a crown high above her head, and two long plaits of tawny red hair, bound with gold braid, descend to her knees.[175] From the wealth of annotation in her rehearsal books, we can believe that she thought more deeply about this role than any of her "easier" ones. Perhaps it *was* her best. In Sargent's painting, she said, "is all that I meant to do."[176]

Of the *mise-en-scène* of the six Shakespeares that Irving brought to America, that of *Macbeth* was praised above all the rest. "It may be doubted," said Jeannette Gilder, "when this tragedy ever before was produced with such pictorial treatment, such appreciation of the spirit of poetry and of fateful portent that pervades it."[177] Irving's *Henry VIII* had been a masterpiece of historical reconstruction—a "documentary play" that faithfully reproduced certain famous sixteenth-century rooms and buildings; but *Macbeth* is all mood and mystery, and as Ellen Terry remarked, "Henry's imagination was always stirred by the queer and the uncanny. This was a great advantage in *Macbeth* in which the atmosphere is charged with strange forces."[178] The buildings and landscapes were "real," of course—"painted with admirable solidity and that subdued richness of tone which is so great a relief from the glare and glitter which fulfil the ordinary managerial concept of splendor."[179] The costumes, too, taken from patterns of the eleventh century—brown leather and fur, woolens of dull bronze color, dark red, green, blue, and purple—and the "Wagnerian" accompaniment music, especially composed by Sir Arthur Sullivan—all blended together to compose a dark, massive, dangerous world.

"It was as if Prospero were producing Macbeth . . ." said Nym Crinkle. "It is like reading Dante's *Inferno* again—by turning over Doré's pictures. . . . I saw the weird sisters for the first time come flickering through the gloom, dusky phantoms, to melt again into nothingness." The play opened on a dark stage, with wind, rain, and thunder crashes. Flashes of lightning from black clouds revealed the witches one by one, seemingly suspended in space. At the end of the sisters' strange cries they vanished in mists (clouds of steam). At their second appearance, said Nym Crinkle, "there burned, low down, that flame of fire in the sodden sky, already staining the blasted heath with the hue of blood."[180] That flaming red would be seen again at the end of the play, hanging over another barren landscape in which Macbeth ("a great famished wolf," Miss Terry calls him) met his death in combat with Macduff.

And between these first and last bloody skies, Irving wrought miracles of chiaroscuro. "Throughout the play," said a critic in the *Dramatic Mirror,* "the scenes are pervaded by that dullness of light so characteristic of the architecture and so symbolic of the half barbarism of the time. Without the walls of the heavy-browed castle, and in its courts, as within its chambers, there are shadows and glooms."[181] In the fifth scene, in a hall of the palace at Inverness, Lady Macbeth read Macbeth's letter, lighted only by the glow of a woodfire at stage right. In this same half-dark hall occurred the scene in which she prompted Macbeth to commit murder and the passage in which she goaded him to the act when his purpose failed. The arrival of Duncan at Inverness ought, of course, to occur by daylight, when we imagine the air alive with "temple-haunting martlets." But Irving made it a night scene, with "torchlight on flashing steel and waving tartans." The general illumination rose just enough to reveal the massive walls and bastions of

Illus. 129. The slaying of Macbeth. Macduff is played by George Alexander. Folger Shakespeare Library.

Inverness palace and its vast arched gateway lighted from within.

The whole of the second act—the murder and its aftermath—was played in a heavy two-story construction that filled the entire stage, the courtyard of Macbeth's palace. At stage right there rose a huge stone pillar; beyond it a winding staircase led to Duncan's chamber. At the left another stair led straight away from the audience up to a gallery surrounding the courtyard. Doors along the gallery gave into the chambers of the multitude of guests accompanying the royal visit. The vast scene was dimly lighted by a single lantern hung on a beam attached to the stone pillar. As the scene opens, sounds of wind and thunder set an ominous tone. When Macduff discovers the murder and sounds the alarm, the scene explodes into life and light as dozens of courtiers, soldiers, and attendants burst through doors above and below, bearing torches, leaning over the gallery railing, crowding down the stairs.

A much-discussed feature of the Banquet Scene was the representation of Banquo's ghost by nothing more than a greenish light shining on an empty stool. This was regarded as a great improvement over the 1888 system by which a figure made of cardboard and gauze, so lighted that it glowed an iridescent blue, rose up through a slit in the floor and convinced nobody.

The Caldron Scene was made "natural," so to speak, by dispensing with the conventional cast iron pot. Flame and steam rose out of a crater in the side of a rocky hill at stage left, and into this hole the witches hurled the ingredients of their hellish brew. The apparitions and the figures of the future kings emerged from a thick mist—that is, came from nowhere and went nowhere in clouds of steam. The Caldron Scene was followed by a dramatically purposeless but wonderfully atmospheric interlude. In a setting of lake and mountains, with a silvery moon floating high, a chorus of white-clad spirits (in London sixty of them) sang a lyric, "Over Woods, high Rocks and Fountains," composed by Middleton, used by Davenant, and long since discarded by nineteenth-century producers.

Immediately after these final passages of the witches, a striking effect was achieved as the scene abruptly changed from night to day: "England—a Country Lane." A charming landscape, brightly painted, brilliantly lighted, it signaled the forthcoming victory over the tyrant, the kingdom purged of poison.

Irving brought his Lyceum productions to America eight times, seven of them accompanied by Miss Terry. In August of 1886, after his second American season, he came again "purely for pleasure"—to entertain fifty friends at Delmonico's (editors, actors, artists, leaders in politics and society), and to enjoy a yachting trip from New York to Maine and back. "No royal progress was never more enthusiastically welcomed nor attended by more lavish hospitalities," it was reported in the *Spirit of the Times*. "He can no longer feel a stranger here, and the plan which we proposed, last season, that he should divide his theatrical business between England and America is now being seriously considered. In that event a new theatre would be built for him in this metropolis."[182]

That plan did not quite work out. No theatre was built for him. Nonetheless, of his next eighteen seasons he spent six in America. And it is plain that he meant as much to America as America meant to him. Through his efforts here he carried off over a half-million dollars, but Americans paid their money gladly in exchange for the most finely wrought productions in the English-speaking world.

How "great" an actor Irving was could never be agreed upon in his own time and of course cannot be settled now. Gordon Crosse, the delightful recorder of fifty years of Shakespearean playgoing, tells us that he was once warned never to argue with the younger generation on the question of whether or not Irving was a great actor. "I never do," he says. "I tell them."[183] That is an amusing flourish, and the attitude it represents was common among the eighty or more aging devotees who contributed to the 1939 volume called *We Saw Him Act*. But it cannot dispose of the considerable body of experienced American critics who thought otherwise. Irving had his partisans in America, of course. Stephen Fiske of the *Spirit of the Times* and his editor, E. A. Buck, used news notes as well as critical columns to promote Irving. But the other Fiske, young Harrison Grey Fiske, could not abide the man. William Winter, who thought Irving could do almost nothing wrong, piled up many a two-thousand-to three-thousand-word review so gushing with praise that one can hardly see or hear Irving (or Miss Terry) through the smoky prose. But Henry Clapp of Boston's *Advertiser*, George Montgomery, and after him E. A. Dithmar of the *New York Times*, John Ranken Towse of the *Evening Post*, and Jeannette Gilder of *The Critic* tried to behave like critics; tried to report facts, analyze them, and distill their significances. Their reviews are genuinely informative because in their writing we can sense live minds seriously examining real theatrical experiences. They do not sound bought and paid for.

These more discriminating critics generally agree that Irving is a man of extraordinary intelligence.[184]

When he studies a role and *plans* what to do with it, they say, he is usually right on target. When he comes to performing it, however, especially if it is a heavy tragic role, he often fails to bring it off. Because he lacks power, both vocal and physical, he cannot execute what his fine brain tells him should be done. He is a light actor, a character actor of consummate genius; but as a tragic actor he cannot rank with Salvini or Edwin Booth of his own time, or with Phelps or Macready of the previous generation.

Of his performances of Shakespeare it appears that the very best was his Malvolio, a role upon which he could lavish his natural gift for eccentric comedy. In Malvolio's late scenes he could "humanize" the character and win sympathy through pathos, and Malvolio's suffering falls nicely short of a demand for tragic passion. Unfortunately, Irving undervalued his own achievement in the role and soon dropped it. His Cardinal Wolsey, though quite unlike the burly and overbearing character that Shakespeare intended, was a neat variant of his sinuous Iago and Mephistopheles. Though "wrong," it was a triumph of consistency. His Hamlet was, so to speak, half a Hamlet: brilliant in the playful parts, touching in the melancholy, thoughtful parts, picturesque, ingenious, inventive, but unable to build up and sustain emotionally powerful scenes such as those with Ophelia and Gertrude. Even William Winter took exception (mild, to be sure) to Irving's application of "natural treatment and colloquial style" to Hamlet, finding this method "enfeebled and inadequate in contact with the towering magnitude of Shakespeare's thought."[185] Both Clapp and Towse, after their first encounter with his Shylock, rated it a failure—Clapp because Irving could not produce Shylock's mighty rages ("nothing more than a little rattle and steam"), Towse for what he took to be inconsistency between the "evil" Shylock of the early and middle scenes and Shylock the martyr in the Trial Scene. But Shylock was a perennial favorite, the one Shakespearean character that Irving never had to shelve. Its record of a thousand and more performances qualifies it for higher place than these early critics would allow.

The sternest of Irving's critics had to acknowledge that, whatever his faults, he projected across the footlights an inescapable charm. Towse reports how on Irving's New York opening in *The Bells,* "the personal fascination of the man—that subtle attribute commonly called magnetism—gradually asserted its power over his hearers, compelling their attention and controlling their sympathies." Ellen Terry, who was in love with Irving, speaks of "that splendid head, those wonderful hands, the whole strange beauty of him."[186] And here in 1884 is Henry Clapp, who could never wholeheartedly endorse any of Irving's work:

> Speaking for myself, I should say that Mr. Irving's face is without exception the most fascinating I have seen upon the stage. Once beheld, it will not out of the memory; and I find, upon sifting my recollections, that, when there is no deliberate effort of my will, his face appears to me, not under the distorting or glorifying transformations of the stage, but with its usual look of quiet and somewhat sad thoughtfulness. . . . There is no impropriety in saying that this peculiar charm seems to grow out of the nature of the man himself,—out of a rare and lofty refinement, a subtile and delicate intellectuality, a largeness and sweetness of nature.

When Clapp reprinted his article eighteen years later, he let stand these generous recognitions, along with many more pleasant notes upon Irving's intellect and character, with the caveat only that his "general summing-up would now be less favorable to Mr. Irving than then it was."

American critics argued endlessly about Irving's worth as an actor, but no one doubted his contribution to our threatre in his function as a manager. As J.M.M said in the *Dramatic Mirror,*[187] "Mr. Irving is of an intensely artistic temperament, and is almost literally the slave of his profession. . . . The happiest hours Mr. Irving spends in his theatre are not, as might be supposed, those in which he receives the plaudits of his public, but those which he devotes to rehearsing a play, explaining his ideas about it and conveying his impressions to his comrades." He assembled supporting companies in whose work, said Towse in 1884, "it would by hypercritical to pick a flaw." He guaranteed the perfection of their work, Edwin Booth tells us, by downright despotic control of their every move and sound: "He sits on the stage during rehearsals, watching every movement and listening to every word. If he sees anything to correct or alter, he rises and points out the fault. . . . From first to last he rules the stage with an iron will, but as an offset to this he displays a patience that is marvellous."[188] He summoned the most esteemed artists of the day, from Pre-Raphaelites like Sir Edward Burne-Jones to academic neo-classicists like Sir Lawrence Alma-Tadema to design scenery; the finest scene-painters—Hawes Craven, William Telbin, Joseph Harker—to execute the designs; Charles Cattermole and Alice Comyns Carr for costumes; Edward German and Sir Arthur Sullivan to compose entr'acte and accompaniment music.

"When was it," cried Towse, "that a legitimate play was presented in which every detail of scenery, external or interior, every bit of property, every costume

Illus. 130. Sir Henry Irving. Courtesy of the University of Illinois Theatre.

was absolutely correct?" It was not that American managers had not spent money: they had spent vast sums on *The Black Crook* and similar trash. They were now taught by Irving that Shakespeare does *not* "spell ruin," that legitimate drama, produced with taste and intelligence, would prove more profitable than all the expensive sensation dramas which vulgar managers assumed the public wanted.

Over and over the critics retrace Irving's scenic miracles—Shylock's Venice, the Hampton Court of Charles I, the solid masonry of *Hamlet*'s Elsinore, the royal London of *Henry VIII,* the terrifying chiaroscuro of *Macbeth*—to bludgeon our American managers and actor-managers into mending their ways. Edwin Booth, as we know, was once an eager producer, but after 1874 when he lost his great theatre, he turned his back on all that and focused on earning money as an actor, not wasting money in putting up grand shows for an ungrateful public. Irving's example did not rouse Booth from his lethargy, but his partner in the mid- and late 1880s, Lawrence Barrett, did respond to the Irving challenge, and, as we have seen, did renovate *The Merchant of Venice, Othello,* and *Julius Caesar* with productional effects worthy of his British rival.

They all arrived at total scenic realism just before the cinema drove them out of that line of business and forced the theatre artists to find new ways to say what the Shakespeare plays truly mean.

Herbert Beerbohm Tree

According to Ellen Terry, during the 1890s it became apparent that dominance of the London theatrical scene by the Lyceum, so carefully built up by Henry Irving in the 1870s and 1880s, was gradually eroding;[189] that fashion was turning toward younger managements, and particularly toward the Haymarket—from Irving to a manager whom Irving had no great respect for, Herbert Beerbohm Tree. (Born Beerbohm in 1853, he added the name of Tree in 1877 when he decided to enter the profession. After his knighthood in 1911 he preferred to be called Sir Herbert Tree. He died in 1917.)[190]

Tree shared with Irving the belief that what makes the difference between great acting and what Irving would call mere mumming was the projection of the actor's "own humanity."

> You cannot imagine a characterless person playing the great characters of Shakespeare. . . . It requires individuality to interpret individuality, to realise the creations of the master brain. Nothing else than the actor's individuality will make the humanity of these characters stand out sharp and clear from the mass of humanities grouped about it and behind it.[191]

He protests too much. Of course we delight in the distinctive voices, faces, and figures of our first actors, but when they play roles of substance we look beyond these personal qualities (the mere tools of their trade) to find what they have made of "the creations of the master brain." And when a Tree offered his "individuality," remarkable as it was—and coupled with an almost uncanny knack for physical disguise—as the equivalent of Falstaff or Wolsey, audiences may well have wondered whether the goods for sale were sterling or plate.

It was Tree's boast, confirmed repeatedly by Maud his wife, that he never "studied" a role (when undertaking a classic role, he never looked into the traditional modes in which it had been played), but rather drifted into a role, improvising business and even language as rehearsals proceeded.[192] Shaw, who called this "creative acting"—as opposed to "interpretive acting"[193]—says that for Tree as for Irving a text was only a literary scaffold on which to hang his own creations. "The author, whether Shakespeare or Shaw, was a lame dog to be helped over the stile by the ingenuity and inventiveness of the actor-producer. . . . His parts were his avatars; and the play had to stand the descent of the deity into it as best it could."[194] Even Tree's friend, the English critic W. L. Courtney, would "admit without reserve that Tree as a personality was greater than anything he accomplished."[195]

Needless to say, Tree's "individuality" was very unlike Irving's. Irving was a formidable person—proud, reserved, domineering, aloof. Tree was a companionable person—carefree, playful, dandiacal, whimsical, witty, boyishly eager to please and to be pleased. Tree's biographer, Hesketh Pearson, says there can be no doubt that Irving was far more impressive than Tree (Pearson's actual words are "a far greater actor"): "Irving enthralled an audience; Tree entertained it."[196] Tree was tall, lean (in later years inclining to the portly), and sandy-haired. Physically he was graceful enough, a little showy of gesture perhaps, but free of Irving's compulsive writhings. His voice was somewhat high and hard, with an occasional lisp. Shaw called it an "un-English voice" like nobody else's. "His feeling for verbal music was entirely non-Miltonic: he had a music of his own; but it was not the music characteristic of English rhetoric; and blank verse, as such, had no charm for him; nor, I suspect, did he credit it with charm for anyone else."[197]

Illus. 131. Courtesy of the University of Illinois Theatre.

In the spring of 1887, after a decade in the profession, Tree "shook himself free of the shackles of other people's authority," as Mrs. Tree puts it, "and took a threatre of his own." This was the Comedy Theatre in Panton Street, where he staged *The Red Lamp,* a melodrama about spy-catching in czarist Russia. Then that autumn he undertook what Mrs. Tree calls his "Great Adventure," the management of the Haymarket Theatre,[198] where for ten years he could mount such a range of new plays and old that would qualify him in popular opinion as the only rival and inevitable successor to Irving. Pearson points out how after a couple of seasons of getting his program running, he began tossing out little challenges to Irving.[199] For one thing, he began to play Shakespeare. *The Merry Wives of Windsor,* which he offered in 1889 (not, to be sure, a play that Irving would have touched), had not been seen in London for fifteen years, and except perhaps for Tree's own debatable Falstaff it pleased greatly. It not only had a fine run but Tree would revive it often, reveling in its stunts, and played it to the end of his career. In 1892 he undertook Hamlet. Irving had given up Hamlet by that time, but in popular estimation it still "belonged to him," so that Tree's assumption of it set another stake into Irving's territory. In *A Man's Shadow* Tree doubled as look-alike hero and villain, similar to Irving's combination of Lesurques and Dubosc in *The Lyons Mail.* Tree's Svengali in *Trilby* became as famous a melodrama villain as Irving's Mathias in *The Bells.* Tree interested himself more than Irving did in contemporary British drama, staging Oscar Wilde and Henry Arthur Jones (Shaw, too, of course, much later). He investigated the progressive new drama coming from the Continent. The scandal of the first London performance of Ibsen's *Ghosts* (1891) had hardly subsided when Tree dared to introduce *An Enemy of the People,* making a fair success of Dr. Stockman. He also staged an adaptation of Maeterlinck's *The Intruder.* By 1895 he was ready to follow the Irving pattern of touring his company to America. And finally in 1897 he achieved what no actor-manager before him had done—he built his own theatre, the handsomest in London and privileged to be called "Her Majesty's."

After 1897 Irving would create only one more Shakespeare at the Lyceum—*Coriolanus,* and that a failure. Tree took up the torch—*Julius Caesar* in 1898, *King John* in 1899, *A Midsummer Night's Dream* in 1900, *Twelfth Night* in 1901, and so on to a total of sixteen Shakespeares by 1912, and every one of them in the Irving tradition of the "grand spectacular." If he was not as great an actor as Irving, he was, as Pearson points out, at least as worthy a pageant-master.[200]

Besides adding a new Shakespeare every year, Tree initiated an annual Shakespeare Festival.[201] In the spring of 1905, he revived in six days six of his own past productions in their full splendor. He repeated these six-day festivals in 1906, 1907, and 1908. In 1909 he extended the festival to two weeks, in 1910 to a month, in 1911, 1912, and 1913 to three months. For these extended festivals he invited the other actor-managers of London to bring their Shakespeares to his stage, including, amazingly, William Poel of the Elizabethan Stage Society, who opposed without compromise everything that Tree stood for in the way of theatre practice. Poel chose to produce *The Two Gentlemen of Verona* (with an actress in the role of Valentine!) and Tree obligingly built him a forestage across the orchestra pit and lighted the play by lamps hung along the front of the balconies, as Poel demanded.[202]

In about the year 1912, the long-burgeoning plans for an English National Theatre were coming to a head. Tree, who in popular esteem had come to be recognized as head of the profession (he had already been knighted) took it for granted that he would be named director of the official institution. Suddenly he was alarmed.[203] Young Harley Granville Barker, who had directed the Shaw plays at the Royal Court, had recently been commissioned by Lord Howard de Walden to produce Shakespeare in the "modernistic" style, and murmurs were in the air that the directorship would fall to him. Tree was furious: "I think that Barker is probably being backed up by some of the Shakespeare Committee, who are naturally jealous of the national work I have done. But I will have no nonsense and shall cut myself adrift from them and start the thing myself if I find any knavish tricks."

In a calmer mood he could justify his faith in his work with these words: "What one wants is sincerity, directness, and a reverence for Shakespeare." He had no idea, of course, how hollowly these words would ring as we read them today, how his methods of pageant-mastering Shakespeare were nearing the end of the road. In any case, the rivalry came to nothing. The war struck before anything could be decided. Tree died in 1917 and Barker withdrew from the producing theater altogether.

For all of Tree's affability, his wit, his desire to please, for all his well-advertised candidacy as successor to Irving, when he first brought his company to America he roused little enthusiasm from the American critics. Opening in New York at Abbey's Theatre on January 28, 1895 he ran off a series of "disguise" roles, calculated to demonstrate his "versatility"—Demetrius, the fat ugly spy-catcher in *The Red Lamp;* Gringoire, a graceful young medieval ballad-monger; and Captain Swift, a rascally Australian highwayman attempting to "go straight" in English society—before coming to his eagerly awaited Falstaff in *The Merry Wives* two weeks later. Towse of the New York *Post* reckoned Falstaff a lively performance, but "more remarkable as an exhibition of the resources of theatrical disguise than as an original or inspired interpretation of the fat knight." With all this cleverness of "making up," Sir John's identity is "not only concealed, it is annihilated." Tree simply had not the inner power to endow the model with life. "Mr. Tree's impersonation is bulk without substance. There is no heat in his love-making, no leering braggadocio in his scenes with Ford, no really comic terror in his adventures with the wives, while in his description of his

Illus. 132. Herbert Beerbohm Tree as Falstaff.

sousing in the Thames the most humorous feature consists in the dilapidation of his garments." In short: "a success of mere mechanism."[204] Twenty years later, Towse would grant him very little more. However clever Tree was, Towse said, however expert in the tricks of his trade, he could claim no place among the truly great actors. Towse could not even rank him with Henry Irving (of whom he had already said harsh things enough); as a reasonably equivalent artist he would suggest Charles Kean.[205]

E. A. Dithmar of the *New York Times* enjoyed describing Falstaff's "very very fat" body, how "his jowls hang over his collar" and "his huge double chin falls below his whiskers." We learn indeed from Howard Ticknor of Boston, who once watched Tree make up and dress for the role (in fourteen minutes!) that those jowls and chin were artificial stuff pasted onto his face along with his beard.[206] Dithmar took note of the ironic circumstance that to preserve the illusion of overall fatness Tree could never remove his huge gauntleted gloves. "Though he complains of the heat, he keeps his hands covered with thick leather indoors, when he is courting Ford's wife, when he is taking his ease at his inn."[207]

Jeannette Gilder insisted that *versatility,* for which Tree was so widely praised, does not consist merely in alteration of physical appearance—"that temperament plays a most important part in every successful impersonation, and is something that cannot be acquired or counterfeited." Tree's "enormous legs and thighs, the colossal body and the red and swollen face, in which every feature except the eyes, is false, contain no suggestion of the actual personage concealed within them."[208] She refrained from describing Tree's "frankly farcical" antics, but we read elsewhere that, for one thing, in his disguise as the fat woman of Brainford he wore so short a skirt that as he scrambled about the stage on all fours while Ford beat him with a slapstick, his boots and his vast bottom clad in red tights were unamusingly visible.[209]

The *New York Times,* among others, recalled Henry James's assessment of Tree's original London Falstaff as mere *scenery:* "Why Falstaff's very person was nothing *but* scenery. A false face, a false figure, false hands, false legs—scarcely a square inch on which the irrepressible humour of the rogue could break into illustrative touches. And he is so human, so expressive, of so rich a physiognomy. One would rather Mr. Beerbohm Tree should have played the part in his own clever elegant slimness—that would at least have represented life. A Falstaff all 'make-up' is an opaque substance."[210] In the *Tribune,* William Winter kept his temper through a discursive paragraph or two, but broke out waspishly at last that "Mr. Tree is really no more fitted for Falstaff than Mr. Jefferson is for Timon of Athens or Mr. Toole for Coriolanus." And he reminded us of Dr. Johnson's observation on the Quaker lady preaching a sermon: it was not remarkable that she did it so well but that like a dancing dog she did it at all.[211]

Tree's Hamlet, which he exhibited at Abbey's a week later (February 21, 1895), was treated somewhat less harshly, though largely because of its elegant appearance. Tree played it in his own person—tall, graceful, handsomely dressed in tones of gray and black. He wore a blond wig, curled up at the sides,

Illus. 133. Tree as Hamlet. Folger Shakespeare Library.

with a lock or two falling prettily across his forehead, and this, with his small blond beard and mustache, raised for many old-timers pleasant memories of Charles Fechter. He was "undoubtedly a youth of royal blood," said Dithmar in the *New York Times,* a royal Dane, and "such a prince as romantic maidens might well dream about."[212] Felix de Fontaine of the New York *Herald* praised "the perfectly sober and colloquial manner in which he spoke his lines." Without rant or shout he brought out the music of the text, and the words sounded not like words committed to memory but the spontaneous utterance of the man's own thought.[213] Arthur Warren of the Boston *Herald* (there is always one reviewer wearing rose-colored glasses) ranked Tree's Hamlet with "the greatest this age has seen."[214]

But encomium stops here. This, after all, was the same Hamlet that Tree's friend W. S. Gilbert had described as "Funny, but not the least bit vulgar."[215] I don't find that Gilbert's witticism had yet penetrated to America (though Tree himself, to take the sting out of it, repeated it far and wide), but the American critics had their own terms of dismissal, of which the commonest was "melodrama." Tree had so far yielded to the fashion of musical accompaniment that he had commissioned George Henschel to compose an extensive score, Wagnerian in manner, with a leitmotiv for each important scene and character.[216] The emotional appeal of this music, together with tricky lighting effects, seemed often to play Shakespeare off the stage, to reduce the text to the status of libretto—in short, to "melodrama."

More damaging still was Tree's inability to conceive and execute a wholly consistent study of Hamlet—imaginative, sincere, dignified, and everywhere expressive of the unique tragic spirit which we identify with this unique character. "It is shallow," said William Winter, "devoid of poetic emotion, finical in fibre, marred by inappropriate alertness and fussy bustle, and hard and metallic in execution. It belongs to that school in England that was represented by Barry Sullivan. It wins respect. It cannot inspire affection."[217] Jeannette Gilder nicely elaborated Winter's idea of "fussy bustle" by pointing out that here, as in Tree's "disguise" parts, he depended altogether on externals. "His Hamlet is one long and hopeless struggle to interpret the poignancy of human emotion by the little ingenuities of pantomime, to stir the heart and convince the intellect by an endless succession of mere attitudes and gestures." He offers us "a superficial cleverness of device, the elaboration of traditional 'points' and the addition of much new and trivial 'business,' most of it being in the nature of that embroidery which confuses and obscures, without improving the original pattern." He fidgets with his sword, his tablets, with the picture of his father which he wears about his neck, and seems always to be saying, "How shall I make the audience understand my view of this passage?"[218]

Tree's response to this critical bombardment was characteristically good-humored. He got up a lecture, "Hamlet from an Actor's Prompt Book," which he delivered at Harvard a month later.[219] The opening gambit of his lecture was a half-playful claim for infallibility. It is something like the Socratic chains of inspiration descending from muse, to poet, to performer. The author Shakespeare was an actor. His Hamlet was an actor. And Tree is an actor. Who then more than an actor, in the white heat of passion, can better explore the giddy heights of Shakespeare's masterpiece? He, the actor, has the privilege of speaking those noble words, of being translated into the higher region of the great poet's imaginings, of soaring on the wings of passion into the rapt heaven of poetic fantasy (etc., etc.). Here then in this (my) actor's prompt book are certain truths about Hamlet which have been revealed to me.

Granting the comical circularity of Tree's reasoning ("these things are right because I have been inspired to do them"), it may illuminate some of the critic's objections to examine a few of the twenty or so items which Tree offers for approval. In the second act, for instance, Tree invented the "double entrance" for Hamlet "reading on a book," thus anticipating by a whole generation that which Dover Wilson would make so much of in *What Happens in Hamlet.*[220] Suffice to say that Tree made little of it. He says only that Hamlet enters slightly before his cue, detects the King and Polonius in their conspiracy, vanishes for a moment behind the curtains, and then enters stark staring mad to encounter Polonius. In short, he used the business only to provide a cue to assume his antic disposition for that particular moment. But *if he had actually listened to the terms of the conspiracy*—to "loose" Ophelia to him on an occasion when king and counselor, hiding behind an arras, could spy upon the encounter—this knowledge would resonate deep into the play, would above all control and restructure the meeting with Ophelia when that meeting did come to pass. He would *know* she was bait to a trap, that he was being spied upon. But Tree was thinking only of the isolated moment, not the total fabric of the play, and so his "double entrance" may well have seemed to Miss Gilder one more "little ingenuity of pantomime."

When the First Player, reciting the woes of Hecuba, spoke of the "mobled" queen, the word "mobled" suggested to Tree, though for no reason that an audience could understand, that Hamlet could expose Claudius through the medium of a play. Out popped his tablets and he began making notes for *The Mousetrap.* A little later, during his soliloquy, when he came to thoughts of his uncle, "Bloody, bawdy villain . . ." he whipped out his sword and began thrusting it at the empty throne chair. One can see some dramatic sense in this "imaginary" killing of the King, but critics of the time dismissed it as showy and distractive. As the soliloquy drew towards its end, daylight waned, the stage darkened, and the act concluded with a long tableau of Hamlet crouched at a fireplace, bathed in red light, as he continued to scribble dialogue for the play that would catch the conscience of the King. Tree half-apologized for this as "a purely pictorial effect," but for the critics it was mere melodrama.

From "To be or not to be" to the end of the Ophelia scene a cluster of Tree's inventions and effects set the critics' teeth on edge. To begin with, Ophelia was placed near enough to overhear "the self-torturings of Hamlet in that great soliloquy wherein he pours out his very heart"—and hearing these words she fell on her knees, appearing to pray for her distraught lover. Tree supposed that her participation in the scene would add pathos to Hamlet's "wondrous words," but of course it only puzzled the audience. As Ophelia approached him to deliver his "remembrances," he appeared about to embrace her; but suddenly he remembered the medallion with his father's portrait on it, raised it and kissed it. This action ws *supposed* to say to the audience that his duty to his father was more sacred than his love for Ophelia. A moment later he was shouting at Ophelia, "Are *you* honest? Are *you* fair? The unusual emphasis on the pronoun was *supposed* to remind the audience that he had earlier declared that "Frailty, thy name is woman!" and now, if he could, he would exempt Ophelia from that condemnation of womankind. He uttered the phrase "get thee to a nunnery" not in the customary tone of cruel dismissal, but *very tenderly,* signifying that among nuns she should find safe haven from himself and from the total corruption of the world. A gust of pity welled up in him: he took her in his arms and was about to kiss her, but just then he discovered the spies in the arras. He asked the fatal question, "Where is your father?" received her lying answer, blew up the rest of the scene in a torrent of rage, and stormed off the stage.

Quite disingenuously Tree then wrote in his lecture, "I have read" (what everyone knows as one of the most famous bits of stage business in the history of *Hamlet*) "that Edmund Kean, in this scene, used to come on the stage again, and . . . smother her hands with passionate kisses." Tree improved upon that. He returned. He found Ophelia kneeling at a couch, sobbing. He wished to console her. But he dared not show her that in spite of all he loves her. She must never again know of or hope for his love. So he stole up behind her, tenderly planted a kiss on a tress of her hair, and stole from the room. This, as the critics noticed, made nonsense of the King's next line, "Love! his affections do not that way tend." But Tree either did not notice the King's line, or, more probably, "soaring on the wings of passion" assumed that the tensions and sentiment of the scene would obliterate the significance of the King's response.

In the Play Scene he introduced a court jester, to whom he could address certain rude lines that Hamlet is supposed to speak to the King; and to whom he could drop aside the line: "It was a brute part of him to kill so capital a calf," thus avoiding insulting Polonius openly. He managed somehow to direct the bawdy responses to Ophelia's questions not to her but to the King.

He restored the heretofore always omitted soliloquy, "How all occasions do inform against me, To stir my dull revenge" (provoked, according to Shakespeare, by the fourth-act transit of Fortinbras), by attaching it to "'Tis now the very witching time of night," after the Play Scene—but how he managed this, or how much of it he could restore, since no Fortinbras appeared to provoke it, is not clear. After the funeral of Ophelia he returned to the churchyard gathering wild flowers and casting them into her grave. He canceled the character of Osric.

At the close of Horatio's benediction line, "Good night, sweet prince, and flights of angels sing thee to thy rest," a chorus of heavenly voices did indeed answer with an appropriate mortuary tune. It was "as if in abeyance to pressure of an electric button," wrote a Boston critic; "it may be in line with modern stage craft, but it jars the sensibilities."[221]

Here then, in the tricked-up, trifling, showily sentimental Hamlet of Beerbohm Tree we may sense a feeble close to the long history of Hamlets in nineteenth-century America. And it is fair to William Winter, so often the dodo-bird in these chapters, that in the year 1895 that he should read the obsequies.

> Within the last forty years two actors—and only two—have appeared, who could truly and greatly impersonate Hamlet. Those were Edwin Booth and Henry Irving. Booth is dead. Irving is now, probably, out of tune with the part, and too old for it. There is no one else. Nobody on the German, Italian, or French stage can act it according to Shakespeare. There are, perhaps, a few tolerable Hamlets wandering about in the provinces of England and America—such actors, for instance, as Haworth, Warde, Whiteside, Willard, Rignold, Mantell, Wilson Barrett, and Creston Clarke—but as Curtis once asked, "Who wants a tolerable egg?" The question is readily answered. Someday, perhaps, a new tragedian may arise, to whom Nature shall have given the soul, the temperament, the passion, the mind, the face, the voice, and the person—together with all the deadly burden of sorrowful spiritual experience essential for his pre-ordination—that are imperative for the true embodiment of that sublime character. Another generation may see another Booth. For the present, Hamlet lives but in the library, and in the heart.[222]

Another Hamlet, though—Forbes-Robertson's—would soon arrive.

Tree returned to America in the autumn of 1896,

while his new theatre was still building, partly to raise money for it and mainly to try out a new play by Gilbert Parker—a dramatization of Parker's novel, about the fall of Quebec, called *The Seats of the Mighty.* The play failed in Washington, and while Parker frantically rewrote scene after scene of it, it failed in New York, in Boston, and in Philadelphia. Finally, after April 28, 1897, when Tree used it in London to open Her Majesty's it failed again.[223] Throughout his second American tour he sprinkled in bits of his standard repertory and, as a novelty, a Falstaff scene out of *Henry IV,* which he had produced the whole of at the Haymarket in May. On that occasion Bernard Shaw had declared that "Mr. Tree only wants one thing to make him an excellent Falstaff, and that is to get born over again as unlike himself as possible" and suggested that he might as well attempt Juliet.[224] In New York William Winter brushed aside this new version of Falstaff as worthless, "for he possesses no more real humor than there is in a section of gas-pipe."[225]

For nearly twenty years—the great years of Her (then His) Majesty's Theatre—Tree kept to London; but once the Great War got under way the London public had less and less use for "serious" theatre, and in the autumn of 1915 Tree accepted a call from Triangle-Reliance of Hollywood, with a ten-month contract at a salary in excess of $100,000, to make a series of Shakespeare motion pictures.[226] In January and February of 1916, teamed with Constance Collier and rehearsed by D. W. Griffith, he completed a film of *Macbeth.* Unfortunately, though it was handsomely reviewed, it failed so dismally at box offices that the company abandoned plans for further Shakespeares and got rid of its obligation to Tree the next autumn by putting him through a role so *infra dig* (an American farmer in *The Old Folks at Home*) that he surrendered the remnant of his contract and put an end to his career in the movies.

Meanwhile, having rented His Majesty's Theatre to Oscar Asche, he renewed his presence on the American stage. The year 1916 was the tercentenary of Shakespeare's death, an occasion calling for lectures, exhibitions, and stage performances without number, both amateur and professional, as tributes to his memory. Since the European nations—especially England and Germany—were totally preoccupied with tearing each other to pieces—it was mainly left to America to do the honors. New York, of course, became the headquarters and clearing house for whatever was to be done, and Tree, eager to participate, arranged with Triangle-Reliance that he could interrupt his film work to join the New York celebration. He would contribute three productions during the spring season. (See below, "Epilogue," beginning on page 291 for a full account of the New York celebration.)

Illus. 134. Tree as Cardinal Wolsey.

Tree's first contribution, which opened March 14, 1916, was a revival of his 1910 production of *Henry VIII,* which he brought from London, lock, stock, and barrel. To offer this "least Shakespearean" of Shakespeare's plays, this "procession of tapestry," seemed to Lawrence Gilman of *The North American Review* rather perverse;[227] but it was a quite in character for Shakespeare's supreme pageant-master to put forward this most flamboyantly pictorial and archaeologically provable production—his ultimate development in what he referred to as "the modern manner."

When Tree speaks of "the modern manner" of staging Shakespeare, and of the "public demand" for it,[228] we recognize, of course, that his point of reference is not to *our* taste but to the taste of high Edwardian times. He was not unaware, of course, of the rising "new movement" in theatre art, of what J. L. Styan calls "the Shakespeare Revolution."[229] He knew of Shaw's and others' attacks on the staging methods of Henry Irving. He knew of William Poel, of Poel's mad notion of abolishing scenery and returning Shakespeare to the unadorned platform stage; even, as we have seen, he brought Poel into His Majesty's and built a Poelesque platform over the music pit for him to play on. He was not only aware of Gordon Craig's demand for simplified stage decoration, but had actually journeyed to Moscow to see Craig's *Hamlet* production there. He claimed to enjoy parts of it, and at one point commissioned Craig to design scenery for *Macbeth.* When he declared that "Ragtime and Futurism are holding carnival on our boards," I assume he was sneering at the Bakst-cum-fantasy-cum-art-nouveau productions of Barker. But all this, he declared, "is only the passing of dead matter" and soon "the fickle public, sated with the ephemeral, may return once more to the ample bosom of the Drama."

It was Tree's contention that if Shakespeare is a living author, we must look at him with the eyes, hear him with the ears of our own generation, and thus he must be presented with all the resources of the theatre of our time. We must apply to him the same care, the same reverence for accuracy, the same regard for stage illusion, for mounting, scenery, and costume, which we devote to authors of lesser degree. We must avail ourselves of those adjuncts which in these days science and art place at the manager's right hand. We must grant him the crowds and armies, the pride, pomp, and circumstance which he calls for everywhere in his work. The public demands that we put Shakespeare on the stage as worthily and magnificently as the manager can afford.

In order further to achieve this "modern manner" Tree cut *Henry VIII* to the quick, reducing it, as was his wont, from five acts to three, and offering, with just enough language to hold it together, a three-and-one-half hour banquet of pictures, processions, music, dance, and pantomime. Of course, as Woollcott of the *New York Times* admitted, "There is no play of Shakespeare you would more willingly see smothered in scenery and rich costumes, for the street crowds, the banqueters, the spectators to court, and the grandly bedecked guests at the coronation play as important a part as the great cardinal or the unhappy queen in what is after all a panorama of the early years of the eighth Henry's reign."[230]

Towse in the *Post* found not only "picturesqueness," but "a very positive realistic and historical value" in "such scenes as 'The Cloisters,' with the procession of monks, acolytes, and choristers preceding the doughty Cardinal; 'The Banqueting Hall' in Wolsey's Palace, with its characteristic ceiling, the long lines of tables, the brilliant array of guests and the scarlet host at his high table, flanked by vested singers in the choir-loft; the menacing 'River Gate,' with the ominous barge on the silent river; 'The Pleasaunce' at Windsor, with its old-fashioned garden, in the shadow of a mighty cedar, the Round Tower rising majestically above, and the silver Thames winding through the meadow-lands below; 'The Hall in Blackfriars,' with the feast in colors offered by the rich costumes, and the final 'Westminster Abbey.'" These, said Towse, all "appeal to the intelligence as well as to the eye, and exhibit extraordinary ingenuity and forethought."[231] And much music was there too—music for the dances originally composed for Irving's production by Edward German, part songs, ballads, and slow music during scene changes and between the acts. Yet Woollcott, having "Second Thoughts" about the show for the Sunday edition of the *New York Times,* confessed exhaustion: "You feel as though you had watched a grand parade during the afternoon, spent the evening at the Hippodrome, and read three novels by Harrison Ainsworth before going to bed." For the most part, he said, the show consisted of "lavish pageants of a scope infrequently attempted on the picture frame stage in the past, and not likely to be attempted there at all when, in the course of theatrical events, the movie screen and the stage settle each to the things it can do best.[232]

During the three and a half hours there was little enough acting to stir deep feelings or deserve praise. Everyone agreed that Lyn Harding's rendering of the King was a superb likeness: "Holbein's portrait quickened to life," said Woollcott, "stamping, snorting, and tossing his head like the beef-fed bull that defender of the faith most certainly was." Only Queen Katherine, played by a long-experienced Shakespearean actress, struck tragic fire. As Francis Hackett declared in *The New Republic,* "Because Miss Edith Wynne Matthison did not take her part as an incident in a pageant, but as an interpretation in a human story, she made the humanity of that story the touching thing it ought to be." She distinguishes herself in virtue and queenliness. "Into Katherine's speech at Blackfriars, Shakespeare has poured all his understanding of her emergency and the depths within her that it stirred. Miss Matthison lived it out for the beholder, a woman very pitiful in her just cause."[233]

The accounts of Tree's own work suggest that in all his long career he had never yet learned to "get inside" a character and act from that character's deep conviction. He still worked from externals. In his vast height, clad in Wolsey's scarlet robes, he easily dominated the stage. But that was not enough. He "would fain be doing," as a fidgety Petruchio would put it. In his first scene, in a manner quite uncalled for, he stalked down to center stage to glare defiantly upon Buckingham. During the banquet in his own hall, he left his place at the table and came to the footlights, said Towse in *The Nation,* "with the apparent purpose of giving Anne Bullen an opportunity of mocking him, and registering his own indignation and wrath in interpolated pantomime." "These are all the bad, old tricks of the actor," said Woollcott, "tricks which the Londoner, accepting them as familiar alloy in the genuinely cherished gold, may no longer notice, but which help to rob the Wolsey of the earlier scenes of any suggestions of the statesman or of the sinister man of reserve power." Most of the critics acknowledged that Tree did read the "long farewell to all his greatness" with dignity and eloquence, though some noticed that he lacked the sense of humility that would render it truly pathetic. His farewell speeches to Cromwell were praised too, though apparently he then overreached for sympathy by taking a seemingly interminable exit through a long-disappearing corridor upstage center.

The final scene contained no Shakespeare at all. We were in Westminister Abbey looking toward the great west windows ("real stained-glass," they tell us). The King on a high perch smiled down on the crowds below as Anne Bullen entered at the west door, attended by "the rich stream of lords and ladies," came forward to the altar, knelt and prayed, rose, bowed to her people. The Archbishop of Canterbury anointed and crowned her, "which performed, the choir, With all the choicest music of the kingdom, Together sung *Te Deum.*" No dialogue was uttered, and the drama of the scene, as the *Tribune* critic observed, "is largely potential; to grasp it, one must look ahead a few years to the day when the head of Anne rolls in the dust by royal command."[234]

In spite of reservations, though, the production ran from March 14 into early May, and it was the talk of the town. After the gala opening the *Herald* published a list of sixty or seventy men and women "well known in all walks of life" who were prominent in boxes and in the orchestra. And one assumes that Colonel Edward House and party (Tree's personal guests), the Vanderbilts and Kahns and Winthrops and Belmonts and Flaglers and Tafts and Gallatins were getting a full portion of what they most expected from Shakespearean theatre.[235]

There were knowledgeable critics there, too, who would not willingly let the old scenic methods go. Towse, for instance, whose judgment of actors and acting are invariably well grounded, had to say that "the methods of the older scenic artists—Mr. Joseph Harker, in this instance—are infinitely preferable to many of the impressionist vagaries of the new." Four years later George Odell would declare in the Epilogue to his *Shakespeare from Betterton to Irving* that this *Henry VIII,* seen in America in 1916, "was a revelation of old-time splendour in theatrical mounting, and still lives in memory as perhaps the most gorgeous thing ever attempted in this country in that line of staging."[236] He would "lay a wreath on the tomb of the brave believer in Shakespeare and the theatre."

Henry VIII prospered for six weeks, but on May 7, having promised New York not only a play but a festival, Tree laid it by and opened a two-week run of *The Merchant of Venice.* Interest ran high for two reasons: New York had never seen Tree's famous Shylock, and for his Portia he chose Elsie Ferguson (1885–1961), a young actress with an enormous following, much admired for her beauty and charm in the newest Broadway parlor and costume drama. Unfortunately she had never played Shakespeare, nor, so far as I can make out from the two dozen plays in which she had made her reputation, had ever played anything else of permanent worth. Her fans greeted her with an ovation almost embarrassingly long, but then had to settle for something less than a satisfying Portia. The critics often spent as many words on the beloved Elsie as on Tree, but their message was one of compassionate regret. Charming, playful, and a joy to behold in her early scenes with Nerissa, lovely in her surrender to Bassanio, yet she had not the vocal style to sustain the role. "This is a voice monotonous in tone," wrote Woollcott in the *New York Times,* "a voice trained too long, perhaps, in the contemporary drama."[237] Montrose Moses thought it "a pity that an actress who is such a favorite should have been put to such a test without adequate preparation. . . . Miss Ferguson should have had a year at least, playing Shakespeare in stock, before making a Metropolitan debut."[238] She never attempted Shakespeare again.

Tree got less sympathetic treatment. Never, said one critic, had a New York audience seen the text of the play "so excised, transposed, and otherwise altered to suit the convenience of an actor whose chief efforts are for the sake of spectacular effect."[239] Another labeled him less an actor than a "showman."[240] Presumably to save time from scene-shifting, he reduced the twenty scenes of the play to eight, chopping and splicing the text in his worst "modern manner." At the same time he plastered over the play with so much extraneous business—a ducal procession across the Rialto bridge, revelers dancing and singing in the streets, sounds of a religious service proceeding from a synagogue, the passage of gondolas, a brawl between Christians and Jews—that the curtain did not fall until after midnight. *Life* magazine complained that the impulse toward "realism"—what Towse called "the illusion of actuality"—so got out of hand in the Courtroom Scene that Portia's key speech forbidding Shylock to "shed one drop of Christian blood" was drowned out by the motion and noise of the stage crowd; and that in many earlier passages

Illus. 135. Tree as Shylock.

"the incidental music and the work of the picturesque supernumeraries was permitted to interfere with the real action as interpreted by the speaking characters. All this may be sugar-coating Shakespeare for popular appreciation, but at points it came very near smothering him."[241]

Brander Matthews, writing in the *Evening Mail,* put the significance of the case with fine clarity: "Each season, it seems to us, we are coming to realize that there can be but little compromise with Shakespeare, if there is to be anything resembling an enjoyment of the text." He had recently seen John Corbin's simplified "Elizabethan" production of *The Tempest* at the Century. "How little does all the fuss and scenery of *The Merchant* amount to in one's enjoyment of the evening; how little real illusion there is in it, and how very much of it denies the steady and consistent sweep of the dramatic story itself!"[242]

Of Tree's own performance, perhaps Woollcott's evaluation is as fair as any. He found it to be "a picturesque and superficially effective performance, something better than mediocre, and less than great, but more admirable by far than his work as Wolsey."[243] By sheer size Tree dominated the scene, and as one critic noticed, "his dislike for the centre of the stage has not increased perceptibly since his previous production."[244] His make-up, expectably, was splendid. "In his brown gabardine and golden yellow headgear as he first appeared he was most picturesque. His hook nose, with his gray and tangled beard, lent him a dangerous look, yet did not exclude dignity or intellect. His gestures were throughout Semitic."[245]

As usual, however, it was Tree's cleverness—not only cleverness in rewriting the play and loading it with gimcracks—but cleverness in his own performance that distracted his best critics and belittled him in their estimation. Thus, for instance, in the passages before the elopement of Jessica, as Shylock bade her goodnight and instructed her to lock up the doors and guard his moneybags, he *removed his earrings and his finger ring* and handed them to her.[246] To anyone who did not know the play it would be senseless for him to undress his jewels before going out to supper. To the majority, who knew the play in every detail, it would be heavy handed, at least, to be shown him giving her Leah's ring, which he would make such a fuss about later when she stole it.

Then came the aftermath of the elopement. We recall Henry Irving's notorious slow, silent return home over the bridge, his approach to the deserted house, his knocking, waiting in "tragic" silence as the curtain fell. Tree would improve on that. He approached the house, he knocked, he entered; he called for Jessica and got no answer. He moaned. He stormed through the rooms and up the stairs, calling and moaning. He stormed out of the house and crossed to stage right, where, as Towse cynically suggests, he had instructed the stage manager to place a pile of sand there so that, with biblical precedent, he could pour "ashes over his head."[247] Here again one recalls Jeannette Gilder's old complaint about his Hamlet, that he is forever thinking to himself, "How shall I make the audience understand my view of this passage?"

Whatever the critics' irritation over this business (some there were, who praised it), popular audiences greeted it with a storm of applause, as if it was the finest passage Shakespeare ever thought of. On the opening night they positively stopped the show and demanded a curtain speech. Tree pled exhaustion after such a tremendous passage of "acting," and persuaded them to wait for his speech until the end of the play, when he could have regained breath and composure.

Although for the most part Tree presented Shylock as "a repulsive, almost unclean old money lender . . . sombre and slinking throughout,"[248] Woollcott notes a dozen odd bits of business throughout the play that "appeal to your sympathy for the lonely, desolate, persecuted Jew," and his stature so grows in the Trial Scene that he is at the end "a deeply pathetic figure."[249] Not so for Montrose Moses: "when the evening was over, in memory we did not conjure up the 'Jew that Shakespeare drew,' but rather Mr. Tree's Svengali and Fagan."[250]

To round off his festival, beginning on May 25 Tree offered a few nights of his *Merry Wives of Windsor,* which the American critics had treated so scornfully in 1895. This was an odd decision, partly because it was so late in the season, and partly because the town had just been treated to a highly delightful *Merry Wives.* James Keteltas Hackett had set up a production of it, starring himself as Falstaff, for late March. But early in the rehearsal period he had fallen seriously ill and could not go on with it. The only available substitute was a popular comedian named Tom Wise, fat and funny, but utterly unexperienced in Shakespeare. He had but ten days to learn the part. To everyone's surprise he was immensely successful, and the play had a healthy run. (See below, *Epilogue,* 301–2.

Probably, remembering the harsh critiques of 1895, Tree wanted to prove his Falstaff to Americans after all. During the last twenty years he had played the role happily in London many dozens of times, and felt he deserved an American reappraisal. He was right. In 1916 everyone agreed that his Falstaff was far superior to either his Shylock or his Wolsey, and even the insatiable perfectionist Towse found *The Merry Wives* the best in pictorial quality, in ingenuity of stage business, and faithfulness to text of all of Tree's contributions to the tercentenary.[251] No one at this time quarreled with his outlandish make-up, and apparently over the long years of playing the part Tree had extended his vocal range. Woollcott could write that "his voice, which in other roles has seemed inflexible, does wonders with the speeches of the paltry knight. It develops hitherto unsuspected depths; it is full of chuckles. It sounds for all the world as though it had been solicitously cultivated with many a flagon of sack at the Garter Inn."[252] He had enriched, or at least expanded traditional farcical business. Years earlier F. R. Benson had worked up the "fight" between Evans and Caius to a "football scrum," but now in Tree's production everyone on the stage fell down, rolled over, banged into each other, emulating knockabout films from the Keystone studios. When Falstaff's wooing of Mrs. Ford was interrupted by the news of Ford's approach, he could not get out of his chair, being too fatly wedged into it. He was too fat for the buckbasket, and the wives had to sit on him to stuff him into it.[253] The multiplication of absurd business—what H. T. Parker would call Tree's "dear infirmity"[254]—which he imposed upon the wives (Contance Collier and Henrietta Crosman) was almost embarrassing to them. At least in his curtain speech Tree felt called upon to remind the audience that these were "merry" wives.

Falstaff's followers were apparently played unusually well. Towse singled out "the true artistry of Bardolph, by G. W. Anson," who lifted one of the smallest parts into prominence by sheer force of impersonation. Having a full grip of the character, he employed just the right measure of exaggeration to give the needed touch of humor to squalid realism. . . . A more vivid portrayal of sodden, greedy, shameless alcoholism has seldom been seen upon the stage. It was indisputably real and Shakespearean." By way of contrast Towse describes Tree's performance as "the work of a skilled comedian, intelligent and amusing, but not in the least inspired."[255] The *Tribune* critic, too, could not refrain from noting that Sir Herbert lacked "the mellowness" that Tom Wise had displayed in the recent Hackett production: Tree "acted the role well, but one remembered that Mr. Wise did not seem to have been under the necessity of acting it."[256]

Thus Tree's contribution to the tercentenary wound down to a brief ending—his "best" work enjoying fewest showings and seen by fewest audience. "Society" seems to have stayed away—at least one notices that the *Herald* did not publish its usual list of distinguished first-nighters, and "Mme. Critic" of the *Dramatic Mirror* complained that quite unlike at usual first nights at the New Amsterdam, many men in the audience wore business suits and women were seen in afternoon dresses or even in lace blouses and skirts. Mme. Critic had her doubts that this season's sudden veering toward Shakespeare, the hitherto "scoffed-at," the "highbrow", would last beyond tercentenary time.[257]

Tree returned to Hollywood to complete his disagreeable duties there, made a quick trip home to London, and returned to America in October for a seven-month tour of *Henry VIII* and *The Merry Wives,* visiting the principal cities of the eastern half of the country. The tour concluded with a month-long stand in New York, at the New Amsterdam, and for this engagement he got up a stage version of Thackeray's *The Newcomes.*

After his return to England he acted no more. He did propose to Shaw that he revive *Pygmalion,*[258] and he was busily planning a production of a play called *The Great Lover.* But suddenly during convalescence after an accident, he died.[259] His death is symbolic of the death of the nineteenth-century way with Shakespeare.

Johnston Forbes-Robertson

By far the finest Hamlet known to Americans in the first decades of twentieth century—the finest since Booth, and presently some would be saying the finest ever—was the English Johnston Forbes-Robertson (1853–1937).[260]

The son of an art critic, Forbes-Robertson aspired to a career as a painter, and between the ages of seventeen and twenty he trained at the Royal Academy; he never wanted to be an actor. By accident rather than choice, and thanks to his rich voice and handsome youthful face, in March of 1874 he was drafted to replace a failed actor in a play about Mary Queen of Scots. By the end of that year he had played a leading role with the young Ellen Terry and toured with her, had played several roles for Charles Calvert at Manchester, and had been engaged at the Gaiety in London, where for some months he acted with and studied elocution under the great classic Shakespearean Samuel Phelps.

From then on he earned a steady living in the profession (he kept up his painting as an avocation), playing many dozens of first- and second-level roles in plays now well forgotten. He became a sort of "actors' actor," sought out by Wilson Barrett for

Romeo to support Helena Modjeska's Juliet; by Henry Irving to play Claudio in *Much Ado* and Buckingham in *Henry VIII;* and by Mary Anderson to tour America as her Orlando. Later he played Leontes in her *Winter's Tale.*

But for twenty years he cared too little about professional advancement to take a theatre of his own and set up as a star. He claimed, indeed, long after his long career ended, that he had never enjoyed acting. "Never at any time have I gone on the stage without longing for the moment when the curtain would come down on the last act . . . and I am persuaded, as I look back upon my career, that I was not temperamentally suited to my calling."[261]

Bernard Shaw would have agreed with that depressing self-estimate when he reviewed Forbes-Robertson's Romeo in 1895. In the autumn of that year Henry Irving was to make his fifth tour of America, and he called upon Forbes-Robertson to keep the Lyceum open for the season. Teaming with Mrs. Patrick Campbell, he led off with *Romeo and Juliet.* Shaw, who had been outraged by so many of Irving's Lyceum Shakespeares, was pleased to study a Shakespeare coming from a fresh hand. On the whole he gave Forbes-Robertson decent marks as a producer, even though the staging was artistic in the wrong sense—still in the old spectacular, over-decorated, "Irvingesque" manner.

As for his Romeo, though, Shaw thought he really ought to let the part alone. He hadn't the passion for it. He was "very handsome," of course, "very well dressed, very perfectly behaved. His assortment of tones, of gestures, of facial expressions, of attitudes, are limited to half a dozen apiece; but they are carefully selected and all of the best." But he was simply too mannerly, too much the gentleman, too devoted to "law and order," to have any sympathy with "Shakespeare's love of a shindy." He was utterly incapable of the "fire-eyed fury" with which Romeo must attack Tybalt. He "fights with unconcealed repugance: he makes you feel that to do it in that disorderly way, without seconds, without a doctor, shewing temper about it, and actually calling his adversary names, jars unspeakably on him." Gentleman to the last, he laid out the dead body of Paris "as carefully as if he were folding up his best suit of clothes."[262]

Two years later Irving opted to tour the British provinces, and again he relinquished the Lyceum to Forbes-Robertson. But what should he do with it? Irving, seconded by Ellen Terry, urged him to play Hamlet. At the age of forty-four and quite unaware of his fine-boned handsomeness, he was reluctant to present himself in a "young man's part"; but he let himself be persuaded.[263] Shaw, hearing of this, was doubtful. But when Forbes-Robertson came to him "in tribulation" over the part, Shaw gradually became excited about the possibilities. "I am certain I could make Hamlet a success by having it played as Shakespeare meant it," he wrote Ellen Terry. "H. I. makes it a sentimental affair of his own, and this generation has consequently never seen the real thing." But was Forbes-Robertson the ideal medium? "I am afraid F. R. will do the usual dreary business in the old way, and play the bass clarinet for four hours on end, with disastrous results. Lord! how I could make that play jump along at the Lyceum if I were manager. . . . I'd make lightning and thunder (comedy and tragedy) of the second and third acts: the people would say they had never seen such a play before."[264] Would it be possible for a modest, recessive, "notoriously gentlemanly" actor, after nearly a quarter of a century of service in the profession, to make himself into a creditable Hamlet? Probably not into the passionate and doom-eager Hamlet that Irving, and probably Miss Terry, expected. But the Hamlet Shaw had in mind was of a very different kind, and for that Hamlet Forbes-Robertson just might do.

We have always known from Shaw's review[265] his glowing approval of the performance, but only lately when William Armstrong of the University of London put together *all* the evidence, did we realize how profoundly Shaw influenced (practically directed) Forbes-Robertson's concept of the role.[266]

When Forbes-Robertson first came to Shaw "in tribulation" over the part, Shaw began by drawing up a cast-list, including, of course, Mrs. Patrick Campbell as Ophelia. Then Shaw sent him a letter—"four pages of foolscap, closely written"—to instruct him, among other things, how to make "lightning and thunder" out of the middle parts of the play. The letter is lost, unfortunately,[267] but from Shaw's note to Ellen Terry, from his own review of the performance, Nesbitt's review in the *Times,*[268] Clement Scott's review[269] and others, we can be certain about a good many points of Shaw's advice. Shaw would have warned him against such traditional stage business as wriggling snake-like across the floor to watch the King during the Play Scene; against leaping into the King's chair when the King vacates it, "with the shriek of a Bedlamite" (Nesbitt); against breaking the pipe that Guildenstern cannot play. Probably he urged the actor in the scene with Ophelia *not* to become aware of the King and Polonius stirring behind the arras, but simply to read in Ophelia's face the fact that she is betraying him. Nesbitt so reported it, but thought it too subtle an effect for the audience to understand. From later accounts I am convinced that Forbes-Robertson even-

Illus. 136. Sir Johnston Forbes-Robertson as Hamlet.

tually reverted to the conventional way of actually seeing the spies' movements. It was Shaw's idea that the fourth act, the scene of Ophelia's madness, should not be set in a gloomy room in the castle but in a flowering orchard. Nesbitt reported that "the trees being loaded with apple-blossom, the pictorial effect was very fine, a welcome variation upon the customary bleakness of Elsinore." Above all else in the way of "business," Shaw insisted that Fortinbras be brought in at the end (for the first time, perhaps, since the days of Betterton) and that Hamlet's body should be borne off on a shield while "the soldiers shoot."

In spite of his forty-four years, Forbes-Robertson certainly appeared youthful. (Nesbitt put his age at about twenty-five, the King and Queen in their forties). Shaw had encouraged him to take almost boyish delight in every opportunity for fun. "See how he brightens up when the players come," Shaw wrote; "how he tries to talk philosophy with Rosencrantz and Guildenstern the moment they come into the room; how he stops on his country walk with Horatio to lean over the churchyard wall and draw out the gravedigger whom he sees singing at his trade." Clement Scott was charmed by Hamlet's disposition to merriment: "Over and over again it bubbles up and bursts the bounds of will-power to subdue it—this keen sense of humour, this deperate, natural, impulsive *joie de vivre*. We have never seen a Hamlet before who has in him such a subtle element of fun or such an appreciation of the whimsical. Where other Hamlets scowl and snarl, Forbes-Robertson only smiles." Lightness, brightness, and precision were high among Shaw's desiderata, for he wanted Forbes-Robertson to retain as much of the text as possible—"every gem, in his own part or anyone else's, that he can make time for in a spiritedly brisk performance." And Forbes-Robertson adopted Shaw's recommended attack on the lines. "He does not utter half a line; then stop to act; then go on with another half line; and then stop to act again, with the clock running away with Shakespeare's chances all the time. He plays as Shakespeare should be played, on the line and to the line, with the utterance and acting simultaneous, inseparable and in fact identical."[270]

The very fact that Forbes-Robertson could *not* sustain "fire-eyed fury" through his duel with Tybalt had convinced Shaw that he was the ideal actor for Hamlet. For Hamlet, in Shaw's eyes, is not dominated by the common passions, like Romeo or Macbeth or Antony or Othello. His passions are intellectual. He is a *thinking* hero—one "whose passions are those which have produced the philosophy, the poetry, the art, and the statecraft of the world, and not merely those which have produced its weddings, coroner's inquests, and executions."[271] Shaw's Hamlet does not suffer passion, he criticizes passion. Even at those rare moments when he breaks into a sudden rant—"Bloody, bawdy villain! Remorseless, treacherous, lecherous, kindless villain!"—at once he rebukes himself, calling himself ass and whore for so unpacking his heart with words. Even, says Shaw, "his instinctive sexual impulses offend his intellect; so that when he meets the woman who excites them he invites her to join him in a bitter and scornful criticism of their joint absurdity."

If it is true that there is a little of Hamlet in each of us, *this* is the Hamlet that was in Shaw, and this is the Hamlet that Shaw believed, apparently successfully, that he could draw out of Forbes-Robertson. Not surprisingly this Hamlet is very like Shaw's own Dick Dudgeon (which Forbes-Robertson would play in 1900) and his as yet unrealized Jack Tanner and Cicely Waynflete and Julius Caesar (which Forbes-Robertson would create in 1906). Dispassionate, except where indignation is called for, humorous, witty, and supremely wise.

In 1903, the word that Forbes-Robertson would bring his Hamlet to America roused no fever of expectation like that which had preceded Irving twenty years earlier. In spite of his long service to the stage, he had only recently emerged as a star. Informed critics and the cognoscenti, of course, were eager for his Hamlet—this Hamlet reputed to be so unlike any other, so picturesque, so untheatrical, sane, beautiful to look upon, so modern in interpretation yet so exquisite in delivery of the poet's poetry. A month before his arrival the *Theatre* published a long account of his career, his art and his ideas, contrasting his with all the well known Hamlets of the day and emphasizing that "the younger generation in England, especially the romantic, pin their faith on Johnston Forbes-Robertson. For them he is the embodiment of all that is poetical in acting."[272]

How then could it have happened that when he sailed in September of 1903 he left his *Hamlet* production in storage and brought as his main piece his latest London success, a sentimentalized dramatization of Kipling's *The Light That Failed,* in which love conquers tragedy and smothers it in a happy ending? And why did Forbes-Robertson announce soon after his arrival that "under no circumstances" would he do *Hamlet* (or *Macbeth* or *Othello*) during this his first American season? It is also to be wondered at that he did not open his American tour in New York—did not, in fact, perform in New York at all until November 9, well over a month after his arrival.

On November 10 Adolph Klauber of the *New York Times,* grumbling over the fact that the "greatest living

Illus. 137. Gertrude Elliott as Ophelia.

Hamlet" should be first exhibited in a made-over novel, hinted that the reason was collusion between supposedly rival managements. In the following Sunday's *Times* Klauber's colleague John Corbin spelled out the "collusion theory" in detail. Forbes-Robertson had been brought to America by the management of Klaw and Erlanger, presumably on account of his reputation as a Shakespearean. But the Frohman brothers were planning a grand Shakespeare revival by the newly established team of Sothern and Marlowe, to open in the autumn of the following (1904–5) season. The Frohmans persuaded their "mighty opposites" (or colleagues?) to hold off Forbes-Roberston's Shakespeare until his second visit, and then to book him into rival theatres in the same towns that Sothern and Marlowe would be playing. This sporting arrangement presumably would stir up competition, breed publicity, fatten box office returns. Whether or not this collusion theory is true, one curious fact plays into it. We know from Forbes-Robertson himself that Charles Frohman visited him in London, and in discussing his forthcoming tour assured him that *The Light That Failed* would be a "cinch" in America.[273] What else was said, hinted at, or agreed upon during that visit is not known.

The Light That Failed was by no means a "cinch." Whatever Forbes-Robertson may have agreed to, early that winter he dispatched his brother Ian to London to fetch the *Hamlet* sets and costumes from storage. After training his "Kipling" company in their more demanding roles and trying out in various cities outside the metropolis, he finally introduced *Hamlet* to New York on March 7, 1904.[274]

It was not the happiest of opening nights. For some reason the stage hands at the Knickerbocker Theatre made a concerted effort to spoil the occasion—bungling the scene-changes, cursing and swearing in the wings, wandering in their shirt sleeves in sight of the audience. It was noticeable, too, alas, that the "Kipling" actors were most of them unworthy of their Shakespearean assignments. Yet of Forbes-Robertson's performance Klauber could declare in his *New York Times* review that "it has been accepted by intelligent playgoers everywhere as the one truly great Hamlet of the modern stage," and "the result was such an evening of Shakespearean enjoyment as comes once or twice in a generation."

Inevitably there were objections, especially from the older critics. J. R. Towse of the *Post* suggested that playgoers of the oldest generation, schooled in the traditions of Macready, Phelps, and Charles Kean—or the younger generation, who cherished memories of the emotional fervor of Fechter, the melancholy grace, brilliant reading, and fiery passion of Edwin

Booth, the extraordinary if much-debated performance of Henry Irving—"might be inclined to deny that Mr. Robertson's conception is that of Hamlet at all."[275] Many "old-fashioned folk" will accuse this "nervous, intellectual, impulsive, and essentially modern actor" of committing "a most deplorable sacrifice—of poetic and romantic elevation—in fine, of those very qualities which most enthrall and encourage the imagination." Towse had to acknowledge that by virtue of rapid speaking, of continuous action (the Shavian doctrine of playing "on the line and to the line"), and of reduction of waits during scene changes, much more of Shakespeare's text was given than he had ever heard before. Yet he had to insist that the actor had overdone mere *rapidity.* Not that the actor had gabbled, but that he had taken everything, indiscriminately, too fast. Certain portions of *Hamlet* must be rendered deliberately or their significance is lost: "owing to the rapid pace which he maintained throughout his performance, he was absolutely least effective in the soliloquies . . . because he succeeded in bringing out about one-half of their full meaning." We were not given time to *see* him think or to reflect upon what has just been spoken. Even so, Towse granted that this Hamlet was "inexpressibly superior to the multiform mimicries of Beerbohm Tree or the affectations of Wilson Barrett." And a year later when for some reason Forbes-Robertson's opening night was scantily attended, Towse positively *scolded* the New York public for neglecting "a player commonly spoken of as the legitimate successor to Henry Irving."[276]

William Winter disliked Forbes-Robertson's Hamlet so hotly that to read the opening sentence of his review of the first performance one might conclude that the had not even been present.[277] "The melancholy Dane has come, exceptionally drear," he wrote, "and persons who have not already been sufficiently steeped in gloom, by the dolorous proceedings of this ghastly dramatic season, can obtain a fresh immersion in solemnity by repairing to the Knickerbocker Theatre and gazing on Mr. Forbes-Robertson in the guise of Hamlet." Winter's long column is a mass of sarcasms, irrelevant and seemingly motiveless. The actor, Winter says, is able and experienced, but after thirty years in the profession he offers us nothing more than imitations of conventional effects. His costume and make-up are handsome—a tribute to the sartorial and tonsorial artists—"and, as everybody knows, a miserable man who sees ghosts and contemplates suicide, necessarily must be, and always is, more than commonly scrupulous about his personal appearance." The actor's voice creaks a little, according to Winter, the tones dry, metallic, gaspy. His most Hamlet-like facial expression is "lantern-jawed tenuity." Bits of text are restored, but only capriciously. The reintroduction of Reynaldo is profitless since Polonius acts his tedious senility so badly. Fortinbras is retained "to point the moral for which nobody cares."

A year later Winter spoke of Forbes-Robertson more generously—as scholar, writer, painter, and so on—but not generously of his Hamlet.[278] It was not poetic, it did not exhibit a great personality, it did not exemplify pitiful man vis-à-vis the boundless and awful universe of God, suffering the "lethal misery from which there is no refuge but the grave." It was cold and uninspired and it no more possessed the temperament of Hamlet than did any of the dozen or so German, French, Italian, or our own tame American Hamlets that have invaded our stages since the passing of Booth.

What was it then that our American audiences—especially the younger generation—saw in Forbes-Robertson that reinforced their notion of what Hamlet ought to be? In reporting an interview with the actor, John Corbin attempted to identify the dramatic character with the man:

> The only wonder is that Forbes Robertson did not venture as Hamlet a decade earlier. Even sitting in a modern drawing room in a frock coat, and smoking the usual cigarette, he suggested more of the royal Dane than many an actor man (good old London term of abuse) gets into an entire performance. His eyes are deep and divining; his large, acquiline features have in repose a pale cast of melancholy that gives way when he talks to an animation restrained only by the inherent dignity of the man of the world and the scholar. Several times, as he talked, he got up and strode about the room as he had done the night before in delivering the famous soliloquy on death, his eyes alight with meaning, his bearing erect and princely, and through it all he seems the soul of indifference. . . . From his youth up he must have been, to invert the old phrase, Hamlet without the play.[279]

Adolph Klauber tells us that this Hamlet is less romantic and vehement than E. H. Sothern's, less picturesque and salient in externals than Irving's, less forcible in imagination and less richly colored in emotion than Edwin Booth's. But what attracts us is that

> it impersonates in the highest degree the modern feeling for simple and flawlessly human art. . . . As Forbes-Robertson sits in a leather arm chair . . . the thoughtful profile, the melancholy luminous eyes, the simple dignified attitude suggest nothing so much as the Prince of Denmark. On the stage these attributes heighten and kindle under the spell of beautiful thought and gracious human emotion, but they retain their quality of exquisitely modulated life-likeness.
>
> Tall and spare is this Hamlet, princely erect in carriage, with hands that bespeak in their exquisite refinement the

soul born in the purple: artistically sparing of gesture, yet eloquent in the least flutter of susceptibility and emotion: with a lean countenance of aquiline profile, and hollow, ascetic cheeks, almost gaunt: with large, sensitive mouth, sad, deep, luminous, eloquent eyes, and a voice—but words fail for that voice, leaving the fattest, most opulent dictionary bankrupt.

If it is less than golden and crimson in its emotional suggestion, it is more than silver. In its moments of repression it mutters sonorously like an organ, and like an organ it swells in passionate utterance with a thousand musical modulations. It caresses, it pleads, it sobs, and it cries out in pain. And every tone is replete with delicate thought and apt meaning.[280]

Forbes-Robertson always believed that Klauber's long and eloquent review was the making of his reputation in America. On this one matter of the beauty and expressiveness of his voice the comments through the next dozen years are legion. "Never," wrote a Baltimore critic, "has the English of Shakespeare sounded more beautiful than it does as it comes from the lips of this actor."[281] It would become common among oldsters in the 1930s and after to declare that the only voice comparable to Forbes-Robertson's is that of John Gielgud.

It was the voice that demanded first attention of H. T. Parker when Forbes-Robertson played Hamlet in Boston in 1907:

Here, at last, is a voice that may speak poetry poetically, that vibrates, and makes hearers vibrate, to each poetic image, that may keep the thought, the feeling and the music of Shakespeare's verse. The clarity, the rhythm, the emotional color, the suggestion of the idea behind go side by side in these tones, and live indeed in them. . . . With his tones alone Mr. Robertson might almost act Hamlet in the dark.

Yet lest it appear that Parker saw in Forbes-Robertson only the superb elocutionist, he hurries on to stress the human reality of this Hamlet, being careful, too, to dissociate it from "naturalism," which was the hallmark of the best modern drama and which some misguided actors were wrong--headedly endeavoring to impose upon Shakespeare.

It is the passionate sensibility and the pervading humanity of this Hamlet that makes it, as it seems to us, so characteristic of our time. No actor may act Hamlet in the naturalistic way, though some have tried, because he is all of idealizing poetry. But our time does ask a Hamlet that shall be neither a poetic abstraction nor the gloom-wrapped protagonist of a tragedy of filial revenge. It bids the actor idealize him humanly, and Mr. Robertson fulfils its bidding. It bids him even touch parts of the play lightly, gracefully, buoyantly, with the humor of a quietly alert mind. It bids him summon tenderness toward Ophelia, compassion toward his mother, affection towards his friends. It asks of him something of the fire and the sweetness of noble youth. Mr. Robertson's Hamlet gives all these, and adds the tragedy of a sensitive temperament that for us is the tragedy of Hamlet.[282]

The next day Parker prepared a second notice, first to praise the comparative simplicity of Forbes-Robertson's scenery, which could be changed so quickly as barely to impede the narrative flow. "Thus, from beginning to end, his *Hamlet* has movement and intensity as a dramatic narrative." Then back again to the "humanity" of the production, for on second thoughts Parker recognized that it was not Forbes-Robertson alone but nearly all in his company (by 1907) who were capable of speaking like men rather than like robots.

Still more, it gains pace from the readiness and the alertness with which each player speaks his lines and does his share in the action. Mr. Robertson has not only humanized the part of Hamlet, but he seeks to humanize the play. He has trained his company not to stalk through some conventional stage ceremony, not to make with portentous deliberation "the points" of stage tradition, not to wring each line to the last slow drop, but to take the play, their parts and their speeches naturally, simply, and humanly. After all Claudius, Polonius, Laertes and the courtiers were very human beings, though they do speak verse in the most hallowed tragedy of our stage, and they are the more interesting and appealing beings when they are kept as human as Mr. Robertson has taught his company to make them. Moreover, as some of the actors prove, it is quite possible to speak the verse briskly and keep its poetic quality. "Hamlet" so acted is a new experience to most of us. As a play it has once more the motion, the vitality, the possessing human interest that stage convention and sluggish pace have long denied it—and most misunderstandingly.[283]

Not long after his New York success in 1904, Forbes-Robertson concluded his American tour with a surprising gesture. For several years George Pierce Baker and other members of the English faculty at Harvard University had been staging Shakespeare and other Renaissance plays (*The Silent Woman, Roister Doister,* etc.) with students on a reconstructed Elizabethan stage in Sanders Theatre. When Baker heard that the great Hamlet was coming to America he invited him to play on "Shakespeare's own stage." Forbes-Robertson replied that he should like it of all things. Accordingly, after special adjustment of text and stage business and some special rehearsals, on April 5 and 6, 1904, for the first time in America *Hamlet* was performed by professional actors in a setting very like that for which the play was written. The audience, a critical one made up largely of Harvard faculty and students and guests from Tufts, Wellesley, MIT, and so on, was impressed by the fact that the absence of modern scenery was no loss at all but served practically to focus attention more firmly than ever upon the figure of Hamlet and to clarify the narrative in which he is involved.[284]

Thereafter Forbes-Robertson came to America frequently—in 1905, 1906, 1909, 1910, and 1911—usually brining his American-born wife Gertrude Elliott, whom he had married in 1900, as his leading lady. He played Hamlet regularly, of course, together with a mixed repertory of modern roles, and along the way he created two famous modern works, *one* of which added many laurels to his crown. Shaw wrote *Caesar and Cleopatra* specifically for him in 1898, immediately after his triumphant Lyceum Hamlet. After many delays he produced it, first in New York on October 30, 1906, for a run of 49 performances, then in London on November 25, 1907, for 40 performances more. The genetic relationship between Forbes-Robertson's Hamlet and Shaw's Caesar is implicit in Shaw's pronouncement just before the London production: "I wrote *Caesar and Cleopatra* for Forbes-Robertson, because he is the classic actor of our day, and had a right to require such a service from me. . . . Forbes-Robertson is the only actor I know who can find out the feeling of a speech from its cadence. His art meets the dramatist's art directly, picking it up for completion and expression without explanations or imitations. . . . Without him *Caesar and Cleopatra* would not have been written."[285]

The second famous new work I wish for the actor's sake we could forget, but we cannot forget—for in its time it far outshone even Shaw's masterpiece in common estimation and rivaled *Hamlet* in popularity. In September of 1908, Forbes-Robertson staged Jerome K. Jerome's *The Passing of the Third Floor Back.* From

Illus. 138. The Elizabethan stage at Harvard, as it stood in 1904–5 for the Forbes-Robertson company to play *Hamlet.* In 1916 Forbes-Robertson performed *Hamlet* three times on the (reconstructed) stage to celebrate Shakespeare's birthday and to close his own professional career on April 26.

then on it was demanded everywhere. It made a fortune for the actor. It was his albatross. A simple-minded morality play, it is a sort of upside-down version of Gorki's *The Lower Depths.* Into a drab but "respectable" London boarding house, filled with various types of poseurs, fakers, hypocrites, and near-criminal types, there comes a poor Stranger, assigned to the last and nearly unlivable quarters at the top of the building. In a series of kindly confrontations with the various inmates, through his gentleness, sweetness, goodness, and wisdom he converts the lot of them into Good People. Then he disappears. Something miraculous, Christ-like, has passed. Audiences craved this play. Ministers of every religious persuasion preached sermons about it. At the farewell banquet for Forbes-Robertson in 1916, one speaker called it "one of the greatest sermons ever heard." Meanwhile the maudlin sentimentality of it palled upon the actor. Hesketh Pearson records how one evening in London just before the Stranger's entrance, Forbes-Robertson turned his eyes upward and was heard to mutter, "Chr-r-rist! Will they never let me give up this *bloody* part?" The door opened, and, Christ-like, he went on stage to play it.[286]

After nearly forty years in the profession, in 1912–13 Forbes-Robertson ran through his major repertory in London and the provinces and announced his English retirement. In June of 1913 King George knighted him, so that when he came to America that autumn to begin his final rounds with us, he came as Sir Johnston.

It was his seventh American visit, counting his season as Orlando with Mary Anderson in 1885; and there would be an eighth, for it was his plan this season to perform in nearly twenty cities of the eastern United States and Canada, and after a rest to come once more in 1915–16 for quick visits to a vast number of smaller towns, especially in the central and western states.

By now a full-fledged and experienced manager, he brought in 1913 a company of over sixty performers and aides, nine carloads of scenery, and a repertory of eight plays, including *Hamlet, Caesar and Cleopatra,* and the inescapable *Passing of the Third Floor Back.* The Shubert brothers had just completed building their palatial Shubert Theatre in New York, and the honors flowed in both directions on October 2 when Sir Johnston dedicated it with a performance of *Hamlet.*[287]

During this visit he gave us two of his Shakespeares which few Americans had ever seen. Shylock, which he offered at the Shubert beginning on November 21, he had played only rarely. Not a favorite with him, he first attempted it in Manchester in 1906, played it in one or two American cities in 1907, and introduced it to London only during his round of farewells in 1913. For many reasons it was a role he could do without. To be sure, he could *look* the part. As the *Philadelphia Inquirer* observed in 1907:

> In appearance his Shylock is ideal. A tall figure, spare to gauntness, crouched from age and an assumed humility, but which rises to something like majesty when defied, taunted or scorned; a head, high-browed and serried with lines that denote an unceasing battle with persecution, religious and commercial, eyes that snap fury or blink cunning . . . such is Mr. Robertson's Shylock externally.[288]

But the role was staled from repetition. Every serious actor of the day—American, English, Italian, German—had it in his repertory, and all of these lived still in the shadow of Henry Irving, whose performance and whose "show" were unforgettable. Yet, as Frederick Schrader of the *Dramatic Mirror* and various other critics suggested, perhaps Forbes-Robertson's Shylock was more nearly "the Jew that Shakespeare drew" than the more majestic and lofty Shylock of Irving.[289] As H. T. Parker pointed out, year by year Irving built his Shylock into an apotheosis of the finer and nobler traits of the Jewish character. He appealed so much for sympathy and admiration, that "before he was done, it had lost nearly all relation to *The Merchant of Venice* and to the Jew that Shakespeare set therein." Forbes-Robertson delivered *only what he found in the text.* He emphasized hatred of Christians, and eagerness for revenge on the unhappy representative who had fallen within his power. He made no apologies; "the part here was stripped of the lofty glamor and set sharply in contrast with the charity of the Christians." Parker noted how in the Trial Scene this Shylock glittered, quivered, and almost writhed with inner vindictiveness, malevolence, and confidence of triumph—then when baffled, shrieked out of black wonder at the turn of fate. There was no dignity, no pathos in his blind, agonized exit: "a figure of dismay and despair, of frenzied fear and frenzied abasement, fleeing he knew not whither or how, his garments flying, his eyes raving, his arms beating vainly. So more than one artist has pictured Judas fleeing."[290]

On December 15 he offered New York his second Shakespearean novelty—Othello, a role that he had played occasionally since 1897. Remembering Shaw's recognition of the actor's lack of "fire-eyed" fury in Romeo's fight with Tybalt, and Shaw's opinion that generally he was deficient in the "common passions," we can anticipate what most professional observers held, that Othello was simply outside Forbes-Robertson's range. Klauber of the *New York Times* put the case almost as Shaw might have:

Illus. 139. Forbes-Robertson as Shylock. Courtesy of the University of Illinois Theatre.

Othello is one of those Shakespearean roles which seems most to demand a definite physical equipment. . . . He is a sort of Shakespearean superman of grand passions. And for his complete interpretation he demands more brawn than brain. Mr. Forbes-Robertson, on the other hand, is essentially an actor of the intellect, with a sensitive, sympathetic organism capable of very definite and beautiful gradations of emotion. And though not without fire on occasion, his best effects are produced through processes that suggest a ruling mentality in the man. That is one of the things that makes his Hamlet extraordinary.[291]

His costume and make-up roused expectations that could not be fulfilled. As Arthur Ruhl of the *Tribune* noted:

There was a certain thrill of surprised satisfaction when the tall white-wrapped Moor [in the first two acts he wore a white turban and a white mantle over deep red underdress; in the later acts robes of white and gold] strode across the stage twilight, silent, sinister, commanding, with a strong suggestion of wild force and fire in the quick flash of white teeth in the dark inscrutable face.[292]

But what followed was rather an "admirable reading" than the tragedy of *Othello.* His eloquent address to the Senate was superb, of course; his loving reunion with Desdemona at Cyprus tender and beautiful; his denunciation of Cassio after the brawl in the street hard and cold as ice; his death-speech deeply moving. But in the third and fourth acts "those cumulative bursts of passion" which as Klauber says, "sweep the spectator off his mental pins" simply could not happen. "One misses here the swift rush of events, the big pulse of passion, the crashing crescendo" with which the play thunders toward its denouement.

The best that Parker of Boston, who would never fault Forbes-Robertson, could make of it was that the actor deliberately rejected the common concept of Othello as a barbarous "elemental," deliberately poeticized him, made him a patrician Moor, who might indeed "fetch his life and being from men of royal siege." The impression, said Parker, is "that of an Othello whom Van Dyck might have painted had he concerned himself with the Venice of Shakespeare's play . . ."[293]

Illus. 140. Forbes-Robertson's Othello.

After his 1913–14 tour and a year of rest he returned to America for his final Farewell—not, as certain American critics feared, in the Sarah Bernhardt manner of doing the same performances to the same audiences for the money that was in it, but to travel 18,000 miles playing one- and two-night stands in 118 smaller towns and cities where he had never been seen. He appeared in every state in the nation except Nevada, Vermont, New Hampshire, and Maine. He carried only three plays—*Hamlet, The Passing of the Third Floor Back,* and *The Light that Failed.* Prices were kept reasonably low, from $2.00 to $3.50, and managements succeeded in selling out in spite of the newly invented competition of 10-cent "moving pictures." He flatly declined many a pressing (and obviously profitable) invitation to major cities along his route (Los Angeles, for instance) on the grounds that he had been there before and that he would not break his commitment to a single one-night stand that had been arranged for him.[294]

His professional tour ended not in New York, but in Brooklyn, where as a gesture of farewell to the history of conventional Shakespeare production he discarded painted scenery and played *Hamlet* on a stage hung only with curtains. "Vast curtains of gray velvet under varying lights inclose the stage and frame the short flight of steps that lead to a smaller inner stage, where the background is of blue." The Brooklyn critic found "these simple, handsome draperies more pleasing to the eye, more unobtrusive, more satisfying to the imagination, more thoroughly suggestive of pomp and circumstance" than any setting for *Hamlet* that Forbes-Robertson had ever used.[295]

Illus. 141. Forbes-Robertson and the Polonius of J. H. Barnes.

But there was an epilogue to this tour. The year 1916 was the tercentenary of Shakespeare's death. Shakespeare's death day and reputed birthday were both April 23. In 1916, April 23 fell on a Sunday. On the Monday, Tuesday, and Wednesday following, Forbes-Robertson and company played *Hamlet* again, as they had done twelve years earlier, on the Elizabethan stage in the Sanders Theatre at Harvard. In his curtain speech on Monday he announced that these three performances marked the absolute end of his stage career. He would never act for the public again.[296]

It would not do to call Forbes-Robertson, this actor who never wanted to be an actor, the greatest Shakespearean to visit America during the generation before the Great War, for his Shakespearean roles were few. But for his Hamlet alone he may surely be called the *finest.* In face and body, and for the extraordinary sensitivity with which these instruments expressed every thought and feeling appropriate to the role, he was the ideal Hamlet to look upon. But above all other instruments of expression was his incredibly beautiful, flexible, sensitive voice. "Hardly a thought, a fancy, an emotion or a mood," said H. T. Parker, "fails to transmute for the instant the speech that utters it. The blind might sit before Forbes-Robertson's Hamlet, and though their eyes are sealed, yet apprehend much of it." And the wonder of it all, which through these decades we have been seeking, Forbes-Robertson achieved that kind of "realism" which belongs to Shakespearean verse—the realism which the Gielguds and Ashcrofts and Oliviers and Pascoes and Richardsons have brought to the stages of our own time. As Parker *then* put it, "This imparting and illuminating speech is flowing with the sensuous beauty of music and as swiftly and easily as though it were no more than ordinary human converse." Parker speaks for our day as well as his own when he declares, "We cannot abide Shakespeare spouted after the manner of the old days. No more will we endure Shakespeare chattered after the manner of drawing room comedy. We ask a speech of beauty in itself, of music in itself, that shall also bear thought and passion and character, and that shall seem a human speech exalted into poetry. Perhaps Forbes-Robertson has taught us to hold this high exaction of our Shakespearean actors. Alone of all of them . . . does he fulfill it."[297]

Chapter V

End of the Tradition: Part I
Mansfield and Mantell

When Edwin Booth and Lawrence Barrett were working in partnership in the later 1880s, they had considerable difficulty, as is well known, in filling their companies with actors truly capable of supporting their high endeavors. Booth himself, who had long been regarded America's leading tragic actor, had been scolded in the early 1880s for acting badly ("shambled about the stage ungracefully"), producing badly (letting his plays be "merely pitchforked upon the stage"), and surrounding himself with "mere sticks" in order to make his own acting look better.[1] As a matter of fact, during their partnership Booth and Barrett hired the best actors they could find. The pickings were slim.

As popular taste for Shakespeare and the classics, classically performed, gave ground to a taste for new plays—parlor drama, sensation drama, spectacle, and farce (Nym Crinkle had been proclaiming at least from the early 1870s that "tragedy was dying or dead"),[2] fewer and fewer young persons coming into the profession concerned themselves much with perfecting the histrionic techniques by which Booth and his father before him were judged great. The new drama, increasingly a prose drama, rarely called for grand gestures and full-voiced word-music. "Realism," "colloquialism," "being life-like" were code-words for the theatre that lay just ahead. The triumphant end-product of these impulses, when major writers arrived to make use of them, would be the brainy actors of the Shaw generation—Granville-Barker, Lillah McCarthy, Mrs. Pat Campbell, Sybil Thorndike, and the like, but in America of the 1880s when Booth and Barrett especially needed strong support, the profession was overcrowded with clothes-horses, affected mannerists, ranters, "superfluous lags," and sticks.

Or if there did emerge from the crowd of mediocrities a reasonably effective and classic-style actor—a Louis James or James O'Neill or Frederick Warde, he would take himself out of the market, assemble his own company, and set off as a "star" in his own right.

And finally the command of the Shakespeare stage in America was shot down for our native actors by the invasion of foreign visitors—Irving and Terry, Salvini, Langtry, Bernhardt, Sonnenthal, Bandmann, Mounet-Sully, and many more. America was the foreigners' gold mine and they came again and again to enrich themselves. Our audiences were attracted by their glamour or notoriety, by the novelty of hearing Shakespeare in foreign languages, or—in the case of Irving and Terry—by their attractive personalities and social reputations, their superior stage productions and excellent acting companies. So we filled their coffers, often at the expense of our own best promising professionals.

Booth and Barrett, as we have seen, looked to Mary Anderson to carry on the classical tradition, but she quitted the stage a year or two before they did. After Anderson perhaps Modjeska, but she was aging, or more likely Julia Marlowe. It is doubtful that they would ever have seriously considered Richard Mansfield, who had not yet attempted Shakespeare, or even "found himself" except as a popular musical entertainer or a character actor in certain spectacular and peculiarly repulsive roles. He first made his mark in 1883 as the Baron Chevrial in Octave Feuillet's *A Parisian Romance*.[3] Chevrial is a degenerate millionaire roué, who attempts in sheer malice to destroy artists and business associates who surround him, but dies in horrible convulsions at the end of the fourth act. Chevrial's performance was an astonishing display, always good to thrill a Saturday night audience, and Mansfield kept it in his repertory all his life, but nothing in it suggested that he would ever qualify as an exponent of the "higher drama." In the words of William Winter, it only promulgated "the well-known specious doctrine—especially rife since the advent of that reprehensible French novelist Zola—that the right way to exhibit, exalt, and inculcate virtue is to portray all that is foul and hideous in vice."[4] In 1887 and 1888 Mansfield created Mr. Hyde, the criminal alter ego of Dr. Jekyll in a dramatization of Robert Louis Stevenson's *The Strange Case.*[5] Here in full sight of the audience and without benefit of make-up but only a bit of green light he could transform himself from the handsome Jekyll into "a carnal monster of unqualified evil . . . remarkable for loathsome reptile-like ferocity."[6] To Booth and Barrett such carryings-on probably seemed more like carnival tricks than serious acting. And if they knew Mansfield personally they may well have disliked him, as many in the profession did, for his vanity, jealousy, rudeness, overweening ambition, and occasional unscrupulousness in professional dealings.

Richard Mansfield

Yet Mansfield (1857–1907)[7] had a remarkable range of talents, and if he had lived a decade longer (and been spared certain meannesses of character) he might finally have fulfilled the Booth-Barrett hopes for the future of classic tragedy. As it was he played only four leading Shakespeare roles, and never touched the "great ones." He was handsome enough—not tall but well-built—with a voice so powerful that it could outroar whole armies in violent combat while he called for "A horse! A horse!"[8] It was also a voice capable of displaying a great variety of tones—or "colors," as he called them: a "blue" voice for prayer, a "yellow" voice for jealousy, a "steel gray" voice for sarcasm, a "livid red" voice for hot rage, and so on.[9]

He practiced many skills. The son of an accomplished violinist and a world-famous soprano (Erminia Rudersdorff, 1822–82), he inherited musical abilities. He played the piano, he composed. Among his earliest accomplishments were performances in the English provinces and in America of Gilbert and Sullivan's Sir Joseph Porter, Major General Stanley, John Wellington Wells, and Koko. He is credited with inventing the tune of (Sullivan was stumped by it) "I am the very model of a modern major general."[10] Educated in England, France, and Germany, he was conversant in three languages, and he delighted in dialect parts. He wrote poetry—"verses" we should call them—and set them to music. He studied painting in England with William Powell Frith (he of *Derby Day* and other celebrated genre pictures), and for a while he contemplated a career as a painter. As a stage producer he was singularly conscious of what the stage looked like, and his "painterly eye" was responsible for splendid stage pictures.

Though not for the most part in sympathy with the directions taken by major modern dramatists, he did permit his wife Beatrice Cameron to play Ibsen's Nora *(A Doll's House),*[11] and he introduced Shaw to America: Bluntschli in *Arms and the Man* and Dick Dudgeon in *The Devil's Disciple.* He ended his career with a production of *Peer Gynt.* He sought constantly for new plays and he propagandized for an American National Theatre.

Illus. 142. Richard Mansfield.

But what he especially sought in the new drama was a gallery of great men of history—Julius Caesar, Frederick the Great, Napoleon, and so forth—all idealized of course, to provide exemplars of high and noble conduct in government. Then too, for good measure, he would have some historic villains—Nero, Ivan the Terrible—to show his own versatility and the reverse of the moral coin. Shaw tried to oblige him. Shaw said that he studied Mansfield and then read up on Napoleon, and that in *The Man of Destiny* actor and character were one and the same.[12] Mansfield, wanting a glorified Napoleon, indignantly rejected Shaw's "vulgar Corsican" and played instead scenes from an innocuous Napoleon play by Lorimer Stoddard. Similarly he dismissed Shaw's *Caesar and Cleopatra* because he could make no sense of a Caesar who was not a glorious world-conqueror but a modest, humorous commonsensical man of affairs.

Somehow, almost unbelievably, he accepted Shaw's *Candida* sight unseen, and with it even contracted and imported Janet Achurch, the actress Shaw had chosen to play the name part.[13] But very early in the rehearsals Mansfield canceled his agreement and sent the manuscript home. He found that there was no "action" in the play, that Marchbanks (poet as hero?) was not for him. Then, too, Miss Achurch out-acted him and by her manners (gin and cigarettes) offended him personally. The event is worth mentioning here because in his letter of rejection Mansfield unblushingly laid out his prescription of what a play should be and mean.

> Candida is charming—it is more than charming—it is delightful, and I can well see how you have put into it much that is the best of yourself—but—pardon me—it is *not* a play—at least I do not think it is a play . . . it is talk, talk, talk. . .
>
> You'll have to write a play that a *man* can play and about a woman that heroes fought for and a bit of ribbon that a knight tied to his lance.
>
> The stage is for romance and love and truth and honor. To make men better and noble. To cheer them on the way.—Life is real, Life is earnest, and the grave is not the goal. . . .
>
> Be not like dumb, driven cattle
> Be a hero in the fight!
>
> Go on, Shaw; Beatrice and I are with you—you will be always welcome as a brother. We want a great work from you.[14]

He got no more from Shaw.

Eventually Mansfield found the play which exactly suited his taste and talents—Edmond Rostand's *Cyrano de Bergerac,* which he played through the entire season of 1898–99 and revived a few times thereafter. Full of action, poetry, wit, irony, sentiment, with "a woman that heroes fought for," and—in lieu of a bit of ribbon on his lance—Cyrano's famous "white plume." Cyrano is almost the only play from Mansfield's repertory, apart from his few Shaws and Shakespeares, that is remembered, read, and performed generations later. Yet, curiously, Mansfield affected to dislike *Cyrano,* and said that he acted it only for the money that was in it.[15] In 1910 William Winter, brushing it off as "the fad of a moment," declared it "as dead to our stage as *Pericles,* or *Alexander the Great.*"[16]

In 1887–88 Henry Irving, spending the season (his third) in America, was so taken by Mansfield's character acting as Chevrial, his charm in a romantic farce called *Prince Karl,* and his astonishing transformations from Jekyll to Hyde—reminiscent perhaps of his own success as Mathias in *The Bells*—that he invited Mansfield to London and reserved a time in the fall of 1888 when Mansfield could occupy Irving's own theatre, the Lyceum. When word got about that Daniel Bandmann had obtained a version of *Dr. Jekyll and Mr. Hyde* and planned to take it to London a month before Mansfield got there, Irving was so intent upon serving Mansfield that he rented the only London theatre that Bandmann could have secured, pretending that he needed it for special rehearsals of a non-existent play of his own. Thus through Irving's generous assistance and certain hurry-up arrangements, Mansfield entered the London scene a few days before Bandmann and beat him at the game.[17]

Yet all of Irving's friendly intentions were wasted. The London audiences soon had enough of Mansfield's extravagant mummery and stayed away. When he had played his limited repertory from August 4 to December 1, he owed Irving £1,675 for rent.

But he would not surrender. Common sense would have sent him scurrying home to recoup his losses with American audiences, but he was determined to conquer London and even to outshine Irving, whom somehow he had come to distrust. He would produce Shakespeare. He rented the Globe Theatre in late December and, to mark time, opened with *Prince Karl.* Unfortunately, his voice fell victim to the foul winter weather and he had to stop playing. He engaged Lionel Brough to take over the Globe temporarily, retired to pleasant Bournemouth to recuperate, to regroup his intentions, and to lay plans for a grand revival of *Richard III.* It was to open in mid-March.

Writing to E. A. Dithmar early in January he was downright exuberant.

> Richard III is to be an interesting production at least. If archæology is the rage, then archæology they shall have—and whereas Mr. Irving is said to be correct (but is really only "effective") I shall strive to be both. For the first time the actual armor—the actual Fechweise of the period of Richard will be reproduced from the most careful tracings in the British Museum and under the supervision of Egerton Castle (the greatest authority here) & all the costumes & scenes under the direction of Seymour Lucas A.R.A. My ideas of Richard III are different I think in many respects to the accepted & usual, and may perhaps on that account be interesting. . . . I shall endeavor to make Richard a man

who *might* perchance be *reasonably* supposed to win a woman under such circumstances as those under which he wins Lady Anne—and as I find that he was inordinately fond of dress, I shall dress him finely. Please God I may be successful.[18]

The planning of the production, as described by Mansfield in *Harper's Weekly,* was pure pleasure. "There is as much delight in producing a play," he wrote, "as in building a great house with many rooms in it of original design and adornment."[19]

When he came up from Bournemouth, the first scene, the Tower of London, happened to be set in place. He and Seymour Lucas called for calciums and tried lighting it for every time of day. They decided upon early morning—"that pale white light that gives atmosphere and mystery, and lifts the towers higher, throws deeper shadows into angles, and helps the eye to imagine the black waters of the moat, the grim teeth of the portcullis, the little door in the warder's tower, and walls and yards, draw-bridge and battlements—real, all real." The second scene, in which King Henry was to lose his life, would promise horror. The doomed King lay in a recessed bed, with one small window dimly lighting his prayer book. From one side a stained glass window glowed faintly on a prie-dieu and crucifix. Overhead one ancient lamp gave flickering gloomy light, and a fire burned low in the chimney cave.

From this ominous picture we move to one dancing with light and life. The King's funeral procession would not be halted in a London street, as was the stage custom, but somewhere south of the Thames, along the road towards Chertsey. Flowers are blooming, hedges are white with May blossom. Silver birches bend over grass and fern that hint of violets and primroses. Across fields stretching back into the summer haze we see far off the roofs and towers of old London. Near at hand on the right is a farmhouse with thatched roof, green with lichen and ivy, on the left a cottage; a deep-rutted road runs between them. In the center foreground stands a broken wall, another birch behind it, a carpet of grass before it, buttercups and daisies growing at its foot. "All shall be brilliant with an atmosphere that vibrates in the summer sunshine, and makes you long to lie back on the grass and hark for the note of the lark out of sight up in the gray-blue." A scene set for love in springtime.

Unquestionably these and all the scenes were splendidly composed, as was especially the camp scene at night, with drifting clouds and uncertain moon, a low-lying, bleak country broken by storm-tossed willows and murky pools. The red glow of campfires near Richard's tent, and far off the higher flames of Richmond's watch-fires. Old William Frith had not made a painter of Mansfield, but he taught him how to make pictures.

But what of the text? "Colley Cibber was to be entirely discarded, and Shakespeare enthroned once more." So Mansfield declared in *Harper's Weekly* as late as 1890, but what he had actually staged was a hodgepodge of Cibber, Shakespeare, and "history." He claimed in a letter to Winter[20] that he used Cibber's structure, Shakespeare's language and the "truth" about Richard Duke of Gloster. The rising curtain exhibited his own quite unnecessary invention of a procession scene outside the Tower of London—Edward IV's Queen Elizabeth and a host of followers taking up residence in the Tower. Then out popped Gloster from the warder's tower to deliver the bulk of Shakespeare's opening soliloquy, including

> I—that am rudely stamp'd. . .
> Cheated of feature by dissembling nature,
> Deform'd, unfinish'd—sent before my time
> Into this breathing world, scarce half made up. . .

But Mansfield knew perfectly well that in 1471 Gloster was by no means the halting, hump-shouldered, middle-aged, growling monster that Shakespeare clearly made him and that actors had always shown him to be. In truth Gloster was then a youth of nineteen, slightly crippled perhaps, but handsome and athletic. So a mere *suggestion* of physical deformity would suffice, and the tone of his lines referring to it would waver between irony, self-pity, and joke. He would take up the role of villain, but cheerily, as a mischief-maker, as one would take up any promising profession.

The scene changed to a gloomy room in the Tower for the customarily interpolated assassination of Henvy VI. Richard entered the King's prison chamber swiftly and gracefully—a sinuous, debonair, smiling, cynical young devil. He leaned lazily against the wall, warmed his hands at the fire, bantered with his victim, tested his sword point with his fingertip. When he had listened to enough of the old man's querulous denunciation, he smiled and, as one critic put it, ran him through as a poulterer might skewer a fowl.[21] Withdrawing his weapon, he wiped it on the curtains without a sign of compunction, and turned toward the audience with his ironic (not snarling) soliloquy.

His wooing of Lady Anne in the blossomy field was such a mixture of seeming earnestness and devotion, spiced with bravado and wit, that as Wilstach says, "Anne found him more irresistible than impossible." And his after-soliloquy, "Was ever woman in this humor woo'd?" was uttered brightly and cheerily, "in light tones of boastful raillery which his sharp tongue clipped off at a merry pace."[22]

Illus. 143. Mansfield as Richard III and his wife Beatrice Cameron as Lady Anne. Folger Shakespeare Library.

He sustained this cheerful pursuit of crime and connivance until he reached the Throne Scene—the point where he, like most actors of Richard, finds his world beginning to crumble, where he gives way to uncertainty, worry, even the beginnings of remorse. Mansfield signaled the change with a bit of stage mechanics that every critic noticed and most deplored as too heavy-handedly theatrical. While he brooded on his throne, sensing the loyalty of Buckingham slipping away, hearing of the defection of other allies, ordering the murder of the little princess, a beam of light shining through a stained glass window fell upon his hand. It was red light. His hand, as it were, was bathed in blood. Shuddering, he slipped down the steps to the foot of the throne, and from that moment, aging, he piled crime upon crime, knowing, as all Richards know, that destiny was driving him toward death. Only in the battle scenes did his strength (bravado) return. Before he shouted the lines

> I think there be six Richmonds in the field;
> Five have I slain today instead of him,

he did, in pantomime, fight and slay five false Richmonds before he encountered the true one. The fatal encounter was no dance-like fencing match, but in true medieval fashion (the history books again!) a mighty whacking of each other with massive swords. When disarmed, wounded, and fallen, Mansfield struggled to his feet again and attempted to fight Richmond with his mailed fists. Finally, exhausted, he fell dead clutching the trunk of a tree.

Of course he cut out vast sections of Shakespeare.[23] Clarence's dream was gone, and the dialogue of Clarence's murderers, and the drowning of Clarence in a malmsey-butt. He dropped out the false reconciliation of Gloster and the Queen's company. Like Cibber before him he of course pulled out the pin that holds the whole play together—old Queen Margaret, who, according to Shakespeare's design, prophesied and so brought to pass the whole series of executions throughout the play, and eventually the destruction of Richard himself. Her marvelous description of Gloster as an "elvish-mark'd, abortive, rooting hog" had to be eliminated: this was Shakespeare's image of Gloster, not Mansfield's conception of him as a handsome youth. He omitted the condemnation of Hastings (though in later revivals he apparently restored this passage). When the ghosts of his victims appeared during the night before the battle, they delivered their curses of Richard, but time was saved by eliminating their blessings of Richmond.

He retained one Cibber scene in which, at Richard's orders, the little princes are torn from their mother and hauled off to be murdered. No one was much pleased with Mansfield's handling of the text—the hacking and chopping and semi-Cibberizing. The critics were grateful to be spared the moralizing death-speech which Cibber had concocted for Richard. On the other hand, they were not altogether sure that he had done well in *suppressing* Cibber's one great contribution to the play—that famous line which actors to this day will not willingly part with:

> Off with his head. So much for Buckingham![24]

The production was at least a nine-day wonder. The London critics were genuinely impressed by the splendor of the spectacle and with the scholarship that had recreated the architecture, the armor, the dresses, and the manners of the fifteenth century. Some wondered whether one in ten in the audience would recognize all these triumphs of archaeological research, but after all, as Mansfield had said, "if archaeology is the rage, then archaeology they shall have," and he certainly gave them their money's worth

Illus. 144. Mansfield as Richard III.

in these semi-relevancies. Edward German's musical score, composed at Bournemouth in collaboration with Mansfield, was so expressive of the play that more than one observer urged that it be reconstituted into an independent orchestral suite.[25]

Everyone, however, condemned Mansfield's use of the "ribald trash" of Colley Cibber. This infuriated Mansfield because, as he claimed in a letter to William Winter, while following Cibber's "scenario" he had restored Shakespeare's lines, and "the fools here" could not tell the difference between the great poet and his perverter.[26] But the fault, I suspect, lay not so much with "the fools here" as with what they heard from the lips of the actors. Mansfield himself was not only inexperienced as a verse-speaker but as *The Era* (and many later critics) pointed out, he had an atrocious habit of dropping his voice at the end of each line "so as to practically omit the last couple of syllables." *The Saturday Review,* too, complained that "several of the Globe players have no ear for verse," that superfluous syllables are often introduced, and that "some of the elder players are sadly loose in their text, and mangle the verse shockingly."[27]

But what must have cut up Mansfield most painfully was the widespread rejection of his characterization of Gloster in the early scenes as an attractive, if vicious, youth of nineteen. "Richard is *not* himself again," grumbled the *Times.* It is all very well to have read and to believe Horace Walpole's *Historic Doubts on Richard III,* and to study the four extant portraits of young Gloster and believe him handsome. "But what have these historical considerations to do with a more or less fictitious character who has been clearly pictured as a monster by his author?" It should be Mansfield's business to enact Shakespeare and not present an historical *tableau vivant.* What, indeed, would become of Shakespeare's Hamlet if one substituted the Hamlet of Saxo Grammaticus?[28]

Mansfield was confident a week into the run that he had greatly succeeded, and yet it is obvious in his first report to William Winter that the curs are at his heels. Suddenly he is declaring, "There are more hypocrites, liars, parasites, and sycophants here to the square mile than in America to the square State."[29] The production did not hold. After the early good box offices, attendance dwindled, and by the first of June when his lease ran out his discouragement had degenerated into fretful peevishness. "The amount of courtesy I have received from my brother actors, etc., here would not fill a pea-nut shell! The lying—backbiting—intriguing—slandering, underhand dealing and robbery would, on the other hand, require a very large store house. No,—the people are not pleasant."[30]

Somehow, too, his debt to Irving had swollen from £1675 to £2675. And the total indebtedness that he brought home with him was about $167,000.[31] For reasons that we do not know, he came to blame Irving for his London failure, to believe that Irving had manipulated opposition to him that had ruined his London adventure. Irving eventually had to take him to court to recover the amount owed him. But it is absolutely unbelievable that at the time Irving intended anything but encouragement and support to Mansfield. For many years, as we shall see, Mansfield harbored outrageous hostility toward Irving, though eventually, with the mediation and counsel of William Winter, he managed to suppress this foolish anger, and to pretend, at least, a friendship with one of his earliest advocates and promoters.

Glad to be home again in the summer of 1889, he was fully confident that his novel production of *Richard III* would win back all that London had cost him, both in funds and critical esteem. He planned to open it in Boston, which had always been kind to him, on October 1, and after a solid run there, to tour it to all the principal cities. As a triumphant Shakespearean he would have "grown out of dramatic knickerbockers, so to speak,"[32] and would deal no more in the melodramas and light comedies of his past. He would take his place at the head of the American profession.

But the Boston reviews were sorely mixed. His most powerful advocates in New York went up to Boston to welcome him, and of course sent back glowing reports of the opening night. According to Dithmar of the *New York Times,* the performance "was one of the worthiest and most original illustrations of Shakespeare that this country has ever seen, and its repetition in all the principal American cities will establish Mr. Mansfield in the public eye as an interpreter of the poet. . . . It is a great and noble example of dramatic work."[33] William Winter was nearly as enthusiastic for his readers in the *Tribune.* He could not quite accept Mansfield's attempt to reconcile Shakespeare and "history," for Shakespeare's Gloster declares early that his own devices, with God's help, will "leave the world for me to bustle in," and no one watching the play would believe that from the 1571 murder of King Henry he would wait nearly a dozen years before beginning his "bustling" moves to take the crown. In short, Shakespeare, mindless of "history," starts his play where he starts it, with a totally ready villain set in motion from his opening soliloquy. Apart from this, however, Winter wrote hundreds of words of praise of Mansfield's own performance, of the company, and of the splendid archaeology that supported his production.[34]

Notable among the friendlier Boston critics was Howard Ticknor, whose eloquent essay in the Boston *Herald* recreates many vivid passages of the play. Immensely pleased with the physical production, Ticknor makes the point that Mansfield has learned the art of stagecraft thoroughly, so that we no longer have to look to visiting foreign productions for handsome settings.[35]

Ironically, though, certain other critics, after years of complaining about the shabbiness of American stagings of Shakespeare, found that Mansfield's staging was *too* beautiful, *too* expensive, too much. Clapp of the *Advertiser* claimed to enjoy it himself, but acknowledged that many of his readers would think the soul of the drama was buried under "the limbs and outward flourishes," the mere externals. Edward Edgett, in the *Transcript,* felt that the care spent on accessories threw the dramatic part into the shade. The scholarly Charles Copeland, writing for the *Post,* damned everything, from Mansfield's mangled text to his characterization, and as for the settings "there is a great deal of frame to very little picture. . . . One cannot help receiving the impression now and then that realism has been carried beyond due limits. . . . When Shakespeare is spectacularly treated he feeds the eye rather than the mind."[36]

"The Boston critics are tearing the flesh from off my bones," Mansfield complained to Winter, yet he claimed fine profits at the box office, and kept the play on for a month.[37] Three weeks in Philadelphia were *not* profitable. "The Philadelphians are very indifferent," he wrote Winter, "and don't care a damn about this fine presentation of Shakespeare's tragedy. . . . I should have done better with "The Rag Baby" or "The Tin Soldier." . . . I begin to think I can bear the Boston critics but not the Philadelphia houses!"[38] Washington and Baltimore did little to improve his temper or bank account, and if New York did not rise to *Richard III* (it did not),[39] he would abandon Shakespeare and revert to the old repertory of popular entertainment. "My success or failure in New York will mean *everything* to my future and the direction it will take; if America wants a new actor—new enterprise—new work, and a man who will spend freely all that is given to him, they may encourage me. If they don't—I shall give them comedy and keep my money to myself."[40]

Richard III may have been his best Shakespeare production, and from time to time he revived it. Interesting notices turn up in 1896 and 1897 and again in 1906. But after 1890 he did revert, as he threatened, to his old repertory of modern plays, occasionally adding a new one, such as Clyde Fitch's *Beau Brummel* in 1890 (one of his *major* successes),[41] Thomas Russell Sullivan's *Nero* in 1891 (a failure), and Joseph Hatton's dramatization of *The Scarlet Letter* in 1892 (partially successful). He toured widely—to the Pacific coast and back in 1892, throughout the South in 1893, ever expanding his reputation until the notion began to grow across the country that in spite of his thin repertory he *was* indeed America's leading actor.

In April of 1893 he was flattered by an appeal from a Mr. G. McBride published in the Chicago *InterOcean* that he put aside the light work and "delve in the Shakespearian drama, the classic, the poetic."[42] Mansfield made the most of the occasion by a long and overly modest disclaimer. He would like nothing better than to gratify his friendly advocate, but the critics would not permit it. "It has been decided by those who are set up upon the seats of judgment that this path is not for me. I have endeavored to present both the heroic and the tragic, and I have been led to believe that I am suited to neither." His Nero, his Richard III, his Don Juan had been condemned almost unanimously by the New York critics, and he must accept their verdict. Besides, he had neither the means nor the desire "to dress up and bedizen the works of Shakespeare" as seemed necessary to draw audiences to them in these latter days.[43]

Yet on October 23 of that same year, at Herrmann's Theatre in New York, he opened *The Merchant of Venice,* he the Shylock and his wife Beatrice Cameron the Portia.[44] The choice of Shylock, if he was to reenter the Shakespeare scene, was appropriate, but the place, the time, and the motive were not. Herrmann's was a very small theatre. Its tiny stage could not properly accommodate the elaborate scenery that (in spite of his disparagement of "dressing up and bedizening" Shakespeare) Mansfield could not resist designing and building. The auditorium at Herrmann's was too small to pay for the production even if filled every night, and because 1893 was a year of financial depression, the auditorium was rarely filled. But the worst aspect of the affair was Mansfield's private motive in choosing this role at this time.

Henry Irving was about to arrive in New York (his fourth American visit) featuring his brace of Cardinals—Tennyson's Becket and Shakespeare's Wolsey—and for ballast, of course, his much-loved production of *The Merchant of Venice.* Mansfield's old jealousy and distrust of Irving, heated up over the years to a kind of crazy hatred, "ran like iron through his blood." He would show up Irving's "false" Shylock by opposing to it his own "true" one. "Irving made Shylock a gentleman," he wrote Winter, "but he had his reasons for that. There can be no doubt at all that Shylock was nothing of the kind. . . . I shall make

Illus. 145. Mansfield as Shylock.

Shylock what Shakespeare evidently intended: a hot-blooded, revengeful & rapacious Oriental Jew."[45]

He performed this "true" Shylock for two weeks, to diminishing audiences, from October 23 to November 4. At the end of November, between major triumphs of *Becket* and *Henry VIII,* Irving offered *one week* of Shylock. In the competition (if anyone besides Mansfield recognized these separate events as a competition) Mansfield lost. As we have seen, Irving deliberately emphasized—even invented—softening and sentimentalizing touches in order to win audience sympathy. Mansfield deliberately suppressed every call for sympathy, and his revengeful, rapacious Jew attracted little public interest or critical favor.

William Winter, assuming that Mansfield meant what he said, undertook in his review to communicate the actor's intention, to "place" it in the stage history of the role, and to praise the actor for his skill in doing what he set out to do. Apart from the no longer tenable notion that Shakespeare meant Shylock as a low comedy character, there are two courses open to the actor of the part, said Winter. He can dignify Shylock as a devout representative of Hebraic law, or he can show him as simply an ignoble and malignant individual, "typical of the passion of revenge and typical of nothing else." Mansfield has chosen this second course, in the tradition of Macklin and Cooke, of Kean and Booth, rather than in the tradition of Macready and Irving. He brought Shylock down to the plane of villainous humanity.

> He made him a vindictive and cruel usurer, and he expressed with great power, and brought into the strongest relief the craft and wickedness of his motives, the malignity of his hatred, and the deadly determination of his passion for revenge. Shylock as a father was scarcely disclosed, and neither was he disclosed as an austere and awful representative of the "sacred nation." The ideal embodied by Mr. Mansfield is an image, simply, of incarnate hate and bloodthirsty malice, veiled, as long as necessity so ordains, under a guise of humor. . . . Mr. Mansfield long ago manifested himself as an actor of exceptional force, both physical and nervous, and of extraordinary vocal power. Entering heart and soul into Shylock, he was completely liberated, and he rose to a noble height of tragic authority. . . . Mr. Mansfield was superb in his expression of concentrated and implacable resolve, based on reptile malice and a settled conviction of success.[46]

Thus, and at great length, Winter expanded Mansfield's idea of "a hot-blooded, revengeful & rapacious Oriental Jew," and praised him for it—for the *correctness* as much as for the execution of it.

Mansfield was not pleased, and as attendance dropped off he blamed Winter (and probably other critics) for driving the trade (the Jewish trade) away. After he closed at Herrmann's he took to the road, still firing back at Winter vituperative complaints, until, Winter says, he had to ask him not to write again. Winter offers us what he calls "a mild specimen of his epistolary productions at that time." It was written in early November, from Chicago, where Mansfield had gone at the end of his New York run:

> Damn your criticisms! *No* man can keep me back for long! You can injure my pocket, and you certainly have—on occasions! I had a deuce of a time getting our only patrons, the Jews, to come and see "The Merchant," because *you* made me out a fiend and a vulture. $8000 more of my hard-earned dollars gone; and you impractical Devil—what do I—am I—can I, live on? Air? Do you think I am eternally to sweat and labor for no earthly return?

Irving had played in Chicago just before coming to New York, and Mansfield's wrath fed upon that. "Irving has been feting the critics here and I have again found the trail of the serpent and its slime!" The word was out, too, that Irving intended to play *Dr.*

Jekyll and Mr. Hyde in London. "That being the play in which I should make my re-entrée there, his Snakeship will, snake-like, forestall me!"[47]

On November 14, he was writing to Winter's wife in California. Business in Chicago, he complained, was wretched. Irving's box office had drawn $36,000 a week; Mansfield's barely $4,000, of which his own share was only $2,400 while his expenses exceeded $3,000.

> The work of the critics is bearing fruit—& it's dead-sea fruit. Irving has as usual left the slime of his trail behind him—he feted, wined and dined the critics—they condemn my Merchant of Venice to please him & send him the articles to read & nod over—& we starve here where we have worked so long. I think I could bear it if he were really great & good & anything but a charlatan & a fraud. I have quarreled with Willie. I can't help it. He must know—he does know—or he can have no sense of sound or sight that Irving is a fraud—& he ought to say so. . . . My friends *cannot* & *shall not* be his friends.[48]

He got from Mrs. Winter exactly what he deserved for such whimpering and for his insulting letters to William. Writing from Mentone, she administered such a dressing down as any stern mother might address to an irresponsible adolescent.[49]

Although disappointed in the reception of his first Shylock, he kept working at the role year after year, adding and subtracting stage business, altering costume and make-up, cutting and rearranging the text, until Wilstach calls it at last "very nearly the finest expression of his artistic potentiality."[50] Winter, who records a good many rather foolish literalisms of stage business that Mansfield used at one time or another, concludes in one place that though it never came near Edwin Booth's Shylock or Henry Irving's, yet it takes "high rank among the memorable Shylocks of the American stage."[51] Elsewhere he calls it "like Aladdin's tower,—unfinished."[52]

Seven years would pass after his first bout with Shylock until Mansfield would come to Shakespeare again. Meanwhile he labored hard, in New York and on the road, with his own successes, and sought constantly for new plays. When he explained to G. McBride in 1893 why he could not afford to do Shakespeare, he pled for support of the modern drama. First of all, though, he said, let us have a national theatre:

> You wealthy men who lose a million at the turn of a hand, who build palatial clubs, vast hotels, and what not else for the glory of the Nation, erect, too, a theatre and endow it nobly, and if you think me in any small way worthy, let us establish a National Theatre together, and when men come to us from abroad, prating of their superior schools of art and their great artists, let the sign-boards point hitherward in triumph. Let us encourage men here at home to write, let us have some Shakespeare of the nineteenth century. Is it impossible; is it beyond belief that genius can burn today? Can no man write? Let us no longer be traditional but original; it is easier to copy than to create, and the tiniest original painting from Nature is by far greater than any imitation of another man's work. I am for wholesome, healthy, virile plays of character; I care not whether they be sombre, eccentric, quaint, or humorous, so that they be true and strong.[53]

Apparently no more was heard from Mr. G. McBride.

During these seven years he was in frequent touch with Bernard Shaw, but, as we have seen, he could not stay the course with Shaw farther than with Shaw's easiest comedy, *Arms and the Man* in 1894 and the popular melodrama, *The Devil's Disciple* in 1897. One daring adventure was a play called *The Story of Rodion, The Student,* an adaptation by Charles Henry Meltzer of Dostoyevski's *Crime and Punishment.* In the climactic scene Rodion falls ill, and in his delirium reenacts the murder in grisly detail. Mansfield played the scene superbly, but too many people took it to be merely an imitation of Irving's Mathias in *The Bells,* and it soon disappeared. In Winter's judgment, of course, it deserved to fail as "a shocking story prosily told."[54] Two or three amiable but insignificant romances died young deaths during these years until finally in the fall of 1898 he lighted upon *Cyrano de Bergerac.* He played it for the entire season and it restored him to prosperity.

By 1900 he had at last achieved the recognition that he had so long striven for, that he was indeed America's leading actor, and he was now ready to cap that reputation by once more attempting to treat Shakespeare to an unforgettable revival. He did not choose *Hamlet* or *Othello,* of course, which depended upon roles beyond his powers. He chose *Henry V,* which could refresh the laurels he had won in *Richard III* as a grand *metteur-en-scène.* In the Preface to his acting edition he laid on the expected moral balderdash about the play's "healthy and virile tone (so diametrically in contrast to many of the performances now current)" and "the lesson it teaches of godliness, honour, loyalty, courage, cheerfulness, and perseverance; its beneficial influence on young and old."[55] A more pressing consideration with him, however, was "a desire to prove that the American stage is . . . quite able to hold its own artistically with the European. The ambition of my stage career has been to prove the superiority of the American stage and the American actor; and I maintain that today against all those who pretend the contrary."[56]

Henry V had not been seen in New York since February of 1875, when Jarrett and Palmer, then managers of Booth's Theatre, imported Charles Calvert's

Illus. 146. Mansfield as Henry V. Folger Shakespeare Library.

production from Manchester and brought a London actor, George Rignold, to play the lead. Thus Mansfield's at the Garden Theatre, opening October 3, 1900, was the only thoroughly American production anyone had ever seen.

Since in Mansfield's previous "serious" work, from Chevrial to Richard III to Shylock to Rodion the Student, he had specialized in villains and villainy, it was startling to see him undertake the role of the hero-king. Yet it turned out to be an ideal role for him. The core of the role is simple manliness—bold, bluff, resolute. Henry has no subtle inner problems, no doubts or fears. From first to last he is King, always in command. He needs only to hold an army together, win a war, and for a comic-kicker, to win a bride. Yet this simple-seeming role contains multitudes. Henry does not grow, but from scene to scene he changes, he plays many roles, and for an inveterate character actor like Mansfield he offers a splendid range of opportunities.

Henry has demanded from the French certain dukedoms. The French respond by sending him a box of tennis balls. Mansfield's well-known "propensity to mordant sarcasm," which often turned audiences against him in presumably amiable characters, here served brilliantly in his response to the French insult

> And tell the pleasant prince this mock of his
> Hath turn'd his balls to gun-stones, and his soul
> Shall stand sore charged for the wasteful vengeance
> That shall fly with them. . . .

Next, like a cunning prosecuting attorney he draws out and entraps the traitors in his company, Cambridge, Scroop, and Grey. Then as stern just judge he condemns them to instant execution. The subtlest acting Mansfield is called upon in the entire play is his condemnation of Scroop: it is heartbreaking, for Scroop has been his dearest friend.

Before the walls of Harfleur he plays two roles: first the charismatic leader, joyous in battle, rallying his men to the attack—"Once more unto the breach, dear friends, once more"; then, when the Governor appears upon the walls, he becomes a sort of blazing God of Wrath, threatening murder, rape, and all the horrors of war. His words, fiercer than gun-stones, take the town. In Act IV [Shakespeare's] occur three very different and very admirable quiet passages, all by night. First, disguised like the good Duke in *Measure for Measure,* he goes among his soldiers, pretending to be one of them—a benevolent spy, hearing their doubts, complaints, and fears, and gently persuading them of the rightness of their loyalty to their King. Left alone then he utters a moving soliloquy on the loneliness of kings and the idleness of Ceremony. As dawn is coming on he turns religious suppliant, praying to the God of Battles to

> steel my soldiers' hearts.
> Possess them not with fear: take from them now
> The sense of reckoning. . . .

Before the battle of Agincourt, again as before the gates of Harfleur, he is the blazing battlefield orator, uttering the most famous call to arms in our literature. Though hopelessly outnumbered by the French, Henry, as it were, converts every man into a hundred men by sheer power of rhetoric:

> This day is call'd the feast of Crispian.
> He that outlives this day, and comes safe home,
> Will stand a tip-toe when this day is nam'd,
> And rouse him at the name of Crispian.

In Shakespeare the battle scenes are spread over four acts, but Mansfield so cut the play that he packed them all into three acts. What he then labels Act IV is a spectacular pantomime.

Just as in the Calvert (and Charles Kean) productions of earlier days, while the Chorus to Shakespeare's Act V describes the homecoming of Henry and his army, hundreds of actors and extras, with musical accompaniment, literally act out this grand celebration.

> London is revealed on a sunny morning in holiday dress. Flags are flying, and festoons of roses drape the housetops. Doors and windows are thronged. Trumpeters announce the Lord Mayor and while guards force the people back, the City's ruler passes in state bearing a golden key of the City. Each regiment of soldiers is headed by its commanding duke, and heralds accompany the noblemen bearing their standards. The troops, marching in battalions, with crossbows, pikes, and lances pass through one of the old city gates at the rear. A girl recognizes a sweetheart, rushes to his arms and marches away with him. A woman runs to a soldier she recognizes, asks him a question. He shakes his head sorrowfully. She faints and is carried senseless from the ranks. Finally the trumpets bray the coming of the King. White-robed girls dance before him, waving laurel-sprays. The King, mounted on horseback passes across the stage while the Westminster choir boys sing a hymn of Thanksgiving. The bells vie with the populace in greeting the King.[57]

Those with long memories assure us that Mansfield's procession exceeded in splendor that at Booth's Theatre in 1875.

The fifth act afforded Mansfield yet one more role to play—a plain-speaking, homely wooer: Marry, he exclaims to the French Princess Katherine,

> if you would put me to verses, or to dance for your sake, Kate, why you undid me. . . . If I could win a lady at leapfrog, or by vaulting into my saddle with my armour on my back, under the correction of bragging be it spoken, I should quickly leap into a wife. . . . If thou wouldst have such a one, take me; and take me, take a soldier; take a soldier, take a king.

The tone is such a comical come-down from that of Henry's "serious" scenes—so Benedick-like or Petruchio- or Falstaff-like—that it is almost as if another character were wearing Henry's costume. Yet for Mansfield, whose forte was comedy, as well as for the audiences, this conclusion of the play was most congenial. It was followed by one more scene, the twenty-second, a wordless celebration of the marriage of Henry and Kate in the Cathedral at Troyes.

The twenty-two scenes took four and a half hours to play, at least at the beginning of the run, but no one complained of that. Henry Clapp did wistfully hope that some day some brave manager would dare to stage it with the simplest possible scenery so that "the text . . . shall have 175 minutes to its own sonorous self."[58] But all in all it was agreed that no more beautiful pictures or better stage management had ever been seen on the American stage, and as Dithmar declared in the *New York Times,* "We need not talk now about the Meininger and the management of crowds at Bayreuth."[59]

There were critical objections to the acting, of course. Winter complained of "a certain sluggishness" in Mansfield's movements.[60] The *Dramatic Mirror* thought him monotonous in the early scenes, but steadily improving, and ending "in a capital recital of the delicious love scene."[61] It was generally recognized that Mansfield never would or could get the hang of blank verse, though here, as ever, we cannot be certain what standard of speaking, between singsong and prosaic flatness, any given critic has in mind. The critic of the Boston *Herald* (Arthur Warren?), whose long review is rapturously, yet one feels discriminatingly, enthusiastic, positively "revels" in the fact that Mansfield has treated with contempt those "niceties of elocution" which "excite the admiration of ancient critics and which are such a burlesque and travesty upon the comprehensible speech of intelligent human beings."[62] One hopes that he means no worse than that Mansfield avoided such archaisms of pronunciation as forcing the word *ocean* into three syllables, or squeezing two syllables out of *-tion* or *-scion* endings in order to "keep the rhythm." A moment later in his argument he praises Mansfield for avoiding "that commonplaceness of speech which one or two English actors [whom does he mean?] a few years ago endeavored to make popular in the reading of the Shakespearean text."

Mansfield played *Henry V* for eight weeks in New York, and throughout the rest of the season toured it in all the major cities of the eastern half of the country. By general consensus it was his finest work to date and altogether the best of his Shakespeares. Or, to draw it mild with Norman Hapgood, "More poetry, more sweetness, and more power might be put into Henry, but Mr. Mansfield had something of each of these qualities, and he had so much spirit, dignity, and humor that no fair person who had built a somewhat different Henry out of Shakespeare could refuse to accept Mr. Mansfield's as fine and just."[63]

In 1902, after a profitable season touring in a pleasant bit of fluff adapted from Booth Tarkington's novel, *Monsieur Beaucaire,* Mansfield turned one last time to Shakespeare. We do not know why he chose *Julius Caesar,* or why he chose the role of Brutus (his natural bent toward sardonic humor, as various critics noted, would have fitted him ideally for Cassius). In any case, *Caesar* was the play and in one way the choice was a lucky one. It happened that a year earlier Sir Henry Irving decided at last to use the Roman settings for *Coriolanus* which he had commissioned from Sir Lawrence Alma-Tadema as long ago as 1879.[64] Neither Irving nor Ellen Terry could bring off their parts, the play was withdrawn, and Alma-Tadema's splendid sets went into storage at the Lyceum.

In mid-summer of 1902, Mansfield, vacationing in England, paid a friendly call on Irving in his rooms at the Lyceum (he had long since learned to suppress his crazy jealousy of Irving, so their relations were cordial). As conversation drifted to Roman plays, and it came out that Mansfield was planning *Caesar,* Irving took him to the storage rooms, showed him sections of Alma-Tadema's work, and sold him the lot of it at a bargain price—scenery, costumes, armor, and all. Thus, without effort or care, Mansfield acquired a superb physical production, designed by the highest authority and painted by such master scene painters as William Telbin, Hawes Craven, Richard Marston, and John Young.[65]

Mansfield opened his *Caesar* in Chicago on October 14, 1902, moved it to New York on December 1, and from January 17 to June 6, 1903, toured it widely and with great profit. Wherever he took it, the scenery was without question the grand attraction of the show.

The Chicago papers made the most of this opening in their city of a major production by the then acknowledged "leader of the American stage." But except for Amy Leslie of the *Daily News,* who burbled in her ecstatic style about the splendor of everything, the critics generally were reluctant to commit themselves to all-embracing praise. Delancey Halbert of the *Evening Post* thought the performance slow—"at times it dragged painfully"—and the best he could say for Mansfield was that "he does vastly better than anyone could have a right to expect." One can make little of James O'Donnell Bennett of the *Record-Herald,* a critic who seems to have worn his heart on the outside and never wrote a harsh word. The mere fact that Mansfield made an inconspicuous entrance, lost in the crowd which was attending Caesar to the games, somehow conveyed to Bennett that the actor's conception of the role of Brutus was a matter of "ineffable pathos"! This was the keynote. "This Mansfield Brutus is the saddest, sweetest, gentlest creature that destiny ever played with and then cast pitilessly aside." The *Tribune* devoted an entire page to the event, with sketches of scenes, a review, and some amusing chit-chat about the marshaling of the hundreds of supernumeraries behind the scenes. The reviewer, however, excused himself from comment on the performers and spoke at length only of Alma-Tadema's "pictures," whose tonal beauty reminded him of Edwin Abbey's grand murals, *The Pursuit of the Holy Grail,* in the Boston Public Library.

> There is not a detail that has been overlooked; not so much as the border on a toga, the drapery on a couch, or the placing of a jewel that has not been considered and arranged with regard to historical fidelity and at the same time to pictorial beauty.

What a feast to the eyes was the capital, he said,

> with its brownish yellow walls and canopy, its tiers of sen-

Illus. 147. Mansfield as Brutus.

ators in their togas of white edged with red, and there in the center, full in the light, the mighty Caesar, crowned with laurels of gold, robed in crimson, and across the steps of his throne a crush of deep red velvet that seems to glow and burn with color.[66]

The Tent Scene of Act IV did not come from *Coriolanus.* Presumably Mansfield himself designed it, and in idea and coloring it blended effectively with the rest. From within its brown walls and roof we looked through its broad entrance at the back into a vista of trees and water bathed in blue moonlight. Mansfield conceived the notion that Caesar's ghost should not be seen by anyone but Brutus: only his voice was heard as he passed "invisibly" through a flood of blue-green light. The battle at Philippi was not, as usual, pictured as taking place on a wide stretch of open field. A forest of cypress trees with their tall trunks and wide-spreading tops surrounded an open center where armies clashed and where Cassius and Brutus died.

Once Mansfield arrived in New York his friend Dithmar paid him a compliment he had long sought—one that had probably never been put so precisely:

Those who last night heard his richly vibrant voice and saw his flexible and powerful mimique were confirmed in their belief that the English speaking stage of today holds only one or at most two actors—Sir Henry Irving and Mr. Forbes Robertson—who are his equals and none who in temperamental vigor is his superior.

For two acts and a half, said Dithmar, he was "intellectually interesting." Then, in the Tent Scene of the fourth act, while Cassius stamped and roared, Mansfield retained throughout the stoic elevation of spirit, yet was "everywhere instinct with suppressed volcanic fire, that gave color and fervor to the deep resonant tones of his voice and majestic force to his almost motionless bearing."[67]

This is gratifying. But what are we to make of the reviewer for the *Theatre* magazine who said at once that this Brutus was "a disappointment," that it was "a degenerate Ibsenish Brutus," that there was no excuse for "the ghastly, sinister, almost grotesque figure Mr. Mansfield presented during the first three acts," that he assumed "the demeanor of a decrepit monomaniac."[68] Or the impression of the *Dramatic Mirror* that he was "a singularly colorless individual, vapid when he is not grotesque . . . far from the notion of a man that might have had influence and distinction. . . . For the most part he stood about, clutching a slim palm branch and casting his eyes up to heaven. . . . He was weak, indefinite, and unconvincing."[69] Or the puzzlement of the reviewer who found his make-up extraordinary—"sicklied o'er with a complexion which betokened severe dyspepsia"—who thought he played his earlier scenes "like stained glass windows."[70] Or the opinion of William Lyon Phelps: "I have never known a Brutus in the famous tent scene walk and talk as badly as he. If one reads Hamlet's advice to the players, and then hears Richard Mansfield in the tent scene he will have the opportunity of observing nearly every fault that Shakespeare condemns."[71]

When he got to Boston, much as his scenic effects were admired (the "effects of light and darkness, of storm and sunshine"), much as his ability as "stage manager and stage-setter" was approved, his actorship drew sharp comment:

Mr. Mansfield has a beautiful voice, which he uses with great skill in the way of tone-production. . . . But if he uses his fine voice well in one way, he uses it mighty ill in another. As a rule, he reads his lines about as badly as they can be read. His delivery is a panorama of misplaced emphasis. . . . It is astonishing how much meaning he will succeed in eliminating from Shakespeare's lines. Last evening he even seemed worse in this respect than ever.[72]

Henry Clapp points out what he calls "straws which way the wind blows." These "straws," he suggests, are examples of what happened when Mansfield endeavored to modernize and colloquialize Shakespeare. *Cassius,* which Clapp insists is a two-syllable name, was expanded into *Cass-i-oose,* with a peculiar fullness given to the final syllable. *Brutus* was regularly called *Brut-oose.* (*Julius* was spared being called Jul-i-oose.) A vast number of two-syllable words ending in *ed*—e.g., the word *graspèd* in Brutus' own line, "For so much trash as may be graspèd thus"—were reduced to a single syllable: *graspèd* became *grasp'd,* thus utterly wrecking the verse rhythm. Clapp heard the actor of Marc Antony pronounce *Lupercal* as *Lupércal.* We need not rehearse here Clapp's further and more serious quarrels with the actor's performances.[73] Another observer, signed "W. F. A.," suggests that the -*oose* endings were a sycophantic nod toward the Classics Department of Harvard University, where, it appears, the Continental, not the English, system of pronouncing Latin still prevailed.

The most interesting, though perhaps the least credible interpretation of Mansfield's performance of Brutus is that of James Huneker in the New York *Sun.* Although many critics found Mansfield's mannerisms of voice, posture, and movement in this role not only faulty but often ludicrous, Huneker found that through exercise of imagination, all his qualities, good and bad, fused into a novel and splendidly intelligible Brutus. He has abandoned the traditional "stalk and stare" of the merely melodramatic hero, had studied his Shakespeare deeply, and had realized that Brutus, with his *folie du doute,* is a preliminary sketch of Hamlet. Yet unlike Hamlet, whose grievance is private, Brutus is a politician, concerned for the welfare of a nation. This adds a sinister note.

His Brutus, gentle, loving, has yet the absent manner of one who suffers from a wasting mental malady. He is the true *Anarch,* the dreamer of mad dreams, the regenerator of universal ills. Loving Caesar, he is yet ready to kill him at a hint from Cassius, because of what Caesar may become! Here is political idealism run to crazy paradox!

He seeks nothing for himself: he is hallucinated by his visions of universal justice. Huneker recalls Mansfield's performance of *Rodion the Student,* and invoking Dostoyevski and the theories of the contemporary criminologist, Cesare Lombroso, he finds Brutus a victim of *folie des grandeurs.* He will kill for the good of the commonwealth. Coleridge could not understand Brutus because he had not the advantage of modern discoveries in psychopathology. But now it is obvious that Brutus is "a study in exalted mania—

a mania that has for its theme no craving after mortal self, but a utopia of justice. The slaying of Caesar has all the deliberateness of one hypnotized by cruel fate. After the act momentary remorse is soon crowded from his face by a rapt joy—the joy of a man who has fulfilled his mission. He is no mere regicide, but an arm selected by the gods to scourge the tyrannical, the unrighteous. Nevertheless he is a fanatic. Consecrated by history we only see the heroic side; transpose Brutus to the twentieth century and we load him down with the opprobrious term of Anarchist and put him speedily out of existence.[74]

This interpretation of Mansfield's performance, suggested perhaps by the assassination of President McKinley by the anarchist Czolgosz a year before, is more likely to have come out of Huneker's head than out of Mansfield's. The actor, in fact, is reported to have said later that Brutus is "an old fool," and Mansfield himself was "an old fool" for playing the part.[75]

It was his last Shakespeare, and as we look back over his Shakespearean roles—Richard III, Shylock, Henry V, and Brutus—we realize that although major Shakespeareans played these roles, they do not, taken

Illus. 148. Mansfield, sometimes a prankster, reading a play to his company. See *Illus. 38.*

together, constitute the repertory of a major Shakespearean. As a *producer* of Shakespeare Mansfield held, from first to last, to the motto that "If archaeology is the rage, then archaeology they shall have." That was the mid-century philosophy of *mise-en-scène,* and Mansfield added nothing to it but a certain polish. As an actor he never achieved the technical proficiency of Booth and Barrett, nor projected the warmth of an Irving, nor was his performing an intelligent anticipation of the best that would be realized in the twentieth century.

Shortly before the end of his career there appeared two formal articles which between them neatly establish the ambiguity of Mansfield's reputation then and forever after. In 1906, in the *Cosmopolitan,* Alan Dale called him "Our Worst Actor"; in *Appleton*'s, in 1907, John Corbin called him "The Greatest." Alan Dale's point is the simple one that Richard Mansfield is really no actor at all but only and always his mannered self. On one occasion his mannered self and a certain dramatic role exactly coincided. This was Beau Brummel. "The charm of Mansfield's Beau Brummel was very great indeed, and nobody realized it more than I did. . . . Since those days Mr. Mansfield has been a modified Beau Brummel in everything."

His Brutus, the worst that has ever been seen, said Alan Dale, "was a cynical, dyspeptic and finicky Brutus, with the chipper intonations of Beau Brummel." All that can be said for his Shylock was his perfect make-up. It was "wonderful to look at, but as a piece of acting it was absurd. It was a mixture of horrible rant and a 'haw-haw' intonation. . . . There was the old Jew, a picture to look at behaving as a sort of frenzied Semitic Beau Brummel." And thus Alan Dale runs down the list, savaging Mansfield's Cyrano, Dimmesdale *(The Scarlet Letter),* and Rodion the Student. "There is no living actor who is so obtrusively the man, apart from the role he essays, as Richard Mansfield. That is why I say he is the worst actor I know." He has, to be sure, his prototype in London—Beerbohm Tree, who also "produces well, has mastered the art of make-up, and acts with lamentable mannerism and ridiculous effect."[76]

After Henry Irving died, declared John Corbin, "Mr. Mansfield has come into his own as the greatest actor on the English-speaking stage, and it is time to say so." Irving, the London-based and much older actor, had by far the greater reputation, acknowledged on both sides of the ocean as first in the profession. Mansfield's work was almost unknown abroad. Yet Corbin found that when compared objectively, the two were not far apart in faults and virtues. Corbin was well aware of Mansfield's defects of speech and movement, and he listed them fairly, but "at his worst it may be questioned whether his defects were more noxious than those of Irving, and in the matter of speech—the crucial point in acting—it is certain that they were not." Both men were short in literary judgment, letting their concern for starring roles and center stage outweigh their concern for drama as drama. Irving never let go of Mathias in the wretched melodrama of *The Bells;* Mansfield clung to Baron Chevrial and Mr. Hyde throughout his career. Irving imported cheap Sardou, took credit for producing Goethe's *Faust* but let it be transformed into a romantic operatic spectacular, and reveled in the feeble Victorianism of W. G. Wills while adamantly rejecting every modern dramatist of genuine worth. Mansfield, too, encouraged many a failed playwright, but he did introduce Shaw to America and brought us *Cyrano de Bergerac.* He revived Moliere's *Misanthrope,* and his Alceste was said to be one of his finest performances. He ended his career with a tour de force of *Peer Gynt.* Irving's big-boned face was the mask of a powerful personality, an actor of strong characters; Mansfield's face, like Garrick's, said nothing in particular—it could be the face of a banker, a school teacher, a green grocer. But it was versatile. "The face of Mansfield portrays at will the fresh charms of youth, the strong passions of maturity, or the seared decrepitude of senility. At will it is radiantly gracious, grotesquely humorous, or scarred by tragical passion and despair." In physical vigor, in strength and variety of voice, in the capacity for growth, change, and self-improvement, Corbin gave all the points to Mansfield.

He regretted Mansfield's announcement that he would retire early, for the New Theatre—that "national theatre" which Mansfield had so firmly advocated—was soon to open, and Mansfield ought to be a part of it. We who know what a disaster that New Theatre turned out to be can be glad that Mansfield escaped it. He was ill and dying in the very year that Corbin's defense of him was in the making.[77]

Robert Bruce Mantell

Probably the fairest thing to be said about Robert Bruce Mantell (1854–1928) is that our theatre historians have treated him most unfairly.[78] For fifteen years or thereabouts, remotely seconded by E. H. Sothern, he was our leading American performer of Shakespeare's tragic heroes. He played with varying degrees of success, a round dozen of the "heavies," from Romeo and Shylock to Macbeth, Othello, and Lear. Between 1904 and 1919 he visited Broadway nine times, his engagements ranging from two weeks to two months, giving (according to Attilio Favorini's count) some 275 performances of Shakespeare. During those years, and before and after, he criss-crossed the country with his companies, and during his whole career played Shakespeare some 4,900 times.[79] In a generation when fashionable American audiences were turning away from the classics and clamoring for musicals, farces, domestic comedies, girlie-shows, and the cinema, Mantell maintained a steady audience of Shakespeare lovers. He profited comfortably from them, too. For many years, according to Wendell Phillips Dodge, he was accustomed to an income in excess of $30,000 a year. He acquired an estate at Atlantic Highlands in New Jersey, complete with mansion, farm, gardens, orchards, a rehearsal barn, and a golf course.[80]

Little mention of his service or his success appears in the history books. Arthur Hornblow's *History of the Theatre in America,* which appeared at about the peak of Mantell's career, contains brief reference to him as "a Shakespearian actor of considerable distinction." Glenn Hughes's *The Story of the Theatre* remarks that "since the early nineties he has been the most consistent exponent of Shakespeare in this country." Garff Wilson's *History of American Acting* does not mention him at all. He lingers in popular memory as little more than an "old school ham."

In a playful attempt to define the word "ham" and to curb our unthinking abuse of it, the late Alan Downer called up his own boyhood memories of Mantell.[81] Every year, as Downer remembered it, "the last of the Old School Tragedians" would come to Syracuse to perform whatever Shakespeares were being taught in the local schools. He was

> A noble-browed Scot with keen, flashing eyes, a nose like the prow of a Viking galley, and close cropped steel-grey curls. . . . When I saw him he was an old man [presumably in his seventies], supporting himself from the Onondaga Hotel to the Weiting Opera House on the arm of his charming wife, Genevieve Hamper, sitting nearly helpless in his dressing room while his valet clothed him and made him up . . . and making his final entrance in *Macbeth* with a drawn sword in one hand and, in the other, a heavy cane.
>
> He was . . . too old to be earning his living touring a strenuous Shakespearian repertory. . . . As he sat in the wings awaiting his cue, the great weariness in his soul was evident; as he huddled through his part for the thousandth time, he was plainly an actor who had lived too long, worked too hard. The theatre had disowned him, he was acting in a dead tradition, living in a dead repertory.

This was indeed "ham" acting—merely going through the motions and noises of Macbeth or Brutus or whatever the school curriculum required. But *watch* him, says Downer:

> watch him as Jaques, clutching a staff, chewing the traditional apple, limps painfully to the footlights and lights into the great "Seven Ages" speech like an operatic tenor wringing the neck of "Caro Nome." And at the end—sans teeth, sans eyes, sans taste, sans everything—he casts the remains of the apple to the ground, and his eyes follow it as it rolls into the wings.

Sans everything! An apple core rolls out of sight, an old man's eyes grow dim. That, too, is "ham" and it is also authentic theatre. The cynical comedy of Jaques's view of life abruptly converts to pity and terror as we watch the aged hero of thousands of tragic performances approaching his own death.

"Let us not then," says Downer, "be too free with our epithets of scorn." It is fair to demand that the actor deal honestly with us and with his author, that he deliver to us the play that the author intended. But when we enter the theatre (or gallery or symphony hall) let us check our moralizing Plato and categorizing Aristotle in the cloak room and submit to what the artists have to show us. An experienced taste will tell us which ham is too ripe or too salty—or beneficent, just right.

Born in Scotland, educated in Belfast, apprenticed to the theatre in England in the latter days of Samuel Phelps, Barry Sullivan, Charles Dillon, and others of the "old school," Mantell came to America in 1882, where he thereafter made his career.[82] Tall, blond, powerfully built, handsome, and with a splendid voice, he swiftly won popular favor as a matinee idol. In 1883—the same year that Richard Mansfield struck fire as the Baron Chevrial—Mantell, acting in support of Fanny Davenport, saved her play and her fortune and made his own mark as the hero-villain, Loris Ipanoff, in an adaptation of Sardou's *Fédora.* During the next five to ten years he developed an envied reputation as the romantic hero in a series of melodramas—*Dakolar, Monbars, Tangled Lives, The Face in the Moonlight,* and so forth. But just as his ambition was carrying him beyond these forgettables into Romeo, Othello, Hamlet, and others of the classic repertory, disaster struck.[83]

Early in the 1880s he had drifted into a marriage with one of his supporting actresses, Marie Sheldon. They stayed together long enough to beget two sons, but as it turned out they were incompatible. Mantell took up with a new leading lady, a (Mrs.) Charlotte Behrens, and for some time their clandestine love affair prospered. Unfortunately one evening in a Saratoga hotel the actress Rose Coghlan came upon them dining in a private room and concluded that they were behaving disreputably. She told her story; the scandal spread. Mrs. Mantell sued for divorce, won her case, and was awarded alimony of $100 per week. The Behrens woman bore Mantell a daughter,

Illus. 149. Robert Mantell.

divorced her own husband, and married Mantell at once.

Since Mantell could not possibly keep up his alimony payments he was judged in contempt of court and subject to arrest any time he set foot in the state of New York. For ten or eleven years, while the debt mounted to $60,000, he lived, so to speak, in exile. So vigilant were the New York authorities that in 1897 when Charlotte died (in Michigan) and her body had to be transported to Philadelphia for burial, the New York police boarded the train at Niagara, certain that there they would catch their prey. Mantell eluded them, of course, by dropping south into Ohio and arriving at the funeral site without entering the forbidden territory.[84]

In May of 1900 Mantell took a third wife, Marie Booth Russell—tall, handsome, Junoesque—who had succeeded Charlotte Behrens as leading leady. It was a lasting marriage, though professionally not an altogether fortunate one. Miss Russell was Amazonian enough to look good against Mantell in his regular round of melodramas, but when he turned to Shakespeare it appeared that she had not the sense or sensitivity or even voice enough to handle the Shakespearean leads—yet it was her prerogative to attempt them. Mantell could not demote her even if his judgment told him he should do so, and for many years he had to accept harsh words from the critics on her account.

In 1901 events took an upward turn when the contempt decree was lifted. By plea-bargaining he got the debt to Marie Sheldon reduced to $10,000, a sum he could cope with. The New York police dropped his name from their "Wanted" list and he could once more enjoy the freedom of the state.[85]

All this sorry domestic matter has to be taken into account because it stalled Mantell's developing career in midcourse. A decade of exile from the metropolis, where reputations were made, nearly ruined him. He never ceased to act, of course, playing cities, towns, and whistle-stops from coast to coast, and although his personal reputation held up across the country, it became increasingly difficult to maintain supporting companies of quality. Failed actors trained in the old style ("superfluous lags") and young actors who knew nothing about vocal projection (did not have "Shakespearean voices," as Mantell would put it) and knew little more about stage movement than how to handle a teacup or swing a cane, made a bad mix. Eventually, too, the isolation from New York and the loss of its imprimatur diminished Mantell's value to the provincial managers, since they could not advertise what Winter, Dithmar, and the other moguls of criticism had said about him. Once or twice he even had to "go broke," disband his company, and scramble for means to start again. On one occasion he sank as low as any great actor could sink—to vaudeville. He got up a quick skit with three other hungering performers, joined the B. K. Keith circuit, and in two months had earned enough to resume his proper place in the "legitimate."[86]

It was all very well, after the alimony settlement in 1901, for Mantell and his new wife to visit New York, even to live there, but he could not work there, for no city manager, battening on the popular demand for parlor drama and musicals, would waste his resources on a half-forgotten provincial stroller specializing in Shakespeare, Bulwer's *Richelieu,* and worn-out melodrama. It happened, however, that in November of 1904 when Mantell and Miss Russell were somewhere between one-night stands in Pennsylvania (or was it Texas?) they received a circular letter from the Shubert brothers offering "three weeks of choice time in a handsome Broadway theatre."[87] The Shuberts' motive was crudely transparent: they would rent their theatre to anyone rather than close it. The three weeks they offered were the three just before Christmas when most people were spending their extra money on everything but theatre. And the "handsome Broadway theatre" was merely the little upstairs Herrmann's, slightly refurbished and rechristened the Princess, where Mansfield had failed to draw much audience just a year earlier.

Yet it *was* a way (apparently the only way) of getting into the city. With desperate misgivings Mantell accepted the challenge and announced himself for Richard III on December 5, 1904.[88]

The event provided one of the livelier yarns about theatrical first nights. When Mantell arrived only a day in advance of the opening he discovered that his drapes and backcloths were much too big for the twenty-five-foot opening at the Princess. When cut and folded, as someone observed, the drops looked like "dirty rags hung on a line to dry." The local stage hands wanted extra men hired and a full day's technical rehearsal, but Mantell, down to his bottom dollar, had to refuse them. They took their revenge. At curtain time Mantell discovered that instead of the Act I Tower set, the Act III Throne Room was in place. The audience waited forty minutes while the actor quarreled with the workers and got the stage in order.

When Mantell appeared for his first soliloquy the audience saw scenery wobbling, heard hammers and stage-braces falling and shouts of "All right, Harry," and "Let down that drop there." Suddenly during the soliloquy Mantell lurched forward. The forestage he was working on was barely three feet deep, and a wicked stage hand, standing behind the Tower cloth, calculated that with a smart push he could dump the star into the pit and bring the entertainment to an early ending. Mantell caught himself inches from the edge and carried on. During the second soliloquy a more determined disrupter took over. But Mantell, alerted now to the perils of "front scenes," became aware of someone feeling his way behind the cloth to find the exact spot from which to launch his attack. It was probably at the lines about "Edward, her lord, whom I some three months since, stabb'd in my angry mood at Tewksbury" that Mantell whipped out his sword and thrust it through the cloth. A yelp of pain was heard, which Mantell covered with an exuberant vocal burst, and backstage the guilty one and his cohorts were shocked into silence.

Illus. 150. Mantell as Richard III.

When Mantell trotted off stage ("Shine out, fair sun, till I have bought a glass")—to all appearances cheerily but inwardly boiling, he was greeted by a blustering stage manager: "Here, you, d'you know you've killed a man?" Mantell's response was firm: "I hope to God I have." The damage to the stage hand was a bloody but not serious leg wound.

Mantell sent his dresser to fetch the iron-clad gauntlet which he wore in the battle scenes, put it on, showed it all around, and promised to use it, even fatally, on any of the crew that disturbed the rest of the performance. There was no more trouble behind the scenes that evening or any evening during the three weeks following.

A small audience on a blizzardy night, a mean little theatre, wretched stage management, a country company led by an *old* old-timer (Mantell, whom this audience had not seen for a dozen years, was exactly fifty), how could this minor event have in any degree renewed interest in Shakespeare in the city? Mantell's intense earnestness, his physical power, the likes of which had not been felt since the last visit of Salvini fifteen years earlier, and his marvelous vocal range worked unexpected wonders.

Many of the leading critics bypassed the occasion. William Winter of the *Tribune* spent the evening at Daly's, trying to immortalize a new biblical drama by his friend Thomas Bailey Aldrich: the *Tribune* acknowledged Mantell's first night in a brief and noncommittal squib that could have been written by anybody. The *New York Times* made fun of the clumsy stage management and concluded that Mantell, laudably ambitious, had overreached himself in attempting Richard. The *Herald,* almost alone among the papers reporting the first night, praised the actor's subtlety and shading of the role. Yet word got about that something remarkable had come to town, and by the end of the week some positive notices came in. The *Dramatic Mirror* spoke of Mantell's "fine original training as a player" and declared that "his magnificent and admirably controlled voice is a delight in these days of stage mumbling and incoherence."[89] The critical fraternity must have been made to think twice when Alan Dale, notorious for his swinging attacks upon public *favorites,* declared that Mantell's Richard had "gripped me hard":

> In all of the "business" of the part Mantell was excellent. There were a dozen little touches that struck intelligent observers as realistic. It was quite astonishing today, when we go for subtlety to Ibsen, to rediscover the possibilities of *Richard III* played in an up-to-date manner. And that is how Mantell played it. There were none of the mouthings and rantings of your old school; there were none of the noise and incoherency of the bumptious barnstormer.

Dale thought Mantell's voice alone was worth the price of admission and he could not resist a typical Alan Dale stinger to the effect that the celebrated voice of Forbes-Robertson—so sensitive, so refined—

Illus. 151. Mantell as Othello.

"is not in it with this actor, who has evidently used 'the road' to good advantage.[90] Compared with the diction of the conventional mummer, said Dale, Mantell's is like a clarion to a penny whistle. Another critic, matching Mantell's voice against Mansfield's, declared Mansfield's "a blaring brass band" compared to Mantell's "symphony orchestra," and added that Mantell's lines even when half-whispered could be perfectly understood throughout the auditorium."[91] Arthur Hornblow's *Theatre* magazine welcomed him (cautiously though), placing him "in history," so to speak: "It is a robustious Richard which he presents. A good, old-time traditional Gloucester, such as was presented every Saturday night by an established favorite and tried performer in the palmy days when Shakespeare had a following on the Broadway and lower Broadway. It is never subtle, but always picturesque."[92]

Othello in his second week and *Richelieu* in his third confirmed that he was gifted with enormous powers of body and voice.[93] He lacked polish, of course. In the long years of barnstorming he had grown careless about language, and it became commonplace to fault him for wrong emphases, for omitting words or substituting wrong words, for mugging, for playing to the galleries. He brought nothing new to the theatre. His nondescript sets and costumes bespoke little concern for the niceties of historical research or for beauty of stage decoration. He was no intellectual: one doubts that his reading went beyond playscripts and the daily papers. Did he even read Shakespeare? He never acted from Shakespeare's texts, but always from old acting editions—usually Edwin Booth's as prepared and published by William Winter.

What he did bring was something half-forgotten during the fifteen years since the death of Barrett and the retirement of Booth, during the "mauve decade" and the rising genteelism of the 1890s—Shakespearean tragedy full-voiced and muscular, driven by masculine power. These three tries in the autumn of 1904 won him all he hoped for—entrée to Broadway. And won him, too, the agent who could keep him there. William A. Brady had been the foremost sports promoter of the past decade, manager of the champion pugilist "Gentleman Jim" Corbett and the wrestler Billy Muldoon. Lately, since Corbett had lost his championship to Sullivan and Jeffries, Brady had begun to speculate in theatricals. He attended Mantell's opening in Richard, and saw in him, one supposes, the kind of raw force that had carried Corbett to success in the ring. At any rate he went backstage at once and is said to have said, "Now Bob, old man, don't you ever worry about anything again as long as you live. I will do all the worrying necessary for you in the future. I am going to be your manager. All I ask of you is to act."[94] Their combination lasted, at first under contract and then informally, until 1917, after which Brady's time was taken up by the presidency of the World Film Corporation.[95] The first need was to improve the supporting company. Brady began by hiring an almost entirely new lot, and every year he made hopeful substitutions—never, of course, managing to put together a company that the critics did not grumble at. Fritz Leiber, who signed on as a raw recruit in 1909 was perhaps the only one to stay with Mantell, learn his art, and emerge in the 1920s as an actor-manager and star in his own right. Brady chose plays for Mantell, provided sets and costumes, secured engagements, planned schedules, handled advertising and public relations, directed new productions, and advised Mantell on his own performing.

During the winter and spring of 1905 Brady led the company through countless rehearsals in Philadelphia, Chicago, and elsewhere, and by autumn he had taken the Garden Theatre in New York for a six-week run. *Richard III* on October 23 was the opening event. An old hand at press-agentry, Brady had spread the word that the play would be produced on a sumptuous scale—the battle scenes, for instance, would be backed by a moving panorama and the battles would be fought by 350 supernumeraries. For the first time, to the amusement of columnists and critics, the town learned that Mantell was "conceded to be the greatest living tragedian."[96]

Mantell brought off Richard (this was of course in the modified Colley Cibber version) with at least conventional success, so that, as the *Herald* noted, "the audience received it with alternating laughter and applause as it passed from grim comedy to grimmer tragedy."[97] Richard was always one of Mantell's best cards, useful to him to the end of his career, its strong, even coarse, histrionic effects providing the actor easy opportunities to catch the attention of and warm up any audience. He would use it regularly to open an engagement. On this occasion he succeeded so well that he did not quite offend William Winter. Herein lies the beginning of a puzzling story.

For reasons we can only guess at, when Mantell returned to New York in 1904, the "Dean of Critics" regarded him with utter contempt. Yet in 1917, the eighty-one-year-old Winter journeyed to Albany to be guest of honor at Mantell's sixty-third birthday party, and when Winter died a few months later Mantell was at his bedside. Their relationship had developed almost to one of father and son.[98]

In 1904, it appears, Winter absented himself from Mantell's hole-in-the-corner performances altogether. But in 1905 he simply could not avoid what Brady so blazingly advertised as a major display of the classics. As chief of the drama department at the *Tribune,* Winter had to see them, judge them for his *Tribune* readers, take a stand. It was a hateful assignment. After *Richard III* he posted a brief notice, unsigned, not daring to damn it, having sensed the enthusiastic response of the audience, yet half-canceling every word of faint approval with a perceptible sneer.[99] The Brady connection put him off.

Naturally he despised Brady as a vulgarian, an associate of sporting types, a blarneying huckster. As he would declare in an angry article a couple of weeks later, "The melancholy truth is that few intellectual men are engaged in the management of theatres," and "In almost all directions the spectacle presented is that of feverish, catchpenny, vulgar shopkeeping—intent to get money."[100] So his notice of *Richard III* opens with a sarcastic reference to "Brady, that distinguished devotee of the classic drama." Brady's much-touted scenery, he declared, would certainly not eclipse Mansfield's. He said of Mantell that he had heretofore enjoyed considerable success "of a sort," but "in the West"; he doubted that this interpretation of Richard would "dim the lustre" of the Richards of many other well-remembered actors. It was commendable, to be sure, that Mantell restrained himself vocally so that "one's fearful expectancy of ranting was scantily justified."

Othello, on November 2, was followed by another unsigned squib, still gunning for Brady: "The truth might as well be told . . . first as last regarding the widely posted laudations of the scenery and supporting company with which Mr. Mantell is this season surrounded. The scenery is not in any way commensurate with the managerial puffery thereof, nor does the supporting company rise at any point above mediocrity." He is not on this occasion harsh on Mantell—"an actor of good voice and presence, trained in the old school, and not without moments of imagination." Yet the performance as a whole provided "not a great amount of artistic enjoyment or emotional excitement."[101]

One would not expect an actor of Mantell's physical dimensions to fit into the commonly held image of Hamlet, but any aspiring tragedian—even in their times Edwin Forrest and Tommaso Salvini—had to submit to the Hamlet test. Mantell had played the part, off and on, for twenty years, but on November 6 he exhibited it to a New York audience for the first time. It was respectfully received, even cordially by many in the audiences. The *Herald* critic called it graceful in attitude and gesture, vocally harmonious, yet lacking in inspiration. Its planning was obvious. "He was a mime enjoying the music of his own voice." At the end of the week the *Dramatic Mirror,* while acknowledging that Mantell was too muscular to make an ideal Hamlet and lacked "the nervous, hysterical temperament of the Danish Prince," yet observed that he suggested through his manner that Hamlet's acts of apparent madness "are the result of logical reasoning, and not impulses of the moment"—an interesting interpretation and "a valuable addition to the line of stage Hamlets."[102]

Illus. 152. Mantell as Hamlet.

But to William Winter, Mantell's very act of undertaking the part was sheer audacity; his execution of it a desecration. Booth was dead; Irving was dead: Hamlet had died with them. Mantell's "respectable talent and ample experience . . . do not seem to have done him much good."

> Hamlet requires a combination of attributes and faculties that Mr. Mantell does not possess,—some of them being spirituality of temperament, imagination, distinction, refinement, feeling, grace, repose, intellectual supremacy, and a copious variety of expressive power. . . . He has plenty of voice, but does not know how to use it. His elocution was execrable. His demeanor and gesture were absurd. He spoke soliloquy (which is thinking aloud) as if addressing a public assembly, and, at various times, leaped like the wild gazelle on Judah's hills. Hamlet is not an acrobat, nor a blacksmith, nor a stump orator. It would be a waste of time to discuss such a performance. There is no

Illus. 153. Mantell as Iago.

> more of Hamlet in Robert Mantell than there is of milk in a male tiger."[103]

Winter's outrage was exacerbated by the news that next week Mantell would attempt Macbeth. And worse and worse might follow. "The awful intimation has been published that Mr. E. H. Sothern will present himself as King Lear! Perhaps Mr. Fortesque would favor the public with 'Ariel'; or Mr. James T. Powers come on for 'Miranda.' "

It had been a dreadful season for Winter. First the moral horror of Bernard Shaw's *Mrs. Warren's Profession,* then a revival of the "unspeakable" *Man and Superman,* then Olga Nethersole in *Sappho,* all these to persuade Winter that his beloved theatre was sinking into the pit. It was no consolation to him that he also had to sit through the American premier of *Peter Pan.* Small wonder then that this ignorant country rudesby, promoted by the Barnumesque Brady, presuming to meddle with Shakespeare, should drive Winter into near-hysteria.

Mantell displayed his Macbeth on Monday, November 13. The *New York Times* acknowledged it in a brief notice, finding this character "more suited to his rather florid and heroic style than Hamlet." The *Herald* headlined its review "Strong Macbeth" and "Virile, Forceful Acting." Noting that "there were graybeards present who, in the lobbies, whispered of Booth, and McCullough, and even Kean, and shook their heads regretfully," the *Herald* pointed out that once upon a time "critics picked at Garrick, so Mr. Mantell need not worry too much." By the adjectives "strong" and "forceful," the *Herald* critic did not mean that the actor ranted, but rather that he discriminated skillfully between the good and the bad in the character:

Illus. 154. Mantell as Macbeth. Folger Shakespeare Library.

Illus. 155. Marie Russell, Mantell's third wife.

"the varying, conflicting emotions that swayed Macbeth were sharply outlined and the telling lines and forceful situations were well brought out, with dramatic intelligence and technical skill." The *Dramatic Mirror* is emphatic on this point: Mantell's interpretation of Macbeth was unique in that "instead of a wild, daring, rampant Macbeth, cowed but momentarily by the terrors of the frightful consciousness of hidden guilt, was portrayed an ever nervous, ever fearing king. Into the most boastful speeches and acts, Mantell read terror, both of the living and the dead."[104]

On Tuesday, November 14, when reviews of Mantell's performance were coming in, Winter published a two-column article about *the play* without reference to Mantell at all. He then let his indignation simmer for a day or two while he fashioned, first, a definition of what it takes to play Macbeth properly; second, a bomb to blow Mantell off the New York stage, and his wife, Marie Booth Russell, with him. Most players who undertake the play, he said, think it a common blood and thunder melodrama. It is far more than that. "The first requisite for a good performance of *Macbeth* is the imaginative perception of spiritual things . . . the power to convey the sense of being . . . impelled by evil incarnations of the spiritual world. . . . The next requisite is the capacity to understand that this tragedy is a poetical fabric . . . dealing with spirits: treating of the relation between the world of fact . . . and the greater unknown world of spiritual life with which it is environed. . . . The third requisite is . . . the ability to impersonate, to speak blank verse correctly, and in all ways to create the effect of perfect illusion." Two-thirds of Winter's second essay are elaborations of these three requisites. Obviously, in Winter's understanding, Mantell possessed none of them:

> Mr. Mantell apprehends the play as a melodrama, and, in even the terrible scene of the murder, which should diffuse silent horror and oppress an audience with awe, he plays it to music: and at the end of that scene he makes a silly tableau of apparent preparation for a sword dance. In his delivery of the text there are many errors, many words misplaced, and still more of words that are marred by wrong emphasis. There was not a particle of poetry in the representation, and there seems not to be a particle of it in the man. Not one of the poetic speeches . . . was spoken so

Illus. 156. William Winter. Mantell's most hostile critic and finally dearest friend.

as to thrill any hearer. The tremendous effects that are in the Banquet were never once liberated. There was one burst of noise—the usual resort of the old stager—at "Take thy face hence." It would be pleasant to praise Mr. Mantell! . . . but there is no opportunity of doing so in presence of such a Macbeth as this. It touches the high-water mark of respectable mediocrity, and that is all. . . . The actors do nothing for [the play] that is worth doing. The Lady Macbeth said that she was "bold," yet could not stand straight, and never left off bleating, in a thin, high, querulous voice, till, in the sleep scene, she began to whine: the words there are to be spoken in a clear, thrilling, horrid, agonized whisper. Strange, when players have the opportunity to deal with these great subjects, that they will not take the trouble to think, to feel, to understand, and to rise to the height of such splendid possibilities!

W.W.[105]

That sharp little "W.W." was Winter's last word to Mantell for the season. November 28 was the normal day for reviews of Mantell's *King Lear,* which Brady had scheduled to conclude the run with a grand climax. Winter delivered it the ultimate snub. He mentioned that the performance had taken place, declined to comment on it (we might guess that he stayed at home), and filled his space with an essay on Shakespeare's play.

Brady was counting not only on the greatness of the play but also on its novelty. No major actor had performed it in New York since Salvini (in Italian) in 1885 and Booth in 1886. Much as the play was admired in the book, it was not in those days regarded as "a good acting play." Though Nahum Tate's absurdities had long since been got rid of, modern meddlers (the latest being Winter himself in the version he made for Booth) had damaged the play in modern ways. It was ruinously bowdlerized. Many supposedly "weak" passages had been lopped out to provide "strong curtains." The blinding of Gloucester being too cruel to be enacted, one never knew how he came to be blind. Gloucester's leap from an imaginary cliff was omitted. The great third act went for nothing because Lear's dialogue was rarely heard, the act being largely given over to the makers of thunder-lightning-wind-and-rain, and Brady could be counted on to whip up the most spectacular storm since the one that ruined Edmund Kean's performance in 1820. Brady's special contribution here was a bolt of lightning that flew across the stage and knocked down a tree. And as the *Dramatic Mirror* acutely noted, the public conception of the relationship between humor and pathos now differed vastly from that of Shakespeare's time. "Today the sublime approaches perilously near the ridiculous when, all simultaneously, we are asked to sympathize with a childishly imbecile king, the son of an earl in the disguise of an insane beggar, and a wise fool."[106]

Nonetheless, Mantell's Lear was immensely successful. He was a virile king, said the *Dramatic Mirror,* magnificent in his rages and maledictions in the early scenes, and deeply moving without being maudlin in his final scenes with Cordelia. So great was the demand for *Lear* that the six weeks' engagement was extended to eight, several matinees of *Lear* being added to the normal schedule. Though Mantell's style was "old school," he satisfied thousands of New Yorkers by restoring to them Shakespeare's greatest tragedy with undreamed of intensity and power.

A year later, in November of 1906, Mantell returned to New York to spend a month at the Academy of Music. He would offer four of his established Shakespeares—*Richard III, Hamlet, King Lear,* and *Othello*—and add three more—Iago, Shylock, and Brutus. It was obvious that he had not been wasting time during his country engagements. In Chicago, for instance, where he played Lear and Macbeth, W. L. Hubbard of the Chicago *Tribune* was delighted to observe that "the months that have passed since Mr. Mantell previously played here have brought improvement to him in his art," and congratulated the American stage that at last it has an actor it can call its own "who is fitted by training and abilities to interpret satisfactorily the great tragic roles in Shakespearean drama." In a long paragraph Hubbard catalogued Mantell's excellences and the former faults he had now rid himself of.[107] Similarly, at the end of the Academy engagement, the *Theatre* magazine observed that "Mr. Mantell as a Shakespearian actor has not only enlarged his following to a remarkable extent, but has also gained in the favor of the critical brotherhood."[108]

And somehow or other, even William Winter had recovered from whatever ailed him: henceforth he would treat Mantell with respect—critically, to be sure, but without the sneers and snarls that colored his writings in 1905. The opening paragraph of his 1906 review of *Richard III* sounds very much as if actor and critic have had a good long conversation and come to an understanding. Winter tells us that Mantell "has assumed a professional position that ought to be cordially approved and earnestly commended—for he has made plans to assume and maintain the leadership of our stage, as the representative of Shakespeare. . . . The plans that he has now formed, if successfully fulfilled, could not prove otherwise than beneficial to the stage and to society. It is a comfort to see an actor who, whatever may be his defects, squarely places the emphasis on acting, and does not seek to attract attention by ministering to an ephemeral taste for fads and follies."[109] He would still blame Mantell for excessive "physical exuber-

Illus. 157. Mantell as King Lear.

ance" and for making Richard a "mugging miscreant"—but these were the result of playing to audiences of coarser taste, outside the metropolis. He scolded him, too, for persisting in wrong emphases and incorrect accentuation, and for starting at too high a pitch so that he was out of breath before he reached his climax. But he had fine moments when he used the hollow whisper; "his sardonic humor and his irony are fortunate and true."

As for Hamlet, Winter still felt that Mantell revealed no affinity for the character, but merely spoke the words in the book, illustrating them with the usual stage business. And his Lear, too, was not "a magnificent old king" who goes mad; he was only "a senile proletarian," "an afflicted old man, whom almost any other venerable name would suit as well." Yet his representation "possesses such solid merit, such sincerity of purpose and such frequent tints of artistic beauty, that it ought to be, and can be, warmly extolled, as honorable to the actor and as entirely worthy of public acceptance and deep respect."

Of Othello:

> There is no reason why Mr. Mantell should not give a really great embodiment of Othello. He has the person, the stature, the face, the temperament, the passion, and above all the expressive voice for exactly this fabric of tragedy. . . . But he can never achieve his full victory as the Moor until he ceases to be declamatory and theatrical—making reverberant sounds for the sake of their reverberancy, and indulging in tricks to catch the gallery.[110]

Of Mantell's Brutus, Winter wrote at great length and enthusiasm. It was very wise of the actor to choose this play for this part, for what he needed most is what Hamlet calls "a temperance that may give it smoothness." Brutus being philosophic and meditative, yet under his cold exterior burning with power and boiling with feeling, needs exactly this repose that Hamlet calls for. Such repose is within Mantell's reach, and the more often he plays Brutus and similar characters, the more surely he will achieve it. "There is a kind of comfort in seeing that an ambitious and talented actor, to whom circumstances seem disposed to afford opportunity, has, in a shopkeeping period of theatrical history, entered on the right road." After extended analysis and praise of the garden scene, the assassination, the address to the populace, and the quarrel scene, he declared this "the finest all-around impersonation that he has ever given."[111]

Early in 1907 Mantell took his Shakespeare to Boston, where in three weeks he played eight parts in seven plays and received both handsome compliments and sharp correctives, especially from H. T. Parker and E. F. Edgett of the Boston *Transcript.* Parker, who covered *King Lear,* was well pleased with Mantell's revival of the "old school" methods. They reminded him of theatre-going in his boyhood: "Mr. Mantell's ways in Shakespeare are the ways of the great generation that our fathers knew and in which he had his training. . . . In the main they are good ways still." The text, in the Winter version, was so

Illus. 158. Genevieve Hamper, Mantell's fourth wife, as Juliet.

unsparingly cut that in parts of it one could hardly follow the story, but all of Lear's scenes were there and all his great speeches. And, as in the old days, one went to the theatre simply to see a great actor play Lear. The subordinate characters were scarcely individualized. Unlike most modern actor-managers (say Tree or Sothern) Mantell and Brady made no attempt to create a Britain of any particular century. The palace halls, the heath, the battlefields were conventional theatrical nowheres, in some semi-barbaric time. Unlike most modern actors, Mantell and his company made no attempt to humanize or naturalize the language, but took it off the spool, so to speak. It was simply poetry in the theatre, and every line of it audible and so justly phrased and emphasized as to disclose its meaning. It was a bit artificial, perhaps even stilted, but the surprising effect was that Shakespeare was speaking for himself.

Parker's one objection, a serious one, which he expressed at great length and in elegant style, is that Mantell had not structured the role of Lear so as to create the maximum of tragic effect. In older days the Lear who begins the play was

> lusty of body in spite of his years and locks, big of speech, masterful of bearing, fiery of temper, domineering of spirit, who used . . . to come stridingly to his throne. Who has forgotten their gusty pride, their swelling wrath? They dominated the scene, they stirred to admiration. They were fit protagonists for a mighty tragedy of pitiless fate, and that tragedy . . . became the more piteous and awesome because half that fate was in the pride, the rage, the rashness, the ungoverned and ungovernable strain . . . that made the old king at the start so masterful and puissant a figure.

Now this, it seems to me, is exactly how Mantell played Lear two years earlier, according to the *Dramatic Mirror* and the New York *Herald* of 1905. Perhaps in the meantime he had overdone the vigorous opening of the play, had fallen into his old country habits of making too much noise, and was now, in Boston, fearful of being accused of rant, held back too much. In any case, Parker is sure of his impressions and drives the point home. Mantell, he says, assumes from the beginning what his sufferings ultimately bring home to, "a very foolish fond old man, four score and upward." His steps totter, his voice quavers and turns querulous, his hands shake and lack the strength to draw his sword. There was no regal grandeur to decline from, nothing for fate to destroy. The last half of the play, however, moved Parker deeply:

> From the first words of madness to Edgar to the exit toward the prison with Cordelia, he made his Lear of a very poignant wistfulness, of a vague and tremulous groping, of age speaking out of a childish mouth, of an exquisite gentleness and longing, of a piteousness that was unconscious of itself. And in all these things was a very perfect and tragic illusion. . . . And the curtains shut as though a flood of pity had closed them.[112]

Parker was again pleased at *Macbeth* "to hear the text spoken with declamatory and rhetorical emphasis, even to the rhymed tags at the end of some of the speeches, and to hear it addressed directly to the audience. Our stage is usually a picture stage. Last night it was often the declamatory stage for which Shakespeare wrote." Again too the scenery was "a serviceable and noncommital background. The costumes signified only a rude and ancient time, and of 'atmospheric suggestion' of a primitive Scotland there was none."

> On other occasions one put himself down before Irving's or Robertson's or Booth's Macbeth and took careful thought of it. We watched an impersonation and stood outside the play. Mr. Mantell's Macbeth, by well-ordered and well-expressed conventionality, leads him into it. Shakespeare, not an actor, dominates the scene, speaks full and clear with his own voice of poetry, drama, and character, and summons "atmosphere" beyond the most persuasive contriving of any actor-manager.[113]

Mantell, as we know, was never quite at home in *Hamlet,* but he had to submit it to Boston. E. F. Edgett covered it for the *Transcript,* and he read Mantell a cautionary lesson which I have not encountered elsewhere. Recalling Mantell's career he noted that in the 1880s when he specialized in melodrama heroes he achieved stardom without question. But he was ambitious. He took on Shakespeare at the highest level, so that now we must judge him as a Shakespearean and tragedian. Further, he now aspires to Hamlet, which "more than any character of Shakespeare is . . . the goal of the determined actor." Now we must judge him as Hamlet. Essentially he fails. He knows the words of Hamlet. He knows the actions of Hamlet. But he does not know Hamlet. He merely considers him "a machine for acting." It cannot be helped, but cannot be disregarded, that unlike Booth or Forbes-Robertson he does not look like Hamlet. Further, there is no consistent reason governing his behavior. In the first act he shrinks from his mother's touch, but later reveals no such aversion to her. "He alternately assumes moods of noise and quietude that have no reason either in the text or situation. His violence reaches such heights at times that he vocalizes in extraordinarily incoherent fashion, interjecting inarticulate sounds into line after line, and pronouncing such simple words as 'cries' in two syllables." At times, to be sure, he touches the words with a fine vocal quality that indicates his sympathetic understanding of the character, but "a moment later he will look and act and speak like nothing better than the crushed tragedian of caricature."[114]

He is overly fond of "illustrative gesture," and suits the word to the action in a sense never intended by Shakespeare. He cannot speak of "the fruitful river of the eye" without pointing to his eye; he cannot speak of 'making his quietus' without drawing his dagger from its sheath; worst of all he must show that he knows a "hawk from a hand-saw" by "indicating the backward and forward movement of that useful carpenter's tool."[115]

So, too Edgett found Mantell's rendering of

Othello both good and bad—wobbly. His appearance was splendid—"an erect, stately, and imposing figure, with face of deep-brown swarthiness, not black nor yet the mere dingy white of more than one actor's representation. . . . By the entire absence of a beard he emphasizes the Moor's complexion, his reddened lips, his gleaming teeth, and the rolling whites of his eyes giving at times, perhaps unintentionally, certain mild Negro aspects to the character." Mantell's use of his voice was what most troubled Edgett in this Othello. Beautiful in the extreme in quiet speaking, it was frequently "torn into fragments by a rapid utterance and a violence of speech demanded neither by the man's innate character nor the situation." At such moments Mantell seems to think that Othello is an unchained beast. "Throughout the 'farewell the tranquil mind' speech he leaves no shred of passion untorn, whereas if Othello ever spoke plaintively, contemplatively and sadly, he spoke so at that moment." Happily at the close of the play he was at his best.

There he was mild, gentle, sorrowful, filled with anguish and suffering, and in every word and every movement poignantly effective. As the curtain fell, he left with us the impression of a powerful, thoughtful, intellectual actor who has all the resources of his art at his command, and who is able to command them at will.

His Othello is a remarkable study, but it will never be satisfactory until he learns that passion and violence are not the same.[116]

It was as Shylock, a far lesser role than Hamlet or Othello, and one that offered obvious temptation to rant and violence, that Mantell astonished Edgett with an impeccably controlled performance. One forgot the actor's towering figure in this "man of haggard aspect, bowed down not so much with years as with the strife to maintain life as an alien in the land of his oppressor. "His voice, restrained in volume, resonated with a wide range of distinct and conflicting passions—"pride, anger, hatred, anguish, power, vengeance, and the lust for gold." Proud of his Jewishness, he never forgets his superiority to the Christians whom he is compelled to serve, and he expresses his contempt for them by maintaining constant dignity. Neither Antonio nor Bassanio can force him to lose his temper.

It is only when Salarino provokes him with his taunts that the tempest breaks, and in a whirlwind of words he swears to feed his revenge . . . upon the hapless Antonio. This and the following scene with Tubal alone tempt Mr. Mantell to physical violence, and they tempt him rightly. The moment and the speech demand it. Mr. Mantell fulfills them, not as he fulfilled them in Othello, destroying the effect of passion by the very force of his passion, but by holding himself under complete control. So perfect is his command of himself that he is enabled to give a quiet and downright restrained earnestness to the single phrase, "I am a Jew," in the midst of a long speech that is aflame with uninterrupted passion and pathos.[117]

These, then, are the major instructions provided him by the critics of Boston. He did well to treat Shakespeare's language as heightened discourse, artful and artificial, and to shun the contemporary fashion of "humanizing" it, bringing it down to the level of everyday conversation. In this respect he was maintaining the better features of "old school" acting—care for vocal projection, intelligibility, and clarity of thought. He was complimented, too, for recognizing that acting was more important than scenery, that a well-dressed stage could be achieved without pedantic concern for "historical accuracy" in scenes and costumes. He must learn, however, especially as Othello, to express passion without violence; and in any tragic character (Lear is the prime example) to "structure" the performance so that the end is not foretold at the beginning and so that movement toward the catastrophe is palpable. He had to be scolded, strange to relate, for indulging in "illustrative gestures," some so naïve as to insult the intelligence of the audience.

During the 1907–8 season Mantell avoided New York and worked the country westward, displaying his ever-growing repertory of classic tragedy to admiring audiences everywhere. *King Lear* had seemed the ultimate major novelty that he could ever find, but Brady, still at his elbow, persuaded him to undertake one more—the rarely performed *King John.* Brady revamped the supporting company to some extent and reverted to full-fashioned historical realism in the matter of sets and dresses. According to Percy Hammond of the *Evening Post,* Chicago had never seen anything more magnificent than *King John* when it opened there on November 18, 1907. Hammond congratulated Mantell for enlarging his repertory, for reviving a little-known piece, and for his own performance of the neurotic, vicious, cowardly, and contemptible King, so very unlike all Mantell's other Shakespeare heroes. He faulted the play itself for ambiguity of structure—the first two acts being "vaguely interrelated" and the interest not rising until the King's villainy emerges, or until the pathetic scene in which Hubert is dissuaded from burning out the little Prince's eyes.[118]

W. L. Hubbard of the Chicago *Tribune* was considerably more enthusiastic. Reversing Hammond's view, he found the early acts lively with movement and animation and the latter section a puzzlement. Mantell had cut out a series of political scenes and jumped

Illus. 159. Mantell as King John.

from the death of Prince Arthur to the death of the King, so that the audience never understood the outcome of England's struggle with France and the Papacy.

> Mr. Mantell, as the weak and weakening King John, has a role on which he expends his finest and maturest powers as actor and impersonator. He has devised a remarkably effective make-up for face and figure—one which suggests the former dignity and manly vigor of the king, and yet in and about the eyes and in the slightly hesitating gait and stooped bearing betrays the weak will and weakened physique of the decadent. There are telling moments—big moments in the part—and these Mr. Mantell handles with unfailingly technical skill and finesse and with more of directness and straight convincing power than he displays in any save his ablest characterizations. The defiance of the papal legate is splendidly done, and the first scene with Hubert, in which is done the plotting for the murder of Arthur, is the finest piece of work yet seen from the actor.

The problem of what to make of Mantell's wife, Marie Booth Russell, became peculiarly vexing during the Chicago run of *King John*. By her right as leading lady of the company she of course chose Lady Constance, the last of many Shakespearean roles she undertook for Mantell, and once more she came to grief. Hubbard in his generous review could write, "The support is of the best," and one by one he praised every actor of a significant role. But he could not suppress the cruel truth about Miss Russell.

> The Constance of Miss Russell was a source of pain to every hearer. A worse exhibition of wriggling, writhing, moaning, gurgling, and mouthing cannot be imagined than she indulged in in the great scenes of the mother's lament. It was so bad it was ludicrous. If only she could learn the value of simplicity and naturalness![119]

It is difficult to imagine the pain Miss Russell suffered from such buffeting, or what it cost Mantell himself, or what strain it must have set up between them. As a reviewer once remarked, "Mr. Mantell is unfortunate in his wives."

He was lucky in his fourth and last, however—the young and lovely Genevieve Hamper, another actress in his company, whom he married in 1912, a year after Marie Russell died. Miss Hamper was a passable if not brilliant actress, who supported him nicely as Desdemona, Ophelia, Juliet, and Portia—even, eventually as Lady Macbeth—and became his comfort, practically his caretaker, during his final years.

On January 12, 1909, William Winter published a furious, and probably uncalled for, diatribe against the New York managers for keeping Mantell out of the city. He probably did not yet know that his own days at the *Tribune* were numbered. His screaming denunciations of plays and performers he did not approve of had become a burden that the *Tribune* management could no longer afford, and at the end of the season they dismissed him. Certainly on January 12 he showed no signs of holding his fire in a cause he believed in. He opened with a shout: "WHY?" What has become of Robert Mantell?" He complained that the New York public could behold many a well-advertized performer but few who had earned their reputations by merit or accomplishment. And the public was denied Mantell. It could not be for financial reasons, for during Mantell's last New York engagement he had drawn $1,000 a performance. Forces more insidious must be at work.

> Has it been ordained that the best tragic actor on the American stage shall not be permitted to act in New York? The race of trained actors in Shakespeare,—those who know the traditions and who are experienced and competent in the legitimate drama—has almost entirely disappeared. No one of them is ever seen here now. . . . Can it be that the entrenched promoters of phantasy, frippery and fad are living in dread lest the standard of true Acting should once more be reared? Is Mr. Mantell excluded because his presence would make the pygmies seem exactly what they are?

He asserted that Mantell applied for a booking the previous season but was denied, that he was now so discouraged that he contemplated removing to Australia.[120]

Perhaps Winter's blast had an effect. Or perhaps he simply had not been informed of Mantell's schedule. In any case, Mantell opened *King John* at the New Amsterdam two months later, on March 8, and occupied that theatre for most of the month. Bulliet says that *King John* did not draw well, bringing in only $5,000 during the week that it played, whereas in the second week the standard Shakespeare repertory earned over twice as much.[121] Reviews of *King John* ranged from tepidly approving *(Herald),* to mixed tending to the negative *(New York Times),* to hostile *(The Nation).*[122] Some which I have not seen goaded Winter to editorialize that if they were not impertinent they would be comic.[123] Winter's own review, analyzing both play and performance, much of it obviously composed in advance, fills two and one-half columns of the *Tribune* (something over 3,500 words) as if by sheer bulk of wordage Winter could hoist the production onto Olympus.

Except for the fact that *King John* was virtually unknown to American playgoers (thirty-five years had passed since the last New York production) Winter might have spared his readers several long paragraphs, yet when he comes down to the specifics of Mantell's appearance and performance he never wrote more vividly or informatively. He tells us that when we first see this King John we know that he is sick, feverish in body and distressed in mind. There is a reptilian fascination about his blanched face, menacing yet attractive. His cruel blue eyes are sometimes cold and stony, sometimes wavering and shifting, bespeaking self-conscious evil. "The lips are full, red, and sensual. The head is covered with a shock of reddish hair. The cheeks are covered, but not concealed, by a red, matted beard." His body stoops, his movements are quick and spasmodic. "A trick of plucking at a single hair of the beard expressly denotes a nervous splenetic temperament, overstrained and with difficulty held in check."

Winter's description of the King's death should be quoted entire:

> The King is dying—poisoned by a monk. "The life of all his blood is touched corruptibly." His agony has been terrible. He has been delirious, making idle comment and pathetically breaking into song. He momentarily recovers his reason, at the last. He will not die within four walls or beneath a roof. His soul must have "elbow room: it would not out at windows nor at doors. He is brought into the orchard of the Abbey. The time is night. A wavering, golden light streams over the form of the dying man, and over the stalwart knights and courtiers who are grouped around him,—some of them in full armor, others in the sumptuous colored raiment that John, like all Plantagenets, liked to see. The body of the King, convulsed with pain, is shrunken and withered. His hair and beard are dishevelled. His face is ghastly, and, as seen in the flickering light, it gleams with the gathering dew of death. He has thrown aside his rich attire, and is clad in black trunks and long black hose, with a white shirt, torn open at the throat; around his shoulders there is a loose robe. A more piteous spectacle—made awful with mysterious, grim, and weird environment,—has not been seen; and Mr. Mantell makes the illusion so complete that the theatre is forgotten. The threadlike, gasping, whispering, despairing voice in which he utters the dying speeches of King John,—the abject, pitiful supplication that his kingdom's rivers may be allowed to take their course through his burnt bosom,—can only be heard with tears. If pity and terror be the legitimate object of tragedy,—touching the heart and thrilling and exalting the mind,—Mr. Mantell, assuredly has accomplished its object.[124]

During the remainder of Mantell's New York run, Winter reviewed *Othello, Macbeth, Romeo and Juliet,* and *King Lear*[125] in terms ranging from honestly critical to glowing enthusiastic, as if by now he knew that his own public voice was about to be stilled and he wished to atone for the abuse he had laid on Mantell when he first offered himself as a Shakespearean.

Mantell returned to New York, to Daly's Theatre in 1911, featuring *King Lear;* to the Forty-fourth Street Theatre in 1915 with a repertory of eleven plays. At that time it was announced that his contribution to the Shakespeare tercentenary would be a world tour of *King Lear.*[126] Unfortunately, that plan had to be abandoned because of the spread of the Great War. His only special participation in the tercentenary was to join Margaret Anglin in St. Louis in the summer of 1916 and play Jaques to her Rosalind.[127] The New York theatres experienced a glut of Shakespeare that year—139 performances of seven different plays, led by nearly a dozen principal actors, American and foreign. But Mantell was not one of them.[128]

That was Shakespeare enough for a while, declared *Life* magazine in 1917: "Shakespeare has again become *persona non grata* in New York."[129] Nonetheless Mantell came in briefly in 1917 with *The Merchant of Venice,* and again in 1919 with other items from his repertory. Thereafter until his death in 1928 he was seen only in the provinces.

Once in 1906 a dinner companion asked Mantell to comment on the common critical charge that he was an "old-fashioned" actor. He rose to the charge with what satisfied his interlocutor as "an admirable argument."

> What else can the acting of Shakespeare be but the acting of the old school? Those are dramas that you can't modernize—and this has been proved time and time again by the failures in Shakespearean roles of modern "naturalistic" performers. No less famous persons than Willard and Charles Coghlan are good examples of what I mean. . . . The so-called "natural" method is impossible. In the modern plays one has merely to copy the people in everyday life. Where can you go into the streets or the restaurants or the homes and find a Brutus? One must draw on the imagination. One must create.

And then he tacked about and modified the direction of his argument:

> Still I do not admit that I am an actor of the old school. The actors of the real old school, if you saw them today, would seem to be devouring the scenery. I am attempting to bridge over the gap, to play the great heroic roles which most players do not even dare to attempt, using as much modern method as possible without forfeiting the tragical elevation of the theme and verse. It is a difficult task to apply modern thought to these mighty characters of other days.

He rose from the dinner table then, lighted a fresh cigar, and fired a playful shot at the whole tribe of fashionable "naturalistic" performers whose methods are ruinous to Shakespeare. "I don't want to hurry you," he said, "but I've got to play Othello tonight. I have to get to the theatre ahead of time. You see, I'm a conscientious actor, and when I play the Moor I always black all over!"[130]

It is a brave stand that Mantell here took. He would restore the art of speaking Shakespeare's verse—indeed, of the still subtler art of speaking high-styled prose, while nine actors out of ten in the profession were determined to pulverize all classic language into the formless chatter of street and drawingroom. Yet in 1909 *The Nation* declared of his production of *King John,* "Perhaps the most noticeable feature was the slovenly and unintelligent manner in which all the players, save two or three, spoke their lines with no apparent understanding of either metre or emphasis. In many instances modern pronunciations were given with excruciating results"; and declared the event "a costly demonstration of the practical hopelessness of interpreting Shakespeare satisfactorily . . . until some sort of training school had been established, where actors shall be able to learn something about the proper delivery of verse and appropriate romantic action."[131] Nor was it merely the supporting actors but Mantell himself who was blamed many times for these same violations of Shakespeare's language. He was blamed for not being able to do the very things he most wanted to do and meant to do and could not. A fair summing up of Mantell's value and significance was that of E. F. Edgett of the *Transcript,* when in May of 1920 Mantell made one of his late visits to Boston.

> A half-century and more ago it was a commonplace of the theatre for an actor to attempt Shakespeare. When Mr. Mantell made his change [from melodrama], and now, it requires courage. The rapidly changing seasons in the meantime do not appear to have daunted him. He is still as daring and ambitious as if the destinies that determine the future and the fate of an actor were his to command. He has acted Hamlet and Shylock and Macbeth and King Lear year after year, and he still acts them to the very evident acceptance of a large portion of the public. He has toured the country from end to end, he has endured the discomforts of one-night stands, he has barn-stormed hither and thither, he has remained a week or perhaps a month in the greater cities of the country, and his annual return after the inevitable three months summer rest offers abundant reason to believe that there is a call for Shakespeare and that he is always able and willing to answer the summons. He has proved himself an ardent and a capable devotee of the ancient masterpieces of the drama, even though he may not be a great master of them.[132]

Not great, perhaps, but steadfast.

Chapter VI

End of the Tradition: Part II
Sothern and Marlowe

It is not the fashion nowadays to idolize E. H. Sothern and Julia Marlowe, to rank them with the Booths and Salvinis, the Rehans and Modjeskas, whose fame as Shakespeareans preceded theirs.[1] Even in 1909, when they were called upon to dedicate the palatial New Theatre on Central Park West, the New York millionaires' Temple of Drama, few New York theatre devotees would have held them equal to the glamorous Irving and Terry, whose American visits were of recent memory. Yet they certainly deserved the best esteem of their contemporaries and deserve now a better remembrance than they enjoy. In their first partnership, between 1904 and 1907, they perfected six Shakespeares, introduced three artistically ambitious modern plays, and became without doubt the most distinguished acting couple in America. Indeed, the English critic Arthur Symons would have it that they were the finest actors in the English-speaking world.

In April and May of 1907 they tested their skills on London and like most American stars who braved English audiences, they found the experiment costly. Since they both came of English parentage, something was forgiven them by any Londoners who knew that fact, but professionally they were American, and it was universally assumed that nothing first-rate in the theatrical way could be expected from Yankeeland. They got off to a bad start by offering two modern plays—one German and one American[2]—of little interest to London critics or audiences. When they turned to Shakespeare the critics awoke to their quality and praised them with considerable enthusiasm; but the approval came too late to rouse the interest of the general public, which preferred the flamboyant Shakespeare productions of Beerbohm Tree anyway.

Sothern had predicted a loss of $40,000: since the adventure cost them only $15,000 they could count it a good investment. They had pleased themselves, gratified the discriminating, brought home a sheaf of solid reviews of their Shakespeares, and above all they had inspired Arthur Symons to write a twelve-page essay about them for *The Monthly Review* (reissued in a collection of Symons's essays published on both sides of the ocean), in which without reservation he placed them at the head of the profession.[3]

A few of Symons's sentences convey the drift and emphasis of his argument:

> Why is that we have at the present moment no great acting in England? We can remember it in our own time, in Irving, who was a man of individual genius. . . . But have we in our whole island two actors capable of giving us so serious, so intelligent, so carefully finished, so vital an interpretation of Shakespeare, or, indeed, of rendering any form of poetic drama on the stage, as the Englishman and Englishwoman who came to us in 1907 from America, in the guise of Americans: Julia Marlowe and Edward Sothern?. . . . Now here are two players in whom technique has been carried to a supreme point. There is no actor on our stage who can speak either English or verse as these two American actors can. It is on this preliminary technique, this power of using speech as one uses the notes of a musical instrument, that possibility of great acting depends. . . . What these two players do is to give us, not the impression which we get when we see and admire fine imitations, but the impression we get from real people who, when they speak in verse, seem to be speaking merely the language of their own hearts. They give us every character in the round, whereas with our actors we see no more than profiles. . . . We have nothing like it in England, nothing on the same level, no such honesty and capacity of art, no such worthy results.

Illus. 160. Miss Julia Marlowe: a portrait executed in 1901 by Irving R. Wiles. Presented to the National Gallery of Art, Washington, D.C., by Julia Marlowe Sothern in 1951. Courtesy of the National Portrait Gallery.

In Symons's estimation Sothern's and Marlowe's acting raises the art of theatre, which most estheticians dismiss as unworthy of consideration, to the level of music, sculpture, dance, painting, and the other fine arts.

Julia Marlowe

Julia Marlowe (1866–1950), born in the village of Caldbeck, Cumberland, was not then Julia Marlowe, but Sarah Frances Frost.[4] Her mother, Sarah Strong, inherited from a long line of North-of-England Presbyterians tough-mindedness, independence, and a sturdy sense of responsibility, and she bequeathed these qualities to Sarah Frances. The father, John Frost, was of a different breed—an amiable but aimless fellow—who kept his family alive by operating a small general store—or letting his wife operate it while he hunted, drank, or followed the races. One day in 1870 he got into a fracas with a neighbor and, fearing imprisonment, he fled the country—all the way to America, in fact, and far inland to Indian country west of Kansas City. There out of old habit he again set up as a storekeeper. Eventually he sent for his family, informing them, by the way, that their name was no longer Frost by Brough, the alias he had assumed to get out of England. So at the age of five Sarah Frances Frost became Fanny Brough.

The store in Kansas failed. The Broughs moved east to Ohio, finally settling in Cincinnati. Fanny's mother became the breadwinner and effectual head of the family by running a boarding house (later a small hotel) and putting out the children (four altogether) to earn whatever they could. John Brough wandered about as whim took him, once to Australia and otherwise to places unknown, until Mrs. Brough sensibly divorced him.

In 1878, during the national craze for *H.M.S. Pinafore,* a local theatrical manager in Cincinnati, Colonel Robert Miles, decided to stage it and tour with it commercially with a company of child actors. Fanny, at twelve, read his advertisement and applied for a place in the company. She was accepted, pending only parental approval. That was no problem. Fanny always knew her mind. She told her mother that she was going, and that settled it. She went.

Her biographer, Charles Edward Russell, maintains that independence, self-assurance, and will power, quite as much as her natural artistic gifts, account for Fanny's ultimate theatrical triumphs; and this decision at the age of twelve is the earliest example of his thesis at work. "Nothing could stand in the way of that steadfast resolution," he writes. "If it is not right now, keep on until it is right and I know it is right and will stay right—this was the controlling idea."[5]

The night after she made up her mind, she was onstage at Vincennes, Indiana, untrained and unrehearsed, singing in the sailors' chorus, her salary $7.00 a week. Soon thereafter, her natural talents showing, she was promoted to the role of Sir Joseph Porter, which she sang throughout the 1878–79 season and well into the fall of 1879. But the juvenile *Pinafore* used up its market, and soon she was at home in Cincinnati, "at liberty."

She attempted various employments—studied telegraphy, took up dress-designing, and even for one day boxed ginger snaps in a cracker factory. But her real life was still in the theatre. Cincinnati was an important theatre town, visited by all the stars. Fanny not only *saw* Booth, Jefferson, Barrett, McCullough, Mary Anderson, Clara Morris, Fanny Davenport, and the rest, but was often on stage with them. Her experience with the *Pinafore* company qualified her, at fifty cents a night, to swell a mob, sing in a chorus, march in a procession. She bought a one-volume Shakespeare from a door-to-door salesman, acquired books of popular plays in the modern repertory, and began to study appreciatively what was best in the best performances of America's best actors, and study critically what they did that was wrong.

It troubled her to realize that the principal aim of many famous actors of the day was not so much to embody the characters they were said to be playing, but to "make points"[6]: that is, in tragedy or serious drama to deliver strong emotional passages so loudly, accompanied sometimes by such extravagant postures or surprising stage business that the audience would automatically respond with roars of applause. One could feel a "point" coming on as the actor's voice began to "ladder"—step by step to expand in volume, rise in pitch, and accelerate until it exploded in a burst of noise, But afterward, in the quiet of her room, when Fanny turned to the book of the play and studied certain speeches she had heard "laddered" that night, it would often seem to her that *noise* was uncalled for. In years to come, when she played her matured Juliet, she had to put up with acres of newsprint scolding her, or pitying her weakness, because she did not howl and gyrate like a maniac in the Potion Scene.

Even more disturbing was her realization that the actors did not understand, hence could not project, the meaning of the words they were so melodiously intoning. By uttering the lines in comfortably managed musical patterns they could let the emphases fall where they merely "felt good," quite failing to stress

Illus. 161. Julia Marlowe as Juliet. Folger Shakespeare Library.

the word or words where the kernel of meaning lay. Thus she would cite one "esteemed bungler" of Juliet who would declare to the Nurse,[7]

"Thou and my bosom *henceforth* shall be twain,"

whereas the keyword is probably *"twain"*. From early days she found ludicrous the reading of a Juliet who said,

"My only love *sprung* from my only hate,"

when she should have, with pause and stress, established the antithesis of *"love"* and *"hate"*. A famous Portia announced that

"The *quality* of mercy is not strained,"

whereas Portia's meaning lies in *"not strained"*. Charles Russell himself, as if to demonstrate the widespread sacrifice of meaning to "music," once published an article entitled "Hamstringing Shakespeare" in which he recorded senseless readings by Henry Irving, Beerbohm Tree, and other major Shakespeareans of the recent and memorable past.[8] All her life Miss Marlowe strove to reconcile meaning *and* music, and she would "keep on until it is right and I know it is right and will stay right." Throughout her promptbooks thousand of "right" words are underscored.[9] And many a time when we find a critic complaining of her "imperfect elocution" or "reading her lines badly," the probable truth is that she was reading the lines correctly *but not as the critic was accustomed to hearing them.*

In 1883, when she was seventeen, Fanny was called to the road again to play minor roles in support of one Josephine Reilly, a Cincinnati amateur who aspired to stardom.[10] The tour collapsed early in 1884, but Fanny profited from it in various ways. As Maria in *Twelfth Night* she received whatever good notices the company received. And over and over again Miss Reilly demonstrated, in posture, gesture, movement, voice level, and line-reading, how *not* to play Juliet or Viola or any other part in her repertory.

Best of all, however, out of this venture Fanny won the sponsorship of an older actress, Ada Dow.[11] Impressed by Fanny's latent talent, Miss Dow "adopted" her, took her to New York, and as a straightforward business arrangement accepted a lien on Fanny's future income, and fed and housed her for several years while she read, thought, memorized, and taught herself how to act. Mornings Fanny walked the paths of Central Park, pondering and reciting to herself the several roles in Shakespeare and modern plays upon which she expected to begin her career. Like Mary Anderson before her, she was self-taught, and she taught herself starring roles. Like Miss Anderson, she never thought of entering the profession otherwise than "at the top."

Afternoons she would rehearse her morning's work for "Aunt Ada"—sometimes a sticky operation, for her independently conceived readings and methods often ran counter to Miss Dow's comparatively "old school" ideas. But Fanny's well-considered explanations usually prevailed. Her only other professional mentor was an old Welsh singing teacher named Parsons Price, whose lessons were of inestimable worth. He taught her diaphragmatic breathing, which she had never heard of, and for many months he compelled her to speak up and down the musical scale until he created her "middle register." Her voice became, says Charles Russell,

an extraordinary organ. Its overtone was a full, rich and faultless contralto with a mezzo range, but its undertones were of an amazing variety and exquisite, smooth liquidity . . . so that they sometimes sounded not so much like the tones of one speaking as some new and perfect musical instrument discoursing melody at once and conveying thought.[12]

Critics called it "vocal velvet," and to the end of her career it was accounted one of the most beautiful voices on the American stage.[13]

In the spring of 1887, when she was twenty-one, Colonel Miles (he who had first staged her in *Pinafore*) and Miss Dow decided that she was ready to try out as a star. Not in New York, of course, but for a three-week run in smaller towns of the New England circuit. Not as Fanny Brough, a name that lacked dignity at one end and pronounceability at the other, but the perfect euphony (which she herself invented)—*Julia Marlowe.*[14] And not in Shakespeare until she had proved herself, but in a pair of well-known romantic "she" plays of nineteenth-century confection. She made her debut on April 26 in New London, Connecticut, as Parthenia in a sentimental melodrama translated from the German, called *Ingomar, the Barbarian.*[15] This once famous but well-forgotten play was so great a favorite of Miss Marlowe's (she kept it in her repertory for over a dozen years) that a brief account of it is in order.

The scene is a Greek province in ancient times. In the mountains above the Greek city of Massilia there dwells a brutal tribe that preys upon the Greeks. The tribe's chieftain, Ingomar, violently despises women, using them only as slaves and breeders. When his tribesmen kidnap an old Greek named Myron, and the Massilians will not pay the ransom, Myron's daughter Parthenia offers herself as a prisoner in exchange. Parthenia is a paragon of beauty, innocence, affection, heart-wisdom, and eloquence, the likes of which Ingomar has never encountered. She responds to his harsh threats with gentle persuasion. She teaches him the beauty of flowers—violets and roses—and enchants him by weaving garlands of them and winding these around goblets. She explains to him the nature of love between men and women. This is difficult to put into words, for though she utterly believes in this kind of love she has never (until now) experienced it. The grand turning point is her recitation of a poem about love which contains a pair of lines still remembered as the epitome of mid-century sentimentalism:

> Two souls with but a single thought,
> Two hearts that beat as one.

Ingomar is aroused, enthralled, converted. He accompanies Parthenia down from the mountain, joins the Greeks, marries Parthenia, and persuades his tribe to abandon their rude mountain life, build a city of their own near Massilia, and live with the Greeks like neighbors. Such is the power of goodness, love, and beauty.

Miss Marlowe's performance was the hit of the season in New London, and all good things for her were prophesied by the local reviewers. "Her career will not close," wrote one of them, "till she has climbed to the diamond ridge [?] of artistic fame."[16]

Her second role, Pauline Deschappelles in Bulwer's *Lady of Lyons,* was a neat companion piece to Parthenia because it exactly reversed the love situation. Pauline, a proud beauty, disdainful of all suitors who are not well-born and wealthy, is brought low by the devoted affection of a lowly gardener's son. The role provided her a wider histrionic range than Parthenia, but it put her in an unsympathetic light, and she would not play it again after this three-week experiment. The run was thoroughly successful. Word of it crept into the Boston papers. The *Globe* congratulated manager Miles on having "drawn a prize."[17]

Miles's next move was to secure the Bijou theatre in New York for the afternoon of October 19, 1887, for a "professional matinee"—a single showing of *Ingomar* to an invited audience of managers, critics, and actors. These "professional matinees" in New York were the bane of the theatre profession. Any tyro with money enough to hire a stage and a scratch company could put out a call, and managers and critics vying in the search for new talent ignored such invitations at their peril. But they arrived bored and more often than not left early. This time they did not leave. One critic called it "the best Parthenia seen in New York in a generation."[18] E. A. Dithmar of the *New York Times* opened his review with a happy challenge: "Julia Marlowe: remember her name, for you will hear of her again."[19] In his analysis of her performance he emphasized her simplicity, clarity, quietness, and charm:

> She had not great moments; she made no conspicuous points. . . . The episode of the song of love was treated daintily and without exaggeration. The defiance of Ingomar was true and affecting and not stagy. She expressed the anger of the girl very vividly and without resort to any hackneyed artifice. . . . In depicting the ingenuousness of the girl she was not too coy; when she wept the tears seemed to be real, and her smiles seemed to be reflections of a sunny temperament. her voice is strong and pleasing, and if she has a singing voice it ought to be a pure contralto. Her tones are never mannish. And best of all, she speaks the English language very well.

At the final curtain the stage was strewn with flowers, tributes from amazed spectators who had hurried out between the acts and raided all the nearby flowershops.[20] Dozens of people crowded behind the scenes, among them the burly-minded critic Nym Crinkle, to congratulate her. Augustus Van Cleef of the *Herald* prophesied for her a high place in the profession. Nine managers came backstage during the afternoon to persuade her to star in new plays they were about to produce. But she declined them all: Colonel Miles had plans far more to her liking.

Two months later, on December 12, 1887, Miles presented her for an entire week at the Star theatre, where she would for the first time reveal her beloved Shakespeare, opening the week with Juliet and closing with Viola, roles which she had been studying and acting to herself, but never to an audience, for years. Between them she would repeat Parthenia.

Two days before the opening of *Romeo and Juliet* the *Spirit of the Times* posted a fair warning: "Julia Marlowe, the Southern actress, who made a promising debut as Parthenia . . . will appear professionally on the much larger stage of the Star, and will, of course, be much more strictly judged."[21] And so it was. The audience for *Romeo and Juliet* was large and enthusiastic, applauding generously and calling her before the curtain after the Balcony Scene and the Potion Scene, at the end of each act, and repeatedly at the finale. Most of the critics that I have read, however, took this audience enthusiasm rather edgily, as if *their* right to pass judgment had been preempted. It was an audience of "friends," declared Dithmar, and he trusted that the actress was sensible enough not to be taken in by cheap flattery. "The path that is strewn with flowers and ready-made laurel wreaths," he wrote, "often leads straight to obscurity." William

Winter in the *Tribune* said the audience was "largely composed of personal friends,"[22] an uninformed remark, for as Charles Russell points out, Miss Marlowe *had* no friends except Aunt Ada and Colonel Miles, was totally unknown except to those who had seen her professional matinee, and in fact was not acquainted with six persons in the audience. Indeed she cherished her anonymity. All her life she was a very private person. Much as she was adored by thousands of spectators, she was extremely selective in her choice of persons with whom she could develop true intimacy. And she almost hated publicity. She would never permit a manager to "puff" her appearances. She rarely gave out interviews and invariably declined invitations to social affairs got up to exhibit her as a visiting star.

Newspaper reporters were often piqued at her refusal to provide them "copy," but on this occasion one sympathetic critic declared that he was delighted to celebrate Miss Marlowe's success because she declined to talk about herself:

> How absolutely novel it seems to see a début made on the stage in the old self-respecting way with the thing turning on whether the débutante has talent or not, rather than on how many dresses she has or how much she has done for orphan asylums or how far she has been scandalized with the Prince of Wales!. . . . We owe her a debt for demonstrating the incredible proposition that it is still possible to succeed on merit.[23]

Of course there were faults in these early performances, and most critics were kind enough to mention them in the way of advice, as easily correctable. Stephen Fiske of the *Spirit of the Times,* for instance, noted that her arms needed make-up so they would not look so brown against her white dresses; that she must not curl her fingers while gesturing; that she must not roll her head about during impassioned speeches.[24] Several critics remarked that she often seemed too studied, lacked spontaneity, as if she were carefully remembering what she had taught herself—to stress *this* word and not *that* one, to raise her hand to her face at *this* precise moment and not before or after. Faults like these would surely disappear once she had eased herself into the role with a few performances.

Astonishing though, in view of her professed devotion to the "true text," is the undeniable testimony that at this stage of her work with *Romeo and Juliet* she was using some of Garrick's old "improvements." Thus, for instance, in the first act Romeo did not sigh for Rosaline, of whom there is no mention, but for *Juliet, Juliet!* In the last act Juliet awoke before Romeo died and they played out Garrick's agonizing-absurd Liebestod.[25] She clung to these bad choices for a year or two, but by 1890 a Boston critic congratulated her for having abandoned them.[26]

Van Cleef thought she gestured too much, indulged in too much byplay, and "her mobile face was made to do too much duty in the way of pretty looks, &c."[27] On this point Miss Marlowe would one day agree with him. In an article of advice to young actors, which she wrote for *Theatre* magazine in 1901, she used her early renditions of the Potion Scene as a telling illustration of the fact that an actor "should not move about the stage for the mere sake of action," should not indulge in "fluttering gestures and swift alternations of expression which degenerate into mere grimaces."[28]

> My earlier interpretations of the [Potion] scene were characterized by an eagerness to discover how many interesting bits of business I could create. I overloaded the reading with bric-a-brac. I went to the window, parted the curtains, and looked out upon the sunrise. I sought fresh air, I sank to my knees more than once; in a word, I was restless, and however interesting I may have been, I cannot now feel that I was in any great degree convincing.

Well before 1901 she had discovered the power generated by economy: "The last time I played the Potion scene . . . I moved only three times—from the seat at the foot of Juliet's bed to the prie-dieu, then to the centre of the stage, where I sank upon my knees, and then back to the bed." She had learned to move only when the impulse drove her to move. No longer was it actory bric-a-brac, but the poet's language uttered passionately that did the work.

But "passionate utterance"? Could she express *passion?* In 1887 many agreed in essence with William Winter's judgment that in the early scenes she displayed the "sentiment of love . . . with girlish sweeetness," but that she was incapable of showing the "passion of love."[29] Or in Van Cleef's terms, that "the hot blood of Italy did not seem to course through Miss Marlowe's veins, but rather the cooler fluid of some more northern clime."[30] Stephen Fiske allowed that she understood and felt what she was saying, but could not make her audience feel it; that she "lacked the subtle sympathy which distinguishes a great actor or actress."[31] The opinion was general among the critics in 1887 that so far she lacked "tragic power" and could not bring off the Potion Scene. (But the *audience,* remember, called her back for a special bow at the end of that scene.)

On this point Miss Marlowe simply recognized that her approach to the scene ran counter to what the critics were accustomed to. She did not resent their preconceptions, yet she would not compromise her own conception to satisfy theirs.

I knew there were many excellent critics and sincere men to whom it had never occurred that a women of Juliet's character might have a passion white-hot in its intensity and still be too fine of nature, and of thought too exalted, to show it in one look or gesture or tone that would be inconsistent with her immaculate purity of soul. But I had much rather play her as she seemed to me and have all the critics dissatisfied with it than play it so that they liked it and feel that I had departed from my conviction about her.[32]

She saw Juliet as a very young girl (she retained Lady Capulet's line, "She's not fourteen"—not Garrick's "not eighteen"), but capable of great strength of character when faced with threats or danger. When her father bullied her and ordered her to marry Paris forthwith, when her mother rejected her, when her only confidante, the Nurse, blithely counseled her to submit, she turned hard as nails, determined, unfrightened, unstoppable. Abandoned and alone Juliet the girl suddenly became a brave woman.

"If all else fails, myself have power to die."

Bravely she visited the Friar, bravely accepted the potion and his instructions. At her return she greeted her father and Paris in seeming cheerfulness. Cunningly she put her father off with a pretense of obedience. In the Potion Scene she *spoke* of death and fearful things but she dismissed them. As the horrid imagery grew, her courage mounted and her rich voice deepened. She knew, as Nym Crinkle once observed, "that her ghosts were in herself."

"Nobody was disappointed to find that she was not the ideal Juliet," Fiske wrote in the *Spirit,* for unlike the saccharine Parthenia, Juliet reaches heights and breadths and depths that take experience to explore.[33] Nearly everyone acknowledged her great promise. The critical faculty welcomed her to the profession—all of them but one, the "Dean of Critics," William Winter.

In perfect innocence Miss Marlowe acquired an implacable enemy in Winter.[34] It happened that at her first performance of Juliet Colonel Robert Ingersoll, avid theatre-goer and devotee of Shakespeare, was present, invited there by his friend and protégé Joseph Haworth, who was playing Romeo. From Miss Marlowe's first scene, Ingersoll became enormously excited. This, he thought, was the finest Juliet he had ever heard or seen. During the first entr'acte he encountered Winter in the lobby and began exclaiming about the "wonderful," "glorious" rendition of the Balcony Scene. Winter, who chose to form his own opinions (and had already done so), responded that anyone could play the Balcony Scene, that the Potion Scene was the test, and that Miss Marlowe would certainly fail it. Ingersoll, angry at being contradicted, declared loudly that "you critics make me tired . . . You sit in your little cells playing with your little fingers on your little yardsticks" and can't recognize genius when you see it.

Winter could not respond to this attack in the midst of the crowd, but from then until press-time his brain must have whirled as he tried to shape a review that would do the actress some sort of justice and at the same time put her (and Ingersoll) down. His review is a muddle.[35] The first rambling paragraph seems to say that beginning actors ought to stay out of sight until they are no longer beginners. Next he blamed Miss Marlowe for presuming to be a star by simply presenting herself in a starring role. In an obligatory show of fairness he complimented her intelligence, sensibility, good looks, and so forth, but he couldn't resist canceling each kind word with a hard one: "She has a good voice, not well trained"; or "Her acting was gentle . . . and quite devoid of fascination." The second half of the review is a patchwork of items he found ridiculous, useless, ignorant, silly. He came down hard on Haworth, too, whom he knew was Ingersoll's friend.

If Ingersoll's attack were not enough to turn Winter against Miss Marlowe, yet another motive, perhaps only half-realized, was at work. As we have seen in an earlier chapter, Winter was a devoted supporter of Augustin Daly and of Daly's leading actress, Ada Rehan. Only a few months earlier Miss Rehan had created her amazing Katherine in *The Taming of the Shew*[36] and was obviously scheduled for a brilliant career as a Shakespearean. Winter was by no means interested in promoting any competition to the Daly-Rehan combination. His hostility to Miss Marlowe, which he maintained for nearly a decade, was one of the reasons she kept out of New York for many seasons. Happily his temper changed about the end of the century (after the death of Daly). He and Miss Marlowe became good friends, and he paid handsome tribute to her in one of his last books of theatrical reminiscences.[37]

Presumably Winter stayed home on December 14 to avoid Miss Marlowe's "starring" in *Twelfth Night:* no notice of it appears in the *Tribune.* Dithmar of the *New York Times* thought the "freshness and spontaneity" of her Viola clearly proved her fitness for the profession.[38] If he granted that she had not plumbed the tragic depths of Juliet, yet he thought her Viola came near the ideal—her elocution unforced, pathetic where "she never told her love" in the great scene with Orsino, happily astonished in the little ring scene with Malvolio, alternately tender and vivacious, and endowed with girlish grace and prettiness. In time her Viola would match Modjeska's and Neilson's.

Van Cleef of the *Herald,* not so easily pleased as Dithmar, offered a more penetrating analysis.[39] It did delight him to watch this "beautiful Byronic boy," and to recognize the intelligence and originality in Miss Marlowe's readings. Every Cesario scene charmed him as it passed. Yet he felt that in the scene with Orsino the love she expressed while concealing it "was but girlish affection and not womanly love." The tones were not deep enough. So too, in the "willow

Illus. 162. Miss Marlowe as Viola. Folger Shakespeare Library.

cabin" scene with Olivia "there was not sufficient heart torture in the love pleading for one she herself loved." Yet unquestionably Van Cleef admired Miss Marlowe and expected her speedy rise. In every way (except the hostility of Winter) her week at the Star foretold success.

Next, in order to capitalize on such reputation as she had won at the Star, Colonel Miles sent her and her company on a whirlwind tour into the midwest—Cincinnati to Chicago to Detroit and half a dozen more cities in Indiana, Michigan, and Ohio. Her Chicago notices were perhaps typical of the best-informed that she received along the way. The critic for the *Tribune*[40] acknowledged that she was a novice whose full powers were yet to be developed, but he admired the courage and cheerfulness with which she went about her work: "she was perfectly at her ease, graceful, and quickly intelligent, and never did anything that displeased." She was truly an original, he declared, "infinitely superior to several manufactured actresses of mechanical methods" who have lately been forced upon the public. From observing her Viola Lyman Glover of the *Herald* concluded that she was possessed of "far more than ordinary dramatic instinct, with a leaning toward comedy altogether delightful in its impetuous and unstudied grace."[41] Manager Hamlin of the Grand Theatre invited her to return to his house annually for the next six years. Her confidence was bolstered. But not her bank account. The expenses of the tour ate everything that came in, and she and Aunt Ada returned to New York to resume their frugal living and plan the future.

For reasons which do not appear—probably financial—Colonel Miles separated from her at the end of this tour and she had to find another manager.[42] Several were eager to have her to star in modern prose plays, in translations of Sardou, and so forth, but she insisted she would deal only in Shakespeare and "similar drama," and she would play "only good women." A. M. Palmer wanted her to join his stock company, but she declined to put her career into someone else's hands, to be cast and directed by "some stage manager." Finally she secured the services of one Ariel Barney, who would arrange engagements and stagings and not interfere with her acting or direction.

It happened just then that Helena Modjeska was retiring for a period of rest, so Miss Marlowe took over her entire supporting company.[43] An excellent group, it contained Charles Barron, who for a season or more had played Othello to Booth's Iago: Mary Shaw, an "actor's acress," whose Celia and Olivia nicely complemented Miss Marlowe's Rosalind and Viola; W. F. Owen, a brilliant low comedian; and Robert Taber, an ambitious young leading man in whose skill and will Miss Marlowe would later, to her cost, trust too much. Unfortunately these and the rest were devoted to Madame Modjeska and resisted taking orders from a young unknown posing as a star after one brief professional season. Every direction Miss Marlowe gave out provoked a grumble, heard or unheard, and nothing seemed to please the actors more than a bad house, of which at first there were many.

Luckily, after a series of unhappy one-night stands, Barney booked an entire week in Washington, D.C. where there was waiting a fine audience, distinguished and sophisticated, and well enough informed about Miss Marlowe's reputation in New York and the Midwest to want to see her. From November 6, 1888, when she played Parthenia to a house well crowded with the families of congressmen, judges, and diplomats, throughout the week of modern plays and Shakespeare, she received increasingly enthusiastic notices. By the week's end the box office showed a pleasant balance. But then a well-meaning but stupid critic spoiled everything. Seeking to praise Miss Marlowe, he committed one disastrous sentence:

> But this young girl, who, after a merely nominal novitiate, seems already, among the conventional dead wood of her support, like a star of heaven fallen among faggots.[44]

The more fiery of the "faggots" assumed, of course, that Miss Marlowe had personally inspired, or even invited, the sentence. Much time and tact were required to avert mutiny and restore workable relations between the little general and her troops.

On December 3, 1888, she opened her first engagement in Boston—a decisive one—perhaps a terrifying one for any newcomer except the likes of Julia Marlowe, who never suffered stage fright in her life. For the audiences and critics of Boston–Cambridge were the most sophisticated, knowledgeable, and discriminating of any in America. At the same time they were sympathetic to excellence, mannerly, and fair. She played Parthenia and Julia (Knowles's *The Hunchback*) and finally Juliet to universal enthusiasm—to standing room only on the last three nights.[45] It was the most prosperous week she had known, and it marked the beginning of her love affair with Boston, her favorite of all American cities. An editorial in the *Globe*,[46] probably written by Howard Ticknor, declared among other things that

> The world theatrical has long been waiting for the appearance of just such a star as she promises to be. . . .
> Miss Marlowe's acting is charming. Someone had said that there is poetry in her every tone and movement, or words to that effect, and that somebody came near to speaking the truth. . . .
> Great is art and Miss Marlowe is already one of its charming prophets. Unlike some of art's priestesses she knows acting from posturing, elocution from mouthing, art from millinery. The *Globe* compliments and congratulates this new and shining star. . . .

The next afternoon Arthur Warren of the Boston *Herald* labeled her "The New American Actress" and prophesied that she would prove "the most important acquisition for several years to the American stage."[47]

It was time to expand her Shakespeare repertory, and she spent most rehearsal hours in December directing the company in *As You Like It,* which she intended to offer at her next stand, which would be Philadelphia. On Christmas Eve she played Parthenia to $67 worth of Philadelphians.[48] Attendance improved during the week that followed and Juliet on New Year's Eve brought not only a very good house but a glowing review in the *Public Ledger.* This had been written by the proprietor himself, L. Clarke Davis, who sent her a corrected copy with a covering note to the effect that having seen all the great Juliets of the last thirty-five years he counted hers among the finest. H. H. Furness, the editor of the *Variorum Shakespeare,* was there also, with his earphone and his daughter Caroline: he saw all her roles this season, and to the end of his life remained her champion and friend.[49]

The great event of the Philadelphia season, as Miss Marlowe hoped, was the new Rosalind, which appeared on January 3. A week before, the critic at the *North American,* George Rogers (apparently not much of a critic), turned in a vaguely negative review of her Viola. Now, for no particular reason, he was enraptured by her Rosalind:

> It was so sweet, so tender, so gentle, so refined in method, so pure in feeling, so elevated in spirit; it was illuminated with such lambent humor, irradiated with such piquant, captivating grace, animated by such innocent and artless gaiety and softened with so true a note of pathos that those that went to make allowances for expected deficiencies remained to wonder at its beauties, and the audience followed its course from first to last with a demonstrative delight.[50]

This is not criticism, of course, mere newspaper padding, its maudlin terms more appropriate to Parthenia than to Rosalind. But at least Mr. Rogers could tell which way the wind blew. Enthusiasm was the order of the day. The entire battery of Philadelphia critics joined in praise of the "new risen star." Manager Barney extended the Philadelphia run a week in order to satisfy the demand to see her, sacrificing several one-night stands in order to do so. The nightly receipts that had begun at $67 rose to $1,400 at the end.

During this climax of good fortune Miss Marlowe acquired another enemy even more dangerous than William Winter, and head of the faction—Augustin Daly himself.[51] And again, as in the Winter affair, she was utterly innocent of giving offense, knew nothing of the matter while it was happening. Daly brought one of his favorite farces, called *7–20–8,* to Philadelphia during Miss Marlowe's engagement there. To his amazement and chagrin he found "crowded houses and long reviews for her; but no such pleasing tributes for *7–20–8*." He challenged his old friend at the *Ledger,* L. Clarke Davis, for making "all this fuss about this Marlowe girl. She is most ordinary." Davis stood his ground. Daly declared her "nothing but a flash," only one of these ambitious schoolgirls that think they can act when they can't." In a year, he declared, she would be forgotten, and he wagered a dinner at Delmonico's for Davis and his friends that events would prove him right. As Charles Russell tells this story, "twelve months later Mr. Daly himself sat every night in the gallery of the Fifth Avenue Theatre" watching Miss Marlowe's every motion "with sedulous care." I doubt that Daly did so, but in any case, that, as we shall see, is not the end of the story.

Illus. 163. Miss Marlowe as Rosalind. Folger Shakespeare Library.

In February she returned to Boston, eager to exhibit her Rosalind there. It was well that she did, for her opening night (February 18) garnered her more applause and critical appreciation than any single night in her young career. McNally of the *Herald* declared that "she is unquestionably the best Rosalind on the American stage today" and promised that a year hence it would be even finer.[52] Edward Fuller in the *Post* found her Rosalind "pitched in the right key."[53] Here at last "after a self-conscious Rosalind" (by which he meant Mary Anderson's, which he had just labeled "ludicrous"), "a fluttering, nervous Rosalind" (he meant Modjeska's), "a merry and boisterous Rosalind" (Rose Coghlan's or Fanny Davenport's), "we have the sweet and bright and womanly Rosalind that Shakespeare drew!"

Mrs. Sutherland of the *Transcript,* who, to be sure, thought her "often too girlish, rather than womanly," and thought at times that "the elements of intellectuality and humor give way too much to the elements of sensibility and emotion,"[54] yet observed that "she has not been two minutes on the stage before you find yourself forgetting all about Miss Marlowe, and your attention rivetted upon Rosalind." If in thinking it over afterward you would like to argue a point with the actress, "at that moment you feel that you have no actress to argue with, but Rosalind herself." Henry Clapp of the *Advertiser,* one of the fairest critics, seems to have agreed with Mrs. Sutherland on the point of excessive tenderness and emotional warmth.[55] He objected that "the mirth and mental force" of Marlowe-Rosalind "were constantly weakened by or subordinated to her sentiment:—that she "had hardly time to make a hearty joke or relish the richness of her own mirth before her tenderness welled up and deluged all her voice and text." I think Miss Marlowe would not have been hurt by that criticism, and she may well have profited from it. For Clapp confessed along the way through his generous and wise review that he was so moved by her grace and charm and fine temperament and taste and quick tender sympathy and physical beauty that, quoting Tennyson, the mere sight of her in her Ganymede costume would "make an old man young."[56]

Throughout the vast lot of reviews of this occasion the main supporting players—Barron as Jaques, Taber as Orlando, Mary Shaw as Celia, Owen as Touchstone—were so warmly praised as to compensate for the mere mentions, or less, that they had often got from less appreciative critics. Word of Miss Marlowe's Boston triumph was noted in various New York papers. The *New York Times* editorialized that "calm, critical, cultured Boston had been captured by her, and her audiences had grown to enormous size. . . . Her name tonight is on the lips of everybody."[57]

By now, quite innocent of the dangers that lay ahead, she knew she must face New York. She had not played there since her little trial week at the Star two years before, so that she was hardly known to the New York public. All through the summer while she was a guest of the Ingersoll family at Far Rockaway, she strove to enlarge her Shakespeare repertory by intensive study of Beatrice and Imogen, but—unable to satisfy herself with either—she laid them by.[58] After all, her new Rosalind, along with Juliet and Viola, should suffice to establish her in the metropolis. She instructed Manager Barney to take the Fifth Avenue Theatre for eight weeks, beginning at the height of the season, in mid-January, 1890.

She spent the autumn playing westward, breaking in a new set of actors. Taber, for instance, had left her. But she arrived in New York on schedule, counting on *As You Like It* as a ten-strike, expecting to fill out the run with all her other tried and true plays in repertory order.[59]

But she was anticipated. In mid-December Augustin Daly staged *As You Like It* with his company of already famous stars—Ada Rehan as Rosalind, John Drew as Orlando, Touchstone in the hands of James Lewis, one of the wittiest actors of Shakespeare's clowns. Daly's production was a very merry one, a frolicsome, "spring time" production, with very green greenery and plenty of sunshine. No gloom was cast by George Clarke's Jaques, who was rather whimsical than sourly cynical. All was keyed to the "gleeful animal spirits" of Ada Rehan and her "happy hearted raillery." It opened just a month before Miss Marlowe was scheduled to come to town, and it entirely captured the attention of the public and the press.

Miss Marlowe did not dare offer her quieter, "autumnal," and comparatively sentimental production in competition with Daly's. Instead, she got out *Ingomar* and repeated it night after night for two weeks, losing money all the while. In desperation she opened *As You Like It* on January 27, lost more money, and closed it two weeks later. In her fifth week she added a few performances of modern plays, then sold the last three weeks of her tenancy to another company. Her total loss was $29,000. She would not attempt New York again, to be outmaneuvered by Daly, for five years.

Certain leading New York critics were so devoted to Daly or intimidated by him that they snarled like Cerberuses whenever they sensed that a newcomer threatened to intrude upon Daly's "property."[60] The critic of the Boston *Post* (Charles Copeland) called attention to this phenomenon.[61] "The New York critics distinguish themselves again," he wrote, "by falling upon the Rosalind of Miss Julia Marlowe with extraordinary severity." He had observed the "lavish praise" heaped upon Ada Rehan's Rosalind and "the equally lavish condemnation of Miss Marlowe's." Dithmar of the *New York Times* had declared that in her scenes of badinage with Orlando she was "merely girlish, shallow and pert." The *Evening Post* had applied the dreadful word "amateur." The Boston *Post* writer concluded sadly that "it is only another case of a performance which aroused enthusiasm among intelligent theatre-goers in Boston sharply disapproved by the superior intelligence of New York. Such an intimation that we have much to learn about the drama is really discouraging."

A glimpse into the duplicitous review by William Winter provides a fair understanding of how Daly's nearest friends on the press did his work for him. Winter always established his *bona fides* as an impartial observer by flattering his victim—in this case "an uncommonly pretty and interesting girl" . . . of "ingenuous manners" . . . "child-like charms," etc., whose pleasing personality "may one day enable this clever girl to invest with the authentic attributes of Rosalind." But—

> For the character of Rosalind Miss Marlowe evinced neither distinction nor brilliancy. Rosalind's speech of resentment to the tyrannous Duke was merely an ebullition of shrill, girlish anger. In the forest scenes Miss Marlowe's Rosalind bore no resemblances to a boy, and her deportment and delivery were languid even to the verge of insipidity. Rosalind is not a listless character. However deep her feeling there can be no doubt of her dash and brilliancy of demeanour.

And then, after another generous dollop of personal flattery, "At present the part is beyond her reach." Of the supporting cast he has little to say. Eben Plympton as Orlando is "a little ponderous," but earnest, and he modified the "burly" manner with which he began. In the scenes of exile "he became animated and even disgraceful [*sic*]." Milnes Levick, as Jaques, employed "an artificial, sephulchral, monotonous style of delivery" and made Jaques into "a sort of ecclesiastical bassoon." The scenery was "fantastic," "rough in composition and eccentric in color." The overall effect of the produciton was that of "conventionality and mediocrity."

Miss Marlowe's next season (1890–91) was nearly a total loss.[62] Early in the fall, while staying with friends in Philadelphia, she was stricken with a fever. It was typhoid, and it nearly killed her. For weeks she lay in a coma or was delirious. Her face swelled and blackened, and the physicians were just about to lance her cheeks (thus ending her career forever) when the fever began to recede. Recuperation was very slow. Not until April was she able to act again, and then but little. In May her mother took her abroad for a long rest and refreshment.

In 1891–92, Miss Marlowe added *Much Ado* and *Cymbeline* to her Shakespeare repertory but not, it appears, very successfully. As a matter of fact, she had played Beatrice for a week at the beginning of the preceding season (before her illness) to dedicate a new theatre named for her in Memphis,[63] but her performance did not satisfy her. Nor was it right this time. In Boston Clapp, for instance, though pleased by her beauty of face, figure, and voice, and by her determination to play Beatrice mirthfully, and pleased that she did not, as in Rosalind, let the mirth go under to sentiment, yet felt that like most modern Beatrices she smoothed the sharp edges of her wit and made Beatrice a figure of easy-going drollery.[64] She did not sting Benedick in that opening passage of taunts, but actually flirted a rosebud under his nose like a common coquette. The marvelous leap of imagination in the line, "there was a star danced and under that was I born" came off with no special lift, no joyous discovery, but "amounted to nothing more than a good-natured pleasantry." Nor did she plumb the depths of Beatrice's emotional side. Her discovery that Benedick is in love with her lighted "no fire in her ears"; she even omitted that line and asked, "Can this be true?" in a casual, superficial tone.

In the *Transcript*, Mrs. Sutherland invoked the word "impressionism" to suggest what was wrong with Miss Marlowe's delivery of the part.[65] In Shakespeare's play, she said, Beatrice is "drawn with the most downright distinctness of outline." She "lives and moves in the clearest dry atmosphere, every detail stands out sharply, and the dominant characteristic of the whole is its pungency of effect." Miss Marlowe surely understands the character well enough, but she shows us the picture through a sort of haze. "The subtlety of innuendo, the caustic tartness of repartee, the bright intellectual keenness with which Beatrice overbrims are all somehow slurred over by her." A year later and yet again in 1894, Mrs. Sutherland hit upon the recognition that Beatrice and Benedick—unique among Shakespeare's *dramatis personae*—are Society Comedy, *comédie de moeurs,* Molièresque.[66] Actors skilled in the sharply drawn characters of Goldsmith and Sheridan are better fitted for Beatrice than Miss Marlowe is, whose poetic aroma and personal charm make her Rosalind and Viola so delightful. Miss Marlowe is refined, every inch a lady, but "the elegant court lady, the finished woman of the world, she distinctly is not!" She struggled on with the character for a few years, then dropped it, and learned to master it only when she joined with Sothern in 1904.

On February 18, near the end of this Boston engagement, she offered a role she deeply loved and had been studying for years—Imogen in *Cymbeline.*[67] The plot is a rather muddled one, and by the time it had been cut and arranged for playing time, various critics complained that it was hard to follow. But certainly Miss Marlowe's performance of Imogen—"The consummate flower of womanhood, superior to everyone of her beautiful sisters"—was superb. For Mrs. Sutherland, "Of all the parts Miss Marlowe has acted here this season, we like her Imogen unspeakably best. Her refinement, intelligence, personal charm, are valuable factors in all her impersonations. . . . But her conspicuous power of dramatic impersonation stands forth even more convincing than ever in Imogen; she is Imogen to the life, Imogen through and through." Or elsewhere Mrs. Sutherland speaks of "the illusion she produces of really being the character she assumes to be." She has said this before, we recall, of Miss Marlowe's Rosalind; and years later Arthur Symons will credit this same power of "identification" to both Marlowe and Sothern in their London performances. Miss Marlowe would deny emphatically that she ever thought she *was* the character she was playing, but the illusion she created was a significant ingredient of her art. Both Henry Clapp and Mrs. Sutherland describe in

Illus. 164. Miss Marlowe as Imogen. Folger Shakespeare Library.

loving detail Imogen's emotional progress through the great scene with Iachimo—her glad receipt of Posthumus's letter, her half-hearing and lack of concern at Iachimo's first dark speeches, her abhorrence as she realizes what foul slurs he is uttering against her husband, her dignified but reserved pardon when he changes his tactics and falls to praising Posthumus, the slow subsidence of her wrath and horror over what she had heard. Both critics are agreed that in the next act she "showed genuine dramatic power, and rose to the height of the text in her furious rejection of Cloten.

At this point, however, these two excellent critics parted company. Clapp said that every further point where passion is called for by the situations and the lines—anguish, terror, indignation, grief—the actress failed. Mrs. Sutherland read all this quite differently. According to her, from the moment that Imogen learns from Pisanio that her husband has ordered her death she is simply stunned into a kind of emotional paralysis. From that moment forward she

> brings one element constantly and very artistically into the foreground: this is Imogen's utter physical and moral weariness; nothing could be more finely conceived nor carried out than the listless, almost automatic part she takes in the further proceedings of the play up to the moment when she recognizes Posthumus in his peasant's dress before Cymbeline and the wounded Iachimo; then for the first time the blood begins to course through her veins once more.

This conception, said Mrs. Sutherland, is fine in itself and finely carried out: "It is unspeakably beautiful."

Perhaps what Clapp was asking for was a conventional, even "old school" exhibition of "points." Mrs. Sutherland understood very well why Miss Marlowe suppressed histrionic fireworks the better to experience and communicate a deeper psychological truth. Just as she had declined to rant and tear up the stage in Juliet's Potion Scene out of respect for Juliet's dignity and "immaculate purity of soul," so now she enacted this Imogen, "the consummate flower of womanhood," suffering infinitely worse dangers than Juliet's passing moment of fear—alienated from her father, separated from his husband, threatened by rape, driven into the wilderness, accused of adultery and sentenced by her husband to be slain—she enacted this noble creature with the steadfastness of a near saint.

Presumably it was the difficulty of the play as a whole rather than disaffection for the role that caused Miss Marlowe to shelve it after this season. She would not attempt it again for thirty years.

The season had been a prosperous one, and so too the next (1892–93). Her leading man was the talented and ambitious young Robert Taber, who now rejoined her company; and under the general management of Fred Stinson, who had arranged the tours of both Neilson and Modjeska, she was for the first time scheduled to the Pacific coast. Taber left her again for another company in 1893–94, but rejoined her at the end of that season.

Here her troubles began. She married him.[68]

It should not have mattered, but it did, that she took his name and accepted him as co-star. The billings read "Julia Marlowe Taber and Robert Taber," and this diminished her popularity. Managers wanted to hire "Julia Marlowe" but the magic went out of it when "Taber" was tacked on. Audiences wanted to see "Julia Marlowe" but not "Mrs. Anybody." At least once she had to go to court to obtain her salary because a local management contended she had violated her contract by change of name. Many people resented Taber, too, suspicious that he had tricked his way to stardom simply by marrying a star.

There was something to that. He took over the stage direction, and to a certain extent he began to choose plays with strong roles for himself. He shone as Valence in Browning's *Colombe's Birthday,* as Joseph Surface in *The School for Scaldal,* as Young Marlow in *She Stoops to Conquer,* as Tito in *Romola.* But his truly astonishing decision was to stage *Henry IV, part one,* because he wanted to play Hotspur. When it was pointed out that except for the small part of Lady Percy there was no role for Miss Marlowe, his response was that Prince Hal is "a wonderful part for a woman." Incredibly she agreed to go through with it. After months of preparation and thousands of dollars spent on the finest scenery and costumes, *Henry IV* opened in Milwaukee in September of 1895. Notices ranged from bad to mixed, but Taber persisted during the year and tried it in eleven more cities. Finally A. M. Palmer, tempted by the novelty of it, invited the production to New York in March of 1896.[69] Of course it was a fiasco. As Jeannette Gilder put it in *The Critic,* "It is a pity that Mrs. Taber ever conceived the notion of trying to play a part so essentially masculine as that of the Prince of Wales. The failure of such an experiment must have been a foregone conclusion." Taber himself Miss Gilder found "more savage than passionate" and, "deficient in the attributes of chivalry and humor." Only William Owen, the Falstaff, came off with full honors—one of the best Falstaffs anyone could remember. In 1897, while the Tabers were vacationing in France, a stunning message came to them from the Theatrical Syndicate: they would welcome Miss Marlowe in their houses, but not with Taber as co-star. That was the end of a bad marriage. He stayed in London, she resumed the name of Julia Marlowe, and by 1899 she divorced him.

Illus. 165. Mr. and Mrs. Robert Taber. Folger Shakespeare Library.

The Syndicate (discussed in some detail in the Introduction) had been officially established only in 1896. Whatever Miss Marlowe knew or thought about the Syndicate and their policies before she went abroad, she was in no position to resist them when she returned.[70] Indeed, needing a manager, she put herself into the hands of Charles Dillingham, a young man who was actually connected with the Syndicate, being a friend and protégé of Charles Frohman. Much as she would have liked to return at once to Shakespeare, that would have been vetoed from on high, so she chose *The Countess Valeska,* a romantic melodrama of life in Poland during the Napoleonic liberation of that land. After her brief and successful country tryout, the Syndicate brought her into New York and set her up in the Knickerbocker, their finest theatre. She was enormously successful. *Valeska* ran for many weeks. She went touring then, and when she returned, the Syndicate permitted her to revive some favorite Shakespeares.

But always there was Augustin Daly, who never gave up a grudge.[71] Back in 1896 when he heard that Miss Marlowe was bringing *Henry IV* to town and would play Prince Hal, he announced *Henry IV* at his own theatre with Ada Rehan as Hal. When Miss Marlowe altered her schedule and opened with *Romeo and Juliet,* Daly was on the road with his company, but he quickly arranged for Mrs. Brown Potter and Kyrle Bellew to do *Romeo and Juliet* at his own theatre. They failed miserably, for Mrs. Brown Potter was quite incapable of Juliet. (Not even William Winter, for all his loyalty to the Daly enterprises, could endure her.) When the Marlowe–Taber *Henry IV* did appear a week later, and failed, as was to be expected, Daly at once canceled plans for his Rehan production. Miss Marlowe revived *Twelfth Night;* Daly matched her Viola with Miss Rehan's. In 1897 Miss Marlowe produced a new play with a Scottish locale, *For Bonnie Prince Charlie;* Daly reached far back into nineteenth-century repertory to revive *Meg Merrilies.* There was nothing he could do to counter her *Valeska,* but when she announced that after her tour she would open with *As You Like It,* he posted Ada Rehan as Rosalind on the same night.[72]

In all this play-by-play contest Daly was in deadly earnest, but in the end he was made the butt of a silly little joke. Wanting to claim absolute authenticity for the scenery of his *As You Like It,* he published a letter from one W. T. Greatbach of Birmington containing a photograph of "the only remaining portion of the forest of Arden," and announced that his scene painter Henry Hoyt would reproduce it faithfully for a scene in the play. Miss Marlowe's press agent at once published a letter from one W. T. Smallbach advising her that he was sending her an *actual tree*—"all that is left of the forest of Arden," wishing that it be featured in *her* production of *As You Like It.*[71] Poor old Daly's fighting days were over. Six months later he was dead.

Yet another nuisance attended Miss Marlowe in the years just before and after the turn of the century—a distraction from the purpose for which she was born, grew up, and trained herself. More and more she was being drawn away from Shakespeare.[74] Taber, as we have seen, chose several non-Shakespearean plays in which she had to support him. And the idea that the people craved novelty, romance, and popular excitements—an idea picked up and propagandized by the Syndicate—was real enough. Charles Russell displays a few pages of financial statistics from her 1896–97 account books showing miserable $200 and $300 houses for Shakespeare and weekly losses running from $100 to nearly $700.[75] Once the Syndicate took her in hand they began pressuring her into various popular romances—first *The Countess Valeska,* then after a brief spell of Rosalind and Juliet, into *Colinette,* Clyde Fitch's *Barbara Frietchie,* and a clownish treatment of *When Knighthood Was in Flower* (which she played for two years without relief, exhausting herself and hating it—and getting rich). In the spring of 1904 she even revived the old chestnut *Ingomar,* in order to be speaking poetry again even at that florid, sentimental level. But she could no longer live without Shakespeare. And there, ready to companion her, was Edward Hugh Sothern. And among the Syndicate gang were a pair of brothers whose vision encompassed art as much as pots of gold, Charles and Daniel Frohman. Charles Frohman took Sothern and Marlowe in hand and planned their future.

E. H. Sothern

Edward Hugh Sothern (1859–1933) was the son of the English comedian E. A. Sothern of Lord Dundreary fame. Though born in New Orleans while his parents were on tour, he was educated in England. He planned to become a painter, but abandoned that career and at the age of twenty joined his father in America to follow the actor's trade. Once he found his metier he was a quick study. After a few months with the Boston Museum company learning the elements, and a brief stint with John McCullough just before McCullough's tragic breakdown, he was discovered by Daniel Frohman and drafted to New York, to Frohman's Lyceum Theatre. From 1886 to 1898 he was Frohman's leading man, specializing in light comedy and dashing cloak-and-sword drama like *The Prisoner of Zenda, The Song of the Sword,* or *The King's Musketeers.*

But like many another romantic comedian he wanted to make his mark in classic drama too. To the astonishment and delight of everyone (except William Winter), on September 17, 1900, at the Garden Theatre, he staged and played so fine a Hamlet that at first blush many observers were ready to place it among the greatest Hamlets in living memory. (Winter's response was, "What can you expect of a man who goes to sea in a teaspoon?")[76] Of course, there had not been many truly great Hamlets of late to compare it with. Charles Fechter's had been startling, but that actor could never quite subdue himself to the character. As W. F. A. of the Boston *Transcript* pointed out, Fechter was so much "a man of petulant temper, a man of prompt and immediate action" that he "made Hamlet's long-continued inaction seem almost comic."[77] Henry Irving, in American eyes, achieved little beyond emphasizing "the sweetness and intellectuality of the actor"; and he read the lines, said W. F. A., "perhaps worse, on the whole, than any other of his Shakespearean parts." There was Edwin Booth, of course, taken for granted by every leading American critic in those days as the true and only Hamlet, the fixed star around which all the others

Illus. 166. E. H. Sothern as Hamlet.

moved. Inevitably, and rather to his annoyance, Sothern was marked up or down according to the degree in which he resembled Booth. "More than any other portrayal of Hamlet in recent years," wrote Dithmar of the *New York Times,* "[Sothern's Dane] resembles the Dane of Edwin Booth in his prime. . . . His clustering dark hair, his handsome, mournful eyes, his broad, pale brow, his fine profile are all reminders of the greatest of our Hamlets."[78] Sothern was graceful, too, "never seems to be posing," and "his gesticulation is restrained, but ample and purposeful. . . . It was a tasteful, indisputably intelligent piece of acting, set in a number of carefully planned and suitable pictures."

These are external marks, however, and beyond the externals neither Dithmar nor most of his colleagues cared to go. They could call it immeasurably the best piece of acting that Sothern had ever done, but they admired it rather than were moved by it. They felt that this Hamlet's melancholy was not profound; that we do not share in his unutterable grief for the death of his father nor in his bitterness when his love for Ophelia has been blighted. His scorn and frenzy do not touch us. It is cunning acting, but no more.

Critic after critic tried his own formula for defining Sothern's failure to realize Hamlet's essential "inner" problem. Perhaps Clapp of the Boston *Advertiser* got hold of it best. In the last forty years, he said, no actors except Booth and Irving did anything to solve the prime question, which is the question of Hamlet's inaction. Sothern comes nearer Booth than any other since Booth's time, but the interval is still considerable.[79]

> A little clearer apprehension of the peculiarity of Hamlet's temperament might bring Mr. Sothern almost up to the point of classic precision. He must throw into far stronger relief the dreamy, self-centered, introverted, and metaphysical temperament of the prince,—that temperament which made sustained effort so distasteful to him, which kept him idle and even incapable of plans of action for nearly three sluggish months that succeeded his interview with the Ghost. . . . Even now he gives evidence in many places of a just conception; but the character in his hands still remains too full of usual youthful blood, too near in temperamental conditions to the mode of men of action. It must be sicklied o'er with the pale cast of thought.

Yet Clapp paid Sothern his due of admiration—praised his reserve, self-control, and freedom from affectation.

The *Dramatic Mirror,* warm, too, in praise of Sothern's effort, faulted it in another set of terms.[80] Sothern could not, said the *Mirror,* "make the moods of the man hang together." He gave us not one Hamlet but a series of Hamlets. After his long years as a comedian, it came easy to him to show Hamlet "a care-free youth of rather jocular disposition." His first playful dialogue with Rosencrantz and Guildenstern, his friendly intercourse with the Players, his quibbling with the Gravedigger were light, merry, colloquial, relaxed. But elsewhere he had to become "a morose egoist," elsewhere "a quiet philosopher," elsewhere a passionate but embittered lover, and so forth. The shifting about among these various and contrasting roles kept up the audience's interest, of course, but when we have known them all we have not known one personality with a dominant purpose.

Relief was general that Sothern did not pester his hearers with "new readings" to show how clever he was, but as a correspondent to the *Transcript* asserted, he "bent his whole mind and capacity" to "elucidation of the meaning of the text."[81] Yet the record does not quite free Sothern of charges on this score. To William Winter, at least, it *was* a "new reading" (and a contemptible one) to bring on Fortinbras at the end of the play and to bear Hamlet's body off on a shield.[82] Presumably Sothern ended the play that way because Shakespeare did, or because Forbes-Robertson had so ended it in London three years earlier. But for Winter it was an error, an anticlimax, merely "productive of tediousness," and he was pleased to note that Sothern abandoned it later on.

A *genuinely* wrong-headed innovation was the following.[83] Sothern cut the speech "Now might I do it pat" when he came upon the King praying; but later, in the scene in which the King is banishing him to England, he seized a sword which happened to be lying nearby and attempted to murder the King then and there. Insofar as I can make out from later reviews he got rid of that idle "rewriting" of the play, perhaps after the opening night.

Dithmar wished that for dignity's sake Sothern would not forever be a-kissing.[84]

> He kisses his father's picture, just after the "Foul deeds will rise" speech, when Hamlet is surely not in a kissing mood. He kisses the tablets after he has set down on them that a man may smile and yet be a villain. He kisses the hilt of his sword after the soldiers have sworn upon it. He kisses Ophelia—but any man would do that with such an Ophelia, if he could.

And he was unnecessarily tearful—a notion he may have got from Mounet-Sully or from various visiting German Hamlets who were heavy weepers. He was about to weep at several points in the first soliloquy, "Oh, that this too too solid flesh would melt." Wept in the scene with his mother in her closet. And for reasons no one could understand, he "had a good cry all by himself over the cadaver of Polonius."

But whatever faults that watchful eyes could detect in Sothern's Hamlet, for the most part they cheered him on. The marvel was that a decade after Nym Crinkle had declared Shakespeare "extinct," in the very midst of the Syndicate's campaign to banish Shakespeare from their stages and load them with unworthy trash, one American actor whose name and reputation was synonymous with light entertainment could bring off a Hamlet that drew full houses, pleased discriminating critics, and proved that the people did want Shakespeare after all.

He did not press on to further experiments in Shakespeare—perhaps because being comparatively light of stature he did not see himself in other major Shakespeare roles. He simply tucked *Hamlet* in among his regular titles and staged it from time to time during the next few years. Most critics felt that he gradually altered it without truly improving it. The *Mirror* found it becoming "more melodramatic," less tender and suggestive.[85] Perhaps he kissed less and wept less and strove more for measures of "old-school" energy and drive. At any rate, until the arrival of Forbes-Robertson, he was unquestionably "the best Hamlet on our stage."

Over the years he improved the work of his supporting company, or found better actors than he began with. (In 1903, for instance, he found a "capital Osric" in a young actor named Cecil B. deMille.)[86] His wife Virginia Harned had been a singularly ineffective Ophelia. In 1902 he replaced her with Cissie Loftus, whose career curiously resembled his own. Beginning as a popular mimic in London music halls, she had emerged as an authentic actress of great charm. According to Norman Hapgood, Miss Loftus brought "poetic glamour" to Ophelia: "it shimmered over all Ophelia's madness."[87]

> It is not easy to recall a lovelier Ophelia, with the true pale loveliness of the north, than she made with her flowers in her hands and her hair. Her scraps of song, her wanderings over old, forgotten, far-off things, and her rueful giving of her posies were gently piteous. Her empty eyes, her hollow laugh and her fitful disordered steps were poignant. The illusion of gentle madness was nearly flawless, and never once did the glamour fade.

But another actress, who had never played Ophelia, was waiting for it.

By 1903 and 1904 Julia Marlowe could no longer endure the "trunk-lining" plays (the phrase is her biographer's) that the Syndicate was thrusting her into. Then for the first time she saw Sothern's Hamlet. She sensed in Sothern not only refined artistry but a professional integrity compatible with her own ideals. At once she proposed to Daniel Frohman, still Sothern's manager, a Sothern and Marlowe tour during the 1904–5 season, doing nothing but Shakespeare. Sothern was flattered, Frohman and his brother Charles were so struck by the novelty and daring of the idea, as well as confident of the quality of the artists, that they offered very generous terms. Charles, as we have seen, was deputized during his spring visit to London to persuade Johnston Forbes-Robertson, already engaged for America by Klaw and Erlanger, to do anything *but* Shakespeare in America until his second season, assuring him that his new play out of Kipling, *The Light that Failed* would delight America and suffice for his first season. Perhaps he wanted to "save Shakespeare" for Sothern and Marlowe, so that they would be first in the field.

Sothern and Marlowe

They made a perfect team. Miss Marlowe was far more deeply read in Shakespeare and the literature about him, and many years more experienced in Shakespearean acting. But Sothern was an apt, eager, and extremely intelligent pupil. As he himself said of the case, "The loving and exhaustive labor which she had bestowed upon Shakespearean plays was now lavished upon [my] own budding endeavor with a generosity and eagerness which [I] was sane enough to receive hungrily and to profit by with enthusiasm."[88]

Their working habits were complementary. Miss Marlowe did not much enjoy directing rehearsals, though she assumed her share of it. Her special joy was planning—preparing the promptbook, which involved cutting the text for time, cutting obscurities, suppressing or modifying Elizabethan vulgarities that offended her or that her audiences would not tolerate, marking words for emphasis, and laying out ground plans, entrances, basic positions and movements. Sothern, on the other hand, reveled in rehearsals—would rather rehearse than act, or, to the distress of his actors, than to take time out for lunch. The partners watched each other direct scenes, making notes for improvement, and seeing eye to eye more often than not. One day an old professional watched a rehearsal in progress, grumbled "There's too much 'if you please' and 'thank you' in this company," and left, convinced that nothing good would come of such lack of friction.[89] Sothern's special aptitude was scenic design, and with his native sense for form and color, together with Charles Frohman's generous budgets, his sets were always good to look upon. They were, of course, fully representational in the time-worn esthetic of the nineteenth century.

They worked together for three seasons, doing only Shakespeare the first two, in the third season adding three modern plays "of literary worth"—Percy MacKaye's *Jeanne d'Arc,* Gerhardt Hauptmann's *The Sunken Bell,* and Hermann Sudermann's *John the Baptist.* For two seasons Frohman booked them from coast to coast. The third season culminated in an engagement in London. By that time they had used up nearly all the Shakespeare plays that afforded them balanced roles, so after London they divided forces

Illus. 167. Miss Marlowe and William Seymour at rehearsal.

and for two seasons (1907–8, 1908–9) went separate ways.

In the late summer of 1904, Frohman sent them out to Chicago to test three plays: *Romeo and Juliet, Much Ado About Nothing,* and *Hamlet.* They opened with *Romeo* at the Illinois Theatre on September 19. Though the audience was cordial, the performance was a nervous, rocky one. Miss Marlowe's Juliet, long out of practice, was sorely stained with tones and mannerisms she had acquired in the modern comedies and society dramas she had been playing for six or seven years. Even in the Potion Scene, where she was partially true to form, James O'Donnell Bennett of the *Record-Herald* blamed her for "melodramatic devices of which she was guiltless ten years ago.[90] She was so ineffective in the Balcony Scene that W. L. Hubbard of the *Tribune* actually awarded the honors to Sothern, praising his "young, hot-blooded, ecstatic lover"—flattery, I fear, for these are terms that Sothern rarely earned thereafter.[91] In the Death Scene, according to Hubbard, he lapsed into "melodramatic boisterousness or 'modern' realistic whininess." Only one Chicago reporter of the event found nothing to blame: headlines in the *Daily News* declared that the stars "Act Brilliantly in Shakespeare Glorified," called Marlowe's Juliet "A Marvel," called Sothern's Romeo "A Spiritual Revel of Youth, Grace, Beauty, and Poetic Force."[92] These ecstatic shouts, and the column and more of hysterical congratulation that followed, were the work of the once famous Amy Leslie, whose giddy logorrhea sank the art of criticism to its nadir, and amused if it did not inform Chicago readers of the *Daily News* for forty years.

Much Ado, in the second week, went much better. Miss Marlowe had not played Beatrice since 1894, when she simply did not understand it and substituted mere amiability and flirtatiousness for wit. But by now, having learned the lessons Mrs. Sutherland had spelled out for her in the Boston *Transcript,* she was ready. Sothern had never played Benedick, but it was his kind of part: he was more easily at home in its bright comedy than in the darker role of Romeo. As Bennett put it in the *Record-Herald,*[93] "The Marlowe-Sothern forces wheeled around with amazing confidence and celerity, and in the teeth of critics who felt that they had botched 'Romeo and Juliet' they flung the pleasant truth that, if they are not yet ready to play Shakespearean tragedy, they can give a deliciously spirited, whimsical, and suave representation of the subtlest of the comedies." Almost the only objection raised was that the first scenes were too slow, with Beatrice especially to blame for bearing down too heavily on her witticisms. No longer would she whisk a rosebud under Benedick's nose on "I wonder that you will still be talking, Signior Benedick," but she had not yet quite mastered the difference between rapier and broadsword. Hubbard thought that her "playing smart" in this scene did not endear her to the audience.[94] But early in the second act she caught the right tone and thereafter was in all things excellent.

The universal question, according to Bennett, was, "How were the two stars in their two scenes in Leonato's orchard, and how in the Church scene?" "Successful in, both, truly," he responded, and he underscored his enthusiasm for Miss Marlowe with prickly comparisons. She was

> fluent, easy, strong and hearty. Miss Marlowe elected to play a Beatrice that was not haughty and hard like Miss Rehan's, who made her only a variant on Katherine the Shrew; nor yet one that minced and simpered and snickered as did the Beatrice of Miss Terry, who made the girl a sly minx who said sharp things as if she meant them only for a veil to her cuteness. . . . Miss Marlowe seems to have chosen a middle ground and explored it safely.

Among other items, Bennett praised Beatrice's poem at the end of the Garden Scene—which in the early 1890s she slid past almost as if the news she had just heard meant nothing to her.

> The soliloquy beginning, "Stand I condemned," was sweetly read, the voice and the dreamy self-questioning attitude betokening a delightfully puzzled state of mind and a delicate prophecy of relenting. Then the cry, "Benedick, love on," was uttered wildly, almost hysterically, but with a peal of laughter behind it and making rare music.

The Benedick was not a blustering soldier, said Bennett, not a blistering railer, not a vulgar braggart, but "a serenely cynical gentleman of the court first and of the camp next. . . . He loved the zest of conflict when the fight was fair, and he loved 'dear Lady Disdain' because she played the game and never cried quits." The high point of his performance was a turn of extraordinary delicacy in the dialogue with Beatrice when "the great declaration came and the supreme surrender was made."

> Mr. Sothern achieved a bit of business that was little less than a stroke of genius. Turning to Beatrice with wide eyes, intent, but tremulous within with feeling, he said in level tones, "I do love nothing in the world so well as you." Then he paused slightly on the "Is that not strange?" Then he laughed—softly, half-ashamed, delighted, pensive. Everything was conveyed, and it is a tribute to that masterly stroke that the gratified house was so impressed that it stayed hands which fairly itched to applaud.

Miss Marlowe, too played this dialogue with Benedick with sweep, maturity, and positiveness. Her "Kill

Illus. 168. Sothern and Marlowe in *Romeo and Juliet.* Folger Shakespeare Library.

Claudio!" rang out like a clarion. But so fierce an attack on that shocking line was a strategic error: *the audience laughed.* This moment, as we have seen elsewhere, is one of the most dangerous in all Shakespeare, and many a fine actress has been thrown into confusion by this unwelcome response. I do not find in later reviews that it often, or ever again, happened to Miss Marlowe, nor do we know what special tone, timing, or volume she used to prevent it. Bennett could not see that the fault was hers, and could only refer it to the "false point of view of the audience."

The third week was *Hamlet,* and it belonged to Sothern, W. L. Hubbard found it a startlingly untraditional Hamlet, and he could imagine a Hamlet worshiper of the "palmy days" rising up in wrath and tearing Sothern's interpretation to bits.[95] As we have observed, in Sothern's occasional repetitions of Hamlet after 1900 he tended to harden the character, to desentimentalize it. As Norman Hapgood put it in 1902,[96]

> The distinctive and impressive characteristics of Mr. Sothern's Hamlet are its vitality and intensity of feeling. At least it lives; and its vitality passes the footlights and possesses the spectator. Poetic glamour, either in outward seeming or inner illumination, it seldom has. . . . He does not enter far into the contemplative, speculative and brooding Hamlet. It is Hamlet when his moods are most disordered and excited, Hamlet in his accesses of sudden and desperate action, that Mr. Sothern most vividly realizes. He is prone to be hectic, even neurotic. The bitter self-reproach and self-abasement yielding to excited resolution in "Oh, what a rogue and peasant slave am I!" Mr. Sothern reveals very pregnantly. . . .

Hapgood had suggested, as earlier observers had said of Fechter, that such a Hamlet might well have killed the King long before the outcome of the Fencing Scene. And Hapgood *liked* this heightened vitality. By 1904 Sothern seems to have raised Hamlet's energy and purposefulness still further, and James O'Donnell Bennett did *not* like it.[97] He knew he ought to accept this "expedient, expert, ingenious, careful actor," but he could not find "profound poetic feeling" in him. So he dropped into his review crumbs of praise for such hints of princeliness, filial affection, etc., as he thought he could detect; but what impressed him most he denounced as "sheer rant." Whenever this Hamlet is left alone to plan revenges or inveigh against fate, his passion, said Bennett, is "given the headlong articulation and the raving voice of Bedlam. The man is alone, to be sure, but the hoarse cries of this maniac would have penetrated the remotest dungeons of Elsinore and would promptly have insured him a resting place in one of them." Bennett produced "evidences of acute mania and robustious fury" and declared them a great blemish on Sothern's reading of the part.

Bennett, in short, subscribed to the "tradition" of Hamlet that grew up during the nineteenth century and was fixed immutably, it seemed, by Booth and Irving—Hamlet as gentle melancholy philosopher and poet: the Hamlet of William Hazlitt, who is "the most amiable of misanthropes," whose "ruling passion is to think, not to act"; the Hamlet of Goethe—a hero without a hero's strength of nerve, who sinks beneath a burden which he cannot bear and must not cast away. Hubbard, on the other hand,[98] confronted by this hard-driving Hamlet, took the position that we should be wary of tradition, lest we "tie ourselves to the past, decry progress, and clip the wings of ambitious effort." If this Hamlet does not answer to the terms of tradition, let us judge him by his own terms. Certainly he is more a man of action than a man of reflection, and what of that? Stopped dead in his

Illus. 169. Sothern and Marlowe in *Hamlet,* the Play Scene.

tracks by the disasters that impeded him, he continues to regard himself a man of action. Then *why* could he not fulfill the Ghost's commands? Whereas Bennett objected to the violence of the soliloquies, Hubbard perceived that Hamlet is using the soliloquies in a new way, as worried, reckless, excited self-examinations, angry self-accusations. He is demanding to know why he cannot do the thing that must be done. His raging against himself is not melodrama but true drama, genuinely motivated agony. And his sorrows, his furies, his despairs grip us and awaken our sympathies. When he encounters that meddling old fool Polonius, he does not make a jolly game of twitting him for our simple amusement—he attacks him almost brutally. His directives to the Players are not an amiable extra-dramatic diversion, but a deadly earnest set of instructions how to perform *The Mousetrap.* In the scene of the Recorders, he treats Rosencrantz and Guildenstern with savage sarcasm, not with princely, half-humorous, noble indignation.

There are, of course, Hubbard finds, moments of warmth in his performance. His affection for Horatio is genuine and endearing. In spite of the savagery of his scene with Ophelia, one knows that the savagery only mirrors a deep love. The agony in which he condemns (and pleads with) his mother touches us deeply. Hubbard's conclusion is, "it was in its entirety a highly colored but an intelligent, well-rounded, unusual portrayal of one of the most grateful characters in all drama." In 1900 the *Dramatic Mirror* had dismissed Sothern's performance as not a credible Hamlet but a haphazard collection of Hamlets.[99] It seems clear that by 1904 Sothern had integrated these disparate impersonations under one clear purpose and created a Hamlet that was new and his own. But would it hold?

Miss Marlowe had never before played Ophelia, and she played it now as no one else had ever done. She had learned long since the effectiveness of repose, how at the climax of a deeply moving scene it was best to *do* as little as possible. Her Mad Scene, as Hubbard described it, was both ingenious and touching.[100]

> She came not elaborately bedecked with flowers. Only a few were in her unbound hair, and when she returned for the closing scene she had in her scarf of lace only white rose petals. She gave her "rosemary" and "daisies" not to characters on the stage, but half kneeling she offered only the rose leaves to some imaginary person—her father or Hamlet?—and strewed them about her.

Russell says that this was the first Ophelia he had ever known to move an audience to tears.[101]

This three-week initiation of the Sothern–Marlowe combination in Chicago was an important event in the stage history of Shakespeare in America, and W. L. Hubbard, sensing it, made it plain in his weekly essays in the Sunday *Tribune,* called "The Playgoer."[102] It marked the end, he said, of a long drought of classic drama in Chicago. It demonstrated that in Chicago at least, and doubtless throughout the country, an audience, weary of Syndicate-sponsored trash, would welcome a revival of Shakespeare. It marked the return of Julia Marlowe, after nearly a decade of "trunk-lining" plays, to the work she was so generously qualified for. It brought with her a worthy companion in the enterprise, the "sometime" Shakespearean Edward Sothern, now confirmed as a "regular" Shakespearean, free to play in the best of comedy or tragedy for which his skills qualified him. Their partnership, guaranteed by Charles Frohman to continue, suggested that a regular supporting company under their direction would recover the almost forgotten arts of classic stage English, including a mastery of verse. It even regained some measure of critical forgiveness and favor for the Frohmans who, as associates of the Syndicate (though not the most barbarous of that gang), had participated in the strangulation of the American theatre, but were now willing to divert some of their dubiously won power to promoting the best available talent to the best theatrical cause.

From Chicago the company carried the same plays to Pittsburgh for further testing, then on to New York, where on October 17 at the Knickerbocker Theatre they submitted themselves to the "choice and master spirits of the age," the New York critics. They came off very well. William Winter, to be sure, remembering old quarrels and uncomfortable under the necessity of acknowledging Miss Marlowe's excellence, attempted to minimize Juliet herself as "not one of the great women of Shakespeare," but only "the emblem and apotheosis of amatory passion (which is not the noblest of human propensities)."[103] Of course, he was pleased to observe that she was superior to the "dapper and laborious Romeo" of Sothern, whose "sexual idolatry of one person for another" rendered him "ludicrous." Poor Winter was so rattled that before he was well into his second column he came close to naming Arthur Brooke greater than Shakespeare for inventing(!) this tragic story.

Other critics, less involved in the Wars of the Theatres, made better sense in fewer words. The *Dramatic Mirror* called this *Romeo and Juliet* "One of the very best and most intelligent productions of a Shakespeare play that the local stage has known in recent seasons."[104] The *New York Times* reviewer doubted "whether the English-speaking stage has any two actors who could surpass the present performance."[105]

Illus. 170. Miss Marlowe as Ophelia.

Everyone placed Miss Marlowe's performance above Sothern's. After all, she had first played Juliet seventeen years ago; his Romeo was barely four weeks old. Then, too, for three-fourths of the play Juliet's is the dominant role; Romeo can take control only in the sword fight with Tybalt and in the doom-and-death speeches in the final act. Sothern could rarely start his fires, as he seems to have done at Chicago, in the second-act Balcony Scene. J. R. Towse of the *Post* called him "dull" and "glum,"[106] and it became habitual over the years for critics to suggest that his Romeo was only a misconceived version of an old-fashioned brooding Hamlet.

Miss Marlowe had first played Juliet in 1887, when she was twenty-one. Her acting version then quite properly retained the Nurse's line, "She's not fourteen." In 1904 New York had not seen her Juliet for a decade (since she was twenty-eight). Now in 1904 she was thirty-eight and the Nurse, yielding a point, said, "She's not sixteen." But as the *Globe* critic remarked, she "is not too old to act Juliet, and will not be for many years."[107] Juliet would be the last role she ever played in public, in 1924, when she was 57. The Nurse then said, "She's of a pretty age," and no one would have minded if she had said, "She's not fourteen." Her girl-like beauty had not yet given way to Time's fell hand.

The beauty of Miss Marlowe's Juliet lay not only in her perfect face, but in her perfect voice. As Henry Taylor Parker once wrote in the Boston *Transcript:*[108]

> The years, actual or imagined, of Juliet vanished in the whole impression of Miss Marlowe's acting. Her ripeness for passion, be it of love or death—under an Italian sun and a young poet's imaginings—abides, and such illusion is finer and more fragrant than mere physical seeming. A chief means to this illusion lies in Miss Marlowe's tones. She is not content to speak Shakespeare's verse with intelligible, rhythmic and sensitive diction. No more does it satisfy her to color those tones with the silvery lightness or the deep golden glow of Shakespeare's imagery of romance and passion. She seeks to make his poetry seem an inevitable, a natural speech for Juliet in the circumstance and the emotions in which the play sets her. Imagine an Isolde reciting the verse of Wagner's opera. Recall her singing it in the changeful flood of Wagner's music. As that music exalts her speech, so may the accomplished, imaginative, ardent actress exalt Juliet's until it seems not only a poetic language but the inevitable voice of her passion. Miss Marlowe exalts it so. Her gestures, her poses, her play of feature are often sparing in Juliet, because she has distilled the essence of the part into her tones.

Illus. 171. Miss Marlowe as Juliet.

In 1904 Towse took exception to *one aspect* of Miss Marlowe's art as a producer that she could well have done with less of—her zeal for dressing the stage with busy supernumeraries, whose function was to create a "real" world out of which the life of the play would seem to grow. Local color. "Realism." Embroidery work.[109] Miss Marlowe was by no means alone in this. Everybody had been doing it—Daly, Irving, Mansfield, Tree—just as they had also been making scenery more obviously three-dimensional and "real"—just as, too, they had been heightening the emotional tone of major scenes and soliloquies with fiddles and drums from the orchestral pit. Miss Marlowe, it seems, conspicuously overdid the busy-work. Towse traced this tendency, and the reasons for it, back to Charles Kean's productions at the Princess's in the 1850s (he could have reached farther):

> It was an evil day for the artistic theatre when Charles Kean demonstrated that public attention might be diverted from the feebleness of the acting to the splendor of the stage trappings. Modern managers have proceeded further in this direction than even he would have deemed possible. Sooner or later there will be a reaction towards earlier and sounder principles, and then more anxiety and care will be lavished upon the play and less upon the scenery.

The reaction was already under way in England with William Poel's fiery protests against standard scenic practice, and his efforts to "return to the Globe." But Towse perhaps had not yet heard of Poel, nor in any case would have taken his method seriously.

From any of the dozen or more surviving Marlowe promptbooks of *Romeo and Juliet* each meticulously typewritten in black and red, we can see exactly what Towse was complaining about. When the curtain rises, the orchestra continuing its overture, we watch a long drawn out pantomime. A group of court ladies is gathered about a stone well at the center of the stage, the women conversing with each other and playing with children. A boy is eating an apple. A woman draws water from the well, pours it into an urn that she lifts to her shoulder; she leaves the stage. Two monks cross the stage. The ladies bow and kneel. The monks bless them, and Samson and Gregory, who have entered, cross themselves. A pair of pages enter, and one of them chucks a court lady under the chin. The other ladies chase the pages away. A military officer crosses the stage and goes out. The children imitate his pompous strut and the ladies laugh and point. Another boy enters, whistling and skipping, snatches the apple from the first boy and runs off, pursued by three children. Four guards, carrying spears, cross the stage and the ladies wave to them. When the fighting begins, the ladies scream and try to restrain the fighters. Although the ninety lines of dialogue, down to Prince Escalus's entry, are cut to fifty, twelve pages of stage directions (typed single-space) cover every cut and slash and blow of fist which make up this fight.

Nothing very novel or clever has gone into this business, but hours of drilling of the fighters and the dozen or fifteen supers have been spent to create for us (needlessly) the reality of a hot summer day in a Catholic town in Italy. And throughout the promptbook acres of single-space typing keep up the busy background life while the play goes on. This account of the opening moments of Romeo and Juliet is a fair representation of Miss Marlowe's staging of *any* Shakespeare.

The New York critics, like the Chicagoans, found *Much Ado* a much more agreeable experience than *Romeo and Juliet,* though both Towse and Winter assure us that the Irving-Terry *Much Ado,* which had last come to America a decade before, was far finer than this, both in the acting and the *mise-en-scène.*[110] To the relief of his old friends and admirers, Sothern could now shed his "nighted color" and play the manly,

Illus. 172. Sothern and Marlowe as Beatrice and Benedick. Folger Shakespeare Library.

witty Benedick in his accustomed comic manner. It is pleasing to see Winter lay by old differences and praise Miss Marlowe's Church Scene without reservation:

> Miss Marlowe's performance of Beatrice becomes, at this supreme point, exceptionally lovely, and in its sincerity, superb. The great moment for Beatrice is that of the outrageous insult to Hero,—the pure, gentle, blameless girl, whom the stronger woman so entirely loves. All levity drops from Beatrice in an instant, and her soul springs, full-statured, to the defense of virtue and truth. Here Miss Marlowe's inherent personal nobility reinforces her decisive emotional power, and she becomes magnificent. Amazement and horror at the infamy of the accusation against

Hero, and detestation of the insensate cruelty with which it is made, culminate in a piteous and furious frenzy, which is half despair at her helpless inability, and half the enthusiasm of resentment and coveted revenge. It is in situations of this kind that the genius of Miss Marlowe is revealed, and this fine performance more than ever demonstrates her peculiar aptitude for the passionate, heroic, robust characters of dramatic fiction.

Strangely enough, she ended the scene with a quite banal piece of business. When Benedick accepted her commission to challenge Claudio, kissed her hand and turned to go, she called him back, stepped down to him, and kissed him on the lips. That action would have the curious effect of ending the tension between them at once—the only really interesting tension in the play. That tension must not end, of course, until all the lesser jugglery of the Hero-Claudio plot is disposed of. It can end only after one last sputtering of firecracker lines when Benedick stops Beatrice's mouth with a kiss and signals with his laughing epilogue that the play is finished.

Although *Much Ado* was a great favorite in the 1904–5 and 1905–6 seasons, the actors then shelved it and did not play it again for several years. In 1913 it was greeted with a flood of welcoming reviews. Although—as somebody in 1913 noted—the play was 313 years old, it was unquestionably the most delightful comedy of the season.[111] Sothern was then recognized as the "best all-Shakespearean actor the American stage has produced since Booth," and Miss Marlowe had "long since worn the mantles dropped by Mary Anderson and Ada Rehan."

The New York performance of *Hamlet* in November of 1904 yielded little critical opinion worth preserving, for the critics who had seen Sothern's performance from time to time since 1900 wasted little time reevaluating it now. William Winter probably stayed away: he transcribed from a Chicago paper a pleasant paragraph about Marlowe's Ophelia and declined to comment upon so "unfruitful" a subject as Sothern.[112] Joseph Clarke of the *Herald* lingered over Sothern long enough to express a dissatisfaction curiously at odds with what we read about in Chicago. Clarke found his Hamlet "dignified, graceful, scholarly, impressive," but it was "uninspired."[113] And it was unbearably *slow.* The curtain rose at a quarter to eight, but the play ran on past midnight. The text was cut rather more than usual, but the actors were unusually deliberate in word and movement and "a good deal of novel dumb show, ingenious enough in conception, was forced into not entirely congenial companionship with the text, to explain this new Hamlet's interpretations of the latter where he departed from the conventional and traditional."

What had become of the raving maniac that so offended Bennett in Chicago a few weeks before, or the furious self-accuser that so pleased Hubbard? And what were these "novel dumb shows"? The only explanation that I can offer is that Sothern could never satisfy himself with any version of Hamlet and experimented with it ceaselessly. Indeed, one L. P. of the Boston *Transcript* found a neat metaphor for it: "Mr. Sothern's Hamlet is one of those Gothic churches where the scaffolding is always up somewhere. The edifice is never finished, and it is not intended that it should be. If any thing, the dignity of the pile is enhanced by the rough timbers that mask some buttress or façade. The work goes on."[114]

In the beginning, in 1900, it was probably conservative, perhaps Boothian, sympathetic or even sentimental. Or it was a collection of various Hamlets, as the *Dramatic Mirror* described it. Then he hardened and energized it, made it violent. Then in New York in the fall of 1904 it was unbearably slow. Later that year a Boston critic complained that he imbued his performance with "fits of inexplicable fury."[115] In London, in 1907, it was a strange mixture that thoroughly gratified the critic for the *Standard:*[116]

Poetical, sincere, and convincing, the Hamlet of E. H. Sothern brushes aside the cobwebs which have been woven around the character, and—as did the Hamlet of Mr. Forbes Robertson—reveals to us the man, sane, though distraught. The Hamlet we met at the Waldorf Theatre last night is a very human Hamlet, quiet and conversational, for the most part, but given to sudden outbursts of uncontrollable emotion, when body and voice seem to shake and scream to express an agony of spirit past all bearing.

In 1908 Henry Shelley of Boston claimed that "his whole interpretation is pitched in a key of unrelieved melancholy" and the "prolongation of emphasis, with its accompanying 'stage business', accounted for the . . . slowness which often amounted to a soporific lethargy."[117] In 1910 the *Daily Advertiser* said, "He has forsaken the bombast that he more recently has brought to the role."[118] When he returned to the stage after the Great War he seems to have exhausted all the variations and settled down to some comfortable middle course. He was then sixty years old. What Henry Parker found in him in 1919 was "a 'sound' performance of Hamlet the play, if ever there were such."[119] And a "sound" impersonation of the character. Yet it had no vitality. "It suggests a Hamlet figured, diagrammed . . . with every emphasis set in place, every transition calculated, every movement foreseen. . . . It lacks animation and ardor, the romantic glow and illusion that ought, as often as *Hamlet* is acted, to make the play strange, new, and irresistible."

For their second season (1905–6) Charles Frohman

persuaded them to lead off with *The Taming of the Shrew.* This would provide them another vehicle with nicely balanced roles and extend their playing into a fresh mode, that of farce. It was a timely assignment, for the last great Katherine, Ada Rehan, having lost her health, had finally retired. There was some risk in the assignment, for Miss Marlowe was utterly unlike what Miss Rehan had been in her prime, and comparisons were unavoidable. Henry Parker spelled out the difference with perfect clarity.[120]

> Miss Rehan's Katherine was of large dimensions. Its dominating trait was an imperiousness that transcended even pride. Who of us . . . can forget the tawny figure that swept into the room in Baptista's house, tense with pride in every motion and every tone—imperious will incarnate? It was too magnificent to be quite human. . . . When Petruchio insulted her with delays and scurvy dress and clownish manners on her wedding day, we youngsters in the house, fresh from our Latin books, used to feel as though he were affronting Juno herself. When he bore her off triumphant on his shoulders we might have been watching the rape of a goddess.

Against this sort of thing, of course, the delicate girlish Marlowe could not compete. She had to play in quite another key, smaller in design and workmanship. "It is rather more human," said Parker, "and much more nervous. It is easy to call it even neurotic, and on that side it is of America here and now, though the scene of the play is Padua three centuries ago."

> Miss Marlowe's Katherine is mainly a neurotic shrew à la mode. It is as far from Shakespeare's in one direction as Miss Rehan's was in the other. Miss Rehan asked us to take hers with tremendous seriousness, and made us take it so. Miss Marlowe's is nervously comical, and she does not try to persuade us that it is anything else. She could not, if she would, when by many a little sign she is smiling herself at her own acting.

"I followed the book," Miss Marlowe insisted.[121] "Here it is, read for yourself. The stage directions . . . explicitly direct that Katherine should be boisterous, emphatic, and unladylike. It says here to beat him, to throw things at him. I do all that." And Parker confirms that "she struggled, she slapped, she kicked, she bit. She pouted, she grimaced, she set her jaw in impotent anger. She shrieked, she snapped." And Sothern responded with like violence—but always as if amused at her and at himself, with a mental wink, with a smile ready to break on his lips. "It was a smile of sentiment as well, for this Petruchio was sentimental over his Katherine in his quiet way." His sense of humor was "adroit, suggestive, imaginative and original and it lifted the part in its finer moments into something very like high comedy."

Illus. 173. Sothern as Petruchio.

In their public statements the actors emphasized that their performance was a "farce," deliberately lightened in obedience to the text, a jolly romp. Moreover, it was nearer to two hours than four hours in playing time. It was far less elaborate scenically than Daly's production had been—adequate, but stripped down "for the road." The text, too, was reduced. Citing the authority of Fleay, Furness, Furnivall, and the like, they dropped the frame-story of Christopher

Sly.[122] They boasted that their text was purely Shakespearean, free of interpolations from Garrick. They did not advertise that they had cut many passages of the Bianca story—so many that some reviewers feared the audience might not be able to follow it; nor that they had revised the order of scenes, rather as Daly had done, in order to reduce the number of changes.

The tone was set visually by the brilliant costuming. In sixteenth-century Italy "you can have gay, picturesque robes and fine bright stockings and plenty of plumed hats."[123] Petruchio came to the wedding in brown and red leather breeches, great dirty boots, a swinging cloak and a wide-brimmed hat topped with a mass of red and green feathers. There beside him was old Baptista in plum-colored hose and purple velvet cloak. The foppish Gremio wore salmon-pink, the women blue and white, Lucentio's skirts and cap were vermillion. Against such blaze of color the wildest fooling could be expected. Petruchio performed on stage the riotous doings that Gremio says happened inside the church. He came waltzing out of the church with his arms around the priest, whirling him about until priest and clerk fell sprawling; he called for a drink, tossed it down, and threw the sops in the sexton's face. When it was time to go, he tossed Kate up onto the rump of a dappled gray horse, leaped into the saddle and galloped away, Grumio following on a speckled ass. (Such was the business described in early performances: later he carried Kate over his shoulder and we read no more about the horse and the ass.)[124]

When they arrived at Petruchio's country place, Kate had been truly rained on, dumped from her horse, dragged through mud. In a burst of tenderness Petruchio removed her shoes and hung her stockings by the fire to dry. Then he bellowed at his servants, knocked them down like dominoes, leaped on the table, smashed dishes. Once at least in a New York performance he hurled the burnt leg of mutton across the stage and squarely onto the white shirt front of a distinguished gentleman sitting in the first box.[125]

When Kate had been sent upstairs (in wooden shoes) supperless to bed, sentiment took over. As Petruchio mused in soliloquy on his progress in the taming process, he knelt to the drying shoes and stockings and kissed them. Hearing her clattering on the stairs, he pretended to sleep in his chair. She came down to search the room for food. Finding none, she snatched off a shoe and made as if to strike him with it, but thought better of it and clattered up to bed again. More sentiment: Petruchio blew kisses toward her behind her back. "How he adores his Kate!" wrote Philip Hale.[126] "Even when he abuses her, when he starves her, when he delivers his address on continence . . . he would yield at any touch." For, as he says, "this is a way to kill a wife with kindness."

Thus a playful irony was set up for the audience. They could laugh unreservedly at every crudity, meanness, and cruelty that occurred, being assured between the lines that the end of the story would be nothing but "love." In his wildest tantrums, Sothern was in effect winking at the audience, and out of his own ingenuity—not from Shakespeare!—he produced the business of blowing kisses and kissing wet stockings. Nor could Miss Marlowe quite submerge herself in the shrew. At one moment when she should have been most shrewish Philip Hale heard a woman in the audience whisper, "How sweet she is!" Her own favorite bit of business occurred in the argument with Petruchio about the time of day. He says it is seven. She says it is two. He says it is seven. She "agrees" by showing the audience seven fingers. He turns his back. She shows two fingers.[127] Such a "cuteness" serves as an appropriate signature to the Sothern-Marlowe way with the play.

Their *Shrew* was vastly popular and it served the box-office very well over many seasons. It opened in Cleveland on September 18, 1905, played several stands throughout the East, opened at the Knickerbocker in New York on October 16 (to condescending notices), and played on tour throughout the season. They kept it in repertory, always to well-filled houses, down to their final season of 1923. Punch and Judy will never die.

The *Shrew* was paired with *The Merchant of Venice,* another play with balanced roles, though, to be sure, Sothern and Marlowe would be on the stage together only during the Trial Scene. It opened in Cleveland on September 21, 1905, and reached the Knickerbocker in New York on October 30.[128] Unfortunately its New York opening coincided exactly with that of *Mrs. Warren's Profession,* and the town was too shaken by that Shavian earthquake—Shaw's exposé of the bawdy house business—to pay proper attention to Shakespeare. *Mrs. Warren* was closed at once, the company was arrested on a morals charge, theatre for once got page one headlines, and the inner pages carried editorials and denunciations galore from "responsible" critics. So a good many reviews of *The Merchant* were delayed until the weekend.

Opinions were mixed and contradictory. William Winter, so often edgy about Sothern and Marlowe, now declared that they "have in many ways achieved the best results so far in their career as twin stars in this revival."[129] If Sothern is not a great Shylock at least he "comes nearer to the tragic stature in this role than in any he has yet attempted. He is a man of intelligence, technical skill, and high purpose, and all this is manifest in his performance." The *New York Times* (was in Adolph Klauber?), on the other hand, could make nothing of him but that he was "the filthiest figure that has yet appeared to typify the great poetic creation, and no sort of argument can justify it."[130] He was "foully, offensively unclean," and Sothern used every element of make-up and garb to express that idea—"a study in indistinct gray—very dirty gray." Klauber, if it was he, could not believe that elegant Venetian gentlemen would do business with such a filthy creature. Against this opinion, strange to say, Joseph Clarke of the *Herald* objected to a kind of *elegance* in Sothern's performance.[131] He "proved himself an excellent elocutionist . . . he was studiously and intelligently careful in his verbal method. The emphasis seemed too apt, the harmony sounded too felicitous, the gesture came in too pat to give the illusion of spontaneousness. But it was a thoroughly acceptable portrayal."

Sometime along the way, however—whether as whimsical experiment or as reasoned attempt to follow the rising tide of "realism"—Sothern introduced a Yiddish accent—"lisping sibilants, catarrhal gutturals, and strange nasal tones."[132] K. M. in the Boston *Transcript* mentioned this in 1910, noting at the same time that Tubal, the other Jew in the play, spoke pure, uncolored English. An unsigned New York review of 1921 noticed that his "native accent" is stressed more than ever and his make-up is more decidedly Semitic. He seems, too, to have been heightening the tragic aspects of his Shylock as he drew toward the end of his career in 1924.

Illus. 174. Sothern as Shylock. Folger Shakespeare Library.

Everyone praised Miss Marlowe's Portia, though perhaps less effusively than her performance of most other roles, and only Clarke of the *Herald* seems to have understood what she wanted to convey in the Trial Scene.[133] There, said Clarke, "she achieved a calm dignity that once in a while and just at the appropriate moment seemed to tremble on the verge of amusement, and so very effectively kept the audience reminded of the dual part she was playing." That came very near to understanding Miss Marlowe's motivation.[134] In her own thinking she could not take the Trial Scene seriously. Being Bellario's representative, she knew perfectly well that Antonio was in no danger, that in fact her whole act of leading Shylock on was a sort of practical joke. Therefore she could not make herself build up the solemnly dramatic crescendo that other Portias were wont to do. Deliberately she introduced into her conduct of the Trial a certain lightness, which the critics, expecting to be harrowed by heavy rhetoric, did not readily appreciate.

At its very best, perhaps, it was "a glorious romantic comedy," as Parker described it in 1905.[135] Not a little of the romantic effect was created by the lovely scenery that Sothern himself designed.

> Our eyes traversed the Venice of romance—not the hackneyed square of the lion and St. Mark's and the doges' palace. They wandered down long irregular canals in the blazing sunshine of a Venetian noon. They left the gray cool of Venetian walls misty in the soft starlit, lamplit night. Here was the striped mooring for a gondola, there a waterside shrine, and there again the great dome of Santa Maria della Salute. The golden red and brown sails of fishing boats closed prospects. The duke and the magnificoes sat in stately and opulent court high in frescoed and sculptured hall of the doges' palace. Their retinue suited their state. Antonio, Bassanio, and all the rest trooped out of roofed bridges, or lounged against some broken old capital. The night tinkled with music and crackled with the laugh of the masquers. There were flashes of color, of dance, of sport and youthful play. Once more there was the Venice of romance on the stage. . . .

It was not the bare stage of Shakespeare's Globe, but the Venice that Shakespeare may have known or may have imagined. And the Belmont that Parker described, Portia's great hall, inspired very likely by one

Illus. 175. Miss Marlowe as Portia. Folger Shakespeare Library.

of Veronese's palatial paintings, set the spectators dreaming. It costs us, who take for granted the verities and the magic of cinema, an intense effort to imagine the excitement painted canvas could arouse in those late heirs of nineteenth-century scenography.

Twelfth Night, which reached New York on November 13, 1905, completing the triad of new productions in this second season, was probably Sothern and Marlowe's finest. Miss Marlowe, praised by everyone, seemed in temperament, said William Winter, "to be more harmonious with the character of Viola than with almost any other character in Shakespeare."[136] In her own person "romantic, tender, passionate, yet self-contained, pensive and sad," she could instantly identify with Viola, who "never told her love," but waited, selflessly, for love to come to her. This praise was predictable, for Winter had made peace with Miss Marlowe. Now, too, he praised Sothern (of whom he had been capable of saying harsh things) with a sort of generosity.

> Mr. Sothern's impersonation of Malvolio is, by far, the best display of a Shakespearian character that he has given. Here again aptitude of temperament reinforces professional capacity. Mr. Sothern is a comedian and likewise an egotist, and Malvolio is an egotistical comedy part.

He goes on to say that Henry Irving was the first in modern times (in 1884) to play the role in exemplary fashion—"a formidable, passionate man, strikingly eccentric, never a buffoon, but capable of acute suffering from injustice, and capable also of bitter resentment." Sothern follows that fine example. His Malvolio

> is serious, capable, experienced, austere—a man to prompt thought as well as laughter. He typifies indurated self-conceit. He is a narrow-minded, complacent, strutting dullard; a pompous ass; and just a little crazed with the overweening sense of his own importance. Mr. Sothern so depicted him,—acting in a vein of suitable repose, and elaborating the delineation with all needful touches of light and shade. The consistent preservation of sour austerity is the pervasive merit of the performance.

The *Dramatic Mirror,* which a week before had thought poorly of Sothern's Shylock, was doubly impressed with this week's achievement as Malvolio, underscoring the *dignity* of the character by likening him to Don Quixote or a princely figure from a Velázquez painting.[137] In London toward the end of the next season (1906–7), Walkley of the *Times* and other London critics were delighted by both Marlowe and Sothern when they caught a glimpse of them in these ideally appropriate roles. "Viola she is," said Walkley, turning then to that same compliment which Miss Marlowe's Viola must have received dozens of times from middle-aged male critics, "a delicious Viola, who sets the heart beating, and the warm blood coursing through the veins."

However successful *Twelfth Night* was, after 1907 one does not hear much about it for several years. Finally in 1919, 1921, and 1923, when Marlowe and

Sothern were concluding their careers together, *Twelfth Night* was one of the staples of their repertory, and it was welcome. On October 12, 1919, Alexander Woollcott wrote for the *New York Times:*[138]

> This week we have been hearing voices. They are two of the loveliest voices that ever fell on mortal ears—Julia Marlowe's and Ethel Barrymore's. Miss Marlowe's has lost none of its beauty in . . . her absence from the stage. Clear, rich, sure, it once more brings priceless music to the speech of the maid who was shipwrecked on the seacoast of Illyria. Hers is of classic regularity and perfection, as though it had been wrought for the poetry of Shakespeare.

Of Sothern, on this same occasion, the *World* reported that "the pompous, strutting, complacent, conceited and austerely comic Malvolio—as acted by Mr. Sothern is also unchanged. . . . Without disparagement of some of his other Shakespearian characters, he is, as Malvolio, at his best."[139]

In the 1890s one of Miss Marlowe's favorite roles had been Rosalind, and during the visit to England in 1907 she was eager to try it in London. Unfortunately Sothern had not prepared any role in *As You Like It,* so on April 29 and 30 she went on without him, supported by Frederick Lewis as Orlando and J. Sayre Crawley as Jaques. The London *Mail* was charmed by the performance and declared Miss Marlowe "born to play in comedy"; the *Sketch* thought "she has more sense of the beauty of sound in language than most players";[140] and the *Illustrated Sporting and Dramatic News* gave the production a whole page with cartoon sketches, and took the occasion to thank "Uncle Sam" for keeping alive the "cult of the Bard," for sending so many American tourists to Stratford for the recent birthday celebration, and for preserving "the art of speaking blank verse" far better than English actors just then were managing to do.[141]

After the second season of their partnership—the season of *The Shrew, The Merchant,* and *Twelfth Night*—they separated from Charles Frohman's management. Frohman did not approve of their plan for the third season, which included, besides repetitions of Shakespeare, the three plays of Hauptmann, MacKaye, and Sudermann, and the London adventure. Apparently Frohman saw too much risk, asked to be excused from his contract, and wished them Godspeed. Only so much Sothern tells us.[142] Charles Russell provides a bit of behind-the-scenes melodrama that prompted the separation.[143] The Frohmans, after all, were part of the Syndicate, and one member of the Syndicate—perhaps Klaw, perhaps Erlanger—wanted from the first to get rid of Sothern and Marlowe. So when Sothern, acting within terms of his contract, began to arrange with a favorite costume firm to prepare the wardrobe for a certain play, the hostile member of the Syndicate attempted to assign the order to a different firm. Sothern called attention to his right by contract, but yielded so far as to put up the order for competitive bidding by all the best firms in the business. The Syndicate's man lost. From then on, through a series of incidents, the actors were pestered and made uncomfortable by the upper management. Their parting with Charles Frohman was perfectly amicable,

Illus. 176. Sothern as Malvolio. Folger Shakespeare Library.

and getting out from under the Syndicate was a relief. By that time, fortunately the Shubert Trust had risen to sufficient strength to compete with the Syndicate, and by shifting allegiance to the Shuberts, the actors expected to improve their opportunities and income.[144]

When their third season ended in London, they realized that the American public had probably seen enough for a while of the limited repertory in which they could co-star with fair distribution of honors. So for the next two seasons (1907–8, 1908–9) they divided. Sothern seems to have had a good time of it, alternating in half a dozen pieces that he enjoyed; but Miss Marlowe was trapped.[145] The Shuberts let her do an occasional Shakespeare, but she spent far too many evenings that first season in a lightweight comedy about the Italian Renaissance called *Gloria* by J. B. Fagan. The second season she was confined to the role of Yvette in Mary Johnston's *The Goddess of Reason,* a play about the French Revolution. It was a bad play, but her personal attractiveness was drawing her $10,000 a month. Money could not hold her, however. As she told the Shuberts, "I am going back to play Shakespeare to the people." She had persuaded Sothern to join her down at the Academy of Music on Fourteenth Street, to do Shakespeare at popular prices.[146]

That brave plan was interrupted, however, when in the spring of 1909 they were called to ready themselves to inaugurate the great new "national" theatre, called the New, in the coming fall. As America's most distinguished team of Shakespeareans, they were asked to lead the New Theatre's stock company in all its productions of classic plays for three years. Their first assignment was to direct and play the leading roles in *Antony and Cleopatra.*

In his biography of Miss Marlowe, Charles Russell entitled his brief chapter XXIII "Disasters of the New Theatre." It would take a very long chapter to rehearse all those disasters, their causes and results, but here we need only take note of some of the more significant turns of events.[147] As we have seen, in 1892 Helena Modjeska, after one full and stable career in the theatre of Poland, and now in the midst of an exhausting second career "on the road" in this country, published in *The Forum* an eloquent appeal for the establishment of at least one permanent, endowed theatre[148] of the sort common in major cities throughout continental Europe, where fine theatre artists could dwell in security, perform in repertory, preserve the dramatic masterpieces of the past, foster modern drama, and train young artists who would serve the next generation. Modjeska's was but one of many such pleas and proposals, before and after, including some from Sothern and from Marlowe, calling for the establishment of municipal theatres or at least one "national" theatre.

In 1891 a Mr. H. B. McDowell established in New York a "Theatre of Arts and Letters": it produced a couple of one-act plays and disappeared.[149] In 1897 the *Criterion* magazine sponsored a series of new European plays, but failed to continue. Early in 1903 Joseph I. C. Clarke, vice-president of the American Dramatists' Club, called a meeting to plan an "endowed national theatre," and many authors, actors, producers, and theatrical editors rallied to his support.[150] By 1904 Clarke was President of the National Art Theatre Society, and at a banquet in his honor he spelled out the Society's plans in detail.[151] Very quickly the club acquired over a thousand members, but not enough funds to take a theatre and initiate a program. An appeal to Andrew Carnegie was flatly rejected. An endowed theatre, Carnegie declared, is a weak theatre: "The only way to endow a theatre is to buy tickets at the box office."[152]

Just when it appeared that the idea of a National Art Theatre was dead, it was "rescued" by an enterprising German named Heinrich Conried.[153] Conried had come to America in the 1870s, had for many years directed the German-speaking theatre in Irving Place, and in 1903 had been elected by the Metropolitan Opera and Real Estate Company to succeed Maurice Grau as managing director of the Opera. Once in that position, he was ringed about by all the millionaires who kept the Metropolitan Opera afloat, and he easily persuaded thirty of them to ante $100,000 apiece to do for drama what they had done and were doing for opera. One of his millionaires was Henry Morgenthau, who happened to own that piece of ground just above Columbus Circle, bounded by Sixty-second and Sixty-third Streets and facing Central Park West—an absolutely ideal position for the kind of palatial building envisioned by the donors, a building to rival in magnificence Vienna's Burgtheater or the Paris Opera.[154]

Eyebrows were raised when it became known that one million of the three million dollars in the fund went to Morgenthau for his real estate, and inevitably it was whispered (but never proved) that Conried had taken a handsome commission for the sale.[155] More eyebrows were raised because of the speed and assurance with which Conried laid out plans for the building and its uses.[156] The stage was 100 feet wide and 50 feet deep; the proscenium opening was about 40 feet wide and 40 feet high; the pit under the stage was 32 feet deep. The capacity of the house was about

2100. The orchestra held about 600; the 23 boxes surrounding the orchestra held 138; two proscenium boxes held 20; above the boxes a set of "foyer stalls" held 256; the long curving first balcony held 736; a narrow top balcony held 280. The program, according to Conried, would be a carefully mixed repertory: two nights a week of Shakespeare or other classic drama, two nights of modern plays both American and European; two nights of light opera *(opéra comique).* Conried himself as overall director would choose what pieces were to be presented and assign directors to those pieces which he himself did not direct. The performing would be done by a permanent stock company, without stars. And so forth. It was all very systematic, authoritarian, Germanic, and unworkable. The worst feature of all, perhaps, was the "golden horseshoe" of private boxes for the very rich. These boxes (show-cases) would do at the Metropolitan Opera, where the Fashionables went to be seen, to be lulled by tunes perhaps, and to hear without the effort of understanding. Plays, however—especially the "classics"—with nothing but words in them, called for closer attention and harder brainwork than many of the Fashionables cared to expend. Then, too, no one seems to have applied simple arithmetic to the system of box ownership. If a play, whether old or new, or a comic opera, however amusing, was to be shown twice a week for, say, twelve weeks, how many box holders were going to see it twenty-four times? The result, of course, was that except on first or second nights most of the boxes were empty. The story went around that the wife of one box holder, hiring a cook, settled satisfactorily every condition but one: "This I will not do," said the applicant, "I will not okkepy yer box at the New Theayter."[157]

Illus. 178. Winthrop Ames, director of the New Theatre.

Illus. 177. Heinrich Conried, director of the Metropolitan Opera and promoter of the New Theatre.

Otto Kahn, one of the millionaires, who knew something about theatre and truly cared for its well-being, tried to salvage the situation, though it had developed too far to be saved by patchwork. He managed to ease Morgenthau off the board of control, though he could not modify the million-dollar purchase of land. He dismissed Conried's claim to the directorship. Unfortunately Conried's plans for the

Illus. 179. The New Theatre.

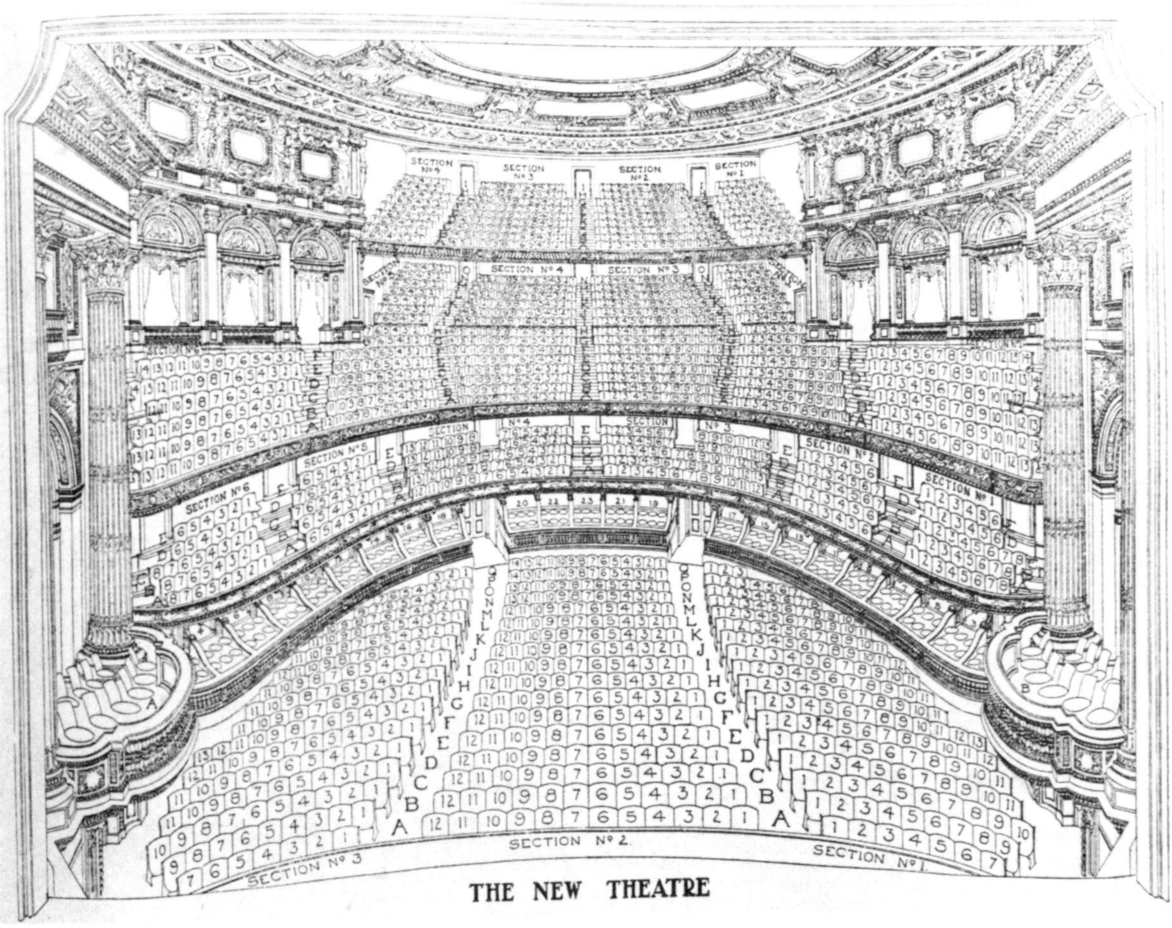

Illus. 180. Auditorium of the New Theatre.

size and shape of the building, his notion that the same house could serve both drama and opera, the overall vastness and elaborate decor of the building had been too firmly embedded in the minds of the sponsors (and the sponsor's wives) to be altered or withdrawn. These plutocrats had paid down their money and they wanted their money's worth. Conried's plans were those which the architects followed.

But who should direct this mighty enterprise? Conried was out of it. As a matter of fact, he fell ill in 1909, returned to Europe and died. The board considered Richard Mansfield, a difficult person to work with, but he also died. David Belasco was too narrowly committed to Belascoism. Having heard of a brilliant young actor-producer in London, Harley Granville Barker, they brought him over for serious discussions. But Barker, who sensed that drama in our century—whether by Shakespeare, Chekhov, Barker himself, or Shaw—depended upon actor-audience intimacy, took one look at the architect's plans and the partly finished building, thanked his hosts, and went home.[158]

Finally they hit upon an ideal choice, a young Bostonian named Winthrop Ames[159]—Harvard-educated, a devotee of theatre who had traveled widely in Europe studying major theatres there, and who had spent a few seasons directing the Castle Square Theatre in Boston. Ames presented himself to the board in the spring of 1908, made several sensible proposals for the building (which mainly went unheeded), and in July was appointed managing director.

Then what play should be chosen to open this great theatre? Shakespeare, of course. And a tragedy, not a lighter play. But nothing so hackneyed as *Hamlet.* Ames offered what appeared to be an ideal choice—*Antony and Cleopatra,* which Coleridge had called Shakespeare's "most wonderful" play, in its giant power a rival of Shakespeare's greatest works. And it had rarely been done, perhaps never worthily.

Ames and his advisers combed the profession to assemble the best possible stock company, flexible actors who could handle modern domestic drama or Shakespeare with equal ease.[160] They found a handful left over from the days of Booth and Barrett when blank verse was a second nature to them; and a good many who perhaps shunned the "old school" but at least were sufficiently strong to make their presence felt in the vast marble halls of the New. Inevitably, though, the management recognized that to open with such a pair of roles as Antony and Cleopatra nothing less than the best Shakespeareans in the country would satisfy the donors. Only Sothern and Marlowe would do.

Of course, Sothern and Marlowe accepted the invitation and even agreed to head the company in classic drama for the future. Caught up in the universal euphoria, they failed to recognize that neither of them was right for *Antony and Cleopatra*—that, in fact, on their own initiative they would never have dreamed of producing it. In stature and personality Sothern no more resembled the triple pillar of the world than he resembled Othello. Miss Marlowe, who had long since declared she wished to play only "good women," probably shared the attitude of Sarah Siddons, who once said that if she played Cleopatra as it ought to be played she would hate herself.[161] But they accepted: the honor of inaugurating America's "national" theatre was one they could not forgo.

It was written into their contract that in all classic plays which they would perform at the New (for their engagement was not for the one play only but open-ended) they were to be responsible for their own stage business. They took this to mean that, as was their custom, they would plan and direct the acting of the whole company. Accordingly, while Miss Marlowe studied Cleopatra all summer, she worked up a complete promptbook.[162] She cut and arranged the text as seemed best for a three-hour presentation. She settled every movement and essential stage business. She marked every line for verbal emphasis. When they came to the first meeting of the company, Sothern was prepared to put Miss Marlowe's plans into effect. For the first time they were introduced to their "stage manager," Louis Calvert, the well known English actor and producer.[163] Miss Marlowe handed him her book. He glanced at it and smilingly returned it with words to the effect that "we won't need that, dear lady." For the first time they realized that Calvert had been brought over to serve as principal stage director, and *Antony and Cleopatra* was his first assignment. The struggle that ensued could not be settled with a few words and apologies. It could not be compromised. Calvert was utterly unsympathetic to the Sothern-Marlowe approach to the play and insisted upon doing what he thought he was hired for. Sothern and Marlowe insisted on the terms of their contract and their artistic integrity. Eventually it was Calvert who withdrew, and Sothern pulled the company through the rehearsals. But this ugly confusion of authority contributed its bit to the ultimate failure of the New Theatre's opening play.

Another impediment to success of the production was the scenic arrangements, over which Sothern and Marlowe had no control whatever. A fine scene painter named Jules Guérin, recently returned from Egypt, was put in charge, and he seems to have thought much more of Cleopatra's palace than of Shakespeare's play.[164] According to John Corbin, Guérin flanked the stage with "huge Egyptian columns in the round, mounted on a base that rose nine steps from the playing space. The woodwork alone cost four thousand dollars. Once set, that vast edifice could not be shifted. The other scenes . . . were perforce set inside this hollow square. Every shift had to be made up and down those steps." Scene shifting took so long that after the initial performance two entire scenes, including that aboard Pompey's galley, had to be dropped in order to end the play before midnight.

The preparations were so difficult that there was never time for a complete dress rehearsal before Saturday, November 6, when there was scheduled a "preview" performance for an invited audience.[165] That afternoon was filled with ceremonies. The builder handed the keys of the building to the architect who handed them to J. Pierpont Morgan who thanked the planners and, in the name of the founders, declared the building open "to the service of the drama and to the citizens of New York." A chorus then sang an ode by Percy MacKaye, celebrating the return of "the Prince of Faery." Brief but high-minded addresses were delivered by Governor Hughes and Senator Elihu Root. And to conclude the dedication program, Johnston Forbes-Robertson de-

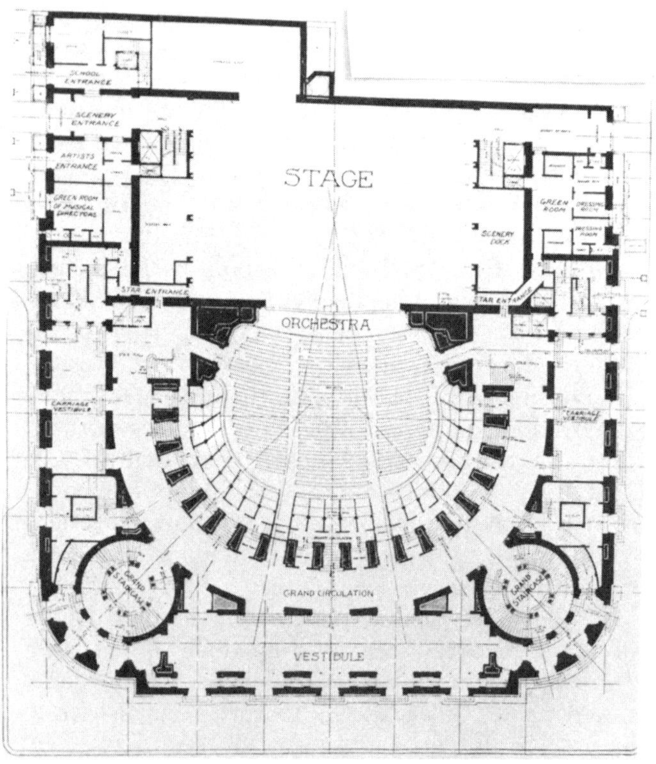

Illus. 181. Ground Plan of the New Theatre.

Illus. 182. The "Imperial Box", the New Theatre.

Illus. 183. Antony and Cleopatra at the New Theatre: the final scene.

livered to the New Theatre company of actors, who were assembled on the stage with him, Hamlet's advice to the players.

At 8:30 that evening the curtain rose on Cleopatra's palace, its huge Egyptian pillars framing a vista of the Nile and its farther shore, a backdrop adapted from one of Guérin's paintings. The invited audience—"a carefully selected congregation of high-brows," said Rennold Wolf of the *Telegraph*—were in for an intensely boring evening.[166] In most parts of the house at least half the dialogue was lost or blurred, and this for many reasons. Most of the actors spoke their lines badly, dropping the end-words, a fatal error in any theatre and especially in so vast and cavernous an auditorium as this one. Many lines were drowned out by noise from the ventilating system. Because of a faulty dynamo the stage lighting could not be brought up to proper intensity, so that from a distance one could not make out facial expression, or even at times know which actor was speaking. The actors, perhaps contending with the accoustical problems, took their speeches at too slow a pace. Difficulty with moving scenery caused long delays between the acts.

Rennold Wolf kept tabs on the audience. Among them he spotted one "dramatic reviewer so grave and serious in his contemplation of stage affairs that his very erudition once cost him his position on a sordid newspaper." This was William Winter, recently fired (though not because of his erudition) after forty-four years service on the *Tribune*. Winter left at ten o'clock.

> A few minutes later William Gillette, Eugene Presbey and other American dramatists . . . walked around the corner to the Hotel Empire and substituted supper for art. Chauncey M. Depew and party surrendered at 11:15. Governor Hughes lasted twenty minutes longer. At midnight but four of the dozens of boxes were occupied. At 12:55, when Cleopatra breathed her last, less than one-third of the original audience survived. David Belasco was true to the end. Daniel Frohman also was game.

Ames and his associates cannot be blamed for the dullness of the play itself, Wolf declared, though they were at fault for having chosen it. The worst fault was that of the actors, whose performance "may generously be described as mediocre."

By Monday, November 8, the stage lighting had been corrected, the noisy ventilating pipes somewhat stilled, and enough scenes had been cut so that the audience was let go at 11:40 instead of 12:55. But still no one was very happy about it. Klauber of the *New York Times* was one of the several critics who acknowledged that Sothern and Marlowe had no rivals in America as "bearers of the classic banner," yet they had not the requisite qualities for Antony and Cleopatra.[167] "By personality and experience, by physique and temperament, their range is not sufficiently expansive" for these roles.

> Miss Marlowe has beauty, it is true, and charm and sympathy; she reads melodiously and her voice falls at times with soothing utterance on the ear; she moves with grace and ease, often with plastic variety of pose. But neither her beauty, grace, nor charm, action or utterance or the power of speech is of a quality to bring Egypt's voluptuous Queen before us.

Since she cannot realize Cleopatra, she attempts to make Cleopatra as nearly like herself as possible. Nothing about her, or Sothern either, would inspire the famous remark of the British matron attending the play: "How very different from the home life of our dear Queen!" Klauber continued:

> One looks in vain for the suggestion of languorous Orientalism, for the warm passions, the quick impulses, the violent changes, now hot; now cold; for the authority and weight of a woman and a queen.

Some critics gave her credit for rising to the heights of passion in the "jealousy" scene, when the messenger brings word of Antony's marriage, but to Klauber she was always more girl than woman, and her bursts of temper were the tantrums of an ingenue.

Sothern got some credit for his explosion of rage when he comes upon Caesar's messenger Thyreus kissing Cleopatra's hand, and orders him whipped, and again for the scene with Eros when he hears of Cleopatra's supposed death, "a scene," said Klauber, "played with a suggestion of sardonic bitterness and disappointment, of sorrow in the face of a last overwhelming calamity that cannot be combatted, of a firm understanding that the end has come, the end of all ambition, and a desire and will for death to close the chapter." But rarely was there a suggestion of the "demi-Atlas of this earth, the arm and burgonet of men." In calm, said Towse, he was not majestic; in sorrow he expressed only a lugubrious melancholy. Whole passages were delivered "in a mournful chant which is sadly depressing."[168] Rennold Wolf declared that he lacked "the dash, the virility of the warrior," and summed up his Antony as "a Hamlet in whiskers."

Unquestionably the play was a failure, and Sothern and Marlowe shouldered their fair share of blame. It may well be that throughout the twelve weeks that they suffered their twice-a-week repetition, they and the other actors improved their speaking somewhat and adapted their voices to the cavernous spaces. But the mark of doom was set by the opening night reviews. Well before the opening, however, Sothern and Marlowe explained to Ames (in confidence) that in spite of their earlier commitment, at the end of the run of *Antony and Cleopatra* they would have to separate from the New.[169] They could not work with Calvert, of course; they did not believe in the mixed program of drama and musicals; they sensed that in spite of all proclaimed intentions this was not a theatre for "the people" but only for the Fashionables, who in the long run would abandon it; that indeed the entire enterprise would fail.

They organized their own company and went on tour in Shakespeare. At the end of the second season Ames himself gave up management of the New and built his own idea of a proper theatre, the Little Theatre in West Forty-fourth Street, designed to seat fewer than 500.[170] The New, thereafter renamed the Century, came under ordinary commercial management, housing musicals, spectacles such as Max Reinhardt's *The Miracle,* and an occasional Shakespeare, including one return of Sothern and Marlowe. In 1930 it was pulled down.

Escape from the New Theatre must have seemed like waking from a nightmare into daylight and sanity. Now, together with Sothern, Miss Marlowe could resume the course she had been diverted from, "to go back to play Shakespeare to the people at popular prices." After a warm-up tour her newly organized company played not one but two engagements downtown at the Academy of Music. The huge old house was packed on Monday, February 7, and the welcome loud and sincere when they opened a week-long run of *Romeo and Juliet.* The second week was devoted to the *Shrew,* the third to the *Merchant,* the fourth to *Hamlet* with a matinee of *Twelfth Night.* After a two-week rest they returned on March 21, the Monday after Easter for a two-week "farewell engagement." The first week was entirely given over to *As You Like It,* this being Miss Marlowe's first Rosalind in New York in a dozen years, and Sothern's debut as Jaques. The second week they ran off all six of their current repertory, always, it appears, to well-filled houses.

The morning after the first *As You Like It* Klauber wondered if the success or failure of Shakespare could be a matter of geography.[171] North of Twenty-third Street he did not flourish, but "down in Fourteenth Street last night's audience testified both to the poet's popularity and that of the two artists who were bringing his much-beloved comedy back on the stage. Arthur Warren of the *Tribune*[172] speculated at length on

> the attraction that Shakespeare has for the great run of playgoers. From the front of the stage to the dim reaches of the gallery the big theatre has been filled with people who manifest a real pleasure in anything that concerns the Shakespeare plays. These audiences are not moved by fad or fashion. They go to the theatre for pleasure, not for mere amusement or to kill time. They are fond of the stars, of course, but they are fond of Shakespeare, too, although managers generally doubt that Shakespeare can bring profit. Mr. Sothern and Miss Marlowe know probably more than any one else about the attitude of the public toward Shakespeare.

The disaster of *Antony and Cleopatra* seems to have been forgotten. It might as well never have happened.

Miss Marlowe had always loved *As You Like It,* but after 1899, except for her two envenings of Rosalind in London in 1907, circumstances had usually kept her out of the role. The play so emphatically belongs to Rosalind that it was difficult to find a place in it where Sothern could shine. Eventually, of course, he obliged by getting up Jaques.

He muffed his chances there, however, by giving it a "new reading," and for his pains got a mixed press. Apparently he took Jaques' major pronouncements as true gospel, and abandoning the traditional oratorical, elocutionary manner, aimed for "naturalism," as if he wanted to be accepted in earnest by his hearers. Klauber of the *New York Times* found him colorless, tedious, "all on one level."[173] The reviewer for the *Dramatic Mirror* thought he reduced the role to an "insipidly watery consistency."[174] On the other hand, when certain Boston critics heard him in the next season, they found "every word of his clearcut orotund speech a pleasure to the ear and to the mind," and were delighted to hear the Seven Ages speech "delivered almost in conversational tone by the speaker to his companions, all seated at a table."[175] The New York critics were right, of course, in calling for pompous histrionics. Jaques' cynicism is the supreme folly in the play, and he *must* be played with some measure of affectation or heightened oratory so that the healthy-minded in Arden—the Banished Duke, Orlando, and especially Rosalind—can bring him down with a palpable thump.

It will be remembered that in 1889 Miss Marlowe's Rosalind was criticized by her best Boston critics as too girlish, too emotional, sensitive to the point of sentimentality; that she hardly dared open her "autumnal" production of *As You Like It* in New York after the "happy hearted raillery" of Ada Rehan's Rosalind in Augustin Daly's "spring-time" production. In those days, we may suppose, she was too near to Parthenia, which was still in her repertory, to clear her spirits for Rosalind.

Since then, however, she had studied Beatrice and Katherine the Shrew and Portia and knew something more about how to set free reserves of comic power. For the critic of the *Dramatic Mirror,* indeed, she let go too much.[176] Her Rosalind's "coquetry is overemphasized, its vivacity is too dynamic. It is purely hoydenish, romping, teazing—a madcap sort of hide-and-seek performance, lacking in the higher elements of poetic refinement and interpretive dignity." The response of the audience at the Academy, however, was better represented by Frank DeFoe's celebration in the *World.*[177]

> Miss Marlowe's return to doublet and hose will be especially welcome to all lovers of poetic drama; it is an auspicious event. There is no comedy role in the Shakespearean repertoire which adjusts itself so well to her intellectual attainments and personal graces, and there is no actress on the English speaking stage who speaks the verse so beautifully or illuminates the character so charmingly as she. . . . The character is tuned to a sustained note of healthy light-heartedness, sparkling vivacity and merry banter. No touch of sadness is permitted to enter the mood of this lovelorn maiden masquerading in Arden in boy's attire. . . . She may be grave, she may swagger in her masculine assumption and she may be wistful in her glowing love passion, but she is never sad. . . . As long as Miss Marlowe continues to romp in the Forest of Arden the spirit of poetry on our stage will live.

So too the Boston critics when she carried her repertory there in November. Thus the *Christian Science Monitor:*[178]

> The arch humor, the brisk wit and above all the bubbling playfulness of Rosalind have delicious expression. . . . We in the audience were enjoying in the perfection of its maturity the art of one who, gifted from the first, has toiled lovingly to search out the depths of beauty in Shakespeare. For beauty is always the keynote of Miss Marlowe's acting, as it is of all poetry, art and music that comforts and inspires.

The Boston *Herald,* too, perceived how in the forest scenes with Orlando, she succeeded in playing at a double level—"making what was most serious to her possess the charm of an exquisite frolic."[179]

When Sothern and Marlowe let it be known, after the catastrophe of *Antony and Cleopatra,* that their next major creation, long thought upon by both, would be *Macbeth,* public credulity was as strained as it had been in the 1880s when the fashionable comedienne Lillie Langtry announced for the same play. Sothern was no more fit in stature to represent Bellona's bridegroom

Illus. 184. Sothern as Macbeth.

than he had been for the Emperor Antony, nor did Miss Marlowe suggest the conventional (though now outmoded) image of Macbeth's lady as a Siddonian Thunderbearer. Yet they had firm precedents to build upon—especially the Irving-Terry production last seen in America fifteen years earlier. If Sothern lacked Irving's height, he at least was gifted with neat physical composition, was well trained in bodily composure, and was capable of speaking Shakespeare's English so that it could be understood. Miss Marlowe had made up her promptbook many years before and examined every critical resource that could enrich her performance.[180]

Their *Macbeth* opened in New Haven, November 4, 1910; in Boston on November 14, and in New York on December 5. A handsome production in every way, it won surprising success. To begin with, Sothern exercised his finest talents on the *mise-en-scène,* handsome deep sets for major scenes and a series of well-painted drops to get the play through the rapid run of early scenes.[181] Following Irving's model, Sothern depended much on mists, shadows, and darkness to enhance the mystery of the play. He took unusual care of lighting, too, so that it seemed always to come from window or moon or fireplace, and not merely from general stage lamps.

In a couple of points he followed Irving's staging too closely. In London (I cannot be certain that Irving brought this effect to America), after the Caldron Scene, Irving introduced a chorus of some sixty white-clad spirits, apparently air-borne, singing a Middleton-cum-Davenant lyric, "Over Woods, high Rocks, and Fountains." Sothern produced a similar musical ballet of angelic figures. Numerous critical voices protested this intrusion of non-dramatic, non-Shakespearean matter into a performance which at 3:35 in length was a touch too long.[182] Sothern also imported the musical score by the late Sir Arthur Sullivan that Irving had requisitioned for his *Macbeth.* By this time the "melodrama" manner which Irving and Daly and others had fostered of underscoring practically every passage of a poetic play with music from the pit was coming to be recognized as a nuisance. Sothern would have done well to silence the drums and fiddles and let Shakespeare do his work. But these objections aside, Sothern's staging was regarded as a triumphant showing of the mood and meaning and action of the play, one of the finest in the last dozen or more years. Yet it was also one of the last in the "old-fashioned" mode of the nineteenth century, and here and there, in subordinate clauses, one hears an echo of wonderment about whether all this expensive illusionism is worth the candle.

As for Sothern's performance, probably Henry Parker of Boston's *Transcript* traces it as clearly as anyone. It was obviously clearly planned. Sothern began as "in the prime of middle age and of rather Viking aspect. The drooping moustache, the thin beard about the chin, the suggestion of beak-like grooves in the nose, the hair falling . . . heavy black about the head and neck all suggested this." As he grew older the aspect changed. In the scene at the castle court (the murder scene) he "had begun to turn haggard and old; the king whom Banquo's ghost confronted at the banquet was distinctly so: while the Macbeth who marked [*sic*] his foes at Dunsinane was wild and worn in aspect, a kind of gross and frenzied phantom of the Macbeth of the beginning."

Macbeth's furious resuscitation for the final fight, after his long steady debilitation of nerve, must have provided a scene unsurpassable. Unlike Irving, who fought Macduff against a bloody sunset in an open field, Sothern staged the last scene inside the castle walls.

> Malcolm and Siward's men battled their way into it over ramparts and through great doors that, falling, revealed a vista of the sea. From other parts of the castle came the din of other storming parties. At last it was carried; the defenders surrendered, the victors appeared here and there amid rejoicing cries. The solitary Macbeth and Macduff fought the final duel. It was a fight to see: for Mr. Sothern made the caught and doomed Macbeth fight like a wild beast; he struck down those who would interfere; he brought Macduff almost to his knees; losing his sword he plied his dagger; and when at last Macduff struck home, he died with the outcry of a wild beast stricken in the full tide of its fury.

This gradation into age, nervous terror, even hysteria (he fainted at the end of the Caldron Scene), and wild resurgence of energy at the end was a clearly worked out pattern of development generally appreciated by the best of critics. Such as took exception to Sothern's Macbeth did so simply because he was too little the stalwart soldier; as Philip Hale of the Boston *Herald* put it, too "irresolute, given to self-introspection and soliloquy, inclined toward hysterial demonstrations"—if not a brother, at least a cousin of Hamlet.[183] The critic of the *Christian Science Monitor* actually picked up the metaphor of his Antony by a New York critic and called his Macbeth "a Hamlet in a beard."[184]

Miss Marlowe's Lady Macbeth was, expectedly, a passionately devoted wife, moved only in all that she says and does to promote Macbeth's rise to the kingship—with no concern for herself, but for his sake alone. One of the most moving effects in the play, expressive of her total devotion to her husband, was her behavior throughout the Banquet Scene:

> It was all for Macbeth that she strove through the scene of the feast; of him she thought and of him only; the alarmed, bewildered thanes were to her almost as much phantoms as Banquo's ghost itself. At last they were gone. Macbeth sits inert and moody in his chair. She sinks to the floor beside him. She reaches out her hand. She looks up at him with a love in her eyes, "You lack the season of all natures, sleep," and the accents are of a compassion and affection that aches for itself because it cannot heal another's woe.[185]

Her Sleep-walking Scene was deeply moving to some, declared ordinary by others. Certainly it was staged beautifully. She emerged from the darkness of an upper room, faintly lighted by her candle as she picked her way slowly down a pillared staircase. She moaned pitifully as she washed her hands. The few lines of the scene were dramatic jewels dropped into the moments of pantomime. "Surely this scene ranks with noblest attainments of Miss Marlowe's long career of accomplishment."[186]

Of the New York critics, many of them too "sophisticated" (by heaven knows what standards of smartness) to accept Sothern and Marlowe as the foremost American Shakespeareans of the day, one reads opinions like these:

> *The Nation:* "An elaborate, conscientious, and, on the whole, intelligent revival of *Macbeth* is a welcome addition in these degenerate days. . . . The interpretation of the tragedy is not especially brilliant in any respect. . . . Mr. Sothern is not a subtle or inspired actor, but he has ambition and perseverance. . . . Miss Marlowe's Lady Macbeth is lacking in sustained tragic intensity and power. . . . [187]
>
> *Life:* "Mr. Sothern's staging, though elaborate, is not spectacular, and there is no reason, outside of its being Shakespeare, and that it is given an adequate presentation, why New Yorkers should leave the fleshpots of slangy farce and the chorus-girl shows to sit through this gory tragedy."[188]
>
> The *Tribune:* The opinion of Arthur Warren is especially interesting. In summary, he would not allow that either Sothern or Miss Marlowe was a great or inspired actor, or endowed with qualities which "enable them to depict the sweep of irresistible passion," and so on. Yet here at a vast new theatre, the Broadway, at prices lower than for the shallowest musical comedy, they are playing poetic tragedy—Shakespeare's *Macbeth*—and making money at it! Commercial managers must be dumbfounded. By hard work these earnest, if not brilliant, actors prove that there is an enormous public hungry for Shakespeare. Their position is honorable and high.[189]

Everyone had reservations, but as Hornblow put it in *Theatre* magazine,[190] "The Sothern-Marlowe production of *Macbeth* will be remembered as one of the most elaborate and satisfying the present generation has seen of Shakespeare's tragedy."[190] The *Dramatic Mirror* recognized the *generosity* with which the team of stars have treated the play.[191] "They have reaped richly from the public, yet they sow as lavishly as they reap. The average manager makes no such experiments as this. In fact, the average manager witnessing this production of *Macbeth,* might cry with a louder voice than ever that Shakespeare spells ruin. Yet the Broadway Theatre was filled Monday night with people and echoed with enthusiasm."

Illus. 185. Miss Marlowe as Lady Macbeth.

Illus. 186. The slaying of Macbeth. Frederick Lewis as Macduff.

As Sothern himself put it, it was not a play for a long run[192] "because of popular aversion to the principal characters," but it served them well in repertory. During the remainder of the season they played it along with their other half-dozen favorites, from coast to coast.

Early in 1911 Sothern finally won a divorce from his first wife, Virginia Harned, who had been his leading lady at the beginning of the century; and in the summer of that year he and Miss Marlowe were married.

Illus. 187. Sothern as war-time entertainer of the troops over-seas.

Thereafter for the next three and a half seasons they toured regularly and widely, reaching into the South, the Northwest, and even Canada. Besides their usual repertory they occasionally added matinees of *Richelieu* and *If I Were King* for Sothern to shine in. In January of 1914, Miss Marlowe fell ill and had to withdraw for the season.[193] Then the Great War broke out, and from 1914 to the fall of 1919 they did not play, Sothern spending most of his time (joined occasionally by Miss Marlowe), entertaining the troops with patriotic recitations and solo scenes from Shakespeare.[194] Thus they were prevented from joining the cluster of Shakespeareans, English and American, who vied with each other in New York in 1916, celebrating the tercentenary of Shakespeare's death.

They returned to the stage in 1919 and thereafter played their repertory in all but one season through the spring of 1924—then retired forever. During these years they revived one more Shakespeare, of which perhaps the less we remember the better. This was *Cymbeline,* at Jolson's Fifty-ninth Street Theatre, October 2, 1923. Miss Marlowe had loved the character of Imogen all her professional life, and thirty years before this, in Boston, her performance had been praised by the finest critics. She could not bear to leave the stage without once more experiencing the love, the shame, the fearless dedication, the terror, and the consummation of that superb role. Unfortunately, as John Corbin of the *New York Times,* a critic who had in earlier times adored her, could not help but observe,

> Of late years Miss Marlowe's mannerisms have steadily grown on her—overwrought and fallacious pathos, alternating with outbursts of false passion. Worst of all is an extreme deliberation in utterance, further retarded by false pauses that destroy poetic rhythm and even rob her scenes of their prime quality of spontaneity and passion. There are times when she seems to be deliberately composing the play, not acting it.[195]

Heywood Broun and Alexander Woollcott both had formerly admired, even loved, her magnificent voice, but now in this role they deplored her abuse of it.[196] Towse of the *Post* defended her as well as he could and turned the blame for the four-hour long tedium on "the dead weight of the plot." In *The Drama* Horace Howard Furness, Jr. defended her in a full-dress review[197] in which he declared that "in her gallery of lovely Shakespearean heroines this is her masterpiece. It is not acting this: it *is* Imogen." But the weight of informed opinion condemned this performance. Insofar as I can make out, through the rest of the season she quite redeemed herself in Juliet (which she had first played thirty-seven years before), in Portia, Ophelia, Viola, and the rest. That was the year that Eleanora Duse declared, "You are in my memory and in my heart. You are *Juliet*—the most beautiful, the most perfect, of the Juliets that I have met in my life."[198]

It is marvelous that Miss Marlowe, at fifty-eight, was so beautiful a Juliet, that Sothern could pass for Romeo or Petruchio at sixty-five. But even more delightful to contemplate is that at their ages they were susceptible to young ideas.[199] "We left the stage in 1914," said Sothern. "When we decided to act again, we studied all the contributions that had been made by the new school of stage decorators in America and abroad." And they put those contributions to work. In 1900 when he and Daniel Frohman first staged *Hamlet,* the theatre was in the throes of the Irvingesque manner of staging. Sothern, caught in the tide, could only emulate Irving, and his 1900 *Hamlet* sets were built solidly of wood—massive platforms, stairways, towers, castles, a church. And four years later when he became responsible for the *mise-en-scène* during the long partnership with Miss Marlowe, there was still only the one way. "Every brick, stone and mortar were there as faithfully reproduced as highly developed scene-painters could depict them. We were so steeped in the process that it would have been heresy for anyone to suggest that we were wrong and that this manner was doomed to failure because it was choking itself out of existence."[200] As late as 1910 he was intent on recreating a "real" Venice for *The Merchant,* doubtful and perhaps scornful of whatever he yet knew of the ideas of Gordon Craig, his imitators and followers.

By 1919 he had been amazed, delighted, and converted by what neat effects had been achieved with the simplest means, especially in musical comedy. For *Twelfth Night,* the play with which they made their reentry, they dressed the stage mainly with drapery.[201] Neutral-toned narrow drapes just inside the theatre's permanent proscenium created a false proscenium. At right center and left center a pair of slender drapes, fluted, resembled classical columns, and whether by accident or design they divided the lateral space of the stage very much as did the stage posts of the typical Elizabethan playhouse. In front of each of these cloth columns stood a low bench facing the audience. At either side of the stage, curtains could be drawn upstage from the proscenium to form side walls, or they could be drawn away, in, say, a garden scene, to reveal topiary bushes. At a little distance beyond the cloth columns one saw at center a low flight of steps leading up to a balustraded walkway crossing the stage; beyond that more topiary, symmetrically arranged; and behind all a blue skycloth. For some scenes, in *Twelfth Night* or other plays, flats or arches might be dropped into this central scenic space or into the side spaces, converting them into separate smaller openings. Any of the openings, at sides or rear, could be filled with "plugs" to repre-

Illus. 188. Sothern's postwar simplified scenery. The lower setting, for Orsino's palace, is easily transformed into Olivia's garden, above.

sent scenic vistas, domestic walls, cupboards, fireplaces, or what you will. Bits of furniture and properties could be moved on or off and scenic changes could be effected with minimal loss of time. Thus for the first time since Forbes-Robertson's farewell Hamlets a smooth, nearly uninterrupted flow of narrative was available, and much fuller texts could be presented in the three to three and a half hours, which audiences accepted as normal playing time. And yet in one further way Sothern and Marlowe's late productions shook loose from the hangman's noose of custom. They banished musical accompaniment to dramatic scenes.[202] "No longer does Hamlet die to a wailing dirge, Malvolio pick his steps to a flowery minuet, Bassanio choose the casket to a dreamy waltz, or Petruchio tame his fiery shrew to virulent, virile strains." Only when someone calls for a dance, or Orsino needs melody to soothe his painful love-longing, would Sothern and Marlowe allow music to smother Shakespeare, and presumably such music as was heard came from dramatically prepared-for, on-stage performers or from the wings. The pit-band was exiled.

So ready, indeed, was Sothern to shake free from the past and join the twentieth century that he paid a very handsome tribute and expression of gratitude to the rise of the Little Theatre movement. The hard-headed, set-in-cement professionals (Belasco, for instance) utterly despised the pretensions of the amateurs gathering forces across the country. But Sothern knew that the wider the Little Theatre spread the more intelligent support it would create for the professional theatre. "The man who does a thing himself grows keen to see how more expert men do it." Beyond that, too, the amateurs could bring out plays—experimental new ones and excellent but neglected classics—that the profit-and-loss minded commercial managers would not dare attempt until their worth was proven by the amateurs. And the Little Theatres had already gone far in advance of the professionals in the new arts of stage decoration.

Julia Marlowe and her partner and eventual husband, Edward Sothern, were a brave and devoted pair of artists, who through a troubled and often drab period struggled to keep Shakespeare alive in America. They could not by themselves break the usurpation of our theatre by the Syndicate, yet with the friendly connivance of Charles Frohman they succeeded for several years in playing Shakespeare and what appeared to them significant modern drama under the cover of the Syndicate. Eventually they had the strength and will to break all false managerial bonds and manage themselves. Late in their careers they even got rid of the plushy overloading of Shakespeare stages. Though never in the forefront of scenographic revolutionaries, they took what was essential from the new schools of "stage decoration" and moved toward the scenic simplicities in which Shakespeare could best do his own work. Down to their last sorry failure in *Cymbeline* they were striving (beyond their strength) to enrich the Shakespearean stage repertory. And even when that failed they were still able actors. Age brought them down, and they could not compete with an aggressive younger, flashy, fashionable Barrymore-ish generation of actors, whose record of Shakespearean achievement, compared to theirs, weighs little in the balance.

Pretty much they are forgotten, or remembered only as lesser leftovers from Victorian–Edwardian days—"old school," artificial, sentimental. Whoever seeks out recordings of their performances will hardly believe the noises that emerge. Alexander Woollcott declared that *her* voice, at least, was the most beautiful that he had ever heard from any stage. We must believe the witnesses.

Epilogue
The Shakespeare Tercentenary

OCCASIONALLY I HAVE REFERRED to the year 1916 as the Shakespeare tercentenary, and to efforts in New York that year to honor Shakespeare's memory. Oddly enough, and conveniently for centenary watchers, his birthday in 1564 and his death in 1616 both fell on April 23. This is one holy day that we have learned not to overlook.

In 1864, the tercentenary of the birth, when the Civil War was at its hottest, New York just barely noticed the occasion.[1] At noon that day the cornerstone was laid for the Shakespeare Monument in Central Park, and the proceeds of two benefit performances that evening were turned over to the Monument Committee. Old James Henry Hackett donated to the cause his Falstaff at Niblo's Garden and Edwin Booth his Romeo at the Winter Garden. Brooklyn, too, paid some minor notice. After the Conways performed *Twelfth Night,* someone recited an "Ode to Shakespeare" and the Stratford Club displayed a series of "Shakespearean Tableaux." Press coverage was minimal and except for an American visitor's report of the festival at Stratford-upon-Avon, no American magazine published anything about Shakespeare.

Only New York's German population, in their Stadt-Theater in the Bowery, showed serious appreciation of "Unser Shakespeare." During almost every month throughout the 1863–64 season they staged a Shakespeare play and gave it a run: *Macbeth, Die Bezähmte Widerspenstige, Ein Wintermärchen, Ein Sommernachtstraum, Der Sturm, Hamlet, Der Kaufmann von Venedig,* and *Richard der Dritte.* Of these eight plays, with their repetitions, the Germans must have enjoyed forty or more evenings of Shakespeare during the 1863–64 season. And, be it noted, their translations were taken from *Shakespeare,* not from adaptations by Davenant or Garrick or Dryden or Cibber.

As for London in 1864, Shakespeare was in the doldrums. Charles Kean, the great pageant-master of the midcentury, would surely have made a fuss over the tercentenary, but he had given up management and taken his wife on a round-the-world tour. The one acknowledged celebrational event was a spectacular *Henry IV* at Drury Lane, featuring Samuel Phelps's famous Falstaff.[2]

Out at Stratford, however—that little farmers' market town—something truly remarkable happened. The Stratfordians, eager to establish that the place of Shakespeare's birth was truly Shakespeare's home, turned to their mayor, Edward Fordham Flower, to take the lead. Flower, already four times their mayor, a man of energy and vision, self-educated, traveled, a self-styled "citizen of the world" (he had spent several years of his youth in America helping run slaves to freedom through the southern Illinois village of Albion)—he seized the initiative. Since there was no proper theatre to accommodate the many events that he planned for several hundred guests, he erected a Grand Pavilion, twelve-sided and wooden, to serve as theatre and banquet hall.[3]

Our American visitor, reporting to *Harper's,*[4] spent at Stratford one of the two weeks that the festival lasted. He went down from London by train with hundreds of others and was cabbed to his quarters in the White Lion Hotel. After a good steak dinner he lounged about the hotel, meeting fellow guests. The next day (Saturday) he passed in visits to sights of the town—first the birthplace and "the room where He was born," then the museum to see the schooldesk at which Shakespeare learned his "small Latin and less Greek," then to New Place where once stood the famous mulberry tree. For the Grand Banquet in the

Pavilion, long lines of tables were dressed with flowers and figurines—saccharine Romeos, pastry Hamlets, and iced Portias on cake pedestals. The guests feasted on capon, duck, and boar-meat, followed by the "queen of curds and cream" and "lyric flagons" of wine. There were speeches by Lord Houghton, Archbishop Trench, the Earl of Carlisle, a German professor, and Mayor Flower himself. Greetings were received from Germany and Russia.

On the second day some of the guests boated on the Avon; most attended one service or another in the Shakespeare church and gazed upon the gravesite and the Shakespeare bust, now nicely repainted in its original colors. Monday morning our American strolled through the "Shakespeare Gallery," where Mayor Flower had brought together four or five hundred of the finest theatrical paintings in England, including some thirty portraits of Shakespeare and the alleged death mask. Queen Victoria had graciously lent Sir Thomas Lawrence's great painting of Kemble as Hamlet, and there, too, was Sir Joshua Reynolds's version (the second) of Mrs. Siddons as the Tragic Muse. Monday's pleasures were musical: in the afternoon Handel's *Messiah,* in the evening songs inspired by Shakespeare, both concerts featuring the great tenor, Sims Reeves.

On other mornings the American strolled through fields of daisies and cuckoo-pints to Ann Hathaway's cottage, which he found sadly decayed; or visited the Red Horse Hotel, made famous by Washington Irving; or took the long walk with a friend to Charlecote Hall and the deer park. For the first time ever the Hall was open to Shakespearean pilgrims. The Hall was well guarded by servants, but the Lucy family had conspicuously absented themselves, for they still bore an unsinkable grudge against the famous youth who had stolen their deer.

The plays that Flower had requisitioned included *Twelfth Night* with John Baldwin Buckstone, *Romeo and Juliet* with the French actress Stella Colas, the Webb brothers' production of *The Comedy of Errors, As You Like It* by the Haymarket company, *Othello,* and *Much Ado About Nothing.* One evening was given over to "a grand Costume Ball of Shakespearean Characters." There should have been a *Hamlet,* of course, but that was prevented by a spat between rival actors. Flower invited Charles Fechter, whose modern man-of-fashion Hamlet was the talk of London; and he asked Samuel Phelps, the last of his generation of great native tragedians, to play the villain in *Cymbeline.* Phelps was insulted, and not only declined Iachimo but let his wrathful claims to Hamlet be known through a broadside that went the rounds in London and amused snickerers from the sidelines. So there was no *Hamlet.* And no *Cymbeline.*

The snob element among the London critics and most of the theatre profession scorned the Stratford affair as insignificant, and Flower did not attempt to convert his festival into an annual event. Fifteen years later his son Charles built the first Shakespeare Memorial Theatre and instituted a two-week program every April. But it would be yet another half-century before the annual Stratford Festival would be regarded by the London establishment as any more than a "country rep" affair.

As the year 1916 approached, the English anticipated it by establishing an Executive Committee, chaired by Lord Plymouth, for Commemoration of the Tercentenary of Shakespeare's death, but almost at once England was caught up in the Great War, so that all plans were held in abeyance. Normally Beerbohm Tree could be counted on to arrange a spring festival of Shakespeare, but the threat of a bomb attack prevented that even in 1915, and by 1916 Tree had gone to America to make films. Forbes-Robertson, who had bidden farewell to the London stage in 1913, was also in America, doing a farewell-tour of the West. Only Martin-Harvey's company, touring in the northern counties and in Ireland, might be able to bring *Henry V* into London in early May.

Meanwhile the Germans, confident of military victory, released messages to taunt the British, announcing their own full-scale Shakespeare celebrations at Weimar, Berlin, and Prague. The English Committee, meeting on January 11, announced that their program would take place as follows.[5] Since April 23 was Easter, the opening event would be a service in the Abbey on April 30. On Monday, May 1, the prime minister would chair a convocation at Mansion House. On Tuesday, at 2:30 P.M. a matinee of *Julius Caesar* would take place in Drury Lane Theatre, the king and queen attending. The Annual Shakespeare Lecture, by Dr. J. W. Mackail, would be delivered to the British Academy on Wednesday, May 3; and that day would also be designated Shakespeare Day in all the schools. William Poel would install a plaque on a building on the Bankside to mark the location of Shakespeare's Globe Playhouse. Ben Greet would direct the complete Hamlet at the Old Vic. Exhibitions of Shakespeareana would be mounted at major libraries throughout England. The Frank Benson company would play its customary two-week repertory at Stratford-upon-Avon, commencing April 24. According to the *Times* the associated Baconians would perform Ceremonies of Derision at a time and place to be announced.

Thus it devolved upon Shakespeareans in America to hold up the honor of the side. The response was all that could be hoped for.[6] A Shakespeare Celebration

Committee was established in New York, headquarters at No. 10 East Forty-third Street, with some twenty-five or thirty persons prominent in society, finance, education, theatre, and the arts responsible for activating Shakespearean lectures, pageants, plays, library exhibits, musical concerts, sermons, study clubs, handicrafts, tree planting, and establishment of Shakespeare gardens all over the city and its environs. The public library at Forty-second Street would lay out a vast collection of famous actors' promptbooks, portraits, and other memorabilia, including the entire collection lately given to them by Ada Rehan. *Theatre* magazine would devote its whole April issue to pictorial material and articles on Shakespeare by famous scholars and critics past and present. The *New York Times* would issue a huge Shakespeare supplement every Sunday for ten weeks.

Here and there as the tercentenary plans shaped up, a voice of doom would prophesy it would all come to nothing. As late as mid-March 1916, Alexander Woollcott was declaring in the *New York Times* that the odds against Shakespeare were very great, for "this is a generation in which theatre audiences have been carefully trained away from him."[7] Ever since Ibsen, he wrote, our significant drama has been prose drama—that of Hauptmann, Shaw, Galsworthy, Barker—and Ibsen's influence is felt even by those who have never read or seen his work: "The most shameless little potboilers on Broadway write their pieces under circumstances Ibsen helped mightily to create." We have invented the convention of the fourth wall, he said, and the actors have been taught restraint—quiet, suppressed playing. Our average American pay-as-you-enter playgoers have learned to eavesdrop on real-life happenings on the stage, life presumably like their own. He quoted Henry Arthur Jones who had observed that "the eavesdropping convention is developing a school of admirable realistic actors, who can render with extreme nicety all those subtleties of the drawing room and the street which are scarcely worth rendering."

Of course, there is much truth in this. Yet surely when Woollcott could find only two praiseworthy Shakespeares—Forbes-Robertson's *Hamlet* and Barker's *A Midsummer Night's Dream*—in recent years, I think he failed to recognize some fine achievements on stage and more responsible attitudes in New York audiences than he gave them credit for. He ought surely to have remembered that between 1904 and 1907 Julia Marlowe, whose voice he adored, had, together with her partner, restored three seasons (six plays) of Shakespeare; that she and Sothern had won high critical honors in London; that, undaunted by the crushing defeat of *Antony and Cleopatra,* they redeemed themselves by delivering a handsome and popular production of *Macbeth,* a play which most observers would have predicted was as far beyond their scope as *Antony and Cleopatra* had been. Miss Marlowe delighted multitudes by reviving her lovely Rosalind, not seen for the last dozen years. By going "downtown," to Fourteenth Street, and playing "to the people at popular prices," they played Shakespeare to packed houses, rivaling the drawing power of the musicals and girlie shows in fashionable theatres uptown.[8]

Woollcott's taste was doubtless too fastidious for him to take much pleasure in the burly masculine playing of Robert Mantell, but year after year Mantell carried the greater tragic heroes all over the country, and brought them to New York repeatedly.[9] Another vigorously masculine performance Woollcott must have remembered was Lewis Waller's *Henry V,* imported from London to Daly's Theatre on September 30, 1912. "His was a very manly, bluff, and regal King Harry", said the Brooklyn *Daily Eagle.* He was majestic in his rebuke of the Dauphin's proffered insult, full of fine fire in those two glorious invocations to England's fighting spirit, . . . earnestly devout in his appeal to the King of Battles, and by turns humorous and passionate in his struggle for Katherine's love in the last act."[10] The *Dramatic Mirror* observed that "the same public which turned thumbs down on a trivial play by Edward Knoblauch could rise to enthusiastic appreciation of a rousing play by William Shakespeare," and credited the success to the artistic acting of Waller himself, to Madge Titheradge who read the choruses, and the whole supporting company.[11] Arthur Hornblow observed in *Theatre* magazine that "There is a Shakespearean following in New York City, and it is a big one too. . . . Be he high-brow or pin-head, he is a foolish theatre-goer who overlooks his opportunity to see "Henry V" so well produced."[12] J. R. Towse, whose standards were demanding, concluded his notice in *The Nation* with, "*Henry V* has not been so well played in the last forty years."[13]

A month later, after a quarter of a century of performing nothing but modern plays for Daniel Frohman, then for Charles Frohman, there emerged a Shakespearean director and actor of extraordinary promise. This was William Faversham, whose *Julius Caesar,* on November 4, 1912, so startled the editor of the *Dramatic Mirror* that he declared, "Frankly, I regard this the best Shakespeare production of two decades."[14] And point by point he went on to justify that bold assertion. For one thing, the scenery was right. It was old-style representational scenery, of course, for Faversham was not interested in the New Stagecraft and firmly held that while *acting* came first, well designed and efficient pictorial backing was a perfectly acceptable addition to theatrical effect.[15] He

Ilus. 189. Lewis Waller as Henry V.

had got hold of superb designs for *Caesar,* done by Sir Lawence Alma-Tadema near the end of his life, and he had them painted by the prince of old-style painters, Joseph Harker. But the central reason for his triumph was the casting and the training of the actors. For Brutus he found Tyrone Power, a big man with a big voice capable of nuances of expression. The *Mirror* critic ranked him with E. L. Davenport "and the best American exponents of the role." Frank Keenan's Cassius was ready with the nervous energy and sharpness, hampered only by excessively modern methods. Fuller Mellish's Caesar was admirable. Faversham, being comparatively slight of stature and trained in romantic and comic material, saved Mark Antony for himself. He played the great speech over Caesar's body brilliantly—not as a set piece of oratory, but a genuine communication with the mob, which itself was the best trained mob since that of the Meiningen Company.

The Boston *Transcript* reviewed this Caesar twice:

Illus. 190. William Faversham as Mark Antony in *Julius Caesar.*

Illus. 191. Tyrone Power as Brutus.

first by H. T. Parker who went down to New York to see it in mid-November, and then by Kenneth Macgowan[16] when the production moved to Boston. Both critics, enraptured, wrote at great length and with such perspicuity as well as eloquence that they deserve to be anthologized. One section of Parker's review, labeled "Speech and Humanity," confronts the problem which Woollcott thought insoluble—how to speak Shakespeare's language in the post-Ibsen era—and settles it more sensibly than any other study of the problem in that day that I have encountered:[17] The keen and pervading pleasure of the revival is the acting, because at last in a classic play it is of the sort that brings illusion and stimulation to us sitting before it in 1912. Parker sets up an amusing analogy between the art of classic acting and the strength of the Catholic Church—its mingling of perpetuity and opportunism. The Church founds some of its virtues on the rock of Peter; it draws others from the ways and standards of the passing day. And so, too, when successful, does the art of acting Shakespeare:

It must keep certain essential attributes; it may adapt its other qualities to the ways of the immediate histrionic time. For example, the actor must speak Shakespeare's verse with

Illus. 192. Frank Keenan as Cassius.

the arts of diction that shall make it readily comprehensible, round its phrases, keep rhythm and movement, vivify its poetic images, intensify, diversify, and color it. In a word, in such a tragedy as *Julius Caesar,* the speech must seem exalted, of large minds and fine spirits in outward and inner stress. Yet at times that same speech must slide lightly through routine interchanges, like the transitional passages in a piece of music. Yet, if it is to work illusion and stir answering emotions in our theatrical generation, it must still seem the speech of human beings. By habit and temperament, we will not abide persistent declamation, large-mouthed grandiloquence. No more, however, will we endure Shakespeare's text babbled like a conversation in a modern comedy. Then it becomes a grotesque, a farcical travesty and mockery of itself. There is one art of diction for *The Concert,*[18] for example, and another for *Julius Caesar.*

One of Faversham's greatest accomplishments in this production was his control over the speech of his actors.

One and all of the principals speak the verse with a rare intelligibility, because they can understand and feel poetry, with a rare impartment of its movement, color and variety, with a sense of its imagery, its emotion, its reflection of spirits in agitation, reflection, and deed. Yet one and all escape the Scylla and the Charybdis on either side of them. They are not quite conversational even in the transitional passages they handle most lightly: and they are never stilted and dehumanized in the old mouthing fashion.

In a later passage, where Parker repeats that "the verse . . . comes worthily and believably off the tongues" of these actors, he insists that "best of all" each character clearly keeps "the mixed mettle of his personality": Brutus his high opinion of himself; Cassius, though heroic, yet not free from envy, malice, and mockery; Antony, his "ingratiating shallows"; Caesar his vanities and obsessions. "And so the more are they men, and do these actors make believable and impressive men of them."

Faversham was greatly excited about Shakespeare—for the moment.[18] He realized the vast opportunities for actors in Shakespeare. He believed that the public appetite for Shakespeare was on the rise, fed incidentally by the enthusiasm of school teachers who were inculcating love of Shakespeare in their students. He had found that success in production lay in finding splendid voices expressing sensitive spirits, and in playing with vivacity and speed. Already he was planning a *Hamlet* for the following year, *if* he could find the voices; or sometimes he spoke of *Henry VIII* for the following year, *if* he could find the voices. But neither came to pass. Late in 1913 he produced *Othello* in San Francisco, gratifying his personal ambition to play Iago.[20] He toured it across the country to the satisfaction of audiences and critics. But the response of New York critics, though not hostile, was sufficiently unenthusiastic to discourage him.

The *Othello* won some favor in New York because of comparison with Forbes-Robertson's recent weak production. Since Othello was rather too weighty a part for Forbes-Robertson, he played it rarely and not too well and staged it indifferently, after which some critics concluded that the play itself ought to be shelved.[21] Faversham provided handsome scenery, again painted by Harker, and he planned his cast with care. His choice for Othello was R. D. MacLean, big-bodied like Tyrone Power, with a powerful voice which Faversham persuaded him to restrain except for those inevitably thunderous passages in the last two acts. Arthur Ruhl of the *Tribune* described MacLean as "thick-necked, deep-voiced and slow, a lowering, dull-witted, very bull of a man."[22] This is exactly what Faversham wanted as a foil to his own Iago. He had been planning this Iago for years: it was a blithe Iago, a merry Iago, laughing at his own cruelties, and thus, theatrically, heightening his viciousness by his seeming innocence (honesty). Now Edwin Booth had played Iago as a "comedian" all his career, but he gave plenty of signs of innate malevolence, so that while all about him believed him "honest," the audience was never deceived. Faversham amused many by his pranks, but for all who remembered Booth's double-play of bright surface over murderous black intentions, Faversham failed. He was not dangerous: he emitted no electrifying flashes of evil, nothing to frighten the audience. To many, therefore, he trivialized the part and the play. The reviews, on the whole, recognized the great skill that had gone into the production. The *New York Times* thanked him for restoring the play to the acting lists.[23] But enough exceptions were taken to frighten Faversham away from further experiments with Shakespeare,[24] so he never revealed what might have been a very attractive Hamlet.

March of 1914 brought to New York one of America's most famous actresses, Margaret Anglin, in three Shakespeare comedies, all produced and managed by herself. Miss Anglin, like Faversham, had come up through the Frohman organization, her specialty being strong emotional roles in society drama. During a visit to Australia she decided to attempt Shakespeare. Returning to California, she created four productions—*As You Like It, The Taming of the Shrew, Twelfth Night,* and *Antony and Cleopatra*—with Livingston Platt, one of the brightest advocates of the New Stagecraft, to design them all.[25] After touring them across Canada, she opened the three comedies on March 17, 20, and 24, at the Hudson in New York. Everyone praised her for her energy, initiative, intelligence, and taste, and for the blessing she brought to

Illus. 193. Margaret Anglin as Rosalind.

Illus. 194. Livingston Platt, American designer in the manner of the "New Stagecraft."

the New York stage by introducing the clean, fresh, uncluttered work of Livingston Platt. Opinions of her acting, however, and that of her company were wildly inconsistent. Her Rosalind, for instance, according to the *New York Times,*[26] was abundantly vital and finely musical to listen to; but according to *Theatre* magazine it was precise, formal, artificial, glib, and unfeeling; according to *Life,* her voice was affected at times with a tremolo, at times she sang rather than spoke; at times words and phrases were mumbled or stuck in her throat. Of her principal clown, Sidney Greenstreet, Walter Prichard Eaton wrote that in *Twelfth Night* he was a rare find, an accomplished artist with an unforced and unctuous comedy sense. . . . His Sir Toby Belch is a rare treat;"[27] but J. R. Towse said he "played the part [Sir Toby] with all the license of burlesque, bellowing throughout like a bull of Bashan and indulging in all the old and some new extravagancies . . . he hopelessly vulgarized and denaturalized the whole character." Miss Anglin's try was a noble one, but like Faversham, she did not extend it into a career.

These are but a few of the notable Shakespeares that New York saw in 1912–14. Meanwhile, Forbes-Robertson was making his farewell tour of the eastern states; Sothern and Marlowe, after playing their whole repertory across the country, were settled at the Manhattan; and the Frank Benson company was touring Canada and America. Walter Prichard Eaton declared in the *American* magazine for May, 1914 that "It is doubtful if even the "palmy days" . . . Shakespeare was so frequently acted as in America during the winter of 1913–14." By squeezing the count a little he estimated that there will have been 1,320 performances of Shakespeare in the United States and Canada during the season just closing. The April issue of *Everybody's* carried a long essay called "This Year It's Shakespeare," and the July *Theatre* magazine another essay called "The Classical Revival."[28]

There were more to come. In November of 1914

Illus. 195. Phyllis Neilson-Terry as Viola.

Ellen Terry's young niece Phyllis Neilson-Terry visited America with a pleasing if not quite matured *Twelfth Night.*[29] In February of 1915 Mantell ran off *King John, King Lear, Macbeth, Hamlet, The Merchant of Venice, Romeo and Juliet, Othello, Richard III, Julius Caesar,* and two or three pseudo-classical heroic plays. Barker's astonishing *Midsummer Night's Dream* was seen in February.[30]

It is a pity that some of these could not have been revived in 1916 to enrich the tercentenary. And that Sothern and Marlowe were in retirement. Forbes-Robertson was in the country, carrying Shakespeare-fever south, north, and west as he played his final farewells, but by previous agreement he could not participate in the New York celebration. One could wish that Miss Anglin had brought in her *Antony and Cleopatra,* for though Eaton thought when he saw her in Montreal that she had not mastered the role, yet Livingston Platt's staging of that play was by far his most beautiful. Not that the tercentenary was starved. Besides the countless amateur and extra-theatrical demonstrations, between February and May it embraced six professional stage productions and an outdoor masque performed by thousands.

When the first major stage production occurred on February 7, Alexander Woollcott might well have snorted, "I told you so." This was the *Macbeth* of James Keteltas Hackett and Viola Allen. Hackett, son of the famous "Falstaff" Hackett of long ago, had been a matinee idol in romantic and melodramatic plays with the Frohmans since 1895, but he had done very little Shakespeare. Now at the age of forty-seven he could sense that his days as a romantic hero were about used up, and it was time if ever to put himself forward as a Shakespearean. He could well afford financially to do so, having lately inherited a million dollars from a distant relative. He decided to splurge some of his wealth on the tercentenary and try for some big parts. He commissioned the fashionable Viennese designer, Joseph Urban, lately arrived in America, to prepare *Macbeth, Othello,* and *The Merry Wives of Windsor,* and announced these for early production. In *The Merry Wives* he would emulate his long-dead father's fame as Falstaff.

Macbeth came first. Everyone recognized that Hackett's physique, his strong clear voice, and his long experience in vigorous *(Prisoner of Zenda)* roles certainly qualified him for Macbeth. But in announcements of the production he stirred up doubts. Both he and his Lady Macbeth, Viola Allen, would introduce certain innovations in their characters, a new treatment which, if not acceptable, would at least provide the charm of novelty. His own principal "innovation" seems to have been to make Macbeth an enlightened modern citizen who will have no truck with the supernatural. His response to the Witches was "jocose." At the appearance of Banquo's ghost at the banquet, Hackett regarded it with "a large leer," which perhaps suggested the oncoming of madness, but in any case was "unfortunate." Miss Allen's innovation was neither to bully Macbeth in the old Cushman way, nor to lure him on with sexy invitation, à la Langtry or Terry, but to "mother" him—to wheedle and patronize him like a weak, spoiled child.

Neither conception pleased, or was even generally understood. Hackett wanted the audience to accept the Macbeths as basically attractive human beings at home in contemporary society, swayed by their pas-

Illus. 196. James K. Hackett as Macbeth.

sions and ambitions, victims of a compelling fate—without the glamor of a halo, or the heroic setting which marks them as demi-gods. What he accomplished was only to destroy the mystery and terror of the play and to reduce the principal characters to a pair of common murderers. The *Evening Mail* said that "nothing more inept than the acting of *Macbeth* has come within our range of vision these many years."[31] One rude fellow interpreted a gesture of Macbeth's to his followers as signifying "Ta-ta, boys; see you later"; and thought the laughing and dancing of the Witches very appropriate to a musical comedy.[32] I doubt that Woollcott covered it at all. Probably Klauber, the regular *New York Times* critic, was responsible for the fair but severe pronouncement: "an ambitious, dignified, magnificently mounted, and quite inadequately acted presentation of *Macbeth*."[33]

Everyone praised the mounting, which Hackett had poured a fortune into. Urban's sets were masterpieces of modeling and painting. The *New York Times* guessed that never in three hundred years had the play been set so handsomely. Apparently, however, the sets were heavy to move and there were too many of them. A good three-quarters of an hour was consumed in intermissions and scene changes while the audience had to listen to inappropriate music played too loudly by the pit band. Someone speculated that in Vienna Urban was accustomed to more modern machinery that moved scenery swiftly, and must have supposed that modern America would have its theatres so equipped, too. The Criterion Theatre was not. In any case, however handsome the scenery, it could not save the play from the faulty conceptions and ruinous acting by the principals. Hackett was wrong, but he was not a fool, and he was sure he had a Macbeth in him. He staged the play again in 1924 (eight years later) and was warmly praised for it, even by Alexander Woollcott.[34]

Hackett postponed the *Othello* he had promised and set to work at once on *The Merry Wives*. He brought in the popular comedienne Henrietta Crosman to play Mistress Page alongside Viola Allen's Mistress Ford, and again engaged Joseph Urban for the scenery. Unfortunately Hackett fell ill about a week into March, and on March 10 it was apparent that he could not carry on. In desperation someone suggested Thomas Wise, a fat comedian much loved along Broadway for the dozens of country storekeepers, bluff sea captains, old farmers, and so forth with which he had amused the town for years. He had *never* played Shakespeare. A phone call caught him at the Lamb's Club. In ten minutes he was at the theatre. In ten days (March 20) he opened in Falstaff.

The first night, one gathers from the notices, was

Illus. 197. Thomas Wise as Falstaff.

pretty rough. "The performance suffered much," said Towse, "from an excess of zeal on the one hand, and a plentiful lack of Shakespearean experience on the other. . . . The individual players strove manfully (or womanfully) to disguise their difficulties with the dialogue by 'rushing' them, as it were, taking refuge in loudness, rapidity, and violent gesticulation." Crosman and Allen were both "over-anxious, over-emphatic, and labored."[35] But Wise, if he had not yet got hold of Falstaff's peculiar style of humor, had plenty of his own to get through a hard night's work:

> Mr. Wise was most amusing in those scenes which gave his natural fun-making abilities full rein. His tremendous stomach, receptacle of uncountable flagons of sack, was encased in a doublet of bright orange. Bright orange were the tights that encased his ample legs, and jackboots of faun decorated his substantial feet. He rolled from scene to scene quivering like a mountain of jelly, as he boozed and guzzled and boasted, and entangled himself in the snares set by those zestful wives, Mrs. Ford and Mrs. Page.[36]

He is said to have been most Falstaffian in the scenes with Ford, especially when he described himself being dumped into the Thames "hissing hot."

The performances improved steadily as the evenings passed, and the audiences grew as the word spread of the fun to be had. Mme. Critic (Marie Schrader) of the *Dramatic Mirror* reported that in mid-April the house was packed to the ceiling; that she had "seldom heard more genuine laughter than at the Shakespearean farce."[37] About the middle of May, when it was playing to full houses, it had to be closed because of contractual obligations. All was not lost, however: on January 8, 1917, one Silvio Hein, a musical composer turned producer, restored Wise's Falstaff to the public with another staging, another set of wives (Constance Collier and Isabel Irving), and the merry farce was off to another run.[38]

It is a pleasure to find one genuine rarity during the celebration—for the first time in three hundred years *The Tempest* was played entire, "as Shakespeare wrote it and on the stage for which he wrote it." *The Tempest* had been very popular in England from 1667 (in America from 1770), but that was the play as "improved" by Davenant and Dryden. After Macready got rid of the "improvements" in 1838, it continued to be fairly popular in England because of the opportunities it offered, like a Christmas pantomime, for elaborate spectacle and tricks of magic. In America it was rare. William Burton staged it in the 1850s because he loved to play Caliban; in 1869 William Davidge dressed it up with an imported ballet troupe; in 1897 Augustin Daly cut the text by half and cluttered the stage with ill-managed scenery.

When John Corbin, an enthusiast for the Poelesque idea of a "return to the Globe," was on the staff of the New Theatre, he produced *The Winter's Tale* on a mock-up of the Globe stage, and he intended to follow it the next season with *The Tempest.* But the New Theatre died and became the Century, and Corbin was out of it. Now during the celebration, the Drama Society of New York rented the Century for a couple of weeks so that Corbin could realize his plan for *The Tempest.* A designer named Thomas Benrimo built on the Century stage the kind of Globe platform and tiring-house that Corbin required. It appears to have been a tall, rather shallow box set. The right and left walls had each a curtained entrance. The central portion of the back wall opened to reveal a curtained inner stage in which furniture could be set and moved freely. Caliban's cave was somewhere—probably in a smaller opening in the back wall. Above the inner stage was a high gallery. Some large rocks and low shrubs were set about the outer stage.[39]

A few ladders in the inner stage created the hold of "the ship." Electric flashes and the shaking of tin thunder sheets created "the storm." When the spirits of the masque disappeared into the inner stage their departure was rendered invisible by a curtain of steam. These few effects we know the Jacobean theatre had the means for—even flash powders in lieu of flashing electricity. The only "advantages" Corbin had over Shakespeare was the ability to darken the stage and auditorium, and he could use an actress instead of a boy to play Miranda. (Following long tradition he also used a girl for Ariel.)

The actors played the play straight through without a single pause for scene-changing. (Two intermissions were introduced to accommodate the habits of modern audiences.) The experiment was regarded as a great success—for once, that is. Few of the critics were ready for regular use of the simplicities of the New Stagecraft, let alone the spartan scenic nothingness of the Globe. Only a very few would acknowledge that Shakespeare's pen was his own best scene painter.

Success of the experiment depended of course on the quality of the actors' acting and especially their speaking. On this matter the critics were mostly generous, but there were dissenters. The *New York Times* could declare that "No cast of such uniformly high excellence has been assembled for a Shakespearean revival in this city in recent seasons."[40] Generally Walter Hampden's Caliban was praised for its fury and power, though an occasional ill-informed observer expected him to be an outright clown. Everyone was delighted and amazed by the Ariel of Fania Marinoff, who "shot through the play like quicksilver, vivacious, alert and spiritual";[41] and everyone praised a popular

Illus. 198. Louis Calvert as Prospero and Jane Grey as Miranda in *The Tempest* on an Elizabethan-style stage built on the main stage of the Century (formerly the New) Theatre.

comedian named George Hassell for his Stephano. Depending on which paper you read, Louis Calvert's Prospero "has an eye-filling figure and a sonorous, ear-filling voice, reads his lines with keen intelligence, and invests Prospero with an immense benevolence"; or he "read his long speeches with a sing-song monotony"; or one "might have preferred a more kindly Prospero"; or he "was peculiarly disappointing: his voice was husky and he quite failed to give Prospero's lines the dignity and sweetness that resides in them."[42]

The scheduling of performances was unusual. The law forbade any theatre to open on April 23, because it was a Sunday. But the Drama Society, being a private club, could stage a "final dress rehearsal" on that evening, and invite its whole membership, its friends and benefactors, without admission charge. The professional critics could use their passes that evening if they wished. One notes in a short guest-list recorded in the *Herald* several of the old sponsors of the New Theatre—the Belmonts, Kahns, Morgans, Winthrops, etc., and a few distinguished critics like Walter Pri-

Illus. 199. Sir Herbert Tree's production of *The Merchant of Venice* for the Shakespeare tercentenary. The Trial Scene, Elsie Ferguson as Portia, Tree as Shylock.

chard Eaton. But *all* the critics were there, and in the main they wrote up the affair enthusiastically in the Monday papers. The production was at once opened to the general public, at low prices, and, at the beginning at least, to sold-out houses. The success of this venture of the Drama Society was one more potent sign that the iron grip of illusionist scenery for poetic drama was loosening.

In chapter IV I have described in considerable detail Sir Herbert Tree's contributions to the celebration: his *Henry VIII* (March 14), a much reduced text but a highly educational display of sixteenth-century costume, architecture, and interior decoration; his *Merchant of Venice* (May 7), generally disliked for Elsie Ferguson's failure as Portia and for Tree's quirky additions of "business" to Shylock; and finally *The Merry Wives of Windsor* (May 25), an exuberant romp, probably improved over what he showed New York in 1895, but rather an anticlimax after the extraordinary Falstaff of Tom Wise in Hackett's production, which had only recently closed. Unfortunately for attendance, Tree's first night coincided with the second night of the great outdoor Shakespearean Masque, which drew 18,000 spectators to its opening, and about that many every night for over a week, leaving no great public for Tree until later.

The grand climax of the New York celebration, especially commissioned and in preparation for many months, was this Community Masque, composed by what one interviewer called "the busiest poet in America," Percy MacKaye. It was called *Caliban by the Yellow Sands.*[42] MacKaye wrote a verse play of sorts, built upon elements of *The Tempest,* and scattered through it pageants illustrating the history of the Western theatre from the Egyptians to the Renaissance.

A Community Masque was a gigantic operation, and for Percy MacKaye it was a kind of lay religion. It was at once the sacred art of poetry and a social function of vast importance. Just as in ancient Athens, it brought poetry to the people, and brought the whole community together to celebrate noble ideals, joining persons of all shades of opinion in a common cause. Or so MacKaye thought his masque-making would do. Two years earlier when he staged such a masque for St. Louis, 7,000 local citizens participated in its five performances and 500,000 persons saw and heard it. When he read it, before it was produced, to assemblies of St. Louis ministers, to Negro high schools, to clubs of advertising men, to I. W. W. meetings, all approved it. It gave them "a sort of spiritual and intellectual meeting place, a common interest." In New York, at a banquet for the Mayor's Committee for the Shakespeare Celebration, the mil-

Illus. 200. Percy MacKaye, author of *Caliban of the Yellow Sands,* a masque composed for the New York celebration of the Shakespeare tercentenary.

Illus. 201. Joseph Urban's stage for *Caliban of the Yellow Sands.*

lionaire Otto Kahn and Morris Hillquit, the leader of the Socialist Party, agreed that in bringing persons of downright opposing opinions into this one noble and high-minded effort, art was producing practical democracy.

MacKaye assumed, naturally enough, that the ideal site for his masque would be found somewhere in Central Park. But this was before reckoning with the Robert Moses of that day. Not for Shakespeare nor all the millionaires in the city would the commissioner and his board permit the hordes of celebrants to defile the property in their trust. The authorities of City College saved the situation by offering Lewisohn Stadium and athletic field, and there Joseph Urban set about creating a vast outdoor theatre. By extending the permanent stadium with wooden bleachers he provided seating for about 20,000 in a sort of half-circle surrounding part of the field, which, covered with sand, resembled the orchestra of an ancient Greek theatre. At the center of the circle stood a low round stage. Beyond the north rim of the circle he built his main stage, flanked by interesting groups of low fat columns, pedestals for statues, and formal hut-like structures used for entrances. Beyond the main stage, curtains opened on a wide inner stage where scenery could be set and changed. On top of this scenic stage, a platform supported a symphony orchestra and a chorus, concealed from the audience by thin curtains. The stage was mainly lighted by a battery of powerful electric lamps located above and behind the audience.

For the principal speaking parts MacKaye obtained the services of forty-seven professional actors known to have strong carrying voices. Among them were Howard Kyle (Prospero), Gareth Hughes (Ariel), Lionel Braham (Caliban), Tom Wise, Edith Wynne Matthison, Eric Blind, Robert Mantell, Margaret Wycherly, Viola Compton, and John Drew. These forty-seven and, of course, all the "citizens," played without wages. The number of dancers, singers, and non-speaking figures is usually given as 1,500, but apparently exceeded 1,600. Robert Edmond Jones made at least 500 costume designs for his crews to render. Arthur Farwell composed and directed hours of music, orchestral and vocal. Barrels of rouge, gallons of liquid make-up, thousands of cakes of soap, hundreds of basins, and thousands of towels had to be kept in supply. Hundreds of volunteers served as wardrobe keepers, traffic directors, ushers, and so forth.

When MacKaye talks about poetry and democracy, about bringing poetry to the people, one expects of him some sort of Sandburg; or at his most fervent a Vachel Lindsay; or a Whitman who would contain multitudes.[44] The book of *Caliban* lets us down. There is no substance here, nor passion, and the "multitudes" are only allegorical gas bubbles. Mac-

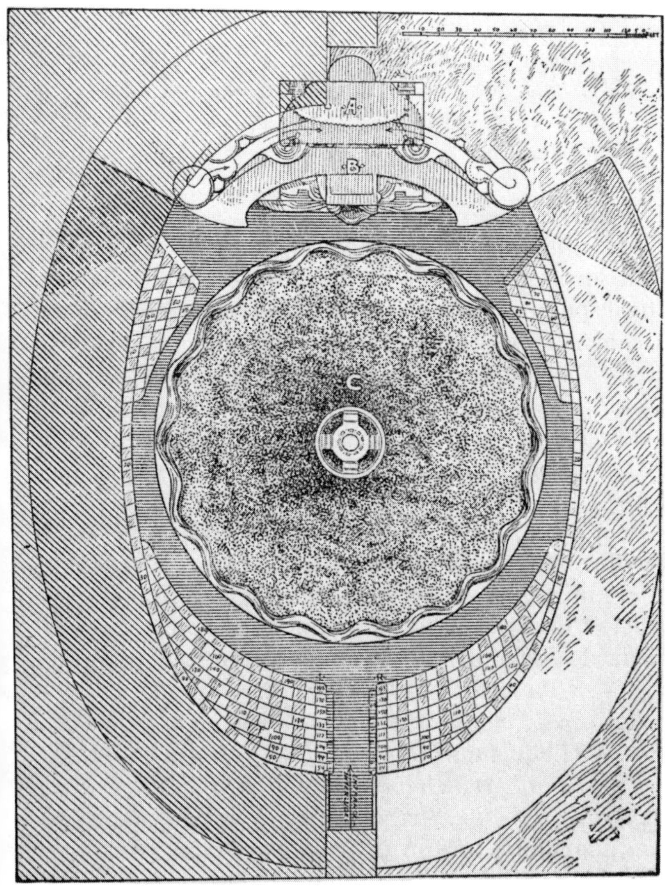

Illus. 202. Ground Plan for auditorium and stage for *Caliban of the Yellow Sands.*

Kaye seizes on the central figures in *The Tempest,* strips them of their Shakespearean habiliments—their poetry and their magic—and reduces them to counters in a banal allegory of Good overmastering Evil. Or perhaps Good educating Evil until it learns how to become good. (Caliban's conversion, if he *is* converted, happens only in one speech and a crouching down before "Shakespeare" at the very end: throughout the play he is driven and guided by Lust, and just before the end he temporarily prevails by War. Even as an allegorist, MacKaye was a bumbler.)

No doubt the whole masque, with its constant alteration from drama to spectacle to drama was an impressive oral-visual experience, a sort of educational circus performance. But the heart of MacKaye's work is his book of *Caliban,* and there we must take his measure—not only his but that of the 135,000 New Yorkers who, we assume, were impressed by it.

Caliban, the ruling inhabitant of a rocky island, is the son of a loathsome mud-monster mother, Sycorax, sired by a bull-like, dragon-like father-monster, Setebos. Attended by three spirits, War, Death, and Lust, Caliban is Evil. He is ignorant, murderous, lecherous, a composite of all that is beastly. The Good spirit of the island, Ariel, who represents Love and Joy, is trapped in the fangs of Setebos, and Ariel's company of attendant spirits are imprisoned in Setebos's belly. After the spirits of Evil perform certain horrid rituals in honor of Setebos, Ariel summons Miranda and her father Prospero. Miranda arrives first—loving, kind, beautiful, and innocent—and for a few pages she is in some danger, for Sycorax urges Caliban to mate with her and produce a race of Calibans. But just in the nick of time, amid thunder, lightning, and choric supplications (tenors for Good, basses for Evil), a winged throne appears bearing Prospero, with scroll and staff. He rescues Miranda and frees Ariel and his spirits, who drive Caliban from the main stage down into the orchestra. The spirits sing and dance there, celebrating their freedom. Then they pelt Caliban with yellow sand and drive him back into his cave. The spirits of War, Death and Lust are seen in pantomime preparing a conspiracy against Prospero.

This much is *Prologue* to the play. Practically speaking it *is* the play. MacKaye had not much knack for

Illus. 203. Joseph Urban's sketch for the monster Setebos in *Caliban of the Yellow Sands.*

plot or action. Through three acts Caliban, driven by Lust, attempts to rape Miranda, but he is always frustrated. In his most spectacular effort he somehow gets hold of Prospero's magic staff, conjures up the world of Caligula, and all but sinks Miranda in a Roman orgy; but just at the height of danger, a fiery Cross appears overhead; priests pass, swinging censers; an image of St. Agnes, haloed, holding a white lamb, is revealed; and Caligula, unmasked, is only a priest of Setebos, and retires—benched, so to speak. By the end of the play Caliban has been exposed to so much Goodness that he capitulates (has been "educated") and kneeling at the feet of *Shakespeare,* who has arrived to speak the Epilogue, begs for "more visions."

> "Yet—yet I yearn to build, to be thine Artist
> And stablish this thine Earth among the stars—
> Beautiful!"

A hasty resolution to play and to allegory.

Auxiliary to this moral fable MacKaye demonstrates through a series of Interludes that the history of theatre mirrors the history of civilization. Each of these Interludes, involving masses of figures, appears to have taken place in the arena, or orchestra, and of course is accompanied by Arthur Farwell's music from on high. They are as follows:

I.	*Egypt:* a ceremony of Osiris worship.	(148 actors)
II.	*Greece:* the noble zenith of Greek dramatic art—chants, athletic dance, the second chorus of *Antigone*	(175 actors)
III.	*Rome:* decadence of art and civilization. Roman mimes act out a pantomime of the Sphinx and Hercules to entertain Caligula. At the end the actor of Hercules is dragged off and whipped.	(150 actors)
IV.	*Germanic:* an austere and grotesque pantomime of the legend of Dr. Faustus.	(150 actors)
V.	*France:* the splendor of medieval France. The meeting of Kings Henry and Francis on the Field of the Cloth of Gold.	(150 actors)
VI.	*Italy and Spain:* Italian *commedia dell'arte* actors pantomime the story of *Don Giovanni.*	(150 actors)
VII.	*Elizabethan England.* Eight episodes of dances, processions, May Pole dancing, Morris dances, etc.	(400 actors)
VIII.	*International.* Procession of theatres, actors, and playwrights.	(300 actors)

The total number of actors as here listed is 1,623.

Also spliced in as inner scenes, each in connection with an Interlude, are brief passages from eleven Shakespeare plays: *Antony and Cleopatra, Troilus and Cressida, Julius Caesar, Hamlet, Henry VIII, Romeo and Juliet, The Merchant of Venice, The Winter's Tale, As You Like It, The Merry Wives of Windsor,* and *Henry V.* But since the masque proved an hour too long several of these passages were omitted after the first performance.

As a poet, MacKaye, "the busiest poet in America," hardly manages the first step up Parnassus. The limits of his imagination are marked, to adapt a phrase of Willard Thorp's, in "knitting up classical images into a poetical robe to drape over the sordidness of modern [1912–15] America." No wonder that in the Peaceable Kingdom of Percy MacKaye, the likes of Socialist Morris Hillquit and millionaire Otto Kahn could, in the name of "art," cheerfully feed at the same table. The subject being Shakespeare, it was inevitable in that generation and in the mind of Percy MacKaye, that the verse should be imitation Elizabethan-Jacobean unrhymed iambic pentameter. Here and there, to be sure, when Ariel and Prospero have no more than straightforward business to conduct, they express themselves quite sensibly in common prose, laid out as verse. But surely MacKaye felt the hot breath of the grim-faced Muse at his shoulder when Caliban breaks out with the following sexually threatening approach to Miranda, "who recoils, half fearful" (as who should not?) with

> Wist where salt water lappeth warm i' the noon
> And shore-fish breed i' the shoals.—Wist where the sea-bull
> Flap-flappeth his fin and walloweth there his cow
> And snoreth the rainbow from his nostrils.

The ichor that flowed through MacKaye's plastic veins was "thee—thou—thy—'tis well—thou canst—falleth—scorcheth—showest—what say'st—an thou wert—couldst—wouldst—tush, fool." No one objected to this, of course, for it was the sound of "poetry;" it was "Shakespeare." The huge audiences knew, for the most part, that Shakespeare talked like that.

Supposed to open on May 23, it was rained out and postponed to May 24th.[45] That meant extending it beyond its five days as scheduled. But popular demand was such that it seems to have run through the second week and accumulated probably ten performances. Some 135,00 people saw it, and it paid off the $100,000 that it cost. The performers, the Committee, and all concerned ended in high euphoria with resolves to make a Community Masque an annual event, to erect a permanent theatre for Shakespeare, to.. . . But the Great War took over. There was no more Shakespeare in New York in 1916, and *Caliban,* except that hundreds of copies stand on library shelves, has long since been forgotten.

Postscript: On March 18, 1916, it was reported in the *Dramatic Mirror* that one Colonel George Fabyan of Chicago, Illinois, and Lake Geneva, Wisconsin, a scholar and menagerie keeper, had declared Shakespeare "a faker." Francis Bacon wrote the plays. William Selig, a film producer, had come before Judge Richard S. Tuthill of the Circuit Court, and asked that Fabyan be enjoined from defaming Shakespeare. Injunction granted. Fabyan vowed to take his case to the Supreme Court of the land. On May 6 it was reported in the *Mirror* that Judge Tuthill had studied all the evidence and lifted the injunction, having concluded, that Bacon *did* write the plays. On May 13, the *Mirror* reported that Judge Tuthill had overruled his own decision, and awarded the plays to Shakespeare after all. "The Shakespeare Tercentenary may now proceed uninhibited."

Notes

Introduction

1. George C. D. Odell, *Shakespeare—From Betterton to Irving,* 2 vols. (New York: Scribners, 1920), II, 463.

2. Ibid., 466–68.

3. George Meredith, *An Essay on Comedy, and the Uses of the Comic Spirit,* ed. Lane Cooper (New York: Scribners, 1918), pp. 118–19 (emphasis added).

4. *Ellen Terry and Bernard Shaw, A Correspondence,* ed. Christopher St. John (New York: Theatre Arts Books, 1931), p. xvi.

5. Krows, Arthur Edwin, *Play Production in America* (New York: Henry Holt and Company, 1916), p. 160.

6. Accounts of the Syndicate and of the Shubert's Independent Movement are numerous and widely scattered. From the beginning, the *Dramatic Mirror* reported the activities of these organizations, then editorialized vigorously against them; but by 1909 the attacks tapered off. *Life* magazine, too, fought them from the beginning. The earliest orderly, detailed (and hostile) account is Norman Hapgood's essay on the Syndicate in the *International Monthly* I (January 1900), 89–122; reprinted in *The Stage in America, 1897–1900* (New York: The Macmillan Company, 1901), pp. 6–38. Krow's book, cited above, has some general commentary on booking systems. Robert Grau's book, *The Business Man in the Amusement World* (New York: Broadway Publishing Company, 1910) contains countless references to Erlanger, Klaw, the Shuberts, and Charles Frohman, all indexed. Grau admired Erlanger and Klaw immensely; his best passages on these two are at pp. 3–12 and 282–92. From Mrs. Fiske's point of view they were The Enemy: see Archie Binns, *Mrs. Fiske and the American Theatre* (New York: Crown Publishers, Inc., 1955), pp. 77–84, 120, 123, 143, 354–55, 397. For an entertaining account of both the Syndicate and the Shuberts and the wars between them see *The Brothers Shubert* by Jerry Stagg (New York: Random House, 1968).

7. Binns, p. 79.

8. Between November 13 and February 26, Fiske published fifteen numbers of the *Supplement.*

9. Most issues of *Life* from ca. 1897 carry cartoons or commentary of extreme hostility. At one point Charles Metcalfe, the editor, was refused entrance to a Syndicate theatre, and had to take his case to the State Legislature.

10. The most recent defense of the Syndicate is an article by Milo L. Smith, "The Klaw-Erlanger Bogeyman Myth," *Players Magazine,* XLIV (December 1969), pp. 70–75.

11. Isaac F. Marcosson and Daniel Frohman, *Charles Frohman: Manager and Man* (New York: Harper & Brothers, 1916).

I. Booth and Barrett

1. A. C. Wheeler, "The Extinction of Shakespeare," *Arena,* I (March 1890), pp. 423–31.

2. Edwina Booth Grossmann, *Edwin Booth. Recollections by his Daughter and Letters to Her and to His Friends* (New York: Century Co., 1894), p. 113.

3. Daniel J. Watermeier, ed., *Between Actor and Critic: Selected Letters of Edwin Booth and William Winter* (Princeton: Princeton University Press), p. 300.

4. Barrett's career and his management of Booth from 1886 to 1891 have been reported in two unpublished dissertations to which I am immensely indebted: James R. Miller, "Lawrence Barrett on the New York Stage" (Tufts University, 1972); and John Chase Soliday, "The 'Joint Star' Tours of Edwin Booth and Lawrence Barrett" (University of Minnesota, 1974). Dr. Soliday has collected reviews and news reports from every visit to every town and city that the partners made during their "Joint Star" tours.

5. Booth to Barrett, June 13, 1867 (The Players). The phrase in quotation marks is the title of the translation of Victor Cousin's essays, *Du vrai, du beau, et du bien* (Paris, 1854).

6. New York *World,* September 6, 1870.

7. New York *Leader,* September 10, 1870. Quoted by Miller, p. 73. See also Melvin R. White, "Lawrence Barrett and the Role of Cassius," *Quarterly Journal of Speech,* L (October 1964), pp. 293–98.

8. Booth to Barrett, November 13 and 20, 1870 (The Players).

9. Booth to Barrett, November 13 and 20, 1870 (The Players). Booth's first offer was $150 and 10 percent of the Saturday nights; at Barrett's insistence he raised it to $250.

10. Booth to Barrett, March 7, 1872 (The Players).

11. Barrett to Booth, November 10, 1870 (The Players).

12. Booth to Barrett, December 26, 1872 (The Players).

13. Barrett to Booth, January 1, 1873 (The Players).

14. William Winter, *Life and Art of Edwin Booth* (New York: Macmillan and Co., 1893), pp. 98–99.

15. Eleanor Ruggles, *Prince of Players, Edwin Booth* (New York: W. W. Norton Company, Inc., 1953), p. 255.

16. *Life,* January 3, 1884; *Spirit of the Times,* December 22, 1883.

17. Booth to Barrett, December 23, 1860 (The Players).

18. Booth's Museum company was praised generously. See *The Critic,* January 24, 1885; *Spirit of the Times,* February 7, 1885; etc.

19. Miller, pp. 119–26.

20. This production has been fully described by Richard Lee Benson in "Jarrett and Palmer's 1875 Production of Julius Caesar: A Reconstruction" (Unpublished diss., University of Illinois, 1968).

21. *Spirit of the Times,* January 1, 1876.

22. *New York Times,* December 5, 1876. See also Barrett's promptbook of *King Lear* (Furness Collection, University of Pennsylvania).

23. Miller, p. 148.

24. Otis Skinner, *The Last Tragedian* (New York: Dodd Mead & Company, 1939), p. 182. Skinner dates letter from Booth to Barrett, accepting Barrett's apology, March 25, 1880. The original of this letter is missing.

25. Watermeier, p. 266.

26. The contract, witnessed by James Osgood and Launt Thompson, is in the Harvard Theatre Collection.

27. Barrett's preference for management over acting is recorded in his obituary, New York *Herald,* March 21, 1891.

28. Clara Morris, *Life on the Stage* (New York: McClure, Phillips & Co., 1901), p. 207; Otis Skinner,. *Footlights and Spotlights* (New York: Blue Ribbon Books, 1924), p. 110.

29. Alfred Ayres [Thomas Embley Osmund], *Acting and Actors* (New York: D. Appleton and Company, 1894), pp. 87–91.

30. Skinner, *Footlights and Spotlights,* p. 111.

31. Morris, p. 206.

32. Barrett to Booth, December 19, 1869 (The Players).

33. Miller, p. 112.

34. The net profits are taken from the *Booth-Barrett Tours Record Book,* which is at The Players. In the first season, when Booth toured alone, he took 80 percent of the profit; thereafter Booth took 60 percent and Barrett 40 percent. This table is adapted from reckonings by James Miller.

35. The itinerary for each of the five seasons is made up from the Frank Lodge files of playbills at The Players and the Harvard Theatre Collection. The Booth tour of 1886–87 is especially richly documented. Besides reviews recoverable from local papers, we have Booth's letters to Barrett; his letters to his daughter and friends as she printed them in Grossmann, *Edwin Booth;* his further letters to his daughter in the Theatre Collection of the New York Public Library; the letters to Barrett from Arthur Chase, the company manager, in the collection of the late Edith Barrett; and the reminiscences of Kitty Molony—see Katherine Goodale, *Behind the Scenes with Edwin Booth* (Boston: Houghton, Mifflin Co., 1931).

36. Goodale, pp. 42–48, 261–63; Chase to Barrett, October 4 and 20, 1886 (Edith Barrett Collection).

37. Chase to Barrett, September 9, 11, 12, 14, 1886 (Edith Barrett Collection).

38. Goodale, pp. 23–25.

39. Chase to Barrett, September 16, 1886 (Edith Barrett Collection).

40. Charles H. Shattuck, *The Hamlet of Edwin Booth* (Urbana: University of Illinois Press, 1969), pp. 302–5.

41. Booth to Barrett, February 11 [1887] (Harvard Theatre Collection).

42. Goodale, pp. 154–75.

43. Shattuck, p. 307.

44. Booth's third most popular role this season was Iago (34 times). Many considered Iago his very best role. After that, Bertuccio in *The Fool's Revenge* (22), Shylock and Petruchio (17 each) in cut-down versions, Macbeth (7), Richard III (7), and King Lear (7).

45. Chase to Barrett, October 4, 1886 (Edith Barrett Collection).

46. Chase to Barrett, October 6, 1886 (Edith Barrett Collection).

47. Chase to Barrett, October 20, 1886 (Edith Barrett Collection).

48. Booth to his daughter, October 21, 1886 (New York Public Library Theatre Collection).

49. Booth to Barrett, November 7, 1886 (Harvard Theatre Collection).

50. Chase to Barrett, November 10, 1886 (Edith Barrett Collection).

51. Goodale, pp. 69–73.

52. Chase to Barrett, November 1, 4, 5, 6, 17, 27 (Edith Barrett Collection).

53. Goodale, pp. 77–80, and Chase to Barrett, December 11, 1886 (Edith Barrett Collection).

54. Chase to Barrett, January 30, 1887 (Edith Barrett Collection).

55. Chase to Barrett, February 2 and 6, 1887 (Edith Barrett Collection).

56. Chase to Barrett, February 15, 1887 (Edith Barrett Collection).

57. Chase to Barrett, March 2, 1887 (Edith Barrett Collection).

58. Chase to Barrett, March 4, 1887 (Edith Barrett Collection).

59. Chase to Barrett, March 13, 1887 (Edith Barrett Collection).

60. Chase to Barrett, April 3, 1887 (Edith Barrett Collection).

61. Goodale, pp. 203–17. Although Kitty Molony remembered it as a "once only" Othello, in fact Booth played it twice, on March 17 and 30.

62. Chase to Barrett, April 30, 1887 (Edith Barrett Collection).

63. Chase to Barrett, April 28, 1887 (Edith Barrett Collection).

64. Booth to Barrett, September 26 [1886] (Harvard Theatre Collection).

65. Chase to Barrett, October 15, 1886 (Edith Barrett Collection).

66. Booth to his daughter, September 19, 1886 (New York Public Library Theatre Collection).

67. Many letters comment on Emma Vaders' brilliance and her eccentricity: Booth to Barrett, September 26 and October 10 [1886] (Harvard Theatre Collection); Booth to his daughter, October 21, 1886 (New York Public Library Theatre Collection); Chase to Barrett, [September 17], 23, 28, October 16, December 4, 1886 (Edith Barrett Collection). Miss Vaders did eventually go mad.

68. Booth to Barrett, February 1 [1887] (Harvard Theatre Collection).

69. Many letters comment on Barron: Chase to Barrett, September 28, October 12, December 4, 1886, and February 6 and 8, 1887 (Edith Barrett Collection); Booth to Barrett, November 17 [1886], January 27 and February 11 [1887] (Harvard Theatre Collection).

70. For comments on Malone, see Chase to Barrett, September 28 and October 12, 1886 (Edith Barrett Collection); Booth to Barrett, November 7 [1886], January 20 and March 7 [1887] (Harvard Theatre Collection).

71. For comments on Ahrendt, see Chase to Barrett, September 28, 1886 (Edith Barrett Collection); Booth to Barrett, October 10, 1886 (Harvard Theatre Collection).

72. For comments on Sullivan, see Chase to Barrett, September 28 and October 12, 1886 (Edith Barrett Collection); Booth to Barrett, October 10, 1886 (Harvard Theatre Collection).

73. For comments on Kitty Molony, see Booth to Barrett, October 10, 1886, "After Lear" [January 20], February 11, and March 5 [1887] (Harvard Theatre Collection).

74. John Chase Soliday in his dissertation (pp. 117–50) gives a description of every member of the company.

75. Arthur Chase labored faithfully all summer on plans for the new season, reporting progress to Barrett in at least forty letters now in the Edith Barrett Collection. On July 2 he completed arrangements for the private car.

76. See Soliday, pp. 298–310, for a full account of the Kansas City fiasco. Much of it is told by Augustus Thomas, *The Print of My Remembrance* (New York: Scribners, 1922), pp. 231–34.

77. After the assassination of President Lincoln, Booth would never play in Washington. Trainloads of Washingtonians would

travel to Baltimore to see him perform.

78. For detailed information on "speculation" in theatre tickets during this tour, see Soliday, pp. 401–7, 416–19, 487–90.

79. For this "circus" event, see Soliday, pp. 552–61.

80. Detroit *Evening News,* September 16, 1887; Toledo *Blade,* November 18, 1887; both quoted in Soliday, pp. 257–324.

81. Watermeier, pp. 286–87.

82. Grossman, pp. 80–81.

83. Cincinnati *Times-Star,* November 8, 1887. Quoted in Soliday, p. 318. Se also *The Enquirer,* November 8, 1887. Booth scrapbook no. 2 (Folger Shakespeare Library).

84. San Francisco *Chronicle,* March 6, 1888. Booth scrapbook no. 2 (Folger Shakespeare Library).

85. San Francisco *Evening Post,* March 6, 1888. Quoted in Soliday, p. 471.

86. Richmond *Dispatch,* January 17, 1888. Quoted in Soliday, p. 394.

87. Montgomery *Daily Advertiser,* February 4, 1888. Booth scrapbook no. 2 (The Folger Shakespeare Library).

88. Charleston *News and Courier,* January 18, 1888. Quoted in Soliday, p. 396.

89. Edwin Milton Royle, *Edwin Booth As I Knew Him* (New York: The Players, 1933), p. 25.

90. Chase to Barrett, March 18, 1887 (Edith Barrett Collection). Booth to Barrett, March 25, 1887 (Harvard Theatre Collection).

91. Cincinnati *Times-Star,* November 10, 1887. Quoted in Soliday, p. 321.

92. *Indianapolis Sentinel,* April 29, 1888. Booth scrapbook no. 2 (Folger Shakespeare Library).

93. Soliday, p. 528.

94. Soliday, pp. 535–56.

95. In the second half of the season they occasionally offered a bill of two "modern" plays—Booth playing a shortened version of *The Fool's Revenge* and Barrett following with *David Garrick* or *The King's Pleasure* or *Yorick's Love.*

96. Grossman, p. 83.

97. This account of the *Merchant* scenery is taken from the Philadelphia *Item,* February 22, 1889. Booth scrapbook no. 3 (Folger Shakespeare Library). See also the Philadelphia *Press* and *Inquirer* of the same date; the Chicago *Tribune,* October 2, 1888; the New York *Star,* November 4, 1888, and *The Graphic* and New York *Sun,* November 15, 1888.

98. For Booth's interpretation of Shylock, see Chicago *Inter-Ocean,* October 18, 1887, and St. Louis *Post Dispatch,* November 5, 1887. Booth scrapbook no. 2 (Folger Shakespeare Library); Chicago *Mail, Journal,* and *Tribune,* all October 2, 1888. Booth scrapbook no. 3 (Folger Shakespeare Library). See also Booth's notes to H. H. Furness in Grossman, especially that of January 31, 1887 (p. 268). See also his notes on Shylock throughout the Furness Variorum, and Toby Lelyveld, *Shylock on the Stage* (London: Routledge & Kegan Paul, Ltd., 1961), pp. 63–77.

99. Clipping from the *Philadelphia Evening Bulletin,* December 24, 1895. See Irving-Terry Scrapbook, II (Folger Shakespeare Library).

100. Philadelphia *North American,* February 19, 1889. Booth scrapbook no. 3 (Folger Shakespeare Library). See also Boston *Globe,* Boston *Herald,* and Boston *Post,* January 22, 1889.

101. Grossman, p. 89. For pictures of these scenes, see Benson, *passim.*

102. Boston *Post,* January 22, 1889. Booth scrapbook no. 3 (Folger Shakespeare Library).

103. Rapturous reviews appeared in the Kansas City *Times,* September 9, 14, 16, and the New York *Star,* September 10 and 14.

104. Grossman, p. 89.

105. A full account of Booth's illness is given in Soliday, pp. 637–60.

106. San Francisco *Daily Examiner,* May 14, 1889. Quoted in Soliday, p. 689.

107. Skinner, *Footlights and Spotlights,* p. 72.

108. Booth to Barrett, October 5, 1889 (Harvard Theatre Collection).

109. Chase to Barrett, October 2 and 9, 1889 (Edith Barrett Collection). Whatever edginess may have existed between the principals during the tour, none of it was remembered by Modjeska. The season was "delightful," Booth was "one of the kindest and pleasantest men of the profession"; and she filled many pages with friendly and affectionate reminiscences. *Memories and Impressions of Helena Modjeska. An Autobiography* (New York: The Macmillan Company, 1910), pp. 496–511.

110. Booth to Barrett, April 1, 1890 (Harvard Theatre Collection).

111. Shattuck, pp. 112, 139–40, 244–47.

112. Booth to Barrett, November 24, 1889 (Harvard Theatre Collection).

113. Chase to Barrett, October 29, 1889 (Edwin Barrett Collection).

114. Miller, pp. 288–95.

115. George C. D. Odell, *Annals of the New York Stage,* XIV (New York: Columbia University Press, 1945), 542.

II. Augustin Daly

1. The standard biography of Daly is *The Life of Augustin Daly* by his brother Joseph Francis Daly (New York: The Macmillan Company, 1917). A critical examination of Daly's work is Marvin Felheim's *The Theater of Augustin Daly* (Cambridge: Harvard University Press, 1956). Daly's productions through the season of 1893–94 are covered in Odell's *Annals of the New York Stage,* vols. VIII to XV. His Shakespeare productions are described at length in William Winter's *Shakespeare on the Stage,* I (New York: I, Moffat, Yard, & Co., 1911; reprint, New York: Benjamin Blom, 1969); II (New York: Moffat, Yard, & Co., 1915; reprint, New York: Benjamin Blom, 1969); III (New York: Moffat, Yard, & Co., 1916; reprint, New York: Benjamin Blom, 1968–69).

2. Odell, *Annals,* VIII, 571.

3. Daly to Winter, June 7, 1870 (Folger Shakespeare Library).

4. Daly to Winter, June 1, 1882 (Folger Shakespeare Library).

5. W. Graham Robertson, *Life Was Worth Living* (New York: Harper and Brothers [1931]), pp. 231–32.

6. *Dramatic Mirror,* February 11, 1888.

7. *Saturday Review,* October 9, 1897. In Shaw, *Our Theatres in the Nineties,* 3 vols. (London: Constable and Company, 1948), III, 209–10.

8. For the most explicit account of the Daly-Rehan relationship, see Cornelia Otis Skinner, *Family Circle* (Boston: Houghton Mifflin Company, 1948), pp. 80–82.

9. Augustin Daly, *Woffington: A Tribute to the Actress and the Woman,* 2d ed. (Troy, N.Y.: Nims and Knight, 1891), p. 15.

10. Rehan to Winter, July 1, 1899 (Folger Shakespeare Library).

11. Otis Skinner, *Footlights and Spotlights* (Indianapolis: The Bobbs-Merrill Company, 1924), pp. 269–72.

12. William Winter, *Vagrant Memories* (New York: George H. Doran Company, 1915), p. 235.

13. See Felheim, pp. 33–36 for details of Daly's influence on the press; also Charles Edward Russell, *Julia Marlowe, Her Life and Art* (New York: D. Appleton and Company, 1926), pp. 274–84.

14. Hapgood reprinted press comments on Daly's attack on him in the New York *Commercial Advertiser,* January 28, 1898.

15. Dora Knowlton Ranous, *Diary of a Daly Debutante* (New York: Duffield & Company, 1910), p. 54. Miss Knowlton did not follow the theatre profession, though her husband William Ranous, was a stage manager. She turned to a literary career, was assistant to the editor of *Century* magazine, translated Maupassant, the novels of Flaubert, D'Annunzio's *Il Fuoco* and other Italian works, and was co-editor of an anthology of Italian masterworks from Cavalcanti to Fogazzaro, much of which she translated.

16. Ranous, pp. 65–66.

17. Ranous, pp. 30–31.

18. Joseph Daly, p. 90.

19. William Winter, *The Wallet of Time,* 2 vols. (New York: Moffat, Yard, & Co., 1913), I, 343.

20. Clara Morris, *Life on the Stage: My Personal Experiences and Recollections* (New York: McClure, Phillips & Co., 1901), pp. 319–20.

21. Daly to Rehan, September 29, 1894 (Folger Shakespeare Library). There are two drafts of this letter reporting her first week's share in the profits as "A Star," or equal sharer. In Joseph Daly, Appendix A, it is clear that Miss Rehan was liberally remembered in Daly's will.

22. For the Scott-Siddons visit, see Joseph Daly, pp. 94–96; Odell *Annals,* VIII, 575–76. For the Booth visit, see Joseph Daly, pp. 198–206; Odell, *Annals,* X, 13–15; Winter, *Shakespeare on the Stage, II,* 445–50; Felheim, pp. 231–32. For the Neilson visit, see Joseph Daly, pp. 227–29; Odell, *Annals,* X, 189–92; Felheim, p. 233.

23. E. A. D[ithmar], *Memories of Daly's Theatres* (Privately printed, 1897), p. 58. See also Odell's *Annals,* IX, 263; Winter, *Shakespeare on the Stage, III,* 398–402; Felheim, p. 230.

24. Odell, *Annals,* IX, 419; Winter, *Shakespeare on the Stage, III,* 268–70; Felheim, pp. 230–13.

25. New York *Herald,* February 22, 1874, quoted in Odell, *Annals,* IX, 396–97; Felheim, p. 230.

26. Odell, *Annals,* X, 184–86; Winter, *Shakespeare on the Stage, II,* 262–65.

27. The number was in fact eleven, counting the production of *Romeo and Juliet* that Daly mounted in 1896 for the company of Mrs. Potter and Kyrle Bellew. Daly published an acting version of *Henry IV,* which he never got round to stage. Graham Robertson, p. 228, mentions that he designed the costumes for a never-produced *Cymbeline.*

28. Several letters from Winter to Daly refer to his work on *The Merry Wives*—e.g., March 25, June 10, and June 18, 1884. In December of 1885 he wrote the Introduction, and on January 5, 1886, he thanked Daly for the $50 payment for it (Folger Shakespeare Library).

29. Winter to Daly, December 14, 1885 (Folger Shakespeare Library).

30. Winter often stated his principles of emendation, notably in the Preface to *Shakespeare on the Stage, III,* 25–28. Felheim cites the most significant of these, p. 221.

31. *The Merry Wives* is discussed in Odell, *Annals,* XIII, 8–9; Winter, *Shakespeare on the Stage, III,* 398–405; Joseph Daly, pp. 393–97; John Ranken Towse, *Sixty Years of the Theatre: An old Critic's Memories* (New York: Funk and Wagnalls Company, 1916), pp. 345–47; Felheim, pp. 235–38.

32. Winter reprinted this Epilogue in *Shakespeare on the Stage, III,* 405.

33. Winter to Daly, June 10, 1884 (Folger Shakespeare Library).

34. Joseph Daly, p. 396.

35. *New York Times,* January 15, 1886.

36. Winter, *Shakespeare on the Stage, III,* 401.

37. New York *Tribune,* January 15, 1886.

38. Towse, pp. 345–47.

39. Joseph Daly, pp. 395–97.

40. Colley Cibber, *An Apology for the Life of Mr. Colley Cibber,* 2 vols. (New York: Athenaeum Press, n.d.), I, 168–69.

41. New York *Herald,* January 15, 1886.

42. *Spirit of the Times,* January 26, 1886.

43. New York *Post,* January 15, 1886.

44. *New York Times,* January 12, 1898.

45. *The Shrew* is discussed in Odell, *Annals,* XIII, 215–16; Winter, *Shakespeare on the Stage,* III, 511–28; Joseph Daly, pp. 426–31; Towse, pp. 347–49; and Felheim, pp. 238–43.

46. Robertson, p. 216.

47. Joseph Daly, p. 428.

48. Robertson, p. 216.

49. Odell, *Annals,* XIII, 216.

50. *Athenaeum,* June 2, 1888.

51. Winter, *Shakespeare on the Stage,* II, 521–52.

52. Towse, p. 348.

53. Robertson, p. 216.

54. Robertson, p. 216. Daly's actors, though, including Ada, were very often condemned as sounding "not at all Shakespearean." Howard Ticknor of the Boston *Daily Advertiser,* May 23, 1887, and the London *Era,* June 2, 1888, were among those especially critical of the actors' speech.

55. It is plain that Daly made his own version. Winter to Daly, November 5, 1887, says, "I have read it carefully and it seems to me that you have made an excellent working version of the comedy" (Folger Shakespeare Library).

56. For photographs of this set and the Veronese painting, see Theodore Shank, "Shakespeare and Nineteenth Century Realism," *Theatre Survey,* IV (1963), Plates VIII and IX after p. 64.

57. New York *Tribune,* January 19, 1887.

58. Boston *Evening Transcript,* May 24, 1887.

59. *New York Times,* January 19, 1887.

60. Ibid., January 23, 1887.

61. Ibid., April 14, 1887.

62. Ibid., January 19, 1887.

63. Boston *Evening Transcript,* May 24, 1887.

64. Boston *Home Journal,* May 28, 1887.

65. *Dramatic Mirror,* February 26, 1887.

66. *Dramatic Mirror,* March 30, 1889.

67. William Winter, *Ada Rehan: A Study* (New York: privately printed, 1891), p. 58.

68. Joseph Daly, p. 428.

69. *The Dream* is discussed in Odell, *Annals,* XIII, 417–19; Winter, *Shakespeare on the Stage,* III, 268–76; Joseph Daly, p. 446; Towse, pp. 349–50; and Felheim, pp. 243–46.

70. Again it is plain that Daly made his own acting version. Winter to Daly, November 5, 1887 (Folger Shakespeare Library).

71. New York *Herald,* February 1, 1888; *New York Times,* February 1, 1888.

72. William Archer, *Theatrical World of 1895* (London: Walter Scott, Ltd. 1896.)

73. Bernard Shaw, *Our Theatres in the Nineties,* I, 178–84; *Theatrical World of 1895,* p. 247.

74. New York *Herald,* February 1, 1888.

75. *The Critic,* February 11, 1888, p. 70.

76. Towse, p. 349.

77. Shaw, *Our Theatres in the Nineties,* I, 181–83.

78. Ibid., 184.

79. Moore's promptbook of the *Dream* is in the Folger Shakespeare Library, numbered MND, 21.

80. Shaw, *Our Theatres in the Nineties,* I, 178.

81. This direction and other stage directions are from Daly's edition, privately printed in 1888.

82. New York *Herald,* February 1, 1888.

83. Shaw, *Our Theatres in the Nineties,* I, 178.

84. *Theatrical World of 1895*, pp. 251–52.

85. Odell, *Annals*, VI, 282–83, 291–92; VIII, 280–81.

86. George Edgar Montgomery, "A Revival of Shakespeare's 'Midsummer Night's Dream,'" *The Cosmopolitan*, V (April 1888), p. 101.

87. The photographs of four stages of the barge's journey are reproduced by Theodore Shank in *Theatre Survey*, IV (1963),Plates XVI–XIX, after p. 64.

88. Dithmar in the *New York Times*, February 1, 1888; Winter in *Harper's Weekly*, February 18, 1888.

89. Archer in *Theatrical World of 1895*, p. 250; Shaw in *Our Theatres in the Nineties*, I, 179.

90. New York *Herald*, February 1, 1888.

91. *Dramatic Mirror*, February 4 and 11, 1888.

92. *New York Times*, New York *Tribune*, New York *Herald*, New York *Star*, all of February 1, 1888.

93. New York *Tribune*, February 1, 1888.

94. *The Critic*, February 11, 1888.

95. New York *Star*, February 1, 1888.

96. Odell, *Annals*, XIII, 419.

97. *Athenaeum*, July 13, 1895.

98. *As You Like It* is discussed in Odell, *Annals*, XIV, 219–23; Winter, *Shakespeare on the Stage*, II, 259–82; Joseph Daly, pp. 491–97; Towse, pp. 350–52; and Felheim, pp. 246–49.

99. Daly was persuaded to this pronunciation by H. H. Furness, who argued from the way it is rhymed in Orlando's verses. Winter, doubtful of it, was offering on November 28, 1889 (Folger Shakespeare Library) to hunt for a sixteenth-century "authority" for it. In 1890 many London critics—*e.g., Globe, Chronicle*, and the *Morning Advertiser* of July 16—noticed it or objected to it.

100. Especially the London critics (of 1890) invoked "womanly" and "womanliness" to define Miss Rehan's quality. See the *Daily Telegraph, Echo*, and *Daily News* of July 16; *St. James Budget*, July 18; *Saturday Review* and *Dramatic Review* of July 19; *Sunday Times*, July 20; *World*, July 23; *Queen*, July 26; *Theatre*, August 1.

101. Winter, in preparing his review, says, "I very much wish to know about your restorations." November 28, 1889 (Folger Shakespeare Library).

102. For Macready's version see Charles H. Shattuck,. ed., *Mr. Macready Produces "As You Like It": A Prompt-book Study* (Urbana: Beta Phi Mu, 1962). Two of Moore's promptbooks of special interest are in the Folger Shakespeare Library, numbered AYL, 23 and AYL, 16. Another of Moore's books and Ada Rehan's souvenir album are in the Theatre Collection of the New York Public Library. The following notes on cuts and arrangements are based on Daly's privately printed edition (New York, 1890).

103. For Helen Faucit's conception of the character and the play, see Helena Faucit, Lady Martin, *On Some of Shakespeare's Female Characters*. (Edinburgh and London: William Blackwood and Sons, 1904), pp. 227–85.

104. The "panoramic" sliding of forest flats was remarked upon by the *New York Times*, the *Sun*, and the Boston *Herald* of December 18, and *The Critic*, December 28. That Daly did not take his panoramic sets to London is confirmed by the *Era* and the *Dramatic Review* of July 19, 1890.

105. Musical accompaniment to the Shakespearean *dialogue* was noticed, and usually denounced, by *The Critic*, December 28, 1889; the Boston *Advertiser*, May 28, 1890; the London *Daily Chronicle*, July 16, 1890; London *World*, July 23, 1890; *Illustrated Sporting and Dramatic News*, August 2, 1890. In 1897 Shaw complained (*Our Theatres in the Nineties*, III, 208) of "slow music stealing up from the band at all the well-known recitations of Adam, Jaques, and Rosalind. " I do not know when Daly began the practice, or whether he invented it, or, as sometimes appears, he followed the lead of Henry Irving. It is of course a throwback to melodrama.

106. *New York Times*, December 18, 1889.

107. New York *Tribune*, December 18, 1889.

108. New York *World*, December 18, 1889.

109. *Dramatic Mirror*, January 4, 1890. Rosalind's forest costume is described in the *New York Times*, December 18, 1889; Boston *Advertiser*, May 28, 1890; London *Daily Chronicle*, July 16, 1890; London *Theatre*, August 1, 1890.

110. *The Critic*, December 28, 1889.

111. New York *Herald*, December 18, 1889.

112. *Spirit of the Times*, December 21, 1889.

113. Boston *Advertiser*, May 28, 1890; London *Star*, July 16, 1890; and *Illustrated Sporting and Dramatic News*, August 2, 1890. Winter was much pleased by the actors' "incessant movement," *Harper's Weekly*, January 11, 1890, and so were the London *Telegraph* and *Globe* of July 16, 1890. William Archer attacked it sharply in the *World*, July 23, 1890.

114. *Theatre*, II (December 1902), pp. 26–27.

115. Copeland's complaint is in the Boston *Post*, May 29, 1890. See also in London, the *Evening News, Star, Echo* of July 16; the *Era* and *Gentlewoman* of July 19; *Observer*, July 20; *Illustrated Sporting and Dramatic News*, August 2, 1890.

116. Robertson, pp. 225–26.

117. New York *Herald*, December 18, 1889.

118. Boston *Transcript*, May 28, 1890.

119. London *Daily Telegraph*, July 16, 1890. Other London papers which include praise of Miss Rehan's speech include the *Globe* and *Daily News* of July 16; *Dramatic Review*, July 19; *People*, July 20; *Man of the World*, July 23, 1890.

120. *Illustrated London News*, July 26, 1890.

121. Robertson, pp. 172–73.

122. Joseph Daly, p. 493, and Irving to Daly (Folger Shakespeare Library Y.C. 4349,20).

123. London *Globe*, July 16, 1890.

124. Winter to Daly, July 15, 1890 (Folger Shakespeare Library); Marie Bancroft to Miss Rehan, July 16, and Squire Bancroft to Daly, July 16 (Folger Shakespeare Library).

125. Emma Hardy to Miss Rehan, July 16, 1890 (Folger Shakespeare Library).

126. Joseph Daly, p. 494.

127. Helen Faucit to Miss Rehan, July 28, 1890 (Folger Shakespeare Library).

128. Joseph Daly, pp. 493–94. For Miss Rehan's "dear letter" of acceptance of the feather, see *Ellen Terry's Memoirs* (New York: G. P. Putnam's Sons, 1932), p. 225.

129. Justin Huntly McCarthy to Miss Rehan, July 15, 1890 (Folger Shakespeare Library).

130. Ada Rehan to Daly, July 20, 1890 (Folger Shakespeare Library).

131. When Robertson saw the production in London he was shocked by what had become of his designs, especially Viola's first dress. Robertson, p. 228.

132. *Twelfth Night* is discussed in Odell, *Annals*, XV, 280–28; Winter, *Shakespeare on the Stage*, II, 64–75; Towse, pp. 356–57; Joseph Daly, pp. 505–6, 574–76; and Felheim, pp. 252–57.

133. New York *Tribune*, February 22, 1893.

134. *The Critic*, March 4, 1893.

135. *New York Times*, February 22 and 26, 1893; *Evening Post*, February 22; Boston *Herald*, April 18, 1893 and September 28, 1894; Boston *Advertiser* and Boston *Transcript*, April 18, 1893.

136. Notably adverse comments on the comics appeared in the New York *Evening Post*, February 22, 1893; Boston *Transcript*, April 18, 1893; Boston *Advertiser*, September 28, 1894.

137. See Odell, *Annals*, XV, 281 and the New York *Herald*, Febru-

ary 22, 1893, for objection to Malvolio's costume. Towse praised Clarke's acting, New York *Evening Post,* February 22, 1893.

138. Daubigny's singing was praised by Towse and by Clapp in the Boston *Advertiser,* April 28, 1893, and September 28, 1894.

139. Miss Rehan's Viola was praised without reservation by Winter, Dithmar, and Nym Crinkle, in the New York *Tribune, New York Times,* and New York *World* of February 22, 1893, and by Arthur Warren of the Boston *Herald,* April 18, 1893, and September 28, 1894. Her limitations of temperament and elocutionary skills were underscored in the New York *Evening Post* and New York *Herald* of February 22, 1893; *The Critic,* March 4, 1893; *Town Topics,* March 2; 1893; Clapp in the Boston *Advertiser* and Mrs. Sutherland in the *Transcript,* April 18, 1893.

140. Walkley in the *Times,* January 9, 1894; the *Athenaeum,* January 13, 1894; Archer in *Theatrical World of 1895,* pp. 22–31; Shaw in *Our Theatres in the Nineties,* I, 25–26.

141. Boston *Advertiser,* September 28, 1894.

142. New York *Commercial Advertiser,* January 27, 1898.

143. New York *Commercial Advertiser,* December 2, 1893. Most critics took exception, from mild to violent, to Daly's high-handed manipulation of the text. The following account of changes is based upon a copy of Daly's edition (New York, privately printed, 1893), with prompter's cuts (Folger Shakespeare Library).

144. Furness to Daly, January 27, 1893 (Folger Shakespeare Library).

145. Norman Hapgood was particularly outraged by this and other of Daly's corruptions of the play. New York *Commercial Advertiser,* January 27, 1898.

146. Winter to Daly, n.d., item 178 (Folger Shakespeare Library).

147. John Philip Kemble printed these two catches in his edition of 1810; his comics had probably been using them for decades before that.

148. Winter, *Shakespeare on the Stage,* II, 67.

149. Bernard Shaw *Music in London,* III, 149 (vol. XXVIII in the Ayot St. Lawrence edition, New York: William Wise and Company, 1931).

150. Furness to Daly, January 27, 1893 (Folger Shakespeare Library).

151. Boston *Herald,* April 18, 1893.

152. New York *Commercial Advertiser,* December 2, 1893.

153. William Archer, *The Theatrical 'World' of 1894* (London: Walter Scott, Ltd., 1895), pp. 22–31; Bernard Shaw, *Music in London* III, 148–9 in the Ayot St. Lawrence Edition (New York: William Wise & Company, 1931)

154. Boston *Advertiser,* September 28, 1894.

155. Hay to Daly, March 29, 1893 (Folger Shakespeare Library).

156. Joseph Daly, p. 504.

157. Shaw, *Our Theatres in the Nineties,* I, 170–76.

158. For an account of Daly's hostility to Miss Marlowe, see Charles Edward Russell, *Julia Marlowe, Her Life and Art* (New York: D. Appleton and Company, 1926), pp. 271–85.

159. The Potter-Bellew *Romeo and Juliet* was condemned by Winter in the New York *Tribune* and by the *New York Times* of March 4, 1896. The New York *Herald* and Boston *Herald* both praised it.

160. New York *Post,* December 24, 1896.

161. *New York Times,* April 7, 1897.

162. New York *Tribune,* April 7, 1897.

163. New York *Commercial Advertiser,* April 7, 1897.

164. *New York Times,* November 27, 1898.

165. Joseph Daly, p. 632.

166. The photographs of six *Merchant* sets were published by Theodore Shank in *Theatre Survey* IV (1963), Plates IX–XIV, following p. 64.

167. Norman Hapgood, *The Stage in America, 1897–1900* (New York: Macmillan Company, 1901), p. 157.

168. New York *Tribune,* November 20, 1898.

169. *Harper's Weekly,* December 3, 1898.

170. Daly to Winter, December 1, 1898 (Folger Shakespeare Library).

III. The Feminization of Shakespeare

1. For Comstock's career see Heywood Brown and Margaret Leech, *Antony Comstock, Roundsman of the Lord* (New York: A. & C. Boni, 1927).

2. New York *Tribune,* November 20, 1876.

3. *New York Times,* December 23, 1877.

4. William Winter, *Shakespeare on the Stage,* III (New York: Moffat, Yard, & Co., 1916; reprint, New York: Benjamin Blom, 1968–69), 459–60.

5. Winter, *Shakespeare on the Stage,* II (New York: Moffat, Yard, & Co., 1915; reprint, New York: Benjamin Blom, 1969). 167–68, 287.

6. Ibid., 288.

7. Boston *Transcript,* October 26, 1886.

8. For the Manchester *plein air* production, see the Boston *Transcript* and the *New York Times,* August 9, 1887, and the *Era* (London), August 27, 1887.

9. For the Castle Point performance, see the Boston *Herald,* the New York *Tribune,* and the *New York Times,* June 17, 1891.

10. New York *World,* January 8, 1889.

11. New York *Herald,* November 22, 1893.

12. Miss Neilson's life was so clouded with mysteries and crossed with scandal that we shall never have a definitive biography of her. The best essay is Albert E. Johnson's "Greatest of Juliets" which appeared in *Theatre Arts* (August 1957). Charles Pascoe's *The Dramatic List* (London: David Bogue, 1880), pp. 271–75, sticks to the facts of her life on the stage. At the time of her death, in mid-August, 1880, the Paris *Figaro* published daily reports of her final suffering (August 16, 17, 18, 19). Countless obituaries appeared, most of them repeating the romantic legends of her origin. Of particular interest is "The Late Miss Neilson" in the London *Era* (September 5, 1880), written by Edward Compton, who was present at her death. Amelia E. Barr contributed an article, "The Early Home of Adelaide Neilson" to *Lippincotts* (December 1882). Laura Holloway Langford published a brief book *Adelaide Neilson, a Souvenir* (New York: Funk and Wagnalls, 1885), and three years later under the name of Holloway, published "A Reminder of Neilson" in the Boston *Journal.* In 1889, Betsy O'Dowd published "A Life's Mystery Solved" in the Kansas City *Journal.* Thanks to spiritualist mediums, information about her poured in from the other world for years after her death. According to the Boston *Sunday Herald* (May 19, 1901), she was accidentally poisoned by a waiter, one Pierre Loreaux, who had been hired by a would-be lover of Miss Neilson to poison Edward Compton. He confused and reversed the glasses. Horrified at his error he fled to London, but in every piece of gold he had been paid he saw Miss Neilson's face. He threw the gold pieces into the Thames, leaped in after them, and drowned. For other accounts, see William Winter, *The Wallet of Time,* 2 vols. (New York: Moffat, Yard, & Co., 1913), I, 544–61; and Clement Scott, *The Drama of Yesterday and Today* (London: Macmillan and Co., 1899), II, 215–30.

13. G. C. D. Odell, *Annals of the New York Stage,* 15 vols. (New York: Columbia University Press, 1927–49), IX, 255.

14. Clement Scott, *The Drama of Yesterday and Today,* II, 216.

15. For details of the Birch divorce case, see the *Times,* May 4, 1874. For Miss Neilson's divorce from Lee, see the New York *World,*

February 20, 1877.

16. *New York Times* and New York *Tribune,* November 19, 1872. The New York *Herald* review of this date was generally hostile, but a correspondent to the *Herald* on December 15 praised her warmly.

17. *New York Times,* April 21, 1874. The New York *Herald,* October 29, 1874. was persistently hostile.

18. On May 4, 1880, the *New York Times,* New York *Tribune,* and New York *Herald* sang her praises. For summary evaluations, see J. Ranken Towse, *Sixty Years of the Theatre* (New York: Funk and Wagnalls, 1916), p. 134; and Winter, *Shakespeare on the Stage,* II, 151–55.

19. Undated clipping from the Boston *Advertiser* (Harvard Theatre Collection). This is Henry Austin Clapp, and probably of February 17, 1880, when Miss Neilson had reappeared in Boston after an absence of seven years. For Clapp's magnificent final tributes to her, see *Reminiscences of a Dramatic Critic* (Boston: Houghton, Mifflin and Company, 1902), pp. 159–72.

20. London *Observer,* February 6, 1876. The *Dramatic Mirror,* May 8, 1880, printed a negative review of *As You Like It* together with a positive review of *Romeo and Juliet.* For summary evaluation, see Winter, *Shakespeare on the Stage,* II, 284–85.

21. New York *Telegram,* October 20, 1874.

22. New York *Herald,* October 20, 1874.

23. *New York Times,* May 8, 1877.

24. New York *Tribune,* May 8, 1877.

25. Undated clippings (1880) (Harvard Theatre Collection.) It is Henry Clapp, in the *Advertiser.*

26. New York *Tribune,* October 28, 1880. For summary evaluation, see Winter, *Shakespeare on the Stage,* II, 41–45.

27. *Advertiser,* February 24, 1880. See also Winter, *Shakespeare on the Stage,* III, 131–34.

28. Boston *Courier,* April 25, 1880.

29. New York *Tribune,* May 25, 1880.

30. Studies of Mary Anderson include J. M. Farrar, *Mary Anderson, The Story of her Life and Professional Career* (London: David Bogue, 1884); William Winter, *The Stage Life of Mary Anderson* (New York: G. J. Coombes, 1886); Mary Anderson de Navarro, *A Few Memories* (New York: Harper and Brothers, 1896); John Ranken Towse, *Sixty Years,* pp. 214–21; Winter, *The Wallet of Time,* II, 1–46; John Shaw, "Mary Anderson's Stratford Production of *As You Like It,*" *Theatre Annual* (1974), pp. 40–58; Raymond C. Sawyer, *"The Shakespearean Acting of Mary Anderson, 1880–89"* (Ph.D. diss., University of Illinois, 1975).

31. Towse, *Sixty Years,* p. 216.

32. New York *Herald,* November 13, 1877.

33. *Spirit of the Times,* November 24, 1877.

34. *New York Times,* November 20, 1877.

35. J. M. Farrar devoted chapter VIII of his *Mary Anderson* to quoting London reviews of her first season, most of them hostile. The first batch of comments I cite are mostly from the *Morning Post,* September 3, 1883.

36. Farrar quoted this from *The Graphic,* December 14, 1883.

37. Winter, *Shakespeare on the Stage,* II, 175.

38. Anderson, *A Few Memories,* pp. 179–82.

39. Philadelphia *Evening Bulletin,* November 8, 1884.

40. *Spirit of the Times,* November 8, 1884.

41. Quoted by Lord Lytton in *Nineteenth Century, XVI* (December 1884), 880–81.

42. *Saturday Review,* November 8, 1884.

43. Lord Lytton, "Miss Anderson's Juliet," *Nineteenth Century,* XVI (December 1884), 879–900.

44. Boston, *Evening Transcript,* December 1, 1885; Boston *Courier,* December 6, 1885; Chicago *Inter Ocean,* March 9, 1886.

45. New York *World,* November 25, 1885.

46. "Mrs. Mary Montague." A clipping of November 15, 1885, from an unidentified Brooklyn paper (Harvard Theatre Collection).

47. Winter, *Shakespeare on the Stage,* II, 176–79.

48. The London correspondent to an unidentified Boston paper (September 1, 1885) names sixteen of the London critics who came down to Stratford on the great Western railroad (Harvard Theatre Collection).

49. *Topical Times,* September 5, 1885. The *Times,* by the way, said she would have done *As You Like It* at the Lyceum, but Irving stipulated that she should not, as he intended to stage it there himself. Of course he never did.

50. E.g., *Topical Times,* September 5, *Referee,* August 29; *Sportsman,* August 31, 1885.

51. *London World,* September 2, 1885.

52. *Era,* September 5, 1885, among others speaks of the devotion of Americans to Stratford, and the number of them attending *As You Like It.*

53. *Sporting Times,* September 5; *The Bat,* September 5, 1885.

54. *Daily Chronicle, Morning Post, Daily Telegraph,* all of August 31, 1885; *Sunday Times,* August 30, 1885.

55. *The Academy,* September 5, 1885.

56. *St. Stephen's Review,* September 5, 1885.

57. Archer's review appeared in the London *World* on September 2, 1885; his essay covering all Miss Anderson's London performances appeared in *The Theatre,* N.S. VI (October 1, 1885), pp. 176–82.

58. New York *Tribune,* September 16, 1885.

59. Anderson, *A Few Memories,* pp. 212–13. The rapturous welcome and general disappointment are clearly expressed in the *New York Times* and the New York *Herald,* October 13, 1885; the *Dramatic Mirror,* October 17; *Spirit of the Times,* October 17, 24, and 31; *The Critic,* October 24. Winter's detailed descriptions of Miss Anderson's production are given in his reviews from Stratford and New York in the New York *Tribune,* September 16 and October 13, and in *Shakespeare on the Stage,* II, 293–302.

60. *The Winter's Tale,* V.2, 35–36: "The majesty of the creature in resemblance of the mother."

61. Among the London reviews are those in the *Daily Chronicle,* the *Standard, Morning Post, Morning Advertiser,* September 12, 1887; *Saturday Review,* September 17; and Archer's review in *The Theatre,* X (October 1, 1887).

62. This remark occurs not in her regular acting edition, but in her souvenir edition of *The Winter's Tale,* 1887. See George C. D. Odell, *Shakespeare from Betterton to Irving* (New York: Scribners, 1920) II, 396.

63. See Archer's review, *The Theatre,* X (October 1, 1887).

64. Anderson, *A Few Memories,* p. 247.

65. See Winter's long appreciation of it in *The Wallet of Time,* II, 27–38. Important reviews appeared in the *New York Times,* New York *Tribune,* New York *World,* and *Press* on November 14, 1888; *Spirit of the Times,* November 17; *The Republic* (J. W. Keller), November 25; in the Boston *Transcript* and the Boston *Advertiser,* December 27; in the Chicago *Inter Ocean,* January 30, 1889. See also Odell *Shakespeare from Betterton to Irving,* II, 382, 403, 407–8, 437–38.

66. New York *World,* November 14, 1888.

67. Boston *Advertiser,* December 27, 1888.

68. Odell, *Annals,* XIV, 18–19.

69. Shaw's review of Mary Anderson's *A Few Memories* (*Saturday Review,* April 4, 1896), reprinted in *Our Theatres in the Nineties,* 3 vols. (London: Constable and Company, 1948), II, 85–91.

70. Shaw to Ellen Terry, November 1, 1895. See *Ellen Terry and Bernard Shaw, a Correspondence* (New York: Theatre Arts Books, 1949), p. 17.

71. Mrs. Mowatt's career is brilliantly developed by Eric Wollencott Barnes, *The Lady of Fashion: The Life and the Theatre of Anna Cora Mowatt* (New York: Scribners, 1954).

72. *Spirit of the Times,* December 24, 1881.

73. *New York Times* and New York *Tribune,* October 14, 1885; *Spirit of the Times,* October 17, 1885; Winter, *Shakespeare on the Stage,* II, 179–83; Odell, *Annals,* XIII, 25.

74. *Spirit of the Times,* October 17 and December 5, 1885.

75. Otis Skinner, *Footlights and Spotlights, Recollections of My Life on the Stage* (Indianapolis: Bobbs-Merrill, 1924), p. 196.

76. Odell, *Annals,* XIV, 592; Winter, *Shakespeare on the Stage,* III, 136–39.

77. Obituary notice in full detail in the *Dramatic Mirror,* April 16, 1898.

78. The biographies of Lillie Langtry include her own reminiscences, *The Days I Knew* (New York: George H. Doran Company, 1925); Pierre Sichel, *The Jersey Lily: The Story of the Fabulous Mrs. Langtry* (Englewood Cliffs, N.J.: Prentice-Hall, 1958); Noel Bertram Gerson, *Because I Loved Him: The Life and Loves of Lillie Langtry* (New York: Morrow, 1971); James Brough, *The Prince and the Lily* (New York: Coward, McCann & Geoghegan, 1975). In 1978–79 a thirteen-part dramatization of her life, made by the BBC and starring Francesca Annis, was broadcast in England and America. It showed her "life," but very little of her life in the theatre.

79. "The Jersey Lily—How she was taught at Pope's Villa—Rehearsing Rosalind on Mr. Labouchère's Lawn" is a two-column newspaper clipping, hand-dated December 8, 1882 (Harvard Theatre Collection).

80. Of the forty or more London reviews of Mrs. Langtry's opening of *As You Like It,* especially favorable reviews appeared in the *Morning Post, Globe, Daily News,* and *Morning Advertiser* of September 25, 1882, and the *Era* of September 30. Reviews in the *Daily Telegraph,* September 25, and in *Bell's Life in London* and the *Illustrated Sporting and Dramatic News,* September 30, were conspicuously hostile.

81. *Sunday Times,* September 24, 1882.

82. *Era,* September 30, 1882.

83. *Daily Telegraph,* September 25, 1882.

84. Helen Faucit's "Imogen, Princess of Britain" is dated October 1882. Her "Rosalind" was completed in September 1884. These and six other essays were collected in *On Some of Shakespeare's Female Characters,* 7th ed. (Edinborough and London: William Blackwood and Sons, 1904).

85. *Bell's Life in London,* September 30, 1882.

86. W. Graham Robertson, *Life Was Worth Living,* p. 71. Ellen Terry testified in her *Memoirs* (p. 112) that Mrs. Langtry was "lovely" and that she was "too well-bred to be hoydenish."

87. *Era.* September 30, 1882.

88. *Morning Post,* September 25, 1882.

89. *Bell's Life in London,* September 30, 1882.

90. *Spirit of the Times,* November 11, 1882.

91. *Spirit of the Times,* November 18, 1982.

92. *Dramatic Mirror,* November 18, 1882.

93. *Spirit of the Times,* November 18, 1882.

94. New York *World,* New York *Herald, Telegram, New York Times,* New York *Post,* New York *Sun,* November 14, 1882.

95. New York *Tribune,* November 14, 1882.

96. *The Critic,* November 18, 1882.

97. Gerson, *Because I Loved Him,* p. 104.

98. *Spirit of the Times,* December 9, 1882.

99. *Spirit of the Times,* December 2, 1882.

100. *Spirit of the Times,* October 23, 1886.

101. *Spirit of the Times,* February 9, 1889.

102. New York *World,* January 22, 1889.

103. *Dramatic Mirror,* January 26, 1889.

104. New York *World,* January 22, 1889.

105. *Spirit of the Times,* January 26, 1889.

106. *Dramatic Mirror,* January 19 and 26, 1889.

107. *New York Times,* New York *Tribune, The Graphic,* New York *Post, Press,* all of January 22, 1889.

108. *Spirit of the Times,* January 26, 1889.

109. *Era,* March 1, 1890.

110. The main facts about Mrs. Brown Potter's career are given in an obituary in the New York *Herald-Tribune,* February 14, 1936. See also Amy Leslie, *Some Players* (Chicago: H. S. Stone and Company, 1899), pp. 329–33; and Emma B. Kaufman, "Cora Urquhart Potter," *Frank Leslie's Popular Magazine* (March 1902), pp. 185–90.

111. *Dramatic Mirror,* January 26, 1889.

112. Chicago *Tribune,* May 22, 1889.

113. "Megargee's" special telegram to Philadelphia *Times,* January 9, 1899.

114. This account of Bellew's acting version is taken mainly from Nym Crinkle's description of it in the New York *World,* January 2, 1889.

115. Cleopatra's dresses are described by Nym Crinkle in the New York *World,* and in great detail by Fanny Edgar Thomas under the title "A Queen in Gauzy Garb" in the New York *Star,* January 20, 1889.

116. Boston *Herald,* February 24, 1889.

117. New York *Sun,* January 9, 1889. See also the New York *Herald* and Philadelphia *Times,* January 9, 1889; *Dramatic Mirror,* January 12 and 19, 1889.

118. Chicago *Tribune,* May 22, 1889.

119. Boston *Herald,* February 24, 1889. The business of exposing her breast is commented on widely and leeringly, with denials that she went quite so far after the first performance. Her husband's presence at that performance is mentioned in the New York *Herald-Tribune,* February 14, 1936.

120. New York *Tribune,* January 9, 1889.

121. Winter, *Shakespeare on the Stage,* III, 461–64.

122. *New York Times,* January 9, 1889.

123. *Spirit of the Times,* January 12, 1889.

124. *Life,* January 24, 1889.

125. "Nym Crinkle's Feuilleton" in the *Dramatic Mirror,* January 12, 14, 26, 1889.

126. Boston *Post,* January 21 and 29, 1889.

127. *The Theatre,* V (January 12, 1889), pp. 39–44.

128. *The Theatre,* V (January 19, 1889), p. 53.

129. *The Theatre,* V (February 2, 1889), pp. 97–100.

130. The acting version, prepared by Bellew, is described in a long review, hand-dated March 8, 1896, in the Harvard Theatre Collection.

131. New York *Tribune,* March 4, 1896.

132. Joseph Francis Daly, *The Life of Augustin Daly* (New York: Macmillan, 1917), p. 591.

133. Her sorry last years are recounted in the obituary in the New York *Herald-Tribune,* February 14, 1936.

134. *The Memories and Impressions of Helena Modjeska, an Autobiography* was published posthumously (New York: The Macmillan Company, 1910). William Winter devoted a chapter to Modjeska in *The Wallet of Time,* I, 359–97. The most detailed and indispensable study is by Marion Moore Coleman, *Fair Rosalind: the American Career of Helena Modjeska* (Cheshire, Conn.: Cherry Hill Books, 1969).

135. In December of 1893 she discovered that Sinnmayer had had another wife at the time he "married" her. See Coleman, *Fair Rosalind,* p. 638.

136. For the final spelling of her stage name, see Coleman, *Fair*

Rosalind, p. 85.

137. See *Memories and Impression,* pp. 45ff. and Index (under Benda).

138. This number includes Desdemona, which she played only twice in English, at the Cincinnati Drama Festival in April 1884.

139. These statistics are derived from Coleman's exhaustive annals of her American performances, in *Fair Rosalind,* pp. 881–968.

140. This account of her Juliet is derived from the *New York Times* and New York *Herald,* October 13, 1878, the New York *Tribune,* October 14, *Spirit of the Times,* October 19, Winter, *Shakespeare on the Stage,* II, 171–72; Towse, *Sixty Years,* pp. 204–5, and Odello's *Annals,* X, 576.

141. Jan McDonald, "Helena Modjeska's Season at the Court Theatre, London, 1880–1881," in *Theatre Research,* XI, 1971, 149.

142. Her social and professional connections in England are recorded in *Memories and Impressions,* chap. 44 and 45.

143. New York *Herald,* December 12, 1882.

144. The family of Richard Watson Gilder and his sister Jeannette were devoted friends of Modjeska. Jeannette's reviews of Modjeska were always sympathetic (and discriminating, too). Often, as this one of her Rosalind in *The Critic,* December 16, 1882, they were vividly detailed. See also Winter, *Shakespeare on the Stage,* II, 291–93.

145. On January 22, 1892, she lectured to the Goethe Club of New York on the subject of Rosalind, and subsequently her discourse was published in various newspapers. It is printed entire in Coleman, *Fair Rosaline,* pp. 575–81.

146. Towse, *Sixty Years,* pp. 205–6.

147. Odell, *Annals,* XII, 23.

148. New York *Tribune,* December 19, 1882.

149. *New York Times,* December 19, 1882.

150. New York *Herald,* December 19, 1882.

151. Towse, *Sixty Years,* pp. 206–7.

152. Odell, *Annals,* XII, 23.

153. *New York Times,* December 7, 1886.

154. Mixed reviews may be noted in the Boston *Transcript,* March 29, 1884; New York *Herald,* February 5, 1888; *New York Times,* February 6, 1888; *The Critic,* February 11, 1888; the Boston *Post* and Boston *Record,* March 30, 1888; Winter, *Shakespeare on the Stage,* III, 135–36; and Towse, *Sixty Years,* pp. 266–68.

155. Objections to the play on moral grounds occur in Towse, *Sixty Years,* pp. 269–70; Boston *Advertiser,* March 28, 1888, and March 8, 1898; Boston *Home Journal,* March 31, 1888; New York *Recorder,* October 12, 1895; and Boston *Journal and Budget,* March 13, 1898. Approval of the morality of the play occurs in the *New York Times,* February 7, 1888; *The Critic,* February 11, 1888; Boston *Post* and Boston *Transcript,* March 28, 1888; and New York *World,* October 8, 1895.

156. *New York Times,* February 7, 1888.

157. New York *Herald,* February 7, 1888.

158. *The Critic,* February 11, 1888.

159. Boston *Post,* March 28, 1888.

160. Boston *Advertiser,* March 28, 1888.

161. *New York Times,* February 8, 1888.

162. Boston *Transcript,* March 27, 1888.

163. Boston *Post,* reprinted in *The Dramatic Year* (Boston: Ticknor and Company, 1889), pp. 203–6. See Towse, *Sixty Years,* pp. 270–73.

164. Otis Skinner, *Footlights and Spotlights,* p. 172.

165. *Dramatic Mirror,* October 26, 1889.

166. Chicago *Herald,* March 20, 1890.

167. Boston *Transcript,* January 22, 1890, Chicago *Herald,* March 20, 1890.

168. New York *Tribune,* October 29, 1889.

169. H. H. Furness, ed., *The Merchant of Venice, A New Variorum Edition* (New York: J. B. Lippincott, 1888), p. 383.

170. *New York Times,* October 29, 1889.

171. Boston *Transcript,* January 21, 1890.

172. Coleman, *Fair Rosalind,* p. 645.

173. *Spirit of the Times,* November 2, 1889.

174. *Dramatic Mirror,* November 9, 1889.

175. New York *Tribune,* November 5, 1889.

176. Boston *Home Journal,* November 16, 1889.

177. *The Critic,* November 23, 1889.

178. Undated clipping of Nym Crinkle's review.

179. Coleman, *Fair Rosalind,* p. 502.

180. Thomas Campbell, *Life of Mrs. Siddons,* 2 vols. (London: Effingham Wilson, 1834), II, 10–34.

181. Winter, in *Shakespeare on the Stage,* I (New York: Moffat, Yard & Co., 1911; reprint, New York: Benjamin Blom, 1969), 510–12, denies that her Lady Macbeth was planned or unified. But the several following points noted by Dithmar in the *New York Times* and Meltzer in the New York *Herald* on November 19, 1889, Gilder in *The Critic,* November 23, and others, together with the fact that she retained the part to the end of her career, suggest that Winter simply misunderstood her "feminine" Lady Macbeth.

182. These statistics are derived from Coleman's annals.

183. Towse, *Sixty Years,* p. 274.

184. Coleman, *Fair Rosalind,* p. 740.

185. Chicago *Tribune,* October 18, 1898.

186. Chicago *Chronicle,* October 11, 1898.

187. Winter, in *Shakespeare on the Stage,* III, 507, describes the acting version he made for her. He approved her performance, but disapproved her attempt to make Constance the central figure of the play.

188. Winter, in *The Wallet of Time,* I, 384, mistakenly states that she played Hermione about 1905 or 1906. She was planning it in 1904, but all that came of her plans was to direct a company of amateurs for a charity performance.

189. *The Forum,* XIV, November 1892, pp. 337–44.

190. *Memories and Impressions,* p. 555.

191. The list of books devoted to Bernhardt is enormous. The latest popular biography in English is Cornelia Otis Skinner, *Madame Sarah* (Boston: Houghton Mifflin, 1967; reprint, New York: Dell, 1968). A serious study of her actorship is Gerda Taranow, *Sarah Bernhardt, the Art within the Legend* (Princeton: Princeton University Press, 1972).

192. Winter, *Shakespeare on the Stage,* I, 428.

193. *Atlantic Monthly* (May 1866).

194. Edward Vining, *The Mystery of Hamlet* (Philadelphia: J. P. Lippincott, 1881).

195. *Era,* May 20, 1899.

196. "Alan Dale Describes Sarah Bernhardt as Hamlet," newspaper clipping hand-dated June 12, 1899 (Harvard Theatre Collection).

197. Rostand's remark is repeated sarcastically by Winter in the New York *Tribune,* December 26, 1900. The review ("Alas, Poor Hamlet") is reprinted in *Shakespeare on the Stage,* I, 431–42.

198. *Times,* June 13, 1899.

199. *Saturday Review,* June 17, 1899. Reprinted in *Around Theatres* (New York: Simon and Schuster, 1954), pp. 34–37.

200. New York *Herald,* December 26, 1900.

201. Boston *Transcript,* December 26, 1900.

202. *New York Times,* December 26, 1900.

203. *The Critic,* February, 1901.

204. All of Bernhardt's objectionable stage business that follows here is recorded in Winter, *Shakespeare on the Stage,* I, pp. 431–42.

205. This "c'est le roi!" is recorded in Gerda Taranow, *Sarah Bernhardt, The Art within the Legend* (Princeton: Princeton University Press, 1972), pp. 81–82.

206. "On Seeing Madame Bernhardt's Hamlet," *North American,* 171 (December 1900), 908–19.

IV. Foreign Visitors and the New Realism

1. William W. Appleton, *Charles Macklin. An Actor's Life* (Cambridge: Harvard University Press, 1960), p. 18.

2. John Hill, *The Actor: A Treatise on the Art of Playing,* rev. ed. (London: R. Griffiths, 1755), p. 151.

3. Reported by Jan Kott in "Hamlet and Orestes," *PMLA,* LXXXII (October 1967), p. 312.

4. The only book-length account of Fechter is Kate Field's *Charles Albert Fechter* (Boston: J. R. Osgood and Company, 1882). Miss Field had earlier published an essay "Fechter as Hamlet," in the *Atlantic Monthly,* XXVI (November 1870), pp. 558–70. William Winter did a brief biographical chapter in *The Wallet of Time,* 2 vols. (New York: Moffat, Yard, & Co., 1912), II, 222–27. For major critiques, see George Henry Lewes, *On Actors and the Art of Acting* (London: Smith, Edler & Co., 1875; reprint, New York: Grove Press, n.d.), pp. 113–42; Henry Austin Clapp, *Reminiscences of a Dramatic Critic* (Boston: Houghton Mifflin, 1902), pp. 113–30; William Winter, *Shakespeare on the Stage,* I (New York: Moffat, Yard & Co., 1911; reprint, New York: Benjamin Blom, 1969), 286–87, 403–10; John Ranken Towse, *Sixty Years of the Theatre, An Old Critic's Memories* (New York: Funk and Wagnalls, 1916), pp. 62–79. A thoroughly researched assessment, generally approving, is John A. Mills's "The Modesty of Nature: Charles Fechter's Hamlet," *Theatre Survey,* XV (May 1974), pp. 59–78. In a long footnote Mills documents Fechter's influence on Henry Irving.

5. Lewes, pp. 146–74.

6. Lewes, pp. 119–21; Towse, p. 72.

7. Undated clipping in the Harvard Theatre Collection. The Boston *Advertiser,* ca. February 22, 1870.

8. *The Galaxy,* IX (April 1870), p. 557.

9. Winter, *Shakespeare on the Stage,* I, p. 404.

10. *The Galaxy,* pp. 557–58.

11. *The Nation,* February 24, 1870, p. 119.

12. Field, "Fechter as Hamlet," pp. 563–64.

13. Clapp, p. 127.

14. Edwin Booth's note. See Charles H. Shattuck, *The Hamlet of Edwin Booth* (Urbana: University of Illinois Press, 1969), p. 236.

15. *The Galaxy,* p. 560; *New York Times,* February 16, 1870.

16. *The Galaxy,* pp. 558–59.

17. *The Nation,* February 24, 1870, p. 119.

18. Boston *Advertiser,* ca. February 22, 1870.

19. Field, "Fechter as Hamlet," p. 56.

20. Boston *Daily Advertiser,* November 26, 1862.

21. Lewes, pp. 117ff.

22. Lewes, p. 130.

23. Charles Dickens, "On Mr. Fechter's Acting," *Atlantic Monthly,* XXIV (August 1869), pp. 242–44.

24. G. C. D. Odell, *Annals of the New York Stage,* 15 vols. (New York: Columbia University Press, 1927–49), VIII (1936), 594.

25. *New York Times,* February 16, 1870.

26. *Turf, Field, and Farm,* February 18, 1870 (signed "Proteus").

27. Winter, *Shakespeare on the Stage,* I, 403–10.

28. Boston *Traveller,* February 22, 1870.

29. Boston *Advertiser,* ca. February 22, 1870.

30. Salvini wrote a volume of reminiscences, *Ricordi: Aneddoti ed Impressioni* (Milano: Fratelli Dumolard, Editori, 1895). A reduced version of this volume, translated anonymously, was published earlier, *Leaves from the Autobiography of Tommaso Salvini* (New York: The Century Company, 1893). William Winter devoted a brief biographical chapter to Salvini in *The Wallet of Time,* I, 283–90. For critical studies, see Edward Tuckerman Mason, *The Othello of Tommaso Salvini* (New York: G. P. Putnam's Sons, 1890); Henry Austin Clapp, *Reminiscences of a Dramatic Critic* (Boston: Houghton, Mifflin and Company, 1902), pp. 142–58; four essays by Salvini himself which appeared in *Putnam's Monthly,* on *Othello* (October 1907); on *Macbeth* (November 1907); on *Hamlet* (December 1907); and on *King Lear* (January 1908); William Winter, *Shakespeare on the Stage,* I; II (New York: Moffat, Yard, & Co. 1915; reprint, New York: Benjamin Blom, 1969); John Ranken Towse, *Sixty Years of the Theatre, An Old Critic's Memories* (New York: Funk and Wagnalls Company, 1916), pp. 157–79. Edward Carroll Powers has recently described the unpublished commentaries on Salvini in the Thomas Russell Sullivan papers at the American Antiquarian Society and the Harvard Theatre Collection. "Tommaso Salvini: An American Devotee's View," *Theatre Survey,* XV (November 1974), pp. 130–42. David H. Fennema, "The Popular Response to Tommaso Salvini in America," *Theatre History Studies,* II (1982), pp. 103–13.

31. Salvini, *Ricordi,* p. 60; *Leaves,* p. 25.

32. *Ricordi,* pp. 77–84; *Leaves,* pp. 40–45.

33. *Ricordi,* pp. 122–25; *Leaves,* pp. 83–86.

34. *Ricordi,* pp. 88–102; *Leaves,* pp. 49–63.

35. *Ricordi,* pp. 114–19; *Leaves,* pp. 75–81.

36. *Putnam's Monthly* (October 1907), pp. 23–28.

37. *Ricordi,* pp. 136–40; *Leaves,* pp. 90–92.

38. *Ricordi,* pp. 221–22; *Leaves,* pp. 116–18.

39. *Ricordi,* p. 139; *Leaves,* p. 93.

40. Towse, p. 158.

41. *The Critic,* October 31, 1885, p. 211.

42. *New York Times,* September 17, 1873.

43. *Spirit of the Times,* December 18, 1880, p. 506.

44. *Ricordi,* pp. 402–8; *Leaves,* pp. 234–38.

45. *New York Times,* September 17, 1873.

46. Mason, p. 3.

47. Mason, pp. 8–9.

48. Mason, p. 17.

49. *New York Times,* September 17, 1873.

50. Mason, pp. 21–23. He was probably referring to the Othello of Edwin Booth, which critics often described as unduly solemn.

51. Mason, pp. 60–61.

52. Mason, pp. 52–53; see also Towse, p. 162.

53. Mason, p. 67.

54. Mason, p. 74.

55. *Othello: a tragedy in five acts by William Shakespeare, as performed by Sig. Salvini and the American Company . . .* (New York: A. S. Seers Engraving and Printing Establishment, n.d.), pp. 108–12.

56. Mason, pp. 76–77.

57. Ibid., pp. 89–91.

58. Towse, pp. 162–63; see also Mason, p. 95.

59. Mason, p. 107; Towse, p. 164.

60. *Dramatic Mirror,* January 26, 1889.

61. *Dramatic Mirror,* October 26, 1889.

62. New York *Tribune,* September 17, 1873. I am tempted to suspect this review was not written by Winter but a substitute.

63. New York *Tribune,* April 27, 1886.

64. Winter, *Shakespeare on the Stage,* I, 291.

65. *Ricordi,* p. 139; *Leaves,* p. 93.

66. New York *Herald,* October 3, 1873.

67. *New York Times,* December 18, 1880.

68. Winter, *Shakespeare on the Stage,* I, 415–16.

69. Winter, *Wallet of Time,* I, 288–89.

70. *Putnam's Monthly* (December 1907), pp. 352–56.

71. *Spirit of the Times,* February 19, 1881.

72. Boston *Daily Advertiser,* April 22, 1881.

73. *New York Times,* February 11, 1881.

74. Winter, *Shakespeare on the Stage,* I, 486–89.

75. Towse, pp. 178–79.

76. *Putnam's Monthly* (November 1907), pp. 211–13.

77. Towse, p. 174.

78. Winter, *Shakespeare on the Stage,* II, 472.

79. Boston *Transcript,* January 16, 1883, and December 9, 1885. The following details of his performance are derived from these *Transcript* reviews, from Winter's account in *Shakespeare on the Stage,* and from Jeannette Gilder's "pre-view."

80. *Putnam's Monthly* (January 1908), pp. 465–68.

81. *The Critic,* February 17, 1883.

82. Towse, pp. 175–77.

83. Towse, p. 161.

84. *The Critic,* October 31, 1885, p. 211.

85. The biographical and critical writing about Henry Irving and Ellen Terry is too vast to account for here. The following titles have been useful in preparing the present essay. Madeleine Bingham, *Henry Irving, The Greatest Victorian Actor* (New York: Stein and Day, 1978); Austin Brereton, *The Life of Henry Irving,* 2 vols. (London: Longman Green and Co., 1908); Carol Jones Carlisle, *Shakespeare from the Greenroom* (Chapel Hill: University of North Carolina Press, 1969); Henry Austin Clapp, *Reminiscences of a Dramatic Critic* (Boston: Houghton Mifflin and Company, 1902), pp. 194–236; Edith Craig and Christopher St. John, eds., *Ellen Terry's Memoirs* (New York: G. P. Putnam's Sons, 1932); Edward Gordon Craig, *Henry Irving* (London: Longmans Green and Co., 1930; reprint, New York: Benjamin Blom, 1969); Richard Foulkes, "The Staging of the Trial Scene in Irving's The Merchant of Venice," *ETJ,* 28 (October 1976), 312–17; Alan Hughes, *Henry Irving, Shakespearean* (Cambridge: Cambridge University Press, 1981); Alan Hughes, "Henry Irving's Tragedy of Shylock," *ETJ,* 24 (October 1972), 249–68; Laurence Irving, *Henry Irving, The Actor and His World* (New York: The Macmillan Company, 1952); Herbert W. Kline, *Henry Irving and the Lyceum Company in America* (unpublished dissertation, University of Illinois at Urbana, 1967); Roger Manvell, *Ellen Terry* (London: Heinemann, 1968); Edward M. Moore, "Henry Irving's Shakespearean Productions," *Theatre Survey,* 17 (November 1976), pp. 195–216 Odell, *Annals of the New York Stage,* XII–XV; George C. D. Odell, *Shakespeare from Betterton to Irving,* 2 vols. (New York: Scribners, 1920; reprint, New York: Benjamin Blom, 1963); Wendy Phyllis Rouder, *Henry Irving's Macbeth* (unpublished Ph.D. diss., University of Illinois at Urbana, 1971); George Rowell, *Theatre in the Age of Irving* (Totowa, N.J.: Rowman and Littlefield, 1981); H. A. Saintsbury and Cecil Palmer, eds., *We Saw Him Act. A Symposium on the Art of Sir Henry Irving* (London: Hurst & Blackett, 1930; reprint, New York: Benjamin Blom, 1969); John Ranken Towse, *Sixty Years* pp. 235–47, 285–317; William Winter, *Henry Irving* (New York: George J. Coombs, 1885); William Winter, *Shakespeare on the Stage,* I, II.

86. Fiske's column in the *Spirit of the Times* is dated October 17; the issue appeared October 20.

87. Brereton, I, 372ff.; L. Irving, pp. 408–9.

88. Brereton, II, 14–16, 33, 35–37, 47–48; L. Irving, pp. 416–34; Winter, *Henry Irving,* pp. 1–2, 115–17.

89. Shaw suspected Irving of more serious attempts to ingratiate critics by paying them to translate plays which he would never produce. He claimed that Irving tried to buy an option on *The Man of Destiny* in order to win Shaw's good opinion in order to shelve the play. See the Shaw-Terry correspondence passim.

90. Brereton, II, pp. 113–14, 129–33, 264–25, 171–73, 276–77, 217–23.

91. *Ellen Terry's Memoirs,* p. 128.

92. L. Irving, Appendix B, pp. 685–709.

93. New York *Tribune,* October 30, 1883; Winter, *Henry Irving,* p. 7.

94. *New York Times,* October 30, 1883.

95. New York *Tribune,* October 31, 1883.

96. J. Hudson Kirby, a flamboyant actor of the 1830s and 1840s, inspired the once famous saying, "Wake me up when Kirby dies."

97. *Spirit of the Times,* November 17, 1883.

98. L. Irving, p. 646.

99. See Stephen C. Schultz, "Toward an Irvingesque Theory of Shakespearean Acting," *Quarterly Journal of Speech,* LXI (December 1975), pp. 428–38. See Brereton, I, 121–22, 342; L. Irving, pp. 499–500, 675–84; *Ellen Terry's Memoirs,* pp. 165–66; Manvell, p. 193; W. L. Courtney, "Momus: A Socratic Dialogue," *National Review* (April 1892), p. 224; Henry Irving, *The Drama* (New York: Tait, Sons & Company, 1892), pp. 10–12.

100. Winter, *Shakespeare on the Stage,* I, 175.

101. L. Irving, pp. 333–34.

102. Odell, *Shakespeare from Betterton to Irving,* II, 353–54.

103. Winter, *Shakespeare on the Stage,* I, 186–87.

104. Brereton, I 306–7.

105. Brereton, I, 311–16.

106. The following account of Irving's performance is derived from Winter's Shakespeare on the Stage, I, 171–97; Brereton, I, 301–8; L. Irving, pp. 339–44; Toby Lelyfeld, *Shylock on the Stage* (London: Routledge Kegan & Paul, 1961), pp. 79–95; *Ellen Terry's Memoirs,* pp. 146–47; and many American reviews. Alan Hughes (p. 233) does not find in English reviews that Irving cried, "No, no, no," after wishing Jessica dead. Very likely this was one of Irving's later "softenings" of Shylock. See Edward Moore, p. 202.

107. Boston *Evening Transcript,* December 13, 1883.

108. New York *Herald,* November 7, 1883.

109. *Spirit of the Times,* November 10, 1893.

110. Odell, *Annals,* XII, 224.

111. *New York Times,* November 7, 1883.

112. Boston *Evening Transcript,* October 24, 1884.

113. *The Fashionable Tragedian* (Edinborough and Glasgow: Thomas Gray and Company, 1877), known to have been written by William Archer and Robert Lowe. On the occasion of Irving's *Henry VIII* in 1892, Lowe apologized for this "sin of youth." See L. Irving, p. 543.

114. *Dramatic Mirror,* November 3, 1883. "Count Joannes," born George Jones, a proper tragedian in the 1830s and 1840s, assumed the title of Count after a sojourn in Europe. Eccentric to the point of madness, in the 1870s he became identified with the "hero" of H. J. Byron's skit called *The Crushed Tragedian.*

115. Craig, pp. 62–69.

116. Clapp's article in the March 1884, *Atlantic,* 53, pp. 413–22 is reprinted in his *Reminiscences of a Dramatic Critic,* pp. 194–236. The fellow-critic who invoked Volapük (the artificial language invented in 1879) to identify Irving's *"patois"* was J. R. Towse, *Sixty Years,* p. 303.

117. *Spirit of the Times,* November 29, 1884.

118. Stephen Schultz, "Toward an Irvingesque Theory of Shakespearean Acting," p. 434.

119. *Dramatic Mirror,* December 29, 1883. I cannot identify "J.M.M." He claims to have seen Irving before 1883 in *Hamlet, Othello,* and *Macbeth,* so he must have spent time in England.

120. *Dramatic Mirror,* April 5, 1884.

121. Boston *Evening Transcript,* February 28, 1884.

122. New York *Tribune,* April 1, 1884.

123. Unidentified Boston clipping (Harvard Theatre Collection).

124. New York *Tribune,* April 1, 1884; Winter, *Henry Irving,* pp. 61–63.

125. Boston *Evening Transcript,* February 28, 1884.

126. *New York Times,* April 1, 1884; *Herald,* April 1, 1884; Boston *Advertiser,* March 14, 1894. Fiske of the *Dramatic Mirror* simply lost his temper and wrote abusively. Irving was "incapable" of playing

Benedick; he was too old, he was ugly, cynical, crusty saturnine, grotesque, absurd, "as playful as the baby elephant at Barnum's" etc.

127. William Winter in the *Tribune,* April 1, 1884.

128. L. Irving, 402. Forbes-Robertson's painting is now at The Players.

129. Clapp in the Boston *Advertiser,* March 14, 1894; and an unidentified Boston clipping (Harvard Theatre Collection).

130. *Ellen Terry's Memoirs,* pp. 127–28; Boston *Evening Transcript,* October 23, 1895. The gag goes back at least to John Philip Kemble's time. Kemble, who probably invented it, inked an extended version of it on an interleaf of his promptbook.

131. Brereton, II, pp. 54–56, 61–62; L. Irving, pp. 438–41; *Ellen Terry's Memoirs,* pp. 179–80.

132. Brereton, II, 55; New York *Tribune,* November 19, 1884; Winter, *Henry Irving,* p. 82.

133. New York *Herald,* November 19, 1884; *New York Times,* November 19, 1884; *Spirit of the Times,* November 22, 1884; *The Critic,* November 22, 1884; L. Irving, pp. 440–41.

134. Boston *Journal,* November 6, 1884; *Spirit of the Times,* November 8, 1884; New York *Herald,* November 19, 1884; *Dramatic Mirror,* November 22, 1884.

135. *Illustrated London News,* July 19, 1884, quoted in Odell, *Shakespeare from Betterton to Irving,* II, 431–32; New York *Herald,* November 19, 1884.

136. *Spirit of the Times,* November 15, 1884; March 28, 1885.

137. Clement Scott in the London *Daily Telegraph,* November 1, 1874, quoted at length in Brereton, I, 171–74. See below, note 141.

138. Russell's long review in the Liverpool *Daily Post* is largely reprinted in Brereton, I, 176–85. See for this note on soliloquies, p. 182.

139. Winter, *Shakespeare on the Stage,* I, 358.

140. L Irving, pp. 432–33.

141. *New York Times,* December 5, 1883. Just as in London in 1874, Irving's first two acts brought no applause. See Alan Hughes, pp. 29–30.

142. Clapp's essay is in the *Atlantic Monthly* 53 (March 1884), 413–22 reprinted in his *Reminiscences,* pp. 194–236. Towse's essay is in the *Century* 27, (March 1884), pp. 660–69.

143. L. Irving, pp. 432–33.

144. *New York Times,* November 27, 1884. A new critic refers vaguely to a previous review in January. Montgomery's review appeared December 5, 1883.

145. Nym Crinkle in the New York *World,* quoted by L. Irving, p. 446.

146. New York *Tribune,* November 27, 1884; Winter, *Henry Irving,* pp. 84–96.

147. *Spirit of the Times,* December 6, 1884.

148. *Dramatic Mirror,* December 6, 1884. Edmund Dantes is James O'Neill's famous role in *Monte Cristo.*

149. New York *Herald,* November 27, 1884.

150. L. Irving, pp. 554–62.

151. Brereton, II, 166.

152. Brereton, II, 166–67; L. Irving, p. 542.

153. *Ellen Terry's Memoirs,* pp. 239–40.

154. *Dramatic Mirror,* December 9, 1893.

155. Brereton, II, 178–85; L. Irving, pp. 554–62.

156. New York *Tribune,* December 5, 1893.

157. Brereton, II, 169.

158. L. Irving, p. 558.

159. New York *Tribune,* December 5, 1893; *New York Times,* December 5, 1893.

160. *New York Times,* December 5, 1893.

161. *New York Times,* October 30, 1895.

162. Irving's lecture on *Macbeth* was first given at Owen's College, Manchester, in December 1894 (Brereton, II, 274). He gave it again, at Columbia University, on November 25, 1895. It is printed in Thomas B. Reed, ed., *Modern Eloquence,* VIII (Philadelphia: John D. Morris and Company, 1900), 724–38.

163. L. Irving, p. 260.

164. New York *Herald,* October 30, 1895; New York *Morning Advertiser,* October 30, 1895; Boston *Advertiser,* April 22, 1896; Towse, *Sixty Years,* pp. 301–4.

165. New York *World,* November 3, 1895.

166. W. Graham Robertson, *Life Was Worth Living* (New York: Harper and Brothers [1931], p. 162.

167. *The Critic,* November 9, 1895; *The Mail and Express,* October 30, 1895; New York *Sun,* November 1, 1895; *New York Times,* October 30, 1895.

168. New York *World,* December 18, 1895.

169. *Ellen Terry's Memoirs,* p. 234.

170. *The Critic,* November 9, 1895; New York *Sunday Herald,* November 3, 1895; Boston *Advertiser,* April 22, 1896; *Life,* November 14, 1895; *Dramatic Mirror,* November 9, 1895; Boston *Globe,* April 22, 1895; New York *Mail and Express,* October 30, 1895; Boston *Advertiser,* April 22, 1896; New York *Sun,* November 1, 1895.

171. For her preparation of Lady Macbeth, see *Ellen Terry's Memoirs,* pp. 231–35; L. Irving, pp. 499–503; Manvell, pp. 191–202.

172. Brereton, II, 137–38.

173. Manvell, p. 194. In his Appendix I, pp. 356–62, Manvell has printed most of the rehearsal notes Miss Terry jotted in her study books of *Macbeth.* See also Wendy Rouder, whose dissertation is a "reconstruction" of Irving's production.

174. New York *Morning Advertiser,* October 30, 1895.

175. The Sargent portrait belonged to Irving. After his death in 1905, Sir Joseph Duveen bought it and presented it to the nation. For over half a century it hung in the Tate Gallery; it is now in the National Portrait Gallery.

176. Manvell, p. 201.

177. *The Critic,* November 9, 1895.

178. *Ellen Terry's Memoirs,* p. 233.

179. *The Critic,* November 9, 1895.

180. New York *World,* November 3, 1895.

181. *Dramatic Mirror,* November 9, 1895. The following notes on major scenes are derived partly from reviews and largely from drawings of scenes collected by Wendy Rouder and included in her dissertation.

182. *Spirit of the Times,* August 14, 21, 28, 1886. These reports were probably written by Stephen Fiske. Both he and his editor E. A. Buck were guests of Irving at the Delmonico banquet.

183. Gordon Crosse, *Shakespearean Playgoing 1890–1952* (London: A. R. Mowbray & Co., Ltd., 1953), p. 15.

184. Most of the following opinions are expressed in Henry Clapp's essay in the *Atlantic Monthly* (January 1884), or in his *Reminiscences of a Dramatic Critic* (1902); or in John R. Towse's essay in the *Century* XXVII (March 1884), or in his *Sixty Years* (1916), pp. 235ff. and 286ff.

185. New York *Tribune,* November 27, 1884; Winter, *Henry Irving,* pp. 86–87.

186. Ellen Terry's *Memoirs,* p. 82.

187. *Dramatic Mirror,* December 29, 1883.

188. Louis Frederick Austin (pseud. Frederic Daly), *Henry Irving in England and America* (New York: R. Worthington, 1884), p. 282.

189. Ellen Terry's *Memoirs,* pp. 249ff.

190. The official biography of Tree is Hesketh Pearson, *Beerbohm Tree, His Life and Laughter* (New York: Harper & Brothers, 1956). An early study is Mrs. George Cran, *Herbert Beerbohm Tree* (London: John Lane, The Bodley Head, 1907). Soon after Tree's death his half-brother Max Beerbohm brought out *Herbert Beerbohm Tree.*

Some Memories of Him and His Art, Collected by Max Beerbohm (New York: E. P. Dutton and Company, n.d.). This contains the reminiscences of his wife, his daughters, Max himself, seven essays by friends and associates, and some of Tree's own writings. A recent biography is Madeleine Bingham, *The Great Lover* (London: Atheneum, 1979). A valuable article is Leonard H. Knight, "Beerbohm Tree in America," *Theatre Survey,* VIII (May 1967), pp. 37–52. Another is Ralph Berry, "Beerbohm Tree as Director: Three Shakespearean Productions," *Theatre Studies* I (May 1983), pp. 81–100. Chapters or sections devoted to Tree appear in John Ranken Towse, *Sixty Years of the Theatre, An Old Critic's Memories* (New York and London: Funk & Wagnalls Company, 1916); Donald Brook, *A Pageant of Actors* (London: Rockliff, 1950); Hesketh Pearson, *The Last Actor-Managers* (London: Methuen & Co. Ltd., 1950); Bertram Joseph, *The Tragic Actor* (London: Routledge and Kegan Paul, 1959); Frances Donaldson, *The Actor-Managers* (Chicago: Henry Regnery Company, 1970). William Winter has described Tree's Hamlet in *Shakespeare on the Stage,* I and Falstaff in III. Reminiscences of Tree occur in the autobiographies of numerous fellow-actors, including Oscar Asche, Constance Collier, Ellen Terry, Seymour Hicks, H. Chance Newton, and Elizabeth Robins. Tree left three volumes of essays, of which the most interesting is *Thoughts and After-Thoughts* (New York and London: Funk and Wagnalls, 1913).

191. Tree, *Thoughts and After-Thoughts,* pp. 201–2.

192. "Herbert and I" in Max Beerbohm, pp. 21, 63, 109, 117, etc. See also Winter, *Shakespeare on the Stage,* I, 387–88; and Pearson, *Beerbohm Tree,* p. 191.

193. For Shaw on Irving, see *Our Theatres in the Nineties,* II, 198–99.

194. For Shaw on Tree, see Max Beerbohm, 241–52.

195. For Courtney on Tree, see Max Beerbohm, p. 258.

196. Pearson, *Beerbohm Tree,* p. 117.

197. For Shaw on Tree, see Max Beerbohm, p. 248.

198. Maud Tree, in Max Beerbohm, pp. 27, 31.

199. Pearson, *Beerbohm Tree,* pp. 59ff.

200. Ibid., pp. 116ff.

201. Ibid., pp. 165ff.

202. Robert Speaight, *William Poel and the Elizabethan Revival* (Cambridge: Harvard University Press, 1954), p. 121.

203. Pearson, *Beerbohm Tree,* pp. 158–161; C. B. Purdom, *Harley Granville Barker: Man of the Theatre, Dramatist and Scholar* (Cambridge: Harvard University Press, 1956), Index (*see* National Theatre).

204. New York *Evening Post,* February 16, 1895.

205. Towse, *Sixty Years,* p. 438.

206. Boston *Journal,* March 26, 1895.

207. *New York Times,* February 17, 1895.

208. *The Critic,* February 23, 1895.

209. *New York Times,* February 17, 1895.

210. James's comment occurred in "After the Play," *New Review* (June 1889). See *Henry James, The Scenic Art,* ed. Alan Wade (New York: Hill and Wang, Inc., 1957), pp. 241–42.

211. *New York Tribune,* February 16, 1895.

212.*New York Times,* February 22, 1895.

213. New York *Herald,* February 22, 1895.

214. Boston *Herald,* February 29, 1895.

215. Pearson, *Beerbohm Tree,* p. 64. Gilbert's actual remark was, "My dear fellow, I never saw anything so funny in my life, and yet it was not in the least vulgar."

216. Pearson, *Beerbohm Tree,* p. 63.

217. New York *Tribune,* February 22, 1895.

218. *The Critic,* March 2, 1895.

219. Tree's lecture is in *Thoughts and After-Thoughts,* pp. 123–54.

220. J. Dover Wilson, *What Happens in Hamlet* (Cambridge: Cambridge University Press, 1937).

221. A review signed by George T. Richardson in an unidentified Boston newspaper, March 29, 1895 (Harvard Theatre Collection).

222. New York *Tribune,* February 22, 1895.

223. Pearson, *Beerbohm Tree,* pp. 94–98.

224. Bernard Shaw, *Our Theatres in the Nineties,* II, 130–31.

225. New York *Tribune,* December 8, 1896.

226. For the complete story of Tree in Hollywood, see Robert Hamilton Ball, *Shakespeare on Silent Film, A Strange Eventful History* (New York: Theatre Arts Books, 1968), pp. 229–35, 362–63.

227. *The North American Review* (May 1916), 763–65.

228. Tree's arguments in support of his "modern method" and his attacks on "the new movement" are scattered through *Thoughts and After-Thoughts.* See especially "The Living Shakespeare," pp. 39–72.

229. J. L. Styan, *The Shakespeare Revolution* (Cambridge: Cambridge University Press, 1977).

230. *New York Times,* March 15, 1916.

231. New York *Evening Post,* March 18, 1916.

232. *New York Times,* March 19, 1916.

233. *The New Republic,* March 25, 1916.

234. New York *Tribune,* March 15, 1916.

235. New York *Herald,* March 15, 1916.

236. Odell, *Shakespeare from Betterton to Irving,* II, 463–64.

237. *New York Times,* May 9, 1916.

238. Unidentified clipping, "The World of Drama" (Harvard Theatre Collection).

239. Unidentified New York paper, May 9, 1916 (Harvard Theatre Collection).

240. New York *Tribune,* May 9, 1916.

241. *Life,* May 18, 1916.

242. New York *Evening Mail,* May 9, 1916.

243. *New York Times,* May 9, 1916.

244. New York *Tribune,* May 9, 1916.

245. New York *American,* May 9, 1916.

246. New York *Evening Mail,* May 9, 1916.

247. New York *Evening Post,* May 9, 1916. Among the many papers that report the scene of Shylock's homecoming are the *Brooklyn Eagle,* the New York *Evening Post,* the *Journal of Commerce, The Nation,* the New York *Sun,* and *Theatre.*

248. New York *Herald,* May 9, 1916.

249. *New York Times,* May 9, 1916.

250. Unidentified clipping, "The World of Drama" (Harvard Theatre Collection).

251. *The Nation* (June 8, 1916).

252. *New York Times,* May 26, 1916.

253. New York *Tribune,* May 26, 1916.

254. *Boston Evening Transcript,* November 1, 1916.

255. *The Nation* (June 8, 1916).

256. New York *Tribune,* May 26, 1916.

257. *Dramatic Mirror,* June 3, 1916.

258. Shaw, in *Max Beerbohm,* p. 246.

259. Pearson, *Beerbohm Tree,* p. 234.

260. The only "formal" biographies of Sir Johnston Forbes-Robertson are the entries in the *Dictionary of National Biography* and *Who Was Who in the Theatre.* During his retirement he published a rambling and chatty set of reminiscenses, *A Player Under Three Reigns* (Boston: Little, Brown, and Company, 1925). Appreciative chapters are devoted to him by Hesketh Pearson, *The Last Actor-Managers* (London: Methuen & Co., 1950); Kenneth Bruce Findlater, *Six Great Actors* (London: Hamish Hamilton, 1957); and Frances Donaldson, *The Actor Managers* (Chicago: Henry Regnery Com-

pany, 1970). Countless notes on him occur, of course, in G. C. D. Odell's *Shakespeare from Betterton to Irving,* in Bertram Joseph's *The Tragic Actor,* and in the reminiscences of the many actors, critics, and friends of his time.

261. Forbes-Robertson, *A Player Under Three Reigns,* p. 320.

262. Bernard Shaw, review of September 28, 1895, in *Our Theatres in the Nineties,* I, 197–204.

263. Forbes-Robertson, pp. 182–83.

264. Shaw to Ellen Terry, July 27, 1897. In *Ellen Terry and Bernard Shaw, A Correspondence,* edited by Christopher St. John (New York: Theatre Arts Books, 1949), pp. 217–18.

265. Shaw, review of October 2, 1897, in *Our Theatres in the Nineties,* III, 200–207.

266. W. A. Armstrong, "Bernard Shaw and Forbes-Robertson's *Hamlet,*" *Shakespeare Quarterly* XV (Winter 1964), 27–31. Forbes-Robertson's *Hamlet* promptbook at the Huntington Library is probably a late one, "for the road." It is very heavily cut.

267. Forbes-Robertson, pp. 183–84.

268. The *Times,* September 13, 1897.

269. *Daily Telegraph,* September 13, 1897, reprinted in *Some Notable Hamlets of the Present Time* (London: Greening & Co., 1960), pp. 152ff.

270. See especially *Our Theatres in the Nineties,* III, 206.

271. See especially *Our Theatres in the Nineties,* III, 201.

272. J. Redfern Mason, "Forbes Robertson's Coming Visit," the *Theatre* (August 1903), pp. 198–200.

273. Forbes-Robertson gives a not very informative account of these dealings, pp. 249–50. For Klauber's suspicions and Corbin's explanation see the *New York Times,* November 10, 1903 and the Sunday edition of November 15.

274. *New York Times,* March 8, 1904; New York *Herald,* March 8, 1904; *Dramatic Mirror,* March 19, 1904; Sunday issue of the *New York Times,* March 13, 1904; *Life,* March 24, 1904; *The Theatre Magazine* (April 1904).

275. New York *Evening Post,* March 8, 1904.

276. New York *Evening Post,* March 14, 1905.

277. New York *Tribune,* March 8, 1904, and March 14, 1905.

278. New York *Tribune,* March 14, 1905.

279. Sunday issue of the *New York Times,* March 13, 1904.

280. *New York Times,* March 8, 1904.

281. Clipping from an undated Baltimore paper (Harvard Theatre Collection).

282. Boston *Transcript,* January 23, 1907.

283. Boston *Transcript,* January 24, 1907.

284. The Harvard performances were generously reviewed in the Boston *Transcript,* the Boston *Herald,* and other papers, and Baker published a formal report in the 1905 *Shakespeare Jahrbuch,* pp. 297–301. The most recent account of Forbes-Robertson's performances of *Hamlet* on Professor Baker's Globe stage (1904 and 1916) is an essay by Jeanne Newlin, Curator of the Harvard Theatre Collection, in a brochure entitled *Shakespeare's First Globe Theatre.* This brochure (a collector's item) was issued by the Harvard Theatre Collection on April 3, 1980, on the occasion of the unveiling of C. Walter Hodges's model of the Globe, which he has presented to the Collection. Dr. Newlin's essay, "An Open Stage for Shakespeare," is preliminary to her forthcoming comprehensive study of Baker's achievements and his influence on open staging in future productions of Shakespeare.

285. Shaw's famous tribute to Forbes-Robertson is part of an article he published in *Play Pictorial* (October 1907) just before the London production of *Caesar and Cleopatra.* The whole article is reprinted in Raymond Mander and Joe Mitchenson, *Theatrical Companion to Shaw* (London: Rockliff, 1954), pp. 63–fl4.

286. Hesketh Pearson, p. 6. It is schocking to realize that the finest Hamlet of his generation was compelled (to make a living?), by the benighted standards of the "best class" of theatre-goers, to repeat "this *bloody* part" endlessly.

287. Descriptions of the new Shubert Theatre and accounts of Sir Johnston's opening performance of *Hamlet* were published in all the leading newspapers (e.g., the *New York Times,* the New York *Herald,* the New York *Tribune* of October 3, 1913). The *Dramatic Mirror,* October 8, carried a piece of Frederick F. Schrader, then its editor, claiming to have been the first in America to have recognized the preeminence of Forbes-Robertson's *Hamlet. The Nation,* October 9, and *Life* October 16, carried interesting reviews of *Hamlet.* Since this was to be Sir Johnston's farewell to the New York stage, the *Theatre Magazine* (December 1913) carried two articles about him, one by Marion Taylor, and one (a long interview) by Ada Patterson. At the end of his run, over one hundred members of the Press Club, J. I. C. Clarke in the chair, feted him; and another banquet by the Civic Forum, Isaac N. Seligman presiding, with four hundred guests, was given the evening before Sir Johnston and Lady Forbes-Robertson sailed for home. Records of these celebrations are preserved in the Seligman-Eisenstein scrapbook in the Folger Shakespeare Library.

288. *Philadelphia Inquirer,* February 1, 1907. New York reviews appear in the *New York Times,* the *Herald,* the *Tribune,* November 22, 1913. A review by N. H. appeared in *Harper's Weekly* 58 (December 13, 1913).

289. *Dramatic Mirror,* November 26, 1913.

290. Boston *Evening Transcript,* January 31, 1914.

291. *New York Times,* December 16, 1913.

292. New York *Tribune,* December 16, 1913.

293. Boston *Evening Transcript,* February 12, 1914. See also the New York *Herald,* December 16, 1913; *Dramatic Mirror,* December 17, 1913; *The Nation,* December 18, 1913; and *Life,* December 25, 1913.

294. Ray Henderson, "On the Farewell Highway with Sir J. Forbes-Robertson," *Dramatic Mirror,* September 9, 1916.

295. *Brooklyn Times,* April 11, 1916; Brooklyn *Standard Union,* April 11, 1916.

296. This event was widely covered. See, e.g., *The Christian Science Monitor,* April 26, 1916; unidentified clippings in the Harvard Theatre Collection, April 25 and April 27, 1916; and *The Nation,* May 4, 1916.

297. Bostion *Evening Transcript,* January 27, 1914.

V. Mansfield and Mantell

1. *Spirit of the Times,* December 22, 1883; *Life,* January 3, 1884; Boston *Gazette,* December 2, 1883. Booth was then in low spirits, exhausted from travel and personal worries.

2. New York *World,* January 9, 1870; A. C. Wheeler (Nym Crinkle), "The Extinction of Shakespeare," *Arena,* I (March 1890), pp. 423–31.

3. Octave Feuillet's *Un Roman Parisienne* was first produced at the Gymnase-Dramatique on October 28, 1882. Mansfield's translation was made by A. R. Cazauron.

4. William Winter, *The Life and Art of Richard Mansfield,* 2 vols. (New York: Moffat, Yard, & Co., 1910; reprint, Westport, Conn.: Greenwood, 1970), II, 14.

5. Stevenson's *The Strange Case of Dr. Jekyll and Mr. Hyde* appeared in 1886. The dramatization, in 1887, was made for Mansfield by Thomas Russell Sullivan.

6. Winter, *Life and Art,* II, 43.

7. Two biographies of Mansfield appeared shortly after his death. Paul Wilstach, his press agent, published *Richard Mansfield, The Man and the Actor* (London: Chapman and Hall, 1908); and William Winter, the "official" biographer, brought out *The Life and Art of Richard Mansfield,* 2 vols. (New York: Moffat, Yard, & Co., 1910; reprint, Greenwood, 1970). Winter's first volume is the biography; the second is reviews of each of his roles, plus a valuable Chronology. Winter reviews Mansfield's roles again in *Shakespeare*

on the Stage, I (New York: Moffat, Yard, & Co., 1911; reprint, New York: Benjamin Blom, 1969), 119–21, 197–200; and III (New York: Moffat, Yard, & Co., 1915, reprint, New York: Benjamin Blom, 1968–69), 618–19. Valuable essays on Mansfield appear in Garff Wilson, *A History of American Acting* (Bloomington: Indiana University Press, 1966), 206–13, and Edward Wagenknecht, *Merely Players* (Norman: University of Oklahoma Press, 1966), 214–38. Unpublished Ph.D. dissertations on "The Acting of Richard Mansfield," by Jack Bibee, (University of Illinois, 1974), and "The Shakespearean Acting of Richard Mansfield" by Alex Pinkston (University of California at Los Angeles, 1980) have been very useful to me. There are of course a vast number of notes and articles on Mansfield written by his contemporaries and by later critics.

8. Paul Case, "The Real Richard Mansfield," *Theatre Magazine* (August 1914), pp. 61–62.

9. John Corbin, "The Greatest English Actor," *Appleton's Magazine,* IX (1907), pp. 288–89. Mansfield described this system of Klang-farbe to students in the Empire School of Acting. See also Wilstach, p. 235; Kenyon West, "Richard Mansfield," *Arena,* XXXV (January 1906), p. 15.

10. Wilstach, pp. 74–75.

11. Wilstach, p. 193; Winter, *Life and Art,* I, 139, 230–31, 310.

12. Wilstach, p. 264.

13. For Shaw's letters to Mansfield, Miss Achurch, and others on the *Candida* affair, see Bernard Shaw, *Collected Letters, 1874–1897,* ed. Dan H. Lawrence (New York: Dodd, Mead & Company, 1965), pp. 494–524.

14. For the full text of this letter see Shaw's *Collected Letters, 1874–1897,* pp. 522–24. Also printed in Archibald Henderson, *George Bernard Shaw, Man of the Century* (New York: Appleton-Century-Crofts, 1956), pp. 438–39.

15. Winter, *Life and Art,* II, 130.

16. Ibid., 136.

17. Wilstach, pp. 156–60.

18. Mansfield to Dithmar, January 26, 1887 (The Folger Shakespeare Library, Y.c. 489 [14a]).

19. Richard Mansfield, "The Story of a Production," *Harper's Weekly,* XXXIV (May 24, 1890), 407–8. The following descriptons of scenery are largely taken from the same source, the actions from various reviews.

20. Winter, *Life and Art,* I, 107.

21. John Ranken Towse, *Sixty Years* (New York: Funk and Wagnalls Company, 1916), p. 326.

22. Wilstach, p. 183.

23. Many critics list major omissions. The Boston *Post,* October 22, 1889, gives as full a reckoning as any.

24. E.g. *Times,* March 18, 1889; *Era,* March 23, 1889.

25. E.g., the *Times,* May 18, 1889.

26. Winter, *Life and Art,* I, 107.

27. *The Saturday Review,* March 23, 1889.

28. The *Times,* March 18, 1889.

29. Winter, *Life and Art,* I, 107–8.

30. Ibid., I, 111.

31. Austin Brereton, *The Life of Henry Irving,* 2 vols. (New York: Longmans, Green, and Co., 1908), II, 129; Winter, *Life and Art,* I, 200, 258.

32. Wilstach, p. 188.

33. *New York Times,* October 22, 1889.

34. New York *Tribune,* October 22, 1889.

35. Boston *Herald,* October 22, 1889.

36. The Boston *Advertiser,* Boston *Transcript,* Boston *Post,* all of October 22, 1889. Mansfield received one letter that probably represented widespread opinion: "Give us more hump." Wilstach, p. 189.

37. Winter, *Life and Art,* I, 114.

38. Ibid., I. 117.

39. For the New York opening, see G. C. D. Odell, *Annals of the New York Stage,* 15 vols. (New York: Columbia University Press, 1927–49), XIV, 237–9.

40. Winter, *Life and Art,* I, 119.

41. Though *Beau Brummel* is officially credited to Clyde Fitch, Winter furiously contested Fitch's claim to it. See Winter, *Life and Art,* II, 301-12.

42. Wilstach, p. 243.

43. Ibid., pp. 243–48.

44. Odell's *Annals,* XV, 614–15.

45. Mansfield to Winter, October 30, 1893 (The Folger Shakespeare Library, Y.c. 489 [137]).

46. New York *Tribune,* October 24, 1893.

47. Winter, *Life and Art,* I, 193.

48. Mansfield to Mrs. Winter, November 14, 1893 (The Folger Shakespeare Library, Y.c. 489 [106]).

49. Mrs. Winter to Mansfield, November 19, 1893 (The Folger Shakespeare Library, Y.c. 489 [106]).

50. Wilstach, p. 252.

51. Winter, *Life and Art,* II, 118.

52. William Winter, *Shakespeare on the Stage,* I, 200.

53. Wilstach, pp. 243–48.

54. Winter, *Life and Art,* I, 240.

55. *The Richard Mansfield Acting Version of King Henry V . . .* (New York: McClure, Phillips & Co. 1901), pp. xi–xiv.

56. Wilstach, p. 349.

57. Derived from Mansfield's "Act Four," pp. 97–99, and from various reviews.

58. Boston *Advertiser,* April 19, 1901.

59. *New York Times,* October 4, 1900.

60. New York *Tribune,* October 4, 1900.

61. *Dramatic Mirror,* October 13, 1900.

62. Boston *Herald,* April 8, 1901.

63. Norman Hapgood, *The Stage in America, 1897–1900* (New York: The Macmillan Company, 1901), p. 177.

64. Sybil Rosenfield, "Alma-Tadema's Designs for Henry Irving's *Coriolanus,*" *Deutsche Shakespeare Gesellschaft West: Jahrbuch 1974,* pp. 84–95. See also Phene Spiers, "The Architecture of *Coriolanus,*" *Architectural Review,* X (July 1901), pp. 3–21.

65. W. A. Stanley, "Richard Mansfield's Real Self," *Theatre* (October 1957), pp. 200–201.

66. Chicago *Daily News,* Chicago *Evening Post,* Chicago *Record-Herald,* Chicago *Tribune,* October 15, 1902.

67. *New York Times,* December 2, 1902.

68. *Theatre* (January 1903), pp. 3–4.

69. *Dramatic Mirror,* December 13, 1902.

70. Unidentified New York newspaper (Harvard Theatre Collection).

71. William Lyon Phelps, "Shakespeare in New York," *Independent,* February 5, 1903, p. 298.

72. Unidentified Boston paper, January 20, 1903, signed W. F. A. (Harvard Theatre Collection).

73. Boston *Herald,* January 20, 1903. Review identified as by Clapp.

74. New York *Sun.* Review identified as by James Huneker.

75. Stanley, "Richard Mansfield's Real Self."

76. Alan Dale, "Who Is Our Worst Actor?" *Cosmopolitan,* XL (April 1906), pp. 683–90.

77. John Corbin, "The Greatest English Actor," *Appleton's Magazine,* IX (1907), pp. 287–94.

78. Only one book-length account of Mantell exists: C. J. Bulliet, *Robert Mantell's Romance* (Boston: John W. Luce & Company, 1918). Bulliet was an agent of Mantell's and Mantell assisted in providing information about his early days. See p. 242. William

Winter discusses Mantell's roles in the three volumes of his *Shakespeare on the Stage.* In I, p. 210 (Shylock); pp. 311–12 (Othello); pp. 493–98 (Macbeth). In II, p. 170 (Romeo), pp. 462–65 (Lear). In III, pp. 508–16 (King John). Several brief articles, some by Mantell himself, appeared in popular magazines during his life. One useful piece is by Wendell Phillips Dodge, "Robert B. Mantell. The Actor who Makes Shakespeare Pay," *The Strand,* XLIII (June 1912), pp. 592–603. The only modern scholarship is an article by Attilio Favorini, "Richard's Himself Again. Robert Mantell's Shakespearean Debut in New York City," *Educational Theatre Journal,* XXIV (December 1972), pp. 402–14.

79. Favorini, "Richard's Himself Again," p. 413.

80. Dodge, "Robert B. Mantell," pp. 602–3.

81. Alan S. Downer, "A Pocketful of Hams," *The Delphian Quarterly* (October 1944), pp. 38–42.

82. For accounts of Mantell's early years, see Bulliet, chapters I to XII.

83. For information about Mantell's early domestic troubles, see *New York Times,* September 11, 1892. See also Bulliet, pp. 140–41.

84. Bulliet, pp. 150–51.

85. Ibid., p. 168.

86. Ibid., pp. 153–56.

87. Ibid., p. 176. See also Dodge, p. 592.

88. For the story of the reentry into New York and the events of the first night of *Richard III,* see Favorini, *passim;* Bulliet, pp. 178–87; and Dodge, pp. 592–96.

89. New York *Tribune,* December 6, 1904; *New York Times,* December 6; New York *Herald,* December 6; *Dramatic Mirror,* December 24, 1904.

90. Dale's comments in the Boston *Journal* are quoted by Favorini, pp. 409–10.

91. New York *Evening Sun,* quoted by Favorini, p. 409.

92. *Theatre* (January 1905), p. 3.

93. Reviews of *Othello* appeared on December 13, 1904; of *Richelieu* on December 20.

94. Brady's remark is recorded by Dodge, p. 596. See also Favorini, 411ff.; and Bulliet, pp. 186 and *passim.*

95. Bulliet, 253–54.

96. *New York Times,* October 24, 1905.

97. New York *Herald,* October 24, 1905.

98. Bulliet, pp. 251–52.

99. New York *Tribune,* October 24, 1905.

100. Ibid., November 10, 1905. He is attacking the Syndicate, of course, but sweeping Brady in with it.

101. Ibid., November 3, 1905.

102. New York *Herald,* November 7, 1905; *Dramatic Mirror,* November 18, 1905.

103. New York *Tribune,* November 7, 1905.

104. *New York Times,* November 14, 1905; New York *Herald,* November 14, 1905; *Dramatic Mirror,* November 25, 1905.

105. New York *Tribune,* November 16, 1905.

106. *Dramatic Mirror,* December 9, 1905.

107. Chicago *Tribune,* March 4, 1906.

108. *Theatre* (December 6, 1906), pp. xx–xxi.

109. New York *Tribune,* November 6, 1906. Winter even mentions that Mantell has added Charles Macklin's Sir Pertinax MacSycophant to his list of roles. This sounds like something Mantell told him he *meant* to do. I doubt that it ever came to pass.

110. New York *Tribune,* November 13, 1906.

111. New York *Tribune,* November 27, 1906.

112. Boston *Transcript,* February 26, 1907.

113. Boston *Transcript,* March 2, 1907.

114. *The Crushed Tragedian,* by H. J. Byron, was supposed to be based on the character of a half-mad tragedian, George Jones, who called himself Count Joannes.

115. Boston *Evening Transcript,* March 12, 1907.

116. Boston *Evening Transcript,* March 5, 1907.

117. Boston *Transcript,* March 7, 1907.

118. Chicago *Evening Post,* November 19, 1907.

119. Chicago *Tribune,* November 20, 1907.

120. New York *Tribune,* January 12, 1909. Again Winter is blasting the Syndicate.

121. Bulliet, p. 223.

122. New York *Herald,* March 9, 1909; *New York Times,* March 9; *The Nation* (March 11, p. 258).

123. New York *Tribune,* March 12, 1909.

124. New York *Tribune,* March 9, 1909.

125. New York *Tribune,* March 20, 16, 25, 1909.

126. New York *Herald,* February 7, 1915.

127. Bulliet, p. 248. He did return to New York in May to be one of the voices in Percy MacKaye's Masque of *Caliban.*

128. See complete figures for 1916 in William Lyon Phelps, *The Twentieth Century Theatre* (New York: The Macmillan Company, 1918), pp. 103–4.

129. *Life,* April 26, 1917, p. 728.

130. *New York Times,* November 25, 1906. Favorini lists the same statement in the New York *Journal,* December 14, 1904.

131. *The Nation* (March 11, 1909), p. 258.

132. Boston *Transcript,* May 11, 1920.

VI. Sothern and Marlowe

1. We have two biographies of Julia Marlowe. The excellent official one, *Julia Marlowe, Her Life and Art* (New York and London: D. Appleton and Company, 1926) was written at the close of her stage career by Charles Edward Russell, her devoted admirer and "chief adviser concerning her business affairs" for more than thirty years. The other, *Julia Marlowe's Story* (New York and Toronto: Rinehart & Company, Inc., 1954) was written by E. H. Sothern as dictated by Miss Marlowe, and left in manuscript. It was edited by Fairfax Downey and published after Miss Marlowe's death. A semi-autobiography of Sothern, called *The Melancholy Tale of "Me": My Remembrances* (New York: Scribners, 1916), is a rambling and chattering lot of reminiscences mainly of earlier years. Many articles and notes about Sothern and Marlowe (besides the thousands of reviews) were published during their careers, of which the following are a sample.

Charles E. Russell, "A Notable Dramatic Achievement" (after their first New York season together) in *The Critic,* XLV (December 1904), pp. 525–31. Elizabeth McCracken, "Mr. Sothern as a Producer," in *The Critic,* XLVII (November 1905), pp. 464–86. Elizabeth McCracken, "Julia Marlowe," in the *Century,* LXXIII (November 1906), pp. 47–55. William Winter has treated some of their roles in his three volumes of *Shakespeare on the Stage,* I (New York: Moffat, Yard, & Co., 1911; reprint, New York: Benjamin Blom, 1969), Sothern's Shylock at pp. 208–10, and Hamlet at pp. 388–92; II (New York: Moffatt, Yard, & Co., 1915; reprint, New York: Benjamin Blom, 1969), their joint Malvolio-Viola at pp. 89–91, Romeo-Juliet at pp. 190–93, their Rosalind-Jaques at pp. 303–5; their Katharine-Petruchio at pp. 534–53. In III (New York: Moffat, Yard, & Co., 1916; reprint, New York: Benjamin Blom, 1968–69), he mentions Imogen at p. 136, and treats Antony-Cleopatra at pp. 464–67. In his *Wallet of Time,* 2 vols. (New York: Moffat, Yard, & Co., 1912), Winter writes at greater length about their *Hamlet, Romeo and Juliet, Much Ado,* and *Twelfth Night.* Oscar W. Firkins, "Sothern and Marlowe—An Estimate" (hostile to Sothern, limited approval of Marlowe), in *Theatre Magazine* (October 1913), pp. 118ff. John Ranken Towse devoted a chapter (limited approval) to "Julia Marlowe and E. H. Sothern" in *Sixty Years of the Theatre, An*

Old Critic's Memories (New York: Funk and Wagnalls, 1916), pp. 390–403. Garff B. Wilson in *A History of American Acting* (Bloomington and London: Indiana University Press, 1966) treats Miss Marlowe at pp. 140–45 and Sothern at 213–16. A. Richard Sogliuzzo's "Edward H. Sothern and Julia Marlowe on the Art of Acting," in *Theatre Survey, XI* (November 1970), pp. 187–200 is a well-thought-out analysis based upon a detailed bibliography. A brief essay of Sogliuzzo's, "Edward H. Sothern and Julia Marlowe Direct Shakespeare," was published in Alpha Psi Omega's *Playbill* in 1972. Sallie Mitchell's University of Illinois dissertation, 1976 (unpublished) is entitled "The Early Career of Julia Marlowe: The Making of a Star."

2. The German play was Gerhardt Hauptmann's *The Sunken Bell,* 1896, and the American was Percy Mackaye's *Jeanne d'Arc,* 1906.

3. Arthur Symons, "Great Acting in English," *The Monthly Review,* XXVII (April–June 1907), pp. 14ff. Reprinted in Symons's *Plays, Acting, and Music, A Book of Theory* (New York: E. P. Dutton & Company, 1909), pp. 182–199.

4. Charles Russell skillfully narrates the first twenty or more years of Miss Marlowe's life, before his association with her, in the first eight chapters of his biography. His source of information was for the most part Miss Marlowe herself. His fastidious accuracy suggests that he "checked his references."

5. For these words, presumably Miss Marlowe's own, see Russell, p. 378.

6. On nineteenth-century actors' addiction to "point-making," see Russell, p. 37.

7. Specimens of false readings that Miss Marlowe took note of are given by Russell at pp. 38–39 and p. 49.

8. *The Bookman,* III (November 1920), pp. 207–12.

9. Specimen pages of her promptbook of *The Merchant of Venice* are reproduced by Russell at pp. 442–43. For locations of her vast number of extant promptbooks, see Index to my guide to *The Shakespeare Promptbooks* (Urbana and London: University of Illinois Press, 1965).

10. For the season with Miss Reilly, see Russell, pp. 40–45.

11. For Miss Marlowe's early study under the sponsorship of Ada Dow, and her voice training with Parsons Price, see Russell, chap. III, pp. 46–65.

12. Russell, p. 58.

13. For Alexander Woollcott's splendid tribute, ("Second Thoughts on First Nights," *New York Times,* October 12, 1919), see p. 275.

14. For the invention of the name "Julia Marlowe," see Russell, p. 65.

15. *Ingomar the Barbarian,* translated from the German by Mrs. G. W. Lovell in 1851, was a standard vehicle for romantic ingenues for nearly half a century.

16. The New London *Telegraph,* April 26, 1887. Quoted by Russell, p. 71.

17. Boston *Globe,* May 15, 1887.

18. Stanley McKenna, quoted by Russell, p. 85.

19. *New York Times,* October 20, 1887.

20. The excitements of this first New York matinee are vividly described by Russell, with a long quotation from Nym Crinkle's review, pp. 80–85.

21. *Spirit of the Times,* December 10, 1887.

22. Dithmar in the *New York Times,* Winter in the *Tribune,* both December 13, 1887.

23. Moody Merrill, in *Judge,* quoted by Russell, pp. 105–6.

24. *Spirit of the Times,* December 27, 1887.

25. *New York Times,* December 13, 1887.

26. Boston *Home Journal,* April 12, 1890.

27. New York *Herald,* December 13, 1887.

28. "The Essentials of Stage Success," *Theatre* (December 1901), pp. 13–15.

29. New York *Tribune,* December 13, 1887.

30. New York *Herald,* December 13, 1887.

31. *Spirit of the Times,* December 17, 1887.

32. As told to Russell, pp. 149–50.

33. *Spirit of the Times,* December 17, 1887.

34. The story of Ingersoll's encounter with Winter between the acts at *Romeo and Juliet,* and Winter's ensuing displeasure, is told by Russell, pp. 94–98.

35. New York *Tribune,* December 13, 1887.

36. Ada Rehan's Katherine in the *Shrew* opened on January 18, 1887, and played to April 30, a record of 121 performances.

37. William Winter, *Vagrant Memories, Being Further Recollections of Other Days* (New York: George H. Doran Company, 1915), chapter X, pp. 447–74.

38. *New York Times,* December 15, 1887.

39. New York *Herald,* December 15, 1887.

40. Chicago *Tribune* (summarizing her Juliet, Parthenia, Viola, and Julia), February 19, 1888.

41. Chicago *Herald,* February 15, 1888.

42. Her difficulties in finding a management are narrated by Russell, pp. 119–25. The remark about playing "only good women" occurs on p. 122.

43. For her problems with the Modjeska company, see Russell, pp. 126–30.

44. Quoted from the Washington Sunday *Herald* by Russell, p. 129.

45. Her Boston engagement opened for a week on December 3, 1888—"success, instant and unqualified." It was about this time that Russell became associated with her as business manager.

46. The Boston *Globe* editorial is transcribed by Russell, pp. 137–38.

47. Arthur Warren, then of the Boston *Herald,* would become critic of the New York *Tribune* in 1909 when William Winter was dismissed from that paper. Russell, p. 138.

48. For the opening night in Philadelphia, see Russell, pp. 146–47.

49. For an account of her friendship with L. Clarke Davis, George Childs, H. H. Furness, and other eminent Philadelphians, see Russell, pp. 148–57.

50. Rogers's rapturous account of her Rosalind is transcribed by Russell, p. 154.

51. Augustin Daly's hostility to Miss Marlowe is spelled out from beginning to end, in great detail, by Russell, pp. 275–85. See also *Julia Marlowe's Story,* pp. 82–83.

52. Boston *Herald,* February 19, 1889.

53. Boston *Post,* February 19, 1889.

54. Boston *Transcript,* February 19, 1889.

55. Boston *Advertiser,* February 19, 1889.

56. Clapp is quoting "a sight to make an old man young" from Tennyson's "The Gardener's Daughter," 1.140.

57. *New York Times,* quoted by Russell, p. 160.

58. Her preparations for Beatrice and Imogen during her summer residence with the Ingersolls are discussed by Russell, pp. 170–73.

59. She opened in the Fifth Avenue Theatre in New York in mid-January, but not in *As You Like It,* as she had intended. Daly's *As You Like It* with Ada Rehan's Rosalind had opened on December 17 and was still running strong.

60. Dithmar in the *New York Times,* Winter in the New York *Tribune,* Alan Dale in the New York *World,* Van Cleef in the New York *Herald,* Towse in the New York *Post* (all of January 28, 1890)

criticized her severely. The *Dramatic Mirror* and the *Spirit of the Times* published their strictures in their next issues.

61. The Boston *Post* critic defended Miss Marlowe against the New York attacks on January 29. Another defense appeared on February 13.

62. For this "lost season" and her illness, see Russell, pp. 184–90.

63. Russell, p. 181.

64. Boston *Advertiser,* February 2, 1892.

65. Boston *Transcript,* February 2, 1892.

66. Boston *Transcript,* March 11, 1893, and April 4, 1894.

67. The Boston *Advertiser* review (Clapp) appeared on February 19, 1892; the Boston *Transcript* review (Sutherland) on February 20. The half-dozen other reviews that I have seen range from favorable to enthusiastic about Miss Marlowe's performance.

68. For her marriage to Robert Taber and its conquences, see Russell, pp. 212ff; for their separation, p. 260; for their divorce, p. 270. The New York *Press* of December 10, 1899, carried an article headlined "Only Heartbreak Made Julia Marlowe Great."

69. For the failure of *Henry IV* in New York see the *New York Times,* New York *Herald,* and New York *Tribune* (all of March 20, 1896), and the *Dramatic Mirror,* March 28, 1896. Miss Gilder's trenchant review is in *The Critic* of March 28.

70. For pressures exerted by the Syndicate, see Russell, pp. 250ff.

71. For Daly's campaign against Miss Marlowe, see Russell, pp. 278–84.

72. The "rival Rosalinds" were much written up at the time. For example, see the New York *World* of January 3 and January 7, 1899.

73. This event, which amused the town, is reported in a clipping entitled "Rival Relics from Forest of Arden" from an unidentified newspaper dated New York, January 7, [1899]. (In the Harvard Theatre Collection). Winter confirms the contribution of Mr. Greatbach in *Shakespeare on the Stage,* II, 275.

74. Between Taber and the Syndicate, Miss Marlowe was mainly prevented from playing Shakespeare at this time. Russell displays on pp. 288–89 financial records that bear out the claim that "Shakespeare spells ruin."

75. Russell, pp. 288–89.

76. The Winter quip is quoted in *Julia Marlowe's Story,* p. 165. It appears in Winter's *Wallet of Time,* II, p. 54.

77. These references to Fechter, Irving, and Booth were made in a review by W. F. A. in the Boston *Transcript,* October 2, 1900.

78. *New York Times,* September 18, 1900.

79. Boston *Advertiser* (undated clipping). Doubtless in Sothern's first season as Hamlet, at the Hollis Street Theatre, with his original company.

80. *Dramatic Mirror,* September 29, 1900.

81. Boston, *Transcript,* October 12, 1900, signed Henry M. Rogers.

82. Winter's review in the New York *Tribune,* September 18, 1900, is brief, general, and sullen. In *Shakespeare on the Stage,* I, 388–92, he denounces these "errors."

83. New York *Herald,* September 18, 1900.

84. *New York Times,* September 18, 1900.

85. *Dramatic Mirror,* January 10, 1903.

86. Ibid.

87. New York *Commercial Advertiser,* December 31, 1902, and Boston *Transcript,* April 7, 1903.

88. *Julia Marlowe's Story,* p. 164.

89. Ibid., p. 174.

90. Chicago *Record-Herald,* September 20, 1904.

91. Chicago *Tribune,* September 20 and 25, and October 9, 1904.

92. Chicago *Daily News,* September 20, 1904.

93. Chicago *Record-Herald,* September 28, 1904.

94. Chicago *Tribune,* September 27 and October 9, 1904.

95. Ibid., October 4 and 9, 1904.

96. New York *Commercial Advertiser,* December 31, 1902.

97. Chicago *Record-Herald,* October 6, 1904.

98. Chicago *Tribune,* October 4, 1904.

99. *Dramatic Mirror,* September, 1900.

100. Chicago *Tribune,* October 9, 1904.

101. Russell, p. 323.

102. Chicago *Tribune,* September 25 and October 9, 1904.

103. New York *Tribune,* October 18, 1904.

104. *Dramatic Mirror,* October 29, 1904.

105. *New York Times,* October 18, 1904.

106. New York *Evening Post,* October 18, 1904.

107. New York *Globe,* October 18, 1904.

108. Boston *Transcript* (undated clipping, probably of 1907).

109. New York Evening *Post,* October 18, 1904.

110. New York *Tribune* and New York *Post,* both of November 1, 1904.

111. Boston *Journal,* May 13, 1913.

112. New York *Tribune,* November 15, 1904.

113. New York *Herald,* November 15, 1904.

114. Boston *Transcript,* February 1, 1910.

115. Unidentified clipping (Harvard Theatre Collection).

116. London *Standard,* May 3, 1907. See also Arthur Symons, *The Nation,* CXI (July 24, 1920), pp. 97–98.

117. Unidentified clipping (Harvard Theatre Collection), January 19, 1908.

118. Clapp in undated clipping (Harvard Theatre Collection).

119. Boston *Transcript,* November 12, 1919.

120. Ibid., December 2, 1905.

121. Ibid., November 25, 1905.

122. *New York Times,* October 22, 1905.

123. Boston *Transcript,* December 19, 1911.

124. The horse and the ass are mentioned in New York reviews in October 1905, but not in Boston reviews in November.

125. *Julia Marlowe's Story,* p. 177.

126. Boston *Herald,* January 25, 1910.

127. Russell, p. 336.

128. Ibid., pp. 337 and 347.

129. New York *Tribune,* November 5, 1905.

130. *New York Times,* November 5, 1905.

131. New York *Herald,* October 3, 1905.

132. Boston *Transcript,* December 19, 1910, and an unidentified New York review of November 28, 1921.

133. New York *Herald,* October 31, 1905.

134. Russell explains Miss Marlowe's dislike of the role of Portia, on the position Shakespeare has put her in, pp. 339–41.

135. Boston *Transcript,* December 15, 1905.

136. New York *Tribune,* November 14, 1905.

137. *Dramatic Mirror,* November 25, 1905.

138. *New York Times,* October 12, 1919.

139. New York *World,* October 7, 1919.

140. London *Mail* and London *Sketch,* both of May 8, 1907.

141. London *Illustrated Sporting and Dramatic News,* May 11, 1907.

142. *The Melancholy Tale of "Me,"* pp. 364–65.

143. See Russell for more details of this arrangment, pp. 354–56.

144. Russell, p. 356.

145. Ibid., p. 452–61.

146. Ibid., p. 461.

147. Masses of writing in newspapers and magazines in the first two decades of the century cover the inception, the planning, the rise and fall of the New Theatre. The footnotes that follow call

attention to those easily available sources that I have used. Many items that I have not documented are derived from an excellently researched doctoral dissertation at Stanford University by John Henry Jennings, 1952: "A History of the New Theatre, New York, 1909–1911." Though unpublished, this Ph.D. dissertation is available from University Microfilm.

148. *The Forum* (November 1892), pp. 337–44.

149. For the *Theatre of Arts and Letters,* see references in the *Atlantic,* LXXV (May 1895), p. 688; *The Literary Digest,* XXVI (April 4, 1903), p. 491; Montrose B. Moses, *The Life of Heirich Conried* (New York: Thomas Y. Cromwell Company, 1916), p. 270.

150. *The Literary Digest,* XXXVI (April 14, 1903), pp. 490–91; *The Independent,* LV (April 9, 1903), pp. 870–72.

151. Clarke's proposals were reported in *Arena,* XXI (June 1904), pp. 641–45. Further proposals are in *Arena,* XXXII (July 1904), pp. 48–53.

152. Arthur Hornblow responded to Carnegie's refusal to subsidize a theatre in *Theatre* (April 1904), p. 87.

153. For Heinrich Conried's involvement in the plans for the New Theatre, see the Jennings dissertation referred to in n.147 and the Moses biography, pp. 227–92. Conried's ideas were announced to the New York *Evening Post* by C. H. Meltzer, and reprinted in *The Literary Digest,* November 18, 1905.

154. Meltzer continued to promote Conried's plans in *Harper's Weekly,* XLIX (December 30, 1905), pp. 1942–44.

155. *Life* (November 23, 1905) commented on Conried's plans and expressed suspicions about Conried's motives and the financial transactions under way. Further suspicions were raised by X. Y. Z. in *Theatre Magazine* (January 1906), pp. 7–8.

156. Elaborate descriptions of the theatre-to-be, with architectural views, appeared in *Theatre* (August 1906), pp, 202–3, and (April 1908), pp. 92–5. Exact figures for the seating capacity are not easy to determine. I have counted the seats as numbered in Illus. 180, but as Jennings explains in his dissertation the builders had to make minor adjustments.

157. See John Corbin, "The New Theatre in New York," *The World's Work* (September 1911), pp. 14840–41.

158. John Corbin disputed Barker's claim that the theatre was too large. Norman Hapgood agreed with Barker. See *The Literary Digest,* XXVI (May 2, 1908), pp. 653–54. For a detailed drawing of the house as seen from the stage, with seats numbered, see *Theatre* (August 1909), pp. 58–60. Elaborate essays on the New are by John Corbin in *Outlook,* XCIII (October 23, 1909), pp. 395–406, and William Lyon Phelps in *The Independent,* LXVII (October 1909), pp. 957–62.

159. The staff is named in *The Nation,* LXXXVI (July 30, 1908), p. 103. They are Winthrop Ames, director; Lee Shubert, business manager; and John Corbin, literary manager. For a modern assessment of Ames, see David MacArthur, "Winthrop Ames: The Gentleman as Producer-Director," in the *Educational Theatre Journal,* XVI (December 1964), pp. 349–59.

160. The actors are described, with photographs, in *Theatre* (November 1909), pp. 144–45.

161. Herschel Baker, *John Philip Kemble* (Cambridge: Harvard University Press, 1942), p. 323.

162. Russell, p. 468.

163. Ibid., p. 469.

164. "Reminiscences of John Corbin," *New York Times,* April 22, 1923.

165. The preview is described by Arthur Warren in the New York *Tribune,* November 9, 1909; by the *Outlook,* XCIII (November 20, 1909).

166. New York *Telegraph,* November 9, 1909.

167. New York *Times,* November 9, 1909.

168. New York *Post,* November 9, 1909.

169. Russell, p. 469.

170. *Theatre* (March 1912), p. 77.

171. *New York Times,* March 22, 1910.

172. New York *Tribune,* March 22, 1910.

173. *New York Times,* March 22, 1910.

174. *Dramatic Mirror,* April 12, 1910.

175. *Christian Science Monitor,* November 22, 1910.

176. *Dramatic Mirror,* April 12, 1910.

177. New York *World,* March 22, 1910.

178. *Christian Science Monitor,* November 22, 1910.

179. Boston *Herald,* November 22, 1910.

180. Russell, p. 477.

181. Ibid., p. 479.

182. Boston *Transcript,* November 15, 1910.

183. Boston *Herald,* November 15, 1910.

184. *Christian Science Monitor,* November 15, 1910.

185. Parker in the Boston *Transcript,* November 15, 1910.

186. *Christian Science Monitor,* November 15, 1910.

187. *The Nation,* XC (December 10, 1910), pp. 560–61.

188. *Life* (December 22, 1910), p. 1152.

189. New York *Tribune,* December 9, 1910.

190. *Theatre* (January 11, 1911), pp. 3 and 12.

191. *Dramatic Mirror,* December 7, 1910.

192. Russell, p. 494,

193. Ibid., p. 507.

194. Withrop Ames, "E. H. Sothern as a War Camp Troubadour," *New York Times,* November 12, 1933.

195. *New York Times,* October 3, 1923.

196. The New York reviews of Brown, Woollcott, and Towse were reported in a Boston paper (unidentified clipping), October 8, 1923.

197. *The Drama, A Monthly Review* (December, 1923), pp. 87–88.

198. Russell, pp. 536–38.

199. In two articles called "Modernizing Shakespeare," *Theatre* (February and March 1922), Sothern explained in considerable detail his version of modernized scenography.

200. Photographs of the *Twelfth Night* sets are given in the February issue.

201. *Theatre* (February 1922), p. 136.

202. Ibid., (March 1922), p. 198.

Epilogue. The Shakespeare Tercentenary

1. G. C. D. Odell, *Annals of the New York Stage,* 15 vols. (New York: Columbia University Press, 1927–49), VII (1931). For Booth's Romeo, p. 556; for Hackett's Falstaff, p. 562; for the Germans at the Stadt-Theatre, pp. 589–93; for the Conways in Brooklyn, p. 619. Further benefits for the statue fund included the Booth brothers' *Julius Caesar,* November 25, 1864, pp. 638–39; lectures by Hackett in January, 1865, p. 690; Mrs. Lander's Beatrice, February 23, 1865.

2. G. C. D. Odell, *Shakespeare from Betterton to Irving,* 2 vols. (New York: Scribners, 1920), II, 257, 299, 361.

3. For a full account of the Stratford Festival, splendidly illustrated, see Richard Foulkes, *The Shakespeare Tercentenary of 1864.* (London: The Society for Theatre Research, 1984.)

4. *Harper's,* XXIX (August 1864), pp. 336–46; T. C. Kemp and J. C. Trewin, *The Stratford Festival* (Birmingham: Cornish Brothers Ltd., 1953), pp. 4–5; Shirley S. Allen, *Samuel Phelps and Sadler's Wells Theatre* (Middletown: Wesleyan University Press, 1971), p. 296.

5. The *Times*, 1916, January 12, the Committee meets; February 21, German events announced; March 2, the Cologne Gazette prints outright ridicule of British efforts to commemorate Shakespeare; March 20, total list of events to take place; May 3, review of the Drury Lane *Julius Caesar*.

6. *Theatre* (February 16) p. 67, gives a full account of the committee for the Shakespeare Celebration and lists many events that will take place. See also *Dramatic Mirror*, LXXV (January 22, 1916), pp. 3–5 and (February 19, 1916), p. 6.

7. *New York Times*, March 12, 1916.

8. See above, chapter VI, pp. 282–3.

9. See above, chapter V, p. 242.

10. Brooklyn *Daily Eagle*, October 1, 1912.

11. *Dramatic Mirror*, October 2, 1912.

12. *Theatre*, November, 1912, p. 130.

13. *The Nation*, XCV (October 3, 1912), p. 315.

14. *Dramatic Mirror*, November 13, 1912.

15. Boston *Transcript*, December 12, 1912 (reprinted from New York *Sun*). Possibly Faversham obtained the *Caesar* sets of the late Richard Mansfield.

16. Boston *Transcript* (undated clipping, Harvard Theatre Collection, signed K. M.).

17. Boston *Transcript*, November 14, 1912. This is Parker's review of the performance in New York.

18. *The Concert*, an exceptionally clever comedy by Hermann Bahr, was produced in New York by David Belasco, October 10, 1910.

19. For Faversham's future plans see New York *Tribune*, November 24, 1912; *Dramatic Mirror*, November 13, 1912; November 18, 1916.

20. "How I Found My Iago," *Harper's Weekly*, LVII (February 28, 1914), p. 22.

21. Forbes-Robertson's *Othello* had been seen in New York during the week of December 15, 1913.

22. New York *Tribune*, February 10, 1914.

23. *New York Times*, February 10, 1914.

24. Other reviews of the *Othello*, friendly but critical, appear in the following New York papers (all of February 10, 1914) the *American, Commercial Advertiser, Evening Post, Evening Sun, Evening World, Sun, World;* and *The Nation*, February 12; *Dramatic Mirror*, February 11; *Life*, February 26; *Theatre* (March), p. 112.

25. The most interesting coverage of Miss Anglin's productions is Walter Prichard Eaton's essay on the current theatre in the *American Magazine* (May 1914).

26. On Rosalind, *New York Times*, March 18, 1914; *Theatre* (May 1914), p. 224; *The Nation*, XCVIII (March 19, 1914), pp. 309–10.

27. On *Twelfth Night*, *New York Times*, March 25, 1914; *Life*, April 9, pp. 654–55; *Independent*, LXXVIII (April 6, 1914), p. 33; *Theatre* (May 1914), p. 225; *The Nation* (March 26, 1914), pp. 340–41.

28. *Everybody's*, XXX (April 1914), pp. 543–53; *Theatre* (July 1914), pp. 15–17.

29. Miss Neilson-Terry was widely reviewed. See (all of November 24, 1914) *New York Times*, New York *Tribune*, New York *World*, New York *Sun;* and *Dramatic Mirror*, December 2, 1914; *The Nation*, XCIX (December 3, 1914), p. 669; *Theatre* (January 1915), p. 8, 32.

30. February 16, 1915. Barker's *Dream* belongs so emphatically to "modern" Shakespeare that I postpone discussion of it to a subsequent volume.

31. New York *Evening Mail*, February 8, 1916.

32. Unidentified clipping, February 9, 1916 (Harvard Theatre Collection).

33. Hackett played his *Macbeth* first in Boston, It was reviewed in many unidentified papers, January 11, 1916 (Harvard Theatre Collection). The quotation from the *New York Times* is of February 8, 1916. Other important New York reviews are in the *Commercial Advertiser, World*, and *Evening Post*, all February 8, 1916; and *Dramatic Mirror*, February 12, 1916; *The Nation* (February 17, 1916); New York *Tribune*, February 13, 1916; New York *Post*, February 17, 1916; *Life*, February 24, 1916; *Theatre* (March 1916).

34. Woollcott reviewed Hackett's later *Macbeth* in the *New York Times*, March 17, 1924; Gilbert Gabriel in the New York *Sun*, March 17, 1924; Laurence Stallings in an unidentified New York paper, March 17, 1924; Frank Lea Short for the *Christian Science Monitor*, March 18, 1924.

35. Boston *Transcript*, March 24, 1916 (transcription of Towse in the New York *Post*).

36. New York *Sun*, March 21, 1916.

37. *Dramatic Mirror*, April 16, 1916.

38. For the 1917 revival, see *Dramatic Mirror*, January 20, 1917; *Theatre* (February 1917), pp. 87–88; *Life*, January 25, 1917.

39. The staging is described in an undated clipping (Harvard Theatre Collection) by H. K. M. (Moderwell) entitled "*The Tempest* Acted: Restoring *The Tempest* to Our Stage."

40. *New York Times*, April 24, 1916.

41. New York *Sun*, April 24, 1916.

42. On Calvert's Prospero: the New York *Herald*, April 24, 1916, called him singsong; the New York *Sun* thought he lacked variety; other opinions are quoted from unidentified New York papers (Harvard Theatre Collection). Moderwell found him husky and short on "dignity and sweetness."

43. Percy MacKaye, *Caliban by the Yellow Sands*, (Garden City, N.Y.: Doubleday, Page & Company, 1916). Published well before the production, it contains in a huge appendix full instructions for later producers. Ground plan and sketches of some of the scenery by Joseph Urban and Robert Edmond Jones are included.

44. A long interview with MacKaye, by Joyce Kilmer, contains many of the playwright's ideas. See also the long introduction to the published volume.

45. The *New York Times* covered every important development of the production. May 19, Robert Edmond Jones and crews building costumes; May 22, the participation by professional actors; dressing rooms and other physical arrangements; May 24, rain postpones scheduled opening on May 23; May 25, long review of the opening; May 26, second performance shortened by omitting some Inner Scenes and speeding up Interludes; May 27, decision to extend the run; June 3, receipts meet expenses; June 6, after final performance, speeches, awards.

Index